W9-BKP-854

■ United States Holocaust Memorial Museum
Center for Advanced Holocaust Studies

Documenting Life
and Destruction
Holocaust Sources
in Context

SERIES EDITOR

Jürgen Matthäus

A project of the

United States Holocaust Memorial Museum

SARA J. BLOOMFIELD
Director

Center for Advanced Holocaust Studies

PAUL A. SHAPIRO
Director

JÜRGEN MATTHÄUS
Director, Applied Research

under the auspices of the

Academic Committee
of the
United States Holocaust Memorial Council

ALVIN H. ROSENFELD, *Chair*

Doris L. Bergen	Alfred Gottschalk	Michael R. Marrus
Richard Breitman	Peter Hayes	John T. Pawlikowski
Christopher Browning	Sara Horowitz	Aron Rodrigue
David Engel	Steven T. Katz	George D. Schwab
Willard A. Fletcher	William S. Levine	Nechama Tec
Zvi Y. Gitelman	Deborah E. Lipstadt	James E. Young

with major support from

The Blum Family Foundation
and
The William S. and Ina Levine Foundation

and additional support from

The Dorot Foundation

The authors have worked to provide clear information about the provenance of each document and illustration included here. In some instances, particularly for journals and newspapers printed in Germany during the 1930s but no longer in print, we have been unable to verify the existence or identity of any present copyright owners. If notified of any item inadvertently credited wrongly, we will include updated credit information in reprints of this work. In the same vein, if a reader has verifiable information about a person's fate that remains incomplete in this volume, it would be greatly appreciated if that data were shared with the authors.

Documenting Life and Destruction
Holocaust Sources in Context

JEWISH RESPONSES TO PERSECUTION

Volume I

1933–1938

Jürgen Matthäus
and
Mark Roseman

Advisory Committee:

Christopher Browning
David Engel
Sara Horowitz
Steven T. Katz
Aron Rodrigue
Alvin H. Rosenfeld
Nechama Tec

AltaMira Press
in association with the United States Holocaust Memorial Museum
2010

WINGATE UNIVERSITY LIBRARY

For USHMM:
Project Manager: Mel Hecker
Contributing Editor: Jan Lambertz
Researcher/Indexer: Ryan Farrell
Translators: Stephen Pallavicini, Gina Tumbarello
Research Assistants: Adam Blackler, Daniel Brewing, Hillah Culman, Doreen Densky,
Melissa Kravetz, Michael McConnell, Julia Schreiber, and Michaela Soyer

Published by AltaMira Press
A division of Rowman & Littlefield Publishers, Inc.
A wholly owned subsidiary of The Rowman & Littlefield Publishing Group, Inc.
4501 Forbes Boulevard, Suite 200, Lanham, Maryland 20706
http://www.altamirapress.com

Estover Road, Plymouth PL6 7PY, United Kingdom

Copyright © 2010 by AltaMira Press

All rights reserved. No part of this book may be reproduced in any form or by any electronic
or mechanical means, including information storage and retrieval systems, without written
permission from the publisher, except by a reviewer who may quote passages in a review.

British Library Cataloguing in Publication Information Available

LIBRARY OF CONGRESS CATALOGING-IN-PUBLICATION DATA

Matthäus, Jürgen, 1959–
    Jewish responses to persecution, 1933–1938 / Jürgen Matthäus and Mark Roseman.
    p. cm. — (Documenting life and destruction: Holocaust sources in context)
    Includes bibliographical references and index.
    ISBN 978-0-7591-1908-6 (v. 1 : cloth : alk. paper)—
    ISBN 978-0-7591-1910-9 (v. 1: electronic)
    1. Jews—Germany—History—1933–1945. 2. Jews—Persecutions—Germany—
History—20th century. 3. Jews—Germany—Social conditions—20th century.
    4. Germany—Ethnic relations—History—20th century. 5. Antisemitism—Germany—
History—20th century. 6. Holocaust, Jewish (1939–1945)—Germany—. I. Roseman, Mark.
II. Title.
    DS134.255.M38 2010
    940.53'18—dc22   2009022613

⊗™ The paper used in this publication meets the minimum requirements of American
National Standard for Information Sciences—Permanence of Paper for Printed Library
Materials, ANSI/NISO Z39.48-1992.

Printed in the United States of America

"I do not want to assert prematurely that we have already reached the last circle of hell, for uncertainty is not the worst thing, because in uncertainty there is still hope."

— Victor Klemperer, Dresden, entry for New Year's Eve 1938, quoted from his diary, *I Will Bear Witness: A Diary of the Nazi Years, 1933–1941* (New York: Random House, 1998), 285.

Contents

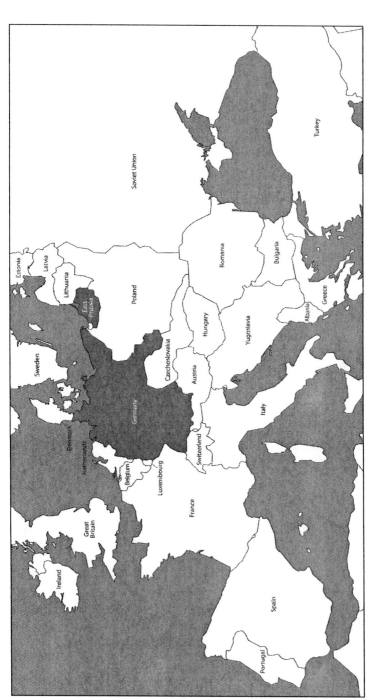

Europe, 1935. Source: USHMM. For a useful map on Germany's territorial expansion 1935–1939, see http://germanhistorydocs.ghi-dc.org/map
.cfm?map_id=2884 (accessed October 16, 2009).

INTRODUCTION TO THE
JEWISH RESPONSES TO
PERSECUTION SERIES

JÜRGEN MATTHÄUS, ALEXANDRA GARBARINI,
AND MARK ROSEMAN

IN A LETTER TO HIS WIFE, written shortly after Adolf Hitler's appointment as chancellor of the German Reich in January 1933, a German Jewish man posed some painful questions to himself:

> What ties do you still have here? How strong are they? What can you
> still hope to get here and how much can you hope for? Is there really no
> possibility at all for a Jew to take part in this? Or, if it's not possible now,
> when might it be so? Is there a chance that you could wait out this period
> of transition? Should you? . . . And what exactly are you giving up here?
> What could you expect to find on the outside? Where do you belong?
> How would you establish yourself elsewhere—and where? What are you
> actually looking for? What is really important to you? Where do your basic
> values lie, what are your talents, your aims, your ideals?

Weeks later, before his departure to Palestine, he observed in pithy notebook form the good, middle-class German Jews around him: "Real collapse. Hard and terrible fall. People could not always see that the planks they were standing on were just balanced on a rickety scaffold. Now suddenly they're seeing every-thing give way beneath them. Where are they falling? Into nothingness."[1]

For Otto Rudolph Heinsheimer, the person who wrote these words, such questions continued to reverberate at least until his emigration in July 1933. His mood was in keeping with that of many German Jews suddenly subjected to persecution. On the one hand, there was shock at the abrupt turn of events; on the other, there still seemed to be time to weigh different strategies for deal-ing with the new situation. This moment has long since disappeared from view. Heinsheimer's uncertainty at the time stands in marked contrast to the long-held family memory of his past, which his daughter, eminent historian Shulamit Volkov, describes as "the Zionist story at its best": the story of a man who quickly realized that he had no place in Nazi Germany and embarked on a suc-cessful life in the *Yishuv* as a father, husband, and lawyer. That version of his life, perfectly suited to the demands of an emerging Israeli society keen to imag-ine itself as the triumphant alternative to an antisemitic Europe, only unraveled when her father's letters from 1933 surfaced after his death. The letters, written from Germany to his wife, who had already left, are evidence of, in Volkov's words, "the pain, the confusion, the imminent depression, the disorientation, and, finally, the hesitant decision to sail after her to Palestine."[2]

Heinsheimer's letters—and his daughter's surprise at their content—remind us of the power of contemporary sources to illuminate the past. That power is of course not limited to documents on the Holocaust. As any history teacher knows, contemporary witness reports are invaluable for conveying a sense of immediacy: if only for a moment, students grasp the reality of a time when the past was still the present, and outcomes with which we are all familiar were still unknown. When it comes to understanding the Holocaust, however, con-temporary documents, particularly those stemming from the hands of victims rather than perpetrators, have a significance and expressiveness that goes beyond this general rule. They can recover the agency and subjectivity of those too often seen merely as the recipients of Nazi policy. They can rescue the diversity and individuality of millions of women, men, and children whom their tormentors tried to treat as the faceless, undifferentiated "Jew." And they can bring to life the uncertainty, confusion, and disbelief of those confronted by measures and

---

1. Letters by Otto Rudolph Heinsheimer, written between April and July 1933, trans-lated from Shulamit Volkov, "Der Einzelne und die Gemeinde: Zwischen Erfüllung und Enttäuschung," in *Das jüdische Projekt der Moderne: Zehn Essays* (Munich: Verlag C. H. Beck, 2001), 187, 199. See also Shulamit Volkov, "Prologue: My Father Leaves His German Homeland," in *Germans, Jews, and Antisemites: Trials in Emancipation* (Cambridge: Cambridge University Press, 2006), 7–9.

2. Volkov, "Prologue," 1–5.

processes that only in retrospect have become an irremovable part of our mental landscape.

Not everyone accepts the power of such documentation. Some have indeed claimed that the singularity of the Holocaust was such that there can be no witnessing of it.[3] The authentic observers, the true victims, so the argument goes, perished, unable under the extreme conditions to articulate their feelings and experiences, while those who survived are by dint of the guilt of surviving, of their temporal and spatial distance from the events of which they now speak, and of our distance from them, rendered incapable of communicating their experiences authentically. This volume and the others in this series would not have been produced had the authors shared such a view. There is no doubt, however, that witness reports on the Holocaust not only offer rewards but also pose challenges beyond those that pertain to historical sources per se.

This stricture applies particularly to *retrospective* accounts of the Holocaust, which probably more than other conventional historical memoirs are colored by the writer's hindsight. For much of the period of Nazi rule, as Heinsheimer's anguished letters remind us, contemporary observers often had no idea where things would lead, even if they might in some cases be gripped by remarkably prescient forebodings. Those observers lucky enough to survive were in later life forever confronted by the knowledge of the enormity of what had befallen them. The sheer fact of being a survivor created a different status, a different way of relating to the world.[4] More than most other memoirists, Holocaust survivors, after their reprieve from Nazi terror, lived and wrote under conditions vastly different from their former lives. Within the context of Palestine and later Israel, it was understandable, for example, that Otto Heinsheimer might conceal even from those closest to him the real story of his hesitancy and anguish in leaving a beloved Fatherland. For these reasons, the volumes of this series emphasize *contemporary* witness statements, that is to say, sources created close to the events by those discriminated against as Jews.

That it has been possible to construct these volumes almost exclusively from contemporary reports, memoranda, letters, diaries, and photographs is a testament to what has survived. Following the opening of Eastern

---

3. See, e.g., Dori Laub, "Truth and Testimony: The Process and the Struggle," in *Trauma: Explorations in Memory*, ed. Cathy Caruth (Baltimore: Johns Hopkins University Press, 1995), 61–75; Giorgio Agamben, *Homo Sacer: Sovereign Power and Bare Life* (Stanford, CA: Stanford University Press, 1998).

4. For some of the most profound reflections on survival and its postwar implications, see Primo Levi, *The Drowned and the Saved* (New York: Summit Books, 1988); Jean Améry, *At the Mind's Limits: Contemplations by a Survivor on Auschwitz and Its Realities* (New York: Schocken Books, 1980).

European archives, recent years have seen the emergence of a huge volume of documentation and a wealth of publications to match. Important new studies explore the course of events that constitute the Holocaust and provide new answers to the questions how, when, and why the perpetrators did what they did. It is all the more surprising, then, that sources generated by the victims, even where available for research since the end of World War II, have found comparatively less scholarly interest. As a result, there is no recently published English-language document collection that university teachers can turn to for a firsthand sense of the breadth and diversity of Jewish responses to Nazi persecution.[5] The aim of this series is to fill that gap. And if these volumes achieve nothing else, they will hopefully convey the sheer richness, vitality, and depth of witness records preserved in archives and libraries across the globe.

Yet, even the reliance on contemporary accounts does not spare us from having to grapple with particular features and difficulties of Holocaust documentation. In some cases, the conditions under which people wrote were indeed so extreme, their survival so in doubt, that the continued devotion to diaries and reports is more revealing for what the very act of writing tells us about how Jews responded to the Holocaust than for any particular details described in the texts. In other cases, particularly, though not only, in Germany in the 1930s, Jewish individuals and agencies operated in a strange environment. For a while they were ironically somewhat freer from institutional pressures than all the non-Jewish groups brought into line with official policy; at the same time, they were increasingly the victims of permanent surveillance and marginalization. To understand a report written under such circumstances, we need to be able to read between the lines of a text that had to be meaningful to its Jewish recipients but whose authors were conscious of the Gestapo's watchful gaze. Because every echo that manages to escape the muffled cellar of Nazi rule is in some way in discord with the reality it depicts, we will need to understand the undertones, the whispers, and the reverberations. In introducing the various texts featured

---

5. Isaiah Trunk, *Jewish Responses to Nazi Persecution: Collective and Individual Behavior in Extremis* (New York: Stein & Day, 1979), presents the first English-language source compilation on the topic but has long been out of print. For different approaches to Jewish responses, see Philip Friedman, *Roads to Extinction: Essays on the Holocaust* (New York: JPS, 1980); David G. Roskies, *The Literature of Destruction: Jewish Responses to Catastrophe* (Philadelphia: Jewish Publication Society, 1988); Monika Richarz, ed., *Jewish Life in Germany: Memoirs from Three Centuries* (Bloomington: Indiana University Press, 1991); Yehuda Bauer, *Jewish Reactions to the Holocaust* (Tel Aviv: MOD, 1989); Saul Friedländer, *Nazi Germany and the Jews*, vol. 1, *The Years of Persecution, 1933–1939*; vol. 2, *The Years of Extermination, 1939–1945* (New York: HarperCollins, 1997, 2007); Dan Michman, *Holocaust Historiography: A Jewish Perspective* (Portland, OR: Vallentine Mitchell, 2003).

in this collection, we have tried to convey a sense of the circumstances of their production and communication.

Beyond the distinctive constraints attendant on the emergence of their testimony, witnesses within the Nazi empire faced another challenge, namely, the huge problem of comprehending the human landscape around them. This problem was not the same at all times and in all German-dominated places, but it was in many cases unprecedented. In the early years of the Third Reich, observers found it difficult to differentiate the strange mix of the normal and the abnormal, of the stable and the revolutionary, of continued orderly rule from above and pressure from the streets. Heinsheimer's troubled musings in that sense faithfully reflected a puzzling, disturbing world. Impelled by the decision of his wife, he was one of the "lucky" ones who drew the correct conclusion that things would continue to go badly and emigrated in time. Others, though, had plausible reasons for reading the conditions before them in a different way.

What made it so difficult to understand their true position? Doubtless, the architects and practitioners of German anti-Jewish policies understood how to conceal some of their intentions. But the fluidity and contradictions of the rapidly changing situation reveal that even the protagonists knew little about the destination: the Holocaust as we know it was not a foregone conclusion and, before the war, certainly not a preplanned one. In later years and other places, the problems of understanding were different. By the time the war had started, precious little normality or stability remained to console those Jews affected by Nazi measures. But in a situation as unprecedented as it was unpredictable, the difficulty of truly understanding (or believing) the direction of the process and still more of understanding why any human being would want to construct and serve such a murderous machine was all the greater. Those problems of comprehension are not ones that vanish in hindsight, and the agonized reflections of witnesses to hell appear as immediate, compelling, and troubling today as when their authors put pen to paper.

The construction of a set of volumes on this scale inevitably involves choices and raises questions. Is it appropriate to limit our vision to Jewish victims of Nazi policy, and how should that group be defined? How do Jewish reactions compare to those of other victims of persecution, especially those also targeted by Nazi racial policy, and what do we lose if we exclude their experiences? Is the term *Jewish* meant to describe only persons who identified themselves as Jews or all those to whom anti-Jewish activists and bureaucrats applied the term, irrespective of their targets' self-definition? This latter, broad definition presents problems of its own; it is after all based on the perpetrators' perception of Jewish identity, one that found its clearest manifestation in the Nuremberg Laws enacted in September 1935. It includes Jews who had converted to another faith, as well as many more who maintained no ties to Jewish traditions and often perceived their enforced Jewishness as a stigma. Restricting the spectrum covered in this series to those who identified themselves as Jews would help avoid a number of problems in defining Jewish reactions and create almost automatically a somewhat more coherent (though still very diverse) group. Yet, can one adopt a narrow definition that excludes Holocaust victims who shared the fate of self-identifying Jews?

The authors of this series have opted for a broader understanding of Jewish responses, partly because the Nazi state and other institutions robbed the individual of the power of self-definition, partly because we would lose sight of important aspects of historical reality if we ignored the responses of those outside the scope of traditional Jewish affiliation. Also, both those who identified themselves as Jews and those forced back on a long discarded Jewish status changed their self-definitions over time in response to their experiences of persecution. The distinction is thus far from absolute and reminds us once again of the diversity and fluidity of a group the Nazis tried to see as uniform and undifferentiated as manifested in the propaganda myth of "the Jew" with its deep roots in racial ideology. At the same time, however, we believe that we can differentiate with sufficient clarity between Nazi policies toward Jews broadly defined and those toward other groups to justify excluding the latter from these volumes. As part of the overall series of source volumes titled *Documenting Life and Destruction*, the United States Holocaust Memorial Museum's (USHMM) Center for Advanced Holocaust Studies plans to present similar volumes on the specific responses and fates of other groups engulfed in the Holocaust.

What counts as a "response" to Nazi policy, and how "Jewish" were the actions here brought into the spotlight? In this series, preference is given to "response" over comparable terms (e.g., "reaction," "experience," "attitude," "perception"), partly because of the breadth of behavior and actions the word can encompass, partly because the accent here is on Jews as actors, not simply as passive witnesses, and partly because "response" carries overtones of reflection and thought. Not every Jewish response was well thought out, and often there was little time for calm rumination on the right course of action. Nevertheless, a great many documents in this volume reveal the victims as thinking, feeling, reflective individuals capable of gaining striking insights into their situation. But how "Jewish," one might ask, were such responses? Some of the statements and actions documented here undoubtedly reveal common behavior patterns displayed by any group or individual under threat. Others, however, reflect Jewish Diaspora life in the first half of the twentieth century with its specific political, religious, cultural, and social aspects. The sources selected for the series are designed to reflect different forms of behavior by different strata, segments, or subgroups within European Jewry at different points in time. Beyond established patterns of internal stratification, the documentation needs to capture the fact that all individuals have their own idiosyncrasies, their specific problems and perceptions. Consequently, in addition to Jewish leadership (e.g., the *Judenräte* in major ghettos or representative organizations in different countries), the series will document the life of a variety of "ordinary" Jews, inside the urban centers of Europe as well as on the periphery.

A note of caution for those who are expecting to find definitive answers and clear-cut messages: within the narrow confines of these volumes, while we seek to draw out some of the insights suggested by the documents under review, we do not offer hard-and-fast conclusions. Instead, we leave these to the reader. We do, however, aim at presenting the material basis, in the form of documentation, contextualization, and annotation, for readers to pursue the subject in its many facets. The narrative presented here consists of many partly dissonant and conflicting voices. Not only does maintaining a certain degree of tension between different sources representing life in extremis seem natural in a source selection that tries to avoid generalizing and glossing over the complexities of the historical situation, but it also offers a chance to highlight the diversity of Jewish experiences, perceptions, and reactions as they changed over time.

We will see how useful standard, often dichotomous parameters for defining Jewish responses—Eastern Jews and Jews in Western Europe, religious and atheist, or more generically, rich and poor, female and male, young and old— turn out to be in the context of the Holocaust, or whether other, more transient and subtle forms of group formation and identification prevailed at times. Because these volumes rely primarily on documentation generated by Jews at the time of persecution, the chronological structure of this series differs somewhat from the periodization of perpetrator-oriented studies. Nevertheless, while the series does not focus on the anti-Jewish measures planned and implemented by the perpetrators, the selected documents naturally reflect the various stages and manifestations of persecution through the perceptions and actions of those subjected to them: Jewish men, women, and children of different backgrounds and orientations.

The massive imbalance in the power relationship between those who victimized on the one hand and the victims on the other implies that the potential for Jewish agency was restricted from the start and increasingly diminished over time. As a result, what constituted resistance under such circumstances needs to be rethought. Armed resistance, the most manifest form of Jewish opposition, required extraordinary women and men willing to face insurmountable obstacles and the prospect of almost certain death. But in keeping with much recent historiography, this series operates with notions of resistance, opposition, and self-assertion that encompass a far wider range of behavior than just armed engagement with the enemy.[6] Many kinds of unarmed resistance also entailed enormous risk. Indeed, given the dangers involved and the minimal chances for even the slightest semblance of success, it is remarkable how many instances of individuals and groups resisting can be documented. We need also bear in mind that while nonviolent practices such as religious observance, diary or letter writing, and artistic or other cultural activities may not appear to us as particularly confrontational, they nonetheless often represented bold expressions of Jewish men and women's will to subvert the authority of their victimizers and to reduce existential pressure. Yet, while these volumes place particular emphasis on recovering such signs of initiative and will, they also attempt to provide sufficient contextual information for the reader to understand that the framework of persecution, its central building blocks, and its driving forces remained completely beyond the reach of Jewish agency. Decisions were forced upon Jewish men and women that lay outside any ordinary parameters of human choice.

In identifying sources, we have assessed their relevance, specificity, and context in terms of type, composition, style, content, and usability.[7] Relevant criteria were, among others, immediacy (the document should provide a sense of the meaning, scope, and quality of Jewish reactions), novelty (show new aspects of historical reality and perception), specificity (reflect unique aspects of a shared fate), clarity (enable readers to understand the particular setting and its broader context), and research value (exemplify key issues and provide stimulus for further study). In selecting sources, the authors tried to take the relative importance of particular settings into account, especially in Eastern and Southeast Europe, where most of the victims lived and where, during the war, the "Final Solution," defined as the systematic mass murder of Jewish men, women, and children, was implemented. This does not mean that the series will deal only with major cities, large ghettos, and death camps; in fact, it is one of the aims of these volumes to present a historical narrative that integrates both centers—urban and otherwise—and periphery.

---

6. For an introduction to the debates, see Robert Rozett, "Jewish Resistance," in *The Historiography of the Holocaust*, ed. Dan Stone (Houndmills, NY: Palgrave, 2004), 344–63; Michael R. Marrus, "Varieties of Jewish Resistance," in *Major Changes within the Jewish People in the Wake of the Holocaust: Proceedings of the Ninth Yad Vashem International Historical Conference Jerusalem, June 1993*, ed. Yisrael Gutman (Jerusalem: Yad Vashem, 1996), 269–300; Nechama Tec, *Jewish Resistance: Facts, Omissions, and Distortions* (Washington, DC: USHMM occasional paper, 2007).

7. These criteria follow Raul Hilberg, *Sources of Holocaust Research: An Analysis* (Chicago: Ivan Dee, 2001).

No compilation of sources can substitute for a monographic analysis of the topic. It can, however, as Isaiah Trunk put it in the late 1970s in a pathbreaking volume from which this series borrows its title, "direct further interest and inquiry into this area."[8] The aim of the volumes in the series is to present select documentation, adequately annotated and concisely contextualized, that reflects different aspects of Jewish responses to persecution during and immediately after the Holocaust. The authors of each volume have tried to provide what they regard as a clear structure that is organized chronologically while allowing for thematic clusters. Chapter introductions, short introductory sketches to the sources, annotations, further reading, and additional information (e.g., glossary, chronology) help place the material in its context. Nevertheless, as much as we have attempted to apply sound historiographic methods, we are aware that the selection of documentation and its representation in these slender books remains subjective. In addition to the print volumes, with their limited number of translated sources and restrictions in scope, we are planning to make more extensive documentation available electronically (e.g., copies of sources in their original languages and formats that can be accessed through the USHMM website).

The volumes in the series have achieved one of their key aims if they convey a better understanding of the openness of the process in the minds of those who—like Otto Heinsheimer and millions of others—lived through it, if they make us more aware of the unpredictability and impact of persecution, as well as of the great diversity of perceptions and reactions by different strata and groups within the Jewish minority persecuted by Nazi Germany or one of its allies. With these volumes we hope to deepen the understanding of Jewish agency under circumstances that increasingly reduced real options to choices between the impossible and the unthinkable.

---

8. Trunk, *Jewish Responses*, xi.

READER'S GUIDE

THE VOLUMES in this series embed original historical documents in an explanatory text by the authors. Our comments provide readers with clues about the context and distinctiveness of the documents presented and locate them in a loose narrative of communal experience and responses. This volume moves for the most part chronologically, allowing readers to gain a sense of how Jewish experience evolved over time, from the initial Nazi takeover in 1933 through the frightening developments of 1938. Within individual chapters, some material is grouped thematically rather than purely chronologically.

The translated documents in this volume have been printed in a distinct format to set them apart from our commentary. We have reproduced the form and content of the originals as faithfully as possible and worked to provide clear information about the provenance of each document. We have standardized emphases used by the authors of the documents by underlining them. In cases where we could not print a document in its entirety, we have marked any omitted text with ellipses ([. . .]).

Many foreign-language terms used by commentators of the 1930s carry multiple, ambiguous, or complicated meanings difficult to capture in English. Sometimes they represent distinct religious concepts or the peculiar, new—often racialized—bureaucratic terms of the Nazi state, but sometimes they simply constitute the distinctive vocabularies of sentiment, identity, mood, and so forth that pertain to every language. The nuances of particular terms can be important for understanding both the rhetoric of public appeals and the language of private reflection, and in some cases we have indicated the difficulty of translation by adding the original word or phrase in brackets after the English version.

A number of names, events, and organizations appear in boldface throughout the volume when they are first mentioned in a chapter. This indicates that readers can find further information on the highlighted term in the glossary at the end of the volume. Using the rich resources of the United States Holocaust Memorial Museum's library and archives, we have attempted to reveal the ultimate fate of each author of a document in the years following 1938. Some of this information appears in the glossary and some of it in footnotes to the original documents. Regrettably, we were unable to unearth information on every individual who makes an appearance in these pages.

Readers will find two other resources at the back of the volume to orient them in the complex events of this period. We have provided a basic chronology of important events that unfolded in the years covered by this volume. The bibliography also offers the reader an opportunity to explore the topics and events touched on here in greater depth.

Forthcoming volumes in the series:

Volume II: Jewish Responses to Persecution 1938–1940
Volume III: Jewish Responses to Persecution 1941–1942
Volume IV: Jewish Responses to Persecution 1942–1943
Volume V: Jewish Responses to Persecution 1944–1946

ABBREVIATIONS

(Bold indicates a glossary term.)

AJDC, AJJDC	**American Jewish Joint Distribution Committee**
AJYB	*American Jewish Year Book*
BDJ	**Bund Deutsch-Jüdischer Jugend** (League of German Jewish Youth)
CV, Centralverein	**Centralverein deutscher Staatsbürger jüdischen Glaubens** (Central Association of German Citizens of the Jewish Faith)
CZA	Central Zionist Archives, Jerusalem
FZGH	Forschungsstelle für Zeitgeschichte (Research Institute for Contemporary History), Hamburg
HIAS	Hebrew Sheltering and Immigrant Aid Society
Hilfsverein	**Hilfsverein der deutschen Juden** (Relief Association of German Jews)
HJ	Hitler-Jugend (Hitler Youth)
H&GS	*Holocaust and Genocide Studies*
ITS	International Tracing Service, Bad Arolsen, Germany
JCA, ICA	Jewish Colonization Association
JFB	**Jüdischer Frauenbund** (League of Jewish Women)
LBIJMB	Leo Baeck Institute Archive at the Jewish Museum, Berlin

LBINY	Leo Baeck Institute Archive, New York
LBIYB	*Leo Baeck Institute Year Book*
NSDAP	Nationalsozialistische Deutsche Arbeiter-Partei (Nazi Party)
RjF	**Reichsbund jüdischer Frontsoldaten** (Reich Association of Jewish Frontline Soldiers)
RM	**Reichsmark** (German currency)
RV	**Reichsvertretung der deutschen Juden** (Reich Representation of German Jews)
RVC	**Reichsverband christlich-deutscher Staatsbürger nicht-arischer oder nicht rein arischer Abstammung** (Reich Union of Christian-German Citizens of Non-Aryan or Not-Purely-Aryan Descent)
SA	Sturmabteilung (Nazi storm troopers)
SAM	Special Archive Moscow (Russian: Rossiiskii gosudarstvennyi voennyi arkhiv)
SD	Sicherheitsdienst ("intelligence service" of the Nazi Party)
SS	Schutzstaffel (Nazi "protective squadron")
USHMM	United States Holocaust Memorial Museum, Washington, D.C.
USHMMA	USHMM Archives
USHMMPA	USHMM Photo Archive
VndJ	**Verband nationaldeutscher Juden** (Association of National German Jews)
WJC	**World Jewish Congress**
WL	Wiener Library, London
YVS	*Yad Vashem Studies*
ZAHA	**Zentralausschuss der deutschen Juden für Hilfe und Aufbau** (Central Committee of the German Jews for Help and Reconstruction)
ZVfD	**Zionistische Vereinigung für Deutschland** (Zionist Association for Germany)

VOLUME INTRODUCTION

Jews and Other Germans before and after 1933

JÜRGEN MATTHÄUS AND MARK ROSEMAN

O LOOK BACK AT the early years of Nazi rule is to gaze across an almost unbridgeable chasm. We cannot escape our knowledge of the later crimes, but in 1933 the world did not yet know these crimes were possible. Our later awareness propels us to view everything that happened in those early years as prelude and antecedent. Yet, when Hitler was appointed Reich chancellor in January 1933, so much was uncertain. No one knew whether the Nazi regime could keep a firm grip on power, and few could be sure that the party's street-fighter rhetoric of the 1920s would become the manifesto for government in the 1930s. Could any party or group in Germany really roll back the achievements of the Enlightenment, remove Jews' legal status, and establish a racial state? Few predicted the enormous military capability that Germany would develop in a few short years or the willingness of its elites to engage in an aggressive war of expansion. And no one could foresee that this advanced nation would soon be deporting and murdering Jewish men, women, and children in every part of Europe dominated by the Reich. Numbed by hindsight, we also fail to see the developments that transfixed the gaze of contemporaries. With our knowledge of Auschwitz, it is hard to be overly moved by a one-day boycott of Jewish stores. Yet in April 1933, that boycott, and above all the symbolic portent of concerted government support for such an unconstitutional measure, sent a shudder through the entire body of German Jews. This volume of documents seeks to uncover the perspective and the proportions of the contemporary world of Jews in Hitler's Germany.

Since the Enlightenment, Jews had become increasingly woven into the fabric of German cultural, social, and economic life. In 1933, roughly 525,000 Germans declared themselves as Jews. While they comprised less than 1 percent of the country's population, most of them belonged to the middle class and identified strongly with their Fatherland. A strong segment—almost one hundred thousand, of whom about 40 percent were born in Germany—did not have German citizenship, however, and belonged to families that had come to the Reich from Eastern Europe. With the exception of these *Ostjuden*, few Jews in Germany maintained strong links with traditional Jewish life. Religious observance was low and the rate of intermarriage high. By the late 1920s, Marion Kaplan notes, "some Jewish leaders actually feared the complete fusion of their community into German society by the end of the 20th century."[1] Disparities remained between the non-Jewish majority's social and demographic structure and that of the Jewish minority,[2] but urbanization, social mobility, and intermarriage continued to erode the differences between the two worlds. Our knowledge of the Holocaust should not conceal the very considerable ties between Jewish and non-Jewish Germans that existed at the time Hitler came to power.

At the same time, hindsight can produce a different kind of blindness. If it is true that little in their previous experience had prepared Germany's Jews for what befell them after 1933, it is also the case that those émigrés and survivors who later claimed that there had been no antisemitism before Hitler had lost sight of their own past experience. Indeed, in pre-Nazi Germany,

---

1. Marion A. Kaplan, *Between Dignity and Despair: Jewish Life in Nazi Germany* (New York: Oxford University Press, 1998), 12. For an overview of the demographic and social situation of Jews in Germany on the eve of the Nazi era, see Kaplan, *Between Dignity,* 10–16; Werner Mosse, "At Home in Germany: The Jews during the Weimar Era," in *Juden im nationalsozialistischen Deutschland: The Jews in Nazi Germany, 1933–1945,* ed. Arnold Paucker (Tübingen: J. C. B. Mohr, 1986), 31–44.

2. In 1933, the majority of Jews in Germany lived in cities with more than 100,000 inhabitants; roughly 160,000 (or more than 32 percent of all Jews in Germany) were residents of Berlin. In 1936, more than 92 percent of Austrian Jewry lived in Vienna. The Jewish birth rate, which had been decreasing since the nineteenth century was considerably lower than that of the German population in total (in 1932, it was 7.2 percent compared to 16.2 percent). A disproportionately high number of Jews were employed in the professions and in commerce though the economic crisis of the late 1920s and early 1930s had increased the tendency toward impoverishment. See Avraham Barkai, Paul Mendes-Flohr, and Steven Lowenstein, *Deutsch-Jüdische Geschichte der Neuzeit,* vol. 4, *Aufbruch und Zerstörung, 1918–1945* (Munich: C. H. Beck, 1997).

even though real differences between Jew and non-Jew were being eroded, antisemitic fantasies and anxieties mushroomed. To believers in racial antisemitism, the visible Jewish minority, equivalent to 0.77 percent of the overall German population in 1933 (the corresponding figure for Austria, albeit from 1934, was 190,000, or 2.8 percent), represented only one side of the "Jewish problem." The other consisted of those more than one hundred thousand persons who did not consider themselves Jews. Some had Jewish ancestry but had lost or actively renounced their religious affiliation by converting to the Christian faith or joining the ranks of Socialists and Communists. Some were partners in so-called mixed marriages (*Mischehen*), and some were the offspring of such marriages, called "*Mischlinge*" ("mixed breeds"). Anti-Jewish activists thus lumped together an extremely heterogeneous body comprising those who regarded themselves as Jews and those merely labeled as being racially Jewish. This group had little to no common identity except in the distorted propaganda figure of "the Jew."

The categories of "*Mischehen*" and "*Mischling*" drew on a discourse of race and interbreeding that had accompanied European colonialism and nationalism since the late nineteenth century. When propagandists of the Jewish racial threat created elaborate subcategories of "three-quarter Jews," "half-Jews," and "one-quarter Jews," based on what antisemites dubbed the "race" (actually the religious affiliation) of individuals' parents and grandparents, they mirrored the way interracial encounters had been treated in the colonies. In this case, however, the combination of the assimilated Jew's relative invisibility, on the one hand, and the antisemites' belief in a global Jewish conspiracy, on the other, gave these categories a particular menace. According to an influential school of racist ideologues, the "hidden Jews" posed a particular danger to the German *Volk*. Greatly inflated estimates of the number of "mixed breeds" (up to 750,000, while their actual number was a fraction of this) attest to the obsession with "racial purity" as a utopian ideal and with "race defilement" as a national threat.[3]

Despite the seeming precision of the antisemites' racial mathematics and the elaborate paranoia wound into their conspiracy theories, confusion in fact

---

3. Kaplan, *Between Dignity*, 74–76. The groundbreaking monograph by Beate Meyer, *"Jüdische Mischlinge": Rassenpolitik und Verfolgungserfahrung, 1933–1945* (Hamburg: Doelling & Galitz, 1999), 25, 465, puts the number of "mixed marriages" in Germany in 1933 at 35,000 and the number of "*Mischlinge*" in 1939 at roughly 105,000: 50,000 "first-degree *Mischlinge*" (according to the Nuremberg Laws, persons with two Jewish grandparents but not belonging to the Jewish religion and not married to a Jewish person on September 15, 1935) and 55,000 "second-degree *Mischlinge*" (persons descended from one Jewish grandparent).

prevailed among proponents of anti-Jewish measures as to what exactly was to be done with the Jews. Even the Nazi Party provided no clear-cut message. While party propagandists ranted against "Jewish Bolshevists," "Jewish race defilers," and the "Jewish republic" as a whole, the program of the Nazi Party's predecessor, passed in early 1920 and declared unalterable by Hitler, stipulated simply that "only persons of German blood, whatever their creed, may be members of the nation [*Volksgenossen*]. Accordingly, no Jew may be a member of the nation."[4] What that meant beyond a new definition of citizenship remained unclear.

Unclear, too, or at least hotly debated among historians, is how widely accepted such antisemitic theories were. No doubt, antisemitism, while rooted in traditional Christian Jew hatred, had been reinvigorated by the infusion of modern ideas about biology in the last decades of the nineteenth century. The belief that there was a "Jewish question" of one sort or another was not restricted to hard-core antisemites; historian Shulamit Volkov has seen it as becoming part of Germany's "cultural code."[5] By cultural code, Volkov meant that even before World War I an increasing section of Germany's upper and middle classes believed that some kind of inalienable difference existed between German and Jew. Above all, to be German one had to be of German ethnic descent; Jews' claim to citizenship was seen as epitomizing the false notion of legally rather than ethnic-culturally defined nationhood.

For a brief period after World War I, German antisemitism exploded— mirroring, though often exceeding, a similar explosion of antisemitic conspiracy theories on the global stage. In many German and, indeed, other European cities, the strains of war had exacerbated tensions against the outsider, while shortages had added bitterness against the speculator. The huge Russian export of Jewish migrants and refugees produced in the postwar world a sense of global Jewry as never before, coupled with the unfamiliar image of Eastern European refugees in every European capital.[6] The wartime diplomatic competition between London and Berlin for Russian-Jewish support had, among other things, helped give rise to the British government's

---

4. Program of the German Workers' Party, February 1920, article 4, cited in Jeremy Noakes and Geoffrey Pridham, eds., *Nazism, 1919–1945*, vol. 1, *The Rise to Power, 1919–1934* (Exeter: University of Exeter Press, 1998), 14.

5. Shulamit Volkov, "Anti-Semitism as a Cultural Code," *LBIYB* 23 (1978): 25–46.

6. Saul Friedländer, "Political Transformations during the War and Their Effect on the Jewish Question," in *Hostages of Modernization: Studies on Modern Antisemitism, 1870–1933/39, Germany–Great Britain–France*, ed. Herbert A. Strauss (New York: Walter de Gruyter; 1993), 150–64.

Balfour Declaration, in which the world's most powerful empire officially endorsed what had been Zionist pipedreams. Once the fighting had stopped, Jews were nominally the beneficiaries of the minority-rights elements in the postwar treaties, toothless though they often really were.[7] Jews, it seemed, had become a global force, capable of manipulating international policy. The overrepresentation of Jews among leading Communists in Russia, Germany, and throughout Eastern Europe lent credence to the claim that Jews were the fomenters of internal sedition. Jews' global visibility in this unsettled time was thus remarkable. Even at this point, however, voices within Germany that called for a complete reversal of Jewish emancipation remained isolated on the right-wing fringe. Moreover, after the immediate postwar crisis had been settled, the threat of revolution contained, and inflation brought under control, the antisemitic panic abated. The **Weimar Republic**'s relatively good years of the mid-1920s saw a sharp decline in the radical Right's political fortunes. In electoral terms, the Nazis remained a marginal force; less than 3 percent of voters favored the Nationalsozialistische Deutsche Arbeiter-Partei (NSDAP) in the 1928 **Reichstag** election.

Since the late nineteenth century, German Jews had reacted and adjusted to the antisemitic challenge in different ways. Many discounted antisemitism as merely the expression of a dying prejudice and took their increasing constitutional rights, improving economic position, and rising social status as proof that anti-Jewish agitation would soon disappear. This not-implausible vision of the future with the accompanying habit of ignoring discordant notes in the present was one reason why many German Jews would find it so hard to take the Nazis at their word. Yet the German Jewish community's reaction to antisemitism before 1933 was by no means ostrichlike. Well ahead of Hitler's rise to power, many responded to signs of prejudice or discrimination by becoming organized, forming a range of associations for Jewish men, women, and young adults that helped express common interests, aims, and desires. Of course, not all Jewish organizations were formed with a view to combating antisemitism. Some, like the League of Jewish Women (**Jüdischer Frauenbund**, or JFB) with its fifty thousand members, saw themselves as part of a larger German, indeed international, organizational environment, in this case as a partner in the bourgeois feminist movement. Others, like the Zionist Association for Germany (**Zionistische Vereinigung für Deutschland**, or ZVfD) drew many of their ideas from German nationalism while accepting

---

7. Carol Fink, *Defending the Rights of Others: The Great Powers, the Jews, and International Minority Protection, 1878–1938* (New York: Cambridge University Press, 2004).

the notion of a "Jewish question" that required Jews in the Diaspora to aim at creating a Jewish homeland in Palestine.[8]

It was certainly the need to fight antisemitism that triggered the formation of the most influential organization within German Jewry: the Central Association of German Citizens of the Jewish Faith (**Centralverein deutscher Staatsbürger jüdischen Glaubens,** or CV) established in 1893. Yet, as its name indicated, the organization epitomized the prevailing desire among German Jews to be both fully accepted as German citizens and at the same time to maintain adherence to the Jewish faith. With its large membership (in the 1920s, between sixty and seventy thousand individuals, and many more through organizational affiliations) and well-established geographical structure (local branches in towns and cities and regional offices for the German states), the CV in many respects embodied the dominant spirit among German Jewry. Until the organization's dissolution in the wake of the November 1938 pogroms, its leadership consisted of predominantly male professionals, mostly lawyers, who decided on policy matters from the head office in Berlin and communicated with members in the pages of the widely circulated *CV-Zeitung.* The recent discovery of the CV's papers in a Moscow archive has shown just how significant it was in coordinating responses to the Nazi Party before and in the first years after 1933. For this reason, considerable space is accorded in this volume to the CV's actions and perceptions.[9]

The CV's interpretation of what it meant to be a Jew in Germany, influential though it was, did not remain uncontested. Challenge came not only from the racial antisemitism of the political Right but also from within the Jewish community itself. The most influential competitor in the struggle to define German Jewish identity was the Zionist movement. Bolstered by the Balfour Declaration of 1917 and the rising antisemitic tide in postwar

8. Marion A. Kaplan, *The Jewish Feminist Movement in Germany: The Campaigns of the Jüdischer Frauenbund, 1904–1938* (London: Greenwood, 1979); Hagit Lavsky, *Before Catastrophe: The Distinctive Path of German Zionism* (Detroit, MI: Wayne State University Press, 1996).

9. See Arnold Paucker, "Jewish Self-Defence," in *The Jews in Nazi Germany*, 55–65; Marjorie Lamberti, "The Jewish Defence in Germany after the National-Socialist Seizure of Power," *LBIYB* 42 (1997): 135–47. For an in-depth study of the CV's history, see Avraham Barkai, *"Wehr Dich!" Der Centralverein deutscher Staatsbürger jüdischen Glaubens (C.V.), 1893–1938* (Munich: C. H. Beck, 2002); on the organization's papers, see Avraham Barkai, "The C.V. and Its Archives: A Reassessment," *LBIYB* 45 (2000): 173–82. On the CV's legal defense work before 1933, see Inbal Steinitz, *Der Kampf jüdischer Anwälte gegen den Antisemitismus* (Berlin: Metropol Verlag, 2008).

Europe, the Zionists grew from a fringe group into a powerful force. True, *organized* German Zionism, with the ZVfD as its main manifestation and the *Jüdische Rundschau* as its leading newspaper, remained comparatively small in terms of membership. However, its challenge to the oligarchic structures of Jewish communal and organizational life enjoyed strong appeal among Jewish youth and non-German Jews, especially those "Eastern Jews" who saw no viable long-term perspective for Jewish life outside Palestine. Partly in recognition of Zionism's appeal, the CV's mission evolved during the 1920s from the "cultivation of German sentiment" enshrined in its statutes toward fostering a more assertive and self-aware Jewish identity. The CV understood Jewishness as encompassing more than just religiosity and thus spoke to the needs of many in search of their cultural roots.[10] Despite its claim to political neutrality and nonsectarian orientation, until 1933 the CV's attitude toward Zionism and its Eastern Jewish supporters remained ambiguous at best and confrontational in times of crisis.

The CV's ability to develop a constructive dialogue with Zionism was further complicated after World War I by the fact that a number of Germany's assimilated Jews were now swept along by the hypernationalism permeating German society. On the right of the Jewish political spectrum, new organizations emerged combining a vehement anti-Zionism with outspoken assertions of German nationalism. Among these groups, the Reich Association of Jewish Frontline Soldiers (**Reichsbund jüdischer Frontsoldaten**, or RjF) had the biggest mass appeal. Fringe groups like the Association of National German Jews (**Verband nationaldeutscher Juden**, or VndJ) went even further in the direction of embracing German ultranationalism (though still trying to keep its distance from *völkisch* racism). While the RjF in particular might cooperate with the CV in the fight against German antisemitism, the CV thus found itself the object of attacks from Zionists on one side and pro–German nationalist Jews on the other, a predicament that persisted into the early phase of Nazi rule.[11]

---

10. Ismar Schorsch, *Jewish Reactions to German Anti-Semitism, 1870–1914* (New York: Columbia University Press, 1972); Barkai, "*Wehr Dich!,*" 370–72.

11. Avraham Barkai, "Between *Deutschtum* and *Judentum*: Ideological Controversies inside the Centralverein," in *In Search of Jewish Community: Jewish Identities in Germany and Austria, 1918–1933*, ed. Michael Brenner and Derek J. Penslar (Bloomington: Indiana University Press, 1998), 74–91.

Flyer by Reichsbund jüdischer Frontsoldaten for the 1932 Reichstag election. Printed from Arnold Paucker, *Der jüdische Abwehrkampf gegen Antisemitismus und Nationalsozialismus in den letzten Jahren der Weimarer Republik* (Hamburg: Leibniz Verlag, 1968), 213.

The seed of hatred and lies

A sower passes through the land, spreads hatred and lies with his hand. **Germans, beware of this poisonous seed!** From it sprouts the slander that during the Great War the Jews were cowards and shirkers. 12,000 fallen Jewish soldiers bear witness for us who defended the Fatherland with their life and property. **Reichsbund jüdischer Frontsoldaten e.V.**

Even so, no organization in Germany acquired as much experience in the fight against Nazi antisemitism as the CV. The CV recognized that the Nazi Party was using antisemitism as only one weapon among many in its political arsenal; it was equally clear, however, that the "Jewish question" represented a firm article of faith for many party members who otherwise disagreed with one another and that it had huge social appeal on which future political success could be built. Traditionally, the CV's main weapons were the law, challenging violations of existing laws in the courtroom, and education, publicly exposing antisemitic myths. In the late years of the Weimar Republic, however, the

CV leadership recognized that the Nazis' increasing political success might call for new measures. The basis for a functioning democracy was being eroded as the political extremes, the Nazi and the Communist parties, battled it out on the streets. German elites turned away from the Weimar consensus toward the Right. In the struggle for equal rights and respect for minorities, only the Social Democrats remained as a staunch ally. Despite reluctance from more traditionally minded CV leaders and pronounced opposition from its right wing, a small group of younger functionaries around **Hans Reichmann** tried to devise new tactics. Antisemitism, they argued, could be best combated by analyzing the sources of Nazi successes among the masses and counteracting their aggressive propaganda with similar means, thus mobilizing a broad audience for anti-antisemitic opposition. Consequently, the CV redirected its efforts to the fields of mass propaganda and political agitation with flyers and publications distributed in large quantities throughout Germany.

The CV's fight against antisemitism failed above all because of German elites' unwillingness to stand up and be counted. The Right's irreconcilable enmity toward the Weimar Republic, derisively dubbed the "Jewish republic" or the "Weimar system," now regained mass appeal during the economic depression of the late 1920s and early 1930s. The result was what Hans Mommsen has called the "dissolution of the parliamentary system from within."[12] In a political atmosphere "heavy with crisis and apocalypse," as Detlev Peukert has characterized Weimar's end phase, "racism and nationalism, anti-Marxism and anti-Bolshevism, anti-liberalism and cults of 'leadership' flourished."[13] In this situation, many public servants, businessmen, professionals, and military men in the Reich found the Nazis' constant calls for a revision of the "Versailles peace treaty of shame" and for the creation of an antiegalitarian "people's community" (***Volksgemeinschaft***) appealing. When in September 1931 roughly five hundred Nazi storm troopers (**SA** men) went on the rampage on the Kurfürstendamm, Berlin's most elegant boulevard, attacking people who in their mind "looked Jewish," the Centralverein protested against what it called the "first serious, outspokenly anti-Jewish eruption" in Germany's capital and deplored the absence of a "front of decent people" (*Front der Anständigen*).[14] There were foot soldiers among the non-Jewish population but no leaders to create such a front; instead of human decency, race hatred became an increasingly accepted part of German politics.

---

12. Hans Mommsen, *The Rise and Fall of Weimar Democracy* (Chapel Hill: University of North Carolina Press, 1996), 303.

13. Detlev J. K. Peukert, *The Weimar Republic: The Crisis of Classical Modernity* (New York: Hill and Wang, 1993), 231, 242.

14. *CV-Zeitung*, September 18, 1931, 457–58, 465–66; quoted in Barkai, *"Wehr Dich!,"* 259.

Having abandoned Weimar constitutional democracy, and with political choices increasingly polarized between a Communist revolution or a Nazi take-over, some key elites moved even closer to Hitler. Nothing attested to this constellation more clearly than his appointment on January 30, 1933, as German chancellor in a coalition government numerically dominated not by the Nazi Party but by representatives of the traditional political Right. Still, the CV did not abandon its efforts to defend Jewish interests, even under the changed circumstance of Nazi rule, and many of the documents in this volume attest to its continued role. Complemented by sources from individual Jews, the documentation generated by organizations such as the CV and featured in this volume offers unique insights into the multiple layers of Jewish reactions to persecution in the first five years of Nazi rule.

This book and the other four volumes in the *Jewish Responses to Persecution* series are not designed to give a comprehensive account of what Germans and others did to Jews, although each chapter in Volume I is introduced by a brief sketch of new developments in Nazi policy making. In retrospect we see an uneven, yet increasingly radical, process of segregation that prior to the beginning of World War II would bring about the "social death" of German Jews[15] and end in the destruction of European Jewry.[16] From the contemporary Jewish perspective, however, this linearity was not so apparent and the outcome anything but certain. The documents in this volume, and indeed in this series, reveal a vast spectrum of Jewish hopes, expectations, perceptions, and actions that evolved unevenly over time. Contemporaries drew hope from their past experiences and the apparent sturdiness of traditional civic values but struggled to reconcile this hope with the violent and rapid changes brought about by Hitler's appointment and the rabid actions of his henchmen. The result was a most confusing kaleidoscope of impressions that prompted an equally diverse set of reactions. Some German Jews, like Otto Heinsheimer whose story opened the introduction to this source series, emigrated early. More followed later. Some, insofar as was possible, resisted, and many accommodated themselves to changing realities while trying to eke out the possibilities for a meaningful and bearable life.

---

15. Marion Kaplan derives the term *social death* from Orlando Paterson's study of slavery and applies it to German Jews to signal "their subjection, their excommunication from the 'legitimate social or moral community,' and their relegation to a perpetual state of dishonor" (Kaplan, *Between Dignity*, 5).

16. For essential overview studies on the Holocaust, see Raul Hilberg, *The Destruction of the European Jews*, rev. exp. ed. (New Haven, CT: Yale University Press, 2003); Saul Friedländer, *Nazi Germany and the Jews*, vol. 1, *The Years of Persecution, 1933–1939*; vol. 2, *The Years of Extermination, 1939–1945* (New York: HarperCollins, 1997, 2007); Leni Yahil, *The Holocaust: The Fate of European Jewry, 1932–1945* (New York: Oxford University Press, 1990).

The sources that document these actions and reactions vary as much as the mental world of the people who produced them. Yet, often they fall short of what a reader looking back with hindsight might expect. Many, perhaps most, published reports produced by organizations read like trite descriptions of facts, abstract reflections, or unrealistic appeals to stay calm during the coming storm; even diary entries and personal letters tend to lack the drama and urgency contained in accounts written later with greater knowledge of what the Nazis were capable of. Often, self-censorship was involved. In 1936, Alfred Wiener, a former leading CV functionary and, since his emigration in early 1933, an active documenter of Nazi anti-Jewish policy, provided the London Board of Deputies of British Jews with a brief synopsis of what he called "the work of enlightenment by German Jewry before 1933." Wiener and the recipients of the report sensed its explosive potential, not because "German Jewry did so little against antisemitism" prior to Hitler's coming to power but because "it would be very dangerous to publish now what it did." "The Nazis," the board of deputies' press department wrote to the organization's president, Neville Laski, "could easily make use of it, and those Jews who still remain in Germany would be made to suffer even more than now."[17]

From the very beginning of Nazi rule, therefore, fears of a police clampdown or denunciation clearly prompted German Jews to avoid leaving a paper trail of critical thoughts until safely beyond the Third Reich's grasp. As the above example shows, even after leaving Germany's shores, fears for those staying behind continued to constrain what the emigrants recorded. Moreover, there was another obstacle to providing rich and stirring descriptions of what was happening. Writers of contemporary accounts may well have had a sense of impending catastrophe in the back of their minds, but the incremental changes to everyday life often did not offer opportunity for such forebodings to find immediate expression in their texts—or seem to justify sharing them with others. Because contemporaries were often simply reacting to the particular challenges of the day, they could not or did not have an eye to the larger picture, although here records generated by well-informed community leaders, as well as reflections from Jews who escaped into exile, offer some correctives. Nevertheless, as we hope this volume shows, some documents do speak to us with great immediacy and show how radically Jewish life was transformed even before "*Kristallnacht*," the nationwide pogrom of November 1938, shattered Jewish lives across the length and breadth of Germany.

---

17. Letter by Gustav Warburg, Board of Deputies of British Jews, London, to its president, Neville Laski, London, July 3, 1936; National Archive of the United Kingdom, Kew, Acc 3121 B04 CE010.

Perhaps more than other volumes, this book would not have come about without the crucial help of far more individuals and institutions than we can acknowledge here. We are grateful to the William S. and Ina Levine Foundation and the Blum Family Foundation for their generous support, as well as to the Dorot Foundation, which funded summer research fellows at the Center for Advanced Holocaust Studies involved in our project. Frank Bajohr (FZGH) and Frank Mecklenburg (LBINY) provided crucial assistance in the form of archival material outside the USHMM. For their good advice, we are greatly indebted to two Museum survivor volunteers, Margit Meissner and Isaac D. Nehama. Jan Lambertz deserves special credit for being the steadiest, most reliable and devoted collaborator we had in the course of the project. Beate Meyer (Hamburg), Marion Kaplan (New York), and Michael Wildt (Berlin) agreed to review an earlier version of this volume; their input was invaluable for getting us on what we hope is the right track. Atina Grossmann (New York) and Pamela Nadell (Washington, D.C.) shared their insights into the usefulness of a source edition for classroom teaching, and Susanne Heim (Berlin) helped out with background checks in Germany. Peter Crane and Gershon Greenberg offered valuable advice. At AltaMira Press we would like to thank Jack Meinhardt, Marissa Parks, Elaine McGarraugh, and Jennifer Kelland Fagan for their dedication to the project.

Within the USHMM, we have received critical support from a range of individuals. Paul A. Shapiro, director of the Center for Advanced Holocaust Studies, conceived of the project many years ago and remained unwavering in his support. Gwen Sherman and Wrenetta Richards maintained their good humor in the face of forms and figures. The staffs of the museum's library, archives, and photographic reference section were of enormous assistance; we would especially like to thank Michlean Amir, Judy Cohen, Ronald Coleman, Rebecca Erbelding, Nancy Hartman, Steven Kanaley, Henry Mayer, Vincent Slatt, Leslie Swift, Holly Vorhies, Caroline Waddell, and Mark Ziomek. Within the Center for Advanced Holocaust Studies, special thanks go to Anatol Steck and Radu Ioanid (International Archival Programs), Victoria Barnett (Church Relations), Patricia Heberer and Severin Hochberg (Historian's Office), and Lisa Yavnai (Fellowship Program). The staff historians on the Applied Scholars team—Martin Dean, Emil Kerenji, Geoffrey Megargee, and Leah Wolfson—enhanced this project in a number of ways, if only by tolerating the series editor's office door being closed on occasion. Our special thanks go to the members of the USHMM's Academic Committee, who supported the project over the years in more ways than one, and particularly to Doris Bergen, Christopher Browning, Steven T. Katz, and Nechama Tec who commented on the manuscript.

PART I
THE BATTLES OF 1933

A SERIES OF ARTICLES on the "Jewish question" dominated the January
26, 1933, issue of the weekly *CV-Zeitung*. Under the headline "Where Are
the Voices of the Wise?" the top of the front page was devoted to a eulogy given
by the Hamburg banker **Max Warburg** for the recently deceased Berlin textile
magnate and philanthropist Dr. James Simon. In the speech, Simon's own life
almost disappeared behind Warburg's condemnation of the anti-Jewish forces
at work in Germany. Where were the men who would go against the tide?
When would veterans of the world war, who had experienced the courage of
their Jewish fellow soldiers firsthand, stand up and be counted? Warburg's angry
lament was followed by a lengthy article entitled "It Will Only Get Worse in
the Future."[1] Responding to a recent Nazi outburst in the **Reichstag** on the
"Jewish question," the detailed, hard-hitting, and alarming article examined the
state of the Nazi Party and enumerated its most recent antisemitic utterances.
This piece in turn was followed by an account of the **Centralverein deutscher
Staatsbürger jüdischen Glaubens'** (CV) educational work across the length
and breadth of Germany as it battled to inform the public of the truth about
the "Jewish question." For the *CV-Zeitung*'s readers the threat posed to German
Jews by Nazi antisemitism could thus not have been clearer, particularly since
the paper had addressed the problem for some time. Yet the January 26 issue
also offered hope: despite the Nazis' recent success in regional elections, their
party faced a financial crisis, a crisis in leadership, and inner dissension.

---

1. *CV-Zeitung*, January 26, 1933.

A week later the *CV-Zeitung* had the unpleasant duty of reporting Hitler's appointment as chancellor on January 30, 1933.[2] "German Jews look into the future," the paper noted, "gravely and with concern." Yet for all the obvious worries, the issue reveals both how difficult it was for contemporaries to make sense of the situation confronting them and how difficult it remains for us as later readers to interpret the sources correctly. Given the powerful exposés of previous months, the *CV-Zeitung*'s readers will have been as alarmed by what the paper did not say as by what it did. The measured approach, the holding out of hope that perhaps some good might just come of the new government, stood in sharp contrast to previous assessments of the Nazi Party. The changed political situation was forcing the paper to be diplomatic. It had to weigh the impact of its words not just on its usual readership but on those who were now in power. Overnight, and before any obvious threat from Nazi thugs forced editors to be cautious, the public voice of Jewry had lost its clarity.

Even if the *CV-Zeitung* had allowed itself the luxury of saying exactly what it thought, the situation it confronted remained hard to read. For all Germans the inclusion of Nazi leaders in the national government on January 30, 1933, was clearly a major development. In the general population, those leaning politically to the Right, though they might harbor some anxieties about the Nazis' socialist posturing, tended to welcome the prospect of a "national revolution" that would restore Germany's internal stability and international status. Germans supporting the Left saw Hitler as a henchman of big capital and a harbinger of militarism and dictatorship. To a certain extent, German Jews, too, were divided along such political lines, but most were also keenly aware of the spreading antisemitic threat. Still, would Hitler's rule turn out to be just as fleeting as the fragmentary cabinets of the **Weimar Republic** that had preceded it? The *CV-Zeitung* pointed out the enormous contradictions contained within the new cabinet. The Nazis were working alongside conservative nationalists whom they had only recently decried as Jewish capitalists. Even if the coalition survived, the question was whether Hitler had triumphed or been tamed. The *New York Times* headline on January 31, "Hitler Made Chancellor of Germany. But Coalition Cabinet Limits Power. Centrists Hold Balance in Reichstag," echoed a perception shared by many. They expected concessions and compromise in a coalition government seemingly dominated by leaders from other parties and dependent on the support of Reich President **Paul von Hindenburg**. Few believed that Nazi programs would serve as the sole blueprint for the cabinet's policy making.[3] Whatever the case, the *CV-Zeitung* surely

---

2. *CV-Zeitung*, February 2, 1933.

3. On the Nazi seizure of power, among a great many other titles, see Peter Fritzsche, *Germans into Nazis* (Cambridge, MA: Harvard University Press, 1998); Ian Kershaw, *Hitler, 1889–1936: Hubris* (London: Allen Lane, 1998), ch. 10.

made one of the truest claims ever to appear in print when it predicted that after the dust had settled, political and social scientists would look back and study the developments of the coming weeks with enormous interest.

By the summer of 1933, however, hopes that the Nazi regime would be just a brief interlude were fading. By dint of emergency decrees and the *Ermächtigungsgesetz* ("Enabling Act"), the government had vastly extended its powers. The president remained in office, but his legislative role had passed to the chancellor. Most of the Nazis' political opponents had been marginalized, while local and regional governments had come increasingly under central control. The other parties had gone into forced or voluntary liquidation, and the trade unions were all shut down. All kinds of groups, from stamp-collecting societies to professional associations, subjected themselves to a process of *Gleichschaltung*: they brought their organizations "into line" with the objectives of the new government. The press followed that trend, and even trustworthy old dailies such as the *Frankfurter Zeitung* grew cautious about what they put into print.[4]

As the Nazi movement threw off the constraints of coalition rule, it moved forward on Jewish policy. After a spate of physical attacks and boycotts at the local and regional levels, a national boycott and purge of the civil service followed in April. But were these just measures to placate its rank and file or the first steps toward achieving racial homogeneity? How committed were the regime and its top leadership to the systematic exclusion of Jews and Jewish influence from German society? Who was in charge of instituting the antisemitic program, what were its concrete goals, and how far would it go? The Nazis never appointed a minister for Jewish affairs; nor did they create a budget for Jewish policy. The exact relationship between their party and the state was never clarified. In the stormy first months of the Hitler era, few could thus discern what answers to the "Jewish question" Hitler and his supporters were going to come up with; indeed, most historians doubt that the party itself had any sense of the extremes that were to follow.[5]

Another imponderable in the early period of Nazi rule was the "institutional conscience" of the nation in the form of the courts and the churches. How far would they go to maintain traditional norms and protections for vilified minorities? The Weimar Republic's violent political climate and the years of unmitigated antisemitic propaganda had certainly left their mark on the general public, the

---

4. On *Gleichschaltung*, see Sebastian Haffner, *Defying Hitler: A Memoir* (New York: Farrar, Straus and Giroux, 2002); Kershaw, *Hitler, 1889–1936*, 435–36, 469, 479–81, (on the *Frankfurter Zeitung*'s stance), 509–10; Martin Broszat, *The Hitler State: The Foundation and Development of the Internal Structure of the Third Reich* (New York: Longman, 1981), 66–67.

5. See Raul Hilberg, *The Destruction of the European Jews*, rev. exp. ed. (New Haven, CT: Yale University Press, 2003), 1:40–43.

middle classes, and especially the military, bureaucrats, and other elites. Like all other state officials, members of the German justice system were now brought into line—if they did not actively sympathize with the Nazi agenda from the start. Given the close ideological affinities between Hitler's party and the nationalist-*völkisch* Right, it was, in retrospect, perhaps unsurprising that judges and lawyers who had not themselves been punitively targeted accepted the view that the exclusionary laws enacted in the spring of 1933 were "for the protection of the German *Volk* and state."[6] At the time, the alacrity with which non-Nazi elites hastened to provide their assent to Nazi measures still shocked Germany's Jews, despite insights by Max Warburg and others about the failure of reputable citizens to stand up and be counted. As it turned out, many bureaucrats surpassed Nazi activists in inventing new tools that could help "cleanse" the Fatherland of potential enemies, most notably Communists and Jews.[7]

After the destruction of the left-wing parties and trade unions in the spring of 1933, the churches remained the last significant social force outside the direct control of the regime that could speak out against racial persecution. For the major Christian churches in Germany, however, the Nazi revolution was at least a welcome alternative to a Communist one. Where they were not actively embracing the Nazi cause with striking zeal—as many Protestant churchmen did—the churches' priority was to defend their institutional integrity against the assault of the racial state and to make sure they would not lose members to organizations created by the new regime. For the rest, they were quiescent, particularly in relation to Jewish policy. Traditional Christian antisemitism had been bolstered by the widespread view that "Jewish influence" dominated important parts of the German economy and culture. Like the population at large, many church functionaries thus had at least some sympathy for a national program to reduce the presence of Jews in public life.[8]

6. For the German judicial system, see Lothar Gruchmann, *Justiz im Dritten Reich, 1933–1940: Anpassung und Unterwerfung in der Ära Gürtner* (Munich: Oldenbourg, 2001).

7. Saul Friedländer, *Nazi Germany and the Jews*, vol. 1, *The Years of Persecution, 1933–1939* (New York: HarperCollins, 1997), 34–36; Claudia Koonz, *The Nazi Conscience* (Cambridge, MA: Harvard University Press, 2003), 163–89. For an overview of studies on German public opinion during the Third Reich, see Ian Kershaw, *Hitler, the Germans, and the Final Solution* (New Haven, CT: Yale University Press, 2008), 3–11.

8. Friedländer, *Nazi Germany*, 1:41–49; Kevin P. Spicer, *Hitler's Priests: Catholic Clergy and National Socialism* (DeKalb: Northern Illinois University Press, 2008); Doris L. Bergen, *Twisted Cross: The German Christian Movement in the Third Reich* (Chapel Hill: University of North Carolina Press, 1996); Michael Phayer, *The Catholic Church and the Holocaust, 1930–1965* (Bloomington: Indiana University Press, 2000); Manfred Gailus, ed., *Kirchliche Amtshilfe: Die Kirche und die Judenverfolgung im "Dritten Reich"* (Göttingen: Vandenhoeck & Ruprecht, 2008).

Under the shock of early events, German Jews began to reevaluate Germany's recent history and their place in German society. Having consigned antisemitism to the scrap heap of outmoded, if residually dangerous, ideas, they now began to see in the Nazi rise to power merely the latest example of a pattern familiar throughout the history of Jews in the Diaspora. As unprecedented as the Nazis' elevation to ruling party was, the threat of increased persecution by rabid antisemites seemed like the recurrence of an all-too-common historical Jewish experience and an expansion of anti-Jewish policies already practiced in varying degrees in a host of countries. A significant number of German Jews decided that the writing was on the wall in a country they could no longer regard as home. In the course of 1933, thirty-seven thousand left Germany, the highest annual number of Jewish emigrants until 1938. Around three-quarters of these went to other, mainly neighboring, European countries; indeed, in this first year of Nazi rule, France alone absorbed one-quarter of all Jewish emigrants.[9] (All figures are somewhat unreliable, however, because many in this first stage crossed the borders illegally or without being recorded.) Around 5,392 emigrated to Palestine,[10] while initially only a tiny fraction went to the United States—in the first six months of 1933, only 72 Jewish immigrants from Germany are recorded as having arrived there.[11]

Yet, for all the uncertainties and the shock at the massive groundswell of anti-Jewish activity that swept the country and found its first, most visible expression in the boycott of April 1, 1933, many German Jews retained some hope. Non-Jewish allies appeared here and there to intervene, be it the old Reich President Hindenburg, who sympathized with calls for special concessions for German Jewish veterans of World War I, mid-level bureaucrats in Berlin ministries who agreed to listen to complaints voiced by Jewish leaders, or nameless members of the public who showed sympathy for beleaguered Jewish shop owners during the boycott. It remained unclear whether these examples of support were indications of opposition to the regime's measures or mere relics of civic decency. Were the main targets of the "national revolution" not the Nazis' political enemies, the Communists and Social Democrats? How long could the Nazis' commitment to anti-Jewish measures be sustained in the economic and diplomatic crisis that marked the early 1930s?

---

9. Herbert A. Strauss, "Jewish Emigration from Germany: Nazi Policies and Jewish Responses," *LBIYB* 25 (1980): 351, 355.

10. See *AJYB* 36 (1934–1935): 403.

11. *AJYB* 36 (1934–1935): 383. In the year from July 1933 to June 1934, however, the figure for the United States had already risen substantially to 1,786, or around 43 percent of all Jewish immigration to the United States in the period; see *AJYB* 37 (1935–1936): 366; *AJYB* 39 (1937–1938): 759.

In the first year after the Nazi takeover, Jewish responses thus spanned the full spectrum, from despair in the face of such aggressive attacks on hard-won civic equality to hope that Hitler's reign would be brief. Some fought for what remained of their rights and status, while others worked to adapt their own or organized Jewish life to the changed situation. The range of responses is even greater if one includes not only self-conscious and devout Jews but also those who had not regarded themselves as Jewish until the regime branded them as such. The sudden and growing external pressure forced German Jews to reevaluate how they perceived themselves, how their institutions should respond, and what opportunities they saw for a future life in Germany.

CHAPTER 1

Confronting the
Nazi Revolution

EARLY WEEKS

A sense of shock, mitigated by the hope that this new government would not last longer than its predecessors, dominated the early reaction of German Jews to Hitler's appointment. The assessment offered by the weekly journal *Der Israelit* (*The Israelite*) in its February 2, 1933, editorial was fairly typical of the Jewish press. Only a brief aside about ritual slaughter offered a distinctive note, reflecting *Der Israelit*'s particular position as the voice of orthodox German Jewry.

Weighing up the dual potential of antisemitism, the editorial's author noted the obvious dangers inherent in anti-Jewish agitation but also implicitly acknowledged that antisemitic rhetoric might function as a safety valve, releasing the pressures of discontent. Beyond the use of temporary enabling acts and the bleak prospect of what he called a "cold pogrom"—most likely he was thinking of state-sanctioned, yet isolated, incidents of violence against individual Jews—the writer was clearly unsure of what the new regime would do. Much depended on how state bureaucrats and law-enforcement agents would react if the Nazi Party program became the road map for government policy.

As a reference to Germany's European great power status reminded the journal's readers, the international situation was another unknown variable in the equation. What pressures could and would foreign powers exert in a world in which the Great Depression and the breakdown of world trade had limited most nations' willingness to look beyond pressing problems at home? How important would it be for Germany to adhere to the rules of the international community? While it reveals the paper's writers wrestling with these issues, this editorial poses, as indeed it posed its contemporary readers, an interpretative challenge typical of many Jewish public statements in the first year of Nazi rule. There is no reason to doubt the author's sincerity; still, we cannot be sure that some of the writer's bleaker assessments or deeper fears were not being suppressed. The paper may well have been wary of sketching out negative scenarios that might alarm readers or, worse, be seized on by radical groups within the ruling party.

DOCUMENT I-I: "The New Situation," *Der Israelit*, February 2, 1933, 1–2 (translated from German).

Hitler's cabinet, established on Monday at midday in Berlin, weighs heavily on the minds of all German Jewry and, in fact, all those circles that view the overheated rhetoric of today's exaggerated nationalistic race fanaticism as an obstacle to human civilization and historical progress.

We do not subscribe to the view that Herr Hitler and his friends, now finally in possession of the power they have desired for so long, will enact the proposals circulating in the *Angriff* or the *Völkischer Beobachter* newspapers[1]; they will not suddenly divest German Jews of their constitutional rights, lock them away in race ghettos, or subject them to the avaricious and murderous impulses of the mob. They not only <u>cannot</u> do this because many other crucial factors hold their powers in check, ranging from the Reich president to some of the political parties affiliated with them, but they also clearly do not <u>want</u> to go this route, for when one acts as a European world power, the whole atmosphere is more conducive to ethical reflection upon one's better self than to revisiting one's earlier oppositional role: operating as a European world power means that one seeks an enduring place in the harmonious exchange of peoples of culture. And beyond that, it is clear that the powers at Wilhelmstrasse[2] no longer see demagogic appeals designed to heat up mass gatherings of the *Volk* as strictly necessary. The new Prussian Minister of the Interior [Hermann Göring] can perform a far greater service to the old comrades in arms and party friends by rejuvenating the huge, state civil service along National Socialist lines than by making open concessions to the brutal manifestations of hatred of Jews.

---

1. *Der Angriff* and *Völkischer Beobachter* were Nazi Party newspapers.
2. This was the site of major government agencies in Berlin.

Not to recognize the gravity of the situation, however, would be inexcusably optimistic. The less the new men in power prove able to perform legislative miracles for the German people as they struggle with hunger and hardship, the more they will find it attractive instead, in order to appear to be doing something, to be seen as at least turning a few sections of the Nazi Party's racial theory program into political practice; this could easily be accomplished—without resorting to the creation of sensationalistic and compromising laws against Jews—rather by staging a "cold pogrom" [*trockenes Pogrom*], by systematically excluding Jews from economic and cultural life, by laying the path for their economic and cultural starvation.

In a National Socialist civil service, to what extent will the old Prussian civil servant's sense of duty prevail over long-nurtured antisemitic instincts and be able to prevent chicanery toward Jews and the abridgment of their legal rights? To what extent will a police force with a National Socialist at its helm be reliable and impartial in every case involving Jews (or even Socialist or Communist citizens)? Only the future will reveal whether these questions and concerns are justified.

The way things stand, it seems to be the lesser evil that—through the Center Party's toleration of the new government and despite a short-term Enabling Act—the foundation on which the parliament and its system of checks and balances rest is upheld (one need only think, for example, of the dangers that might otherwise threaten the *shechitah* [ritual slaughter]). This status quo is more desirable than a vote of no confidence that would bring about dissolution of the Reichstag and, with it, dictatorship without bounds and the introduction of government experiments under the mantle of a state of emergency.

If mainstream German Zionism as embodied in the Zionist Association (**Zionistische Vereinigung für Deutschland**, or ZVfD), presented a more upbeat assessment, this was not because of any positive expectations associated with the Nazi takeover as such or with German public opinion. Indeed, Zionists took the "seizure of power" as proof that it was futile to expect that antisemitism would ever disappear in the Diaspora. But the hope for Zionists was that the political changes would help to crystallize a new kind of Jewish revival, above all, the clearer emergence of a Jewish national consciousness.

In his first article after Hitler's appointment, **Robert Weltsch**, the editor of the ZVfD's weekly *Jüdische Rundschau*, offered an eloquent and influential German Zionist response. He left the reader in no doubt about the challenges that lay ahead and showed awareness of one of the distinctive features of the new situation: Nazism was not organized along the lines of traditional political parties, limited to a narrow group of formal members. Instead, it was a broad social movement whose influence reached well beyond the limits of those who held a party membership card. Nevertheless, contained within the threat confronting Germany's Jews was also an opportunity. Jews could no longer forget who they were.

DOCUMENT 1-2: "Inner Security," *Jüdische Rundschau*, February 3, 1933, 45–46[3] (translated from German).

Overnight the event that no-one wanted to believe would happen has become fact: Hitler is chancellor of the German Reich. This new development forces us to confront the reality of our underlying situation. [. . .] The truth is that pressure from the National Socialists has affected life in Germany for some time. Quite apart from the fact that Jews are being systematically shut out of economic and cultural life, antisemitism has come to dominate the psychological atmosphere. This actually also has the effect that the Jew again knows that he is a Jew, for no one lets him forget it. But the feeling of being completely surrounded by people who take their spiritual cues from the *Angriff* and the *Völkischer Beobachter*, with their infernal agitation against Jews, is hardly a cheering thought. We were always convinced—and the *Jüdische Rundschau* repeatedly emphasized this—that the National Socialist movement, for some time now no longer a mere political party, has become the authoritative source for public opinion and would in the end also seize positions of power. [. . .]

It would be ridiculous for us to say that Jews are perfect or that they have no faults. It is we ourselves who suffer most from certain phenomena in Jewish life. Zionism clearly recognized forty years ago that our community needed to renew from within. We know that we are dragging remnants of the old ghetto along with us. And likewise—perhaps even worse—we are burdened with the by-products of assimilation, an assimilation that gave us "freedom on the outside, but a feeling of servitude within." But we do now also have a <u>new Jewry</u> that seeks to free itself both from the remnants of the ghetto and also from the damage brought on by assimilation; a Jewry that has found its way back to itself, that knows its own worth, that fearlessly defends itself, that knows how to maintain distance and keep its composure, that confronts its enemies not with envy and arrogance but with

---

3. Also printed in *Ja-Sagen zum Judentum: Eine Aufsatzreihe der "Jüdischen Rundschau" zur Lage der deutschen Juden* (Berlin: Verlag der "Jüdischen Rundschau," 1933), 154–58.

a clear countenance. This new Jewry, internally secure, ignores all insults and assaults and keeps its head held high. To make this work, everything depends on freeing the Jews from their atomization and self-estrangement and drawing them together for the Jewish cause.

The *Jüdische Rundschau*'s criticism of the remnants of assimilation was aimed at the German Jewish majority, most notably its biggest organization, the **Centralverein deutscher Staatsbürger jüdischen Glaubens** (CV). On the night of Hitler's appointment, the CV came out with a statement by its presiding board expressing the conviction that, despite good reasons to mistrust the new government, "no one will dare to touch our constitutional rights" and asked its members to stay calm.[4] Of course, this was less a confident prediction of what lay ahead than a strategic statement that sought both to allay German Jews' fears and to exhort the new government to exercise moderation. The CV had waged a protracted fight against the Nazi Party in the late 1920s and early 1930s, and clearly many CV leaders must have felt far more serious foreboding in private. Yet, even the pessimists among the Jewish leaders were probably as little prepared as rank-and-file members for the avalanche of disturbing events that followed. Many of those who emigrated early on did so with the expectation of returning after a period of temporary exile.[5]

After the burning of the **Reichstag** building and the restriction of personal rights in late February, Nazi activists began to switch their sights from Communists and others on the political Left toward Jews. The *völkisch* identification of Jews with communism, irrespective of actual facts, abetted this process. In conjunction with the national election on March 5, the CV issued a statement assuring German Jews of its tireless fight against "unwarranted attacks" on Jews and "that Germany will remain Germany and that no one can rob us of our native soil and our Fatherland."[6]

The March election consolidated the Nazis' position without bringing them their hoped for absolute majority. A wave of anti-Jewish measures subsequently swept through German cities. In many localities, Jews were barred from public employment, shops owned by Jews were boycotted, and antisemites unleashed their hostility on the streets with impunity. These disturbing and increasingly frequent incidents did not form a coherent, nationwide pattern. Hitler officially called for "the strictest and blindest discipline" and prohibited "isolated actions"

---

4. *CV-Zeitung*, February 2, 1933, 1.

5. Salomon Adler-Rudel, *Jüdische Selbsthilfe unter dem Nazi-Regime, 1933–1939 im Spiegel der Berichte der Reichsvertretung der Juden in Deutschland* (Tübingen: J. C. B. Mohr, 1974), 72.

6. *CV-Zeitung*, March 9, 1933, 1.

(*Einzelaktionen*) as an affront "against the national government."[7] Yet the state apparatus followed its own anti-Jewish agenda, especially on issues that had long been contentious like *shechitah* (German: *Schächten*). Hans Kronheim, a rabbi in Bielefeld in Westphalia, wrote to his fiancée about the first tangible changes he experienced after the Nazi takeover.[8]

DOCUMENT 1-3: Letter by Hans Kronheim, Bielefeld, to Senta Wallach, Hannover, March 21, 1933, USHMMA Acc. 2008.292 box 3 (translated from German).

Dear Senta:

So that you get the news at once: I had barely finished getting ready this morning when the doorbell rang. It was the ritual butcher [*Schaucher;* *shochet*] Rosenbladt.[9] I immediately suspected something bad: ritual slaughtering [*Schächten*] has been prohibited. The ban was applied as soon as he showed up yesterday at the abattoir. And today the paper has the official notification, in bold print, on the first page of the local news.[10] Otherwise the little town is very quiet, except for the Goldbach [street in Bielefeld] showing its first swastika flag, diagonally across from me. I wonder what will come next! [. . .]

---

7. Radio speech by Hitler, March 12, 1933, quoted in *CV-Zeitung*, March 16, 1933, 1.

8. Hans Kronheim (1885–1958) served as a rabbi in Bielefeld, Westphalia, for over two decades until his emigration in 1938 to the United States with his wife, Senta (née Wallach), and two daughters (born 1934 and 1936). See *Year Book of the Central Conference of American Rabbis* (Central Conference of American Rabbis, 1960), 208; Monika Minninger, Joachim Meynert, and Friedhelm Schäffer, eds., *Antisemitisch Verfolgte registriert in Bielefeld, 1933–1945: Eine Dokumentation jüdischer Einzelschicksale* (Bielefeld: Kürbis, 1985), 119–20.

9. This may have been the *shochet* Hirsch Rosenblatt (1879–1942?). A Polish citizen, he and his wife, Frieda (née Schwarzbart), were deported out of Germany in late October 1938 with other Polish Jews. They were later sent to Auschwitz, where they perished. See Minninger, Meynert, and Schäffer, *Antisemitisch Verfolgte*, 183.

10. Since the early twentieth century, agitation against Jewish ritual slaughter had been appropriated by German antisemites as part of their agenda, often dressed up in the guise of animal protection. Already in 1926, the Bavarian diet had passed a law that outlawed ritual slaughter based on the vote of members from the Nazi, Communist, and Social Democratic parties, causing widespread protest by German Jewish organizations. After the Nazi takeover, prohibiting *shechitah* was one of the first measures enacted across Germany. See Avraham Barkai, *"Wehr Dich!" Der Centralverein deutscher Staatsbürger jüdischen Glaubens (C.V.), 1893–1938* (Munich: C. H. Beck, 2002), 193–94; Havi Ben-Sasson and Amos Goldberg, eds., *Years Wherein We Have Seen Evil: Selected Aspects in the History of Religious Jewry during the Holocaust*, vol. 1, *Orthodox Jewry in Germany under the Nazi Rule* (Jerusalem: Yad Vashem, 2003), 67–82.

As it turned out, the new regime did nothing to suppress anti-Jewish measures initiated by eager activists or bureaucrats. In fact, higher-level Nazi leaders used the evidence of local unrest to build up the pressure for more concerted policy, culminating eventually in the nationwide boycott on April 1, 1933. Foreign protests had little impact; indeed, as we will see, they could inflame rather than moderate tempers. And likewise, the protests of German Jews themselves remained largely ineffectual (though the very powerlessness of the Jews should have been evidence enough to disprove as pure fantasy the antisemitic claim that an organized Jewish conspiracy controlled world events).

DOCUMENT 1-4: Jewish war veterans march in protest against the Nazi persecution of German Jews, New York City, March 23, 1933, USHMMPA WS# 11152.

Four thousand Jewish war veterans and other supporters protest against the Nazi regime's antisemitic platform and policies. Ten thousand spectators attended their march to New York's city hall on March 23, 1933. Printed with permission by the Jewish War Veterans of the USA.

Even at this early stage, the leaders of the large Jewish organizations faced a balancing act that in coming months and years would be increasingly difficult to maintain. They had to provide their members with realistic guidance while attempting to stave off a sense of panic; they had to defend their interests without creating pretexts that would unleash further antisemitic actions. They knew that at times they should speak out; yet, at times it seemed more opportune to comply with the pressure exerted by the government and to hope that developments would—as CV president **Julius Brodnitz** wrote with satisfaction, describing a recent meeting with **Hermann Göring** in March—take "a different turn than intended" by the regime.[11] In a confusing and highly charged situation, Jews both within and outside Germany looked to the CV for guidance because it had the longest experience in fighting for Jewish rights. Behind-the-scenes negotiations involving the top German Jewish functionaries seemed as important for achieving some kind of positive effect as did carefully worded public proclamations.

The growing Nazi pressure on Jewish leaders to condemn anti-Nazi protests abroad provided an early example of these dilemmas. On the one hand, German Jewish leaders knew that much of the foreign protest was justified; on the other, they took pains to establish their loyalty credentials and fend off the risk of a pogrom. In an address to the participants of a protest rally organized by Jewish organizations in New York, CV vice president Ernst Wallach exhorted them to "refrain from stirring the emotions of the audience against Germany."[12] Requests flooded into the CV head office in Berlin from German Jews, members as well as nonmembers, calling on the organization to speak out against anti-German propaganda abroad. Jewish activists differed on how best to help their fellow German Jews. From London, Albert Einstein, not normally a believer in pandering to government authorities, sent a telegram urging the CV to come out with a "public warning against foreign boycott movements"[13]—by which he meant those aimed at German exports abroad and not the anti-Jewish boycott planned by Nazi activists in Germany. By the time Einstein's appeal reached Berlin, the CV had already issued the following statement to the German and international press.

---

11. Julius Brodnitz, handwritten note, Amsterdam, April 28, 1934; USHMMA Acc. 2008.189.1 Brodnitz collection.

12. "250,000 Jews Here to Protest Today," *New York Times*, March 27, 1933, 4.

13. Telegram from Albert Einstein, London, to CV Berlin, March 23, 1933; USHMMA RG 11.001M.31, reel 100 (SAM 721-1-2292, 324). This telegram stands in marked contrast to a well-publicized letter by Einstein addressed to the CV in 1920 in which he attacked its leaders for their "softly-softly" approach (*Leisetreter*) and for not being more forceful in asserting their Jewishness vis-à-vis the antisemitic threat (printed in *Jüdische Rundschau*, December 10, 1920).

DOCUMENT 1-5: **CV press release dated March 24, 1933, *CV-Zeitung*, March 30, 1933, 2 (translated from German).**

[. . .] The CV, the largest organization of the 565,000 German Jews and faithful to the Fatherland, hereby responds to the events of recent days:

According to German press reports, a variety of foreign newspapers claim, for example, that mutilated Jewish corpses are being regularly deposited at the entrance of the Jewish cemetery in Berlin-Weissensee,[14] that Jewish girls have been forcibly rounded up in public spaces, and that hundreds of German Jews have arrived in Geneva, of whom nine-tenths— many of them children—were victims of severe abuse. All such claims are pure fiction. The CV emphatically declares that German Jewry cannot be held accountable for such irresponsible misrepresentations, which should be roundly condemned.

The German people have experienced enormous political changes in the past weeks. Acts of political revenge and violence have occurred, some of them against Jews. Both the Reich and the state governments have successfully taken steps to restore law and order as quickly as possible. The order issued by the Reich chancellor [Hitler] to refrain from all isolated actions of this nature has proven effective.[15]

Recently in particular we have seen very clearly antisemitic goals being articulated in diverse arenas of economics and life, and this naturally fills us with grave concern. As before, the CV considers the struggle against these goals to be a domestic German matter. However, we are convinced that the equal rights of German Jews, which they have fully earned in war and peace by sacrificing life and property, will not be abrogated. Bound inseparably to the German Fatherland, German Jews will continue to work with all other Germans of goodwill for the advancement of the Fatherland.

These and similar pronouncements published by German Jewish organizations—among others, by the Union of German Rabbis[16]—not only failed to have any effect on the Nazi Party and its leaders but also confused concerned observers abroad and alienated their own clientele. For some German

---

14. One of several in Berlin, this large Jewish cemetery in the district of Weissensee was designed by architect Hugo Licht and dedicated in 1880.

15. See note 7.

16. See declaration by "Allgemeiner Rabbiner-Verband in Deutschland," printed in *CV-Zeitung*, March 23, 1933, 2.

Jews with nationalistic leanings, the Jewish organizations were not going far enough in expressing their unconditional loyalty to the Fatherland. For others, like the writer of the following letter, who were experiencing the direct effects of anti-Jewish aggression or reading about it every day in Jewish newspapers, these declarations ignored grim warning signs about the future.

DOCUMENT 1-6: **Letter by Enni Hilzenrad, Berlin, to CV head office Berlin, March 25, 1933, USHMMA RG 11.001M.31, reel 100 (SAM 721-1-2292, 316–17)[17] (translated from German).**

> [. . .] Although it is true that the lives of our Jewish coreligionists have not yet been disturbed here, bit by bit every German Jewish man and woman will be robbed of any means of subsistence. [. . .] What is to become of German Jews who can no longer earn a living here? [. . .] If people of other faiths stage boycotts against us, then we Jews need to hold fast together and support each other. The Union of Rabbis[18] calls for German Jews to remain loyal to the German Fatherland. Don't they see the writing on the wall? Are we to go back into the ghettos of old? Unspeakable misery awaits us. [. . .]

BOYCOTT

As in other countries, the call for a boycott of Jewish businesses had been a familiar item on the wish lists of German antisemites. With the Nazis' rise to power, the threat for Jewish entrepreneurs became real. Preceded by local actions all over the country, the boycott movement reached a first high point in a centrally organized Nazi Party campaign that had been planned to last several days but in the end was limited to one Saturday, April 1, 1933. While the Nazi storm troopers (the **SA**) figured prominently, the success of anti-Jewish agitation depended on the reactions of the larger population. An early example from the western German town of Wesel shows that German Jews initially perceived appeals to nationalist values as a successful card with which they could trump Nazi activists.

---

17. Shorthand typist Enni Hilzenrad, born 1900 or 1901, arrived in New York via Southampton, England, in early October 1938 with her father, Mechel (a businessman), and her mother, Birtha (a housewife), as stateless Polish Jews. Enni was born in Berlin, and the family had formerly lived in the city's Pankow section. It is unclear whether they remained in the United States.

18. "Allgemeiner Rabbiner-Verband in Deutschland"; see note 16.

DOCUMENT 1-7: Letter by CV regional office Rhineland-Westphalia (Ernst Plaut)[19] to CV head office Berlin, March 20, 1933, USHMMA RG 11.001M.31, reel 101 (SAM 721-1-2321, 67) (translated from German).

Our member, Mr. Heinrich Leyens of Wesel, sends us, per our request, some flyers related to the following: SA men had taken up positions in front of the much esteemed firm Leyens and Levenbach in Wesel with large posters bearing the slogan "Don't buy from Jews." Thereupon Mr. Erich Leyens placed himself next to an SA man with the flyers and distributed them personally. In doing so he was wearing the uniform of his old regiment and his medals of honor. While the SA man was patrolling the block where the store is located, Mr. Leyens accompanied him. Soon a gigantic crowd of people gathered who grabbed the flyers and clearly expressed their sympathy. After sixty to ninety minutes, Mr. Leyens was asked by the police administration to go into the store and to distribute the flyers only inside the building. Despite the fact that even then SA men wanted to prevent customers from entering the store, an exceptionally large number of customers soon turned up and forced their way in. The visitors consisted to a large extent of ladies and gentlemen of the well-established bourgeois circles in Wesel, the wives of former officers in the Wesel regiments, etc.—thus mainly people who politically lean to the right. In the days that followed, the Leyens business received a continuous stream of visits from persons standing on the right who expressed their regret about the incident and distanced themselves firmly from the boycott. We also attach some newspaper cuttings[20] about the incident that show, among other things, that such firm interventions can be successful even today. Of course it is not always possible to proceed in this way.

The suggestion for the flyer probably came from the Jewish veterans' organization, the **Reichsbund jüdischer Frontsoldaten** (RjF), because similar versions circulated in Germany at that time.[21] Document 1-8 shows the flyer handed out by Erich Leyens.

---

19. Ernst Plaut (1899–1945) was on the board of the CV's regional office Rhineland-Westphalia. In 1939 he emigrated to London with his wife and son, where he died shortly before the end of the war. See Hermann Schröter, *Geschichte und Schicksal der Essener Juden: Gedenkbuch für die jüdischen Mitbürger der Stadt Essen* (Essen: Stadt Essen, 1980), 683.

20. *Weseler Volksblatt*, March 11, 1933, a newspaper run by the Catholic Center Party, with reference to the "just defense" put up by Jewish families in the city "to prove their Germanness [*Deutschtum*] and their patriotic sentiment."

21. See Marion Kaplan, ed., *Geschichte des jüdischen Alltags in Deutschland: Vom 17. Jahrhundert bis 1945* (Munich: C. H. Beck, 2003), 398 (not reproduced in the English translation of this book: *Jewish Daily Life in Germany, 1618–1945* [New York: Oxford University Press, 2005]).

DOCUMENT I-8: Antiboycott flyer by H. and E. Leyens, USHMMA RG 11.001M.31, reel 101 (SAM 721-1-2321).

Unser Herr Reichskanzler Hitler

die Herren Reichsminister Frick und Göring haben mehrfach folgende Erklärungen abgegeben:

„Wer im 3. Reich einen Frontsoldaten beleidigt, wird mit Zuchthaus bestraft!"

Die 3 Brüder Leyens waren als Kriegsfreiwillige an der Front, sie sind verwundet worden und haben Auszeichnungen für tapferes Verhalten erhalten. Der Vater Leyens stand in freiwilliger Wehr gegen die Spartakisten. Sein Großvater ist in den Freiheitskämpfen an der Katzbach verwundet worden.

Müssen wir uns nach dieser Vergangenheit in nationalem Dienst jetzt öffentlich beschimpfen lassen? Soll das heute der Dank des Vaterlandes sein, wenn vor unserer Tür durch große Plakate aufgefordert wird, nicht in unserm Haus zu kaufen? Wir fassen diese Aktion, die Hand in Hand mit verleumderischen Behauptungen in der Stadt geht, als Angriff auf unsere nationale und bürgerliche Ehre auf, und als eine Schändung des Andenkens von 12000 gefallenen deutschen Frontsoldaten jüdischen Glaubens. Wir sehen darüber hinaus in dieser Aufforderung eine Beleidigung für jeden anständigen Bürger. Es ist uns nicht bange darum, daß es in Wesel auch heute noch die Zivilcourage gibt, die Bismarck einstmals forderte, und deutsche Treue, die gerade jetzt zu uns steht.

Heinrich und Erich Leyens
zugleich als Verfasser und Herausgeber.

Our Reich Chancellor Mr. Hitler, the Reich Ministers Frick and Göring have repeatedly made the following proclamations:

"In the Third Reich, whoever offends a combat veteran will be punished by incarceration!"

The three Leyens brothers served at the front during the war as volunteers, were wounded, and received medals for their bravery. The Leyenses' father volunteered against the Spartacists. His grandfather was wounded in the war of liberation at the Katzbach.[22]

After serving in the military, must we suffer public abuse now? Is this the reward of the Fatherland: posters in the front of our door demanding that no one do business at our establishment? We regard this action, which goes hand in hand with slanderous claims in the city, as an attack on our national and civic honor and as a desecration of the memory of 12,000 fallen German frontline soldiers of the Jewish faith. We also see in this demand an insult to every decent citizen. We have no doubt that in Wesel, even today, the civic courage once demanded by Bismarck[23] still exists and that especially now German steadfastness stands by us.

Heinrich and Erich Leyens, simultaneously as authors and publishers.

Erich Leyens left Germany in 1935 and later settled in the United States; several members of his family who remained were murdered during the war.[24]

Across Germany Jews felt dismayed and humiliated by the public spectacle of the nationwide boycott on April 1 and its massive orchestration by the Nazi media. In the Silesian city of Breslau, the SA and SS had behaved earlier, as one

---

22. This sentence refers to the war against Napoleonic troops in 1812–1814; the previous sentence makes reference to civil disturbances between left-wing ("Spartacists") and right-wing groups in Germany after World War I.

23. Otto von Bismarck, chancellor of the German Reich, 1871–1890.

24. See Erich Leyens and Lotte Andor, *Years of Estrangement* (Evanston, IL: Northwestern University Press, 1996), 10.

Breslau Jew observed, "worse than the hordes during the Thirty Years War."[25] Grim images of age-old persecution appeared also in the diary of **Willy Cohn,** a Jewish teacher and historian in that city.

DOCUMENT 1-9: **Willy Cohn, diary entries for March 31 and April 1, 1933, translated from Norbert Conrads, ed.**, *Kein Recht, Nirgends: Tagebuch vom Untergang des Breslauer Judentums*, **1933–1941 (Cologne: Böhlau Verlag, 2006), 1:24.**

March 31, 1933

Breslau, Friday. Woke up very early this morning. Dreamed about Herr Göring. Even if one doesn't want to think about these things, it's hard to get them out of your head. Taught at the school for two hours! The morning papers announced that the Nazi Party had proposed cutting back the number of Jewish and "bastardized" [*bastardisierten*] teachers and limiting the proportion of Jewish high school teachers to 1 percent. After school I performed the most humiliating task of my life up to now: I went to the police to get a stamp in my passport, a stamp for us Jews that makes our passports valid for domestic use only.[26] The official was very civil and friendly during this procedure, but we had to stand in a long line, which was exhausting; even much older people such as Counselor [*Geheimrat*] Rosenstein! Even my 73-year-old mother had to stand in line for an hour! A complete assault on our human dignity! But one also has to put up with this! Our ancestors had it much worse! We can't let this wear us down. But it's not easy! The whole world is in an uproar about what's happening to us—not because we have set off alarm bells about the latest outrages but because it's become clear what they're doing to us! Everything is just an excuse that they can use to annihilate us. Countless livelihoods have been destroyed. There is an outcry going all through the civilized world!

It's impossible to describe all the things one feels, especially after sacrificing oneself for Germany over so many years. One is now reduced to hoping that one's children will have a better future in Palestine.

---

25. Walter Tausk, *Breslauer Tagebuch, 1933–1940*, ed. Ryszard Kincel (Berlin: Aufbau Taschenbuch Verlag, 2000), 26 (diary entry for February 10, 1933).

26. Beginning on April 1, 1933, Germans needed visas to leave the country; around the same time, municipalities started refusing to issue new passports to Jews and recalling existing ones "for review." The *J*-stamp in passports issued to Jews was introduced in early October 1938. See Joseph Walk, ed., *Das Sonderrecht für die Juden im NS-Staat: Eine Sammlung der gesetzlichen Maßnahmen und Richtlinien—Inhalt und Bedeutung* (Heidelberg: UTB, 1996), 8–9, nos. 28, 32; 224, nos. 556, 557.

April 1, 1933

Breslau, Saturday! I got up quite early today and did some writing; it is the best diversion because if one opens the newspapers nowadays, one becomes simply outraged at the way we're being treated. We witness the final loss of human dignity.

Spent two hours at school; I took the streetcar line 26 in order to avoid the downtown area. The boycott got underway today at ten o'clock. Some see it as a great success that the action will be interrupted from at least Monday to Wednesday. In some classes many of the Jewish students stayed home. Incidentally, one gets the impression that decent Christian circles are increasingly keeping their distance from such events. In the end not everything is gloom and doom! You have to pull yourself together and try to stay calm. They were standing in front of shops and businesses today holding signs on which they had painted yellow patches. "Jew" and similar things were painted on them! Darkest Middle Ages! At least they didn't start a riot. Trautner's [store in Breslau] closed at one thirty in the afternoon. Toward evening the caretaker of our building phoned to say that nothing had happened there. [. . .]

I'm feeling fairly depressed today. I usually take refuge in my books, but it's not working entirely. Finding some diversion outside is no longer possible. I cannot and do not want to think about the future at the moment. One has to wait and see! If only our Jewish people in Germany would learn from this that all attempts to assimilate lead nowhere and thus learn to live their own Jewishness!

Stigmatizing Jews—attempting to shame them in public and marking them as separate to convey dishonor—had been a staple of Christian antisemitism in the Middle Ages. Plastering Jewish-owned shops and offices with posters, stickers, painted slogans, and signs during the April boycott, Nazi Party activists worked to ensure that their message was not lost on the general public. The tool kit of the Nazi boycott provoked defiance among German Jews, but it also deepened their disillusionment with fellow Germans. The Leyens brothers and many other German Jews attempted to diminish the effects of Nazi attacks by displaying their war medals on the day of the boycott; others tried to outmaneuver the party's tactics on the day of the boycott by closing their businesses voluntarily or even by advertising their identification with Germany in larger letters than the Nazis had used. What might have appeared as pandering inside the Reich could be seen outside of Germany, as illustrated by the photograph in document 1-10 published in France, as an attempt to defy Nazi pressure.

DOCUMENT 1-10: Poster from *Der Gelbe Fleck: Die Ausrottung von 500.000 deutschen Juden* (Paris: Editions du Carrefour, 1936), 29.

Photo of shop window with boycott posters, April 1933: One printed by NSDAP boycott committee reads, "It is prohibited to buy in this Jewish shop." Another, hand-painted most likely by the owner, reads, "In protest against the foreign atrocity propaganda, we are closing our store for today."

Caption in *Der Gelbe Fleck*: Two revealing posters from the days [sic] of the April 1933 boycott in the window of a department store in West Berlin.

The Zionist response found its sharpest expression in an article by Robert Weltsch, editor of the *Jüdische Rundschau*, entitled "Wear the Yellow Badge with Pride," in which he reiterated his hope for increased Jewish self-esteem in the face of ostracism by non-Jews.[27] As we have seen, Weltsch and the Zionist press had made similar calls before. But this particular text acquired iconic status because its publication coincided with the highly visible drama of the boycott. **Mally Dienemann**, the wife of a rabbi in the western German city of Offenbach, was particularly sensitive to the historical echoes that resonated throughout the experiences of these early weeks.

---

27. Robert Weltsch, "Tragt ihn mit Stolz, den gelben Fleck," *Jüdische Rundschau*, April 4, 1933, 1–2; also in *Ja-Sagen zum Judentum*, 24–29.

DOCUMENT 1-11: Mally Dienemann, diary entry for April 3, 1933, LBINY MM 18, 11a (translated from German).

Offenbach, April 3, 1933.
On Saturday there was a boycott of all Jewish stores, doctors, lawyers. Black slips of paper with white dots were posted on Jewish stores and SA men stood in front of the buildings and stopped people from entering the stores or going to lawyers or doctors. [. . .] I thought, how unvarying is our fate; now we are [supposedly] harming Germany with fairy tales about atrocities, while in the Middle Ages it was we who were supposed to have poisoned wells, etc. I felt like my own ghost wandering the streets. Were we dreaming, or was it real? Could people really do this to each other? And why, why? Did any of those in power really believe that these Jews were to blame for spreading this so-called atrocity propaganda? [. . .]

The Nazi assault destroyed established networks of solidarity, sometimes by force, but more frequently because non-Nazi groups adapted to the new regime's preferences and demands. Jewish women's organizations, for instance, increasingly found themselves shut out of their traditional partnership with the German women's rights movement. The **Jüdischer Frauenbund** (League of Jewish Women or JFB) decided to preempt exclusion from the umbrella group by formally cutting its ties to its old associates.

DOCUMENT 1-12: Letter by Jüdischer Frauenbund to the Bund Deutscher Frauenvereine, May 10, 1933, *Blätter des JFB*, May 1933, 12 (translated from German).

To the League of German Women's Associations [Bund Deutscher Frauenvereine, or BDF]
Attn.: Frau Dr. von Zahn-Harnack, Director[28]
Berlin W[est]
Motzstrasse 22

---

28. Agnes von Zahn-Harnack (1884–1950), an advocate for women's rights and women academics, became head of the *Bund Deutscher Frauenvereine* in 1931 until the organization dissolved itself in 1933, reluctant or unable to conform to Nazi prerequisites. Zahn-Harnack may have given some public lectures against antisemitism, but other non-Jewish activists in the organization proved less willing to speak out. See Claudia Koonz, *Mothers in the Fatherland: Women, the Family, and Nazi Politics* (New York: St. Martin's Press, 1987), 103; Richard J. Evans, *The Feminist Movement in Germany, 1894–1933* (London: Sage Publications, 1976), 237–38, 255–59.

Dear Frau Dr. von Zahn-Harnack,

Our board meeting of May 9 focused on our work in the interdenominational women's movement up to now. As a result of our deliberations, we decided to resign from the League of German Women's Associations. Working together has ceased to be beneficial or rewarding under the present circumstances, and continuing this collaboration would only negatively affect both of our organizations. The most recent newsletters [by the BDF] provided ample proof of this.

We are withdrawing from the organization that has up to now embodied the German women's movement. But at heart we will retain our inward ties to that movement, for it has also been a fundamental bedrock of our League [i.e., the Jüdischer Frauenbund]. I need hardly remind you in this context that Jewish women have been a part of the German women's movement from its earliest days, helping not only to fill its ranks but to steer it on its course. Names such as Henriette Goldschmidt, Jeanette Schwerin, Lina Morgenstern, Josephine Levy-Rathenau, Jenny Apolant, and Alice Salomon are inseparable from the story of the German women's movement.[29] They live on in our thoughts as well: as women who paved the way for women's education, learning, and professions.

Our decision to leave the League of German Women's Associations has not been taken lightly. It is a painful moment for us.

With best regards, signed on behalf of the Jewish Women's League, we are [signed] Bertha Pappenheim, Bettina Brenner, Paula Ollendorff, Dr. Marg. Berent, Hannah Karminski[30]

Despite shedding its Jewish members, the League of German Women's Associations did not fare well under the new order either. According to an editorial note printed on the same page of the JFB's journal, the league, founded

---

29. Henriette Goldschmidt (1825–1920), Jeanette Schwerin (1852–1899), Lina Morgenstern (1830–1909), Josephine Levy-Rathenau (1877–1921), Jenny Apolant (1874–1925), and Alice Salomon (1872–1948) were Jewish women who played a leading role in the German women's movement of the nineteenth and early twentieth centuries. See Marion A. Kaplan, *The Jewish Feminist Movement in Germany: The Campaigns of the Jüdischer Frauenbund, 1904–1938* (London: Greenwood, 1979).

30. Bertha Pappenheim (1859–1936), Bettina Brenner (1887–1948), Paula Ollendorff (1860–1938), Margarete Berent (1887–1965), and Hannah Karminski (see glossary) were all leading figures in the JFB. See Kaplan, *The Jewish Feminist Movement*, and Gudrun Maierhof, *Selbstbehauptung im Chaos: Frauen in der jüdischen Selbsthilfe, 1933–1943* (Frankfurt am Main: Campus, 2002).

in 1894 and in early 1933 comprising more than eighty women's groups with roughly 750,000 members, dissolved itself on May 15, 1933.[31]

It was not just German Jews who pondered the best strategy for responding to the Nazis. While the solidarity expressed by their brethren abroad in the first weeks of the Hitler government had been reassuring for Jews in Germany, it was far from clear what external intervention could achieve—particularly for the vast majority of German Jews who did not want to leave the country. Would agitation from abroad in fact cause more harm than good, as the intense Nazi reaction to so-called foreign atrocity propaganda had suggested? Existing and newly created relief agencies tried to alleviate the plight of refugees and the most vulnerable in Germany; yet, despite the economic challenges posed by Nazi policies, observers both inside and outside the Reich believed that for the time being German Jewry was still sufficiently well equipped to provide for its own ranks. Conditions in Germany in 1933 seemed less dire than those confronting Jews in Eastern European countries, with their long tradition of state-sponsored discrimination, ranging from segregation to boycotts to pogroms and murder.[32]

International Jewish organizations also faced the dilemma that pushing too hard in support of German Jews might ignite the "Jewish question" elsewhere. Zionist institutions such as the **Jewish Agency for Palestine**, for example, possessed a solid organizational basis with which to support German Jewish settlement in Palestine; yet, tensions in the British mandate limited Zionists' ability to promote such emigration. Nevertheless, some hoped that Zionists might still be able to strike a deal with the new German regime that would benefit both German Jews and the Zionists' settlement plans in the Middle East.[33]

PHYSICAL THREATS

Despite organized efforts to provide both psychological and financial support for Germany's Jews, many felt desperate, their distress aggravated by the fear that the Nazi takeover, in addition to its psychological and material consequences, would threaten the lives of family and friends, if not their own. As part of the hunt for Communists and in line with propaganda stereotypes about Jews as Bolshevists, criminals, and public enemies, Jewish men were among

---

31. *Blätter des JFB,* May 1933, 12.

32. See David Kramer, "Jewish Welfare Work under the Impact of Pauperization," in *Juden im nationalsozialistischen Deutschland: The Jews in Nazi Germany, 1933–1945,* ed. Arnold Paucker (Tübingen: J. C. B. Mohr, 1986), 173–88.

33. See Francis R. Nicosia, *Zionism and Anti-Semitism in Nazi Germany* (Cambridge: Cambridge University Press, 2008).

the first to experience Nazi brutality. Mobs assaulted Orthodox Jews in Berlin and beat them up; similar attacks took place elsewhere in Germany, sometimes with deadly results. While censorship in Germany concealed information about atrocities and replaced it with hearsay and rumors, reports by emigrants and correspondents found their way into foreign newspapers, journals, and books.[34]

Men being dragged off to Nazi torture cellars and concentration camps provided the most gripping images of life in the Third Reich, but Jewish women and children also suffered psychological as well as physical harm from their peers. Serious assaults on children that formerly would not have been tolerated suddenly became acceptable and were indeed sometimes encouraged by grown-ups in positions of authority. In a school system that labeled Jews as the "enemy," school yard bullies and their followers had an easier time unleashing their hostility on Jewish children, who in turn were forced to develop their own coping strategies.[35]

DOCUMENT 1-13: Else R. Behrend-Rosenfeld, diary entry for September 2, 1939, reflecting on events up to October 1933, translated from Else R. Behrend-Rosenfeld, *Ich stand nicht allein: Leben einer Jüdin in Deutschland*, 1933–1944 (Munich: C. H. Beck, 1988), 23–24.[36]

Already, at the end of October of 1933, I noticed that the children [her daughter Hanna and son Peter] had gotten quieter than usual and no longer talked about their day in school. The children from the village, some of whom had always picked up Peter and Hanna on their way to school, no longer did so. Peter came home one day with a small, bleeding head wound and, when we asked what had happened, told us, very embarrassed, that he had fallen. And so I spoke to both children alone after dinner. I soon learned what had happened; Hanna began to sob, and it

---

34. For examples reported in the United States until mid-1933, see *The Jews in Nazi Germany: The Factual Record of Their Persecution by the National Socialists* (New York: American Jewish Committee, 1933), 18–36.

35. In September 1933, eugenics and racial science were officially introduced as part of the curriculum in German schools. See Marion A. Kaplan, *Between Dignity and Despair: Jewish Life in Nazi Germany* (New York: Oxford University Press, 1998), 94–99.

36. In 1933, Else R. Behrend-Rosenfeld was living with her family in Bavaria in the vicinity of Schönau am Königssee. In the spring of 1944, she escaped across the Swiss border and survived the war. Her children spent part of the war years in England, Hanna working as a nurse and Peter, at least initially, on a farm near Oxford. See Else R. Behrend-Rosenfeld, *Ich stand nicht allein: Leben einer Jüdin in Deutschland, 1933–1944* (Munich: C. H. Beck 1988), 12, 248ff; USHMMA, Acc. 2000.227, Herbert Cohn collection, folder 2, 223.

cost Peter, the twelve-year-old, a great effort not to begin crying too. And then, little by little, he told us that the teacher had been unfriendly to him since the beginning, ranted against the Jews on a daily basis, and that he had pointed at them and said, "Those two are also Jews; do we want to put up with such a thing? You must defend yourselves against them." The [other] children had yelled at them on their way to school and thrown stones at them, and today several of them had attacked Peter and tried to throw him in the Ache River. He had fallen in the process and gashed his head slightly. Because some people happened to be passing by, the boys ran away. They [Peter and Hanna] had not wanted to tell us about their difficulties because they knew that we had enough cares and they much preferred dealing with the problem on their own. I reassured them both by telling them that even children who were older could not have coped with this on their own. This incident weighed heavily on us; fortunately, though, we did not yet suspect that life would become more and more difficult until the weight of events would bring us both [Else and her husband] close to the point of collapse.

Jews arrested by the SA and SS units acting on their own initiative or as auxiliary policemen faced less publicly visible, but ultimately more systematic and harsh, assaults than those falling victim to simple mob violence. The arrests were made on the basis of a host of charges to legitimize the so-called *Schutzhaft* ("protective custody"), as envisaged by the presidential decree "for the protection of *Volk* and state" enacted on February 28, 1933. Given the dangerous lack of clarity about what was legal or illegal—an uncertainty that became a constitutive element of the Nazi system in general—no Jew could be sure when he or she was crossing the line or might be arrested. Although the SA in particular rapidly found its power on the street reined in, protective custody orders continued to be issued by the secret state police, the **Gestapo**, which emerged as the most influential branch of the executive apparatus once SS chief **Heinrich Himmler** had reorganized it on a national basis.[37]

Those Jews caught in the dragnet of police arrests and concentration camp incarceration found their ability to act, even simply to see and understand what was happening around them, drastically reduced. Already at this early stage, the Nazi terror system subjected them to massive and arbitrary violence from their SS guards. Many of the concentration camps that mushroomed all over Germany in the first weeks after Hitler's accession to power served as temporary

---

37. Michael Burleigh and Wolfgang Wippermann, *The Racial State* (Cambridge: Cambridge University Press, 1991), 60–63.

prisons for Jews. Dachau, near the city of Munich, established in late March 1933 as one of the very first concentration camps, housed several Jews among the hundred political prisoners initially taken into "protective custody." Once SS men had taken over as guards, they immediately singled out the Jewish prisoners; by the end of May, twelve of the Jewish men had been tortured to death or driven to commit suicide.[38] The more Jewish prisoners tried to retain or defend elements of their Jewish identity, the greater their chances of being targeted for abuse, torture, or murder.

Cantor and Jewish community teacher **Max Abraham**, from the small Jewish community of Rathenow in the province of Brandenburg, was arrested in June 1933 and transferred in September with a dozen other Jews to the northern German concentration camp Papenburg. He survived to record his camp experiences and, after escaping from the Reich, published his account in Czechoslovakia in 1934.

DOCUMENT 1-14: **Max Abraham on his incarceration in the Papenburg concentration camp, fall 1933, first printed in Max Abraham, *Juda verrecke: Ein Rabbiner im Konzentrationslager* (Templitz-Schönau: Druck- und Verlagsanstalt, 1934)[39] (translated from German).**

[. . .] When I heard from a friend for the first time in March of 1933 what he had seen from the window of his apartment in Berlin, Alte Schönhauser Strasse 33—how Nazis beat Jews terribly with rubber truncheons and cut off their beards—I just could not believe it, even though I was convinced that my friend would never lie. He went on to tell me that Nazi thugs had forced their way into a nearby synagogue, forced those who were praying to lie down on the benches, and mistreated them. I could not and would not believe it, despite the fact that other friends living nearby confirmed his account.

Soon I experienced physically, firsthand, the terrible barbarism that had befallen Germany. Had I not been forced to "study" the conditions in the brown [i.e., Nazi] torture hell at firsthand, perhaps I would have

38. See Barbara Distel, "Dachau Main Camp," in *United States Holocaust Memorial Museum Encyclopedia of Camps and Ghettos, 1933–1945*, vol. 1, *Early Camps, Youth Camps, and Concentration Camps and Subcamps under the SS-Business Administration Main Office (WVHA)*, ed. Geoffrey P. Megargee (Bloomington: Indiana University Press, 2009), 442–46.

39. Reprint in Irene A. Diekmann and Klaus Wettig, eds., *Konzentrationslager Oranienburg: Augenzeugenberichte aus dem Jahre 1933* (Potsdam: Verlag für Berlin-Brandenburg, 2003), 124–55. On the Papenburg camp, see Joseph Robert White, "Papenburg [a.k.a. Emsland]," in *The USHMM Encyclopedia of Camps and Ghettos, 1933–1945*, 1:152–54.

agreed with the German propaganda minister, Herr Dr. Joseph Goebbels, that in Germany no Jew and no opponent of the regime had "had a hair touched on his head" and that those who had been spared [abuse] were now showing their gratitude by promulgating "atrocity propaganda" [*Greuelhetze*] against Germany. It is the Third Reich's leaders' tactic to "prove" to the world and a completely uninformed German public through radio speeches, solemn assurances, and newspaper articles that on April 1 a boycott had been conducted without causing Jews any harm and that concentration camps had been created for the sole purpose of educating opponents to become members of the people's community [*Volksgenossen*]. I will discuss here this education in concentration camps.

I did not write this book to take revenge or to be vindictive, but to show my Jewish friends and all freedom fighters around the world the tortures that Jewish and political prisoners in "protective custody" have to endure; I want to make visible to them what I have experienced and seen for myself.

[. . . ; after the author's arrest and transfer to the Papenburg concentration camp:] The Jewish High Holidays were approaching. We debated anxiously whether the SS people knew the dates of the holidays because we feared worse cruelties. We thus agreed to avoid any hint about the upcoming holidays. I was initially determined to ask the camp commander whether the Jewish labor detail could be exempted from work. However, my comrades had to persuade me that such a request would not only be futile but could also have alarming consequences.

We had not reckoned with our relatives, who sent their greetings for the Jewish New Year, unaware of events in the camp. Because the letters were read by a censor, the SS learned of the dates, and there was nothing left to conceal. Thus I ended up going to the camp commander after all to request a work exemption and permission to conduct services. Answer: "That isn't done here!"

The first day of the holiday: at six o'clock in the morning, we Jews who were newcomers in the camp were assigned to a special detachment [*Sonderkommando*]. We were chased across the yard at a quick marching tempo. We were ordered to stop in front of a manure pit. We had to climb down into the pit and get into formation at the bottom. I was yanked out of the line of my comrades and positioned in the middle of the pit. SS NCO [*Scharführer*] Everling screamed at me, "Here you go, Rabbi. You can hold services here!"

Everything in me rebelled against dragging our religion—so literally— into the dirt. I remained silent.

Everling: "Are you refusing to follow the command?"

"I'm not holding services in a manure pit!"

Everling hauled me out of the pit—rubber batons and gun butts rained down on me. I was brought to my bunk unconscious. I lay there for two hours before regaining consciousness.

In the afternoon we were brought into the same pit in which the others had been forced to work in the late morning. And now Everling asked me to deliver a speech on Judaism and the other religions. I started, "Like other religions, Judaism sees the Ten Commandments as fundamental principles, as well as the most beautiful biblical saying, 'Love thy neighbor as thyself.'"

At this point Everling interrupted me. "Stop, you swine. We will teach you what it means to love your neighbor!"

Then I was so terribly mistreated that I got a high fever and severe cramps. My body was beaten raw; I could neither sit nor lie down. I spent a terrible night having confused and horrible feverish hallucinations. I was brought to the sick ward the next morning in a terrible state. My companions here were only non-Jewish comrades, Social Democrats and Communists, who looked after me in a self-sacrificing manner. I will never forget their comradely help. When I fasted on the Day of Atonement [*Versöhnungstag*; Yom Kippur], they gave me food at the close of the day despite my weak state. I stayed in the ward for two weeks. Later I learned that I had been in a critical, life-threatening state for some days. [. . .]

For those deprived of all sense of purpose and confronted with insurmountable obstacles, suicide could appear as the only remaining way out. Already, during the Weimar period, the number of Jews who took their own lives had been disproportionately high. The Nazi takeover and the April boycott pushed the figure throughout the Reich up to three to four hundred in the months of April and May alone.[40] Some Jews wanted to send a signal with their deaths. The following final letter was written by thirty-one-year-old Fritz Rosenfelder of

---

40. Konrad Kwiet and Helmut Eschwege, *Selbstbehauptung und Widerstand: Deutsche Juden im Kampf um Existenz und Menschenwürde, 1933–1945* (Hamburg: Christians, 1984), 194–200. While between 1924 and 1926 in Berlin 68 out of 100,000 Jews committed suicide, for 1932 to 1934 the figure was 70.2, compared to 48.8 for non-Jewish Berliners; for the period 1933 to 1945, Kwiet and Eschwege estimate that at least 5,000 German Jews (or around 1 percent of the 525,000 Germans of Jewish faith registered in 1933) committed suicide (Kwiet and Eschwege, *Selbstbehauptung*, 199, 201). See also Anna Fischer, *Erzwungener Freitod: Spuren und Zeugnisse in den Freitod getriebener Juden der Jahre 1938–1945 in Berlin* (Berlin: Text Verlag, 2007).

Bad Cannstadt near Stuttgart after his sports association (*Deutsche Turnerschaft*) decided to exclude **"non-Aryans."**

DOCUMENT 1-15: Final letter by Fritz Rosenfelder to his friends, April 1933 (translated from German).

My beloved friends!

With this I bid you a last farewell! A German Jew could not bear to live, knowing that the movement in which the people of Germany [*das nationale Deutschland*] place their hope for the future [*die Rettung erhofft*] views him as a traitor to the Fatherland! I depart [from this earth] without hatred or rancor. A deeply felt hope stirs in me that reason may soon return! As I see it, there is nothing left for me to do until that day, and thus I am attempting through my suicide to jolt [*aufzurütteln*] my Christian friends into awareness. The step I am taking will show you how things look for us German Jews. How I would have preferred to sacrifice my life for my Fatherland! Do not mourn. Rather, let the truth be known; help the truth to triumph.

In so doing you would pay me the greatest tribute!

Yours F. [. . .]

Rosenfelder's desperate act did indeed register, first in the *Jüdische Rundschau*, which printed his letter anonymously as testimony of the Jewish plight, and later in the local Nazi press, where an author gleefully recommended that other Jews follow Rosenfelder's example.[41]

---

41. See Christian Goeschel, "Suicides of German Jews in the Third Reich," *German History* 25, no. 1 (2007): 22–45; see also Kwiet and Eschwege, *Selbstbehauptung*, 200; Kaplan, *Between Dignity*, 179–84.

DOCUMENT 1-16: "Personal Tragedy," *Jüdische Rundschau*, April 25, 1933, 163 (translated from German).

Persönliche Tragödie

Aus Stuttgart wird uns geschrieben:

Unter den Fällen, in denen die Geschehnisse unserer Zeit jüdische Menschen dazu treiben, ihr Leben wegzuwerfen, ist durch seine Begleitumstände einer bemerkenswert, der sich in Stuttgart abgespielt hat. Ein junger Kaufmann von 31 Jahren, begeisterter Anhänger des deutschen Turn- und Sportwesens und Riegenführer eines Turnvereins, in geordneten Verhältnissen lebend, hat sich erschossen. Unter seinen Papieren fand man angestrichen eine Pressenotiz über den Beschluß der deutschen Turnerschaft, den Arierparagraphen einzuführen und außerdem folgenden an seine Freunde gerichteten Brief.

Ihr lieben Freunde!

Hierdurch ein letztes Lebewohl! Ein **deutscher** Jude konnte es nicht über sich bringen, zu leben in dem Bewußtsein, von der Bewegung, von der das nationale Deutschland die Rettung erhofft, als Vaterlandsverräter betrachtet zu werden! Ich gehe ohne Haß und Groll. Ein inniger Wunsch beseelt mich — möge in Bälde die Vernunft Einkehr halten! Da mir bis dahin überhaupt keine — meinem Empfinden entsprechende — Tätigkeit möglich ist, versuche ich durch meinen Freitod, meine christlichen Freunde aufzurütteln. Wie es in uns deutschen Juden aussieht, — mögt Ihr aus meinem Schritt ersehen. Wie viel lieber hätte ich mein Leben für mein Vaterland gegeben! Trauert nicht —, sondern versucht aufzuklären und der Wahrheit zum Siege zu verhelfen.

So erweist Ihr mir die größte Ehre!

Euer F....*)

Dieser Fall und dieser Brief kennzeichnen eine in diesen Tagen immer neu zu beobachtende Erscheinung: Schutzloser als der irgendwie metaphysisch, sei es gefühlsmäßig oder bluthaft, ist in dieser Zeit schwerster Erschütterung der inneren und äußeren Existenz **der** Jude preisgegeben, dessen Leben um einen Mittelpunkt kreist, aus dem er die Tatsache seines Judeseins **ausgeschaltet** hat. F. wollte als Zeuge für sein Deutschtum sterben, aber durch seinen Tod ist er, über sein Wissen und Wollen hinaus, auch zum Zeugen für die Sache des Judentums geworden.   m.

*) Auf Wunsch der Familie soll der Name nicht genannt werden.

Personal Tragedy

From Stuttgart we receive the following:

Among the cases in which present-day events have driven Jewish people to throw away their lives, one instance from Stuttgart stands out due to its circumstances. A young salesman, aged 31, an enthusiastic fan of German sports and captain (*Riegenführer*) of his gymnastics club, living an orderly life, shot himself to death. Among his papers, a marked-up press clipping was found concerning the decision by the German gymnastics association to introduce the Aryan clause, as well as the following letter addressed to his friends:

[. . .]

[See above document 1-15; note added by *Jüdische Rundschau* that the name has been withheld according to the wish of the deceased's family.]

[. . .]

This case and this letter highlight a phenomenon that has become all too common nowadays: in this time of severe disruption to one's inner life and external existence, those Jews who have excluded any reference to their Jewishness from their lives are less protected than those who are somehow metaphysically—either through beliefs or blood (*bluthaft*)—tied to [their] Jewishness (*Judentum*). F. [Fritz Rosenfelder] wanted to die as witness for his sense of Germanness (*Deutschtum*), but through his death he has become—even beyond what he could have known or wanted—also a witness to the Jewish cause.

CHAPTER 2

EXCLUSION AND
INTROSPECTION

EMBATTLED IDENTITIES

By the summer of 1933, Hitler had substantially consolidated his position. Many Jews continued to hope the new regime would founder, but they were forced to take the idea seriously that the Nazis were there to stay. Jewish organizations began to move beyond coping with the initial shock and tried to develop longer-term structures to manage the new situation. That would not be easy. The future remained hard to read, and the shocks kept on coming. Moreover, the idea of *the* Jew or *the* Jewish community was a shibboleth, invented by the Nazis despite the prevalence of fragmentation among Jews. True, to some extent, the Nazis had indeed turned the Jews as they imagined them into a reality since their blanket policies brought a heterogeneous group under one definition. Even when no physical violence was involved, the increasing political and social pressure exerted by the Nazis left a strong mark on all those subjected to their power. Yet the sense of sharing a common fate could not create the basis for a unified response overnight. For one thing, the experience of powerlessness left many feeling isolated, unable to believe that anything could be done collectively. For another, the bewildering complexities and seeming inconsistencies of the Nazis' actions could trigger new divisions. Nazi policy was applied unevenly in different regions and by different bodies. The very diverse circumstances of those affected meant that Nazi actions struck different sections of the Jewish community in different ways and at different times. Even identical Nazi measures might be interpreted differently, depending on the group or individual. Jewish organizational leaders, with access to information from many sources and a sense of the larger picture, could often scrutinize new measures using a different lens than average members of the community. Ordinary people who felt themselves discriminated against as Jews had only their own experiences, exchanges with the people closest to them, and the heavily censored information provided by the Jewish press and Jewish organizations or gleaned at social gatherings to go on.

The Nazis' anti-Jewish policies targeted not only those who viewed themselves as Jewish but also those who felt no ties with Jewish tradition and were branded as Jews solely because of their parents' or grandparents' religious affiliations. Nazi regulations would eventually create an entirely new class of people, the so-called mixed breeds or "*Mischlinge*," a "third race" consisting of persons with mixed Jewish and non-Jewish backgrounds whose racial status ranked somewhere between Jews and the newly constructed "**Aryans**." Until the 1935 **Nuremberg Laws** introduced a normative definition, it was unclear exactly who belonged to this group and where the Nazi racial state drew the line. Even after these laws took effect, decisions about who should be regarded and treated as a Jew and who qualified as "Aryan" often required investigations and decisions on an individual basis. These procedures inevitably created insecurity and a sense of permanent threat in many families.

Luise Solmitz and her husband, Fredy, a retired major and decorated pilot who fought with the German army during World War I, lived in Hamburg in what came to be termed a "mixed marriage." Because of Fredy's Jewish ancestry, their daughter, Gisela, became a "non-Aryan" as defined in the first supplementary decree to the Law for the Restoration of the Public Service issued on April 11, 1933. The designation "non-Aryan," the decree ruled, included any person with a Jewish parent or grandparent. Because racial theorists and racial testing were incapable of identifying phenotypical markers distinguishing Jews from non-Jews, the 1933 decree defined Jewishness on the basis of the religious affiliation of a person's grandparents. Not only was this predicated on cooperation on the part of the Christian churches that administered birth and baptism records—a cooperation that was readily forthcoming[1]—but it also, unsurprisingly, resulted in confusion and forced many to confront aspects of family history that had mattered little until the Nazi takeover.[2]

---

1. See Gailus, *Kirchliche Amtshilfe*.

2. For this decree and other Nazi racial laws, see Yitzhak Arad, Yisrael Gutman, and Abraham Margaliot, eds., *Documents on the Holocaust: Selected Sources on the Destruction of the Jews of Germany and Austria, Poland, and the Soviet Union* (Jerusalem: Yad Vashem, 1981); Karl A. Schleunes, ed., *Legislating the Holocaust: The Bernhard Loesener Memoirs and Supporting Documents* (Boulder, CO: Westview Press, 2001).

Luise and Fredy Solmitz, stalwart German nationalists, had welcomed Hitler's appointment and in early February felt "intoxicated with enthusiasm" when they watched a Nazi procession in Hamburg, despite the fact that some of the marchers were chanting the Nazi epithet *Juda verrecke* (equivalent to "death to the Jews" or "Jews rot in hell").[3] Soon enough they discovered that antisemitism would not be a propagandistic sideshow but, rather, a central feature of Nazi rule. Particularly in the case of mixed Jewish-Christian ancestry or families with converts, it was the schools' treatment of the children that first forced families to confront the "racial" status ascribed to them by the regime. Children who had seen themselves as regular Germans, just like their neighbors, discovered from one day to the next that they had become pariahs.

DOCUMENT 2-1: **Luise Solmitz, diary entries, late May 1933, FZGH 11 S 11 (translated from German) (stray punctuation in the original).**

May 20, 1933

It proved to be a fateful day for us. Gis. [Gisela, her daughter, born 1920] had already told us that other schools had conducted an ancestry survey; I shook my head [. . .] Then Gis. came home from school: "Am I an Aryan?" and gave Fredy [Luise's Jewish husband] a certificate to fill out: "My daughter Gisela S. is of Aryan descent (Cross out where applicable)." An accompanying booklet for messages to parents [*Verkehrsheft*] explained: "A non-Aryan is a person who is descended from non-Aryan, especially Jewish, parents or grandparents. It suffices if one parent or one grandparent is non-Aryan. This can be assumed particularly in cases where one parent or grandparent belonged to the Jewish religious faith." Fr. and I have known each other for 20.5 years; not once, strange as it may seem, have we ever discussed this. . . . He then withdrew into his room. . . . Thus I did not know that Gis. had stormed into his room; one glance: "You're crossing out the wrong thing!"

May 21, 1933

. . . In the morning he showed me the fateful slip of paper, which he had already signed—with his lifeblood—and I added my name to it. We were now revealing to the school, to the public, a thing that we had not touched on in our relationship for 20.5 years. [. . .]

---

3. Luise Solmitz, diary entry for February 6, 1933, FZGH 11 S 11. For the similar case of "*Mischling*" Sybille Ortmann, see Peter Crane, "*Wir leben nun mal auf einem Vulkan*" (Bonn: Weidle Verlag, 2005), 73.

Miss Evers [Gisela's school teacher] was tactful enough to demand the answer in a sealed envelope. In the class next door, a teacher had already conducted an oral survey—an act of unimaginable crudeness and unnecessary because many of the children knew as little about race and ancestry as Gisela.—Fr. said, "I'll leave it up to you if she should know about it or not"—maybe it was an act of providence that she had seen him [filling in the form]; she hammered me with questions and so I told Fr. to tell her the truth. He took her to his room; I tried not to think. He called me [in]. The child had gone pale as snow. Fr. said to her, "You can and should keep holding your head high, you should & can be proud. And now, give us a kiss." [. . .]

May 28, 1933

. . . Fr. said, "For all eternity, what has been done to Gisela cannot be made right again. Did you see her frightened eyes when Miss Krueger [neighbor] started talking about the questionnaire again yesterday? . . . And have you heard how little Heye [neighbor's child] said that half-Jewish teachers are also going to be dismissed? . . . What good does it do for her to work hard at school; she can't achieve anything, can't become anything; all paths, all doors are hopelessly closed for her. . . . They can take everything away from us. . . . What else would there be for us to do than to put an end to it all; and Gis. must join us. It's terrible to have to say something like this, but the three of us now have no home on this earth." . . . Gis. woke up, happily, in high spirits, mischievous, and with an irrepressible youthful enthusiasm.

Racial attacks against Jews and "*Mischlinge*" went hand in hand with the stigmatization of sexual relations between "non-Aryans" and "Aryans." Though rules forbidding such relations were not yet on the statute book, local Nazis enacted public spectacles, putting alleged offenders in the pillory. For Jewish observers, these medieval displays of communal ostracism reinforced their sense of how dangerous and threatening the public sphere had become. **Kurt Rosenberg**, a Jewish lawyer living in Hamburg, recorded such events whenever they came to his attention.

DOCUMENT 2-2: Kurt Rosenberg, diary entries for August 20 and 31, 1933, LBINY AR 25279 (translated from German).

August 20, 1933

Day by day the assault on human rights and the human dignity of Jews continues, fragmented into a thousand individual affronts [*Einzelaktionen*], while much noise is made for passage of an animal protection law that will outlaw vivisection and promotes kindness to animals. It is impossible to count all the small incidents that daily plague us. In Cuxhaven an Aryan girl and a non-Aryan man are led through the city wearing signs around their necks, "I am a pig because I took up with a Jew," etc. In other locales the names of Aryan girls who have been seen in the company of Jews are published. And elsewhere Jews are prohibited from entering streets and town squares. Aryan and non-Aryan physicians, including war veterans, are in general prohibited from filling in for each other, may not work together, may not consult with one another. [. . .]

August 31, 1933

A female cook, who is reprimanded for peeling the skin off eels that are still alive, answers, "Does no harm. That sort [of fish] is used to it." It's not a good thing to be an eel. [. . .]

A Professor Lessing [Theodor Lessing; see document 2-3] has been murdered in Marienbad. He was a former university teacher in Braunschweig and most recently a journalist for the *Prague Tageblatt* [daily German-language newspaper]. In Austria a Nazi in prison was freed, and he escaped over the Italian border. Now he wants to take part in the annual [Nazi] party rally in Nuremberg.

The fallout of the revolution can be seen in hundreds of ways.

Alongside these changes, the skirmishes continue: people dismissed from jobs and official positions—and no day goes by without new stories cropping up. Because I'm an attorney who was dismissed, everyone [meaning non-Jews critical of the regime] feels safe around me in venting their feelings—albeit cautiously and with a ghastly fear of being sent to a concentration camp. I've learned to keep my mouth shut. [. . .]

It has gotten very quiet in my own office. I have too much time for brooding over things. Again and again plans crop up, vague and uncontrollable: running a children's home on the Italian or French coast. One finds oneself perpetually wrenched back and forth between planning and persevering. Not much space is left for major diversions. One feels tired and unnerved. One longs above all for peace. You avoid others in the same boat, those who are all too ready to unload their cares and pessimism on you. You end up waiting but don't know for what. One almost wishes that fate would force you to make decisions.

Some Jews who associated themselves primarily with socialism or communism had officially renounced their membership in Jewish religious communities before Hitler came to power. Among them was Theodor Lessing, a radical critic of German nationalism during the Weimar Republic whose death Kurt Rosenberg noted in his diary. In his article on the "Jewish question," written during his Prague exile shortly before his assassination by Nazi sympathizers in August 1933, Lessing reflects on antisemitism and its consequences after Hitler's coming to power.

DOCUMENT 2-3: **Theodor Lessing, "Germany and Its Jews," 1933, translated from Jörg Wollenberg, ed., "Wir machen nicht mit!" Schriften gegen den Nationalismus und zur Judenfrage (Bremen: Donat Verlag, 1997), 225, 239–40.**

[. . .] How did those respond who were pushed aside? I will remain quiet about the undignified answer of the Reichsbund jüdischer Frontsoldaten [RjF], about the whining and the secret ways of the CV, about the declarations of submissiveness by learned German professional Jews, none of whom wanted to miss out on the "big moment." [. . .]

Thus we German Jews leave our native place [Heimat] [. . .] with no army of men marching behind us? No, that's not how it is! Behind us is the army of our fathers: Abraham, Jacob, Moses. But behind us are also all the German guardian spirits [Schutzgeister]. With us, all those who have a native place in our heart are leaving Germany. As are those who perhaps have no other home on earth than in ourselves: Goethe with his world wisdom and clear humanism, Schubert with his comforting song. Dürer's true childlikeness, Hölderlin's lyrical bliss. And you, too, beloved teachers of my youth: Johannes Scherr, Wilhelm Jordan. I will remember you and remain true.[4]

And in this way we are German and will remain German. And in this way we are Jews and will remain Jews. But we are something entirely dif-

---

4. Lessing makes references here to a number of German writers and artists who influenced him, the best known being Albrecht Dürer (1471–1528), painter and printmaker from Nuremberg renowned for his innovative woodcuts and engravings, and Johann Wolfgang von Goethe (1749–1832), a major figure in German literary tradition.

ferent and much more than just Jews and just Germans! We are carriers of
the world's conscience, vessels of divine spirit, thanks to whom humanity
exists and humanism, and purpose and quality and victory. Beyond all
hells of nature and life, "lo bechail, welo bekoach, ki im beruach" [Hebrew
for "neither with force nor power, only with the strength of the mind"].

Another category of victims created by the application of race laws were the
"non-Aryan" Christians, persons of Jewish ancestry who had converted to the
Christian faith. Most had turned to Protestantism (around ninety thousand)
and fewer to Catholicism (some twenty-six thousand).[5] Reasons for conversion
varied widely but reflected the trend toward assimilation that had characterized
German Jewish history since the nineteenth century. When the first anti-Jewish
regulations began to take effect in 1933, many of these Christians found themselves stranded between a community of faith that showed little or no Christian
solidarity, Jews skeptical of apostates, and a notion of being Jewish enforced
from above with which they could not identify. In their desperation, many, such
as Richard O., nevertheless turned to their churches for help.

DOCUMENT 2-4: **Letter from Richard O., Berlin-Lichtenberg, to Protestant bishop
(Reichsbischof) Friedrich von Bodelschwingh, May 29, 1933, translated from Eberhard
Röhm and Jörg Thierfelder, eds., Juden-Christen-Deutsche, vol. 1, 1933–1935 (Stutt-
gart: Calwer Verlag, 1990), 256.**

I personally arranged to have myself baptized by the Protestant [*evange-
lisch*] church in 1908 because [like his father] I also married a Christian
woman and because I wanted the children that we expected to have
some day to be raised as Christians; I wanted my wife to be buried in a
churchyard when the time came, and above all, I wanted to belong to
the Protestant religion because of my deep-seated convictions, which
according to my assessment and experiences were the right ones. . . .
My daughter married a Protestant, and her child was also baptized in
a Protestant church. In spite of my growing Christian ties, red markers
printed with the slogan "Don't buy from Jews!" were glued to the windows of my business on the day of the boycott [April 1, 1933]. When
I protested, they explained to us that we were "half Jews!" in spite of

5. Eberhard Röhm and Jörg Thierfelder, eds., *Juden-Christen-Deutsche*, vol. 1, *1933–1935*
(Stuttgart: Calwer Verlag, 1990), 262–64; Meyer, *"Jüdische Mischlinge,"* 96–105; Aleksandar-
Saša Vuletić, *Christen jüdischer Herkunft im Dritten Reich: Verfolgung und organisierte Selbsthilfe,
1933–1939* (Mainz: Verlag Phillip von Zabern, 1999), 57–145.

our baptismal certificates and the fact that we had been members of the Protestant church for several decades.

Dear Pastor! Those of us who converted and became Protestants are doubly hard-hit because we now belong to "no one." We are neither Jews nor recognized by the state as Christians. So, dear Pastor, what are we? Am I a Jew or a Christian? Am I a member of the *Volk* [*Volksgenossen*] or an outcast? Is my baptismal certificate an inviolable document or not?

These questions fell largely on deaf ears. Although the traditional mission to convert Jews continued for a while, the Christian churches in Germany placed higher priority on protecting their core institutions. Finding themselves shunned by their religious communities, the "non-Aryan Christians" tried to establish their own self-help network. On July 20, 1933, an organization was formed, the awkwardness of its very name—Reich Union of Christian-German Citizens of Non-Aryan or Not-Purely-Aryan Descent (**Reichsverband christlich-deutscher Staatsbürger nichtarischer oder nicht rein arischer Abstammung**, or RVC)—revealing the absurdity of the state's racial categorization and highlighting the many obstacles this small outsider group within the larger Jewish outsider group faced in daily life.

For those who had already strongly identified with their Jewishness, the onset of Nazi persecution did not bring about the same crisis of identity. But particularly for religious Jews (after mainstream Zionism, Orthodoxy represented the most important of the minority orientations within German Jewry) the Nazi onslaught often seemed just as arbitrary as it did to those who did not practice Judaism since the Nazi notion of Judaism was so alien to that of the conservative Orthodox. Not only was the Nazis' way of defining racial identity illogical (despite the Nazi rhetoric, it rested ultimately, as we have seen, not on "race" or "appearance," but on the religious affiliations of grandparents), but it differed from Jews' matrilineal approach to religious descent. Thus, persons Nazis referred to as "full Jews" might not count as Jewish as far as the Orthodox were concerned, while Nazi-defined "*Mischlinge*" could be fully Jewish in religious terms. But more important was the fact that the Nazis paid so little heed to what Germany's Orthodox Jews saw as the religious core of their identity.

At the same time, Orthodox Jews, like the Zionists, could also see some positive aspects to the exclusion being enjoined on Germany's Jews. With the temptations of assimilation removed, more Jews might return to religious practice. Moreover, some Orthodox Jews still hoped that, presented with the authenticity of Jewish religious practice rather than half-hearted efforts at acculturation, Nazis might find Jews acceptable as a different, but loyal, religious minority within their nation.

DOCUMENT 2-5: Letter by Alex Lewin, Hoppstädten (Southwest Germany), to Ismar Elbogen,[6] April 25, 1933, LBINY MF 515, reel 1 (translated from German).

[. . .] I no doubt see the current situation for German Jews differently than you. We have committed a terrible sin. One only has to think of *shechitah* [ritual slaughter]. All that I have experienced here and in these environs is beyond description. Before I got here, Hoppstädten was a total *Kabboloh* factory.[7] People came here from all over the southern Rhineland to get a dose of K. [. . .] Needless to say, *bedikot*[8] was not being practiced. In rural areas there seem to be little difference between orthodox and liberal *shechitah*. [. . .] This whole German Jewry—not Jewry per se—needs to be reformed from top to bottom. But as long as the matter of defining Jewry [*Judentum machen*] is left to the pseudorabbinical or public health or legal and other councils and business people—and the rabbis stand meekly and piously by and do nothing—Jewry in Germany will continue to be defamed as a racial community. I recently had a very intense discussion with a National Socialist. These people know absolutely nothing about religious Judaism. And small wonder. One finds either academics heading up the Jewish communities—basically business people because they allow the Sabbath to become another workday and they know very little about the history of their community. Or they are in business and—as we say here—only show up for evening services in the synagogue once or twice a year. [. . .]

Even where the symbolic displays orchestrated by the regime and its followers targeted a broad range of groups, the specifically anti-Jewish message was not lost on German Jews. Book burnings aimed against what their organizers called an "un-German spirit" took place in many German cities on May 10, 1933. In the United States, alarmed Jewish leaders sponsored parades protesting the burning of books in the Reich and also joined the boycott of German goods.[9] Within Germany, as he did with the boycott, **Robert Weltsch** interpreted the May bonfire of

6. Likely to be Alex Lewin (1888–1942?), a resident of Hoppstädten, who was deported to Auschwitz in 1942 and died there. See www.bundesarchiv.de/gedenkbuch/directory.html. For Ismar Elbogen, see the glossary.

7. This is a derogatory reference to kabbalah as a superstitious aberration from Jewish religious practices; originally, "kabbalah" described a body of mystical Jewish teachings based on an interpretation of the Hebrew scripture as containing hidden meanings.

8. Hebrew; sing.: *bedikah*. Under Jewish purity law, this refers to testing by a woman to determine that she has finished her menstrual period.

9. See, e.g., "100,000 March Here in 6-Hour Protest over Nazi Policies" and "50,000 Jews Unite in Chicago Protests," *New York Times*, both May 11, 1933.

books on Berlin's Opera Square as an ominous sign. Like the previous correspondent, however, in document 2-6 Weltsch too, perhaps, betrays the hope that an authentic Judaism—in his case the emphasis is on national and cultural identity rather than religiosity—may yet earn the Nazis' recognition as a distinct entity characterized by integrity and self-respect.

DOCUMENT 2-6: "Beacon and Reflection," *Jüdische Rundschau*, **May 12, 1933 (translated from German).**

[. . .] For us <u>Jews</u> too this is a memorable night. The large spotlights on Opera Square [in Berlin] also illuminate the intertwining [*Verschlungenheit*] of <u>our</u> existence and <u>our</u> fate. Not only Jews, but also men of purely German blood stood accused. They are judged individually based on their actions. For Jews, however, no individual reasons are necessary; instead, the old slogan applied: "The Jew will be burned." [. . .] But for us Jews, it is the <u>symbolic nature</u> of the event that matters. It is a beacon that calls us to our senses.

<u>Jew, reflect on your own self.</u>

This is what for us is written in flames into this night's sky. [. . .]

What we see being played out here is not just an enormous <u>human</u> tragedy, in which writers of greater and lesser stature are branded by the very community for which they had been writing. It is also the tragedy of an entire <u>Jewish generation</u>, which given the objective conditions under which it lived had no choice but to pursue the goal of inner and external assimilation. And now the very sphere that this generation saw as the high point of successful integration is the place from which it has most painfully and ruthlessly been expelled. But we must recognize that not even this fire has destroyed the connection between Jews and German culture. [. . .]

But what is cast out [*ausgesondert*] here is not work of central Jewish value [*positives Gut des Judentums*]. We refuse to designate literature as Jewish based purely on the <u>negative</u> criterion of being "not German." With few exceptions, German Jewish writers did not write from a *Jewish* consciousness and a sense of <u>Jewish</u> responsibility. Most of these Jews did not take Jewry seriously! Instead, only when <u>both</u> sides have a vibrant feeling for ancestry and people [*Stammes- und Volksgefühl*] can the separation desired by national Germandom [*nationales Deutschtum*] become fruitful.

<u>The emergence of Jewish pride [*jüdischen Selbstbewusstseins*] is our business, not that of those non-Jews who reject us. [. . .]</u>

It was difficult to convey to the outside world the true character of the Third Reich. Not only did the new police state impose restrictions on free expression and communication, but even those with the liberty to write found it hard to capture the unprecedented, contradictory, and often surreal character of everyday life. Document 2-7, written in the summer of 1933 by an unknown author, did find its way into the files of the **World Jewish Congress** office in Paris and addressed the basic options that seemed available to Jews in Germany.

DOCUMENT 2-7: **Anonymous report on the situation of German Jews sent to the Office of the Executive Committee of the World Jewish Congress in Paris, no date (ca. June 1933), USHMMA RG 11.001M.36, reel 193 (SAM 1190-3-7, 172–78) (translated from German).**

[. . . ; following a litany of anti-Jewish measures:]

29. Far more serious than the material hardship of today is the crisis of morale and despair. All German Jews have seen their lives turned upside down. Their whole world has collapsed around them, and they feel they have no future.

In this desperate situation, they [i.e., the Jews in Germany] have three alternatives:

1. to accept the situation
2. not to accept it
3. to emigrate
They will choose the first alternative. [. . .]

32. I am convinced that German Jews prefer to resign themselves to the present situation and will attempt to fit into the new state in some fashion.

Those who follow this route are neither cowardly nor bad Jews. On the contrary, the[ir] best leaders think this way. The non-national [i.e., non-Zionist] Jews—who are expected to renounce individual emancipation, that great achievement of their fathers—must strike a compromise because they cannot cut themselves off from Germany. And the destruction of [Jewish] emancipation is already a fact, not just a threat that might yet be stopped if they mustered enough resistance.

For the national [Zionist] Jews, this idea is even closer at hand. They were always skeptical that individual emancipation [for Jews] would endure, and they believe they have so much inner strength that even when they strike compromises with the National Socialist state (however this entity [*Gebilde*] might look), they will be able to assert their Jewish dignity and human dignity. [. . .]

36. [. . .] We can also ask ourselves, how far one should be willing to compromise.

But, above all, one must ask, does another path even exist?

37. They can choose to fight.

This path is in theory by far the most attractive. But one should contemplate what this would entail.

It would mean fighting to reestablish a construction [*Gebilde*] that has already been destroyed, the individual emancipation of Jews, which is completely at odds with National Socialist ideology as a whole. It would mean taking on the whole current system, a system that has defeated the Catholics, the Socialists, and the Communists and that is supported by the [German] people and has all the weapons at its disposal, as well as the determination to use them. [. . .]

Of course this is all idle speculation. German Jews, including the younger generation, are primarily bourgeois and petit bourgeois in their orientation. Had they not actually been Jews, they would have been as receptive or unreceptive to National Socialism as all other Germans, and they will not wage a heroic revolutionary fight against the new state order. [. . .]

In a situation where German Jews faced a hostile majority all around them and a lack of unity within their own ranks, many found it difficult to demonstrate much empathy with those beyond their immediate circle of family, friends, and community. Solidarity with other groups targeted by hostile Nazi measures was often lacking; old stereotypes about other minorities could still kick in. In a letter to CV president **Julius Brodnitz**, a Berlin rabbi expressed his deep dismay that Jews, "the bearers of the purest insights into deity," had been ranked by the Nazis behind "gypsies" in the racial hierarchy.[10] However, the plight of anti-Nazi groups on the political Left resonated particularly with those German Jews who had shared their political orientation. And there were Jews such as **Willy Cohn,** who could feel sympathy even for traditionally marginal groups, like the Romani people he encountered on a tour of the Silesian countryside.

---

10. Letter by Rabbi Link to Julius Brodnitz, February 23, 1933; USHMMA RG 11.001M.31, reel 114 (SAM 721-1-2562, 7–8).

DOCUMENT 2-8: Willy Cohn, diary entry for August 30, 1933, translated from Norbert Conrads, ed., *Kein Recht, Nirgends: Tagebuch vom Untergang des Breslauer Judentums, 1933–1941* (Cologne: Böhlau Verlag, 2007), 1:72.

August 30, 1933

Hohndorf, Wednesday. [. . .] In the afternoon some pretty gypsy ladies [*Zigeunerweiber*] came by. I made them a present of 10 Pfennig[11]; also talked to them for a while. One feels somehow connected to them. They are also an ostracized people. They were pleased when I tried out my few Slavic words. They told me that they speak *Wendisch* with one another.[12] One wanted to tell my fortune, but I didn't want this. Don't look into the future.

JEWISH LEADERSHIP AND THE "JEWISH SECTOR"

When it came to legal advice and relief work within their own ranks, German Jewry could still rely on experience gained over decades. Especially in the area of social self-help, newly founded organizations such as the Central Committee of German Jews for Help and Reconstruction (**Zentralausschuss der deutschen Juden für Hilfe und Aufbau**, or ZAHA) could draw on a rich tradition of Jewish activism as well as a highly skilled and devoted staff.[13] More questionable, however, was whether in this new era the entrenched framework of so many separate Jewish organizations could provide sufficient leadership and representation. The leaders of the established bodies argued that the existing institutional infrastructure was flexible enough to weather the new challenges. But in the summer of 1933, there were increasingly strident calls from the provinces for a clear and strong Jewish voice vis-à-vis the outside world. The more society, the bureaucracy, and the economy in Germany were restructured along the lines of the so-called **Führer** principle, with its focus on Hitler's charismatic leadership and devoted followers, the more it seemed that German Jews were ill equipped to present a united front against the regime.

The only body at Reich level with any claim to presenting a united leadership was the Reich Representation of the Jewish State Associations (Reichsver-

---

11. One Reichsmark equaled one hundred Pfennig.

12. *Wendisch* (also: *Sorbisch*) is a western Slavic language spoken mostly by members of the Slavic minority living in the German states of Saxony and Brandenburg.

13. See Clemens Vollnhals, "Jüdische Selbsthilfe bis 1938," in *Die Juden in Deutschland, 1933–1945: Leben unter nationalsozialistischer Herrschaft*, ed. Wolfgang Benz (Munich: C. H. Beck, 1989), 314–411; Trude Maurer, "From Everyday to State of Emergency: Jews in Weimar and Nazi Germany," in Kaplan, *Jewish Daily Life*, 271–373.

tretung der jüdischen Landesverbände), a loose association of Jewish communal institutions founded in January 1932. In February 1933 their top five leaders, among them Rabbi **Leo Baeck**, consistuted a small group entitled to "take at any time without any delay the steps deemed necessary" for the interests of German Jewry as a whole.[14] Despite adopting the promising title of "Reich Representation of German Jews" in March 1933, the group enjoyed little real authority and found it hard to make its voice heard alongside influential Jewish institutions like the **CV**, **RjF**, and **ZVfD**, as well as the Berlin Jewish community. Probably the early Reich Representation's most significant legacy was that it provided the core personnel and structure for the later, very similarly named but more representative and authoritative, new **Reichsvertretung der deutschen Juden** (RV) formed in September 1933.[15] During the spring and summer of 1933, appeals like the one circulated by the Jewish community in the eastern German border town of Görlitz gave voice to the prevailing pressure from the middle and lower echelons.

DOCUMENT 2-9: Circular issued by the board and representatives of the Jewish community of Görlitz, May 28, 1933, USHMMA RG 11.001M.31, reel 191 (SAM 721-1-1989, 1-2) (translated from German).

[. . .] Resolution by the Jewish Community of Görlitz on May 28, 1933

The Jews of Görlitz hereby notify the Reichsvertretung der deutschen Juden,[16] all state communal organizations [*Landesverbände*], communities, and all Jewish organizations of the following resolution, which has been unanimously approved:

The national upheaval in Germany and the course it has taken have not met with adequate, unified representation and leadership from German Jews. Thus a fundamental restructuring of German Jewry is now imperative. We urge all of the aforementioned organizations to avoid a drawn-out process of fragmentation by subordinating themselves to an authoritarian leadership that enjoys the unequivocal trust of all circles within German Jewry. This leadership should consist of one or a small number of personages and an advisory board consisting of people who

---

14. Günther Plum, "Deutsche Juden oder Juden in Deutschland?" in Benz, *Juden in Deutschland*, 51.

15. See Otto Dov Kulka, ed., *Deutsches Judentum unter dem Nationalsozialismus*, vol. 1, *Dokumente zur Geschichte der Reichsvertretung der Juden, 1933–1939* (Tübingen: Mohr Siebeck, 1997).

16. This refers to the earlier Reich Representation, that is, the precursor to the "new" Reichsvertretung formed in September 1933.

are genuinely capable of action and drawn from all positive Jewish camps within German Jewry.

This new, single authorized leadership for German Jews should not leave any stone unturned in order to instigate a discussion of the Jewish problem in an upright Jewish manner with the Reich government and to remedy the spiritual, cultural, and economic difficulties facing German Jews on the basis of reciprocal loyalty.

We call for all Jewish communities in Germany to join our appeal without delay and without regard for their membership structure up to now.

Board and representatives of the synagogue community Görlitz.

As the Görlitz appeal indicates, such calls were not always simply about ensuring that the Jewish community enjoyed strong leadership. Many German Jews on the political right argued that Jewry needed to restructure its organizational framework along the lines of the new state's corporate-authoritarian model. Here was yet another variant—complementing the Orthodox and Zionist ones we have already seen—of the hope that a reformed German Jewry might earn the new regime's respect and recognition. This emphasis on firm leadership and proving German Jews' national loyalty was far from restricted to what could be called German Jewry's lunatic fringe, namely, extreme right-wing, marginal organizations such as Max Naumann's **Verband nationaldeutscher Juden** (VndJ) or the Schwarzes Fähnlein (literally, "Little Black Flag").[17] In addition to the World War I veterans represented by the RjF, a significant faction within both the CV and the Jewish mainstream communities wanted to use the crisis to stage a massive shift to the right, if possible by using the existing organizations, and if necessary, by creating new ones.

The intense, often bitter debates about how to present a united Jewish front suggest that such intracommunal exchanges may have served to compensate for Jews' increasing isolation from the outside world and their much reduced possibilities for implementing effective defenses against all that now beset them. But they also revealed the rift between those who demanded complete—and as we know now, completely unrealistic—identification with the national cause and those who argued that Jews must accept the fact of their

---

17. On right-wing fringe groups within the spectrum of German Jewish organizations, see Carl J. Rheins, "The Schwarzes Fähnlein, Jungenschaft, 1932–1934," *LBIYB* 23 (1978): 173–97; Carl J. Rheins, "The Verband nationaldeutscher Juden, 1921–1933," *LBIYB* 25 (1980): 243–68; Carl J. Rheins, "Deutscher Vortrupp, Gefolgschaft deutscher Juden, 1933–1935," *LBIYB* 26 (1981): 207–29.

exclusion. Kurt Rosenberg described in his diary his reaction to a particularly controversial display of zeal by an ultranationalist German Jewish faction.

DOCUMENT 2-10: Kurt Rosenberg, diary entry for June 1, 1933, LBINY AR 25279, folder 6 (translated from German).

June 1, 1933

I was in Berlin yesterday. The transformation of street life is deeply disturbing. Hardly any respectable [*gepflegte*] people—many unkempt individuals in their place—a noticeable proletarianization can be seen on the streets.

Huge notices are posted on the Berlin billboards:

"German citizens of the Jewish faith! Did you know that your so-called leaders are now very openly making deals with the Zionists? Do you realize that the path that these leaders are forcing you down will inevitably lead to the ghetto (as a national minority or the like)? Is this what you want? Or do you wish to remain nationally minded German nationals [*Nationaldeutsche*], regardless of all discrimination [*Zurücksetzungen*]. For those who choose a future in Germany, read our newspaper, *Der Nationaldeutsche Jude* and our pamphlets, in which we have fought for Germandom and against all things un-German for the past twelve years. Verband nationaldeutscher Juden."

The CV took exception to this poster in a sharp polemic that appeared in [its newspaper,] the *CV-Zeitung*, on June 1, 1933. But no polemic can be sharp enough when speaking out against such a publicly conducted demonstration of Jewish divisiveness—the Jews of all people should look beyond their internal disputes and close ranks in this bloody defensive battle. The posters are so thoroughly offensive that I was tempted to spit on them. [. . .]

As the CV stressed in its rebuttal to the poster published by the Verband nationaldeutscher Juden, this kind of Jewish factionalism and infighting would give "pleasure to all those who want to strike the heart of German Jewry in its entirety"; it decried "Jewish self-destruction" (*jüdische Selbstzerfleischung*) and instead called for an increase in organized self-help, already manifest in the creation of the ZAHA and, it contended, in the growth of the CV's ranks by one thousand members since February 1933.[18]

---

18. See "Der Kampf an der Anschlagsäule," *CV-Zeitung*, June 1, 1933, 199.

A report on the founding meeting of what turned out to be the stillborn New Front of German Jews in Berlin, sent to the CV main office by a member who attended the event, sheds further light on the atmosphere and the many divisions prevailing within the Jewish population in these months.

DOCUMENT 2-11: Report sent to the CV head office on the inaugural meeting of the New Front of German Jews held June 13, 1933, in Berlin, USHMMA RG 11.001M.31, reel 191 (SAM 721-1-1985, 1–8) (translated from German).

Report on the Inaugural Meeting of the New Front of German Jews, held in the building of the Society of Friends on June 13, 1933, at 7:30 p.m.

The meeting took place in the Great Hall of the Society of Friends (*Gesellschaft der Freunde*), which was initially filled with approximately 350 to 400 people. During the first uproar, the hall slowly emptied. Audience members drifted out continuously throughout. At most, 75 people were still present during the final speech.

The chairman of the meeting was Friedländer the auditor [*Bücherrevisor*]. The first official speaker was

Mr. Donig, son of the attorney Donig, deemed the future leader of the youth by the chairman.[19] He said,

["]Our program is this: we believe in Germany, but it cannot continue like this. Fighting antisemitism, nationalism, is unnecessary. Originally, nationalism was not at all antisemitic. It only became antisemitic when Jews fought against it because of the boycott, etc. National socialism's antisemitism was aimed against Jewish capitalism. This is no longer necessary, which is why the fight against antisemitism in the NSDAP seems promising. We are Germans and have no reason to relinquish German culture. The idea of fascism is not in opposition to our feelings. We have to reconcile ourselves to national socialism and have to support the new government. It is to be hoped that the new government will work with us. Hope in this direction can especially be drawn from the fact that in the last weeks some improvement has taken place.["] Voice from the audience:

19. Likely to be Dr. jur. Arthur Donig (1881–?), who emigrated to Argentina in 1939 with his wife, Regina, and son Curt Günther Donig (1913–?). See List 226 (published April 4, 1941) in *Expatriation Lists as Published in the "Reichsanzeiger," 1933–1945*, ed. Michael Hepp (Munich: K. G. Saur, 1985), 1:482; Berlin address books, 1933, 1935, 1938 (http://adressbuch.zlb.de); *Datenbank zur Liste der jüdischen Einwohner im Deutschen Reich, 1933–1945* (Berlin: Bundesarchiv, 2008). No reliable information could be traced on the other names mentioned in this document.

"We already held talks with top people and received assurances; more on this later." (But this did not happen.) [Donig continues: "]We have the chance to establish a good working relationship with the new system if we apply ourselves for a long time, as happened in the similar case of Hungary.[20] The Zionists do not have this opportunity. The CV cannot take the leading role because until now it has always fought national socialism. Thus, new men have to come forward. The new Reichsvertretung is also not suitable because it is divided into so many different factions. After the poster affair [*Plakataffäre*], the Naumann movement has no right to lead and has given ammunition to our opponents.[21] For all these reasons it is necessary to have a new organization that will not end up fighting any of the existing factions, but rather, will unite all of them.["]

The 2nd official speaker,

Schwab the pharmacist:

"We are searching for a path to Jewish renewal. In the last months, German Jewry has appeared to be a helpless ship, exhausted from the fight between Zionists and German-minded Jews. We don't want the world's pity; we can take on our enemies ourselves (applause). In the last months German Jews have been defenseless because of their mentality, their sensitivity, and their kind Jewish hearts. A path must be found into the heart of the Aryan *Volksgenossen*, no matter at what cost. Reconciliation is necessary. Anyone who leaves and goes abroad is a traitor. Only some of the German *Volksgenossen* are against us. Recently we had ample proof of German faithfulness." The speaker then recited the many well-known demands for how Jews have to change. For instance, we have to take part in sports; not all sports are dangerous (laughter [from the audience]). One can take everything away from the Jews, but not their belief in Germany. We will never become renegades. We have not always remained dignified enough. We subscribe to the idea of authoritarian leadership [*autoritären Führergedanken*] and the fight against parliamentary liberalism. We should not miss out on Germany's rejuvenation. The leadership generation of Germans and Jews is too old. We do not want to push youth into the foreground, but we should insist, Take us with you! Parents will be a moral example to their children again. Children will respect their parents again. Women should not use makeup. We

---

20. On the antisemitic movement in Hungary, see Ivan T. Berend, "The Road toward the Holocaust: The Ideological and Political Background," in *The Holocaust in Hungary: Forty Years Later*, ed. Randolph L. Braham and Bela Vago (New York: Social Science Monographs, 1985), 31–41.

21. See document 2-10; Rheins, "The Verband nationaldeutscher Juden."

reject cultural bolshevism as practiced especially by Jewish writers and stage directors now living abroad. [. . .]

Naphtali (?) [meaning: name uncertain] "I am speaking as a non-aligned Jew." He speaks against the second official speaker, Schwab, who attacks writers who went into foreign exile. At the conclusion, the speaker makes statements in support of Zionism. Because the speaker looks very bad—Jewish—Schwab declares him to be a Jew from the east [*Ostjude*] who should not have a voice in this setting. (Huge uproar, pronouncements for and against Jews from Eastern Europe, for and against Zionists. The speaker is unable to continue.)

A further speaker supports Naphtali. One should not insult Jews from the east since they are also people with Jewish blood. "I lost my job because of my Marxism. As a Marxist, I fought for equal rights for Jews. Our problem is that there are too many intellectuals in Jewish gatherings. No one bothers with the workers and the clerks, or with the unemployed in the dole queues. That's why there is no community encompassing all of us. A fundamental problem is the constant efforts by parents to give their children a higher education and academic degrees. German Jews are always accused of this. But there are no ties to the masses.["] The speaker demands a new election of the community leadership. [. . .]

The meeting ended in disarray; nothing was heard again of the "new front." The report shows, however, that in the turmoil of the summer of 1933, the small right wing within German Jewry tried to force a redefinition of the organizational agenda. More than the extreme Right spearheaded by the Naumann movement, it was the veterans' organization RjF that had gained ground, acquiring additional members and achieving success in interceding with the regime. As a result of its lobbying in the circle around Reich President **Hindenburg**, the RjF managed to have exemptions included in the Civil Service Law and other regulations, which for the time being protected former soldiers and their families from the full force of anti-Jewish policy. Until their revocation with the passage of the Nuremberg Laws in September 1935, these exemption clauses were to be vital to many Jews in their efforts to retain their jobs and make a living. The evidence that its leadership had gotten a more favorable reception in the halls of power boosted the RjF's standing within German Jewry.

Emboldened by such political success and by the hope that the regime's propaganda focus on "soldierly qualities" might override its antisemitic agenda, the RjF chairman Leo Löwenstein proposed a "leaders' council" (*Führerrat*) to incorporate the new national trend toward more authoritarian leadership. He immediately ran into opposition from Zionists, as well as more moderate mainstream Jewish functionaries, many belonging to the higher echelons of the CV. While agreeing on the need for a nationwide German Jewish umbrella organization, they saw the dangers of overstepping the mark in adapting to the new circumstances. **Ignaz Maybaum**, a rabbi from the eastern German city of Frankfurt an der Oder, former soldier and a member of the RjF, voiced some of these concerns in the pages of the Zionist *Jüdische Rundschau*. His eloquent appeal had an immediate effect, prompting Löwenstein to withdraw his *Führerrat* suggestion until some unnamed later date.[22]

DOCUMENT 2-12: **Ignaz Maybaum, "Rejection of the RjF,"** *Jüdische Rundschau,* **June 16, 1933 (translated from German).**

As a former soldier I am a member of the Reichsbund jüdischer Frontsoldaten. I believe in the need for this organization. As part of German Jewry's struggle to secure its proper place within Germany, the RjF has a particular task which legitimates its right to act alongside other Jewish organizations. It never occurred to me that through my membership in the RjF, I might find myself in conflict with other Jewish organizations, be it the Zionist Organization, be it the CV. [. . .]

The national leadership of the RjF published an "Appeal to the Jews of Germany" in *Schild* on May 25, 1933.[23] [. . .] What can be the reason for lines such as the following: "While certain Jewish institutions go behind the RjF's back and seek to undermine its efforts, our organization [Bund] will not stoop to such behavior." We become even more uncomfortable when we go on to read, "Through our efforts, we (printed in bold) have saved thousands of Jewish livelihoods." It is embarrassing enough in our current distress to read such vainglorious sentences, as though German Jewry had won back all the rights of which it has been deprived. [. . .] Why is the "we" printed in bold? The next sentence follows suit. There we read,

---

22. See letter by Löwenstein to CV and other German Jewish organizations, June 17, 1933; USHMMA RG 11.001M.31, reel 101 (SAM 721-1-1986, 11–27). Leo Löwenstein (1876–1956) was a trained chemist and World War I veteran who, in 1919, founded the RjF. From 1933 he also served as president of its sports organization, Der Schild, which merged in 1934 with the Zionist Makkabi sports clubs to become the sole Jewish sports association in Nazi Germany (1935: 185 clubs with roughly 20,000 members). The RjF and Der Schild were dissolved in 1938; in 1940, Löwenstein was drafted for forced labor in Berlin and managed to leave Germany in 1943, going first to Sweden and later to Switzerland. See Barkai, *"Wehr Dich!,"* 307.

23. *Der Schild* was the name of both RjF's journal and its sports organization.

"We will continue on behalf of our Jewish brothers in the German Fatherland to fight for every inch of ground, and to hold on to every position that can be defended." Both sentences speak of "we" and not the others. By the others, they mean the other Jewish associations. [. . .]

The RjF's appeal speaks of the organization's positive attitudes towards Germandom. Let us first agree that there is not a single Jewish organization in Germany that was not always conscious of its ties to Germany, that did not earnestly enjoin its members to fulfill their full duties as German citizens, and that did not simply assume it to be self-evident that every German Jew would feel love for Germany. By dint of their unceasing struggle against the dogmas of political liberalism, the Zionist group among German Jews might even hope to meet with the most understanding—both in terms of their Jewish aspirations and their relationship to Germany—from the national circles that have come to power in Germany. There is no German Jew—be it Zionist or CV member, such distinctions are irrelevant here—who does not experience the exclusion of Jews in the new German state as a deep misfortune and who is not trying to think of everything possible—what, however, is possible?—to avert this fate. [. . .] The same appeal that, with its proud "we" language, distances itself from the other Jewish associations at the same time declares its ties to Germandom. It must give rise to the false impression that in this respect, too, the other Jewish associations fall short in the RjF's eyes and that in its loyalty to Germany, the RjF stands above them. To have conveyed this impression, the impression that not all German Jewry stands united in its commitment to Germandom and that some of its representatives—among whose ranks the RjF would like to see itself—are to be particularly commended in this respect, is an unforgivable step against which we must protest in the sharpest terms. [. . .]

Resistance to the formation of a united Jewish leadership came not only from nationalist groups like the RjF, with its demands for a more prominent role, but also from regional and local Jewish communal bodies, particularly the large Jewish community of Berlin and its outspokenly anti-Zionist leadership spearheaded by **Heinrich Stahl**. But in the end, a small group of moderate functionaries was able to resolve the issue of national representation. In the absence of a charismatic leader with universal appeal, the focus had to be on consensus building; Leo Baeck and **Otto Hirsch**, the latter representing the Jewish communal bodies in Württemberg, seemed the two persons best qualified to head a body authoritative enough to lead—as two prominent German Jewish functionaries put it—"the positive forces of German Jewry."[24]

On September 17, 1933, months of discussions and negotiations culminated in the formation of the new Reichsvertretung, with Baeck as its president and Hirsch as its director. Most major organizations and communities joined. Reports in the Jewish press on the formation of German Jewry's first representative national body ranged from matter-of-fact to critical in tone, suggesting that no one faction could claim to have won an outright victory. No doubt, the muted reaction reflected the fact that in the current climate there was no guarantee of success, for all the historic achievement in creating a strong national representative body. In their inaugural address, Baeck and his team of leaders struck a solemn note, outlining to the Jewish public the Reichsvertretung's mission.

DOCUMENT 2-13: Appeal at the inauguration of the Reichsvertretung, *Bayerische Israelitische Gemeindezeitung*, October 1, 1933 (translated from German).[25]

[. . . ; following introductory remarks by *Bayerische Israelitische Gemeindezeitung*.] In days that are harsh and bitter, as only days in Jewish history can be, but also significant as few have been, the Jewish regional associations, the large Jewish organizations, and the large [Jewish] communities of Germany have together agreed to entrust us with the leadership and representation of the German Jews.

This decision was neither the product of partisanship nor a desire for advancing special interests. Rather, it grew solely out of our recognition that the life and future of the German Jews today depend on their unity and ability to lend each other support. Thus, the first task will be to breathe life into this unity. The vitality and independence of every organization and group should be respected, but in all large and decisive matters, there can be only one community, only the one collectivity [*Gesamtheit*] of German Jews. Those who today choose a separate path, those who today cut themselves off, act against the German Jews' imperative to survive. The position of individual groups—even those that are much larger and stronger than our own—has become very dif-

24. Letter by Ernst Herzfeld and Willy Katzenstein to Otto Hirsch, August 1, 1933, printed in Kulka, *Deutsches Judentum*, 61; Plum, "Deutsche Juden," 55.

25. The appeal was published in numerous Jewish journals; see also Kulka, *Deutsches Judentum*, 71–72. On the formation of the Reichsvertretung, see Kulka, *Deutsches Judentum*, 10–14; Jacob Boas, "German Jewish Internal Politics under Hitler, 1933–1938," *LBIYB* 29 (1984): 3–12.

ferent under the new government. Legislation and the organization of the economy have been put on a particular path, both inclusive and exclusionary. We need to acknowledge this fact without deluding ourselves. Only then will we be alert to every honorable opportunity that opens up and be equipped to fight for every right, every place, every sphere of life [*Lebensraum*]. By working and providing work, by accomplishing something as a community, German Jews will be able to prove themselves in the new state.

The opportunity to realize our ideas and carry out our duties has been granted to us in only one realm, but it is a crucial one: that of our Jewish life and our Jewish future. Here our tasks have been set down most clearly.

We face new obligations in providing Jewish education; Jewish schools need to cover new subjects, while preserving and protecting traditional subjects, so that we can equip the young generation with a foundation of spiritual strength, inner stamina, and physical vigor. We need to give our youth new options to be trained and retrained [*umgeschichtet*] in jobs oriented to the future so that they have some prospects for securing their existence. The existing sources, together with everything that has already been started and attempted, should be brought together to assist and protect [our youth]. We need to counteract all that threatens to undermine [*Zersetzenden*] and to devote all our strength to reinforcing and building upon the religious foundations of Jewry.

German Jews have been stripped of nearly all of the economic security that they once enjoyed. We should lead the individual out of his isolation with the resources still available to us. Corporate ties and alliances—to the extent that they are allowed—can increase our existing strength and provide some security for the weak, can convert experiences and relationships into something useful for everyone.

Many will lose their foothold in their work and professions on German soil. All questions and opinions aside, we have to face the clear historical necessity of breaking new ground [*Neuland*] for our youth.[26] It has become a huge undertaking to find positions for them and pave the way for them—be it on the holy ground of Palestine, to which destiny has given a new era, or anywhere that German Jews can show their character, wherewithal, and willingness to exert themselves, not by taking away anyone's bread but by producing bread for everyone.

---

26. The term *Neuland* has connotations beyond "new opportunities"; see Theodor Herzl's novel *Altneuland* ("Old-New Land").

For this, as for everything else, we hope for the understanding support of state agencies and for the respect of our non-Jewish fellow citizens, whom we join in love for and allegiance to Germany.

We build not only on the foundation of a lively sense of community and the German Jews' sense of responsibility but also on the self-sacrifice and helping hand of our brothers everywhere.

We want to stand together and work, trusting in our God, for the honor of the Jewish name.

May the essence [*Wesen*] of the German Jew emerge anew from the suffering of today.

Reichsvertretung der deutschen Juden [The names of signatories follow.][27]

Not all German Jews accepted the call for unity. While the ultranationalist VndJ publicly rejected the new Reichsvertretung as a "ghetto creation" dominated by "alien Jewry" (*Fremdjudentum*),[28] some Orthodox groups also refrained from joining the umbrella organization until 1937. In carrying their concerns to the regime separately, they were not alone; in this early phase, even Reichsvertretung member organizations like the ZVfD or the RjF did so.[29] Orthodox functionaries tried to convey Orthodoxy's particular virtues while at the same time addressing more general features of German Jewish experience.

DOCUMENT 2-14: **Letter by the Free Association for the Interests of Orthodox Jewry to Hitler, October 4, 1933, quoted in translation from Marc B. Shapiro, *Between the Jeshiva World and Modern Orthodoxy: The Life and Works of Rabbi Jehiel Jacob Weinberg, 1884–1966* (Portland, OR: Littman Library of Jewish Civilization, 1999), 225–33.**

[. . .] The undersigned Orthodox Jewish organizations, representing that section of German Jewry which considers the Jewish religion as the sole ground and justification of the historical existence of the Jewish people, feel compelled, Herr Reich Chancellor, to set forth openly and honestly their attitude to the Jewish question. [. . .]

---

27. In addition to Baeck as the Reichsvertretung president, eight men representing different German Jewish organizations and bodies, including Otto Hirsch and Heinrich Stahl, signed the appeal.

28. See the flyer of the Verband nationaldeutscher Juden, printed in Kulka, *Deutsches Judentum*, 82–83.

29. See early petitions to Hitler and other government agencies in Klaus J. Herrmann, *Das Dritte Reich und die deutsch-jüdischen Organisationen, 1933–1934* (Cologne: Karl Heymanns Verlag, 1969).

The present situation of German Jewry, as created for them by the German people, is a completely intolerable one, in respect of their legal position and also of their economic existence, their good name, and their scope for religious activity. [. . .] The situation of German Jewry must therefore strike the objective observer throughout the world as plainly desperate, and it is understandable that the German national government is only too easily suspected of deliberately planning the destruction of German Jewry. This mistaken view must be refuted with concrete evidence, if any attempt to enlighten the outside world is to prove successful.

Orthodox Jewry has no wish to abandon its conviction that the German government does not seek the destruction of German Jewry. Even if some individuals do have this objective, we do not believe that it meets with the approval of the Führer or of the German government.

VII. But if we are wrong, if you, Herr Reich Chancellor, and the national government you lead, if the responsible members of the Reich leadership of the NSDAP [Nazi Party] should indeed have made it their objective to eradicate German Jewry from the German body politic, then we would rather cease nurturing illusions and learn the bitter truth. [. . .] If we have to, we shall have the courage to shoulder our tragic fate and leave the outcome confidently to the God of history.

The urgent needs of the moment that had led to the creation of the new Reichsvertretung also prompted the emergence of a much more extensive Jewish "sector," a network of cultural, professional, and welfare associations designed to provide a separate Jewish living space within the new Reich. In fact, well before the national leadership question was settled, a variety of Jewish organizations had already begun to coordinate their relief and assistance work, most notably through the ZAHA.[30] Building on existing ties, and with an eye to enhancing the education, training, and material benefit of German Jewry, especially its youth, communal leaders forged internal alliances that also helped in representing the interests of their clientele vis-à-vis the new regime. The Reich Committee of Jewish Youth Associations (Reichsausschuss der jüdischen Jugendverbände), formed in 1924, was one such Jewish organization that managed to obtain accreditation from the authorities. As a result it was able to boost its activities and provide its members with some level of protection.[31]

---

30. See Adler-Rudel, *Jüdische Selbsthilfe*; Vollnhals, "Jüdische Selbsthilfe," 314–30; Maurer, "From Everyday to State of Emergency," 271–373.

31. See also Friedrich S. Brodnitz, "Memories of the Reichsvertretung: A Personal Report," *LBIYB* 31 (1986): 267–77, regarding the practical usefulness of the identification document (*Führerausweis*) reprinted here.

DOCUMENT 2-15: "Führerausweis" Heinz Kellermann; USHMMA Acc. 2007.96 Kellermann collection, box 2.

[Front:] FÜHRERAUSWEIS Nr. 4
Reichsausschuss der jüdischen Jugendverbände
    [Inside left: facsimile reproduction of letter by Reich Youth Leader (*Reichsjugendführer*) Department Associations (*Abteilung Verbände*), Berlin, November 28, 1933]
    "I confirm the Reich Committee of Jewish Youth Associations [Reichsausschuss der jüdischen Jugendverbände] as the only responsible central organization of Jewish youth that has the right to give out leadership identity cards [*Führerausweise*] to its youth groups."
    [signed:] Der Jugendführer des Deutschen Reiches, Leiter der Abteilung Verbände
    [Inside right: photograph and personal information on Heinz Kellermann]
    "Association [Bund]: member of the leadership council [*Führerrat*] of the Reichsausschuss der jüdischen Jugendverbände e.V."
    [printed:] "This organization has been registered with the Reich Youth Leader and belongs to the sole responsible central organization of Jewish youth."
    Berlin, February 8, [19]34
    [signed:] Reichsausschuss der jüdischen Jugendverbände e.V.

Postwar historiography identified this attempt at, in the words of Ernst Simon, "construction during destruction" (*Aufbau im Untergang*) as the defining feature of German Jewish life after 1933.[32] Indeed, the boom in communal activities

---

32. Ernst Simon, *Aufbau im Untergang: Jüdische Erwachsenenbildung im national-sozialistischen Deutschland als geistiger Widerstand* (Tübingen: J. C. B. Mohr, 1959).

that started in the first year of the Nazi rise to power is particularly striking when juxtaposed with the simultaneous erosion of Jews' social and legal status. The greater the difficulties in sustaining a realistic perspective for a future existence in Germany, the more important became attempts at providing relief and lifting spirits. The attitude of the regime and the non-Jewish population to this project was highly ambivalent. The regime could only welcome the fact that Jews were being forced back upon their own resources, but it was unclear how far it would tolerate genuine autonomy for Jewish organizations or any steps that in the longer term would make life in Germany more livable for its Jews.

Theatrical and musical performances under the auspices of the **Kulturbund deutscher Juden** (Culture League of German Jews) provided one of the key channels still open to creative energies. While many top artists had fled with the first wave of emigration, others remained and eagerly embraced the chance to perform. Created in October 1933 in Berlin as the model for cultural associations in roughly one hundred German cities, the Kulturbund was supported by a sizeable though greatly fluctuating membership. Subject to the supervision of **Joseph Goebbels**'s Reich Propaganda Ministry, its aim was to provide a forum for Jewish performers and a separate space in which Jewish audiences could be among themselves.[33]

In the anonymity of the big cities, Jews were initially often able to attend mainstream performances, but the more they were excluded from such venues or made to feel uncomfortable in them, the more central the Kulturbund's activities became in their cultural calendar. Many of its performances aimed simply to offer a reprieve from reality with distraction and entertainment in the safety of an all-Jewish environment. But some, such as a production of Lessing's famous play *Nathan the Wise*—the very first event staged by the Kulturbund— offered a powerful commentary on current events.[34] Before the curtain went up at the premiere, the theater's director placed the evening ahead in its broader context.

---

33. Akademie der Künste, ed., *Geschlossene Veranstaltung: Der Jüdische Kulturbund in Deutschland, 1933–1941* (Berlin: Akademie Verlag, 1992); Alan E. Steinweis, "Hans Hinkel and German Jewry, 1933–1941," *LBIYB* 38 (1993): 209–19.

34. Gotthold Ephraim Lessing (1729–1781) was a German writer and philosopher best known for championing the need for religious tolerance through his play *Nathan the Wise* as well as his theoretical work *The Education of Humankind*.

DOCUMENT 2-16: Speech by Kurt Singer[35] on the opening night of the Kulturbund-production of *Nathan the Wise*, October 1, 1933, translated from Herbert Freeden, *Jüdisches Theater in Nazideutschland* (Tübingen: Niemeyer Verlag, 1964), 28.

[. . .] When the curtain is raised in the theater of the Kulturbund today for the first time, there is something that all of us will know: more is at stake here than the staging of a play. When the curtain rises we will have a sense that a community cobbled together out of necessity has become a community of productive labor. Only in this way does the theater, otherwise simply enjoyed as a site of entertainment and improvement, become a site of consecration and of a spiritual community in a time filled with pain. Never have the ties that bind stage and audience, the ties between the upper and lower tiers of the theater, been as strong as now. Never has the giving and the receiving been merged into one to such an extent as today, when every breath taken, every word, every gesture spent, seems to imprint onto our very soul the sense of being a community of fate. [. . .]

The image of spiritual community conjured up by Singer in the Berlin gala, powerful though it was, may have struck a jarring note in the ears of those Jews struggling against the odds in remote areas of the Reich. Berlin, with its large Jewish community, provided a unique sense of security, despite the proximity of Nazi centers of decision making. It was the recognition of this advantage that led to an exodus from smaller cities and towns and an ever greater concentration of Germany's Jews in the capital. The difficulty of small-town life in Germany became evident from the countless letters sent to the CV, whose writers voiced their sense of utter isolation and their experience of steep economic decline. From Bensheim in southwestern Germany, a CV member and avid reader of its newspaper observed bleakly that "the many Jews living in rural areas cannot stay if they want to keep from starving" and asked the Berlin head office whether they had "any idea of what is really happening???"[36]

The CV was just one organization within a growing network of institutions for relief, vocational retraining, and emigration efforts that had its roots

---

35. Trained as a doctor and nerve specialist, Kurt Singer (1885–1944) became a conductor, musicologist, and music critic. He cofounded the Kulturbund in 1933 and nurtured Jewish cultural activities after the Nazi rise to power. He emigrated to the Netherlands in 1939, was arrested in 1940 after the German invasion, and was eventually deported to Theresienstadt, where he died in January 1944. See Herbert A. Strauss and Werner Röder, eds., *International Biographical Dictionary*, 2:1088; Kulka, *Deutsches Judentum*, 530.

36. Letter by A. Reiling, Bensheim, to CV head office Berlin, October 30, 1933; USHMMA RG 11.001M.31, reel 121 (SAM 721-1-2675, 189).

in earlier decades of Jewish welfare work in- and outside Germany and was now being coordinated by the new Reichsvertretung. The ZAHA played the lead role in relief work, while a great variety of organizations focused more on training youth and retraining the unemployed for new occupations. The long-standing **Hilfsverein der deutschen Juden** (Relief Association of German Jews) handled requests for emigration to countries other than Palestine, while emigration to Palestine was the domain of the ZVfD-controlled **Palästina-Amt**. From abroad, Jewish organizations attempted to assist by providing funding and help, especially for emigration purposes. The early and amicable division of labor between different organizations in the Reich, despite their different histories and orientations, stands in marked contrast to the bitter debates between those who continued to emphasize German Jews' strong ties to *Deutschtum* and their German Fatherland on the one hand and those who advocated a primarily Jewish religious or Jewish national identity on the other. The new coordinated efforts in the welfare sector showed that despite all ideological differences, organized German Jewry was, even in this early phase of Nazi rule, already grappling for practical solutions to the existential problems created by German *Judenpolitik*. The commitment to working together also revealed at least some understanding that the outside pressures on them were likely only to increase.

CHAPTER 3

STRATEGIES FOR SURVIVAL

EMIGRATION, HOPES, AND REALITIES

To stay or to leave? Up and down the country, day in and day out, German Jewish families agonized about what to do. Husbands and wives were often torn in different directions. Parents and children disagreed about the proper course of action. For those not lucky enough to have well-informed contacts abroad, reliable information about conditions in potential destinations was hard to come by. Armed with our knowledge, we are of course struck by the fact that, despite the Nazi onslaught, over 90 percent of the Jewish community resolved to stay, at least for the time being. Yet, given the challenges facing any would-be emigrant, we might instead be surprised that in 1933 alone well over 5 percent of the German Jewish community quit their homeland.[1] At the **Palästina-Amt** in Berlin, according to its statistics, 1933 saw over thirty thousand Jews seeking information and assistance.[2]

While the implications of the decision to stay or to leave were huge, the thinking of those who stayed and those who left was often not so dissimilar. Many of those who turned their back on their homeland did so amid great uncertainty, as Otto Heinsheimer's letter, with which this volume opens, makes clear. Could all that was familiar, all that had been collectively fought for, be abandoned? Could one start over somewhere completely new? *Should* one start over somewhere new? For those who stayed, doubts about whether ordinary

---

1. See the section on "the emigration quandary" in Kaplan, *Between Dignity*, 62–74.
2. See Adler-Rudel, *Jüdische Selbsthilfe*, 81.

life was possible in Nazi Germany did not go away, as **Kurt Rosenberg**'s diary has already indicated.[3] Often tipping the balance and inducing people to leave were simple everyday things, such as whether one could continue to earn a living or whether one had experienced firsthand some particularly threatening or disturbing episode.

While the ultimate decisions had to be made by families and individuals, for Jewish organizations the debate was difficult as well. Within Germany conflicts between Zionists and non-Zionists continued. Indeed, with the stakes now so high, sometimes the battles were even more caustic than before. But on the question of emigration, the anti-Zionist positions were not as rigid as they had once been. As early as August 1933, **Eva Reichmann**, a **CV** official and staunch adherent of its ethos, wrote in the *CV-Zeitung* that there was virtually no German Jew "who does not draw the strongest consolation from the fact that Palestine is there, and from the positive developments currently taking place there, at a time otherwise very short on consolations."[4] Even so, she argued, deciding to go to Palestine would sever the deep bonds that a large majority of German Jews had to Germany, bonds that would be incredibly difficult to break. The German "Jewish question" would have to be solved above all within Germany.

For many observers in- and outside Germany, it was indeed inconceivable that so robust and important a segment of the international Jewish world should just up and leave. Zionists, true enough, might well quibble about the reality, or at least the validity, of the deep ties to which Eva Reichmann referred—but they could scarcely argue that Palestine, or any other place in the world for that matter, was ready to absorb over half a million German Jews.[5] In an era of unemployment, depression, and the associated anti-immigration politics, including latent or open antisemitism all over the advanced world, no one could imagine a mass open-door policy anywhere.

For the Zionists, Palestine was the most important and desirable destination. A League of Nations mandate since World War I, Palestine was controlled by Britain. As a result of Arab unrest, Britain had introduced quotas on Jewish immigration in the mid-1920s. The restrictions were imposed in part through requirements for evidence of financial health. The £1,000 (15,000 **Reichsmark**) required of those with no particular skills, "capitalists" as they were called, was a princely sum, equivalent to more than five years earnings for a top-paid industrial worker at the time. For those with relevant skills, smaller fees were to be

---

3. See document 2-2.

4. Eva Reichmann-Jungmann, "Unsere Stellung zum Palästina Problem," *CV-Zeitung*, August 3, 1933, 311.

5. Abraham Margaliot, "Emigration—Planung und Wirklichkeit," in Paucker, *The Jews in Nazi Germany*, 303–6.

paid (£500 for professionals and £250 for craftsmen in desirable fields), but even these were still very substantial amounts, generally out of reach.

Even before 1933, a number of organizations had existed at home and abroad to encourage emigration to Palestine and to help defray the costs of doing so. In September 1933, as a result of a decision by the Eighteenth Zionist Congress, new offices for German Jewish emigration were created in London and Palestine. Zionist negotiations with the Nazi regime meant that Palestine gained one particular financial advantage over other destinations. One of the barriers to leaving Germany for any foreign country lay in the strict controls imposed on capital and currency export. This was initially neither antisemitic in intent nor Nazi in origin but reflected Germany's dire, and indeed worsening, shortage of foreign currency at a time of very limited international trade. Of special importance for emigration to British-administered Palestine, therefore, was the **Ha'avara Agreement** concluded in August 1933 between the Reich Economics Ministry and the **ZVfD**. This arrangement used an ingenious device, enabling emigrants to take more of their wealth with them and to pay for the "capitalist visas." No actual money was transferred abroad, but in return for leaving their assets behind, emigrants benefited from the export of a substantial amount of German goods to Palestine; the goods were then sold in Palestine, and the receipts used to pay the emigrants' visa fees and provide start-up capital. For the Nazis, the agreement provided an instrument to speed up Jewish emigration and also created a market for German exports (even if it did not furnish the regime with valuable foreign currency since the exports were paid for with the Reichsmark that the emigrants left behind). German Zionists viewed this as a way for at least a limited number of German Jewish émigrés to retain some of their assets. Moreover, a part of the migrants' remaining property in the Reich could be used for Jewish welfare work. Until the beginning of the war, and despite growing opposition from German officials, thousands of German Jews benefited from this agreement. However, at the same time it increased tensions within international Zionism because it offered further evidence of the privileging of German Jews over other would-be migrants from countries, above all Poland, where the domestic prospects were not particularly rosy either.[6]

Despite this new advantage, the decision to go to Palestine was by no means an easy one, even for committed Zionists. Life there was tough, accompanied by often primitive conditions and conflicts with local Arabs that would only

---

6. On the Ha'avara Agreement and its context, see Francis R. Nicosia, *The Third Reich and the Palestine Question* (London: Tauris, 1985); Francis R. Nicosia, *Zionism and Anti-Semitism in Nazi Germany* (Cambridge: Cambridge University Press, 2008).

worsen over the course of the 1930s. Moreover, for many adults, such as **Willy Cohn**, it was not obvious that the skills they had acquired in Germany would be of any use in Palestine.

DOCUMENT 3-1: **Willy Cohn, diary entry for June 27, 1933, translated from Norbert Conrads, ed.,** *Kein Recht, Nirgends: Tagebuch vom Untergang des Breslauer Judentums, 1933–1941* **(Cologne: Böhlau Verlag, 2007), 1:56.**

June 27, 1933

Breslau, Tuesday. [. . .] We wanted to visit Arthur Wiener in the evening. He now lives on Viktoriastrasse. He returned from *Erez* recently and shared his impressions and practical information with us during the evening. Bildhauer was also there.[7] In short, there are many opportunities for a person with a head for business in a country that is still developing; everyone is content to be there. The Wiener family is quite determined to emigrate and start over with the limited capital that they have left. But, in their case, one knows that he will make a go of it, even under the most difficult circumstances.

The conversation then turned to more personal matters; Trudi [Cohn's wife] is always pushing for us to emigrate; I don't think that the prospects for leaving are very good for us, not with my background. As a result, I'm already a little tired of this discussion, particularly since I feel that for now one should wait to see how things develop. All of these discussions produce a lot of stress, and I always feel enormous regret that Trudi and I are so divided on this question; it's very sad. I don't want to start all over again. Here, I can do something, and here I am someone, but whether I can still make it down there remains to be seen! Of course some intelligent people view the prospects here as quite dismal. But I feel that I have very deep roots here. Experiencing terrible strain, all one's inner strength is needed just to pull through. It's particularly this silent battle with Trudi—who no doubt means well and may well be right from her perspective—that has affected me even more deeply than the whole affair with being put on leave at work [*Beurlaubung*]. [. . .]

---

7. Arthur Wiener, a businessman and friend of Willy Cohn's from Breslau, left for Palestine with his family in October 1933, intending to move there permanently. Erich Bildhauer (1881–1941) edited the *Jüdische Zeitung* in Breslau. He was apparently deported on November 25, 1941, to the Kovno ghetto, where he was murdered on arrival. See Norbert Conrads, ed., *Kein Recht, Nirgends: Tagebuch vom Untergang des Breslauer Judentums, 1933–1941* (Cologne: Böhlau Verlag, 2007), 1:52, 56, 349, 393–94; www.bundesarchiv.de/gedenkbuch.

Those who made it into Palestine certainly felt relief at having escaped Nazi Germany's oppressive atmosphere. Images advertising life in Palestine painted a rosy picture of happy people breaking new ground. Yet immigrants often remained anxious about their own futures and those of the people they had left behind. In sharing their experiences with families back in the Reich, émigrés tried to navigate between, on the one hand, raising anxieties by stressing the fragility of their economic prospects and, on the other, raving about life abroad in a way that might further depress those unable to join them. In a letter to his father, **Julius Moses**, in Berlin, Erwin Moses describes life in Tel Aviv amid violent conflict.

DOCUMENT 3-2: Erwin Moses, Tel Aviv, to Julius Moses, Berlin, November 5, 1933, translated from Dieter Fricke, *Jüdisches Leben in Berlin und Tel Aviv, 1933–1939: Der Briefwechsel des ehemaligen Reichstagsabgeordneten Dr. Julius Moses* (Hamburg: von Bockel, 1997), 115–19.

[. . .] In recent days, dark, foreboding clouds gathered over the land and we did not know what might lie ahead.[8] Now that the skies are clear again, the cares that afflicted us will soon be forgotten. Curious, how this big, fun-loving, lively city in this little country always stands its ground; while every street in both Jerusalem and Haifa trembled, confronted with mass Arab demonstrations as well as English tanks and cannons, nothing changed in Tel Aviv. A tight police cordon was set up on the street going to Jaffa, and Jewish police carried rifles on their shoulders, and—only so that no differentiation was made between Jaffa and Tel Aviv—a state of emergency was also declared here, during which no one could go out on the street between 6:00 p.m. and 5:00 a.m. The feeling of safety is quite complete in Tel Aviv, come what may; this is the Jewish city and strong, ideologically motivated, working Jews protect and defend their accomplishments so well that no one dares to start a fight here.

From a political perspective, things are very bitter; there is no prospect in either the question of immigration or that of land purchases of achieving agreement between Jews and Arabs, for the goals of both people are so diametrically opposed and there can be no compromise. England holds sway, and this time it opted for Jewish rights; it was particularly

---

8. Moses is referring to Arab anti-Jewish and anti-British violence in Jaffa in October and early November 1933. See Dieter Fricke, *Jüdisches Leben in Berlin und Tel Aviv, 1933–1939: Der Briefwechsel des ehemaligen Reichstagsabgeordneten Dr. Julius Moses* (Hamburg: von Bockel, 1997), 111n8.

significant that the English government (on the occasion of the opening
of the harbor in Haifa)—this during the period of unrest—announced its
determination to adhere to the Balfour Declaration.[9] [. . .]

But the most important thing is always that you, dear Papa, are healthy,
that your diabetes is kept in check, and that you don't sink into a depression
that drains you, body and soul. Each of us, young and old, has to persevere
in our given place for as long as it is ordained. It's a good thing that we
humans don't know how long our lives will last and shall thus always hope
for a better future. No rational argument can counter this. There is a god.

Trude [Erwin Moses's wife] has now completely recovered after a
serious illness. It seemed that she would need to have an operation, but
fortunately it was unnecessary in the end. She has to work a great deal
and acquits herself wonderfully in all tasks. Apart from Gad, who speaks,
reads, writes, and understands Hebrew perfectly, she is the person among
us who has mastered the language best, and she is learning very assidu-
ously.[10] Gil also can already speak it fairly well; they are naturally both
model students. I am unfortunately way behind in my studies, due to lack
of persistence and eagerness. [. . .]

And now let me turn to business. The address is Allenby Road 30.
Those who know the area say that it is across from the Moghrabi opera
house. I will send business cards as soon as they are ready—and also some
advertising flyers. The name of the shop is "The Gentleman" [English in
the original], and the title underneath it is "Everything for Men." As the
trademark I will put up a big electric clock outside, which will be the first
public clock in Tel Aviv. [. . .]

There is one more thing that I want to say so that there are no misunderstandings: no one can possibly be more positive about this land,
these people, and the Jewish world than I now am. But I don't want to
look through Zionist-tinted glasses, of whatever hue; I want to stick to the
facts and can't yet believe in a future state, one that has not been created
anywhere else.

With warmest greetings from all of us, yours truly,

Erwin

Educators like Beate Berger, who was running the Beith Ahawah Children's
Home in Berlin, started looking abroad for places of refuge where the children

---

9. See glossary for Balfour Declaration.

10. Gert (later Gad), born 1924, and Günther (Gil), born 1925, were Julius Moses's
grandchildren and the children of Erwin and Gertrud (Trude).

in her care might have a future.[11] Shortly before the Nazis came to power, first efforts were made by **Recha Freier** to establish a youth *Aliyah* offering German youth education and training in Palestine. Until 1933 the results were modest, hindered both by parental concerns and by a policy in Palestine of giving preference to Polish applicants. In the course of 1933, however, international recognition of young people's dire plight in the Third Reich led to greater priority being given to German youth (not always without tensions with Eastern European representatives worried about opportunities for their own youth).

DOCUMENT 3-3: **Beate Berger (center right) and youth from the Beith Ahawah Children's Home on an excursion near Berlin, 1934, USHMMPA WS# 48874.**

Jewish women involved in these relief efforts sent reports back to Germany and, as in document 3-4, their communications could be read in Germany's Jewish press. Siddy Wronsky's account was characteristic both in reminding German Jewish readers of Palestine's foreign and exotic character and, at the

11. Berta "Beate" Berger (1886–1940) was trained as a nurse in Frankfurt am Main and in 1922 became the director of the Beith Ahawah Children's Home. Although she and a number of the children under her care were able to emigrate to Palestine in 1934, she continued to secure the escape of those juveniles still in Berlin until her death in Kirjat Bialik in 1940. See Bargur Ayelet, *Ahawah heisst Liebe: Die Geschichte des jüdischen Kinderheims in der Berliner Auguststrasse* (Munich: DTV, 2006).

same time, in reassuring parents that social pedagogy and proper education were being given due emphasis.[12]

DOCUMENT 3-4: Siddy Wronsky, published diary entries, Haifa, September 1933 and January 1934; *Blätter des JFB*, December 1933, January 1934 (translated from German).

[*Blätter des JFB*, December 1933, 10:]
Berlin, September 7, 1933, written on the train:
Departure from Anhalter train station in Berlin around 10:28 a.m. Bidding farewell to my friends from work, from groups I belong to, from my circle of personal friends. Ending a chapter and moving toward a new phase: working to build our homestead [*Heimstätte*] in *Erez Israel*. My gratitude to our loved ones, who remain in our hearts whether near or far. And a farewell to our home [*Heimat*], where we came of age and which remains with us. [. . .]
[. . . , after her arrival in Haifa on September 16, 1933:]
Meeting with Henriette Szold[13] to discuss the tasks lying before us. Introducing productive methods designed for family welfare work. More than ever, the new *Aliyah* will require training and recruiting people for social work, to create a basic framework for social pedagogical training. Carefully allocating monies for use both here and abroad is a pressing priority if we want to maintain and develop the health of our people [*Volks-körper*]. We need to foster social awareness as widely as possible; the duty of individuals to the common good must also become a fundamental principle for social work. [My] first weeks in Haifa will be devoted to studying the conditions and the language.
[*Blätter des JFB*, January 1934, 10:]
[September 25, 1933:] A beautiful young Yemenite woman appears in the welfare bureau asking for legal protection for her children from her husband, who has left her. Referral of the matter to the rabbinate should bring her relief. Syrian refugees ask for a place to stay. A Vien-

---

12. Siddy Wronsky (1883–1947), an education reformer and Jewish women's activist, published a number of books on social welfare and social work. After her emigration to Palestine in 1933, she continued to write for *Jüdische Wohlfahrtspflege und Sozialpolitik* published in Berlin.

13. Henriette Szold (1860–1945), a longtime Zionist activist from Baltimore, Maryland, and founder of the women's organization Hadassah, worked during the 1930s with Recha Freier to bring Jewish women to Palestine, where she had lived since 1920. See Erica B. Simmons, *Hadassah and the Zionist Project* (Lanham, MD: Rowman & Littlefield, 2006).

nese man with tuberculosis comes in search of medical treatment. German immigrants ask for assistance in securing property they exported from the Reich. A Sephardic father wants his morally endangered daughter locked up for her protection. Visitors bring in all the problems of life in an oriental mandate during office hours at the welfare bureau. [. . .]

While many parents continued to balk at the thought of sending the children off on their own, increasingly that seemed the only way to guarantee the youngsters a decent future. In early April 1934, Beate Berger took a first group of thirty children from Berlin to Palestine; until her death in 1940, she managed to bring dozens more to safety. Recha Freier's work with the Youth Aliyah was complemented by the Children's Emigration Section (Abteilung Kinderauswanderung) within the Reichsvertretung, led by **Käthe Rosenheim**. Between 1933 and 1941 an estimated twelve thousand Jewish children and adolescents, unaccompanied by parents or family members, would emigrate to a range of different countries.[14]

DOCUMENT 3-5: List of youth from the Beith Ahawah Children's Home in Berlin emigrating to Palestine, 1934, USHMMPA WS# 48876.

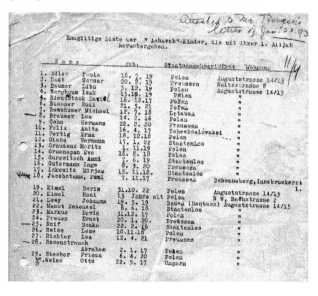

The list is broken down by name, date of birth, citizenship (*staatenlos*: "stateless"), and place of residence. The Beith Ahawah Children's Home was located in Berlin, Auguststrasse 14/15.

14. See Recha Freier, *Let the Children Come: The Early History of Youth Aliyah* (London: Weidenfeld and Nicholson, 1961); for a focus on the late 1930s, see Mark J. Harris and Deborah Oppenheimer, *Into the Arms of Strangers: Stories of the Kindertransport* (London: Bloomsbury Publishing, 2000).

Perhaps implicit in Siddy Wronsky's references to the health of the *Volks-körper* (a racially loaded term, familiar on the German Right and referring to a metaphysical "body of the people"), though not always visible to the outside world, was the fact that until well into the war, the Zionist priority remained to get the best people to Palestine, people who would contribute to building a better society and who would remain there. It was not to bring as many Jews as possible at any price. Zionists were well aware that even apart from British controls, the capacity of Palestine's agriculture and economy to absorb newcomers was limited. Small wonder that in an April 1933 article, the *Jüdische Rundschau* condemned hasty, unplanned emigration and called on German Jews to perform their duty by remaining in their home country. For Zionists, preparation, selection, and training were key, particularly in training centers for skilled trades and agriculture. This was a philosophy that in later years led to conflicts between increasingly desperate applicants on the one hand and selective administrators on the other.[15]

Over the period 1933 to 1938 as a whole, Palestine would be the largest single destination, absorbing perhaps one-quarter of all German Jewish refugees from 1933 to 1935 and a little less than one-fifth from 1936 to 1938.[16] While these figures attest to Palestine's significance, they also show that the majority of German Jewish emigrants in fact went elsewhere. In 1933 around three-quarters opted for European countries. (The distinctive character of this first year's emigration is evinced by the fact that the share of German Jewish emigrants going to European destinations would fall to 35 to 40 percent in 1934 and to just 20 to 25 percent in 1936.) In particular, the first weeks and months of the regime saw an uncontrolled dash across the borders of neighboring countries, with some ten thousand passing through one frontier railway station alone, the Badischer Bahnhof in Basel, Switzerland.[17] At this stage, crossing the French or Swiss borders (often illegally) was comparatively easy. The challenge, however, was to make a go of it in the new country. Having left much of their property behind them, usually lacking any prearranged job opportunities in an era characterized by very high unemployment, and in many cases having

---

15. Margaliot, "Emigration—Planung," 303–6. See also Brian Amkraut, *Between Home and Homeland* (Tuscaloosa: University of Alabama Press, 2006). For Zionist attitudes toward emigration to escape Nazi persecution in the later period, see Dina Porat, *The Blue and the Yellow Stars of David: The Zionist Leadership in Palestine and the Holocaust, 1939–1945* (Cambridge, MA: Harvard University Press, 1990).

16. Margaliot, "Emigration—Planung," 307n34, has slightly different percentages. Those quoted here are calculated from the emigration figures in Strauss, "Jewish Emigration," 326, and the Palestine immigration figures from the respective volumes of the *AJYB* 35 (1933–1934) to 41 (1939–1940).

17. Strauss, "Jewish Emigration," 351, 357.

entered the country of refuge illegally, the emigrants often landed in desperate straits. Even at the end of 1935, the **ZAHA** still believed that only a minority of these emigrants were managing to make a living.[18]

Despite the efforts of German Jewish organizations, it fell largely to wealthier Jews remaining in Germany and increasingly to Jews in other countries to provide assistance, a doubly difficult task given the continuing world economic crisis and high unemployment levels throughout the world. An international support infrastructure for Jewish refugees had been in existence for some years, with relief efforts in Paris, New York, London, and Berlin coordinated by the **HICEM** (an acronym drawing on the participating relief organizations) in Paris. By the fall of 1934, the HICEM prided itself on having helped over seven thousand German Jewish emigrants.[19] For individual refugees such as Lea Folk, the assistance of Jewish refugee committees in finding opportunities to make a living or, as in her case, in obtaining official permission to work was absolutely vital.

DOCUMENT 3-6: Letter by Lea Folk,[20] Amsterdam, November 30, 1933, to the Jewish Refugee Committee in Amsterdam, WL 049-EA-0623, 2–4 (translated from German).

I have been in Holland since June of this year. I was forced to come here because my parents and siblings escaped from Germany.

My father had been employed at the *Adass Jisroel* community in Berlin as a *shohet* [*schauchet*, ritual butcher].[21] Following the prohibition of ritual slaughter, he lost his job on May 1; as a result, he had no possibilities for income.

Our family is dispersed in all directions. My father is in Holland; he is staying with a family we know in Enter. My mother and four smaller siblings are in Poland with relatives, a brother with the *Comité* in Paris,[22] a sister is in Antwerp, a brother in Berlin.

---

18. See "Arbeitsbericht der ZAHA 1935," 9. Available online at http://deposit.d-nb.de/online/jued/jued.htm (last accessed June 18, 2009).

19. "Die Tätigkeit der HICEM für die jüdischen Auswanderer aus Deutschland," *Jüdische Wohlfahrtspflege und Sozialpolitik* 4, nos. 9/10 (1933–1934): 229–37.

20. The authors have been unable to locate conclusive additional information about the future fate of Lea Folk.

21. *Adass Jisroel* (Hebrew: "Community of Israel") was an Orthodox community association formed in 1869 in Berlin.

22. *Comité des Délégations Juives* (Committee of Jewish Delegations) formed in the aftermath of World War I and continued to champion Jewish rights before being absorbed by the World Jewish Congress in 1936. See Kulka, *Deutsches Judentum*, 468.

Currently I am in Amsterdam where I have been offered a job in a home. It is a supervisory position in a strictly religious orphanage, Plantage Middenlaan 80 [street address], that is especially interested in hiring me to make sure they have a person responsible for rituals [*rituellen Menschen*] in the house.

I would personally benefit immensely from this job as it would offer me at least a place to stay; I am completely without means and don't know what to do. [. . .]

In a third of the cases where the HICEM provided assistance, however, its help consisted of paying for transport back to Germany of refugees who had failed to find a foothold in the new countries. And, indeed, one of the resolutions of a HICEM meeting held in May 1933 was to persuade the Jewish relief organizations within Germany to do all they could to restrict Jewish emigration until those who had already crossed the border had found work and permanent places to stay. Around the same time, ZAHA in Germany came to similar conclusions.[23] Reporting on the refugee situation since March 1933, the chairman of the London-based Jewish Refugee Committee, Otto Schiff, noted that despite the dual problem of immigration laws and lack of funding, his organization had found a way to aid fifteen thousand refugees in more than ten countries, six thousand in France alone. Dealing with this burning problem efficiently in the future would hinge on the ability "to discourage the flow of uncontrolled emigration from Germany" and ensure that departures took place in a controlled manner. On the other hand, no international relief effort could afford to ignore the plight of the many German Jews who had not left the country and were facing increasingly difficult circumstances at home.[24]

TARGETS OF THE "PEOPLE'S COMMUNITY"

If emigration took many German Jews into uncharted, sometimes troubled waters, the fate of those who stayed behind in Germany was equally unpredictable as Nazi pressures and policies constantly jeopardized the fragile equilibrium. A case study in persecution and self-help emerges in documents 3-7 and

---

23. ZAHA meeting on April 29, 1933, cited in Margaliot, "Emigration—Planung," 303.

24. Otto Schiff, Jewish Refugees Committee, "Report of the Refugees Sub-Committee," London, October 31, 1933, "private & confidential; not for publication," CZA RG S25 file 9742 (facsimile reprinted in Henry Friedlander and Sybil Milton, eds., *Archives of the Holocaust: An International Collection of Selected Volumes* [New York: Garland Publishing, 1990ff], doc. 60, 3:231–33).

3-8. They tell a story of the arrest of Jewish youth in June 1933 at a training home in the Brandenburg town of Wolzig and the boys' later fate in the Oranienburg concentration camp.

The home, the only one in Germany for troubled youth run according to Jewish religious rules and equipped with modern facilities, had existed since 1929. After the Nazi takeover, relations with neighbors had grown tense, both for ideological reasons and because of the surrounding community's concerns about the home's potentially negative impact on the tourist trade. In early 1933 local officials decided to move against the institution and dislodge the Jewish owners by fabricating charges of Communist activities. Initially unsuccessful, they struck again in early June 1933 and subjected the young inmates to a storm of abuse.[25]

DOCUMENT 3-7: CV report on a search by SA and police in the Wolzig Youth and Training Home, June 1933, USHMMA RG 11.001M.31, reel 151 (SAM 721-1-3071, 370–72) (translated from German).

Report
On Wednesday, the 7th of the month, around five thirty in the morning, some 150 SA men from Friedersdorf, Storkow, and the surrounding areas, as well as six policemen [*Landjäger*] led by a police officer [*Oberlandjäger*] showed up at the Jewish youth and training school [*Jugend- und Lehrheim*] in Wolzig.

The SA men went into the locked villa, which is rented out to staff members of the school. The villa was searched thoroughly, but nothing was found.

In the room of the instructor Fritz Hirsch,[26] one of the SA men put a briefcase on a cabinet. Mr. Hirsch's wife noticed this. She told an SA man that she had seen the briefcase being put on the cabinet. In the meantime,

---

25. See Joseph Walk, *Jüdische Schule und Erziehung im Dritten Reich* (Frankfurt am Main: Hain, 1991), 168–69; Klaus Drobisch, "Überfall auf jüdische Jungen im Juni 1933. Dokumente," in *Brandenburg in der NS-Zeit: Studien und Dokumente*, ed. Dietrich Eichholtz and Almuth Püschel (Berlin: Verlag Volk und Welt, 1993), 168–206.

26. Fritz Hirsch (1903–1982) was a (non-Jewish) youth worker and sports teacher at the Wolzig youth home and was held in a series of Berlin prisons. He continued his work with Jewish youth and adult education students until 1934 in Germany and in the Netherlands, where he then sought refuge. His wife, Charlotte Hirsch (1907–1987), had a two-year-old daughter at the time of the Wolzig arrests. See Eichholtz and Püschel, *Brandenburg in der NS-Zeit*, 169, 172, 173, 179; Lutz van Dick, *Oppositionelles Lehrerverhalten, 1933–1945* (Munich: Weinheim, 1988), 138–62.

other SA men had discovered the briefcase and wanted to keep it as evidence. When asked to whom this briefcase belonged, Mrs. H. answered that it had been placed there by the SA men.

After searching headmaster Oskar Friedmann's apartment, which was located in the villa, two SA men reappeared in a room carrying a briefcase and wanted to search the apartment again.[27] One of them had already been in the apartment. Headmaster Friedmann's wife attempted to stop the two SA men by pointing out they had already conducted a search.

A similar briefcase later turned up in the school building and was withheld as incriminating material because it contained blank membership books of the Communist Party.

During the visit to the villa, SA men rang the bell of the school; they fanned out immediately throughout the entire house. First, they had the office unlocked by the gardener Goldschmidt. He could not be present in the office during the search because he was called by other SA men. In the meantime, a firearm (army pistol) was found in a drawer of the desk in the office. Miss Armer, the clerical assistant, was interrogated. She stated emphatically that she had been in the office the previous evening around midnight, had pulled open the drawer, and at that time there had not been a weapon in the drawer. She was told, "Then someone must have put the weapons [sic] there, and we know who it was." Thereupon Goldschmidt, the gardener, was brought into the office. He denied equally emphatically and insistently having brought the weapon into the office.

When the search of the school started, the students (*Zöglinge*) were ordered to line up and forced to do exercises. After great efforts the staff managed to get permission to distribute breakfast to the students and to keep the female school staff members at work in the kitchen. At first, the students were forced to eat their breakfast on the run.

Meanwhile, the school was searched. A firearm was found under the pillow of the student Werner Treuherz.[28] Treuherz was summoned and asked how long he had been sleeping in the bed in which the weapon was found. He replied, "One year," to which the response was, "And you never noticed that there was a pistol under your pillow?" According to some

---

27. Possibly Oskar Friedmann (1903–?) who later emigrated to England. We have been unable to locate conclusive information about the fate of Betty Armer and Oskar Friedmann's wife. Richard Goldschmidt, identified as the gardener, was detained for a time and later emigrated to South America.

28. Possibly Werner Treuherz (1916–1942) who was deported to the Łódź ghetto on October 18, 1942, and on May 8, 1942, to the Chelmno extermination camp, where he perished. See www.bundesarchiv.de/gedenkbuch/directory.html and http://adressbuch.zlb.de.

of the staff that had stayed behind, additional writings were found and confiscated.

The student's welfare records and some office files were taken away. These items are supposed to be with the county office [*Gemeindevorsteher*] in Wolzig. When the search of the school and villa seemed at an end, a second search took place of the room of the instructor [*Erzieher*] Max Gebhard.[29] The first search led to no results, but during the second, a firearm was found in Gebhard's bookshelf behind some books. Asked where it had come from, Gebhard was completely taken aback and said that he had never had a weapon in his room.

After the head official [*Landrat*] of the responsible district Beeskow-Storkow had been notified via telephone, the following people were arrested:

Director, Oskar Friedmann
Gardener, Goldschmidt
Clerical assistant, Betty Armer
Instructor, Max Gebhard
Instructor, Fritz Hirsch
Student, Werner Treuherz

The arrestees mentioned and all students of the school were loaded onto a truck at 10:30 a.m. and, according to SA men, transported to the concentration camp in Oranienburg.[30]

In order to get students and staff released, the CV and other Jewish officials repeatedly approached local and regional authorities as well as officials in Berlin. They also managed to get their story into the foreign press, including the *London Times*.[31] By the end of June, the authorities had released most of the teachers and administrators.

However, the thirty-nine students remained incarcerated in Oranienburg for another month. One of them, Manfred Benjamin, born in September 1919, may have been the youngest prisoner held in any of the early concentration

29. Possibly Max Gebhardt (1866–1944), who was deported to Theresienstadt in January 1944, where he died on March 3, 1944; see *Datenbank zur Liste der jüdischen Einwohner im Deutschen Reich, 1933–1945* (Berlin: Bundesarchiv, 2008).
30. On the Oranienburg concentration camp, see Bernward Dörner, "Oranienburg," in *USHMM Encyclopedia of Camp and Ghettos*, 1:147–49.
31. "Life in a Nazi Camp: A Farm Student's Experience," *London Times*, September 19, 1933, written by a non-Jewish student in Wolzig who describes his incarceration in Oranienburg concentration camp from June 20 to August 22, 1933.

camps.[32] Though arrested on charges of Communist activities, the following account by **Max Abraham** (who had been transferred from Papenburg camp to Oranienburg) shows that their guards treated Benjamin and his fellow students as Jews.

DOCUMENT 3-8: **Max Abraham, "The Jewish Company," first printed in *Juda ver-recke: Ein Rabbiner im Konzentrationslager* (Templitz-Schönau: Druck- und Verlags-anstalt, 1934)[33] (translated from German).**

The Jewish Company [*Die Judenkompagnie*]

[. . .] The Jewish Company consisted of about 55 people, among them 39 boys from a Jewish education facility near Berlin. The Benjamin[34] among the boys was indeed called Benjamin, and he was thirteen years old. [. . .] The children were beaten for hours on end in the cruelest manner and forced to perform extremely hard physical labor.

Thirteen-year-old Benjamin was naturally spared nothing. The school had accommodated physically weak and mostly psychopathic children with severe learning difficulties. The weakest was the thirteen-year-old, but he was mentally advanced enough to understand what was going on. The children often lamented their suffering and pleaded for help from me, their spiritual counselor. But how was I supposed to help, I, who was under the control of sadistic oppressors myself? My caring had to be restricted to comforting and occasionally supporting them in their physical hardship. [. . .]

The children from the school were incarcerated for six weeks. As a result of their experiences in the Oranienburg camp, many of them would be psychologically damaged for life. Even on the day prior to the release, a nineteen-year-old who was "parlor maid" [*Stubenmädchen*] for an SA man was severely abused. He was accused of having stolen a mark [1 Reichsmark] from the SA man. He was first brought into Room 16, where he was supposed to make a confession. When he was beaten almost uncon-

---

32. Manfred Benjamin (1919–?) moved to Berlin after his release from the Oranienburg concentration camp and emigrated to the Netherlands in April 1939; see *Datenbank zur Liste der jüdischen Einwohner im Deutschen Reich, 1933–1945* (Berlin: Bundesarchiv, 2008). His later fate is unknown.

33. See reprint in Irene A. Diekmann and Klaus Wettig, eds., *Konzentrationslager Oranienburg: Augenzeugenberichte aus dem Jahre 1933* (Potsdam: Verlag für Berlin-Brandenburg, 2003), 119–67; partly also printed with a few slight orthographic changes in *Der Gelbe Fleck: Die Ausrottung von 500.000 deutschen Juden* (Paris: Editions du Carrefour, 1936).

34. A common German expression for the youngest among a group or family.

scious, he confessed to everything of which they accused him. He claimed to have buried the money in the yard, where he had to look for it for half an hour. He could not find the money there—since he had neither stolen nor hidden it. As he assured me later when I talked to him very seriously, he had only made this "confession" to gain time and to recover from the dreadful blows. I believed him; he was certainly not lying to me in that moment. He latched onto my encouragement like a drowning person onto a helping hand.

Since the mark was nowhere to be found, the boy was further brutally beaten and now said that he had hidden the money in a different place in the yard to be spared for half an hour longer. This was repeated three to four times. We older protective custody prisoners could not watch this martyrdom any longer and slipped him a mark so that he could return the "stolen" mark and finally be freed from his torments. The last abuse of the boy happened in the evening. SA men entered the dorm around nine o'clock, asked for the location of the bunk of the "thief," and hit the bare body of the weak young lad with rubber truncheons. We heard the cries of pain and the groans—and were powerless to intervene. [. . .]

Successful interventions with state authorities, such as those leading to the release of the Wolzig prisoners, helped alleviate German Jews' pervasive feeling of powerlessness. They created hope that some vestiges of civilized life would continue or return and that the violent aspects of the Nazi regime would not necessarily become the norm. Moreover, viewed from the perspective of late 1933, the balance sheet of Hitler's government was not entirely negative. Its foreign policy seemed to be on the path to overturning the irksome terms of the hated **Versailles Treaty**. When called upon to participate in the Reichstag election of November 12, 1933, an election that was above all a plebiscite on the government's proposed withdrawal from the **League of Nations**, German Jews found themselves torn in different directions. On the one hand, they were aware that the election was a sham, offering no real choices.[35] On the other hand, Jews also hoped it would give them a chance to affirm their loyalty to the nation—as opposed to the regime—and endorse Germany's struggle to reestablish its international status.

Documents 3-9 and 3-10 are taken from the CV's extensive correspondence about the November elections. They offer a potent reminder of the wide disjuncture between perceptions then and now. What we can easily identify as

---

35. For expressions of dissent during the "elections," see Peter Crane, *"Wir leben nun mal auf einem Vulkan"* (Bonn: Weidle Verlag, 2005), 120–22.

a rigged event with at best symbolic connotations—a vote that presented German Jews with a no-win choice—at the time appeared to many German Jews
as an opportunity to participate in one of the few manifestations of collective
will from which they were not yet excluded. It allowed them to support, in the
words of a **Reichsvertretung** proclamation calling on Jews to vote with the
government, "the equal standing of Germans among nations [. . .] the reconciliation of nations, and [. . .] world peace [. . .] despite everything we have experienced."[36] The following extracts from letters that reached the CV, from the
organization's internal reports, and from its official public statement exemplify
German Jews' conflicting perceptions and attitudes as the November election
approached.

DOCUMENT 3-9: **Letter by Dr. Rudolf Löwenstein,[37] Soest (Westphalia), to CV head
office, October 20, 1933, USHMMA RG 11.001M.31, reel 137 (SAM 721-1-2942,
138) (translated from German).**

To the heads [*Vorstand*] of the CV Berlin
     German Jewry is sorely in need of a decisive statement from its lead-
ers on the burning foreign policy issues of the day and the elections to be
held on these issues. Come what may, we feel that we are bound to our
German Fatherland. We feel most painfully all exclusionary laws that the
Reich government has issued against us and that the ruling party enforces
with even greater vigor.
     All of that has to take a backseat, however, in the interest of the
nation's fight against foreign defamation and oppression. We do not want
to conceal the fact that we differ from other Germans by our religious
beliefs and ancestry. But we want to demonstrate and to put on record as
strongly as we can that we are united as one with them in our deep, fanati-
cal love for our German Fatherland, for the native soil of our German
home, and for the German people, our comrades in destiny. We feel as
keenly as our Aryan brothers [*unsere arischen Volksgenossen*] the humiliation that our heavily armed enemies are again seeking to inflict on us. And
in this moment we stand with pride, confidence and without qualification

---

36. Proclamation by the Reichsvertretung, *CV-Zeitung*, November 2, 1933.
37. Rudolf Löwenstein (1900–?) worked as a doctor in Soest until 1938. When his license
to practice was withdrawn, he moved to Essen and on April 22, 1942, was deported from
there to Izbica with his wife, Margareta. They perished, as did their son Klaus Martin and
daughter Klara. See Hermann Schröter, *Geschichte und Schicksal der Essener Juden: Gedenkbuch für die jüdischen Mitbürger der Stadt Essen* (Essen: Stadt Essen, 1980), 644; *USHMM
ITS Collection Data Base Central Name Index.*

behind the leadership of the new German Reich, behind the chancellor, Adolf Hitler. We have rock-solid confidence in his ability to achieve equality for Germany and to win our Fatherland its rightful place in the sun. Every German Jew must without reservation opt to support the government on November 12. We are determined to put our blood and life and our whole being on the line to become proud and free German citizens with equal rights in a proud and free German Fatherland, a Fatherland built on a foundation of equal rights.

We expect that the leadership of the CV will telegraph the Reich chancellor as soon as possible and convey this firm and implacable conviction and that German Jewry stands united with the will of the people and its leadership. In this moment of danger, we expect that a declaration of loyalty to the Third Reich will also be made by the Reichsverband [presumably the author is referring here to the Reichsvertretung], and that these declarations will be made known to all Germans as quickly as possible via the daily press.

We hope that the CV's leadership will at last openly and courageously recognize the spirit of the times and the will of German Jewry and do what is necessary without bowing to other interests. The charge that at this most fateful juncture the CV has failed to measure up, a charge leveled by very many Jews, including those from the best circles of German Jewry, will thereby be rebutted.

In this spirit we say, Heil Hitler!

DOCUMENT 3-10: **Letter by Willy Rosenfeld,[38] Konstanz, to CV head office, November 6, 1933, USHMMA RG 11.001M.31, reel 137 (SAM 721-1-2942, 86–87) (translated from German).**

Konstanz, November 6, 1933

To the CV Berlin.

In your newspaper [*CV-Zeitung*], number 42 from November 2, 1933, you issued a call to support the policy of the current government with a "yes" vote. As a German Jew, I feel myself obliged to remind you

38. Willy Rosenfeld (1904?–?), son of Rosa (née Guggenheim) and Samson Rosenfeld, lived in Konstanz until he emigrated to Ecuador in 1939 with his mother. Both remained in South America until their deaths. His father had owned part of a family wholesale firm specializing in fabrics or textiles in Konstanz. See Erich Bloch, *Geschichte der Juden von Konstanz im 19. und 20. Jahrhundert* (Konstanz: Stadler, 1996), 190–91, 260, 264, 290; *Datenbank zur Liste der jüdischen Einwohner im Deutschen Reich, 1933–1945* (Berlin: Bundesarchiv, 2008).

of what the current government has been doing to us German Jews. Is it your duty as the representatives of German Jewry to support these hateful measures! Do you have the right to offer a beaten Jewish youth robbed of all prospects a "yes"! Do you want to be people so lacking in character that they ignore injustice and practice cowardliness and deception! If you feel you are Jews, you have to fight with more just means to bring about equality!

Fight, for all the Jewish youth who today are unemployed in all sectors; fight for what is right and use the truth for our honor; then the youth will gladly stand by you to lead a worthy fight.

Have you forgotten that in the year 1914, Jewish children died for their parents and Jewish fathers died for their families for their German Fatherland! And today, 20 years later, you approve with conscious *lies* a policy that doesn't even acknowledge these sacrifices.

You will accuse me of forgetting that I am a Jewish German! To that I reply to you that I was in the first place born as a Jew and secondly found my home [*Heimat*] as a German. However, I cannot forget a cultural outrage that has been committed on us German Jews and that has eaten itself into my heart.

Do you actually believe that the present government, with this dishonest invitation [i.e., the CV's published call to vote "yes"], will after November 12 see you as German citizens; or do you have the feeling that the excited populace will change their minds in our favor!! Until today I felt a great deal of allegiance to the CV and saw myself as a German citizen of Jewish faith. But once I recognized how your position deliberately leads Jewish youth astray, I was forced to join the opposition.

In conclusion, I would like to bring to your attention the fact that here in Konstanz the CV has never put any effort into instructional activities—lectures, etc.—for local youth, even though particularly at a time like the present such measures would have been sensible and appropriate.

Respectfully,
Willy Rosenfeld

As document 3-11, a diary entry by Kurt Rosenberg, makes clear, many Jews were aware that while their own situation was particularly difficult, their non-Jewish neighbors were also often under considerable pressure to conform. It was thus very hard to know exactly which signs of enthusiasm were genuine and which were coerced.

DOCUMENT 3-11: Kurt Rosenberg, diary entry for November 11, 1933, LBINY AR 25279 (translated from German).

The *Volk* is again all stirred up because of the election. Yesterday during Hitler's speech work was halted for one hour, and traffic came to a standstill for a minute—an odd sight, like a scene in a film where everything suddenly freezes. All traffic. For one minute people on the street stood completely still—then the street became almost empty—everyone went inside to listen to the radio. Seemed like a dead city. Countless posters pasted up all over, hung over the streets, from tree to tree. "Hitler stands for Honor, Equality, and Peace." "Down with the Armaments Madness" [*Gegen den Rüstungswahnsinn*]. And now at this moment all the windows are brightly lit up. One has never seen more flags. Residents were told in advance to display flags. Those who don't hang out flags or light up their homes as a show of support do it out of fear.

An SA man came to the door and said that the girls [*Mädchen*][39] had to take part in the parade today—it's all the same whether it's Saturday and their employers are thus having a Sunday [meaning, having the day off]. Six thousand police and SA people are on the move and will force the girls to come out of their houses if necessary. The girls are terribly frightened. The printouts of songs that the girls were given include the lines "Traitors and Jews are making a profit" and "Germany, awake! Death to the Jew!" Cars are driving through the streets carrying trumpeting and screaming SA men who are trying to rally the *Volk*. Drums are beating. For days there has been speech after speech—tents set up on the heath—speeches on the radio—when Hitler begins speaking on the radio about parasites feeding on the *Volk*, one hears someone cry, "Jews," in the background. Huge numbers of us fear that voting won't be done in secret—fantastic rumors are circulating.[40] I was told that in one factory someone threatened the others that they would find out who hadn't voted for Hitler and they would be fired. An unbelievable amount of commotion and propaganda—creating perhaps more a feeling of intoxication than deliberation—creating a frightening state of agitation.

Everything is in motion: cars drive past with models of air defense guns mounted on top of them, accompanied by fire engines and mobile billboards with sirens howling, making propaganda for antiaircraft defenses.

---

39. *Mädchen* refers to the (non-Jewish) female employees of the family.

40. For one report (of several in the CV files) on Jews in Halle/Saale being prevented from voting on November 12, see USHMMA RG 11.001M.31, reel 136 (SAM 721-1-2942, 75).

All Jews fear the new constitution that is being introduced. What will it mean for the future?

The new constitution that Rosenberg and others anticipated was just a rumor; the Weimar Republic's constitution essentially remained in place, but with the *Ermächtigungsgesetz* and other special ordinances having nullified vital clauses and protections.

TAKING STOCK AFTER ONE YEAR

With the regime gearing up to mark the first anniversary of its ascent to power, many German Jews felt moved to reflect on the changes in their situation since January 1933. The threats to one's personal well-being, the speed with which all they had once taken for granted was now being called into question, and the uncertainty about where things were headed triggered existential reflections on what had taken place. Some drew lessons about human existence in general, others about the Jewish fate throughout history. Writing for the members of the **JFB**, Margarete Susman tried to connect the present with past challenges.[41]

DOCUMENT 3-12: Margarete Susman, "On the Edge," *Blätter des JFB*, **April 1934, 1–2 (translated from German).**

In this moment of unimaginable historical shifts, during which human lives have been thrown into complete turmoil, everyone affected has been forced to reflect on the value and meaning of a human life.

Such reflections have led countless German Jews to end their lives. Was that evil of them? Was it good? Today, it no longer makes sense to pose this question, if it ever did. The only people who may judge such actions are those who took this road to its endpoint: the dead. Men cannot sit in judgment over this deed. [. . .]

A few months ago a great Jewish scholar—already on his deathbed but reflecting back on life—laid out the following in his last letter to a friend, thoughts that came from his deep store of knowledge about the

---

41. Margarete Susman (1872–1966) was a German philosopher, essayist, and poet forced to leave Germany for Switzerland in 1934. Despite being placed under a publishing ban by the Swiss authorities, she continued to publish articles condemning the Nazi regime. See Herbert A. Strauss and Werner Röder, eds., *International Biographical Dictionary of Central European Émigrés, 1933–1945*, vol. 2, *The Arts, Sciences, and Literature* (Munich: K. G. Saur, 1982), 1146–47; Charlotte Ueckert, *Margarete Susman und Else Lasker-Schüler* (Hamburg: Europäische Verlagsanstalt, 2000).

meaning of being alive: "It is good not to run away, but to stand and fight tenaciously; even the smallest step then becomes a valuable building block and somehow manages to bring blessings to counteract every drop of anguish. I know this with such certainty that it could have been delivered from the mouth of a godly vision. I see its imprint in the eyes and lines of old faces and in the beauty of old trees, and great music conveys this lesson with mathematical power of conviction."

He knew the truth. He himself gave emphasis to the word "know." He knew it as only those standing on the precipice know and understand, from a place where one can see clearly, unimpeded by the flurry of complexity thrown up in everyday life, a place where the word no longer obscures law. [. . .]

It is through this dogged, hard-fought battle that humans have their true encounter with the divine. Reenacting Jacob's struggle[42] is the primal experience of human existence. Even where victory is out of grasp, waging the battle must be viewed with true awe. But the blessedness of a power revealing itself in its godliness rests only in those who overcome.[43]

In family letters and diaries, reflections on the past year were often triggered by the recurrence of an anniversary or annual event, though now in very changed circumstances. Correspondents waxed nostalgic, remembering all that had changed or been lost and sometimes worrying about what might yet come. During birthdays and holidays—including Christmas, celebrated by many German Jews, among them Julius Moses—the absence of family members and friends, as well as the inability to give presents to loved ones, overshadowed what should have been festive events.

DOCUMENT 3-13: **Letter by Julius Moses, Berlin, to Erwin Moses, Tel Aviv, December 23, 1933, translated from Dieter Fricke,** *Jüdisches Leben in Berlin und Tel Aviv, 1933–1939: Der Briefwechsel des ehemaligen Reichstagsabgeordneten Dr. Julius Moses* **(Hamburg: von Bockel, 1997), 133–34.**

D[ear] o[nes]! Tomorrow night things will look a little different at our place compared with a year ago: only grandma will be with us and, apart from that, no one. And none of the many friends we had, to whom we

---

42. This is a metaphorical reference to the story in Genesis 32:24.

43. The last text passage presents translation problems; in the original German, it reads, "Auch wo der Sieg ausbleibt, gebührt dem Kampfe letzte Ehrfurcht, aber der Segen der sich als Gott entschleiernden Gewalt ruht nur auf dem, der überwindet."

owe so much, will send a note. And as for Christmas presents, I want to show Frieda [Julius Moses's non-Jewish partner] once again my most generous side; so [instead of being able to give her a present,] I'm going to offer up my steadfast love on the table of Christmas presents once again and—so I hear—she will return the favor by contributing 10 cigars. *Sic transit gloria mundi!*[44] Yes, indeed, the things we have to endure! If only these were our only worries! [. . .]

Though the losses and setbacks of the past year loomed large, the message spread by German Jewish organizations at the end of the first twelve months of Nazi rule was one of hope. Leading functionaries of the large Jewish organizations voiced some mildly positive overall assessments of things to come.[45] **Hans Reichmann**, a man rooted in the ideological world typical of moderate CV leaders, had been intensively involved in combating Nazi antisemitism before January 1933 and was privy to the numerous reports of Jews' daily struggles. He was thus well placed to comment on what lay ahead. Though determined to send a positive message to the Jewish public, Reichmann's piece tried to do more than dress up a bleak future in rosy colors.

DOCUMENT 3-14: H. Rn. [Hans Reichmann], "After One Year," *Der Morgen* 1934– 1935 (April 1934): 1–3 (translated from German).

Now that a year has passed, we may be permitted to examine the experience and position of German Jews in what has been the most decisive and difficult period of their history since emancipation. The large majority was completely unprepared for what hit them. Both the indifferent and the strictly intellectual had equally little sense for practical politics. They stood either too far above or too far removed from day-to-day confrontations—confrontations whose trajectory and tone had, for some time, signaled to those in the know how anti-Jewish theories would be executed in reality.

And now they stood stunned in the face of radical change. No better prepared were those others, who here and there had felt the animus

---

44. Latin proverb: "Thus passes the glory of the world."

45. See, e.g., letter by Julius Brodnitz, CV president, to the members of the CV directorate (*Präsidium*) and board (*Beirat*), December 15, 1933, USHMMA RG 11.001M.31, reel 224 (SAM 721-1-25, 183–85); circular letter by ZVfD (A. Kramer, B. Cohen), Berlin, to its branch offices and representatives, February 8, 1934, CZA RG L13 file 138 (facsimile printed in Friedlander and Milton, *Archives of the Holocaust*, doc. 29, 3:145–50).

of their opponents, but who had always hoped that their protected and secured sphere would remain unscathed, no matter what happened.

Because what took place struck the great grandchildren of the generation that was emancipated circa 120 years ago, the historic memory of similar events and therefore also any tradition of reacting to such experiences were missing. People's intellectual and emotional reactions might fall anywhere in the full range from heroism to flight, from celebrating protest to boastful affirmations, from selfish cries of "To the lifeboats!" to a readiness to dedicate one's energies to the community. People were on the verge of reacting in a way that could have severely damaged the reputation of the German Jews in the eyes of the German people and of history.

Today, a year later, we can say with some satisfaction that while many individuals may have left the straight path and gone astray, the German Jewish community has lived through this year and its many decisions with the right attitude. When debasement and accusation were voiced [by anti-Jewish activists] here and there in a manner that went beyond the bounds of the racial-political differentiation favored by the government, the [Jewish] community bore it with stoical pride. It reacted with silent superiority and the security of an inwardly invulnerable people. It was hard hit by exclusion from German cultural developments and indeed often more deeply wounded by this than by the loss of an economic existence. Irrespective of any concerns about their own prestige or egotistical interests, German Jews had the oppressive experience of no longer being allowed to participate in the spiritual, the artistically creative, and the nurturing aspects of German life, and thus in the socially and politically formative life of the nation. Where shared fate in battle had most closely interwoven human bonds, their untying was hard and painful. Little has so affected the current Jewish generation of adult men as the dissolution of bonds and organizations that were once meant to ensure the maintenance of a comradely spirit and tradition. The rootedness in such communities, which embody the shared experience and will of the German people, is a gauge for the closeness of the relationship in which the overwhelming majority of German Jews felt themselves to the German people.

For the majority of German Jews, this sense of belonging to the German people went without saying. It seemed to them too strongly affirmed through the reality of their lives to be shaken by any racial theory. But when such theories began to produce real concrete results, when they [the theories] were presented to the German people and the German Jews repeatedly and with great urgency, when Jewish papers themselves enlisted them to confirm national-Jewish [i.e., Zionist] positions, the responsible German Jew also had to take up the struggle. It was not surprising that some would make a 180-degree turn out of bitterness and injured pride, that indifferent deniers that there was any kind of Jewish problem would suddenly become supporters of radical national-Jewish attempts at solutions. But the number of those who made such instant conversions remained small. The tradition of five generations, the German experience of each individual, the immersion in [German] culture were facts that prevented a violent, inorganic rupturing of social relationships [*Umweltsbeziehungen*]. Indeed, it is fair to say of the majority that their ties to their homeland [*Heimat*] became all the more palpable, the more pressing was a decision about whether they could live in Germany in the future. Where German Jews were forced for the first time to separate from Germany, a separation that they had never imagined they would have to make, one is shaken by the feeling of homelessness [*Heimatlosigkeit*] that resonates through their letters.

Even if Palestine becomes the [German Jews'] country of choice, it cannot compensate for [their] loss of a spiritual homeland. The non-Zionist German Jews lack the years of spiritual preparation and education for Palestine that the Zionists have systematically practiced. People of such emphatically Western European and German character were thus not ready to see in Palestine a replacement for their lost homeland. Still, they gratefully accepted it as a refuge, a refuge that had once been viewed as having been created only for "unfortunate Eastern Jews." In this single year, the majority of German Jews have changed their attitude toward Palestine. At least one now considers it as a possible place to build a new life; many friendships and family relationships reach across from one country to the other. Even if this overwhelmingly practical perspective does not fulfill the ideal that the pioneers of the Zionist idea strove for in their formative work, it should not be castigated as ungrateful. Rather it corresponds with the spiritual attitude of people who, despite everything that has happened and even when personal necessity compels them to turn their backs on their homeland, are determined to preserve the tradition of their German past.

Where people's livelihoods were taken away, dire necessity compelled them to look toward foreign countries. Therefore, several thousand German Jews and many thousand foreign Jews resident in Germany, in total approximately 40,000 to 50,000, went abroad. Most of them had clung as long as it was possible to the slightest chance of an existence in Germany. The manner in which especially the youth made this hard choice was admirable. Without depression and without lamentation, they accepted as an unalterable fact that the paths they had chosen had been blocked, and they looked to forge a new life through retraining for a trade or agricultural job. They and the mass of German Jews were able to bear their hard fate because of a new Jewish consciousness, which more urgently than all the exhortations and challenges of former times gave every one of them the inner security to fight their way through. Those who draw up the spiritual balance sheet of a year full of decisions will include on the profit ledger this rediscovery of inner values, this path back to Judaism. It is in reality a path forward, one that guarantees the continued existence of a Jewish community that, while materially weakened, has gained in self-confidence and in its human worth.

"Non-Aryan" Christians, though facing challenges similar to other Jews, were even less sure about where to find solace. In many cases, they continued to draw some hope from Christianity, the religious affiliation they shared with the majority of the German population. Some hoped that the artificial and arbitrary nature of racial categories, including racial definitions of who was a Jew, would become transparent to the German populace. In early 1934, during the first public meeting of the RVC, its chairman, Richard Wolff, could point not only to successes in finding members new jobs but also to the strength derived from an identity rooted in the Christian faith and its martyrs and from the fact that they shared the same uncertain fate as one another.[46]

DOCUMENT 3-15: **"Aims and Tasks of the Reichsverband," speech by RVC chairman Richard Wolff to RVC members, February 21, 1934, translated from Richard Wolff, _Wir nichtarische Christen: Drei Reden vom Vorsitzenden des Reichsverbandes der nichtarischen Christen_ (Frankfurt an der Oder: [no publisher], 1934), 7–19.**

[. . .] I am aware of my great responsibility. Therefore I see it as my obligation to make very clear that it would be a fatal delusion for us to believe that the regime of Adolf Hitler would be willing for our sake to remove the cornerstone of its renewal program: namely, the notion of race [_Rassegedanken_]. Whether we deplore this or not is immaterial and also unimportant. But it is necessary to face up to this grim fact and for each of us to come to terms with it.

---

46. Richard Wolff (1885–1958), a doctor also employed in a variety of other disciplines, joined the RVC in the fall of 1933 and was its president from early 1934 until late 1935. In 1938 he fled Germany and lived in Nairobi, Kenya, until his death. See Werner Cohn, "Bearers of a Common Fate? The 'Non-Aryan' Christian 'Fate-Comrades' of the Paulus-Bund, 1933–1939," _LBIYB_ 33 (1988): 334, 339–40; Vuletić, _Christen jüdischer Herkunft_, 83–84.

This fate has come crashing down on us with the might of an avalanche during a thaw. We are, and feel ourselves nothing less than, Germans, and [yet] the Aryan laws cut us off from our Aryan fellow Germans [*arischen Volksgenossen*] and thrust us into the same category as our fellow citizens of the Jewish religion in Germany. Many of us who perhaps have inherited some Jewish blood from one grandparent and first learned of it through the all too familiar questionnaire, who do not know even subconsciously anything about Judaism, are now suddenly being seen and treated in public and private life—every day and every hour—as Jews because of the [racial] laws. Clearly we feel loyalty to our Jewish fellow citizens, but it is utterly impossible for us Christian Germans who have some Jewish blood ever to find our way back to Judaism. We must therefore rely completely on ourselves. Our Jewish fellow citizens, who like ourselves were seriously affected by the legislation, can call on the widespread organizations of world Jewry for aid and support; these remain closed to us, although we happily and gratefully acknowledge that transdenominational generosity also occasionally extended from adherents of the Jewish faith to those sharing our fate. But, on the other hand, it is also clear that the Jews, hard hit by current measures, have turned more inward than ever and view us largely as renegades and reject us.

<u>We are Christians</u>, Christians by conviction, not merely because we wanted to acquire baptismal certificates. I encounter people very often who are not prepared to listen to what our organization has to say, and they insist, "You're nothing but a club of Jews in disguise." We need to argue forcefully against this claim. Looking through the card file of our members, I was able to determine that more than three-quarters of them have been Christians since earliest childhood, that is, since their birth, and that only a fraction of our members chose to convert from Judaism to Christianity themselves. [. . .]

Even if we conclude that taking the path back to Judaism is impossible for us, this is hardly a value judgment about Judaism, but rather, a simple statement of unalterable fact. Yet nothing could be more dishonorable or contemptible than for one of us to dare deny the existence of our ancestors or to besmirch the homes of our parents. <u>I will vigorously fight against any antisemitic tendency in our ranks</u>.

Something else should be mentioned in this context. The further our members and those sharing our fate are removed from Judaism by blood, the more likely it seems that they will occasionally expect their lot to improve. They might expect us to grant them a place of privilege. The quarter Jew might conclude that he is better than the half Jew or even the full Jew. This game of percentages is not only futile but also dangerous. On the one hand, those who think in this fashion will have come to realize recently that their view does not coincide with the racial conception of our government, and on the other hand, this kind of thinking presents a serious danger for our organization. [. . .][47]

Our organization is completely apolitical. It strives exclusively for the goal and cause of bringing together those who share our fate and lending them spiritual and economic aid. We see it as our most serious obligation to pass up no opportunity that arises to ease and improve the lot of our members and those who share their fate. To meet the ever growing burden, it is the duty of all those who are still economically better off than most of those sharing our fate to make common cause with us. Or if this is impossible for reasons that we of course will respect, they should at least lend financial support for our work to the extent that they can. My only chance of succeeding in this difficult work is if everyone commits himself to meeting these large moral and ethical responsibilities.

I would not be able to stand before you, ladies and gentlemen, if I myself—and my wife and children—had not been acutely affected by the terrible suffering inflicted on us non-Aryan Christians and had I not forced myself to nurture high hopes for a better future. Thus I call on you again: fight against our worst enemy, one who has crept into the ranks of our children—namely, the feeling of being inferior. Do not let your children live a lie; teach them to hold their heads high; teach them that we carry our worth within ourselves, that we must fight defiantly and vigorously to take charge of our fate.

There is nothing that I wish for more fervently than that our organization could, having fulfilled its purpose, dissolve itself. But until we reach that far distant point, a time as yet unknown, we must stand fast and try to do the utmost to alleviate the lot of those who share our fate, each according to his position and each according to his opportunities.

I hope never to see the day when the German people are again called to arms. But if it comes to that, I would appeal to our youth: show yourselves worthy of your comrades at Langemarck.[48] For the older members of our community, I have this message: let no one outdo you in performing work in a charitable Christian spirit and in your devotion to our beloved

---

47. The "game of percentages" refuted by Wolff in 1934 in fact became increasingly important after the Nuremberg Laws codified the concept of "*Mischlinge.*"

48. This refers to a subsequently highly idealized battle at the beginning of World War I when young German volunteers attacked enemy lines in Belgium and suffered heavy casualties.

German Fatherland, a Fatherland that belongs to us, not only in the past
or present, but evermore.

From the vantage point of American contemporaries, German Jewish prospects looked bleaker, yet far from catastrophic. In the United States as elsewhere,
however, Jews were concerned not just about the events unfolding within Germany but also about how the Nazi model might impact non-Jewish majorities
in their own countries. In a book published in 1934 on the challenges and
future of German Jews, Jacob R. Marcus concludes by raising questions on the
international ramifications of German anti-Jewish policies.

DOCUMENT 3-16: Jacob R. Marcus,[49] "Will German Jewry Survive?" in Jacob R.
Marcus, *The Rise and Destiny of the German Jew* (Cincinnati, OH: Union of American
Hebrew Congregations, 1934), 300.

Only recently (1934), Max Liebermann was asked if he did not believe
that German Jewry had a future, if he did not think that the courageous
activity of the older and newer Jewish organizations was a symptom that
augured well for the future. The artist's ironic answer was typical: "German Jewry is like a man who is mortally wounded—and in addition, has
a cold. So he calls the doctor in to stop his snuffling."[50]
    Liebermann's bitter skepticism is hardly justified. German Jewry has
the will to survive. It is exerting every effort possible to human beings to
maintain its vitality in the face of overwhelming odds. World Jewry is
united as never before, if not as to the methods, certainly as to the urgent
necessity of bringing every resource, financial, political, and moral, to

49. Jacob Rader Marcus (1896–1995) was an American Reform Jewish leader and prolific
chronicler of Jewish history, with academic training in the United States and Germany. He
long served on the faculty of the Hebrew Union College and directed the American Jewish Archives in Cincinnati, Ohio. See Jacob Rader Marcus, ed., *The Concise Dictionary of
American Jewish Biography* (Brooklyn, NY: Carlson, 1994), 2:416; obituary, *New York Times*,
November 16, 1995. The extract from his book is printed with permission of the Jacob Rader
Marcus Center of the American Jewish Archives.
    50. Max Liebermann (1847–1935) was a Berlin-based painter known for his impression-
ist works and his influential role in the 1898 Berlin Secession. He served as the president of
the Prussian Academy of Arts from 1920 until he resigned in protest against the Nazi ban
on Jewish artists in 1933. Liebermann's death in 1935 saw the last large-scale Jewish funeral
in Berlin; in 1943 his wife, Martha, committed suicide. See Emily D. Bilski, ed., *Berlin
Metropolis: Jews and the New Culture, 1890–1918* (Berkley: University of California Press,
1999); Bernd Schmalhausen, *"Ich bin doch nur ein Maler": Max und Martha Liebermann im
"Dritten Reich"* (Hildesheim, NY: Olms, 1994).

the aid of its stricken brethren. The lesson of Jewish history lends us further assurance that, barring wholesale expulsion or massacre, which seem rather remote even under the implacable hatred of the National Socialists, what has been called the "Jewish genius for survival" will manifest itself in Germany.

To be sure, there are problems and difficulties which, taken separately, seem well nigh insurmountable. But taken in the aggregate, and balanced against the elements of strength, it does not seem that their weight can be sufficient to turn the scales against survival.

However, one cannot hide this fact: a most distinguished Jewish group has been brutally crippled by the National Socialist German Workers' Party.

• • •

Is the influence of the National Socialist Party confined to Germany? Has this renaissance of German antisemitism had any effect on the status of the Jew in other European lands? Is it at all possible that German antisemitism can affect the life of the Jew in the United States?

PART II
FEELING ONE'S WAY
JANUARY 1934 TO AUGUST 1935

I N THE SUMMER OF 1933 **Leo Baeck** predicted to a colleague that the
Left would have staged a revolution by winter.[1] Six months later, though
Jewish observers might still venture some cautious optimism, they could not
fail to notice how successfully the regime had consolidated its power, and, even
more unnervingly, its legitimacy among the German population. President Paul
von **Hindenburg**'s death in August 1934 further reduced the possibility of a
viable challenge to Hitler and removed from the political scene the last figure
with enough national prestige to rival the Nazi leader. Hitler, styling himself as
Führer and Reich chancellor, now inherited the prerogatives formerly vested in
the office of president. Moreover, the army, once seen as a potential restraining
force, had already proved itself more than willing to whistle the new regime's
tune. In February 1934, for example, the Reichswehr leadership made the Civil
Service Law's "**Aryan** clause" applicable also to military recruitment.[2] Following
Hindenburg's death and pleased with its elevated place in the new order, the
army voluntarily swore an oath of loyalty to Hitler as supreme commander.

But even if serious threats to the Nazi movement had disappeared, many
observers both Jewish and non-Jewish, remained unsure where things were
headed. For one thing, a tug-of-war between party and state continued. In the

---

1. Conversation between Leo Baeck and a representative of the AJJDC, June 11, 1933,
LBIJMB MF 129; quoted in *Die Verfolgung und Vernichtung der europäischen Juden durch das
nationalsozialistische Deutschland, 1933–1945* (Munich: Oldenbourg, 2007), 1:169.

2. See Joseph Walk, ed., *Das Sonderrecht für die Juden im NS-Staat: Eine Sammlung der
gesetzlichen Maßnahmen und Richtlinien—Inhalt und Bedeutung* (Heidelberg: UTB, 1996),
72, no. 350.

summer of 1933, Hitler proclaimed that the revolutionary phase had ended, but for many Nazi Party figures and particularly the **SA**, the revolution had not gone far enough. While many civil servants on all levels pursued an anti-Jewish agenda, for example, the party's influence within the highest government departments remained very uneven. And down in the localities, many Nazi Party members were disgruntled that the new era had failed to enhance their power, wealth, or status. The result was an increasingly discontented party rank and file, whose demands and claims were most explicitly articulated by the SA. True, during the so-called Night of the Long Knives on June 30, 1934, Hitler ordered the SA leadership imprisoned and murdered, settled a few other old scores, and ended any possible threat of an internal party challenge to his leadership. In the months and years that followed, however, Hitler took steps to ensure that the state bureaucracy could not override the power of the Nazi Party. This was not a good omen for Germany's Jews. Local party branches were not only enthusiastic antisemites but also found that pushing the envelope in Jewish matters was often a good way of extending their authority in relation to society as a whole.[3]

Continuing economic fragility, by contrast, tended to work against anti-Jewish initiatives. In retrospect we can see that Germany rapidly recovered from the Great Depression during the years 1934 and 1935, but to contemporaries the world looked rather different. Viewed from the street, the economic outlook continued to appear uncertain. Industrial output did not regain 1928 levels until 1935, and most importantly, mass unemployment persisted, averaging around three million out of work in 1934. Even for those who were employed, the recovery initially brought only limited benefits. The real wages of many workers fell quite sharply in 1933. In 1934, a foreign exchange crisis led to draconian controls on capital export and foreign trade and created a great deal of public anxiety. Only after 1936 would a sturdy mood of economic confidence buoy Nazi Germany.[4] Not surprisingly, therefore, many in the regime, most notably Reich Bank president and (beginning in August 1934) Reich Economics Minister **Hjalmar Schacht**, avoided doing anything they thought might imperil the creation of new jobs. That concern exerted a powerful brake on Nazi action against Jewish businesses. Decrees issued in the summer and fall of 1933 by senior state and party figures that officially ended all boycott actions against Jewish firms were reissued even more forcefully in 1934 and early 1935.[5] However, these restraints coexisted,

---

3. On competition between different groups to influence Nazi policy, see Saul Friedländer, *Nazi Germany and the Jews,* vol. 1, *The Years of Persecution, 1933–1939* (New York: HarperCollins, 1997, 2007), 23–24.

4. See J. Adam Tooze, *The Wages of Destruction: The Making and Breaking of the Nazi Economy* (London: Allen Lane, 2006), 71–86, 138–65 ("*Volksgemeinschaft* on a budget").

5. See Walk, *Sonderrecht* 50, no. 236; 52, no. 250; 57, no. 276; 68, no. 329.

as noted above, with other more radical and ominous pressures on the Jewish business community, often emerging in the localities.

In the course of 1933, most non-Nazi institutions in Germany had been dissolved or brought in line with new strictures. The press censored itself even before it was compelled to do so. The few elections that took place offered no real choices, and ballots were no longer secret. The Nazi Party grew rapidly after the seizure of power in 1933, as millions of Germans decided it would be advantageous to become a member of the winning side. Party uniforms became fashionable in every town and village. The young were inculcated with the regime's messages, and new grassroots activists emerged all across Germany.[6] This mass involvement gave the regime a power and reach well beyond even the extensive formal prerogatives of the central state, while the ubiquitous presence of brown shirts (Nazis) created the impression of even more massive popular support than the regime was in any case getting.

What was the German population really thinking and feeling in 1934 and 1935? When Germany's Jews looked at their non-Jewish neighbors, it was very hard for them to distinguish between forced compliance and genuine enthusiasm or between party demands and popular initiatives. Indeed, because the free expression of opinion was not possible, the regime itself could not be certain how enthusiastically the population at large supported it. Historians continue to disagree to this day about the breadth and depth of the loyalty commanded by Hitler and his party among the wider population. To understand Jewish responses to Nazi persecution in this period, therefore, we will need to bear in mind contemporary uncertainties about the regime's vision for the future and the strength of its social roots.[7]

Indeed, both Nazi Party activists and Jews were, to a certain extent, feeling their way in this period. The activists continually tested how far the

---

6. In January 1935, the party had about 2.5 million members; in the spring of 1934, the SA had roughly 3 million members. See Michael H. Kater, *The Nazi Party: A Social Profile of Members and Leaders, 1919–1945* (Cambridge, MA: Harvard University Press, 1983), 157–58, fig. 1; Richard Bessel, *Political Violence and the Rise of Nazism: The Storm Troopers in Eastern Germany, 1925–1934* (New Haven, CT: Yale University Press, 1984), 97.

7. For the most sophisticated recent examinations of the various opinion sources that exist on Nazi Germany, see Peter Longerich, *"Davon haben wir nichts gewusst!": Die Deutschen und die Judenverfolgung 1933–1945* (Munich: Siedler Verlag, 2006); Ian Kershaw, *Popular Opinion and Political Dissent in the Third Reich: Bavaria, 1933–1945* (Oxford: Oxford University Press, 2002); Eric A. Johnson and Karl-Heinz Reuband, *What We Knew: Terror, Mass Murder and Everyday Life in Nazi Germany—An Oral History* (London: John Murray Publishers, 2005); Bernward Dörner, *Die Deutschen und der Holocaust: Was niemand wissen wollte, aber jeder wissen konnte* (Berlin: Propyläen, 2007); Frank Bajohr and Dieter Pohl, *Der Holocaust als offenes Geheimnis: Die Deutschen, die NS-Führung und die Alliierten* (Munich: Beck, 2006).

center would allow them to go and what the wider population would bear. For radicals, throwing their weight about in the "Jewish question" meant not only attacking a hated enemy but also deploying a convenient tool with which to impose their stamp on German society more generally. Jews, for their part, were testing whether they could still count on residual loyalties within German society and on established norms on the part of the state. Could one live in this new Germany?

CHAPTER 4

STRETCHING THE LIMITS
OF INFLUENCE

CENTRAL AND REGIONAL PERSPECTIVES

After an initial period of frantic activity, the regime's anti-Jewish drive slowed down. From December 1933 to the summer of 1935, the government enacted no major national legislation on Jewish matters. Even at lower levels, the flood of new ordinances narrowed to a modest stream. If we include all relevant policies and decrees from the national on down to the local level, we find that Berlin Jews, for example, had been subject to some eighty new laws and directives in 1933. But in 1934 the number of such regulations amounted to just fifteen, with only two further measures introduced in the first half of 1935.[1]

With the tide of new prohibitions seemingly ebbing, leading Jewish figures hoped that they might be able to establish some kind of agreement with the new regime. In this they were encouraged also by some verbal gestures on the government side. **Alfred Hirschberg**, a leading **CV** board member and advocate of a continuing belief in a future for Jewish life in Germany, was also one of the closest collaborators of the CV's chairman, **Julius Brodnitz**. Here he reports

1. Wolf Gruner and Stiftung Topographie des Terrors, eds., *Judenverfolgung in Berlin, 1933–1945: Eine Chronologie der Behördenmassnahmen in der Reichshauptstadt Berlin* (Berlin: Hentrich, 1996). For other parts of Germany, see Walk, *Sonderrecht*; Diemut Majer, *"Non-Germans" under the Third Reich: The Nazi Judicial and Administrative System in Germany and Occupied Eastern Europe with Special Regard to Occupied Poland, 1939–1945* (Baltimore: Johns Hopkins University Press, 2004).

to Brodnitz on recent conversations with **Joseph Goebbels**'s legal advisor in the Propaganda Ministry and later a leading figure in the Reich Chamber of Culture, Section Head Hans Schmidt-Leonhardt, occasioned by the antisemitic Reich Law on Editors due to come into force on January 1, 1934. Since the Propaganda Ministry was a new institution and more nazified than many of the other ministries, this access will have seemed particularly noteworthy.

DOCUMENT 4-1: Memorandum "Concerning the Law on Editors" by Alfred Hirschberg for Julius Brodnitz, November 11, 1933, with a letter to the Reichsvertretung, USHMMA RG 11.001M.31, reel 116 (SAM 721-1-2595, 41–44) (translated from German).

[. . .] The conversation with Ministerial Counselor [*Ministerialrat*] Schmidt-Leonhardt was very satisfactory.[2] It showed that even in the ministry of Herr Goebbels, there is clear understanding and recognition of the extraordinarily tragic situation in which German Jews now find themselves. The point was made repeatedly, however, that the biggest problem for German Jews is caused by those who, every time the government makes an accommodating gesture, loudly announce that it is showing signs of weakness or anxiety. Claims of that kind then strengthen radical elements within the party and thus make the job difficult for the "steadier forces" (I am quoting the *Ministerialrat*'s expression). The Propaganda Ministry, or at least this section, also holds the view that the regime's measures toward the Jews were necessary to create a clear position at the outset, in which the German element, as the regime defines it, is the sole power in charge. Once this position has been reached, then it will be possible to talk about integrating long-established, settled Jewish elements. [. . .]

In the accompanying letter to the **Reichsvertretung**, Hirschberg also noted that the Reich propaganda minister had no intention of endangering the existence of the Jewish press and asked for an opportunity to give a verbal report on

---

2. Hans Schmidt-Leonhardt (1886–1945) was a lawyer, member of the NSDAP, and close collaborator with Nazi propaganda leader Joseph Goebbels. When Goebbels became head of the newly established Reich Propaganda Ministry in early spring 1933, Schmidt-Leonhardt was appointed his chief legal advisor. Involved in drafting the Law on Editors promulgated later that same year, he became director of the Reich Chamber of Culture (*Geschäftsführer der Reichskulturkammer*). See Alexander F. Kiefer, "Government Control of Publishing in Germany," *Political Science Quarterly* 57 (March 1942): 72–97.

the "very wide-ranging conversation," which was "understandably not restricted to the specific topic" of the law on press editorship.[3]

Hirschberg most probably could not see the degree to which Schmidt-Leonhardt's restraint was tactical in nature, driven by Hitler's desire for calm in international relations after Germany's withdrawal from the **League of Nations** and by continuing concern about the domestic economic situation and international financial relationships.

Alongside the grounds for cautious optimism, there were also ominous signs on the horizon. While some Jewish businesses were beginning to benefit from economic recovery, many Jews found themselves in dire financial straits. Restrictions increasingly blocked Jews from access to higher-level professional qualifying exams, and significant new exclusions prevented Jewish participation in many spheres of German life. Moreover, despite the official national position that the boycott of Jewish stores was over, municipal authorities, in conjunction with local party officials and district economic advisors (*Gauwirtschaftsberater*), kept up the pressure by continually reviving local boycott actions, illegally barring Jews from entering contracts, and discriminating against Jewish welfare applicants.[4] Among the many Nazi organizations involved in such boycott actions, the Nazi women's organization, or NS-Frauenschaft, played an important role because it had access to a key group of consumers, German women.

Since the beginning of 1934, members of the NS-Frauenschaft in different regions of the Reich had grown increasingly active in the local boycotts of Jewish-owned shops and other small businesses. Were it not for meticulous monitoring by the CV, these local anti-Jewish actions in defiance of official state and party policy would have gone unrecorded. Hoping that Nazi rhetoric of motherhood might yet trump the race divide, Jewish women's activists formulated careful pleas to Gertrud Scholtz-Klink, the head of the German women's organization, as well as to her superiors in the Office of the Deputy

---

3. This Law on Editors (*Schriftleitergesetz*), enacted on October, 4, 1933, sought to align the German press with the tenets of National Socialism by requiring all journalists and editors to join the Reichspressekammer, the regime's print media organization. The legislation, echoing the "Aryan paragraph" of the Civil Service Law passed earlier the same year, effectively barred Jewish citizens from working in Germany's mainstream media by requiring all journalists and editors to be of non-Jewish descent. See Walk, *Sonderrecht* 55, no. 264; Majer, *"Non-Germans" under the Third Reich*, 142.

4. Avraham Barkai, *From Boycott to Annihilation: The Economic Struggle of German Jews, 1933–1943* (Hanover, NH: Brandeis University Press and University Press of New England, 1989), 63–69.

of the Führer.[5] The coordinator of the CV's women's work, Margarete Fried, penned one of these requests in the spring of 1934.[6]

DOCUMENT 4-2: Letter by Margarete Fried to the Reich leader of the Nazi Women's League, Gertrud Scholtz-Klink, April 21, 1934, USHMMA RG 11.001M.31, reel 128 (SAM 721-1-2809, 132–34) (translated from German).

[. . .] I have come to the decision, dear Madam, to present my worries to you. I am a mother of seven children and two years ago I lost my husband. I try to meet the demands of maintaining a household to the best of my ability. My efforts allow me to sympathize deeply with others similarly struggling to meet the demands of daily life.

I know that as a mother, even as a Jewish one, I may speak to you, and I thank you for reading these lines. I don't know to whom I could otherwise turn with my worries. I have always been active in social work, and I currently direct women's work for the CV. I am submitting some brief reports to you taken from letters from around the Reich, letters that trouble me deeply. Limitless misery emerges from these lines. The thought keeps coming to me that only you, dear Madam, can help here. You have taken the concerns of so many upon yourself, and it is that concern for others that prompts me to appeal to you.

The Reich government has granted every German the right to secure a livelihood, and yet members of the National Socialist Women's Association are forbidden to buy in Jewish shops.

My heartfelt request goes out to you now to instruct the leadership of the NS Women's Association to abstain from taking special measures in the economic sphere. I hold firmly to the belief that even if fate separates women, our original purpose still lives in all of us: to give life and to nurture and maintain it! [. . .]

Fried received no response. Toward the end of the year, the **JFB**, too, approached the NS-Frauenschaft leader.

---

5. Gertrud Scholtz-Klink (1902–1999) was a female functionary for the NSDAP during the later years of the Weimar Republic and, from 1934, Reich leader (*Reichsführerin*) of the Nazi Women's League (NS-Frauenschaft). See Claudia Koonz, *Mothers in the Fatherland: Women, the Family, and Nazi Politics* (New York: St. Martin's Press, 1987).

6. Margarete Fried (née Levy; 1885–1958) was a teacher by training and worked in educating Jewish youth from 1923 to 1938. Active in CV relief work, she became coordinator of the CV's women's group for Greater Berlin before emigrating to Palestine in 1939. See Elke-Vera Kotowski, ed., *Juden in Berlin: Biografien* (Berlin: Henschel, 2005), 86.

DOCUMENT 4-3: Letter by Jüdischer Frauenbund to the Reich leader of the Nazi Women's League, Gertrud Scholtz-Klink, November 8, 1934, USHMMA RG 11.001M.31, reel 128 (SAM 721-1-2809, 57–58) (translated from German).

Berlin—Bochum, November 8, 1934

To the Reich leader of the NS-Frauenschaft, Frau Gertrud Scholtz-Klink: [. . .]

In the name of the League of Jewish Women of Germany, on whom the responsibility for Jewish youth is incumbent as the organized voice of Jewish mothers, we take the liberty of presenting to you, the leader of the German women's organizational network, our worries about the fate of this youth.

We Jewish mothers have always, and in full recognition of the burden assigned to us, expressed our unanimous commitment, to the extent that we can, to raise our children to be upstanding people, courageous adherents of our religion, and people who love Germany and are ready to make sacrifices for her. We are aware, however, that this can only be achieved if our children are allowed to grow up in an environment that does not present insurmountable barriers to the development of their moral selves [*Entfaltung ihrer sittlichen Persönlichkeit*]. When honest effort and ambition are met with contempt and misunderstanding, when quality of achievement and goodness of character are not accepted as the criteria by which the individual should be judged, then those barriers are indeed in place.

We know that the NS Women's Association is inseparably bound to all the demands of National Socialism. Therefore, we would never invoke motherly solidarity by asking the NS Women's Association to exert influence on our fate as citizens—whatever that may turn out to be—insofar as that is decided by the principles of national socialism and the authorities of the National Socialist state. But when in front of a hundred thousand German boys and girls, hate and contempt for the Jewish people are praised as virtue and national duty, as happened at the rally for youth in Aachen on July 22 and in Cologne on October 13, we cannot remain silent. Therefore, we, the mothers of the children whose right to live [*Lebensrecht*] is threatened in this way, come to you, the mothers of the children who, from the seed planted in them today, shall some day build German life and the German state.

We have no recommendations to make or plans to present to you, but we call upon the shared motherly responsibilities for the dignity and protection of every living being. In your speech at Nuremberg, you said, dear Mrs. Scholtz-Klink, "To be a mother unifies the women of all strata and all ranks." We hope therefore that you will also sympathize with our motherly worries and will bring to bear your great influence in the service of inculcating a more balanced viewpoint. [. . .]

As far as we know, the Nazi women's organization did not reply; nor did other sections of the Nazi Party leadership respond to interventions by Jewish officials in this matter.

According to reigning official government policy in 1934, Jews were free to pursue a living within Germany (except in the many proscribed professions). However, regional or local measures often made normal life impossible. Moreover, ever since April 1933 businesses, even those owned by Jews, had been under pressure to fire their Jewish employees. Despite legal rulings in favor of Jewish employees, the National Socialist Organization of Factory Cells (*Nationalsozialistische Betriebszellen-Organisation*), a Nazi creation designed to replace the disbanded labor unions, pressured employers to let them go.[7] An astute overseas observer captured this strange mixture of calm and menace, tolerance and exclusion.

DOCUMENT 4-4: "Brief Notes on Recent Stay in Berlin" by David J. Schweitzer, AJJDC European Executive Offices, Paris, to Bernhard Kahn, March 5, 1934, AJJDC Archive AR 3344/628.[8]

Outwardly Berlin presented during my recent stay there a normal appearance, unchanged from that presented during my last stay there early in January of this year. The air is not charged, general courtesy prevails. The feeling of fear and the fear of violence, so characteristic of the earlier days, is gradually disappearing. One hears little of acts of violence. Even though it was openly threatened that returning emigrants suspected of anti-German propaganda abroad would immediately be put in concentration camps, such cases have not actually come to my attention, although a good many émigrés returned to Germany. So much is this the actual situation or so well masked is it that I heard an American, one who has just spent a week passing on to a neighboring country, remark that he could not see that anything has actually happened that so stirred the outside world. This, of course, is grossly exaggerated. In the first place there is still the sharp contrast between the

---

7. Barkai, *From Boycott*, 32–33.

8. David J. Schweitzer (1886–?) was active in a number of American Jewish advocacy groups and an important figure in the AJJDC from 1920 until 1940. For Bernhard Kahn, see the glossary.

Hauptstadt [capital] and the province. The leaders in the province still see fit to make and interpret laws and regulations that are in clear contradiction to those that emanate from the highest authorities. Here and there speeches are made that are full of venom and are clear anti-Jewish attacks. But even in the province, I have heard from a prominent leader who had just returned from other parts to Berlin, that even there contrasts can be observed; whereas in one town a decree might be issued that after a certain date no Jew would be permitted to remain in the town, in the next town the small Jewish population continues to live side by side with their neighbors and pursue their occupations as best they can unmolested. What our friend had failed to see from outward appearances is the tragedy that is befalling daily the job holders who are gradually losing their positions. While on the one hand one can observe a Jewish department store crowded as usual with non-Jews and Jews alike, one can observe in the very next department store the total absence of a single Jewish employee. What is to become of those? [. . .]

With most foreign visitors gleaning contradictory nuggets of information, the U.S. press was able to paint only an incoherent and sketchy picture of the situation in the Reich.[9] German Jewish organizations, however, had access to a broader spectrum of sources and saw the interplay between periphery and center at work on a daily basis. Among the more worrisome regions registered by the CV, the rural districts of East Prussia loomed large. Here Nazi **Gauleiter** Erich Koch had carried out a particularly ruthless and effective purge of the administration, installing his own henchmen, some of whom, like Koch himself, would later play a key role in the mass murder of Jews in the occupied Eastern European territories. The Nazis had been successful in recruiting large numbers of followers in the small rural towns and villages throughout the state.[10] As regional CV officials recognized, they were contending not only with

9. See Deborah E. Lipstadt, "The American Press and the Persecution of German Jewry: The Early Years, 1933–1935," *LBIYB* 29 (1984): 27–55; Deborah E. Lipstadt, *Beyond Belief: The American Press and the Coming of the Holocaust, 1933–1945* (New York: Free Press, 1986). For the revealing insights gained in the early phase of Nazi rule by League of Nations High Commissioner for Refugees James McDonald, see Richard Breitman, Barbara McDonald Stewart, and Severin Hochberg, eds., *Advocate for the Doomed: The Diaries and Papers of James G. McDonald*, vol. 1, *1932–1935* (Bloomington: Indiana University Press in association with the USHMM, 2007).

10. The NSDAP had achieved one of the highest electoral results in 1932 in East Prussia, and the party had grown to more than 5 percent of the entire national membership at that time; see Christian Rohrer, *Nationalsozialistische Macht in Ostpreussen* (Munich: Meidenbauer, 2006), 198–99; Ralf Meindl, *Ostpreussens Gauleiter: Erich Koch. Eine politische Biographie* (Osnabrück: Fibre, 2007), 153, 156.

local administrations and a hostile body of state functionaries but also with the active participation of substantial sections of the population.

DOCUMENT 4-5: Letter by CV regional office East Prussia (Angerthal)[11] to CV head office, March 24, 1934, USHMMA RG 11.001M.31, reel 128 (SAM 721-1-2808, 288–89) (translated from German).

[. . .] When traveling through the provinces, the undersigned was repeatedly informed that it is by no means just a small minority that is organized [in Nazi formations] and therefore supports the efforts toward shutting out the Jews. It may well be in fact that the majority of the inhabitants are organized in one or another of a range of associations whose leaders are anxious to instill National Socialist ideas in their members. In our experience, the main point of this indoctrination is to persuade the members that Jews' continued presence is harmful. The members are therefore called upon to fulfill the [Nazi] Party program's mission of removing the Jews by avoiding Jewish businesses. Once the majority of the inhabitants have been influenced by such propaganda, the Jewish businesses are, in fact, condemned to close. [. . .]

In the view of the section of the population we represent, government decrees will be effective only if they are really enforced on the Party and other association members. Until government officials feel themselves to be in a position to intervene, government measures will not have the hoped-for results. For the Jewish population in the provinces, this fact is increasingly clear and extremely depressing. [. . .]

In its response, the main office in Berlin assured its branch in East Prussia of its commitment and support but stopped short of guaranteeing a positive outcome. Jewish businessmen should hold their ground, they counseled, "for as long as is at all possible."[12] Within East Prussia this advice could be tested almost every day: in the town of Lötzen, a Nazi Party official had publicly com-

---

11. Max Angerthal (1886–1943) was a leading figure in the CV's branch in Königsberg, East Prussia. He remained involved in Jewish relief work both in his native state and later in Berlin until 1943, when he was deported with his wife Vera (née Engel, born 1916) to "the East" ca. 1942. See Stefanie Schüler-Springorum, *Die Jüdische Minderheit in Königsberg/Preussen, 1871–1945* (Göttingen: Vandenhoeck & Ruprecht, 1996), 322, 366; *USHMM ITS Collection Data Base Central Name Index.*

12. CV head office (Rubinstein) to CV regional office East Prussia, March 29, 1934, USHMMA RG 11.001M.31, reel 128 (SAM 721-1-2808, 286–87).

plained that "women in particular are still buying much too much from the Jew" and demanded that everyone should pitch in to "ruin the Jewish-owned shops." Berlin CV officials, **Hans Reichmann** wrote, knew this problem well.

DOCUMENT 4-6: Letter by CV head office (H. Reichmann) to CV regional office East Prussia, April 10, 1934, USHMMA RG 11.001M.31, reel 101 (SAM 721-1-2335, 181) (translated from German).

> [. . .] What you say about the contradiction between orders from govern- mental agencies and those from other functionaries who are not autho- rized to give them is absolutely correct. Ninety percent of our current work is consumed with this problem. This is without a doubt the central obstacle to securing the well-being of German Jewry, and we consequently emphasize it clearly and at length in all our consultations with the appro- priate authorities. The relevant officials, particularly in the Reich Ministry of Economics, are absolutely clear about the meaning of the materials we have presented. We should point out that the materials we are providing to the Reich Ministry of Economics reveal much more strongly and bla- tantly the exclusion of Jews from economic life than the statements that were challenged in Lötzen [i.e., the town on which the CV regional office East Prussia had reported].

Jews' ability to influence local developments varied enormously. Regional CV leaders often placed their hopes in intervention from higher authority. One would assume, the head of the CV office in East Prussia wrote, that leading state agencies would intervene to ensure compliance with government policy and its ban on "wild" or "special actions" (*Sonderaktionen*).[13] And certainly, where local officials appeared hostile, higher authorities could sometimes be prodded to act. Yet confusion reigned about how and when this was best done. Even when local boycotts involved a clear breach of the law, state officials at the Reich level were often hesitant when it came to enforcement, particularly on Jewish mat- ters. Even they were sometimes unsure which agency was responsible for issues affecting Jews and which guidelines applied. Established rules of bureaucratic procedure and administrative action seemed to have been replaced by more slippery realms of responsibility and special assignments. The less Jewish orga- nizations were able to communicate with government agencies, the more they

---

13. CV regional office East Prussia to CV head office, March 29, 1934, USHMMA RG 11.001M.31, reel 101 (SAM 721-1-2335, 182, 185).

had to second-guess what had caused particular problems and how they could be resolved. All this contributed greatly to the general sense of uncertainty that marked German Jewish existence in this period.

CONSTRAINED COMMUNICATIONS

While the CV's attention was occupied by the conflict between ministerial directives and local initiatives, another threat began to raise its head. Until the summer of 1934, the **Gestapo**, the secret state police that hunted down political opponents of the Reich, had played a relatively small role in the persecution of German Jews. The first chief of the Prussian Gestapo, Rudolf Diels, had even arranged for a meeting between **Hermann Göring** and the CV leadership in early March 1933.[14] Empowered to detain suspected opponents indefinitely in *Schutzhaft* ("protective custody") and freed from many of the state controls that constrained it, the Gestapo grew more active in Jewish affairs after SS chief **Heinrich Himmler** took it over in April 1934. Himmler delegated the running of the Gestapo to his most feared and effective right-hand man, **Reinhard Heydrich**, who simultaneously headed the SS intelligence agency, the *Sicherheitsdienst* (SD, or Security Service). Almost immediately after Heydrich's appointment, Jewish individuals and organizations felt a chill new wind blowing from the Gestapo's Berlin headquarters.[15]

On June 13, 1934, the CV's main office in Berlin received an order from the Gestapo's central office for Prussia (the **Gestapa**). The Gestapo had intercepted a CV circular asking regional CV offices whether they had observed antisemitic propaganda or songs in their part of the country. Heydrich's policemen now forbade such circulars and warned of strong sanctions should such enquiries take place in the future. On July 13 the Gestapo intervened again, and this time the CV head office was forced to instruct its members to desist, at least temporarily, from passing on any reports to the authorities about attacks on Jewish individuals or property. The CV tried to negotiate with the Gestapo and

---

14. Julius Brodnitz, diary entry for March 3, 1933; USHMMA Acc. 2008.189.1 Brodnitz collection.

15. With Himmler's appointment as chief of the German police in 1936, the Gestapo, together with the Criminal Police, was reorganized into the Security Police (Sicherheitspolizei) under Heydrich. On the role of the political police in Nazi Germany, see Robert Gellately, *Backing Hitler: Consent and Coercion in Nazi Germany* (New York: Oxford University Press, 2001); George C. Browder, *Hitler's Enforcers: The Gestapo and SS Security Service in the Nazi Revolution* (New York: Oxford University Press 1996); Michael Wildt, *Die Judenpolitik des SD 1935 bis 1938: Eine Dokumentation* (Munich: Oldenbourg, 1995).

protect at least some of its ability to continue communicating with its members and the outside world.

DOCUMENT 4-7: Circular letter no. 8 by CV regional office Brandenburg with a directive by CV head office (Brodnitz, Hirschberg) to its branches, August 8, 1934, USHMMA RG 11.001M.31, reel 97 (SAM 721-1-47, 21) (translated from German).

On July 27, the leadership of the CV sent the following letter to the Gestapa in Berlin in response to an instruction from July 13, 1934. The letter said, among other things:

> It goes without saying that the activity of the CV is conducted with the most precise adherence to the legal regulations and, above all, in a spirit of loyal adherence toward the authorities. The CV, its regional offices, and local leaderships act according to these basic guiding principles set by the association's leadership.
>
> The Gestapa's wishes as regards CV activity emerged from the closing section of the instruction of July 13, in conjunction with the instruction 11 1 B 2 20154 of June 11, and gave us occasion to consult with the section head of II 1 B 2, Dr. Hasselbacher.[16] Based on that consultation we may presume that the following guidelines for our work correspond to the wishes of the Gestapa:
>
> 1. The CV or its branches are not to conduct any surveys concerning anti-Jewish incidents. Should the central economic authorities request material concerning the economic situation of German Jews within certain regions or economic sectors, the CV will issue this request to the head of the economic department of the Gestapa and conduct the survey only with their approval.
>
> 2. Reports that reach the CV or its branches of incidents directed against Jewish people or property should be passed on to the local authorities or, in more serious cases, to the central authorities. If the persons sending in the notices are known to the CV branch to be trustworthy and if the content of the notice seem inherently credible, the information will be forwarded to the authorities with an accompanying note expressly stating that the report contains no commentary [*Stellungnahme*] by the CV. If the sender of the notice is unknown to

---

16. Dr. Karl Haselbacher, Gestapa officer in Berlin since 1934, became head of Department II B (dealing with "Churches, Freemasons, Jews, Emigrants") in 1936 (Wildt, *Die Judenpolitik*, 13–14).

the CV or the content of the notification is not coherent or appears confused, the CV and its branches, respectively, are entitled to clarify the actual circumstances through further inquiry.

We have recently taken the opportunity to provide our branches with guidelines on the basis of these principles and to require, as before, strict compliance.

Sincerely,
[signed:]

Counselor of Justice Dr. [Julius] Brodnitz   Dr. Alfred Hirschberg
President [*Vorsitzender*]   Syndic

You are asked to strictly observe these instructions.

As a result of the new climate of surveillance, CV leaders had to bear in the mind the possibility that information they collected might be used against them by the regime's security apparatus. Even in written private exchanges and internal organizational communications, Jewish officials often kept their stance on key issues deliberately vague so that, if intercepted by the police, they could not be deemed expressions of opposition or subversion. And even where they were not worried about prosecution, they were also mindful of not wanting to provide any arguments that their opponents could exploit.

The CV was hindered from speaking openly in its communications due to threats from a variety of sources. Concern for its members' morale and psychological well-being was also at issue, both for humanitarian reasons and for the preservation of the community's resilience. In October 1934, an article in a non-Jewish newspaper for home and landowners (*Allgemeine Deutsche Haus- und Grundbesitzer-Zeitung*) pointed out that the Nazis were extending the scope of eminent domain in such a way that "racial" grounds might suffice to expropriate these assets from existing owners.

DOCUMENT 4-8: Internal CV memorandum for the editorial board of the *CV-Zeitung*, October 6, 1934, USHMMA RG 11.001M.31, reel 101 (SAM 721-1-2987, 205) (translated from German).

[. . .] I attach the journal for home and landowners with the article "Expropriation in the New Reich." Dr. Reichmann is of the opinion that any mention of this article in the CV newspaper or in the Jewish press could have a strong, unintended impact in Jewish circles. I am therefore drawing special attention to the article. Perhaps the Jewish press could also be alerted accordingly.

The CV leadership appears to have agreed to the proposal and encouraged the Jewish press to avoid airing this topic.[17] Such communications show that public statements issued by the CV and other Jewish bodies cannot be taken at face value. At the time, ordinary Jews found it difficult to evaluate the pronouncements issued by the CV and other organizations. Canny observers could spot the "professional optimism" that flavored many proclamations by Jewish officials.[18] The sturdy, upbeat tone of Jewish voices may have provided some occasional reassurance, but could it be trusted? It was clear that these bodies alone were looking after Jewish interests in a hostile world. But it was equally clear that ordinary Jews had no transparent and reliable guide to the true situation. Small wonder that many, among them **Julius Moses**, grew frustrated and wondered whether their leaders really understood the problems facing the common man and woman.

DOCUMENT 4-9: Letter by Julius Moses, Berlin, to Erwin Moses, Tel Aviv, March 24, 1934, translated from Dieter Fricke, *Jüdisches Leben in Berlin und Tel Aviv, 1933–1939: Der Briefwechsel des ehemaligen Reichstagsabgeordneten Dr. Julius Moses* (Hamburg: von Bockel, 1997), 138–39.

[. . .] Talk about these academics! They're the ones now playing a big role again in all the Jewish organizations and in so-called Jewish politics. They also want a big role where you are [i.e., in Palestine]! The main Jewish leadership here also set up an advisory council [*Beirat*] made up of representatives from all over Germany: the CV newspaper describes this as a "circle of representative people!" Fifty altogether, of whom forty are academics (that's 80 percent!!). Three women and five from the world of business![19] That's our version of Jewish politics and Jewish politicians!!!

17. Note from Hirschberg to the Reichsvertretung Press Office, October 8, 1934; USHMMA RG 11.001M.31, reel 141 (SAM 721-1-2987, 203).

18. See Marjorie Lamberti, "The Jewish Defence in Germany after the National-Socialist Seizure of Power," *LBIYB* 42 (1997): 135–47.

19. When the Reichsvertretung was formed in September 1933, its leaders announced the creation of an advisory council (*Beirat*); however, this council, comprising members from different leading German Jewish organizations, came into being only in February 1934. See Otto Dov Kulka, ed., *Deutsches Judentum unter dem Nationalsozialismus*, vol. 1, *Dokumente zur Geschichte der Reichsvertretung der Juden, 1933–1939* (Tübingen: Mohr Siebeck, 1997), 127–28, 461–62.

There you have the age-old inflated love for Jewish intellectuals! Our patrimony!! And add to that the Jewish war veterans! And only academics at the top! And so who's representing Jewish clerks? The little people, who have such a hard time of it nowadays!! What we really need for Passover is for a Moses to come and free us from the clutches of these Jewish academics. Lend a hand over there! [. . .]

Jews living in small communities doubted that their main representatives in the big cities really grasped what was happening. In fact, however, the CV's records make clear that Jewish leaders quickly caught wind of the situation in the provinces. The following example from Sandersleben in the state of Sachsen-Anhalt shows that at both an individual and institutional level, Jewish businessmen fought hard to assert their rights, in this case even concluding with a mocking reference to the omnipresent *Deutscher Gruss* or the so-called Hitler salute. When it came to the make-or-break issue of earning a living, many Jews proved unafraid to solicit the aid of public institutions. For as long as humanly possible, they doggedly continued to assert their rights.

DOCUMENT 4-10: Letter by Adolf Adler,[20] Sandersleben, to CV head office, July 9, 1934, USHMMA RG 11.001M.31, reel 102 (SAM 721-1-2397, 104–5) (translated from German).

I am contacting you today for the first time as a member [of the CV], since I do not know if the Reichsvertretung is responsible for such matters and I also do not know their address.

I have been a member of your organization for some time, not just since the revolution [*Umsturz*, i.e., the Nazi takeover], and thus hope that you can be of assistance in the matter that follows.

During the night of June 23, the two large display windows at my father's business were completely plastered over with huge red pieces of paper; enclosed you will find two posters that we tore down elsewhere. The two photos that I have enclosed will also give you an "impressive" picture of what happened [photos not included here]. The following Sunday we covered the display windows and went straight to the police early Monday morning to report the incident and lodge a complaint, and I personally went

---

20. Possibly Adolf Adler (1908–1938), who died in January 1938 in Berlin; see *Datenbank zur Liste der jüdischen Einwohner im Deutschen Reich, 1933–1945* (Berlin: Bundesarchiv, 2008). The authors have been unable to find any further information on him or his father, who is mentioned in this document.

to complain to the mayor in his capacity as the local police official. In the meantime I took photos of the display windows on Sunday morning, which surely did not go unnoticed because this resulted in further unpleasantness. I will describe this at greater length in what follows.

Early Tuesday morning I was hauled out of bed and arrested around eight thirty and was told that everything would be set right if I turned over my camera and the photos. However, I could no longer comply with this request since on Monday I had already sent the film to my brother, who was spending time at the home of relatives in northern Germany. When I told the police officer this, he searched my house and then and there took me off to see the mayor. But I could only tell him the same thing and was then released.

The film was later impounded by the local police in Blumenthal (Unterweser [region]), where my brother was staying.

And now to the second case: During the night of July 3, 1934, the display windows and this time also three display cases were vandalized in the same fashion as before. This time it clearly looked as though the scoundrels [*Halunken*]—I can't think of a better term for them—ran out of the larger posters and then took small slips of paper and repeatedly smeared the word "Jew" with brown oil paint on the window, as well as a huge swastika. These same scoundrels then finally also emptied a can of paint in the entry door, or rather on the step leading inside. In the end they must have decided that the [hand-drawn swastika] would give away who was responsible, so they painted it closed like this: [hand drawing depicting a small square divided into four equal spaces]; still, the sign was still very visible afterward.

On that same day in the morning, I went to the police again, namely to the mayor, and informed him that I would photograph the windows this time and complain to some higher-up officials and that we had no intention of removing the graffiti and damage. I told him at the same time that I was there in the name of the "Jewish community" [*Israelitische Gemeinde*] because the vandals had managed to hit another Jewish business for the second time. And I stated that I was also there on behalf of my father. The other Jewish store owner in town is already 79 years old and can no longer make a complaint himself, and my father suffers a heart condition and would no doubt have become too upset, so he sent me in his stead.

I also made an official complaint with the police about this second incident.

But now here is the centerpiece of the affair: on the night of July 5, a window grill of the local synagogue was torn down, and three windows were broken. A grill was damaged on the other side of the building (that is to say, someone tore a hole in it), and there, too, a window was broken with a stone the size of a fist. After learning about this my father himself went to see the mayor on Friday morning, namely in his capacity as head of the local "Jewish community," complained, and also filed charges on the incident. I attach a cutting from the local newspaper from which you can use the advertisement [see document 4-11].

On the occasion of my father's visit to the mayor, this same mayor brought up the vandalism to our shop windows and recommended that we clean them in our own interest, which we did on Friday; I need not tell you the effort this cost, particularly since the graffiti had been done with oil paint. The job took us hours . . . and early Sunday morning a little slip of paper had again been stuck up.

This happened despite the fact that the mayor had promised some remedial action.

My father's business has suffered enormously because of the previous boycott, like all the other small Jewish businesses hereabouts. The new attacks are bringing us closer and closer to the brink of ruin. You will hardly understand from where you are sitting what dire effects all this has in a small community.

And now, let me come to my main reason for writing you today: I intentionally gave you such an extensive and detailed report so that you could get as clear a picture of what has happened here as possible. I would have truly been very happy to come and report in person but unfortunately lacked the funds to do so; I'm just barely making ends meet as a sales representative and couldn't survive if I weren't at least getting my meals at home and living with my parents. And this despite the fact that I am now 26 years old.

I ask you to possibly publish something in your *CV-Zeitung* with respect to the attempted break-in and vandalism at the synagogue so that the wider public actually hears about what is happening.

With regard to the graffiti on our windows, I ask if you could possibly intervene on our behalf with some higher-up officials. However, please only make "discreet" use of the photographs.

I would greatly appreciate hearing from you about what you have been able to do and accomplish for us in this matter.

I send you my regards with Jewish greeting [*mit jüdischem Gruss*]
Yours respectfully,
Adolf Adler

DOCUMENT 4-11: "Wanted" ad published by Jewish community Sandersleben, July 1934, USHMMA RG 11.001M.31, reel 102 (SAM 721-1-2397).

10 Mark Belohnung

zahlen wir demjenigen, der uns die ruchlofen Täter nach-
weift, die in der Nacht vom Donnerstag zum Freitag an
unferem Gotteshaus die Fenfterdrähte abgeriffen und
Scheiben eingefchlagen haben.

Jfraelitifche Cultus-Gemeinde
Sandersleben.

Cutout from the *Sanderslebener Zeitung*, July 7, 1934.

We will pay a reward of 10 Reichsmark to the person who identifies the reckless perpetrators [*ruchlose Täter*] who, in the night from Thursday to Friday, have torn down window grills from our house of God [*Gotteshaus*] and smashed the windows.

Jewish community [*Israelitische Cultus-Gemeinde*] Sandersleben.

Following receipt of this letter, the regional representatives dispatched by the CV to Sandersleben confirmed all of Adler's observations. It appears that although there had been some witnesses, they were too nervous to testify. Despite some hesitation about citing such an isolated, small-town case, the CV forwarded the details to the Reich Economics Ministry, noting that not a single official body in the Anhalt Province had declared itself willing to intervene. The CV also approached the Gestapo and asked it to address the problem.[21] At this stage in 1934, it was evidently still conceivable that the Gestapo might be more committed to upholding the law than attacking Jews. Neither institution, however, seems to have acted. As a result of this kind of exclusionary pressure, by 1935 and 1936 in some small towns across Germany, up to 80 percent of the Jewish population had sunk into destitution.[22]

---

21. See Michael Wildt, *Volksgemeinschaft als Selbstermächtigung: Gewalt gegen Juden in der deutschen Provinz, 1919–1939* (Hamburg: Hamburger Edition, 2007), 139–44.

22. See David Kramer, "Jewish Welfare Work under the Impact of Pauperization," in *Juden im nationalsozialistischen Deutschland: The Jews in Nazi Germany, 1933–1945*, ed. Arnold Paucker (Tübingen: J. C. B. Mohr, 1986), 182–83.

CHAPTER 5

EVERYDAY LIFE IN AN
ERA OF UNCERTAINTY

BREAD ON THE TABLE

While Jewish leaders pondered how best to intervene on behalf of their core-ligionists, individual Jews and their families tried to assess how things stood. How bad was their situation now, and what would it be like in the future? The stories told by relatives, friends, and the press seldom added up to a consistent picture. There was no doubt that a revolution had taken place and that, for most Jews, life had become noticeably worse. Yet, unlike the Russian Revolution in 1917, when so much from the old regime had been torn down, the Nazi tornado had rattled every building but left most visible structures standing. Even institutions that had, in reality, already been fatally compromised, such as the German judiciary, still seemed from the outside to be the same robust bodies they had long been. Would the winds of change eventually die down with little lasting ill effect? Almost every German Jew experienced periods of calm that allowed him or her to entertain some cautious optimism, at least for a while. For a privileged few, life still appeared relatively normal. Yet, for most, some renewed event, above all the periodically revived boycotts and incidents of harassment and violence aimed at Jews, would stir up unease and uncertainty again.[1]

The primary question for most families was whether they would be able to continue earning a living. The first group that urgently confronted this question

---

1. On conflicting experiences in this period, see, among other works, Barkai, *From Boy-cott*, 54–109.

comprised the Jewish civil servants, the victims of the Civil Service Law of April 7, 1933. Because the number of Jews in government employ was small, at most some five thousand or so, and because around half of these received exemptions as a result of their military service, the law initially had only limited effect. Those who were dismissed also received modest pensions (although, in the course of the 1930s, these would be scrapped with the same efficiency as the exemptions from dismissal for Jewish veterans). The law had a larger indirect impact since it provided a model for enacting employment discrimination more generally, and so professionals such as doctors and lawyers were affected. True, many professionals slipped through the law's provisions by virtue of their military service in World War I: more than half of Jewish lawyers initially enjoyed exemptions on this basis. Nevertheless, overall, the discriminatory employment legislation of spring and summer 1933 affected some twelve to thirteen thousand people, or 5 percent of all gainfully employed Jews.[2]

Moreover, even those professionals allowed to continue working were often subjected to increasingly severe discriminatory measures. Many of the approximately nine thousand "non-**Aryan**" doctors in Germany lost their ability to work for public hospitals as early as April 1933. Access to other publicly funded medical positions—medical supervision in schools, for example, or care provisions for patients on state welfare—was progressively closed to them, including accreditation to work for Germany's public health-insurance schemes. As early as summer 1934, the number of "non-Aryan" doctors had decreased to seven thousand, of whom three thousand were not accredited with public health insurance. Well before the **Nuremberg Laws** of 1935, those doctors still practicing medicine were increasingly forced to rely on income from treating their Jewish patients alone.[3]

Outside the government sector and the legal and medical professions, Germany's Jews had already suffered badly from the Great Depression, much like the rest of the population. Unemployment among blue- and white-collar workers in general reached between a quarter and a third in the early 1930s. While employment opportunities in general improved after the Nazi seizure of power, Jews' prospects stagnated or fell. In mid-1933, for example, when 21 percent of all German white-collar workers were without work, the equivalent figure for their Jewish peers stood at 28 percent. National unemployment levels fell steadily in coming months and years, but Jewish unemployment and under-

---

2. See, e.g., Günther Plum, "Wirtschaft und Erwerbsleben," in *Die Juden in Deutschland, 1933–1945: Leben unter nationalsozialistischer Herrschaft,* ed. Wolfgang Benz (Munich: C. H. Beck, 1989), 286–88; Michael H. Kater, *Doctors under Hitler* (Chapel Hill: University of North Carolina Press, 1989), 177–221.

3. Plum, "Wirtschaft und Erwerbsleben," 291; Barkai, *From Boycott,* 31.

employment remained high. Jewish jobless figures in Berlin, for example, were higher at the end of 1933 than they had been in the economically disastrous year of 1932. And the number of out-of-work Jews would rise still further in the course of 1934.[4]

Many Jews turned to the German labor courts to help them fight layoffs on grounds of race. The courts provided some satisfaction, ruling that employers could not fire employees without due notice. However, these same courts refused to ban new, racially tinged employment discrimination as a whole. For example, a Wiesbaden firm fired a Jewish woman employed as a purchasing agent in December 1934 after the Nazi Party's district leadership threatened to boycott the company. The woman, sole breadwinner for a family that included her 71-year-old father and a brother with serious disabilities from service in World War I, turned to the factory-disputes mediation council for assistance. When the council turned down her grievance, she applied to the labor courts for redress, but the labor court in Wiesbaden also rejected her petition. At this point the *Jüdische Rundschau* took up her story.

DOCUMENT 5-1: **"Interesting Judgment of a Labor Court,"** *Jüdische Rundschau*, **March 15, 1935, 4 (translated from German).**

[. . .] The plaintiff lodged an appeal against this judgment at the regional labor court [*Landesarbeitsgericht*] in Frankfurt, but here, too, without success. The appeal was <u>dismissed</u> after the firm declared that the letter from the [party] district leadership had provided only the final impetus to dismiss the plaintiff. Many customers had already threatened that they would no longer shop with the company if it retained the Jewish employee. The company was not willing to put its existence and the livelihoods of hundreds of employees in danger in order to keep one employee at her post.

Among the <u>grounds</u> on which the regional court rejected the appeal was <u>the following</u>:

It is certainly recognized within the law that there are motives for dismissals that render them unethical and legally invalid. In the present case, however, the dismissal took place for economic reasons to avoid the threat of serious negative consequences for the company. A dismissal that is based on appropriate considerations is not unethical. The understanding of what constitutes the <u>ethical feeling</u>

---

4. Clemens Vollnhals, "Jüdische Selbsthilfe bis 1938," in Benz, *Die Juden in Deutschland*, 371–72.

of the decent and right-thinking people's comrade [*Volksgenossen*] is changing and is now significantly shaped by the National Socialist ideology. Today the majority of German people's comrades do not find it unethical when, in the current situation of high unemployment, an Aryan firm removes the single Jewish employee—an employee earning a high salary and occupying a post denied to a German unemployed person—to replace her with an unemployed, nationally reliable German *Volksgenossen*. [. . .]

Since there is no further chance of appeal, the decision is now legally binding.

We are always hearing that the aim of National Socialist Jewish policy is to end "the Jews' disproportionate influence in state and culture" while allowing the Jew who has done nothing wrong the chance to be economically active in order to earn a living. In the present case it seems that it did not involve a person who had sought to influence "state and culture," and evidently she had nothing against her other than her Jewish affiliation. If even such a relatively unimportant and politically truly irrelevant post cannot, for "ideological" reasons, be held by a Jewish woman (although she was supporting a brother wounded in the war), then this is a very restricted interpretation of the scope of economic activity that is allowed to Jews.

Beginning in the nineteenth century, special, Jewish organizations, so-called *Arbeitsnachweise* ("employment bureaus"), had assisted Jews in finding new jobs.[5] During the **Weimar Republic** some sixteen of these bodies had enjoyed official state recognition, as part of the national vocational guidance centers and labor exchanges, in their efforts on behalf of Jewish job seekers. After 1933 their work was more important than ever, but they were increasingly denied access to the non-Jewish job market. The only remaining group of potential employers for Jewish workers, Jewish business owners, faced ever greater pressure to close their shops or yield to non-Jewish opportunists eager to **"Aryanize"** the property of Jewish neighbors.[6] The situation in some smaller towns across Germany became particularly dire; in 1934 the Berlin employment bureaus, by contrast, could place over 30 percent of their male

5. On the history of the *Arbeitsnachweise*, see Vollnhals, "Jüdische Selbsthilfe," 370–71.

6. See Martin Dean, *Robbing the Jews: The Confiscation of Jewish Property in the Holocaust, 1933–1945* (New York: Cambridge University Press in association with the USHMM, 2008); Frank Bajohr, *"Aryanization" in Hamburg: The Economic Exclusion of Jews and the Confiscation of Their Property in Nazi Germany* (New York: Berghahn Books, 2002).

applicants and over 42 percent of the women who sought their help. That still left many without suitable work, particularly men with commercial training or business backgrounds. Thus, the **CV** also sought to offer aid to the unemployed, above all by prodding Jewish employers to hire Jewish staff. The exchange in documents 5-2 and 5-3 reveals the desperate attempts made by some Jews to find any kind of work and the challenges confronting the CV in its efforts to help.

DOCUMENT 5-2: **Letter by Karl Cohn-Biedermann,[7] Berlin, to Alfred Hirschberg, CV head office, May 9, 1935, USHMMA RG 11.001M.31, reel 190 (SAM 721-1-1592, 2–3) (translated from German).**

I, along with many others who were at the CV gathering on the 8th of this month at Lehniner Platz [in Berlin], was truly pleased to hear your urgent appeal to Jewish business owners who have managed to continue providing jobs for Jewish youth. The failure of similar appeals that have been made to the Jewish public unfortunately suggests that your heartfelt words too will have reached the ears of those for whom they were intended, but not their hearts. [. . .]

Urgent help is needed. For the past two years, I have been bitterly confronted with this [fact].

[What follows is a barebones description of the author's professional experience:] Completed training at a bank; long employment experience in a department store; legal training and apprenticeship as a junior barrister with much greater than average success. Managed still in 1935 to attain my doctorate magna cum laude essentially to numb the pain of unemployment in disadvantageous circumstances (my father is a doctor, 71 years old). Good skills, with years of experience in shorthand and typewriting; certification with top marks available on request. A willing worker without academic arrogance—willingness to take on any available work at a fair wage. Shouldn't one be able to find some kind of fitting post in a Jewish-owned business with these qualifications? And yet, it is apparently impossible for people such as me who lack "influence" [*Beziehungen*]. I have advertised for positions and lobbied for them, pursued leads and begged. All my attempts brought no results, which was

---

7. Karl Cohn-Biedermann (1905–?), a German Jewish law student, emigrated to the United States in 1935 and after the war worked for the Library of Congress. See Ernst Stiefel and Frank Mecklenburg, eds., *Deutsche Juristen im Amerikanischen Exil, 1933–1950* (Tübingen: Mohr, 1991), 11–12.

perhaps unavoidable given the indifference and lack of readiness to make sacrifices prevailing among Jewish circles.

My case is by no means special. Rather, it is a typical example of the duress experienced by Jews who have lost their positions, who do not want to leave Germany or cannot leave because of their ideals or for material reasons—but also do not want to sink into dire poverty or, more importantly, completely lose hope. [. . .]

DOCUMENT 5-3: Response letter by Alfred Hirschberg to Karl Cohn-Biedermann, May 13, 1935, USHMMA RG 11.001M.31, reel 190 (SAM 721-1-1592, 5–7) (translated from German).

I received your detailed letter of May 9, for which I sincerely thank you. I am conveying my gratitude to you above all [. . .] because your letter has very incisively described the particular lot of the so-called middle generation [*Zwischengeneration*].[8]

Please believe that the CV is not limiting its efforts to locating jobs for people through general verbal or written appeals. Much more than before, we have recently begun to provide immediate practical assistance in individual cases in this arena. Nonetheless, I ask you not to underestimate the difficulties of such efforts. In part they stem from the fact that invoking the slogan "create work for Jewish youth" can too often be easily misunderstood by non-Jews: they might conclude that we are somehow advocating that non-Jewish workers be deprived of employment opportunities. I need hardly tell you that this is not our intention. [. . .]

I think that it would be extremely effective if we circulated your letter widely, for it depicts the position of Jewish youth and the difficulties they face in a very complete and realistic manner. I intend to send it to a number of Jews who are active in economic life as a symptom of our situation. [. . .]

The racial clauses restricting access for newcomers to professional training and accreditation proved even more ominous than the handicaps imposed on those already in established positions. By early 1935, virtually all professional careers had closed their doors to young Jews. Girls in particular faced a severely limited range of options. At most, they had an advantage over boys when it came to taking up domestic work and service, arenas for which Jewish families that were

---

8. Hirschberg presumably used this term to describe those who had been able to complete their training but were not yet established.

weathering the economic storm but had lost their non-Jewish servants now created a growing demand.[9] As opportunities evaporated, anguished debates broke out within the Jewish community about how best to assist its youth.[10]

These debates overlapped with a call predating 1933 for the "normalization" of the "distorted" Jewish occupational structure. In response to widespread antisemitic accusations that Jews were concentrated too heavily in particular trades, a variety of Jewish groups tried with some limited success to steer youth away from the professions and toward farming and other skilled trades, a process often described in the sources of the time as "professional restructuring" (*Berufsumschichtung*). Yet state law and the discriminatory practices of many craft guilds barred Jews from access to many of these careers as well. As long as Jewish training schools and apprenticeships could be found, skilled trades and agricultural training might yet prove valuable for those seeking to emigrate, particularly to Palestine. But for those remaining in Germany, the challenge of finding an acceptable occupation was an uphill battle.

NEGOTIATING PUBLIC SPACES

For Jewish adults, the biggest uncertainty apart from earning a living was how to negotiate a shared public space, be it walking down the street, visiting public institutions, going shopping, or using public transportation. Given our knowledge of what was to come, it is hard to remember that contemporaries could not see the nature and trajectory of the new order clearly. Only in day-to-day life could Jews test out whether they truly remained safe, whether normal life was possible, and whether even old, established state institutions would protect Jewish citizens. German Jews for the most part did not yet realize that, for the Nazis, targeting the Jews constituted not only an important goal in itself but also a means of imposing their stamp on society as a whole. As the historian Michael Wildt has written, "Asserting the politics of the people's community meant above all implementing policy against Jews."[11] Thus, in fact, for both Jews and Nazis, the period 1934 to 1935 tested the limits of what was permissible and how far Jews could be excluded from the "people's community" (*Volksgemeinschaft*).

One recurrent experience of these years was that Jews were no longer welcome in locations that had once been their regular haunts. Revisiting such

---

9. See Marion A. Kaplan, *Between Dignity and Despair: Jewish Life in Nazi Germany* (New York: Oxford University Press, 1998), 54–57.

10. See Barkai, *From Boycott*, 86.

11. Wildt, *Volksgemeinschaft*, 172.

familiar public places, when even possible, brought back painful memories of what often seemed a remote and barely imaginable past.

DOCUMENT 5-4: **Letter by Julius Moses, Berlin, to Erwin Moses, Tel Aviv, for the week of January 28 to February 3, 1935, translated from Dieter Fricke, *Jüdisches Leben in Berlin und Tel Aviv, 1933–1939: Der Briefwechsel des ehemaligen Reichstagsabgeordneten Dr. Julius Moses* (Hamburg: von Bockel, 1997), 288.**

[. . .] It was midday—it had just turned two o'clock and so we—that's Kurt [Julius Moses's 10-year-old son] and I—went into Kempinski's.[12] Yes, indeed, we went into Kemp[inski's]. To enjoy a meal with a good bottle of wine?? No way!! That was the plan, but no chance. Oh, well—one makes do. We just had a walk through the place to at least reawaken some old memories. And to catch a whiff of the offerings. The place was unbelievably crowded. Bursting with people [*Knüppeldicke voll*]!! Not a single free table. Yup—hardly an empty chair. Remarkable [*merkwürdig*], very remarkable!! So we left the old landmark of old Berlin without paying a cent, but full with all the aromas and the sight of the fantastic cold buffet, which has been spruced up, and the illusions of a bygone day—as though there really were a bygone time to remember. So we saved some money, which can be used for the big trip to *Erez Israel*, which will eventually happen. Only God knows if that will happen before my trip to *Gan Eden* or *Gehinnom*.[13] By the way, you can't get Jaffa oranges at any of the delicatessens or fruit and vegetable shops, only great quantities of cheap and extremely juicy, tasty oranges from Spain and Messina.[14] But no Jaffa! Time to get organized, Zionist Gentlemen. Anyways, quite remarkable.

One sign of the Nazis' incursion into the public sphere was that many Jews now felt unsure how to behave even in those venues to which they still enjoyed access. Most notably, the rapidly growing use of the ***Deutscher Gruss*** ("German greeting"), a raised right arm combined with the slogan "Heil Hitler," presented the dilemma of how to respond and what alternatives remained. Jews thus had to devise strategies not only for contending with the regime and its policies but also for their encounters with a non-Jewish population that, with

---

12. Famous hotel-restaurant in Berlin.

13. *Gan Eden:* Hebrew for the Garden of Eden. In Jewish tradition, the Gehinnom valley near Jerusalem is associated with the gate to hell; see Fricke, *Jüdisches Leben*, 288–89n5–6.

14. Jaffa is a city in Palestine/Israel and also a well-known brand name in Germany for oranges.

varying degrees of enthusiasm, had begun incorporating new practices into its daily rituals.

DOCUMENT 5-5: Letter by Helmuth Bernhard,[15] Berlin, to editors of *CV-Zeitung*, February 7, 1934, USHMMA RG 11.001M.31, reel 113 (SAM 721-1-2553, 6) (translated from German).

Dear editors!

If one is a Jew, and especially if one is a businessman, one will have experienced recently the ever more common German greeting, "Heil Hitler," also often being used toward Jews. It is open for debate whether the person giving the greeting is aware that he is addressing a Jew, although it is not unusual for the greeting to be directed toward people with a typical Jewish appearance as well. But as a Jew one is always in a quandary about how one should reciprocate this greeting without injuring the national feelings of the other person, but also without injuring one's own Jewish dignity and, beyond that, without running afoul of National Socialist [Nazi] authorities. This is especially difficult for the businessman when customers are involved.

Conversely, though, when entering the offices of state authorities and especially of judicial agencies and courthouses, one usually has the feeling that the old greetings—"good day" or "good morning"—are not going over well. And nowadays, "With German greeting" has almost completely replaced "Respectfully yours" at the conclusion of business letters. [. . .]

Surely the opinions in Jewish circles on these issues will diverge in one way or another, particularly since the government has not yet taken a clear position. Consequently, I think it would be worthwhile for your paper to address and discuss this whole complex of questions.

Perhaps even an official statement from the Reichsvertretung about the following questions would be desirable:

Can or should a German Jew ever greet and/or reciprocate a greeting with

1. raising one's arm?
2. "Heil Hitler"[?]
3. "Heil"[?]

---

15. Helmuth Bernhard (1889–?) lived in Berlin until he emigrated to the United States in June 1939; see *Datenbank zur Liste der jüdischen Einwohner im Deutschen Reich, 1933–1945* (Berlin: Bundesarchiv, 2008).

4. "With German greeting"? [*Mit deutschem Gruss*] (in correspondence)
My own purely intuitive, but not authoritative, response to the questions would be as follows:
(1) yes, (2) no, (3) yes, (4) yes.
Respectfully,
Helmuth Bernhard
P.S. I request that if you publish [this letter], you only provide my initials or an alias.

In its response to Bernhard, the CV's head office agreed that "a Jew is permitted to greet people with a raised hand; when it is in accordance with his views, to add the word 'Heil' and to close his correspondence using 'with German greeting.'" However, the organization found it "impractical" to publish its response "for reasons easily understandable, given the present situation."[16]

Jews thus had to balance their sense of integrity with what they thought the outside world would tolerate. Document 5-6, a letter from a long-standing member of the CV and the **RjF**, Friedrich Eppstein, must have touched CV leaders to the core. The issues raised here went to the heart of the question of Jews' relationship to the German homeland and mirrored the problems posed by the transformation of the German public into a racial community.

DOCUMENT 5-6: Letter by Friedrich Eppstein,[17] Mannheim, to CV head office, March 9, 1934, USHMMA RG 11.001M.31, reel 128 (SAM 721-1-2813, 154) (translated from German).

[. . .] Until now I have closed my correspondence principally with "respectfully" [in communications addressed] to the authorities as well. I know of course that in doing this I will attract attention, undoubtedly damage myself in business. I nevertheless have the feeling that I cannot do otherwise.

When I then read the reasoning of the higher regional court Karlsruhe, whereby the marriage of an Aryan with a non-Aryan is described as being, among other things, "unnatural & perverse," then

---

16. Letter by CV head office (Rubinstein) to Helmuth Bernhard, Berlin, February 12, 1934; USHMMA RG 11.001M.31, reel 113 (SAM 721-1-2553, 4–5). In late 1937, Jews were forbidden to use the "German greeting" at court; prohibitions regarding written correspondence by Jewish business persons had taken effect earlier (see Walk, *Sonderrecht* 204, no. 371).

17. The authors have been unable to find further information on the fate of Friedrich Eppstein.

must not the most German feeling of the RjF and CV member—I belong to both organizations—become unsteady in his love to his homeland [*Heimat*]? [. . .]

No one is more attached to his German homeland than I. Day and night I mull over the problems that result & can find nothing to say; & then visions come to me when I am very clear, visions that ever more plainly say, Your love is unhappy, your partner does not deserve you, tear yourself loose, turn yourself toward a worthier object, instead think nostalgically back on your earlier "beloved," & become happy in the circle of your "family." [. . .]

Responding on behalf of the CV, **Eva Reichmann** expressed her sympathy with Eppstein's troubles but assured him that "it would be an unnatural reaction to tear from your heart that love for your homeland." Furthermore, she advised using the phrase "with German greeting" because it "did not indicate a lack of dignity."[18]

In the absence of an unfettered exchange of information and opinions in Nazi Germany, the press functioned as an important register of the official mood. Mirroring trends in state policy, Nazi newspapers in 1934 generally kept antisemitism on the back burner, although coverage of an inflammatory speech by Goebbels in May proved an exception.[19] For much of the year, the key Nazi organs reduced their coverage of the "Jewish question" to one or two anti-Jewish articles each week. Non-Nazi papers such as the *Frankfurter Zeitung* restricted coverage simply to recording new government measures against Jews. Indeed, in December 1934 the *Frankfurter Zeitung* even ventured to criticize the silent boycott being perpetrated in contravention of official government policy against Jewish business concerns.[20]

The Nazi paper *Der Stürmer* proved an important exception to these media trends. Edited by the Franconian Gauleiter **Julius Streicher**, the newspaper used the tagline "The Jews Are Our Misfortune" on the front page of each issue. In lurid style, the paper mounted a series of campaigns against Jews, the Catholic Church, and other institutions that it regarded as enemies of the "people's community." *Der Stürmer*'s attacks on Jews combined traditional popular superstitions with more modern "racial" arguments against Jews based on their supposed prescriptive inferiority. The paper marketed its messages aggressively,

---

18. Letter by CV head office (E. Reichmann) to Friedrich Eppstein, Mannheim, March 21, 1934; USHMMA RG 11.001M.31, reel 128 (SAM 721-1-2813, 147–48).

19. Peter Longerich, *Politik der Vernichtung: Eine Gesamtdarstellung der nationalsozialistischen Judenverfolgung* (Munich: Piper, 1998), 68; Wildt, *Volksgemeinschaft*, 156–57.

20. Longerich, *Politik*, 69.

using special display cases (so-called *Stürmer* boxes mounted in many public places), as well as street vendors and an eye-catching design. On May 1, 1934, *Der Stürmer* published a special edition on "ritual murder," invoking one variation on an old antisemitic theme.

DOCUMENT 5-7: Kurt Rosenberg, diary entry for May 13, 1934, LBINY AR 25279 (translated from German).

[. . .] I read *Der Stürmer's* special issue on ritual murder. It uses the most outrageous material that I have ever seen in a publication, the most scurrilous illustrations—it invokes superstitions from the Middle Ages and before and has turned individual murder cases into ritual murders, etc. News criers sell the paper on the streets in Hamburg, but according to eyewitnesses, few buy it here—except for Jewish customers. It is shattering to see the lack of rights for Jews—as well as the moral crisis of the German people. [. . .]

Since *Der Stürmer's* first appearance in 1923, the CV had been more active than any other Jewish organization in combating the paper's lies.[21] Armed with this experience, CV officials in Berlin may now have viewed any protest against the outrageous paper as a lost, though worthy, cause. But Jews outside a major city such as Berlin still believed the state would come to their aid in fighting the crude insults and fearmongering of Nazi papers.

DOCUMENT 5-8: Letter by CV regional association Rhineland (left bank) to CV head office, November 3, 1934, USHMMA RG 11.001M.31, reel 100 (SAM 721-1-2303, 118) (translated from German).

We have been receiving news from various small localities of our regional association that *Der Stürmer* is very widely disseminated, especially in the rural communities. For the most part it is displayed in wooden cases.

   In order to convey a sense of the atmosphere to you, let us quote directly from the report of the chair of our [CV] local group, Zell an der Mosel:

   "Where are the rabbis when it comes to responding to the new blood-baiting [*Bluthetze*] of *Der Stürmer* (in Xanten despite a

---

21. See Avraham Barkai, *"Wehr Dich!" Der Centralverein deutscher Staatsbürger jüdischen Glaubens (C.V.), 1893–1938* (Munich: C. H. Beck, 2002), 180–85.

clear court judgment)?[22] Now, surely, the Catholic and Protestant clergy will create a unified front with German rabbis against these endless insults against religion and the Bible. Otherwise Streicher could make his threat a reality. Don't treat this warning lightly. *Der Stürmer* is now being read all over the country, and its lies, which of course no one contradicts, unfortunately seem plausible."

Messages of hatred began to contaminate the public spaces of Nazi Germany. They were disseminated throughout German society not only in public speeches and the media but also via seemingly innocuous acts such as singing. The files of the CV from 1934 and 1935 reveal an outpouring of concern about the songs regularly heard on the streets. Graphic verses about "Jews' blood spurting from the knife," belted out by local Hitler Youth, storm troopers, and other groups, aroused anger and anxiety. Most Jewish contemporaries took the offensive lyrics not as literal declarations of their fellow citizens' murderous intentions but rather, disturbing enough in itself, as the way rowdy Nazi groups let off steam. Jewish reactions to Nazi songs remind us that the character of public space changed only gradually. Particularly after the end of the Nazi "revolution," violence in everyday life had been put on hold to a certain extent, and these songs were often the most blatant threat to the more orderly climate that had succeeded the revolutionary phase.[23]

DOCUMENT 5-9: Letter by Bernhard Taitza,[24] Merseburg, to Alfred Hirschberg, CV head office, August 22, 1934, USHMMA RG 11.001M.31, reel 112 (SAM 721-1-2499, 77) (translated from German).

[. . .] Were you ever able to undertake anything in the matter concerning the loathsome song [containing the following lines]: Put the Jews, put the

---

22. This refers to the 1891–1892 trial of Adolf Buschoff, a resident in the town of Xanten (Lower Rhine area) and Jewish butcher, falsely accused of murdering a Christian child for ritual purposes. See Barkai, *"Wehr Dich!,"* 22–23; Christhard Hoffmann, Werner Bergmann, and Helmut Walser-Smith, eds., *Exclusionary Violence: Antisemitic Riots in Modern German History* (Ann Arbor: University of Michigan, 2002), 92.

23. See Jürgen Matthäus, "Antisemitic Symbolism in Early Nazi Germany, 1933–1935," *LBIYB* 45 (2000): 183–203.

24. Bernhard Taitza (1886–?) and his wife, Ida (1892–?), apparently managed to leave Germany, for they had been formally stripped of their German citizenship by March 1939. See Michael Hepp, ed., *Expatriation Lists as Published in the "Reichsanzeiger," 1933–1945* (Munich: K. G. Saur, 1985), 1:135.

bigwigs up against the wall, when Jewish blood spurts from the knife, then all is twice as nice?

I have been informed by a quite reliable party that even though this text is officially forbidden, here in Merseburg it is sung by special request every time they [i.e., Nazi formations] march past the known Jewish apartments. As a result, many local Jews are understandably so upset that their health has suffered. [. . .]

Otherwise they leave us Jews here alone, and we keep to ourselves because no one spends time out on streets or in the taverns. On Sundays everyone heads out of the city for the country, and in the evening we are usually together with family. In business, too, the Jews are extremely cautious so that there is no reason to behave aggressively toward us Jews.

For Jews, the disappearance or reappearance of such songs served as a weather vane for gauging the way the political wind was blowing more generally. Such indicators had a palpable impact on their sense of security.

DOCUMENT 5-10: **Letter by CV regional association Rhineland (left bank), Cologne, to CV head office, October 22, 1934, with copy of letter by the chairman of the CV local branch Meckenheim, Benny Juhl,[25] October 14, 1934, USHMMA RG 11.001M.31, reel 150 (SAM 721-1-3070, 254–55) (translated from German).**

[. . .] Although up to now we have been almost untouched by antisemitism and its terrible effects in peaceful Meckenheim, of late it appears that a different, more malicious spirit has seized the local district [Nazi] party group leadership as well as local officials. Friends on the Aryan side have informed us confidentially that the head of the local district NSDAP returned from the Nuremberg party rally [*Parteitag*] with a new attitude towards *Risches*.[26] [. . .] The local SA stopped singing that horrid song with the lyrics "when Jewish blood spurts from the knife"[27] over a year ago on its own initiative—out of consideration for us and because of the

---

25. This was probably Benedikt Juhl, born in 1868 in Meckenheim (Rhineland). After emigrating to the Netherlands, he was deported from Westerbork to Sobibór on May 18, 1943, along with his wife, Lina (née Hirsch, b. 1875), where both perished. See www .bundesarchiv.de/gedenkbuch; *USHMM ITS Collection Data Base Central Name Index.*

26. This is a Yiddish term meaning "trouble," used by German Jews to describe antisemitic acts. See Werner Weinberg, *Die Reste des Jüdisch-Deutschen* (Stuttgart: W. Kohlhammer, 1969), 92–93.

27. Line in the antisemitic song "Lied der Sturmsoldaten"; in German, "Wenn's Judenblut vom Messer spritzt, dann geht's nochmal so gut."

objections of our more decent Christian fellow citizens. Of late, however, apparently with orders from above, they have again begun serenading us at bedtime with the strains of "hang the Jews." [. . .]

For the author of the previous letter, Jews were not alone in disapproving of the ugly intrusion into the calm and decency of public streets. Thus not just for Jews but for German society as a whole, the question of whether the more raucous and offensive voices could be silenced was an important test case: to what degree could the remaining rules of civility be maintained and how far would the Nazis be able to transform the public sphere? In the case presented in document 5-11, a timid school official evidently implicitly invited Jews to put a halt to bad behavior themselves.

DOCUMENT 5-11: Letter by N. Michelsohn,[28] Minden, to CV regional office East West-phalia, November 27, 1934, USHMMA RG 11.001M.31, reel 112 (SAM 721-1-2499, 37) (translated from German).

[. . .] Last Friday here in the Marienstrasse [street in Minden] I encoun-tered a unit of roughly 30 upperclassmen, who sang the lovely song about "Jewish blood spurting from the knife." Yesterday I visited the headmaster and discussed the occurrence with him. The matter was very uncomfort-able for him, and I really had sympathy for the man. He is unfortunately powerless and could not hold out the prospect of any success from a com-plaint, since he has already stirred up a hornet's nest himself. I believe it would not be at all unwelcome to him if we were to take the matter into our own hands. Perhaps the headmaster will respond accurately to enqui-ries by his superiors. [. . .]

There was in fact good reason in early 1935 for the Jewish organizations to imagine that they were winning the fight and helping to eradicate disturbances from the streets. In early March 1935, the CV's regional association from cen-tral Germany sent back word of a recent conversation with the police chief in Magdeburg that seemed extremely promising. The CV's central executive was delighted and eager to disseminate the report.

---

28. Most likely Nathan Michelsohn, head of the CV local branch in Minden in 1934. He no longer appeared in the registry of Minden residents in 1939, and the authors have been unable to find further information about his fate. See listings in Karin Kristin Ruter and Christian Hampel, *Die Judenpolitik in Deutschland 1933–1945 unter besonderer Berücksichti-gung von Einzelschicksalen jüdischer Bürger der Gemeinden Minden, Petershagen und Luebbecke* (Minden: Gustav Brinkjost, 1986), 21, 34, 89.

DOCUMENT 5-12: Letter by CV regional association Central Germany to CV head office, March 11, 1935, USHMMA RG 11.001M.31, reel 112 (SAM 721-1-2499, 24) (translated from German).

[. . .] In a meeting in the government offices in Magdeburg, the head of the political and police division, former police president von Klingoström, informed me, the undersigned, that a decree had been issued to the regional head of the SA stating that derogatory songs should no longer be sung to the Jews. Mr. von Klingoström declared that this decree had been a great success, for there were no doubt forces in the [Nazi] party that would not welcome such a decree.

DOCUMENT 5-13: CV memorandum for Hans Reichmann and Alfred Hirschberg, March 14, 1935, USHMMA RG 11.001M.31, reel 112 (SAM 721-1-2499, 23) (translated from German).

The news received from the regional association for central Germany is extremely welcome. I would like to pass it on in a circular letter to the other regional associations and recommend not only that the regional associations make use of this but also that we make an appearance in person at Gestapo headquarters [to achieve a similar outcome]. However, other urgent matters demand our attention, so I would like to wait three weeks before proceeding with this.

The CV leadership's brief reference to other, more urgent matters, however, hinted that, just at that moment, new developments were emerging that would profoundly alter Jewish perceptions and experience in Germany. A handwritten addition to the memo said, "Review in three weeks." And by the time April 9 had been reached, an additional note added, "Overtaken by events." The disturbing developments of these weeks will be explored in chapter 6, "Segregation and Exclusion: Spring and Summer 1935."

JEWISH CHILDREN IN THE SCHOOLS OF THE "PEOPLE'S COMMUNITY"

Public schools presented another important test case for Germany's Jews. Initially, most Jewish children, adolescents, and young adults remained students in the public education system, from elementary school, to the classical German high school (*Gymnasium*), to the university. At the end of 1933, only some 25 percent

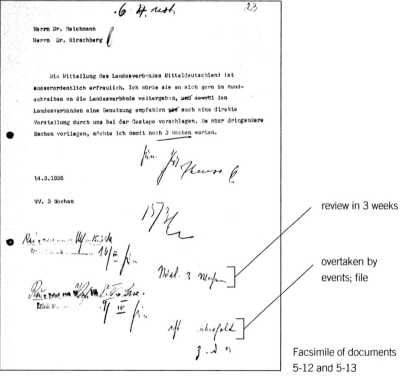

review in 3 weeks

overtaken by events; file

Facsimile of documents 5-12 and 5-13

of the sixty thousand school-aged Jewish children attended some kind of Jewish school. The number of Jewish educational institutions, whether they were schools or teacher-training institutions, thus remained limited, particularly at the secondary level. In the whole of the Reich, there were only ten Jewish secondary schools in 1933, only five of which had the right to award the *Abitur* exam. Even in 1935, around half of Germany's Jewish children remained in public schools, slightly more at the secondary level, slightly fewer in the primary grades.[29]

These children were subjected to the authority and discipline of a German public institution on a daily basis at a time when every public institution had adapted itself to Nazi rule. Patterns of discrimination against Jewish schoolchildren varied from city to city, even from school to school. As in many other social contexts, segregation was at first achieved informally, for instance, through insults made by teachers and classmates inside and outside school. An increasing proportion of their classmates now joined the Hitler Youth (Hitler-Jugend, or HJ), which added a new political dimension to older rivalries and cliques at school. Sharing classroom space with a group stigmatized by the highest state authorities sometimes enticed non-Jewish boys and girls to discard basic rules of behavior and decency.[30]

Traditional markers of popularity among schoolchildren, such as success at sports or good looks, often played a role in determining how aggressively a school's "in group" enacted the theatrics of racial warfare. Popular athletes who happened to be Jewish were often the last to be exposed to the shift in climate, while chubby bookworms suffered ostracism almost from the beginning. Added to this, many teachers joined the Nazi Party and were eager to demonstrate their enthusiasm for the new political order. Teachers not infrequently belonged to those "entrepreneurs of ethnic hatred" anxious to push forward the line excluding Jews beyond even accepted legal limits. In 1934 and particularly 1935, Jewish organizations received many letters from concerned parents and local Jewish leaders complaining about the stance of particular teachers and seeking intervention.

---

29. Vollnhals, "Jüdische Selbsthilfe," 331, 349. *Abitur* is the German equivalent of the high school diploma in the United States.

30. On school experiences, see Vollnhals, "Jüdische Selbsthilfe," 330–41; Kaplan, *Between Dignity*, 94–106; Werner T. Angress, "Jüdische Jugend zwischen nationalsozialistischer Verfolgung und jüdischer Wiedergeburt," in Paucker, *The Jews in Nazi Germany*, 211–32; Ruth Röcher, *Die jüdische Schule im nationalsozialistischen Deutschland, 1933–1942* (Frankfurt am Main: Dipa, 1992); Mark Roseman, *A Past in Hiding: Memory and Survival in Nazi Germany*. (London: Penguin, 2000), 53–86.

DOCUMENT 5-14: CV copy of a letter by the executive of the Jewish community Sterbfritz to the county school officer in Schlüchtern, Kassel region, November 14, 1934, USHMMA RG 11.001M.31, reel 119 (SAM 721-1-2667, 378–79) (translated from German).

As the executive of the Jewish community [*Israelitische Gemeinde*], we take the liberty of forwarding to you a letter we received from members of our congregation.

It is clear from this letter that the treatment of Jewish pupils by the teacher Lukas is not consistent with the existing legal regulations. To illustrate the point, allow us to refer to some of the statements which Herr Lukas is said to have made to the class.

"The Jews are cheats. It is because of the Jews that we now find ourselves in a battle for the Saar.[31] The Christian children should tell their parents not to buy anything from the Jews. The Jews pulled out the Christians' legs and arms.[32] The Jews should pack up their bundles and go to Africa or Spain with their Jewish teachers. He would much rather teach without any Jews."

These statements correspond roughly to repeated remarks made by teacher Lukas. We ask you to address the matter as soon as possible, particularly as the children involved are aged 7–8 and must suffer heavily from such behavior on the part of their teacher.

Yours most respectfully,

The Executive of the Jewish Community

---

31. Under the terms of the post–World War I treaties, after fifteen years as a League of Nations mandate under French rule, the Saar population had the right to choose its future affiliation. At the time this letter was written, the campaign to win the hearts and minds of the Saar population was in full swing. See chapter 6, "Segregation and Exclusion: Spring and Summer 1935," for more details.

32. This seems to have been a Lukas original. Yet, it indicates how Nazi antisemitic rhetoric blurred the literal and the figurative. The accusation was, on one level, meant literally. At the same time, it invoked a standard reflexive German expression, "pulling out the legs and arms," meaning "to pull out all the stops" or "make every effort." This figurative phrase gives the word combination in the teacher's accusation a certain linguistic familiarity that provides power and cohesion, despite the bizarreness of the literal claim and the fact that making an effort is clearly not what was meant here.

DOCUMENT 5-15: Group portrait of German school girls, 1935, USHMMPA WS# 97273.

Group portrait of German girls posing outside their school in front of a Nazi flag. Among those pictured is Lilli Eckstein six months before she was expelled from the school for being Jewish. The daughter of Gustav and Bertha (née Speier) Eckstein, Lilli was born in Heldenbergen near Frankfurt am Main in 1921. In 1937, the Ecksteins moved to Frankfurt after being forced to sell their home and their business. The family resettled in South Africa in late 1938.

Parents wrestled with the challenge of providing their children with some protection while not endorsing the logic of exclusion. What were Jewish children to do when confronted with the insidiously antisemitic lessons of a state that constructed everything in racial terms? Should Jewish boys and girls sit through lessons now taught through the Nazis' racist political lens? The CV's regional association in East Prussia counseled parents to have their children exempted from certain parts of the curriculum; in other cases, however, some officials argued that the presence of Jewish children even during offensive classroom lessons might have a moderating influence.[33] Yet, what influence did the teachings at school ultimately have on Jewish students? Where the option was available, would the children have been better off at Jewish schools from the start? Documents 5-16 and 5-17 provide a glimpse of the dilemmas facing Jewish families.

---

33. CV head office to CV regional association, East Prussia, December 31, 1934; USHMMA RG 11.001M.31, reel 224 (SAM 721-1-24, 369).

DOCUMENT 5-16: **Letter by Alex Blumenau,[34] Wuppertal-Elberfeld, to CV head office, April 14, 1935, with attachment, USHMMA RG 11.001M.31, reel 119 (SAM 721-1-2667, 36, 42) (translated from German).**

[. . .] I am sending you copies of some essays that a now 11-year-old girl with Jewish parents wrote at her Leipzig school because they cause me such concern [*aus bedrücktem Herzen*]. I have reproduced the passages exactly as they were written. [. . .] The parents, good Jews—the husband is from Hanover, the wife was raised in Berlin, both from well-established families in the west of Germany—are friends of mine.

I call your attention to these things, on the one hand, to offer you and the teachers in your circle some firsthand cases that show where we are heading and what is happening to Jewish youth. On the other hand, I want you to tell me how we might effectively counteract the dangers that can be seen between the lines here. [. . .]

Sol-month[35] 8, 1935
Our School Celebration
    We wear our school colors [*Schulkluft*] when we have a celebration. A celebration is held in the school hall with lots of pennants and flags. Usually Miss ——— [name omitted in the original here and subsequently] gives a speech. Sometimes only grades one to six take part, sometimes the lower grades also join in. The teachers all sit on the left-hand side when you come into the hall, and the girls sit in the middle. Miss ——— or Miss ——— usually plays the piano, e.g., the Badenweiler March, while the flags are being carried in, or at the end, the German national anthem.[36]
    We have had very different celebrations, e.g., the celebration of the founding of the empire. It was an hour commemorating the second German empire. Miss ——— told us about Versailles and how it was when Bismarck was finally able to fulfill the burning hopes of the German *Volk* and forge together an empire.[37]

---

34. The authors have been unable to find further information about the fate of Alex Blumenau.
35. The pupil here uses the new Nazi Germanicism *Hornung* for the month of February.
36. During the Nazi era, the *Badenweiler Marsch* was played during public events upon Hitler's arrival.
37. The passage refers to the creation of the (second) German Reich in January 1871 and its longtime chancellor Otto von Bismarck (1815–1898).

Then we had a commemoration for the national revolution. They told us about the Third Reich, the world war, and all about now and how the Führer was appointed to be Reich chancellor.

Then we listened to the broadcast of the results of the referendum from the towns in the Saar region. The announcer was from Holland. There were three ballot options to choose from: one was the status quo, the other one Germany, and the third one, France. We sang various songs before that. After that we raised our flag in the schoolyard when Dr. Goebbels gave the signal on the radio, and Miss ——— gave a speech. Before and after our holidays, we also always had a ceremony, which never fails to make us eager to be good learners. Occasionally we have an event to dedicate a new pennant, at which we are told to whom the pennant is awarded and of what we should be thinking as we march underneath it. After that, two pennant bearers come forward and say thanks. One is the main bearer, and the other is the substitute.

Our school ceremonies are always very interesting.

Teacher's grade: 2 [good]

[teacher's comment:] Nicely detailed work

DOCUMENT 5-17: Letter by CV head office to Alex Blumenau, May 2, 1935, USHMMA RG 11.001M.31, reel 119 (SAM 721-1-2667, 33–35) (translated from German).

[. . .] The articles and the letter that you kindly sent us were of great interest. We also agree with you completely that the conditions revealed by these reports represent a very profound problem for present Jewish life in Germany. However, we are convinced that this problem—precisely because it is so extraordinarily difficult—cannot be solved by a general response issued from one side alone. Whether a child would be better off being educated at a public school for all children or at a Jewish school will in fact always depend on the conditions surrounding each individual case.

Accordingly, the CV cannot take a one-sided stance on the school question. It goes without saying that the CV—especially after the radical change [*Umschwung*, i.e., the Nazi revolution] in places where this seemed necessary and useful—has supported the creation of Jewish schools. On the other hand, we should not ignore that in many cases the parents see no grounds for removing their children from public schools where they get on well with the teaching staff and other pupils. Admittedly, though, education in public schools raises a great many questions, as you rightly point out. It is just as problematic when teachers and other pupils continually draw attention to the fact that the student is different as when a student is simply slotted into the National Socialist way of looking at things, a viewpoint that rejects him as a Jew. [. . .]

Some Jewish children in this period may have still imagined that the new "people's community" included them to some degree. **Elisabeth Block**, born in 1923, lived with her parents and two siblings in rural Niedernburg, Bavaria, where the family ran a greengrocer's business. Her diary is most remarkable for its almost complete lack of references to her own Jewish situation (the Block family celebrated Christmas and the Catholic church holidays commonly marked in Bavaria). Elisabeth's diary also speaks little about political events that surely touched on her or her family's life. In March 1934 Elisabeth Block was just completing elementary school, and for her—at least for the self that she allowed to speak in her diary—the world had not yet established a dividing line that excluded her from the mainstream.

DOCUMENT 5-18: Elisabeth Block, diary entry for March 28, 1934, translated from *Erinnerungszeichen: Die Tagebücher der Elisabeth Block*, ed. Haus der Bayerischen Geschichte (Rosenheim: Bayerische Staatskanzlei, 1993), 66–67.

We had a very nice party celebrating the end of the school year. As we entered the classroom on this day, we saw before us an amazing sight. The teacher's desk was draped with a white and blue cloth [Bavarian colors] and decorated with fragrant primroses. Beautiful green garlands and little flags had been hung around the picture of Hitler and the picture of Hindenburg, which hung on the two blackboards. The handicrafts that we had made were laid out on the school benches near the windows. Little by little, more and more people came in, and our celebration soon began. There was first a speech delivered by three boys from the sixth grade: a look back on the year of the German turnaround [*Wende*, i.e., the Nazi revolution]. Then we sang a song in praise of Germany ["O, Deutschland hoch in Ehren"; roughly translated, "O, Germany, Most Esteemed"]. Then two students in the seventh grade recited a poem, "Rising Up" ["Erhebung"]. After this our head teacher gave a nice speech, followed by a chorus reciting "The German Spring." I was also in this group, along with many girls, and we all wore flower wreathes on our heads and held staffs in our hands. This chorus also sang the song "Longing for the Spring." Then three girls from the continuing education school recited the poem "Vow."

The song "I Gave Myself to the Cause" ["Ich hab' mich ergeben"] followed. When that was over, the head teacher again gave a speech. Finally, the songs "Raise the Flag" [also called "Horst Wessel Song," the anthem of the Nazi Party] and "Deutschland, Deutschland über alles" [first stanza of the German national anthem] were sung. And that is how the school year of 1933–1934 ended.

The wording in Elisabeth's diary leaves open whether she also sang the last two songs; her use of the passive voice implies a certain distance from these emotionally charged performances. It is unclear whether the diary itself was a work of exclusion, marginalizing all emblems of ostracism. Certainly, many Jewish children in Germany fantasized that they would someday be accepted into the larger community.[38]

With greater or lesser vigilance, parents and teachers noted the impact of their children's experiences at school. Jewish publications also sporadically attempted to address the problems facing families and to give troubled parents a feeling that they were not alone.

DOCUMENT 5-19: Betty Schleifer,[39] "School Kids Today," *Frankfurter Israelitisches Gemeindeblatt* **(September 1935): 508 ("women's page") (translated from German).**

The events of the last years shook not only the adults of our community out of their complacency and transformed them. They also had a serious effect on our children and changed them.

One can continuously observe these changes in all age groups, beginning with 6- and 7-year-olds in primary school and extending on up to students in the highest grades. They are particularly visible in the younger children. They no longer seem as innocently happy and full of spirit as they should be at their age and as used to be the case in years

---

38. On children's experiences, see Deborah Dwork, *Children with a Star: Jewish Youth in Nazi Europe* (New Haven, CT: Yale University Press, 1991); Nicholas Stargardt, *Witnesses of War: Children's Lives under the Nazis* (New York: Alfred A. Knopf, 2006); Patricia Heberer, *Children during the Holocaust*, forthcoming in 2010 as part of the USHMM Documenting Life and Destruction series.

39. Betty Schleifer (later Rand-Schleifer; 1902–?) was a teacher at the Philanthropin Jewish school in Frankfurt am Main from 1922 to 1938. Married to a man with Polish citizenship, she was deported to Poland with other Jews in October 1938 but managed to emigrate to Palestine in 1939. See Kommission zur Erforschung der Geschichte der Frankfurter Juden, *Das Philanthropin zu Frankfurt am Main: Dokumente und Erinnerungen* (Frankfurt am Main: Verlag Waldemar Kramer, 1964), 47–64, 114–24, 144, and photos I, VII, and XIV.

past. This does not in fact mean, for instance, that they have entirely stopped laughing and romping around and doing naughty things. But they are also aware of the events unfolding in the world of adults and carry some of this burden on their own shoulders. At age six they already understand that there are many things which they may no longer do; the fearful among them have grown more fearful, and those who are particularly spirited constantly run up against conflicts. Their faces become serious and anxious when one of them begins to talk, and the others also cannot hold back their stories: they recount what they have heard from their parents and siblings, what they decipher from the newspapers, what they have seen on the street or experienced themselves. On days when some new alarm or worry hits the community as a whole, the behavior of schoolchildren between ages six and eight serves as a very good indicator for the situation at home. And the adult who is privy to all these developments is appalled to discover how many manifestations of fear and an inferiority complex have already taken hold of these youngest children. [. . .]

Changed economic and social circumstances have had an effect on children that is even more drastic than the events taking place on the larger stage. I well remember two experiences involving pupils in the first grade: one concerns a small, pale boy who rarely confided in me. But one day during lessons he came running up from his desk and said hastily, "Our furniture and our linens are being auctioned off now, and my mother needs to be there!"—And the other story concerns a student from northern Germany who joined our school. In response to a question about what his father did for a living, he answered, "Unemployed." When I asked for a second time, "Can you perhaps still remember what your father did before he became unemployed?" he answered, "No, I can't remember anymore. But the nameplate on our house said, 'Dr. X., Medicine Counselor' [*Medizinrat*; garbled spelling for *Medizinalrat* ('medical counselor'), an honorary title for a doctor]." [. . .]

The difficult external pressures and the heavy intellectual and mental strains on our youth present the Jewish school with growing challenges. It must attempt to create a lively, consciously Jewish milieu in order to help students feel stronger and happier and to compensate for all the things that they must live without nowadays.

Outside school, whether or not they had identified themselves openly as Jews, Jewish children found themselves rapidly excluded from all non-Jewish clubs and organizations. This turn of events prompted a divorced woman who had been in a "mixed marriage" and was struggling to maintain her car-repair business to write to the CV about her daughter's predicament.

DOCUMENT 5-20: Letter by Erna Rehberg,[40] Malchow, to CV head office, August 13, 1934, USHMMA RG 11.001M.31, reel 144 (SAM 721-1-3012, 116) (translated from German).

My daughter, who is Christian, 13 years old, but not Aryan, was in the German gymnastics club, which is now connected to the Hitler Youth. At a local parade of the club, they gave her the gymnastics flag (not the swastika flag) to carry. A few days later I was told by the board that they very much regret having to remove my daughter from the gymnastics club. She was in the club for about 6 years, but they had received a strong reprimand from Schwerin [major city in the region] that my non-Aryan daughter, who by the way is blond and blue-eyed and is the only non-Aryan child in the place, had carried the flag and that she was still in the gymnastics club at all, and she is to be let go, which hurt me very much for my child, since because of this she is excluded from everything and was very much attached to the gymnastics club. Were they actually entitled to expel the child? I was told that because of the 1936 Olympics, no differences between Aryan and non-Aryan are being made. Is that true? I ask you once again politely, please inform me before you undertake anything because, you will understand, in no case do I want to bring any harm to myself. I look forward to your answer and thank you.

DOCUMENT 5-21: Response letter by CV head office to Erna Rehberg, Malchow, August 17, 1934, USHMMA RG 11.001M.31, reel 144 (SAM 721-1-3012, 114–15) (translated from German).

[. . .] There is nothing to be done against the exclusion of your daughter from the gymnastics club. The gymnastics club is completely free to set its own rules. The Olympic committee has merely agreed to the participation of Jews at the Olympics but cannot force the individual clubs to accept

---

40. Erna Rehberg (née Hahn; 1898–?) lived in Malchow in August 1934 but moved to Berlin-Charlottenburg with her "*Mischling*" daughter Ursula Rehberg (1921–?) in the late 1930s. Ursula emigrated to Britain in August 1939; the fate of her mother could not be traced. See *Datenbank zur Liste der jüdischen Einwohner im Deutschen Reich, 1933–1945* (Berlin: Bundesarchiv, 2008).

Jews. Jewish participants will therefore be chosen primarily from Jewish sport associations of Germany.[41] [. . .]

Increasingly, Jewish youth and sports clubs provided opportunities for temporary escape. From twenty-six thousand in 1932, the number of girls and boys belonging to Jewish youth groups, supported by a wide spectrum of organizations from the RjF via the CV and the **ZVfD** to Orthodox, grew to roughly fifty thousand by 1936.[42]

---

41. On the Berlin Olympics, see Susan D. Bachrach, *The Nazi Olympics: Berlin, 1936* (Boston: Little, Brown, 2000).

42. Kaplan, *Between Dignity*, 109–12; Chaim Schatzker, "The Jewish Youth Movement in Germany in the Holocaust Period (I)—Youth in Confrontation with a New Reality," *LBIYB* 19 (1974): 157–81; Chaim Schatzker, "The Jewish Youth Movement in Germany in the Holocaust Period (II)—The Relations between the Youth Movement and the Hechaluz," *LBIYB* 33 (1988): 301–25.

CHAPTER 6

SEGREGATION AND EXCLUSION
SPRING AND SUMMER 1935

REACTING TO EXCLUSION IN THE SPRING OF 1935

Although the September **Nuremberg Laws** are often seen as the major turning point of 1935, Jewish experiences and perceptions had in fact already changed markedly during the spring and summer of that year. The year began with two major public demonstrations of the Reich's new confidence in relation to its neighbors: the plebiscite about the **Saar**'s future in January and the reintroduction of military conscription in March. Both briefly raised Jews' hopes of being able to demonstrate their allegiance to the German nation, but both turned out to be significant symbolic moments in the ongoing story of their exclusion. Indeed, both events helped to generate a new bout of antisemitic agitation that would grow to unprecedented proportions in coming months. The agitation in turn triggered a sequence of segregation measures by the state and prepared the ground for the Nuremberg Laws.[1]

---

1. Historians have long disagreed about the degree of improvisation involved in the deliberations surrounding the September 1935 Nazi Party conference that led to the enactment of the Nuremberg Laws. It is now certain that preparations had long been underway. We will see below that the CV itself was aware of public pronouncements within informed Nazi circles that anticipated the contents of the Nuremberg Laws by some months. However, the precise timing may still have been rather last-minute (some hasty final drafting took place after the Nuremberg party rally), and the increased antisemitic agitation of the preceding months appears to have played an important role in accelerating the process of formulating the laws. See Friedländer, *Nazi Germany*, 1:137–44; Karl A. Schleunes, ed., *Legislating the Holocaust: The Bernhard Loesener Memoirs and Supporting Documents* (Boulder, CO: Westview Press, 2001); Uwe Dietrich Adam, *Judenpolitik im Dritten Reich* (Düsseldorf: Droste, 1972), 124–44; Wildt, *Die Judenpolitik*, 23–24; Wildt, *Volksgemeinschaft*, 260ff.

France had administered the Saar region since the end of World War I under a **League of Nations** mandate, and the plebiscite held in January 1935 would determine whether the territory should return to Germany. In the run-up to the vote, a **CV** newspaper editorial in December 1934 revealed anew the complex balance the CV sought to maintain between arguing the case for Jewish emigration and still asserting that Jewish life in Germany remained possible. On the one hand, the CV carefully noted the transitional arrangements, including emigration under international law, that were guaranteed to Saar minorities whatever the outcome of the election. On the other hand, the organization nevertheless took to task an article in the *Basler Nachrichten* newspaper implying that, in the event of a German victory, all the Saar's Jews would want to leave the region. The CV instead urged the region's Jews to "join the ranks of the community of German Jews" should the Saar become German.[2]

On January 13, 91 percent of the Saar population voted for a return to Germany. At least privately, some Jews greeted this enthusiastic endorsement of the German option with dismay. Once again, events in the international sphere had bolstered Hitler's standing. Publicly, many German Jews joined in celebrating the plebiscite outcome alongside their non-Jewish counterparts, some with genuine enthusiasm and others as a result of pressures from neighbors, fellow traders, or employees. Increasingly, however, the pressure went the other way, shutting Jews out of communal celebrations.

DOCUMENT 6-1: CV copy of a letter by Gebr. Alsberg & Georg Blank Company,[3] Witten, to Reich Economics Ministry, January 19, 1935, USHMMA RG 11.001M.31, reel 141 (SAM 721-1-2980, 311–12) (translated from German).

[. . .] I. On the occasion of the nationwide "Saar Celebration" held on January 15, the management instructed the head of the council of trust [*Vertrauensrat;* the Nazi-instituted worker's representative body] to fly the flag without hesitation, just as all the other businesses in the city were doing. The council of trust, having repeatedly experienced difficulties in

---

2. "Zum Saarabkommen," *CV-Zeitung,* December 20, 1934. In 1927, roughly four thousand Jews lived in the Saar region (Hilberg, *Destruction,* 82n2).

3. Established in 1928, Gebr. Alsberg & Blank became one of Witten's leading department stores until 1938 when ownership was transferred to the city of Witten as part of the "Aryanization" of German Jewish assets. See Hans-Christian Dahlmann, "'Arisierung' und Gesellschaft in Witten: Wie die Bevölkerung einer Ruhrgebietsstadt das Eigentum ihrer Jüdinnen und Juden übernahm," *Politische Soziologie* 14 (2001): 75; Irene Guenther, *Nazi Chic? Fashioning Women in the Third Reich* (Oxford: Berg, 2004), 374n141.

similar cases with the party or party members, first consulted the NSDAP district headquarters [*Kreisleitung*] in order to prevent similar problems. In earlier cases—for instance, after the death of the Reich president, General Field Marshal von Hindenburg, the thanksgiving pageant [*Ernte-Dank-fest*], and on other general occasions—the party leaders and also the police ordered the flags to be taken down again as soon as they were raised. Each of these incidents caused surprise and agitation among the two hundred employees and, as we were repeatedly told, also among the majority of our customers. In light of these earlier incidents, the council of trust wanted to check back with party leaders to see whether district headquarters would have any objections.

The deputy district leader [of the Nazi Party] replied:

If the flag were displayed, it would be lowered within a few minutes!

Because of this, no flag was displayed [by our business] for the "Saar Celebration."

II. Yesterday we received a call by the German Labor Front's district business association [*DAF Kreisbetriebsgemeinschaft Handel*] to hold the Reich company rally [*Reichsbetriebs-Appell*] on January 21 (see enclosed [not reprinted here]). According to the general order as well as the final paragraph of the enclosed order relating to this, all businesses were supposed to fly the flag on the day of the rally. When consulted on this matter, the district party chief, Kreisleiter Weber, stated that Jewish businesses were not allowed to fly the flag and that Jewish company directors should not attend the parade.

We urgently request that the necessary steps be taken in this matter. Please note that during all of the occasions mentioned, non-Aryan businesses in the surrounding towns flew the flag and that, to our knowledge, it was prohibited only in Witten. It is obvious that this measure is part of the ongoing boycotts, the effects of which have been growing. Customers are kept under constant pressure and do not dare to enter our store for fear of being denounced or being harmed in other ways.

The CV's main office in Berlin wrote the Blank Company that they had not heard of similar restrictions elsewhere. Because the town of Witten in the industrial Ruhr region had proved to be a flashpoint for boycott efforts in the preceding weeks, they concluded that it was an isolated incident in a particularly difficult neck of the woods. An order issued by the Berlin **Gestapo** on February 19, 1935, proved them wrong: it declared that because Jews did not belong to the German people's community, they no longer had the right to fly the national black, white, and red flag.[4] This symbolic gesture of exclusion touched a raw nerve. Morale reports gathered in by the Nazis from across the country noted that the Gestapo decree "caused great dismay in Jewish circles. These circles cannot understand that even Jewish veterans, officers, and so on should be forbidden from raising the black, white, and red flag."[5]

The shared memory of military service in World War I provided the most important means by which older male Jews in particular continued to feel in some ways members of a wider German community. One of the last acts performed by Reich President **Hindenburg** before his death was the creation of a new medal, the *Ehrenkreuz* ("Honor Cross"), for participants of World War I. The ceremonial conferral of these medals was slated for early 1935, although the precise arrangements varied from region to region. Jewish organizations viewed these ceremonies as an important chance to remind Germany of Jewish sacrifices for the Fatherland.

DOCUMENT 6-2: Information sheet no. 3 for members of the CV regional association Central Germany, November 2, 1934, USHMMA RG 11.001M.31, reel 223 (SAM 721-1-20, 36–41) (translated from German).

[. . .] It is the duty of each and every Jew who served on the front or is a war veteran or surviving dependents of a fallen serviceman to apply to his local police administration for the medal conferred on veterans of the front or the war. No exclusion or discrimination of Jewish war veterans shall occur. [. . .]

---

4. Wildt, *Volksgemeinschaft*, 178. During the Weimar Republic, the national flag (*Reichsflagge*) had been black, red, and gold, but the black, white, and red flag (the national flag of the second German empire from 1871 to 1918) continued to be used as a trade and naval flag.

5. Stapostelle Düsseldorf, report for February 1935, and other reports cited in Wildt, *Volksgemeinschaft*, 178.

DOCUMENT 6-3: Honor Cross certificate issued "in the name of the Führer and Reich chancellor" to David Schwab,[6] Lörrach, 1935, USHMMPA WS# 01234.

 Jm Namen des Führers und Reichskanzlers

Kaufmann

David   S c h w a b   L ö r r a c h

ist auf Grund der Verordnung vom 13. Juli 1934 zur Erinnerung an den Weltkrieg 1914/1918 das von dem Reichspräsidenten Generalfeld= marschall von Hindenburg gestiftete

Ehrenkreuz für Frontkämpfer

verliehen worden.

Lörrach , den   3. Mai   1935.

Der Landrat:

Nr.   4206   /35 .

Certificate issued to David Schwab by the Lörrach district office for having earned the *Ehren- kreuz für Frontkämpfer* during World War I; May 3, 1935.

Such public recognition for past services to the country stood in marked con- trast to the government's recent anti-Jewish policy. Yet even men with strong Zionist leanings, such as **Willy Cohn**, felt stirrings of an old esprit de corps—if only briefly—when the award ceremony brought back memories of shared com- bat and sacrifice.

DOCUMENT 6-4: Willy Cohn, diary entry for February 5, 1935, translated from Norbert Conrads, ed., *Kein Recht, Nirgends: Tagebuch vom Untergang des Breslauer Judentums, 1933–1941* (Cologne: Böhlau Verlag, 2007), 1:208.

February 5, 1935
    Breslau, Tuesday. Yesterday around seven o'clock I also took part in the
teachers' meeting at the Jewish school am Anger [address in Breslau]. But

6. David Schwab (1888–1960) emigrated with his family first to Switzerland, then to France and the United States. His son Gerald (Gerd/Gerhard, b. 1925) was drafted in 1944 into the U.S. Army and after the war worked as interpreter and researcher for Allied prosecu- tors of Nazi criminals.

later I was angry that I had gone because I let them know my fairly radical views on Jewish education, views that of course did not go over at all well with these people, who are very oriented toward assimilation. Jacoby [teacher at Anger school] began by invoking feelings for one's homeland and the like, even though nowadays in Klettendorf and other places that we call our "home," Jews encounter the worst kind of abuse. [. . .]

Then went to the police to receive the medal for World War I veterans of frontline combat; you had to sign that you had gotten back your passport. Then the chief of police gave a short speech, in which he pointed out that we should wear the medal with honor; he was conferring it in the name of the Führer and on behalf of the police president. The whole war period came rushing back and everything that we had experienced since. The police chief then handed each of us the certificate and shook hands. You responded, "Here!" when your name was called—the way we used to do it in the service—and clicked your heels! That's just how you respond automatically! [. . .]

Though local government officials in some regions simply dispatched the medals to Jewish recipients in the mail, in many areas Jews attended public award ceremonies, just as Willy Cohn did in Breslau. While taking pride in the events, the irony of doing so amid the general climate of exclusion was not lost on many Jews. The letter presented in document 6-5 not only confronted the local police chief with this irony, but parenthetically revealed that the Jewish storekeepers themselves were being forced to clean up the graffiti defacing their storefronts.

DOCUMENT 6-5: CV copy of a letter by CV regional association Pomerania to the Stettin chief of police, March 20, 1935, USHMMA RG 11.001M.31, reel 145 (SAM 721-1-3019, 220–21) (translated from German).

To the honorable police chief of <u>Stettin</u>:
During the night of March 16 to 17, the sidewalks in front of the Jewish businesses in the Old Town were marked up with graffiti such as "Jew," "traitor to the people," and similar slogans.

By chance the phrase "traitor to the people" was painted next to the Hoffmann furniture store, Breitestr. 31, whose owner had that very morning received the medal for frontline veterans.

The graffiti could only be removed with an acid solution. It is a cause for concern that the sidewalk will suffer great damage from multiple applications of acid solution should these incidents be repeated.

With reference to our meeting with the police president, we most humbly request measures be taken to prevent such occurrences.

On March 16, 1935, in close chronological proximity to the distribution of the medals of honor, Hitler announced that he was introducing general military conscription. The German public reacted with an outpouring of enthusiasm. "All Munich is on its feet," noted a Social Democrat observing Hitler's triumphant visit to the city the next day.[7] The lack of international protest about this violation of the **Versailles Treaty**, coupled with an Anglo-German naval treaty in June, essentially legitimated German rearmament. This enormously enhanced both Hitler's prestige and public confidence in his judgment. His announcement about the draft offered another chance for Jews to underscore their national loyalty in a major moment of national revival. The followers of the far right-wing German Jewish *Vortrupp* around **Hans-Joachim Schoeps** (prohibited later in 1935) were not alone in their hope of serving in the new army and reasserting their patriotic credentials.

DOCUMENT 6-6: Letter by German Vanguard, German Jewish Followers (Der Deutsche Vortrupp, Gefolgschaft Deutscher Juden) to CV head office Berlin, March 22, 1935, USHMMA RG 11.001M.31, reel 181 (SAM 721-1-3221, 253) (translated from German).

Permit us to inform you of the following declaration:
In this important moment in world history, in which the German Reich has reclaimed its military sovereignty, we young German Jews also feel the urge to express our support for this development. Just as our fathers fulfilled their clear duty to the Fatherland between 1914 and 1918, we also declare our willingness to serve, in line with our motto: Ready for Germany!

It is difficult now to reconstruct how pervasive Jewish expectations were that this might offer a renewed opportunity for their young men to demonstrate national allegiance. The fact that the German army had already proven disappointingly amenable to Nazi racial ideas must have given many pause.[8] In any case, the law ultimately passed on May 21, 1935, which established the Wehrmacht on the basis of national service, excluded all "non-**Aryans**" from

---

7. Friedländer, *Nazi Germany*, 1:115.
8. See Friedländer, *Nazi Germany*, 1:117–18.

active military service, though it did leave open the question of using them in the event of war. However serious Jewish expectations may or may not have been, there was no doubting the disappointment occasioned by this new exclusion, particularly among former career officers who had hoped to serve the Fatherland.

As a decorated former officer and a convert to Christianity, **Luise Solmitz**'s husband, Fredy, might have had the best hopes for reintegration into the army. Shortly before the reintroduction of universal conscription, Solmitz learned definitively that he would not be allowed to serve in the military again. His wife's diary makes clear the enormous symbolic and psychological impact of this exclusion. It shows also how far even Jews in so-called mixed marriages who had moved almost exclusively in non-Jewish circles found the walls going up around them. The army's decision, she felt, had now provided the last brick in the wall. Doubly cut off as a non-Jew married to a converted Jew, Luise Solmitz was convinced she could not find a place even in the "ghetto" of Jewish cultural life.

DOCUMENT 6-7: **Luise Solmitz, diary entry for August 13, 1935, FZGH 11 S 11** (translated from German) (stray punctuation in the original).

[. . .] The terrible thing for us three is that they want to take away our claim to being part of the German people [*Volk*] & Fatherland, & we have no ideal to put in their place. The alternative is something alien, a people & body of thought that certainly has cultural and historical value, but that's it. This is all quite different for non-Aryans who are conscious of their heritage and who regard their own people as holy and venerable. It is defiant & brave when Luther declares—& I am reminded of this so often—"And take they our life, goods, fame, child and wife, the Kingdom ours remaineth."[9] Yes, and what remains for us? [. . .]

Bolstered by the major demonstrations of public confidence associated with the Saar plebiscite and the reintroduction of the draft, a number of institutions and groups within the regime began to move against Jews with greater vigor. For those targeted, this new wave of antisemitic activism turned the spring and summer of 1935 into a transformative experience. On the one hand, a new round of local party agitation against Jews emerged, inspired in part by the hope

---

9. The Luther quote is an abridged excerpt from the fourth verse of the hymn "A Mighty Fortress Is Our God"; Solmitz skips a line here. An alternative translation of the two lines in question is "Let goods and kindred go, this mortal life also/His kingdom is forever."

that the Saar plebiscite would be the catalyst for more radical Nazi measures issued from the top.[10] In January 1935 the **Reichsvertretung** had felt called upon to respond to a speech by *Der Stürmer* editor and **Gauleiter** of Franconia **Julius Streicher** implying that Jews had tried to persuade the Saar population to vote against German rule.[11] In the coming weeks and months, *Der Stürmer* and other Nazi papers worked to heat up agitation on the streets.

On the other hand, Jews also found themselves exposed to more disciplined and regulated persecution in the form of intensified police and Gestapo measures. These had been increasing slowly since the previous summer, but beginning in 1935 Gestapo offices set their sights on severely restricting "assimilationism," while they continued to treat Zionist groups relatively leniently. In February, in addition to the ban on flying the national flag, another decree prohibited all Jewish meetings that advocated Jewish identification with Germany or promoted the view that Jews should stay put rather than emigrate. The following month the **Gestapa** in Berlin added to this radical step by instructing its branches that they should justify the restrictions by reference to some particular local conditions. (This was presumably designed to conceal the evidence of a national directive. It is unclear whether this was to keep Jewish organizations guessing or to veil police practices that at that stage had no legal justification.)[12]

The Gestapo regulations were deeply worrying for anyone who still hoped that the Jews might have some place in the new Reich. The CV central office acknowledged the "fundamental significance" of the Gestapo's edict against a continued Jewish presence in Germany, but upheld its reigning principle not to yield any ground voluntarily until forced to relent by the regime.[13] At the same time, the CV's Berlin leaders tried, based on the limited information they had about the Gestapo's ultimate intentions, to guide local officials concerned not to increase anxiety among ordinary members. Responding to a communication from its regional office in southwestern Germany at the end of March, for example, the CV's Berlin leadership presented a cautiously optimistic reading of the Gestapo measure and stressed the importance of providing relief to troubled Jews.

---

10. Friedländer, *Nazi Germany*, 1:113–17; Wildt, *Volksgemeinschaft*, 180.

11. "Die Ehre der deutschen Juden" (declaration by Reichsvertretung), *Jüdische Rundschau*, January 29, 1935, 1.

12. On these developments, see Wildt, *Die Judenpolitik*, 17–18.

13. Letter by CV head office (Hirschberg) to Max Lissner, Parchim, March 2, 1935; USHMMA RG 11.001M.31, reel 147 (SAM 721-1-3032, 329).

DOCUMENT 6-8: Letter by CV head office (Hirschberg) to CV regional association Baden, March 29, 1935, USHMMA RG 11.001M.31, reel 147 (SAM 721-1-3032, 96–98) (translated from German).

[. . .] We can very well imagine that the [Gestapo] regulation has created some disquiet among members. One can say with certainty, however, that there is no reason for such disquiet. Any time the matter comes up in conversation, it should be reiterated that most of the local branches continue to hold their meetings and that there has been no reduction in the number of these meetings. In the case where no meetings are being held, this is mainly the result of a voluntary decision of the regional or local office in question to avoid putting an undue burden on the police in the monitoring of these meetings; moreover, the winter season [of CV meetings and events] will soon come to an end.

In addition, it should be stressed that the regulation does not reflect on the overall Jewish situation. One could point in this respect, for instance, to the fact that one local branch head, who had asked whether all Jews had to emigrate from Germany, was told that this was not the purpose of the regulation. Instead, what mattered was to avoid putting an all too strong <u>emphasis</u> on remaining in Germany.

It must further be pointed out that daily business continues in all respects and that we continue to have the opportunity to confer with individual ministries and other state offices in our day-to-day tasks. Thus, there are no restrictions whatsoever that go beyond what the regulation stipulates.

We would be much obliged if you could convey this information to the local branches. As soon as we are able to pass on further details about the regulation, we will do so.

MOUNTING PRESSURE, CHANGING PERSPECTIVES

As pressures mounted, some retreated ever further into their own private spheres. Yet, even here, they often found little respite or pleasure.

DOCUMENT 6-9: Letter by Julius Moses, Berlin, to Erwin Moses, Tel Aviv, for the second week of March 1935, translated from Dieter Fricke, *Jüdisches Leben in Berlin und Tel Aviv, 1933–1939: Der Briefwechsel des ehemaligen Reichstagsabgeordneten Dr. Julius Moses* (Hamburg: von Bockel, 1997), 302–4 (stray punctuation in the original).

[. . .] In a short essay about alcohol, Thomas Mann[14] once said, "Being in a good mood doesn't mean intoxication. A good mood means feeling fully awake, vigor [*Frische*], one's daily work, going for a stroll, clean air, having few people around to bother one, good books, tranquility, tranquility [*Friede*]." . . . All the prerequisites that Thomas Mann lists for creating a good mood are pretty unobtainable for me. Can only dream of them.

Perhaps there is some reciprocal interaction at work here; one could just as well say fresh air, daily work (which also helps establish an inner equilibrium), taking walks (but only if they aren't a chore), having few people around (that's how it is for me now), good books (yes, but in these times and under these conditions, it's hard to enjoy them fully), etc., etc.: all these are preconditions for establishing the right frame of mind in which one can also use, should also use, a letter as a means to "bare the soul" [*seelisches Offenbarungsmittel*].

And tranquility, tranquility?? Where can one truly find a few hours of peace for the soul? Peacefulness? The nerves never stop humming. Even sleep doesn't bring real relief. The nerves keep humming even when you're asleep. Yes, one definitely needed to have a sound constitution, especially at my age, to survive everything that came our way during the last few years, at least to survive it all physically. Especially if one continuously uses stimulants for that purpose—tobacco, coffee, etc.—which of course give one's nerves an ever greater boost instead of calming them. But you keep taking them, you continue to indulge, in the belief—or perhaps one doesn't really believe—that you can thus find easy escape from brutal reality. Magically transporting oneself to a different place. Usually with negative consequences. And so, more and more drugs [*Rauschgifte*], more and more cigars, ever more blue smoke—incidentally, let me point out: stupidity along the way, even of great import: my stash is rapidly running out,

---

14. Reference to Thomas Mann, "Über den Alkohol," in *Thomas Mann: Gesammelte Werke*, ed. Peter de Mendelssohn (Frankfurt: S. Fischer, 1973), 17:479–80. Thomas Mann (1875–1955) was a major German writer who went into exile in 1933; his books were among those publicly burned in May 1933 in Germany. He and his brother Heinrich staunchly opposed Nazi rule. See Nigel Hamilton, *The Brothers Mann: The Lives of Heinrich and Thomas Mann, 1871–1950 and 1875–1955* (New Haven, CT: Yale University Press, 1978).

if you can [get me more cigars]—but only if you can—else I'll have to do without, have to cope: well, you know how it is.

One uses the intoxicant to push away or pull the plug on brutal reality, or even to deceitfully distort it, fantastically distort it, put a spell on it, to lose it behind a cloud of blue smoke. [. . .] As for coffee, that black drink of the Moor, I'm very grateful to both. [. . .]

Some preferred to dwell on a past with fewer sorrows and greater certainties and to gently remind others of the pleasures that memories might bring.

DOCUMENT 6-10: **Bar Mitzvah note by Max Rosenthal to his grandson, Hans Rosenthal, USHMMPA WS# 28738.**

A card written in German and Hebrew by Max Rosenthal to his grandson, Hans, on the occasion of his Bar Mitzvah on April 13, 1935. The dedication reads, "To my dear Hans on his Bar Mitzvah and to the everlasting memory of his loving grandfather Max. Memories are the only paradise from which we cannot be expelled. Max Rosenthal 13/4 1935." The card was inserted in a book, *Das Ostjüdische Antlitz* [*The Face of the Eastern European Jew*] by Arnold Zweig published 1920 in Berlin, that Rosenthal gave to his grandson for his Bar Mitzvah.

Committed Zionists may have found it easiest to adjust psychologically to the new circumstances. They could feel justified in their earlier skepticism about the possibility of genuine Jewish acculturation in Germany and in their fundamental assumption that life in the Diaspora was essentially hostile to Jews. Radicals on the margin, like the small Staatszionistische Organisation led by **Georg Kareski,** a breakaway from the Zionist Revisionist World Organization, were even publicly willing to declare their satisfaction at the humiliation now experienced by their "assimilationist" opponents. In reality, few Zionists had predicted the speed and aggression with which the authorities were now pushing Jews out of the public sphere. But, after getting over the initial shock, mainstream Zionists could, with hindsight, adjust the story of their own earlier expectations a little and, if only in retrospect, now produce a coherent and meaningful story to explain their current predicament. This is clearly evident in the *Jüdische Rundschau*'s celebration of its fortieth anniversary.

DOCUMENT 6-11: "The Spirit of Work," *Jüdische Rundschau*, **May 10, 1935, 1–2 (translated from German).**

The kind words that we received from friends and organizations to mark the *Jüdische Rundschau*'s fortieth anniversary—so many that we cannot acknowledge them individually—show how the relationship between the Jewish public and its Jewish newspaper has changed, a change that surely also reflects the enormous, more general transformations in our time. The exclusion of Jews from German life has forced Jews to create a life of their own, a life that first and foremost serves to protect and keep sacred our Jewish spiritual and ethical values [*Güter*], carries forward our old traditions, and helps give new shape to a Jewish future, above all in Palestine. This has left its mark on the diverse tasks of a Jewish newspaper as well. There is an unmistakable and profound difference between the Jewish newspaper of today and what one often used to call the "Jewish press." The Jewish newspaper of today can easily be identified as a Jewish paper; its name makes that clear. It speaks for Jews and to Jews and does not set itself up as an arbiter of non-Jewish affairs. This is not a development simply of the last two years, for the *Jüdische Rundschau* is forty years old. If the paper expresses an opinion or passes judgment on cultural or human affairs, it is clear that the viewpoints being expressed are Jewish; there is no pretense that we are presenting a German or other sort of perspective. And thus, in this realm, we have arrived at a situation that not only complies with German *völkisch* demands that have already been proclaimed in the past but also upholds the dignity of Judaism. Some people do not yet comprehend this new state of affairs. The fact that Jews identify and meet their obligations exclusively as Jews and nothing else is the result of their occupying an exceptional position, a position brought about by the objective attribute of race. It is Jews conscious of being Jewish who welcome this result. [. . .]

Those Jews who believed in a Jewish future on German soil were, by contrast, harder pressed to find any solace or vindication in recent developments or to challenge the validity of Zionist claims for a more prominent role within the Jewish organizational sector. While they continued to hope that at least a modest lifestyle might still be sustainable in Germany, they recognized increasingly that emigration constituted an important lifeline for many, particularly younger, Jews. At least among senior figures within the Jewish organizations, it was clear in the spring that the eventual Nuremberg Laws of September were already looming on the political horizon. Two confidential letters sent out by the CV in April and May 1935 show how the rapidly evolving political landscape was changing the organization's outlook. In its April communication, the CV leadership tried to define a viable middle path between illusionary escapism on the one hand and undue pessimism on the other.

DOCUMENT 6-12: Local branch circular (*Ortsgruppenrundbrief*) no. 4 by CV head office "only for personal information of board members and CV persons of trust. Publication, also of extracts, prohibited," April 15, 1935, USHMMA RG 11.001M.31, reel 97 (SAM 721-1-67, 1–10) (translated from German).

Our Reality.
It is particularly difficult today to paint a comprehensive picture of German Jews' situation. Things are in constant flux; problems vary in different parts of the country and within the different spheres of German Jewish existence. While the Jewish population's employment situation is bleak in some areas, Jews elsewhere are able to continue operating without special restrictions; while in individual professional fields—especially those falling within the direct or indirect purview of the Reich Chamber of Culture (Reichskulturkammer)[15]—there is an ever stronger tendency toward exclusion, in others no restriction either in legal or actual terms can be detected.

Our judgment of the situation will be unduly clouded if we approach it with preconceived notions. Some believe that they can simply look away and forget that difficulties cannot be overcome by ignoring them.

However, far worse than sticking one's head in the sand is the willful pessimism that leads some to record our difficulties with a certain satisfaction, seeing in them ostensible confirmation of their own Jewish view of

---

15. The Reichskulturkammer was formed in September 1933 for the purpose of nazifying German cultural policies under the auspices of Propaganda Minister Joseph Goebbels. It consisted of subchambers covering all branches of artistic production and excluding "non-Aryans," who were forced into the Kulturbund.

the world. Such a stance cripples any action. We emphatically reject exaggerating the worries that already exist.

In any case, no Jewish worldview exists that supports the theory that German Jewry is condemned to impoverishment. Before the dramatic changes [*Umschwung*], German Zionism made use of political equality and intellectual and economic upward mobility within Germany in the same way as Zionism abroad continues to do in those countries in which these possibilities still exist. Why do some people choose to profit from the inherently difficult present-day situation? Why do some adopt a downright joyful undertone in speeches and essays about our difficulties and explicitly or implicitly conclude that nothing can be done? [. . .]

It would be irresponsible to ignore all the issues that today trouble German Jews. Nevertheless, they need not and should not lead to the sense of despair that has befallen some of our friends. Our friends, especially those throughout the country, should know that it is not a matter of cheap, soothing slogans but that our position is dictated by a deep sense of responsibility for German Jewry.

We must insist that our insecurity not be heightened through careless slogans about emigration. No one should be criticized for deciding to emigrate when conditions force them to do so. But to argue that emigration and the liquidation of everything that pertains to German Jewry [*Liquidation des deutschen Judentums*] is the only solution would be out of line with the current situation both within and outside of Germany, as well as running against the interests of the German economy.

We will do our job in the service of the Jewish community in Germany free of illusions but also free of crippling or interest-driven pessimism.

The CV's May circular, addressed to a very small group of the CV's most important backers tried to quell fears among its leading members, suggesting to them that the increased legal discrimination planned by the Nazi regime would in fact only codify what was already German Jews' daily reality. The CV's approach here reflected its basic position that it was vital to maintain morale as long as possible and that nothing should be abandoned until there was no alternative. At the same time, the CV articulated a key insight into how the Nazi system operated: laws might be the catalyst for new discrimination, but sometimes they merely sanctioned what had already happened on the ground; in other cases, events rapidly overtook them. Law thus formed but one component of an escalating process that often started with local activists pushing the envelope of anti-Jewish harassment and discrimination. In such cases, top Berlin

officials would then enact national laws to legitimize retroactively what had
in fact already become common practice. This interaction between periphery
and center played a crucial role in radicalizing Nazi anti-Jewish policy. The CV
was thus well aware of something that it would take historians some decades to
recognize.

**DOCUMENT 6-13: Confidential letter (to supporters) by CV head office (Hirschberg),
May 31, 1935, USHMMA RG 11.001M.31, reel 97 (SAM 721-1-69, 338–41) (translated from German).**

Attitude [*Haltung*]

I

Recently a series of leading figures has made remarks regarding the future
regulation of German citizenship rights, above all Reich [Interior] Minister Dr. Frick and Ministry Director [*Ministerialdirektor*] Dr. Stuckart, the
head of the Division for Constitutional Questions (*Verfassungsabteilung*)
in the Reich Ministry of the Interior.[16] According to a statement made
by Minister Dr. Frick (late evening issue [of *Völkischer Beobachter*] for
April 27, 1935), the granting of citizenship rights will be linked to certain
conditions "among which, in line with our principles, will also be the
condition of racial membership in the German *Volk*." According to Dr.
Stuckart, "The new laws stipulate that only persons of German blood may
be granted Reich citizenship [*Reichsbürgerschaft*] as members of the German people's community, with all rights and duties." [. . .]

   Part of this future regulation has been incorporated in the Civil Service Law, which is already in force. Jews are barred from holding higher
state offices [*Repräsentationsstellen des Staates*] and from any new civil service
appointments. It is occasionally overlooked in Jewish circles that Jews have
already lost their state, political, cultural, and civil rights [*Ehrenrechte*]. Thus,
the future codification of the rights of citizenship will confirm on paper
an already existing reality. The comments at hand differentiate between
the right of citizenship [*Staatsbürgerrecht*], which is required to hold both
civic [*Ehrenstellungen*]and state positions [*politische Repräsentationsstellen*

---

16. Wilhelm Stuckart (1902–1953), state secretary of the Reich Ministry of the Interior
under Wilhelm Frick. Stuckart played a key role in the preparation for, and administration of, the Nuremberg Laws and in January 1942 attended the Wannsee Conference where
he proposed the compulsory sterilization of "non-Aryans" and the annulment of marriages
between "*Mischlinge*." He was indicted and tried by military tribunal in 1948 and sentenced
to four years in prison, of which he served three. See Mark Roseman, *The Wannsee Conference
and the Final Solution: A Reconsideration* (New York: Metropolitan, 2002).

des Staates], and the status of a state subject [*Staatsangehörigkeitsbegriff*]. There is no suggestion in recent pronouncements that Jews would, for example, lose their status as state subjects, and thus their protection under state and international law, their economic opportunities, or their formal inclusion within the state (passport).

II

Regarding the Zionist resolutions that we published in the *CV-Zeitung* of May 9, 1935, and that we dealt with in general terms at the time, we add the following observation that we passed on to a small circle of colleagues a few days ago:

What has prompted the Zionist Association [ZVfD] to push itself forward at this very point in time is not entirely clear. One can deduce that the radicalization of Zionism, which has manifested itself in the splitting off of the revisionist union from the Zionist World Organization, has produced a need for more intense propaganda. On the one hand, this increase in propagandizing is meant to disguise the grave difficulties facing Zionism as a whole within Germany. On the other hand, it serves the purpose of demonstrating the strength of Zionist demands to the [Zionist] revisionists. Added to this, the wishes of some individuals for posts in the Berlin Jewish community and other central boards may have prompted the stepped-up efforts. Finally, it is an expression of the desire to provide Jews, particularly the intellectually and culturally advanced Jews of Germany, with a land in the Diaspora apart from Palestine that is completely under Zionist control. Installing Zionists in community positions, etc., would have the effect of strongly mobilizing general Jewish financial resources for Zionist goals and thereby also put less emphasis on the work in Germany. Objectively speaking, the Zionists' claim to leadership within German Jewry and especially the Berlin community has no practical justification. Among other things, this is evident in the fact that the resolutions express no concrete demands at all but merely assert rhetorically "[. . .] that the Zionist viewpoint should serve as the basis for reshaping the whole of Jewish life."

This situation, which naturally can be only touched on here, prompts us to resist emphatically the Zionist claims to power. We have made contact with the other organizations taking a stand on the German Jewish position—the Religious-Liberal Union [Religiös-Liberale Vereinigung], the RjF. Our opposition to the Zionist offensive will be based primarily on the fact that, at the present time, any internal Jewish conflict must be vigorously resisted, that we indeed are prepared to participate in joint efforts in any form, even a new form, but that we are not prepared to give in to a completely unjustified claim to leadership. In making our case we will have to emphasize particularly strongly our commitment to constructive [*positive*] Jewish work, which gives us the ideological right to resist the Zionists' interventions. Our argument will also have to differentiate between Palestine, whose development we support now as before, and Zionist partisanship [*Parteizionismus*], which we are currently fighting.

THE ONSLAUGHT OF THE "PEOPLE'S COMMUNITY"

For many Jews, the most disturbing aspect of late spring and summer 1935 was the almost complete inaction by law-enforcement agencies in the face of growing violence from party thugs and street mobs.[17] Violence was hardly something new, for even in the supposedly calm year of 1934, the CV had compiled comprehensive evidence of incidents targeting individuals and property. Now, however, it attained a quite different intensity.

The causes of this violence were complex. Frustration was widespread among grassroots circles both at the way popular agitation had been reined in during the previous summer and at continuing economic problems in many regions and commercial sectors. Hitler had a keen eye for the need to maintain an ongoing standoff between the civil service and the Nazi Party. Now that the worst excesses of the **SA**'s "go-it-alone" radicalism had been contained by the "Röhm purge," Hitler felt he could afford to make concessions to his rank-and-file supporters again and ensure that government bureaucrats did not always have the upper hand. Local activists liked to see themselves as pushing forward where a timid, stick-in-the-mud bureaucracy was holding back. In reality it was the alacrity with which the civil service had enacted antisemitic measures that created the moral climate in which even more radical demands became thinkable and desirable.

In this general climate, *Der Stürmer* positioned itself in the vanguard of increasingly abusive attacks on Jews, leading in January and February to a number of assaults on people and property. By April other voices in the Nazi Party press had gotten in on the act, targeting not only Jews but also "white Jews" (*weisse Juden*)—non-Jews suspected of sympathy toward the racially persecuted—or

---

17. For special emphasis on this period, see Michael Wildt, "Violence against Jews in Germany, 1933–1939," in *Probing the Depths of German Antisemitism: German Society and the Persecution of the Jews, 1933–1941*, ed. David Bankier (New York: Berghahn, 2000), 181–209; for a broader perspective, see Wildt, *Volksgemeinschaft*.

"women oblivious of their racial identity" (*artvergessene Frauenspersonen*), that is, women who associated with Jews.[18]

Local anti-Jewish violence snowballed. In most cases it remains difficult to reconstruct the exact extent to which high-level planning was implicated, though most of the attacks did carry the mark of at least local Nazi Party organizations. Astute readers of the gleeful reports and hateful incitements in the German press saw a "hundredfold signs" that these incidents were being "led by a central will."[19] The sizable mobs that formed on city street corners and village squares, however, included not just Nazi Party activists but also sympathizers and voyeurs. Intent on creating fear and disruption, the mobs dragged Jews through the streets and smashed up shops and homes. While the SA had been in the forefront of the earlier anti-Jewish boycotters, now Hitler Youth members often played an active role. Although in many cases the police eventually intervened to restore order, they did so at a very late hour, after great violence and destruction had already occurred. Occasionally, "protective custody" saved Jews from further public abuse but branded them with the mark of criminality that could trigger further victimization. Even when the perpetrators' identities were known, as was often the case, they rarely faced legal consequences and thus had little incentive to stop such behavior.

Violence continued to meet with public, and in some cases very open, disapproval.[20] Increasingly, however, the streets belonged to Nazi activists. Particularly in small communities, Jews were left reeling by the experience of suddenly finding themselves completely without protection. The extracts in document 6-14 from a report produced by the CV on events in the Hessian town of Gelnhausen show the threats hanging over Jews from the beginning of 1935. The report also reveals the mixture of motivating factors and the range of people involved.[21]

---

18. See Friedländer, *Nazi Germany*, 1:121–28; Longerich, *"Davon haben wir nichts gewusst!"* 76.

19. Kurt Rosenberg, diary entry for March 4, 1935, LBINY AR 25279.

20. Friedländer, *Nazi Germany*, 1:125. On the attitude of the German public, particularly in the war years, see also Ian Kershaw, *Hitler, the Germans, and the Final Solution* (New Haven, CT: Yale University Press, 2008); David Bankier, *The Germans and the Final Solution: Public Opinion under Nazism* (Oxford: Blackwell, 1992).

21. For an extensive account of conditions in Gelnhausen and the importance of violence in the 1935 anti-Jewish campaigns, see also Wildt, *Volksgemeinschaft*, 167–69, 170–71, 184–85, 186–90.

DOCUMENT 6-14: **Memorandum by CV head office Berlin, July 16, 1935, USHMMA RG 11.001M.31, reel 102 (SAM 721-1-2345, 4–6) (translated from German).**

The boycott of Jewish businesses in Gelnhausen/Kurhessen has taken on dimensions rarely seen in German towns. The majority of the indigenous Jewish businesses—many of which have operated for decades and to some extent even several generations—are poised to go under. Only thirty Jewish families remain in Gelnhausen out of the fifty that once lived here, and they are for the most part threatened with financial ruin. [. . .]

For quite some time windowpanes, including the shop windows of Jewish-owned houses, have been smashed, and the houses have also suffered damage: door locks have been tampered with, acid has been poured into door locks, foul-smelling liquids have been sprayed into houses through the door. And in recent days Jews have also suffered bodily harm. For instance, at the end of June the physician Dr. Schwarzschild[22] was struck in the face by the leader of the *Jungvolk*,[23] Schmidt, as he was on his way to deliver a child. Had Dr. Schwarzschild not continued on his way to the woman giving birth, she could have bled to death.

Wooden slats were used to wreck the windowpanes and display windows. In some cases paving stones and bricks were used to smash the windows.

A number of Jewish residents in Gelnhausen, Alt-Hasslau, and Somborn were taken into protective custody during the past weeks. In some cases a crowd of people pushed their way violently into the houses, dragged out the people living there, and brought them to the prison in Gelnhausen, in some instances after subjecting them to severe mistreatment.

On May 31, the 65-year-old Arthur Meyer was coming out of the synagogue and suffered an acid attack. Three young men, whom he and his two accompanying sons recognized,[24] poured acid in his face, which

---

22. This was most likely Max Schwarzschild (1880–?), a doctor who worked in Gelnhausen and by 1938 had moved to Frankfurt am Main with his wife, Julie (née Strauss; 1890–?). They were deported from there to the Łódź ghetto on October 19, 1941, and did not return. They may have been killed in Auschwitz. At least one son and one daughter survived abroad. See www.bundesarchiv.de/gedenkbuch; *USHMM ITS Collection Data Base Central Name Index.*

23. The *Jungvolk*, part of the Hitler Youth, comprised boys aged ten to fourteen.

24. This was probably Arthur Meyer (b. 1870), who by 1938–1939 had moved to Frankfurt am Main with his wife, Gitella (née Weiskopf, b. 1875), their sons Manfred (b. 1905) and Robert (b. 1908), and another relative, Wilhelmine Meyer (b. 1863), possibly his sister. The authors have been unable to determine the fate of Arthur Meyer. His wife and Wilhelmine were deported to Theresienstadt in September 1942, where they both died. Manfred Meyer was incarcerated between November 10, 1938, and February 2, 1939, in Dachau, but his later fate is unclear. His brother Robert perished in September 1942 in the Majdanek concentration camp. See www.bundesarchiv.de/gedenkbuch; *USHMM ITS Collection Data Base Central Name Index.*

resulted in burns on his skin and eye irritation. Charges have been filed with the prosecutor's office [*Amtsanwaltschaft*] in Hanau.

In addition to this, a number of Jewish residents have been knocked down and ill-used.

Events in other parts of Germany reveal that the crescendo of local anti-Jewish action in these months came not only from the street but also from city officials, who often acted in tandem with the rowdies outside. In the small town of Andernach (10,000 inhabitants in 1930) on the left bank of the Rhine Valley, for example, the Jewish community—with roughly 140 members—had just finished building a new synagogue before Hitler came to power. Consecrated in late May 1933, the building soon became the target of state-sponsored segregation efforts when the mayor ordered the heads of the Andernach community to remove a mural engraving from the synagogue's outside wall.

The Jewish community leaders declined to comply with this order and stressed that the inscription, which had been in clear public view ever since the synagogue was built, presented a "provocation toward neither the state nor a state agency." The community heads appealed to the mayor's superior, the Mayen district administrator (*Landrat*), to have the order revoked, citing assurances from the "highest government representatives that no measures would be taken against any religion, that the right to practice any religion was guaranteed, and that churches and cemeteries would be protected."[25] Pressed for time and searching for support, the Andernach community leadership also informed the CV's regional office but asked them to refrain from publishing the matter in its newspaper while the Reichsvertretung tried to get the backing of the Interior Ministry in Berlin to have the mayor's order revoked.

DOCUMENT 6-15: CV copy of letter by Reichsvertretung (Berliner) to Reich and Prussian Interior Ministry, July 2, 1935, USHMMA RG 11.001M.31, reel 113 (SAM 721-1-2555, 155–58) (translated from German).

Urgent

Re: inscription over the entrance of the synagogue in Andernach. Removal by July 5.

Engraved over the entrance to the synagogue in Andernach is a passage from the Bible (Malachi 2:10):

---

25. Letter by CV regional office Rheinland Linkrheinisch to Berlin head office, July 17, 1935, with copy of appeal letter by the Jewish community of Andernach to the district magistrate Mayen, June 27, 1935; USHMMA RG 11.001M.31, reel 114 (SAM 721-1-2555, 149, 151–53).

"Are we not all children of the same Father? Are we not all created by the same God?"

The mayor of the city of Andernach, serving as the local police authority, has instructed the synagogue community through the attached order to remove this inscription because it is liable to disturb public peace, security, and order. The case concerns a contravention of police regulations, which the Jewish community must remedy. If the community fails to act upon the order by the deadline, the mayor will implement it.

Roughly eight days prior to the issuing of this order, a troop of youth, aged 8 to 15, marched through the city cursing the Jews and finally lined up in front of the synagogue shouting:

"We demand the removal of the inscription on the synagogue. We do not have the same god as the Jews."

The chairman of the synagogue has made verbal appeals to the local police authority but without success. He then filed an appeal with the administrator for the Mayen district. Since the written order explicitly stated that any appeal would not delay its execution, and since the deadline prior to enforcement already ends on July 5, we find ourselves obliged to direct the attention of the minister to this matter now and to voice a request that the local police authority's order be repealed.

In his oral representations [to the authorities], the chairman of the synagogue declared himself unable to effect the inscription's removal. Consequently, it is to be expected that the [local] police authority will itself have the inscription removed. We regard it as our duty to alert you to this because we believe that such an action must severely injure the religious feelings not only of the Jews but of all those for whom the Bible is the basis of their faith.

In view of the impending deadline, we request immediate intervention. We would be grateful if you would inform us of the action taken.

The protest was to no avail. In mid-July the Reich Interior Ministry informed the Reichsvertretung's **Cora Berliner** that it saw "no reason to take issue with the order made by the local police authority."[26] Over the following

---

26. Letter by Reichsvertretung (Berliner) to CV head office Berlin, July 19, 1935, with copy of letter by Reich Ministry of the Interior, July 16, 1935; USHMMA RG 11.001M.31, reel 114 (SAM 721-1-2555, 148).

years, the Andernach Jewish community dwindled, and the synagogue was later burned down on "*Kristallnacht*" by anti-Jewish activists.

Until 1935 much of the anti-Jewish violence had been a by-product of the boycott of Jewish stores. True, local vigilantes had also targeted Jews accused of sexual relations with non-Jews, but in many parts of Germany, it was only in 1935 that the campaign against "*Rassenschande*" ("race defilement") gathered momentum. Indeed, in a major recent collection of Nazi reports on popular morale between 1933 and 1939, between 40 and 50 percent of all references to "*Rassenschande*" date from this one year of 1935 alone.[27] One of the many seeming contradictions of racist thought was that fantasies of predatory Jewish men lusting after innocent German maidens coexisted with the charge that Jewish men were effeminate. In a similar mode, while Jews were seen as cowardly, as *Der Stürmer* never tired of stressing in its articles and images, their blood was deemed potent enough to forever pollute the blood of a German woman.

The trail of violence would often start with a rumor or an anonymous denunciation of an ostensible racial defiler. From there, it might well be picked up by the local or party press, which would name and shame the accused. This in turn would become the pretext for brutal street violence. SA and other groups organized so-called *Prangerumzüge*, processions of shame (the name derived from the public shaming enacted in medieval times). The Nazi Party press, displayed prominently in many German towns and villages, triggered many a witch hunt and mobilized local incidents that sometimes drew hundreds or even thousands of participants and spectators. Not only Jews but also their non-Jewish partners could fall victim to such events. Here, too, however, the attackers did not get their own way all of the time. This was particularly true in the early months of Nazi rule, when Jewish victims still had a chance of gaining a sympathetic response from bystanders or some support from town officials. Even if violence was averted, massive pressure was applied to couples who wanted to uphold what was still their right to marry.[28] The cases presented in documents 6-16 and 6-17 demonstrate both how great the odds against them were and the risks of appealing for help.

---

27. Calculation based on Wildt, *Volksgemeinschaft*, 226n22. The reports are published in Otto Dov Kulka and Eberhard Jäckel, eds., *Die Juden in den geheimen NS-Stimmungsberichten, 1933–1945* (Düsseldorf: Droste, 2004).

28. See Wildt, *Volksgemeinschaft*, 219–66. For images of abuse directed against persons accused of "*Rassenschande*," see Klaus Hesse and Philipp Springer, *Vor aller Augen: Fotodokumente des nationalsozialistischen Terrors in der Provinz* (Essen: Klartext, 2002).

DOCUMENT 6-16: CV copy of letter by CV regional association Central Germany (Sabatzky)[29] to regional government head (*Regierungspräsident*) in Magdeburg, March 15, 1935, USHMMA RG 11.001M.31, reel 130 (SAM 721-1-2845, 56–57) (translated from German).

We received a report from Gardelegen concerning the following incident: Siegbert Marcus, a Jewish businessman in Gardelegen, intends to marry Miss Schernikau there. She is of Aryan ancestry. The two have already been engaged for four years. These circumstances led to an incident on the night of Saturday the 9th going into Sunday the 10th of March, during which the graffiti "I am a race defiler" and "I continue to defile" appeared in big letters on two display windows of the Marcus firm, of which Siegbert Marcus is a co-owner. The same paint was used for graffiti declaring "A Jew's whore lives here" on the house of his [prospective] father-in-law, the master locksmith Paul Schernikau, where the bride also resides. In addition, the newspaper *Der Mitteldeutsche* published the attached article [not attached here] denouncing Miss Schernikau and Mr. Marcus in its issue Sunday, March 10.

First of all, the matter concerns Siegbert Marcus, not Louis Marcus, as the article incorrectly states, and the marriage has not yet taken place but is expected to take place quite soon. In connection with this story, the newspaper *Der Mitteldeutsche* has called for an illegal boycott against Marcus's business.

Both partners joining in this marriage are guided by completely pure motives. The marriage will follow Jewish religious principles so that any children will be raised as Jews. There are no grounds to believe the claims of *Der Mitteldeutsche* that either Mr. Marcus [or] Miss Schernikau is marrying for money. The conclusion that the newspaper reaches—that the Marcus business is seeking an upswing in its economic fortunes because the future spouse of the owner is a Christian—is completely absurd, for the owners of the business have had no intention of using the ethical institution of matrimony as some sort of advertising ploy. The owners are very respected and solid business people who would under no circumstances stoop to such advertisement.

---

29. Kurt Sabatzky (1892–1955) was a World War I veteran who served as the legal representative for the CV in East Prussia in the 1920s and as a CV official in Leipzig, Saxony, from 1933 to 1938. Sent to Buchenwald concentration camp after the November 1938 pogrom, he left for England in 1939 and lived there until his death. See Margarete Limberg and Hubert Rübsaat, eds., *Germans No More: Accounts of Jewish Everyday Life, 1933–1938* (New York: Berghahn Books, 2006), 45–47, 188; catalog of the LBINY.

Apart from this, the display windows were defaced over a series of several nights with slogans calling for a boycott. Master locksmith Schernikau, who has only a very modest income, has lost one contract because a [Nazi] party member blocked it. At the same time, warnings were sent from various quarters yesterday—some were also sent to some of our friends—indicating that Mr. Schernikau would be driven into ruin and prevented from receiving even one single further commission.

Mr. Siegbert Marcus has already gotten in touch with the mayor in his capacity as the local police official, and one hopes that this will hinder any further excesses [*Ausschreitungen*] in this affair. Nevertheless, because of the fundamental importance of this matter and because the newspaper *Der Mitteldeutsche* has issued defamatory statements and calls for a boycott in its pages, we have decided to approach you, President of the Regional Government [*Regierungspräsident*], with a respectful request that you take measures to restore a lawful state of affairs.[30]

DOCUMENT 6-17: Letter by CV local branch Aachen (Löwenstein)[31] to CV head office, April 30, 1935, USHMMA RG 11.001M.31, reel 113 (SAM 721-1-2555, 131–32) (translated from German).

Permit me to inform you of the following case:

Ernst Falk,[32] the son of a well-respected butcher, had a relationship with a young Aryan girl that was not without consequences. The young girl on a number of occasions asked Falk for money to arrange an abortion, and he gave it to her. As the girl nonetheless admits, Falk

---

30. By 1938, Siegbert (Karl) Marcus (1900–?) had married a Jewish woman, Marie Marcus (née Friedlein; 1904–?); both lived in Nuremberg with her parents. Siegbert and Marie Marcus were deported on November 29, 1941, to Riga, where they were murdered. Siegbert Marcus's in-laws were deported to Theresienstadt in 1942 and later died. See www.bundesarchiv.de/gedenkbuch; Michael Diefenbacher and Wiltrud Fischer-Pache, eds., *Gedenkbuch für die Nürnberger Opfer der Schoa* (Nürnberg: Stadtarchiv Nuernberg, 1998), 82, 217, 317.

31. This was probably the lawyer Karl Löwenstein (1883–?), a married man with one son born in 1923. He still resided in Aachen in mid-1938 but may have managed to emigrate. See Herbert Lepper, ed., *Von der Emanzipation zum Holocaust: Die Israelitische Synagogengemeinde zu Aachen, 1801–1942* (Aachen: Verlag der Mayer'schen Buchhandlung, 1994), 2:1589, 1645.

32. This may have been Ernst Falk (1913–?), an unmarried butcher living in Aachen in 1935, son of the butcher Moritz Falk and Emma Falk (née Meyer). They do not appear in the recent memorial book for German Jewish victims of the Holocaust, suggesting they may have survived. See Lepper, *Von der Emanzipation*, 1548.

never encouraged her to take this path but, on the contrary, even tried to discourage her.[33]

Charges were filed against the girl and Falk on the grounds of abortion and aiding and abetting [in procuring an abortion]. At the same time, charges were filed against the abortionist, who performed the abortion. I was Falk's lawyer. The abortionist was sentenced to one year in prison, and the young girl and Falk each received a sentence of six weeks, although the judge indicated a possibility that the sentence might be deferred.

Afterward, the *Westdeutsche Beobachter* newspaper issued a report about the case, which was false inasmuch as it claimed that Falk had seduced the girl and induced her to have the abortion. The girl in fact comes from a family that does not have a good reputation. A younger sister recently gave birth out of wedlock.

As a result of the article, a display window and a glass sign were smashed at the business owned by Falk's father. Furthermore, on the following day, signs appeared in various places accusing Falk of racial defilement and calling upon people to take their business elsewhere. In the evening workers from various factories gathered in front of the house. Because the Falk son could not be found on the premises—he had in the meantime left town—the Falk father was taken into protective custody. I contacted the head of the Gestapo, Regierungs-Assessor Seezen [*sic*],[34] on the following day, and he informed me that the protective custody order would be suspended that evening, which indeed was the case.

The circumstances created a considerable stir in Aachen. The public's attitude revealed itself by the fact that on the day after Falk [the father] was released, his shop was bursting with customers, more than he had ever had before.

Incidentally, unrelated to this affair, a few days earlier—namely on Holy Saturday [the day before Easter]—a series of Jewish businesses in the

---

33. Except for narrowly defined exceptions, abortion was a crime in Germany at the time. On the utility of abortion and sterilization laws for Nazi social policy, see Gabriele Czarnowski, "Women's Crimes, State Crimes: Abortion in Nazi Germany," in *Gender and Crime in Modern Europe*, ed. Margaret L. Arnot and Cornelie Usborne (London: UCL, 1999), 238–57; Gisela Bock, "Ordinary Women in Nazi Germany: Perpetrators, Victims, Followers, and Bystanders," in *Women in the Holocaust*, ed. Dalia Ofer and Lenore J. Weitzman (New Haven, CT: Yale University Press, 1998), 85–100.

34. Heinz Seetzen, at this time a probationary government official at the Gestapo in Aachen, became commander of a mobile killing squad during the war. See Lawrence D. Stokes, "From Law Student to Einsatzgruppe Commander: The Career of a Gestapo Officer," *Canadian Journal of History* 37 (2002): 42–73.

middle of the city here in Aachen were defaced with graffiti, such as "dirty Jew, Jew-man" [*Judenlümmel, Judenmann*], etc. The windows were in some cases seriously damaged by slogans scratched into them with acid. Those business owners who suffered damages informed the Gestapo. No further incidents occurred.

Anticipating a ban on "interracial" marriages, the courts in some regions began preventing them despite the absence of any direct legal injunctions to do so. In May 1935 Reich Interior Minister **Wilhelm Frick**, however, did advise the registrar's offices (*Standesämter*) throughout the country not to conduct "unwanted" (*unerwünscht*) civil marriages between Jews and "Aryans."[35] In September the situation would change dramatically when the Nuremberg Laws outlawed both future marriages and sex out of wedlock between Jews and non-Jews.

While many areas witnessed an unprecedented level of intimidation and violence, in some regions the situation for Jews grew particularly bad. According to a report from the Reichsvertretung to the Reich Interior Ministry in July, these included East Prussia, Mecklenburg, and Berlin.[36] In places like these, local CV officials were no longer persuaded "that anything significant could be gained either through personal appearances or written pleas."[37] In response, the CV head office could only point to its tireless efforts to influence and solicit help from Berlin government officials. It urged its regional representatives "to continue fulfilling our duties and thereby support our friends in their efforts to secure Jewish livelihoods"[38] as long as was humanly possible.

In some places, including the Hesse-Nassau region, the boycott took an ominous turn in the summer. There was nothing new about shoppers being hindered from entering Jewish businesses, but now Jewish consumers found themselves prevented from buying goods in non-Jewish stores. As was brought home to a delegation from the regional Jewish welfare office (Provinzialverband für Jüdische Wohlfahrtspflege in Hessen-Nassau) and the CV consisting of **Curt**

35. Cornelia Essner, *Die "Nürnberger Gesetze" oder die Verwaltung des Rassenwahns, 1933–1945* (Paderborn: Schöningh, 2002), 106.

36. CV copy of letter Reichsvertretung to Reich Interior Ministry, July 26, 1935; USHMMA RG 11.001M.01, reel 183 (SAM 721-2-172, 64–70).

37. Letter by CV regional association East Prussia (Angerthal) to CV head office, August 8, 1935; USHMMA RG 11.001M.31, reel 228 (SAM 721-1-172, 51–53).

38. Letter by CV head office (Reichmann) to East Prussian Syndikus Dr. Max Angerthal, Königsberg, August 12, 1935; USHMMA RG 11.001M.31, reel 228 (SAM 721-1-172, 50).

Bondy and Hilde Meyerowitz,[39] Jews were being starved out of their communities. Sober and clear-eyed though the report is, it is noteworthy that the writers still had no conception that elderly Jews might in coming years find themselves in acute physical danger.

DOCUMENT 6-18: "Report on a Trip to the Jewish Communities of Schlüchtern and Gelnhausen on August 19, 1935" by Hilde Meyerowitz and Curt Bondy, USHMMA RG 11.001M.31, reel 99 (SAM 721-1-98, 1–6) (translated from German; appendices not attached).

The trip was prompted by a growing number of reports about the extremely difficult situation facing the Jewish population of Hesse-Nassau.

The trip's mission was to attain an objective overview of the situation in order to make informed suggestions for immediate or eventual remedial measures. [. . .]

Fourteen visits to twelve different Jewish communities were made, above all to smaller communities in Vogelsberg to which only a few families belong, as well as to larger communities such as Birstein, Schlüchtern, and Langenselbold. We visited the head of the Jewish community in most of these locales.

Our discussions chiefly revolved around the general situation rather than individual relief efforts.

After conducting all these visits, we have come to the following conclusions:

I. General Conditions:

1. In recent weeks, in part only in recent days, signs have been put up prohibiting Jews from entering certain localities, homesteads, and shops. In addition, signs have been posted identifying the houses of Jews.

---

39. Hilde Meyerowitz (1906–?) trained as a social worker in Berlin and worked for the Social Democratic Party's welfare organization, the Arbeiterwohlfahrt. In 1933 she was arrested and, after her release, worked for the Reichsvertretung. In 1934 she became executive director (*Geschäftsführerin*) of the Jewish regional welfare office for Hessen-Nassau until her emigration to the United States in 1938, where she continued her career as a social worker for Jewish organizations. See Renate Knigge-Tesche and Axel Ulrich, eds., *Verfolgung und Widerstand in Hessen, 1933–1945* (Frankfurt am Main: Eichborn, 1996), 349. Monica Kingreen, ed., *"Nach der Kristallnacht": Jüdisches Leben und antijüdische Politik in Frankfurt am Main, 1938–1945* (Frankfurt am Main: Campus, 1999), 148n7; USHMMA Acc. 2000.227 Herbert Cohn collection, folders 2–3.

2. Assaults on Jews have occurred solely in Lichtenroth; we have only received a report from a family member about alleged assaults in Schenklengsfeld, but she was not an eyewitness.

3. Incidents of Jews being roughed up a bit [*kleine Anrempeleien*], stone throwing, and name-calling have occurred in various locations.

4. Reports are coming in from various locations about stringent ordinances that forbid conducting business or associating with Jews.

5. Individual Jews—those who have left their hometowns and come to Frankfurt after traveling through neighboring localities—have succumbed to a significant degree to the understandable hazard of exaggerating these incidents in their memories and accounts. A large proportion of the Jewish population is frightened and may act rashly and imprudently in an emergency.

6. In various localities where Jews are banned from shopping in non-Jewish businesses, it has become difficult for them to buy groceries. However, nowhere has it become completely impossible for Jews to buy groceries by one means or other.

7. There is no immediate danger at present, but there are tensions on both sides. Assaults on Jews could happen at any time, including from strangers to the community. The clear marking of Jewish houses, in part through yellow signs marked "Jews" and in part through Jewish nameplates, makes their ability to identify the Jewish population easier.

8. The opportunities for the Jewish population to earn a living have been further reduced. Cattle dealers have lost virtually every avenue of obtaining an income, owing to the introduction of Jew-free markets—for instance, in Wächtersbach—and through the barring of Jews from entering localities and homesteads, as well as the bans on doing business or associating with Jews. The remaining tradespeople, whether they have businesses in fixed locations or travel with their wares and services, depend solely on their earnings from the small Jewish populace. It looks as though business with the non-Jewish population has come to an almost complete halt.

Because people in part still have land and gardens, it is unlikely that in general a real food emergency will arise. It has been difficult to establish clearly what financial reserves and opportunities for tapping relatives for aid exist.

II. Aid Measures:

A. Immediate, extraordinary local aid measures are not necessary.

1. Providing food supplies is not necessary because, although shopping has become much more difficult, nowhere has it been rendered

completely impossible. There are either still Jewish shops or non-Jewish traders and vendors who will sell groceries to Jews.

2. There are no homeless Jews. Jews have either found lodgings in the homes of other Jews or returned to their own communities. The men to some extent appear to have, for a time, lived apart from their families or slept elsewhere.

3. There is little evidence that schoolchildren, of whom there are very few left, face special difficulties. It remains to be seen what the situation will be after the school year begins.

B. Immediate general measures:

1. Above all, the Reichsvertretung must inform the [Reich] Interior Ministry immediately that the new antisemitic wave brings with it the danger of excesses that could lead to very serious consequences that are surely highly undesirable for all. Some general regulations must be set on how far exclusion can go regarding personal and economic measures taken against Jews. Otherwise, there will be no limit in the competition to be the most antisemitic ([for instance, in the form of] propaganda tours by the SA; measures taken by junior officials).

2. Akin to this report on two districts, we must obtain a picture of how things stand in all of Germany. Depending on whether we find the problems confined to certain areas or widespread, to be short-term or chronic, we need to create a general plan [*Generalplan*] that can serve as a basis for adopting more specific measures [*Einzelmassnahmen*] in a purposeful manner.

(A word about the measures that have already been instituted or are planned: the withdrawal of school-aged children and emigration of Jews in midlife has already taken place to a large extent. On the basis of a general plan, it will then be necessary to investigate very carefully what aid can and must be extended in individual cases: through direct support, through emigration aid—particularly the *Aliyah*, the transplanting [of people] into larger communities. A small sector of the Jewish population, particularly older people, may be relatively safe from harm and can and must remain in villages. They will be able to support themselves to some extent from their land and their gardens.

C. We recommend that the following direct measures be carried out immediately:

1. Allocation of resources and, as far as needed, arrangements for providing groceries immediately [for Jews] in endangered communities.

2. Preparation of lodgings in the event that one or more locales must be evacuated and relatives and friends are unable to house evacuees on short notice.

3. An increase of systematic visits in the near future to emergency areas [*Notgebiete*] by the regional associations [*Provinzialverband*], CV, etc., to gain clear oversight of the situation on a long-term basis. These visits should offer some reassurance to the Jewish populace to the extent that is possible.

At the beginning of 1935, it had still been possible for Jewish leaders to be surprised at how well Jewish establishments were holding out. When Jewish organizations had prevented the singing of the "Horst Wessel Song" in public spaces, it had seemed as if real progress was possible. Now the tone was changing, and the level of confidence had declined. According to **Bernhard Kahn**, the European representative of the **American Jewish Joint Distribution Committee** (AJJDC), by the end of 1935 one-quarter of the Jews of Germany had become destitute and in need of welfare. Many Jewish businesses were being sold off at ridiculously low prices.[40]

Yet Jewish experiences in rural and small-town Germany remained very mixed. A sign of the robustness of part of the Jewish sector was that in the winter of 1935–1936, the Jewish Winter Relief (Jüdische Winterhilfe) campaign raised over RM 3.6 million, or 50 percent more per member of the Jewish community than the equivalent Nazi campaign for the Reich as a whole. While in fall 1935, 20 percent of the Jewish community as a whole desperately needed assistance (in some towns and villages the proportion was as high as 84 percent), a substantial sector was managing to weather the storm, and a smaller group was actually prospering.[41] In some regions and occupations Jews could still go about their business relatively easily, and in many towns and neighborhoods, public order had not yet been transfigured by violence. Where things were more difficult, the CV hoped that it might at least make life more bearable, for example, by making provision to supply local Jews through Jewish stores. In a typical arrangement, cars would drive to homes of Jews to take orders and deliveries would be made the following day.[42] Thus, even though stripped of its traditional functions of providing legal help and fostering "German sentiment," the CV had not completely given up hope of being able to do some good. Irrespective of interorganizational rivalries and the problems the CV was facing in its work every day, members reassured leaders that the organization was needed and that

---

40. Barkai, *From Boycott*, 108.

41. Kramer, "Jewish Welfare Work," in Paucker, *The Jews in Nazi Germany*, 183–86. On the Jüdische Winterhilfe, see Vollnhals, "Jüdische Selbsthilfe," 399–406; Kaplan, *Between Dignity*, 30–32.

42. CV head office (Rubinstein) to CV regional office East Prussia, August 28, 1935, USHMMA RG 11.001M.31, reel 101 (SAM 721-1-2335, 79).

it was worth continuing the struggle. The memorandum presented in document 6-19, however, suggests how quickly attitudes among many of those who had traditionally believed in a German Jewish symbiosis were changing. Evidently, the CV leadership had been worrying about whether it should change its mission statement on the "cultivation of German sentiment." The locals interviewed here were surprised this was even an issue.

DOCUMENT 6-19: Memorandum by CV head office (possibly Hans Reichmann), August 28, 1935, USHMMA RG 11.001M.31, reel 117 (SAM 721-1-2605, 509) (translated from German).

On August 28 of this year, I attended an important meeting in Göttingen, about which I will provide a separate report.

Word soon got around that I was in town, and as a result, fifteen people gathered by and by to discuss various unsettled questions with me in the late afternoon. In the end I raised several questions myself, particularly what members thought about changing the name of the organization, as well as rephrasing its statement of purpose [*Tendenzparagraphen*, referring to the preamble in the CV bylaws on the "cultivation of German sentiment" among its members]. Everyone without exception was surprised that this issue would even present a problem for the organization's leaders. It was seen as being far more important that we are able to carry on with the work than that we maintain old "regimental" traditions [*seelische Haltung a la "Traditionskompagnien"*]. Members expect us to keep the functions of the CV intact; beyond that, nothing else matters.

As far as the general attitude is concerned, it should be noted that, despite great hardship, particularly among cattle and grain dealers, the mood is by no means defeatist or pessimistic. People see the situation without any illusions [*vollkommen nüchtern*] and not only understand, but fully accept, the need to make adjustments.

PART III
SUBJECTS UNDER SIEGE
SEPTEMBER 1935 TO DECEMBER 1937

FOR MANY ORDINARY Germans, the years between the late summer of 1935 and early 1938 formed the most settled and comfortable phase of Nazi rule. The economic recovery proved robust and enduring. For the first time since World War I, the country experienced a sustained sense of economic security. By 1937, Germany had returned to full employment, and a year later there were more jobs than people to fill them. True enough, many of the exaggerated hopes held by Hitler's more ardent supporters in 1933 remained unfulfilled. Yet those small businessmen, for instance, who had voted Nazi in the mistaken belief that their big competitors would be crushed in favor of the little man, still profited from the recovery. For manual workers, the fruits of recovery were more modest. Real wages rose only a little above 1913 levels. Given the booming economy, this limited increase was a sign both that the relative share of national income in wages was falling substantially and that the "German Labor Front" would not fight for workers' interests as the disbanded unions had done before 1933. As the armaments industry expanded, some consumer goods and foodstuffs grew scarce. However, with the **Weimar Republic's** experience of hyperinflation followed by mass unemployment in recent memory, none of this dampened labor's relief and gratitude for full employment and economic stability. Moreover, the rapid professionalization of the workforce meant that in the course of the 1930s, a large number of working-class families saw their boys enter into an apprenticeship after school, for many a significant improvement in status.[1]

Almost universal satisfaction prevailed at Germany's changed position in world affairs. The **Saar** plebiscite of January 1935 and, above all, Hitler's reintroduction of conscription in March without a significant negative reaction abroad were seen as significant milestones of Germany's return to the international stage. The heady successes of 1935 were then trumped in March 1936 by Hitler's gamble in allowing German troops back into Germany's Rhineland territories in defiance of a clause of the **Versailles Treaty**. Once again, Hitler's risk taking proved its worth. At minimal cost (and despite having been completely unprepared to withstand any French military action) Germany asserted its prerogatives and independence. The prestige gained during the Berlin Olympic Games in 1936 and the growing number of foreigners coming to visit the new Reich added to the German public's sense that their Fatherland was once again a respected member of the club of great nations.[2]

Some expected the regime, having consolidated its appeal and found jobs for a new generation of youth, to go soft. Many businessmen and leading conservative figures were looking for a return to world markets and more cordial international relations. But for Hitler, securing his position at home was merely the first step toward achieving more ambitious goals. The Wehrmacht's expansion in manpower and material proceeded apace. In 1935 the military absorbed 70 percent of all central government spending on goods and services; by 1938, the share would be 80 percent. In the course of the 1930s, Hitler recognized that continued military expansion would require far more ruthless prioritization of imports and investment. In the fall of 1936, he outlined a four-year plan to control the import and consumption of nonmilitary goods and to direct investment toward military projects.[3] In a secret meeting with military leaders in November 1937, he mapped out his belief that Germany's need for living space would inevitably bring it into conflict with the other great powers; thus, it would be good for any confrontation to take place between 1943 and 1945, after which Germany's rearmament efforts would begin to be eclipsed by those of the rest of the world. As evidence grew to those in the know that economic activity was being pushed and constrained to meet tough military objectives

---

1. For the most recent survey of incomes, see J. Adam Tooze, *The Wages of Destruction: The Making and Breaking of the German Economy* (London: Allen Lane, 2006), 138–47. On professionalization, see John Gillingham, "The Deproletarianisation of German Society: Vocational Training in the Third Reich," *Journal of Social History* 19 (1986): 423–32.

2. Saul Friedländer, *Nazi Germany and the Jews*, vol. 1, *The Years of Persecution, 1933–1939* (New York: HarperCollins, 1997, 2007), 180–81.

3. Tooze, *Wages*, 207–24.

and that Hitler was ready to take great foreign policy risks to achieve expansion, some more cautious economic and military figures wavered. As a result, Hitler began to discard the conservative elites who had until then helped to establish the Nazis in power.[4]

Under the surface of Nazi Germany's seeming stability, then, the focus on war grew ever sharper. The more Hitler prepared for the conflict ahead, the more he fretted about the threat ostensibly posed to Germany's plans by international Jewry. At the same time, and equally ominously for Germany's Jews, important changes were taking place in the regime's security apparatus, most notably **Heinrich Himmler**'s official appointment as chief of German police on June 17, 1936. The intermingling of **SS** bodies, including the SS security and intelligence branch (the SD), with police departments, such as the **Gestapo**, created a new set of increasingly hybrid institutions.[5] Combining state authority with SS ethos, the police apparatus became an even more efficient instrument for executing the regime's policy and influencing public reactions, be it through the use of terror or the mere threat of surveillance and denunciation.[6] Between late 1933 and 1936, the concentration camp system had contracted. Now, in 1936, Himmler began aggressively expanding it again, while at the same time shifting the attention of his SS police apparatus from left-wing opponents to the Reich's supposed racial enemies. Yet, at least until the foreign policy crises of 1938 (which form the backdrop to Part IV), many ordinary citizens chose to believe that the regime was pursuing a reasonably peaceful and stable course, albeit one with demonstrated commitment to national conscription and a strong army.

In contrast to their non-Jewish counterparts, few German Jews experienced the mid-1930s as either settled or remunerative. Instead, they were confronted with a radical discrepancy between the increasingly comfortable lives of those around them and their own ever more unsettled existences. These two very different trajectories were sometimes directly connected since depriving Jews of

---

4. Schacht, one of the regime's conservative leaders, was increasingly sidelined by Göring from 1936 and lost his position as Reich economics minister in late 1937. For an overview of Nazi politics at this time, see Ian Kershaw, *Hitler, 1889–1936: Hubris* (London: Allen Lane, 1998), 4–60; Richard J. Evans, *The Coming of the Third Reich* (New York: Penguin Press, 2004), 358, 632–45.

5. See George C. Browder, *Foundations of the Nazi Police State: The Formation of Sipo and SD* (Lexington: University Press of Kentucky, 1990); Edward B. Westermann, *Hitler's Police Battalions: Enforcing Racial War in the East* (Lawrence: University Press of Kansas, 2005), 20–123.

6. On the role of denunciations, see Robert Gellately, *Backing Hitler: Consent and Coercion in Nazi Germany* (New York: Oxford University Press, 2001).

their livelihoods turned many non-Jews into beneficiaries. Most Jews found, like Victor Klemperer, that neighbors and others with whom they might briefly interact had no comprehension of how differently Jews were situated.[7] Yet, even among Jews themselves, the picture remained mixed. As we saw in Part II, such indicators as the ability of Jewish organizations to raise charitable donations and the relatively stable numbers of those needing charitable support all pointed to the surprising robustness of many German Jewish businesses until 1937.[8] Jewish reactions still showed a remarkable range from the cautiously optimistic to the downright depressed. However, even those who remained relatively upbeat increasingly accepted that for Jewish youth, all hopes for the future lay outside Germany.

In terms of anti-Jewish policy, the period under review was dominated by the **Nuremberg Laws** of September 1935, the first major national legislation on Jewish affairs since 1933. The laws included two simple but programmatic measures, one of which reduced Jews from legal citizens (*Staatsbürger*, or in its new nazified version, *Reichsbürger*) to legal subjects (*Staatsangehörige*) and the other of which denied them the right to marry or have sexual relations with non-Jews. Important directives followed that clarified and codified the laws and helped the state apparatus enforce them. Thereafter, anti-Jewish measures enacted on the national level again decreased in terms of both quantity and visibility. The Olympics year 1936 in particular saw no eye-catching initiatives—and, indeed, the next major acceleration in Jewish policy did not occur until 1938. A recent compendium of new national, regional, and local policy measures affecting Berlin Jews noted just fourteen in 1936 and nineteen in 1937 as opposed to seventy-four in 1938.[9]

So, how did the Nuremberg Laws impact Germany's Jews, and how did this group experience the years following their passage? Within a spectrum of historical interpretations, three propositions feature prominently. Until recently many historians assumed that the laws resulted from last-minute measures,

---

7. See Victor Klemperer, *I Will Bear Witness: A Diary of the Nazi Years* (New York: Random House, 1998), 1:1933–41.

8. The authors include this statement with the caveat that as the Jewish population dwindled through emigration, stable absolute numbers implied that a growing *proportion* of the remaining population was impoverished. Charitable donations also reflected an enormous effort on the part of organizations in Germany and abroad, as well as a growing sense of communal responsibility on the part of all. See Salomon Adler-Rudel, *Jüdische Selbsthilfe unter dem Nazi-Regime 1933–1939 im Spiegel der Berichte der Reichsvertretung der Juden in Deutschland* (Tübingen: J. C. B. Mohr, 1974).

9. Wolf Gruner and Stiftung Topographie des Terrors, eds., *Judenverfolgung in Berlin, 1933–1945: Eine Chronologie der Behördenmassnahmen in der Reichshauptstadt* (Berlin: Hentrich, 1996).

drafted in haste to be codified in subsequent regulations. As we saw in Part II, however, Nuremberg was long foreshadowed by official discussions well-known in informed Jewish circles.[10] In addition, conventional wisdom has it that in the aftermath of the legislation, the regime's desire for a public relations success at the Olympic Games caused it to backpedal on Jewish affairs, returning to a tougher line only in 1937. Historian Uwe Adam has characterized 1936 as a "period of outward calm and a certain degree of legal security" for Jews.[11] Consequently, German Jews are seen to have misread the laws and Hitler's statement at the time of their announcement as providing for the peaceful, if unequal, coexistence of "**Aryans**" and Jews rather than as the harbinger of coming disaster. Certainly, though higher than in the previous year, emigration remained in 1936 below the level of 1933. Yet all these assumptions turn out to be misleading in one way or another. As the documents in this part will demonstrate, radicalization, while uneven, was far more continuous, and German Jews were far more realistic in recognizing this, than has been supposed.

---

10. See Cornelia Essner, *Die "Nürnberger Gesetze" oder Die Verwaltung des Rassenwahns, 1933–1945* (Paderborn: Schöningh, 2002); Peter Longerich, *Holocaust: The Nazi Persecution and Murder of the Jews* (Oxford: Oxford University Press, 2009), translated from his *Politik der Vernichtung: Eine Gesamtdarstellung der nationalsozialistischen Judenverfolgung* (Munich: Piper, 1998).

11. Uwe Dietrich Adam, *Judenpolitik im Dritten Reich* (Düsseldorf: Droste, 1972), 153 ("Periode äusserer Ruhe und einer gewissen Rechtssicherheit").

CHAPTER 7

THE NUREMBERG LAWS AND THEIR IMPACT

IMMEDIATE REACTIONS AFTER NUREMBERG

After the war, the Reich Interior Ministry's race expert, Bernhard Lösener, recalled that on the evening of September 13, 1935, he and a colleague had been urgently summoned from Berlin to Nuremberg. On his arrival, ministry officials informed him that in just two days' time, Hitler wanted to announce a law dealing with marriage and extramarital relations between Jews and "**Aryans**." A day later, the task had doubled: now Hitler wanted a citizenship law to provide a clear basis for the marriage legislation. Disagreement between Interior Ministry officials and party radicals about what should happen with those of "mixed race" prompted Hitler to ask for four alternative drafts of the citizenship law; in the end he plumped for the most generous one toward "***Mischlinge***" while at the same time struck from the draft the Interior Ministry's preamble that the law applied only to full Jews. This left the floor open for later debates about the treatment of those of mixed descent.[1]

Lösener's account certainly gives a flavor of the kind of undignified scramble that constituted lawmaking in Nazi Germany. Hitler disliked sober procedures and often saw the strategic value of surprises. In this case, as Peter Longerich has argued, the concrete stimulus to legislation may have been, surprisingly, the third and usually ignored element of the Nuremberg legislation,

---

1. Friedländer, *Nazi Germany*, 1:145–51. For an in-depth analysis of Lösener's account, see Karl A. Schleunes, ed., *Legislating the Holocaust: The Bernhard Loesener Memoirs and Supporting Documents* (Boulder, CO: Westview Press, 2001).

namely the Flag Law. Angered by the forcible removal of the swastika flag from the steamship *Bremen* by New York longshoremen, and still more by their subsequent acquittal by a (Jewish) New York judge, Hitler wanted the swastika to become the national, not just the party, flag, which was why he called a special meeting of the Reichstag to take place in Nuremberg directly after the party rally. The desire to define clearly who would be allowed to fly the flag, as well as to ramp up the legislative program of this specially convened Reichstag, in turn prompted passage of the other Nuremberg Laws.[2]

But Lösener's account, which influenced a generation of historians, was also highly misleading, shaped by his postwar desire to present himself as the surprised draftsman in a chaotic procedure and not as the diligent contributor to a much longer process. In reality, while the final details may have been drafted overnight in fevered sessions in Nuremberg, both the citizenship and the race laws were widely anticipated. Ever since 1933, ministerial initiatives and pronouncements by Hitler had suggested that a new definition of citizenship was on its way. In the spring of 1935, as we have seen, registrar's offices were advised not to conduct "mixed marriages" in anticipation of a coming law. Both the burgeoning popular attacks on "race defilers" and the CV's insight expressed in late May 1935 that "the future codification of the rights of citizenship will confirm in writing a situation which today already actually exists"[3] indicated that "law" emerged on the ground before it entered the statute book. In this way the Nuremberg Laws expressed understandings, expectations, and practices already firmly established in government and acquiesced to by the populace.[4]

We have already encountered **Luise Solmitz**, the national conservative wife of converted Jew and decorated war hero Fredy Solmitz. Having experienced her family's increasing social isolation over the last couple of years, Frau Solmitz now described in her diary the moment of their legal exclusion. Like others who had never enjoyed any affiliation to Judaism or the Jewish community but now found themselves in the circle of the damned by dint of the Nazis'

---

2. Longerich, *Politik*, 102ff.

3. See document 6-13.

4. The importance of gradual radicalization, as opposed to central planning, has been stressed particularly by historians of the so-called functionalist school. From a broad spectrum of publications, see, e.g., Hans Mommsen, "The Realization of the Unthinkable: The 'Final Solution of the Jewish Question' in the Third Reich," in *The Policies of Genocide: Jews and Soviet Prisoners of War in Nazi Germany*, ed. Gerhard Hirschfeld (Boston: Allen & Unwin, 1986), 97–144. While capturing the evolutionary character of the process, the functionalists are criticized for underplaying the degree to which Hitler, from time to time, provided clear signals, often well in advance of eventual legislation. For a summary of the debate, see Ian Kershaw, *Hitler, the Germans, and the Final Solution* (New Haven, CT: Yale University Press, 2008), 303–40.

racial definitions, she was particularly conscious of the extraordinary line that fate had drawn between, on the one side, herself, her Jewish husband, and her *"Mischling"* daughter, and, on the other, her seemingly oblivious non-Jewish contemporaries enjoying late summer in Hamburg.

Luise Solmitz instantly grasped the key elements of the new legislation: loss of citizenship, loss of the right to marry an "Aryan," and the ban on employing non-Jewish servants younger than forty-five. It was evidently not clear, however—and there was nothing in the bare-bones legislation announced at Nuremberg to enlighten her—that mixed-race Jews, including her daughter, Gisela, might not be subject to the full impact of these prohibitions. Since the Civil Service Law of 1933 had defined as Jewish even those with just one Jewish grandparent, Solmitz was evidently resigned to the same procedure now.

DOCUMENT 7-1: Luise Solmitz, diary entry for September 15, 1935, FZGH 11 S 11 (translated from German) (stray punctuation in the original).

[. . .] Today meeting of the Reichstag in Nuremberg, the first time [held there] in 400 years. I've been waiting for it to begin for days, feeling afraid. I'm jealous [of our acquaintances] & the cheerful people in the beer gardens: they can calmly look forward to the evening of this beautiful autumn day as much as they did its beginning. Today our civil rights were cut to pieces, the black, white, and red flag—far too holy for the reactionaries[5] to hide behind—has been sullied for the second time & survives only in the form of our national colors.

I was sitting anxiously by the radio around 9:00 p.m. The Führer himself was speaking; his voice is clear, much clearer than before the operation.[6]

1. We don't meddle in foreign affairs.

2. Strong words against the humiliating treatment suffered by our fellow Germans in Lithuania.[7]

---

5. Generally, the German term *die Reaktion* used by Solmitz describes the ultraconservative political Right; in this case, it is not clear to which groups she is referring.

6. Hitler underwent a minor procedure in late May 1935 to remove "an unusually large vocal polyp." (Ulf Schmidt, *Karl Brandt: The Nazi Doctor, Medicine, and Power in the Third Reich* [London: Hambledon Continuum, 2007], 82–83).

7. With increasing intensity during the second half of the 1930s, the German government propagandized the real or imagined plight of "ethnic Germans" living outside the Reich for foreign policy purposes. See Valdis O. Lumans, *Himmler's Auxiliaries: The Volksdeutsche Mittelstelle and the German National Minorities of Europe, 1933–1945* (Chapel Hill: University of North Carolina Press, 1998).

3. New laws.

They are apparently only being announced later. I am in an agony of expectation. One lovely piece of music came after the next & made the wait even more painful. When I went upstairs at one point, Gis. [her daughter, Gisela] was still awake: "Did he already say anything? I am so frightened. . . . I'm not only thinking of myself," Gis. continued, "but also of the others who will be hit."

And how it hit. The new laws were announced around midnight, our civil death sentence. . . .

Our black, white, and red flag is sinking for the second time. Whoever marries my daughter will be sent to prison & so will she. We will have to let the servant girl go. We're no longer allowed to fly a flag. We [don't have] a Jewish flag to fly. . . . Here only on sufferance, I can live as a foreigner in the Fatherland. . . .

I feel fortunate that we will carry these burdens together. . . . And in the end we three have a last resort.[8] On days such as this, you get an inkling of what a comfort this final possibility offers. This awareness of being together & the determination no longer to avoid facing the fact, inwardly or outwardly: we are no longer part of you, and aren't allowed to be. This awareness & this determination were the final results of the Reichstag for me.

It may be easy to think and write this, but living with it is harder. . . . Our child is an outcast, excluded, despised, deemed worthless. A mother has to suffer this. No career, no future, no marriage. Whatever the children of relations and acquaintances or [even] our domestic help are entitled to do, the things they aspire to and can achieve—these are things that G. has no chance of attaining. The school wants to know what the children are planning for the future, and G. says bitterly that she in fact can't become anything; it isn't permitted. If she is sitting among [the other] little girls, with all their hopes and dreams—G. is excluded. . . . We feel as though we are interlopers & even former convicts [*Strafgefangene*] who can never escape the stigma. We still have our house and retirement savings & are grateful for that. Let's live in a cocoon.

Striking, however, and a sign of the fascination Hitler exerted, was that throughout the 1930s Luise Solmitz would repeatedly forget her pariah status and enthuse about the regime's latest diplomatic triumphs.[9]

---

8. This is evidently an oblique reference to suicide.

9. See Richard Evans, "The Diaries of Luise Solmitz," in *Histories of Women, Tales of Gender*, ed. Willem de Blécourt (Amsterdam: AMB Press, 2008), 207–19.

Another anxious citizen glued to the radio during the (interrupted) broadcast of Hitler's speech was **Willy Cohn**. In some respects Cohn's ideological
world mirrored that of Solmitz. A forcibly retired grammar school teacher of
history, he, like Solmitz's husband, was a proud war veteran with deep ties to his
Fatherland, including a bond to German letters that made the idea of emigration hard to contemplate, despite repeated brave talk about *Aliyah*. But in other
respects, Cohn's perspective was very different. His Social Democrat sympathies
in the 1920s had left him with little love for the old national colors and far
fewer illusions than Luise Solmitz about what Hitler's "national" government
would stand for. More significantly, he was both a religiously observant Jew and
an enthusiastic Zionist within the substantial Breslau community—pre-Nazi
Germany's third largest Jewish community[10]—who had long been critical of the
more assimilatory strands in German Judaism.

Unlike many of his peers, Cohn thus welcomed the "racial" separation proposed by the laws (or at least he possessed an intellectual framework that could
rationalize acceptance and imbue it with a positive aspect). Cohn initially had
some hopes that the laws could provide the basis for a future modus vivendi
between Jews and "Aryans." At the same time, Cohn's comments about the local
sports ground reveal his keen awareness of the continuing discrepancy between
any possible positive interpretation of the laws and what was happening on the
ground. While his understanding of the promises made in relation to the Olympics was inaccurate (as the CV pointed out in an earlier document, Germany's
Olympic committee had agreed only to the participation of Jews at the Olympics and not made any commitment about local arrangements),[11] there was no
contesting the larger point that the continued steady removal of possibilities for
a normal life belied the talk of peaceful coexistence.

DOCUMENT 7-2: **Willy Cohn, diary entries for September 1935, translated from
Norbert Conrads, ed.,** *Kein Recht, Nirgends: Tagebuch vom Untergang des Breslauer
Judentums,* **1933–1941 (Cologne: Böhlau Verlag, 2007), 1:275–78.**

[September 16, 1935]

  [. . .] We heard the Führer's speech that opened the "Reichstag" in
Nuremberg around nine o'clock [on September 15]. It centered completely
around the fight against Jewry [*Judentum*] and Marxism; the laws against
Jews were also announced, and these were read following the Führer's
speech. However, the broadcast was interrupted, so as I sit here writing, I

---

  10. Abraham Ascher, *A Community under Siege: The Jews of Breslau under Nazism* (Stanford, CA: Stanford University Press, 2007).
  11. See document 5-21.

don't yet know what they say. In any event, he didn't rail against us in the extreme way that his underlings usually do; although he said that the Jewish people had caused all the problems plaguing the German people, he believed that the Reich government had taken measures that would lead to a tolerable relationship between the German and Jewish people.[12] On the whole, much was left unclear, but the papers will clue us in by and by later this morning. You certainly won't be disappointed if you were expecting things to get worse. [. . .]

In the meantime I've read the new laws; for the most part these are things one already knew in advance: a prohibition on mixed marriages, no Aryan female domestic servant under 45 years [allowed to serve in a Jewish household]; civil rights in the Reich. Jews only legal subjects [*Staatsangehörige*]. If one has watched the National Socialist movement closely, one has to have seen these things coming; they're quite consistent in this respect. Coming from a Jewish point of view, I completely welcome the ban on mixed marriages. [. . .]

[September 19, 1935]

[. . .] Bought the *Jüdische Rundschau*. It appears that the laws announced last Sunday have had a certain calming effect on German Jewish relations. On an uplifting note, Jews [*Judentum*] were recognized as a people. And with this any future for assimilationists in Germany has definitively disappeared. Hopefully they'll get the message from these developments. [. . .] Frau Reich,[13] with whom I discussed Yom Kippur; it really gave me a huge amount of pleasure! Frau Reich is still Lutheran, but she is returning to Judaism out of her deepest inner convictions, even though she was never a member of the Jewish religious community. [. . .]

Dictated a large number of letters to Trudi [his wife] in the morning, including a letter to the Hitachdut Olej Germania[14] concerning our *Aliyah* to

12. In his Nuremberg speech, Hitler had talked about his "hope of possibly being able to bring about, by means of a singular momentous measure, a framework with which the German *Volk* would be in a position to establish tolerable relations with the Jewish people," followed by the threat that, should his "hope" fail, "a new evaluation of the situation would have to take place" (quoted in Friedländer, *Nazi Germany*, 1:141–42).

13. She is the wife of Willy Cohn's college mate Joseph Reich; both emigrated to the United States in the spring of 1937. See Norbert Conrads, ed., *Kein Recht, Nirgends: Tagebuch vom Untergang des Breslauer Judentums, 1933–1941* (Cologne: Böhlau Verlag, 2007), 1:176, 383.

14. Hitachdut Olej Germania (Hebrew; later: Hitachdut Olej Germania we Olej Austria): this was an association advising Central European immigrants in Palestine. See Hitachdut Olej Germania, ed., *Die deutsche Alijah in Palästina—Bericht der Hitachdut Olej Germania für die Jahre 1936/1937* (Tel Aviv: Palestine Publishing Co., 1937).

Jerusalem!—I read in the daily paper that even though the leadership [in Germany] is attempting to reestablish a tolerable relationship between Germans and Jews [*Deutschtum und Judentum*], the little deputy Führers are doing whatever they feel like; Jews can no longer use the athletic fields in Oswitz[15]; but how can that be reconciled with the decision to hold the Olympics here?

Not all German Jews saw the new legislation as an incentive for a stronger Jewish identification. Some, like **Kurt Rosenberg**'s wife, found it hard to discount the laws' message that they were somehow inferior (*Suggestion der Minderwertigkeit*) and struggled with depression.[16] Parents and grandparents, **Julius Moses** among them, who had seen their children and grandchildren emigrate to Palestine could find comfort in their families' relative safety. In a remarkable letter, Moses already anticipated as a certainty the disappearance of German Jewry (though not the physical liquidation of German Jews), but he took comfort in the vision of a settled Israel and of his own grandchildren becoming respectable grandparents in *Erez Israel*. For them, he mused, Germany would be simply a memory of their birthplace and nothing more.

DOCUMENT 7-3: Letter by Julius Moses, Berlin, to Erwin Moses, Tel Aviv, September 1935, translated from Dieter Fricke, *Jüdisches Leben in Berlin und Tel Aviv, 1933–1939: Der Briefwechsel des ehemaligen Reichstagsabgeordneten Dr. Julius Moses* (Hamburg: von Bockel, 1997), 370–71.

Berlin, Rosh Hashanah 1935

[. . .] There is so much I still want to do. For now I want to carry on writing down my many memories! As you see, I've started up again and hopefully won't stop. This time I'm doing it to give you something to read for the New Year!! Well, enjoy!! [*Wohl bekomms*!!] I imagine my grandsons Gad and Gill [Erwin Moses's sons] sitting together in brotherly fashion 50 years from now on the evening of Rosh Hashanah, already retired, respected and established contributors to the building of *Erez Israel*, surrounded by their own children and grandchildren. And I imagine the conversation turning to their grandfather and one of the brothers going into the next room and quietly returning with the "Memoirs." And Gad would begin to recount aloud to his grandsons the story told in these pages, almost as though it were the night of Passover. Yes, he would tell the stories in these pages aloud, for his grandsons are unlikely to be familiar with the German language and won't be able to read the "Memoirs" themselves: yes, it is thoughts such as

---

15. Oswitz (Polish: Osobowice), a town located near Breslau.
16. Kurt Rosenberg, diary entry for December 29, 1935; LBINY AR 25279.

these that give me a certain inner feeling of satisfaction, of well-being. I begin to indulge in them, embrace them, if I picture how Gad, somewhat quiet and calm, Gill more temperamental—like his father and grandfather—tell their grandkids how they were still born in Berlin, why and how their parents emigrated, and also giving their grandchildren a picture of the bygone century through the "Memoirs." And I can picture how the grandkids will sit there with hot faces, hearing of the many battles and works performed by their forebears, their grandfather Gad and Gill, their great-grandfather Erwin, and their great-great-grandfather, who wrote down these "Memoirs," and to which the writings of their great-grandfather Erwin, their own grandfather Gad and Gill, then added and expanded upon, and to which the family archive assembled by their own father in turn added and supplemented. And then they will see for themselves from these stories that their forebears did not fight and suffer and battle in vain, and they will see why they have fought and suffered.

And if they compare the earlier stories with what has been achieved, they will see that the world has marched forward and how that happened, and how their own forebears did their part in bringing about that progress. And that will become an incentive for my great-great-great-grandchildren— I mean the grandkids of Gad and Gill—to seize the opportunity, in the spirit of their forebears, also to contribute to the great project of promoting progress in the world. And through this they will also contribute to the building of *Erez Israel*, this *Erez Israel*, which will at that point—around the year 2000 or so—look quite different from today: a free people on a free soil. [. . .]

In public, Jewish institutions were keen to offer as positive an interpretation of the Nuremberg Laws as they could. They wished not only to raise German Jews' morale but also to remind the Nazis themselves that Hitler's remarks accompanying the announcement of the laws had contained conciliatory (though in retrospect entirely illusory) notes about the peaceful coexistence of Jews and non-Jews. The **Reichsvertretung** issued a careful statement at the end of September expressing its hope "that by being no longer defamed and boycotted, the Jews and the Jewish communities in Germany will be able to sustain themselves spiritually and economically."[17] The Jewish intellectual jour-

---

17. Otto Dov Kulka, ed., *Deutsches Judentum unter dem Nationalsozialismus*, vol. 1, *Dokumente zur Geschichte der Reichsvertretung der Juden, 1933–1939* (Tübingen: Mohr Siebeck, 1997), 236. A draft version of the resolution had directly referred to the Reich government and the Nazi Party as those responsible for sustaining Jewish life in Germany by eradicating discrimination (Kulka, *Deutsches Judentum*, 236n9).

nal *Der Morgen*, which appeared every two months, echoed the Reichsvertretung's hope and urged German Jewry to gather behind an "autonomous Jewish
leadership."[18]

Historians, and indeed some survivors, have taken such statements as proof
that Jewish institutions failed to see the real situation. And it is certainly possible to question whether the attempt to avoid undermining morale sometimes
backfired in terms of creating an illusion of security.[19] Even so, the Reichsvertretung was not silent about the negative assumptions that underlay the racial laws.
Echoing earlier protests voiced at the height of the antisemitic wave of the summer of 1935, during *Kol Nidre* Rabbi **Leo Baeck** condemned "the lie that turns
against us, the libel directed against our religion and its testimonies."[20] Moreover, the same public statement issued by the RV on September 22 expressing
hopes of coexistence also strongly emphasized the importance of emigration
and links to Palestine. The RV's new guidelines (*Arbeitsprogramm*) acknowledged that "the fact that the emerging Jewish generation will almost entirely
(*ganz überwiegend*) have to take the path of emigration will be the determining
factor shaping our work in all areas,"[21] a radical break from the past. In effect,
for all the morale-boosting tones, the striking conclusion must be that the RV
leadership already knew in September 1935 that there was no future for Jews in
Germany,[22] an assessment reflected in the great urgency the organization placed
on fostering emigration.

---

18. "Umschau," *Der Morgen*, November 1935, 329–30.

19. See, for example, Juliane Wetzel, "Auswanderung aus Deutschland," in *Die Juden in
Deutschland, 1933–1945: Leben unter nationalsozialistischer Herrschaft*, ed. Wolfgang Benz
(Munich: C. H. Beck, 1989), 412–98 (here, 414). Wetzel cites the testimony of Auschwitz
survivor Hans Winterfeldt, given in Monika Richarz, ed., *Jüdisches Leben in Deutschland*. Vol.
3 (Stuttgart: Deutsche Verlagsanstalt, 1982), 339.

20. Kulka, *Deutsches Judentum*, 245. The printed address, signed by Leo Baeck and Otto
Hirsch, was sent to all Jewish communities in Germany, but the Gestapo prohibited its dis-
tribution. As a result of this address, Baeck and Hirsch were briefly arrested (Kulka, *Deutsches
Judentum*, 244–45).

21. "Arbeitsbericht des Zentralausschusses für Hilfe und Aufbau bei der Reichsvertretung der Juden in Deutschland für das Jahr 1935." Viewed online at http://deposit.d-nb.de/
online/jued/jued.htm (accessed June 18, 2009).

22. For an assessment of the impact of the Nuremberg Laws on the work of Jewish
organizations, see Abraham Margaliot, "The Reaction of the Jewish Public in Germany to
the Nuremberg Laws," *YVS* 12 (1977): 75–107; Herbert A. Strauss, "Jewish Emigration
from Germany. Nazi Policies and Jewish Responses," *LBIYB* 25 (1980): 313–61; *LBIYB* 26
(1981): 343–409.

DOCUMENT 7-4: Jewish schools in Germany; ZAHA calendar for 5696 (1935–1936), issued September 1935.

[Left:] "Only in Jewish schools can our children form a relationship with that kind of Jewish tradition and history, with the Jewish present and with Jewish creativity, that will enable them to go forward on their difficult life path as upright people."
[Map of Germany with dots indicating Jewish schools.]
[Right:] "Current locations of Jewish schools" in German regions and cities.

Away from the public sphere, another sign of the decisive significance ascribed to the laws by at least some influential Jews was the swift reaction of **Julius Brodnitz**, the CV president. Ever since its creation in 1893, the CV had stood for a German Jewish symbiosis. The balance between the two adjectives had undoubtedly shifted over time, with the "Jewish" element attaining more prominence in the 1920s. But even after 1933, as we have seen, the belief in some kind of distinctive German Jewish fusion persisted. In a laconic telegram, Brodnitz now proposed changes to the organization's name and statutes that with a stroke of the pen would remove any German element (except that the CV's clientele would continue to be the Jews living in Germany). It is no longer clear exactly what considerations prompted Brodnitz's proposal. Was he simply adopting the only name and goal that he felt the regime would accept, given the new legal framework? Or did he go beyond what the law required, reflecting a clear renunciation of any notion of symbiosis by Jewish leaders who had upheld it for decades? Irrespective of motive, the proposed change represented a dramatic break with tradition.

DOCUMENT 7-5: Letter by CV president Julius Brodnitz to the members of the CV central executive (*Hauptvorstand*) with a copy of an application regarding changes to the CV bylaws for submission to the Berlin district court, September 16, 1935, USHMMA RG 11.001M.31, reel 97 (SAM 721-1-69, 23–24) (translated from German).

I will be submitting this application, of which a copy is enclosed, on Tuesday, September 17 of this year at 6:00 [p.m.]. I do not believe I need to provide an explanation to our friends as to why I think the application necessary. One can quarrel with many details, but we cannot keep soliciting advice about whether we need to submit it. In the event that you have not registered your objections before Tuesday at 5:00 p.m. by sending a "reject" via telegram, I will assume you concur. If we do not hear from you, we will instead assume that you support the declaration here enclosed and, in addition, grant me all the rights of the central executive [*CV-Hauptvorstand*] and board [*CV-Hauptversammlung*] inasmuch as they are required to approve such measures. With collegial regards,

Counselor of Justice [*Justizrat*] Dr. Brodnitz

[From the application to be submitted by Brodnitz on behalf of the CV to the District Court (*Amtsgericht*) Berlin-Mitte:] Based on the Reich Citizenship Law of September 15, 1935, I feel obliged to change the name of the CV and the following provisions of its bylaws.

1. Name: § 1. "Jewish CV [Jüdischer Centralverein] e.V."[23]

2. Purpose: § 2. "It seeks to bring together Jews in Germany without regard for their Jewish religious affiliations. Its purpose is to foster Jewish life in Germany, as well as to provide legal and economic support for Jews living in Germany."

3. § 5, section 1 is deleted and replaced with: "Any Jew who is a subject [*Staatsangehörigkeit*] of the German Reich can become a member."

Brodnitz's proposal had, however, gone further than many CV members were yet willing to accept. Instead of his proposed title of "Jewish CV," board members voted to retain a claim to German allegiance with the new name Central Association of the Jews in Germany (Centralverein der Juden in Deutschland). Similar compromise formulas were adopted by the Reichsvertretung and other organizations. Yet Brodnitz, as soon became clear, had understood the regime's requirements better: in 1936, under

---

23. "e.V." (*eingetragener Verein*) denotes the CV's status as a registered association under German civil law.

direct pressure from the authorities, the CV changed its name again, this time to Jewish CV.[24]

The legislation enacted in 1933 had used the term "non-Aryan" without properly clarifying what was meant. In a similar vein, the Nuremberg Laws—the Reich Citizenship Law, the Law for the Protection of German Blood and German Honor, and the Reich Flag Law—now deployed the term "Jew" without defining it either. Only on November 14, 1935, after several meetings between state and party agencies at which Hitler hesitated to come down on one side or the other, were supplementary regulations published (the first of a long series of increasingly sinister codifications or additions to the basic laws designed to make discrimination work in practice) that sought to answer the question of who was a Jew.[25] On the face of it, the Nazi definition was simple: a Jew was a person who descended from three or four Jewish grandparents. A mixed-race Jew was defined as someone descended from one or two Jewish grandparents. In fact, however, the regulations' complexity revealed the multiple forces and political considerations determining where the Nazis drew the line between Jew and non-Jew and, thus, between outsiders and insiders.

Although the same term, "*Mischlinge*," was used for people with either one or two Jewish grandparents, the law and the regulations implicitly introduced a strong distinction between the two categories since the latter could, under certain circumstances, be treated as Jewish. (In later regulations, mixed-race Jews with one and those with two Jewish grandparents would be more clearly distinguished by the separate categories of "second-" and "first-degree *Mischlinge*.") For example, if "*Mischlinge*" with two Jewish grandparents had in some form demonstrated allegiance to the Jewish religion (e.g., paying their state-collected church taxes to the Jewish community), or if, on September 15, 1935, they were married to a Jew, then they would be deemed Jews themselves. In its attempt at disentangling the "mixed-race" issue, the regime applied a hotchpotch of "racial" (ancestry), religious (signs of Jewish practice), and social criteria (marriage to a Jew). In a similar vein, a particular oddity of the law was that, although it talked of the grandparents' "race," paragraph 2 (2) of the First Supplementary Decree to the Reich Citizenship Law determined that any grandparent would be counted as racially Jewish if he or she had belonged to the Jewish religious

---

24. See "Vorlage an die außerordentliche Hauptversammlung am 21. Oktober 1935" (Brodnitz, Rosenstock), USHMMA RG 11.001M.31, reel 99 (SAM 721-1-140, 4–7); Avraham Barkai, "*Wehr Dich!" Der Centralverein deutscher Staatsbürger jüdischen Glaubens (C.V.), 1893–1938* (Munich: C. H. Beck, 2002), 343–44. For the Reichsvertretung, see Kulka, *Deutsches Judentum*, 233–34.

25. For a compilation of supplementary decrees based on the Nuremberg Laws and other documentation, see Schleunes, *Legislating the Holocaust*.

community. As Raul Hilberg has noted, given the key importance this placed on the grandparents' *religious* affiliation, "there was nothing 'racial' in the basic design of the definition" at all; yet, it "remained the basis of categorization throughout the destruction process."[26]

The amendment to the "blood and honor" law offered an equally complex set of regulations on proscribed marriages and reinforced the distinction between mixed-race Jews with one Jewish grandparent, who were not permitted to marry either Jews or other "*Mischlinge*" (marriage to "Aryans" was not forbidden), and mixed-race Jews with two Jewish grandparents, who needed special permission before they could marry either non-Jews or mixed-race Jews with only one Jewish grandparent. The law did not make it illegal for mixed-race Jews with two Jewish grandparents to marry Jews, but, as noted above, under the supplementary decree to the Reich Citizenship Law, doing so would then redefine them as fully Jewish.

The first supplementary regulation to the Reich Citizenship Law also laid down that those Jewish veterans who had kept their positions in the civil service would now lose their posts. A second supplementary decree in December 1935 extended the forced dismissals to other Jewish state employees who had previously enjoyed exemption. To complicate matters further, both laws included provisions according to which Hitler, as Führer and Reich chancellor, could grant exemptions in individual cases. Other laws enacted subsequently allowed, as we will see in Part IV, for a legal reevaluation of the question whether a person was of "German blood" or "Jewish blood," based on the dubious criteria of racial science and national interest.

While Nazi propaganda portrayed "the Jew" as a collective threat, Jewishness as codified in the Nuremberg Laws thus appeared as anything but uniform: the laws created differentiations between "full Jews," "half Jews," and "quarter Jews," between those who adhered to the Jewish religion and those who did not, those who were married to Jewish spouses and those who were not, and—based on Hitler's discretion—those who became upgraded in their racial status to "*Mischling*," those who by way of some exemption became "regarded as Aryans" ("*Geltungsarier*"), and those who hoped in vain for exemption. Given the gradations in discrimination that the authors of the Nuremberg Laws had created, a sense of shared fate could hardly be expected to emerge among those they affected.

For Luise Solmitz, some of the Nuremberg codifications represented a positive surprise compared with what she had feared.

---

26. Raul Hilberg, *The Destruction of the European Jews*, rev. exp. ed. (New Haven, CT: Yale University Press, 2003), 77, 79.

DOCUMENT 7-6: Luise Solmitz, diary entry for November 15, 1935, FZGH 11 S 11 (translated from German).

The implementation regulations [for the racial laws] are out. We never listen to the news anymore, so we were taken by surprise. And that is actually good. It happened that Gis. [her daughter, Gisela] had gone to the city with Fr. [Luise's Jewish husband, Fredy], and I was alone in my snug Biedermeier room and contemplated our fate in the light of the green lamp. At first I just skimmed it & tried—as anyone would—to perhaps find some consolation [in the document]. And there is something: the Führer can make exceptions.

Gis. isn't a Jew, but rather a *"Mischling"* & can thus only marry someone of German descent [*Deutsch-stämmigen*] or someone who only has one out of four Jewish grandparents with special permission. No maid to be employed, if the male head of the household is a non-Aryan (but the age limit of those [maids already employed in Jewish households] "permitted" has been lowered from 46 to 35).

Those who are war veterans, have certain character or other qualities, or have roots in Germany may be subject to special considerations. I write all this down haphazardly, without a source, because Fr. needs the newspaper [with the printed regulations] for his letter to the Führer. If only he would have success. Public servant already before the war, participated in 33 battles, Iron Cross 1st class, etc. All Jewish public servants will be retired, but with full salary, without being promoted, until they reach retirement age, and then receive a pension! A very pressing burden has thus been lifted from our shoulders. What my actual status is [as "Aryan" wife to a Jewish husband] is not mentioned. Enough remains that's burdensome: no voting right for Fr., whether for me I don't know. No job prospects for Gis. Still, it sounds a little different than [at] Nuremberg. [. . .]

While Fr. was writing his letter to the Führer, I was listening to Beethoven's Sixth Symphony in the living room. I sat in the dark; the light of the moon and lantern fell on the white curtains, a wondrous atmosphere; & a heart caught up in a hundred thoughts & cares did not know whether it should sink into bitterness or hold out hope, whether it can in fact breathe a little more easily. Indeed, yes, it should.

The treatment of "Aryans" in mixed marriages would evolve substantially in later years. Although the process was complex and regionally central decisions were variably interpreted, for most such mixed marriages conditions steadily worsened. Fredy Solmitz was alone neither in writing a letter to Hitler nor in failing to achieve anything by it. Despite the laws' provision for them, exemptions were rarely made, and only a few very prominent individuals or those in vital positions were allowed any alleviation of their status.[27]

Few channels remained open to Jews in Germany and fewer still to German Jewish leaders through which they could report to the wider world on the situation in the Reich; nevertheless, information did cross the border.[28] The **World Jewish Congress**'s correspondent captured the laws' impact on Jews' social interaction. Whereas the months before the Nuremberg party congress had seen violent assaults on the grounds of interracial marriage reach a peak, now, following the laws, denunciations to the Gestapo took over as the principal means to attack those suspected of such disregard for racial propriety. In the Franconian city of Würzburg, for example, in 1934 there were only three denunciations to the Gestapo on grounds of race defilement or friendliness to Jews, but there were thirty-one in 1936, twenty-one in 1937, and twenty-eight in 1938. Neighborly spying became a vital part of the terror apparatus.[29] In addition to noting that Jews returning from abroad were arrested and incarcerated in concentration camps for at least six months, the correspondent offered a trenchant description of conditions in Germany in the "Olympic year" of 1936.

DOCUMENT 7-7: Report sent to the WJC Paris office on "The Situation of the Jews in Germany (January 1936)," USHMMA RG 11.001M.36, reel 193 (SAM 1190-3-7, 140–58) (translated from German).

The situation of the Jews in Germany appears outwardly calm. The winter Olympics that are about to begin in Garmisch-Partenkirchen and the big summer Olympics have affected everything that is happening in Germany. In the present treatment of the Jewish question—as with all other controversial topics—one sees clear efforts to avoid anything and everything that might provoke a bad public image, particularly abroad. As a result, attacks on individuals have all but ceased in recent weeks.

---

27. Luise Solmitz, diary entry for November 15, 1935; FZGH 11 S 11. See Jeremy Noakes, "The Development of Nazi Policy towards the German-Jewish '*Mischlinge*,' 1933–1945," *LBIYB* 34 (1989): 291–354.

28. For a postwar account by Reichsvertretung official Friedrich Brodnitz on his clandestine links to foreign journalists and the U.S. consulate in Berlin, see Friedrich S. Brodnitz, "Memories of the Reichsvertretung: A Personal Report," *LBIYB* 31 (1986): 267–77.

29. Robert Gellately, *The Gestapo and German Society: Enforcing the Racial Policy, 1933–1945* (Oxford: Oxford University Press, 1990), 163–64. Interestingly, in the Würzburg case, over half of those doing the denouncing were not party members, and in 30 to 40 percent of the cases, the Gestapo was unable to make the charges stick.

Nonetheless, it has been anything but quiet in the centers of such incidents such as <u>Hesse and Franconia</u>. For instance, a few days ago we received reliable reports that in the now sufficiently well-known case of <u>Gunzenhausen</u> in Franconia—where some Jews were shot as early as 1934[30]—Jews can no longer use a particular train that is popular with workers. Before the train left the station recently, groups of workers who had clearly been put up to it went from compartment to compartment insulting and harassing Jewish passengers in the crudest way imaginable.

[. . . ; after a long list of examples of anti-Jewish measures, the author addresses the impact of the Nuremberg Laws:] It is deeply disturbing to see the human tragedies that arise as a result of these racial laws; they must touch anyone who is used to looking a little below the surface. Relationships between men and women, some of which stretch back for decades, are being torn apart. Even if they manage to survive all the laws, they are poisoned by the fear of every ring of the doorbell, of every letter that might become fodder for a spy to open and to read. The times teem with blackmail and threatening letters of every sort imaginable. Informers and the purveyors of denunciation and human baseness have found fertile ground on which they eagerly sow jealousy, hatred, and resentment. [. . .]

[The report continues with a discussion of new economic measures enacted against Jews; . . .] The curtain appears to have fallen on that tragedy known as "German Jewry" [*Deutsches Judentum*] with the very effectively staged proclamation of the Nuremberg Laws. The naive theatergoer sits in the auditorium, and because the curtain is now down and he no longer hears sounds emanating from the stage, he may come to believe that this tragedy has played out to its conclusion. A nasty misapprehension: those who are more clued in know what is still being acted out behind the curtain. <u>The next act is being assembled</u>, quickly and energetically, albeit without any noise, without disruption to the theatrical illusion. [. . .]

The curtailing of these crude antisemitic weapons—which, incidentally, will reemerge with redoubled intensity after the Olympics—must not mislead one into thinking that the merciless battle of economic extermination against Jews has somehow ceased; it carries on undiminished. Only the methods have changed and gotten subtler, quieter, yet they remain just as effective. They have their effect behind the curtain without arousing much attention. What has become evident is that the Jews can

---

30. On the murder of two Jews in Gunzenhausen in 1934, see Michael Wildt, *Volksgemeinschaft als Selbstermächtigung: Gewalt gegen Juden in der deutschen Provinz, 1919–1939* (Hamburg: Hamburger Edition, 2007), 174; Kershaw, *Hitler, the Germans, and the Final Solution*, 159–60.

be ruined [*zu Grunde richten*] even without the laws and decrees that only provoke negative publicity abroad. One can reach the same goals through administrative methods. Notice was given of laws that would regulate the economic activities of Jews, but they have not appeared. Most likely they have been held back until after the Olympics. But in the meantime, one can achieve whatever one desires. [. . .]

Other outside observers, such as the German Social Democratic Party in exile, concurred. Despite the apparent calm, as the Social Democrats learned through their network of underground informants, the everyday war against the Jews continued with little interruption.[31]

COULD ONE LIVE IN THE NEW GERMANY?

Was it still possible for Jews to earn a living in Germany? Here, as the WJC report and the following examples show, experience continued to be mixed. In some areas a reduction in street violence allowed a certain improvement in trading conditions; however, many were still selling up or were held back from doing so only by uncertainty as to whether they would be able to transfer their capital abroad. In some areas in Germany, particularly in East Prussia and other eastern territories, conditions were so bad that Jews found it hard to enter shops as customers, let alone run a business.

DOCUMENT 7-8: Letter by Rabbi Dr. Karl Rosenthal,[32] Berlin, to CV head office, quoting anonymous letter from Preussisch-Holland, East Prussia, September 26, 1935, USHMMA RG 11.001M.31, reel 183 (SAM 721-2-172, 35) (translated from German).

[. . . ; quote from anonymous letter:] One encounters signs on all the grocery stores and in many other shops announcing that we are not allowed to shop there; being forced to come by a bit of food through some illicit source is only the lesser evil, even though this is not particularly conducive to one's feeling of human dignity or self-

---

31. See the reports compiled by the German Social Democratic Party in exile cited in Longerich, *Politik*, 116–17.

32. Presumably this is Dr. Karl Rosenthal (1889–1952), Reform rabbi in Berlin and World War I veteran. Active in the CV and B'nai B'rith lodge, he was arrested several times before moving to England. His wife, Trudie (née Schuster), and one son fled to Amsterdam before being arrested; his wife survived Bergen-Belsen concentration camp. Karl had followed one of their sons to the United States, where he settled in North Carolina after the war. See USHMMA RG 10.087 Karl Rosenthal family papers; LBINY catalog.

worth. Most [Jewish] travelers—if they do not by chance have a friend who will put them up—can neither find a place to stay overnight nor get a warm meal in the smaller towns. Please do not take this the wrong way; this is not intended as one long whining letter—it will take a great deal more to make us lose heart, and we can still hold our heads high despite the demoralizing effects of [our] enforced idleness. I am writing to let you know how things stand. And so, if the opportunity arises, you can use it for something, such as when you next meet up with someone who has influence. In the end, it is not just about us. [. . .]

I am forwarding this letter, which came in from Preussisch-Holland, a small town in East Prussia, to you with the hope that the "tolerable relationship" of which the Führer spoke a short time ago,[33] will soon bring an improvement in the situation. [. . .]

Even in comparatively quiet cities like Bielefeld, Westphalia, Jewish community leaders warned against congregating, implying that gathering in front of the synagogue could trigger the ire of local antisemites.

---

33. This refers to Hitler's speech in which he announced the Nuremberg Laws. See Chapter 7, note 12.

DOCUMENT 7-9: Flyer handed out by Jewish community Bielefeld, November 7, 1935, USHMMA Acc. 2008.292 Kronheim collection, box 2.

Zur Beachtung !

Dringend ersucht

wird, das Stehenbleiben vor dem Gotteshause

nach dem Gottesdienst zu unterlassen.

Dringend widerraten

wird, den Weg zum und vom Gotteshaus in

größerer Gesellschaft zurückzulegen.

Der Gottesdienst am Tage des **Versöhnungsfestes,** Montag, den 7. Okt., findet **ohne Pause** statt.

Take note!

It is strongly recommended to refrain from standing in front of the synagogue [*Gotteshaus*] after the service.

It is strongly advised not to walk to and from the synagogue in larger groups.

The Yom Kippur service on Monday, October 7, [1935,] will be held without intermission.

DOCUMENT 7-10: File note by CV head office Berlin for department heads (*Dezernenten*), November 6, 1935, USHMMA RG 11.001M.31, reel 127 (SAM 721-1-2807, 7) (translated from German).

The regional branch in Pomerania has sent a report detailing the trip made by several of their officials through the province:

The outlook among [Jewish] retail shop owners has become more confident. Sales have increased. In some cases we learned that sales lagged only slightly behind last year's figures. In two cases we even heard that October sales levels were identical with those seen in

October of 1934. Bear in mind that October of 1934 was characterized by hoarding. Explanations for this pleasing state of affairs vary:
first, some point to the waning of attacks on single Jewish businesses
[*Einzelaktionen*]. Beyond this, the population appears to have gotten
used to seeing the remaining [anti-Jewish] banners. And finally, it is
no longer so noticeable when people go into Jewish shops because
it gets dark much earlier now. Because business has picked up, the
atmosphere of panic and the urge to sell at any price have disappeared. People are judging the situation more calmly, recognizing
the difficulties that crop up if one rents out or sells off one's means
of making a living. They realize that transferring one's property
abroad is impossible and are sitting back for the time being to watch
how things develop, albeit without—at least in most cases—having
completely dropped the idea of selling their businesses. Where owners have decided to give up their enterprises entirely, the liquidation sales have been surprisingly successful. On several occasions we
heard that customers fought over the sales items.

This relatively upbeat assessment of the situation was soon outdated. In
very small communities with no communal resources and no affluent Jews in
the locality able to provide support, life had become impossible—CV officials
called one region in Pomerania an "emergency area" (*Notstandsgebiet*).[34]

At the end of October 1935, the CV ventured yet another intervention
with the economic authorities under Hjalmar Schacht, pointing out the massive discrepancy between the ostensible toleration of Jews' economic activity
and the increasing hindrance in every sphere. The CV's petition was dead on
arrival since Reich Economics Minister Schacht, though outspoken against violent attacks on Jewish business, in fact favored the "**Aryanization**" of all Jewish
businesses over the next five to ten years.[35] Thus, when the CV complained that
local authorities were interpreting the 1933 ban on unauthorized local actions
merely as an injunction against *violent* measures, the CV was, in fact, criticizing
the Reich minister's own tacit position. Most likely the CV's leaders did not
know about Schacht's endorsement of Nazi economic antisemitism, though in
their petition they tried to exploit his pride as much as his sense of principle.

---

34. CV office Schneidemühl to CV head office, July 30, 1936; USHMMA RG
11.001M.31, reel 101 (SAM 721-1-2316, 103–6).

35. See Albert Fischer, *Hjalmar Schacht und Deutschlands "Judenfrage": Der "Wirtschafts-
diktator" und die Vertreibung der Juden aus der Wirtschaft* (Cologne: Böhlau Verlag, 1995).

After all, it was his earlier decrees calling for the "pacification" of the German economy and the end to boycott measures that were being so blatantly disregarded. In any case, whether they had an inkling of his views or not, the CV's leaders had no other person in a position of power who offered even the vague appearance of being willing to listen.

DOCUMENT 7-11: Letter by CV head office Berlin to CV regional offices and officials with a copy of a petition to the Reich Economics Ministry, October 30, 1935, USHMMA RG 11.001M.31, reel 135 (SAM 721-1-2915, 567–72) (translated from German).

[. . . ; petition starts with examples of boycottlike exclusion of Jews from the economy.]

Of great importance, however, is the fact that since the Nuremberg Laws Jewish entrepreneurs have been urged <u>very insistently</u> to sell off their businesses. A number of significant [press] articles have supported these suggestions, and a great many rumors have promoted the idea that even the Reich Economics Ministry is reckoning on the complete exclusion of Jews from the German economy within a year. We know that press notices to this effect have been declared untrue. Nevertheless, we feel obliged to draw attention to these and more radical utterances, which render the pressure [on Jewish businesses] to sell-out even more acute. [. . .]

The uncertainty about whether businesses can really carry on without interference has increased due to the fact that, despite the ban on individual actions [against Jewish establishments], <u>none</u> of this summer's <u>boycott measures has been rescinded.</u> The ban on individual [anti-Jewish boycott] measures [*Einzelaktionen*] has repeatedly been interpreted as referring only to <u>violent</u> interference with the public's business freedom.

[. . .] If the current level of mental and economic stress continues for a longer period of time, Jewish entrepreneurs will no longer be able to conduct their business responsibly and the collapse of numerous economically viable businesses will be inevitable. This danger can be averted only if the current tensions [*Spannungszustand*] subside. <u>One way to do this would be an announcement that reinstitutes the former economic guidelines.</u>

The decrees for economic pacification [*Wirtschaftsbefriedungserlasse*][36] all remain in effect, but the practices we have seen in the past months sharply deviate from them. The public no longer believes they are valid but rather must conclude that the state wants to discontinue economic intercourse [with businesses owned by Jews]. Economic pacification can be achieved only if customers are publicly (i.e., in newspapers and on the radio) reminded that these regulations remain effective; in other words, if they are told along the lines of the regulation issued on September 1, 1933, that in regard to economically active persons no difference is made between Aryans and Jews.

Banning individual measures—which were, as mentioned above, furthermore interpreted narrowly as violent measures—produces at best passive behavior: the photo service [surveillance of customers who frequented Jewish-owned shops by taking their photographs and publicizing their "un-German" behavior] ceases; pickets are no longer being posted outside shops [to enforce the anti-Jewish boycott]. Yet instead of economic vitality, the quiet of the morgue [*Friedhofsruhe*] has fallen over the businesses. The crippling pressure exerted on customers continues; they fear fallout from the measures put in place during the late summer. These prohibitions have never been rescinded and thus remain in effect.

Consequently, in addition to again publicizing the regulations on the economy, only a general lifting of all economically restrictive measures (boycotts, prohibitions for public servants and employees, interventions by the German Labor Front or the National Socialist People's Welfare Organization [Nationalsozialistische Volkswohlfahrt, or NSV] and the branches of the Reich Farmers' Guild [Reichsnährstand], exclusion from public bids, dismissal of staff due to their Jewish ancestry, investigations into the origin of sales items) can eliminate the disruption to economic life.

In the most difficult conditions that Jewish entrepreneurs have faced since April 1933, we feel obliged to present this statement of facts both in the interest of those affected and because of the inevitable repercussions for the economy as a whole.

---

36. On September 1, 1933, the Reich Economics Ministry issued a regulation disallowing boycotts or related measures against legal enterprises. A regulation issued on November 24, 1933, by the Reich labor minister criticized the laying off of Jews employed in private companies and confirmed the nonexistence of "exclusionary laws" (*Ausnahmegesetze*) for Jews. See Joseph Walk, ed., *Das Sonderrecht für die Juden im NS-Staat: Eine Sammlung der gesetzlichen Maßnahmen und Richtlinien—Inhalt und Bedeutung* (Heidelberg: UTB, 1996), 50, no. 236; 62, no. 296.

Signed:

Counselor of Justice Dr. Brodnitz   Dr. [Hans] Reichmann

President   Syndic

Document 7-12 appears particularly revealing of the times, in part because it expresses characteristic uncertainties and tensions and in part because of its idiosyncrasy. It reminds us how difficult it was for individuals to gauge the best way to respond to current economic challenges. What skills should young people who were thinking of emigrating acquire? Should they try to complete formal education or training within Germany so as to present a more rounded list of accomplishments to a receiving country? Or should they try to get out now and complete their training abroad later, when finances allowed? During an era in which skilled craftsmen might find themselves better placed to emigrate than businessmen or professionals, farm workers might be more desirable to recipient countries than craftsmen, and women willing to work as domestic servants might have better prospects than any men, none of the old rules applied.[37]

The closure of most traditional educational and professional-training opportunities to young Jews in any case challenged conventional ideas about how to prepare for life ahead. The unpleasant novelty of the situation led many children to doubt the relevance of parental wisdom and experience. Moreover, since such training options as existed were increasingly concentrated in Jewish-operated institutions—for example, the *Hachsharah*, or farms that offered agricultural training prior to emigration to Palestine—Jewish children were often removed from the parental tutelage to which, under normal circumstances, they would have been subject. This, in turn, allowed tensions and anxieties to come to the fore as parents battled to preserve their authority. If few fathers can have been quite so directly judgmental as Georg Rosenberg, his predicament would have been familiar to many German Jewish parents reduced to offering wisdom via letter to distant offspring.

DOCUMENT 7-12: **Letter by Georg Rosenberg, Frankfurt am Main, to Kurt Rosenberg, Wetzlar (Hesse), March 2, 1937, translated from Oliver Doetzer, "Aus Menschen werden Briefe": Die Korrespondenz einer jüdischen Familie zwischen Verfolgung und Emigration, 1933–1947 (Cologne: Böhlau Verlag, 2002), 36–37.**

Dear Kurt,

We have your nice letter from "Saturday at noon" and were as always pleased to hear from you. But this is not to say that we necessarily agree

---

37. See Adler-Rudel, *Jüdische Selbsthilfe*, 73.

with all your opinions. Stylistically, I think it is manlier to date letters. Noting the weekday and time gives a childish, even feminine [*weibisch*] impression. But that is only an aside, not worth starting an argument over. If you disagree with me, you can do it differently. Are we worrying *too much* about you? You are no better a judge than we are, for only the future will tell. But, of course, just because things develop one way, that doesn't prove a different path wasn't possible.

You are certainly wrong, though, if you think that I want to persuade you to emigrate as soon as possible. I thought I had made my view on this issue sufficiently clear, so clear, in fact, that now Hermann [Kurt Rosenberg's older brother] feels he has to advocate the complete reverse. I think we all have to stay calm and should not make any life-altering decisions just because of pressure or some impression derived from the news or a worry, which hopefully will turn out to be unfounded tomorrow. I have always said to you that for the time being you have to pursue only one goal, that of learning a useful skill [*etwas tüchtiges*]. And I agree with you that there is no better place to do this than in your own business. Didn't I make the same point in the letter to Hermann I sent you?

Why in your last letter (Saturday at noon) did you suddenly decide to adopt the opposite position and make yourself out to be a hero, which, given the situation, is hardly appropriate? But let's say that everything was the way you assume it is—and the views of other people so different from yours[38]: then who has to bear the final consequences if you are wrong??!! Turning 21 and becoming a legal adult is usually just a day passing on the calendar and reveals nothing about how mature you are. I would no longer have played with a toy car when I was 16 or 17 [implication: as you did]. But even leaving aside this particular case, which I certainly don't want to blow up in importance, you generally seem rather immature. The fact that you don't acknowledge it yourself is yet more proof and one more reason why we should not rush your emigration until your character has formed more fully. Unfortunately, I am all too happy to believe what you say, even without your fervent declarations that you indeed still have <u>very, very, very</u> much to learn. And I am less likely to overestimate you than you apparently believe. But expressing such contempt for the businessman [*Kaufmann*] is hardly a sufficient qualification for becoming a competent specialist [*tüchtigen Fachmann*].

Do not make too much of the purposeful, systematic propaganda you encounter nowadays. Don't let it cloud your view of what is actually happening. If you think about it, the technical specialist today is as overrated

---

38. This passage remains obscure because the German text is not clear in its meaning.

as the worker in general or the farmer, just because we have great need of their services. Those who can think back a little longer might remember with how much contempt we used to speak about—and particularly think about—"specialists" or farmers and workers. That was of course as wrong as doing the opposite nowadays. But during relatively normal conditions a really capable businessman can provide for himself at least as well as a competent specialist. He is never as vulnerable to economic cycles, though, and he is also more independent in terms of his time and where he has to be. And so, for a young man such as yourself, the goal you ought to pursue very earnestly and conscientiously should be finding a way to combine your talents and becoming both a specialist and a businessman. The people who manage to do this will surely achieve something in life most easily. [. . .]

Love,

Your father[39]

The dismal situation could cause family strains of quite a different kind too. For many women, pregnancy was too much of a burden. While the Jewish birthrate, already comparatively low before 1933, further decreased, the number of abortions rose.[40] In early 1939, as a result of what appears to have been a denunciation, the thirty-year-old Jewish woman Hanny R. was dragged into a criminal investigation against Meta H.,[41] a non-Jewish midwife who by that time was already serving time in a Berlin prison on another matter, for having performed an abortion on Hanny R. three years earlier. Though abortion was a criminal offence in Germany until well after World War II, Nazi revisions to the law permitted exceptions (e.g., for eugenic reasons to prevent the birth of racially "unwanted" children). In this case, Hanny R., a mother of two desperate not to have another child, became a codefendant used by German law-enforcement agencies as evidence against Meta H., the midwife. No source exists that speaks directly to R.'s predicament; instead, her voice reaches us only through the distorted and sterile format of a Gestapo interrogation report.

---

39. Georg Rosenberg (b. 1878) died after having been deported to the Łódź ghetto in August 1942. Kurt Rosenberg, born in 1916, emigrated to the United States in February 1938 and was killed as a U.S. Army soldier in April 1944. His brother, Hermann Rosenberg (1915–1984), had emigrated to the United States in December 1936. See Maierhof, Schütz, and Simon, eds. *Aus Kindern wurden Briefe*, 276–77.

40. See Marion A. Kaplan, *Between Dignity and Despair: Jewish Life in Nazi Germany* (New York: Oxford University Press, 1998), 82–83; Cornelia Usborne, *Cultures of Abortion in Weimar Germany* (New York: Berghahn Books, 2007).

41. Last names are rendered anonymous by the authors.

DOCUMENT 7-13: Gestapo interrogation protocol of Hanny R., Berlin, January 24, 1939, regarding her abortion performed by an "Aryan" midwife in the spring of 1936, USHMMA RG 14.070M, reel 416 (LAB A Rep. 358.02), case 22666, frames 816–17 (translated from German).

[. . .] I have been made aware of the purpose of my interrogation. I am ready to tell the pure truth.

I admit to having had a miscarriage, which was induced by an illegal intervention. In February 1936 I failed to get my period and concluded that I was pregnant. I already had two children and no longer wanted to deliver a third because for us Jews there is really no prospect of getting on. I turned to a known midwife, Frau H., at the time a resident of Mendelsohnstrasse 16, today Rombergstrasse, and asked if she would like to help me. Frau H. refused at first but sent me away by saying I should come back again. She made objections, saying that she did not like to do it because it carried severe punishments. A day later I again went to Frau H., and now she was willing to perform the procedure [*Eingriff*]. [. . .] The midwife asked for and received RM [Reichsmark] 10 for the procedure.

I cannot identify any further other women who went to H. and allowed the fetus [*Leibesfrucht*] to be aborted. I have also sent no women to Frau H. for the purpose of obtaining an abortion.

I have read this document in person, approved and signed it: [signed Sara Hanny R.[42]].

In another interrogation by the Berlin state prosecutor, Hanny R. confirmed what she had told the Gestapo but added that at the time of the abortion, her family's economic situation had already been dismal and that Meta H., who knew R. as a child, had performed the abortion to help her. Hanny R., her husband, Kurt, and their children, Fred and Helga, born 1930 and 1933, were deported to Auschwitz-Birkenau in March 1943 and murdered there.[43]

For Jewish children, the new racial barriers had closed off almost every career path. In the weeks after the Nuremberg Laws, the Jewish careers advisory

---

42. A directive issued on August 17, 1938, required Jews within the Reich's territory to add a middle name, either Israel or Sara (depending on their gender) by January 1, 1939. See Walk, *Sonderrecht* 237, no. 524, and below. Note the reference in the document to the renaming of streets honoring prominent German Jews, in this case Jewish philosopher Moses Mendelsohn (1729–1786).

43. See www.bundesarchiv/gedenkbuch.de.

service in Frankfurt am Main carried out a survey of 135 Jewish children—67 girls, 58 boys—who were preparing to leave their (Jewish) school and look for work. The article in document 7-14, which discusses the survey results, is revealing on a number of levels. Along with other information generated, the statistics on the children's youth group affiliations offer an insight in miniature into the lack of appeal of any kind of avowedly German Jewish movement—at least for those attending a Jewish school. No doubt the picture might have been somewhat different if the survey had included Jewish pupils still in normal state schools. Even so, the strength of the Zionists' appeal was striking, since, traditionally, Zionist groups had enjoyed much more resonance among Eastern Jews. Furthermore, the special challenges of living in the Third Reich did not shape everything in the survey results. The collision between young people's dreams (or sometimes their lack of clear ambition) and the hard realities of the labor market had, after all, been a phenomenon familiar to career advisors long before 1933. Nazi discrimination aside, the girl who wanted to be an airline pilot would probably have ended up with a desk job under any circumstances. New, however, was that pupils at the higher schools, most of them from middle-class homes with parents working as businessmen or professionals, now contemplated leaving school at fifteen or sixteen.

DOCUMENT 7-14: Dr. Rudolf Stahl,[44] Frankfurt am Main, "Job Wishes of the Youth," *Jüdische Wohlfahrtspflege und Sozialpolitik* 5 (1935): 185–89 (translated from German).

I. Between the beginning of September and the end of October 1935, at the instigation of the Jewish career counseling center, some 130 male and female pupils in Frankfurt am Main wrote essays on the following questions: "What career do I want to pursue? How did I arrive at my choice? What do I think the work will be like?"

Pupils from the graduating class of the Frankfurt Jewish primary schools [*Volksschulen*] contributed to the study, as did the two tenth grade

---

44. Dr. Rudolph F. Stahl (1899–1996), a lawyer and World War I veteran, was active in many youth and Jewish organizations before becoming a functionary of the Reichsvertretung in 1933. He lived in Frankfurt am Main and emigrated to the United States in 1937 with his wife and children. See Kommission zur Erforschung der Geschichte der Frankfurter Juden, *Dokumente zur Geschichte der Frankfurter Juden, 1933–1945* (Frankfurt am Main: W. Kramer, 1963), 551; Werner Röder and Herbert A. Strauss, eds. *Biographisches Handbuch der deutschsprachigen Emigration nach 1933*, Bd. 1, *Politik, Wirtschaft, Öffentliches Leben* (Munich: K. G. Saur, 1980), 719.

classes [*Untersekunden*] of the Jewish high school, whose pupils would
with few exceptions be leaving the school at Easter. [. . .]

II. The social composition of the graduating classes [*Abgangsklassen*]
was evaluated in a special statistic based on questionnaires filled in by
65 male and 70 female pupils; 91 of the 135 children went to primary
schools, 44 to high schools. Of the 135 parents [heads of households],
85 have professions in trade, 24 as artisans, and 13 are self-employed or
officials [*freie und Beamten-Berufe*; the latter presumably with Jewish orga-
nizations]. For 13 parents, no profession was noted, partly due to unemployment or as the father was already deceased. [. . .]

The following breakdown shows the pupils' nationality:

Nationality	Primary School	High School	Total
German	45	42	87
Polish	30	1	31
Stateless	11	1	12
Other foreigners	5	—	5
	91	44	135

The sense of community [*Gemeinschaftswillen*] among the children
is typically revealed by their membership in a youth organization. The
breakdown for the 135 children is as follows:

Youth Groups[45]	Primary School	High School	Total
Aguda	4	1	5
Mizrachi	14	1	15
German Jewish	1	1	2
State Zionists [*staatszion.*]	7	7	—
Various Zionist groups	2	17	19
Sports clubs	6	6	—
Not members	57	24	81
	91	44	135

III.

The careers which these students desire often conflict with the wishes
of their parents; this is particularly the case for girls, whose essays often

45. *Aguda* refers to the orthodox Agudas Jisroel; *Mizrachi* to religious Zionists; German
Jewish to the BDJ and similar mainstream Jewish youth organizations; state Zionists to the
Staatszionistische Organisation under Georg Kareski.

mention or reject their parents' viewpoint. While the parents often plan for the girls to become seamstresses or go into some kind of domestic work, their daughters prefer to become kindergarten teachers or office workers.

In thinking about possible occupations, many children cling to an imagined ideal career that they are reluctant to jettison for more realistic options. They look for a compromise, some solution that will offer a limited measure of satisfaction. Instead of a legal career, they might choose a career in sales; instead of medicine, they might opt for work in a chemical laboratory; and instead of learning languages, the girls opt to become photographers or librarians. A girl who actually wanted to become a pilot writes of other possibilities after weighing up various factors: "I will probably end up in an office after all, since one needs a well-ordered life."

Career counselors face a particularly difficult challenge in the case of students who are completely undecided about which careers to pursue. [. . .]

This indecision mainly crops up among children in high school, while the children who were in primary school almost without exception mentioned a very specific career choice. The indecisiveness among students in high school naturally stems in part from the fact that the children until very recently had no intention of leaving school and already entering the working world. Many essays from this segment of students in particular makes very clear that the children were caught almost completely off guard by the question about careers.

The career choices can be broken down as follows:

BOYS			
CAREER CHOICES	PRIMARY SCHOOL	HIGH SCHOOL	TOTAL FIGURE
Locksmith/metalworker	1	—	1
Auto mechanic	5	—	5
Pilot	1	—	1
Carpenter	7	1	8
Electrical engineering technician	4	2	6
Precision tools mechanic	1	1	2
Artisan/skilled worker, various types	12	3	15
Landscape gardener	6	1	7
Chemist	—	1	1
Sales personnel	1	5	6
Undecided [*Unbestimmt*]	2	4	6
	40	18	58

GIRLS			
CAREER CHOICES	PRIMARY SCHOOL	HIGH SCHOOL	TOTAL FIGURE
Seamstress	17	—	17
Milliner	3	—	3
Gardener	7	—	7
Hairdresser	1	—	1
Home economics	7	3	10
Photographer	1	1	2
Nurse or baby nurse	1	2	3
Kindergarten teacher	2	2	4
Sales personnel	6	1	7
Gymnastics teacher	—	1	1
Pilot	—	1	1
Undecided	—	10	10
	45	21	66
Boys, see above	40	18	58
[Overall total:]	85	39	124

IV.

One sees that most of the essay writers are clearly conscious that Jewry [*Judenheit*] is experiencing occupational restructuring and that the Jewish occupational profile has been unhealthy for a long time. A boy who wishes to make youth *Aliyah* to Palestine as a worker expressed this in the following words: "This is precisely our unnaturalness [*Unnatürlichkeit*]; we always think about the liberal professions and management positions and find it difficult to imagine that someone could be a worker for his entire life."

Even those who are most indecisive are conscious of the fact that they are caught up in a larger process of social restructuring. This was stated most explicitly by a boy who wishes to become a salesman and who ended his essay with the following: "I am a Jew and must share the fate of Jews and—I want to share it." Particularly those youth who want to go to Palestine are very conscious of being able to take a part in building up a society and definitely wish to realize this goal. Even the girl who wants to become a pilot expressed this wish; she hopes to work in this career in Palestine.

Many of the young people see their careers as a means to make a life for themselves and earn a living. In only a few cases do the pupils indicate that the career choice is also a real vocation. Many do not yet see the purpose of careers and avoid any discussion by resorting to a general philosophical statement, using phrases such as "the real world will soon come knocking" or "when school ends, a person's real life begins." [. . .]

VI.

When we asked pupils what they thought working in their career of choice would actually be like, many of the essayists naturally indicated the country in which they hoped to pursue their career choices. In this case the girls deviate markedly from the boys. While only around 40 percent of the girls mentioned a country, the percentage of boys was around 80 percent. Among those who in any way mention the country where they will take up their future occupation, Palestine unquestionably appears first on the list. Among the 58 boys, 27 want to go to Palestine, but only 20 of the 67 girls do. The high school students generally tend to be less inclined to go to Palestine as opposed to other foreign countries, for which they hope in many cases to use family ties. But these are often quite vague ideas, as evidenced by a sentence written by a boy who wants to take a ship heading for Palestine "or to other countries that you can find in the atlas." [. . .]

In concluding, Stahl noted that it could "be taken as a given" that "educational training will need to be geared mainly toward career paths abroad." Once again, here were Jewish representatives in 1935 stating quietly but clearly that there was no Jewish future in Nazi Germany.

CHAPTER 8

BONDS AND BREAKS
WITH GERMANY

EMIGRATION REVISITED

Did the **Nuremberg Laws** leave Germany's Jews dismayed at their legal exclusion or reassured that their status had been codified? As we have seen, historians have often assumed the latter. For many Jews, they argue, the twelve to eighteen months following the 1935 laws were reasonably settled. According to the **Gestapo** and SD's account of Jewish opinion in Nuremberg's aftermath, Jews were indeed relieved that a firm legal framework had replaced arbitrary terror and hoped that they would enjoy protection as a recognized minority.[1] The fact that emigration levels remained below those of 1933 seems also to point in this direction of illusory security. Some later survivor memoirs look back sadly on the alleged complacency of these years. But when we turn to the evidence in detail, the story looks rather different. As the **World Jewish Congress** report in January 1936 (Document 7-7) indicated, the situation was far from calm. What is striking is how German Jews, far from being settled, were now ready to move. In addition to emigration, there was a remarkable tendency to quit the smaller communities and seek safety in numbers. Many moved to Berlin, not only due to its still-large Jewish community but also because of important institutions—foreign consulates, for example, as well as Jewish organizations—capable of giving emigration assistance. In its 1936 report, the **ZAHA**, now a part of the **Reichsvertretung**, offered a poignant example of this process by singling out a random representative community.

---

1. Friedländer, *Nazi Germany*, 1:167.

215

DOCUMENT 8-1: **ZAHA progress report for 1936, 10; source: http://deposit.d-nb.de/ online/jued/jued.htm (translated from German).**

[. . .] As an example for the fluctuation in demography, we can add here some figures on the [Jewish] community [*Gemeinde*] of Crailsheim located in Württemberg; we need to stress that this is not an extreme example, but one randomly selected.

Membership in the Crailsheim community amounted to

In the year	1925	196 souls [*Seelen*]
In	July 1933	160 souls
In	November 1936	96 souls

This represents a decrease of 40 percent. In the last 3.5 years the community counted

0 births

11 deaths

Fifty-eight individuals left the community. Of these 58 individuals, 38 with an average age of 43 years remained in the country; 20 individuals with an average age of 28 emigrated.

Just as in almost all small municipalities, a major portion of the younger members emigrated, and a large portion of people with a higher age settled in larger communities.

Since the persons involved are often destitute, this development, as stated in the report about internal migration [*Binnenwanderung*], represents an additional burden on the social work in the receiving communities. Both movements, emigration and internal migration, lead to a growing depopulation of the smaller communities, which are increasingly less able to fulfill their tasks without material assistance provided by central institutions. [. . .]

For both the writer of the report and his readers, these were not dry figures but the alarming vital signs of a dying people. A growing number of local communities were declared areas of particular need (*Notstandsgemeinde*), defined by the Reichsvertretung as being no longer able to meet their share of communal financial commitments. By the end of 1936, some 276 out of around 1,400 surviving communities fell within this category. Others had been forced to close completely and sell off their buildings. During 1937 the process accelerated markedly. By the end of 1937, half of the Prussian Jewish communities had fewer than fifty members. In East Prussia, an area, as we have seen, subject to particular persecution, almost three out of four communities had fewer than fifty members, and over half were in the process of liquidation.[2]

Beyond the willingness to move internally, well-informed contemporary observers like **Bernhard Kahn** registered an almost panicked search for chances to emigrate.

DOCUMENT 8-2: Confidential report by Bernhard Kahn, AJJDC, European Executive Council, Geneva, titled "Jewish Conditions in Germany," November 29, 1935, AJJDC Archive AR 3344/629.

1. General Condition

At the setting up of the Jewish Laws issued in September, the German Chancellor declared at Nuremberg, that these laws were purposed to establish a tolerable relationship between German and Jew. Irrespective of whether this statement was in earnest, it must be clearly stated that the condition of the Jews since the issuance of the Nuremberg Laws becomes daily more difficult, for the reason in fact that even at the very issuance of the Laws there were definite notifications that these would be executed to the full. About four weeks after Nuremberg, the Minister of the Interior Frick declared in an address that the not too distant fixing of the execution of the Laws would also limit the position of Jews from an economic standpoint.[3] As of today, the execution of these Laws has not been set. What this will mean, when it does happen, one can hardly say. But the state of things which has in the meantime been created, becomes daily less bearable. Jewry is living in a state of the greatest insecurity and nervous unrest.

[. . . ; Kahn refers to a multitude of other difficulties for German and foreign Jews; emigration becoming more pressing and difficult for all groups.] If new and grand scale emigration possibilities are not quickly opened up, we fear that those countries bordering on Germany will be flooded with new refugees. The Jewish organizations are making every effort to quiet the excited, over-wrought, and alarmed people, and to warn them of imprudent flight into foreign countries; with the catastrophic deterioration of conditions these warnings will not have any permanent effect. [. . .]

---

2. "Arbeitsbericht der Reichsvertretung für das Jahr 1937," 2. Viewed online at http://deposit.d-nb.de/online/jued/jued.htm (accessed June 18 2009).

3. This sentence and the first in the document make reference to the supplementary decrees (*Ausführungsbestimmungen*) announced at Nuremberg to be issued later.

The report concludes by stating that "fear, insecurity, nervous unrest are the characteristics that describe the condition of the Jews in Germany today." Indeed, German Jewish authorities felt that 1936 represented the first time in which emigration was being decisively constrained not by subjective reluctance to take on the risks and costs of leaving but by a shortage of available opportunities.[4] (It is not entirely clear on what basis they made this calculation, but it undoubtedly reflected the huge numbers of German Jews seeking assistance to quit the country.) In recognition of the new mood, the **CV**, once the embodiment of German Jewish symbiosis, now saw a role for itself in offering business and other technical courses, especially for those whose skills needed retooling to boost their emigration prospects.

DOCUMENT 8-3: Internal CV head office note for Alfred Hirschberg, June 20, 1936, USHMMA RG 11.001M.31, reel 99 (SAM 721-1-113, 53–54) (translated from German).

Dr. Hirschberg,
    For the continued functioning of the CV, it is vital, as has already been mentioned, to provide the CV with new tasks that constantly legitimize it vis-à-vis its members and other agencies.
    The Kulturbund covers the area of art and culture.
    Religious questions and questions of Jewish learning are handled by the teaching houses [*Lehrhäuser*].[5]
    The Hilfsverein and the Palästina-Amt address questions of emigration.
    Consequently, what remains for the CV is mostly giving legal advice [*Rechtsberatung*], an area of work it has to share with other agencies ([Jewish] communities).
    There is one area which so far no organization has paid any attention to: the fields of scientific, economic [*volkswirtschaftlich*], and business training in the general sense. While doctors' and lawyers' associations have arranged training courses, it has only been accomplished piecemeal, given that the entire eligible group has not been included. The CV should therefore consider whether to include Jewish adult education into its activities.
    It will not be easy for such an organization [*Einrichtung*] to elicit approval from the authorities, since the task it is taking on is not an essentially Jewish

---

4. "Arbeitsbericht des ZAHA 1936," 10. Viewed online at http://deposit.d-nb.de/online/ jued/jued.htm (accessed June 18, 2009).
    5. On the *Lehrhäuser* formed for the training of adults, see Volker Dahm, "Kulturelles und politisches Leben," in Benz, *Juden in Deutschland*, 178–80.

one. On the other hand, it should cater only to Jewish people, a fact that can be expressed in a suitable manner. It should also impart some degree of knowledge and education to émigrés as they will need it in order to make a living in their new countries. In general, Jews are barred in Germany from attending the relevant public [education] institutes. [. . .]

Given the narrowing range of activities permitted by the regime and the concentration of the Jewish public's interest on a few key issues, not many options remained for Jewish organizations to take on new tasks. In September 1936, the Lower Silesian regional branch of the CV, responding to an enquiry about the possibility of increasing lectures and other CV activities, noted that only one topic was guaranteed to find an audience.

DOCUMENT 8-4: Letter by CV regional association Lower Silesia (Breitbarth)[6] to CV head office, September 14, 1936, USHMMA RG 11.001M.31, reel 99 (SAM 721-1-113, 18–20) (translated from German).

[. . .] We think the number of lectures held in local branches [*Ortsgruppen*] should be increased. Police concerns weigh most heavily against this [proposal]. For months we have sought permission to host an event in Münsterberg and in Löwen; although months ago the head of the Gestapo [*Staatspolizeistelle*] in Breslau promised us his approval, our written request again triggered a negative response.

Regarding the issue "Palestine or Diaspora," I would warn against presentations that are too theoretical. Our friends demand—by the way, not only from us, but also from the other organizations—that we address their prospects in life [*Lebensmöglichkeiten*]; they are not interested in scholarly-philosophical problems and the like. A few days ago, Herr Kellermann spoke here in front of a small audience [. . .] despite the fact that the event had been sufficiently publicized by way of advertisements and circular letters.[7] We think that in medium-sized and smaller cities, this problem is even more marked. Only the most current lecture topics draw any attendance. Reports from South Africa and from North and South America always guarantee fully occupied lecture halls. [. . .] We must consider in this context that we have no young men at our

---

6. Dr. Rudolf Breitbarth (1901–?) was an official at the Dresdner Bank in Breslau and syndic for the CV regional office Lower Silesia. His fate after the mid-1930s is unclear. See Conrads, *Kein Recht*, 1:229–30, 357; *Datenbank zur Liste der jüdischen Einwohner im Deutschen Reich, 1933–1945* (Berlin: Bundesarchiv, 2008).

7. For Heinz Kellermann, see the glossary.

disposal. In cases where these youthful and energetic men have not emigrated, they have moved to the larger cities. This is different from the Zionists. A topic like "Diaspora or Palestine" can only be discussed on the approximate level of [the journal] *Der Morgen*. This level is too high. At the same time you cannot descend below this level because then the issue turns into a polemic. Several times already I have discussed the issue of "Diaspora and Palestine" in lodge meetings along the lines of *Der Morgen*. There, too, the audience wasn't always in the position to follow the argument. [. . .]

Taken together, the results are as follows: as necessary as the intensification of our work is and as surely as we can no longer afford the luxury of conducting heroic work silently away from public view, we can be certain that our work will fail and our friends will regard it as superfluous if we deviate too far from our area of special expertise. [. . .]

CV officials from Pomerania concluded gloomily that the time for lectures in many areas had passed. The exodus, especially to Berlin, had reached "a catastrophic scale," while the intellectual life in the region had dropped to "below zero."[8] But if the will to leave Germany was evident, the will to accept German Jewish refugees elsewhere was limited and, indeed, in some cases declining. In 1933, once the initial rush over the border into France, Belgium, and the Netherlands was over, Palestine had become the most important destination for German Jews, with some twenty-six thousand traveling there in the first three years of Nazi rule.[9] As outlined earlier, the preference for Palestine was bolstered by the **Ha'avara Agreement** concluded in 1933 between the German government and Zionist organizations, which was maintained despite its many Jewish critics outside of Germany. As late as December 1935, the executive of the Jewish **Agency for Palestine** still felt it had to defend the Ha'avara deal to the rest of the Jewish world as a "practical and effective way of preventing the wholesale destruction of German Jewry."[10]

---

8. Letter by CV regional office Pomerania to CV head office Berlin, September 12, 1936; USHMMA RG 11.001M.31, reel 99 (SAM 721-1-113, 24).

9. Abraham Margaliot, "Emigration—Planung und Wirklichkeit," in *Juden im nationalsozialistischen Deutschland: The Jews in Nazi Germany, 1933–1945*, ed. Arnold Paucker (Tübingen: J. C. B. Mohr, 1986), 307n24.

10. Jewish Agency for Palestine, "Statement of the Executive of the Jewish Agency on the Subject of 'Haavara' (German Transfer)," December 10, 1935, CZA RG S53, 1626-A; facsimile reprint in Henry Friedlander and Sybil Milton, eds., *Archives of the Holocaust: An International Collection of Selected Volumes* (New York: Garland Publishing, 1990ff), 3:364–69, doc. 92.

However, as the political situation inside Palestine worsened, so too did the prospects for German Jewish immigration to the British mandate. The British announced to Jewish agencies in 1935 that in the future far fewer newcomers would be allowed into the country.[11] The number of immigration certificates (*Zertifikate*) allocated to Jews in Germany after their application had been accepted by the **Palästina-Amt** in the winter of 1935 fell to little more than 50 percent of summer 1933 levels, despite the much higher demand.[12] Few ways remained to circumvent restrictions. As spouses could enter Palestine on one certificate, some married for the sole purpose of emigration. The result was a grey marriage market more or less discreetly advertised in the German Jewish press.

DOCUMENT 8-5: Marriage ad in *Jüdische Rundschau*, September 24, 1935, 16.

Palestine ads

Marriage Pharmacist with license and certificate [*Zertifikat*] in Palestine, single, 33 years, [seeking] female in establishing pharmacy with production and sanitarium, offers [to] Pardess Tunes for Dr. Julius Ness-Ziona, Palestine

---

11. Overall Jewish immigration to Palestine from all countries fell from 61,854 to 29,727. *AJYB* 38 (1936–1937): 580; *AJYB* 39 (1937–1938): 775.

12. "Arbeitsbericht des ZAHA 1936," 30.

Overall some 60 to 80 percent of all applications to emigrate to Palestine were rejected, bringing the number of German Jews entering the British mandate down from eighty-seven hundred in 1936 to thirty-seven hundred in 1937. Over the following years, levels of German emigration to Palestine would remain reasonably constant, but it was clear that Palestine was not going to be the answer in the struggle to find a home abroad, particularly for those over age thirty.[13] As the implications of this reality sank in, it was too much for some.

DOCUMENT 8-6: Letter by CV regional association Central Germany to CV head office, August 14, 1936, USHMMA RG 11.001M.31, reel 102 (SAM 721-1-2397, 243) (translated from German).

Re: Bachmann Weissenfels.

Our liaison person from Weissenfels, the teacher Rau, informs us about the following tragic case.

Siegmund Bachmann,[14] formerly deeply committed to our cause, went over to the Zionist camp with great enthusiasm some time ago. He had firmly counted on being able to emigrate to Palestine. When he saw this possibility disappear, he was gripped by such despair that he threw himself in front of a moving train at the Weissenfels train station. He was killed instantly.[15]

The bitter irony of German Jews' situation in the 1930s was that the mounting pressure to leave was met by ever-new counterpressures to stay. Just when the worsening economic situation might have made the conclusive argument to quit the country, for example, new financial and other disincentives to emigration were put in place.[16] Currency controls were steadily tightened. This was not just perversity on the authorities' part. The Nazis' economic policy was so focused on rearmament, with so little production targeted for export, that

---

13. Strauss, "Jewish Emigration"; Adler-Rudel, *Jüdische Selbsthilfe*, 85.

14. Siegmund Bachmann was born in 1882 in Gleicherwiesen, Thuringia. See Reinhard Schramm, *"Ich will leben . . . " Die Juden von Weissenfels* (Cologne: Böhlau Verlag, 2001), 183; *Datenbank zur Liste der jüdischen Einwohner im Deutschen Reich, 1933–1945* (Berlin: Bundesarchiv, 2008).

15. Reasons for suicide often remained unclear to outsiders. On July 8, 1936, Walter Lachmann, a twenty-eight-year-old, took his own life in Zittau, Germany; the CV report attributed his suicide to "an attack of mental confusion." See USHMMA RG 11.001M.31, reel 102 (SAM 721-1-2397, 291).

16. The continuing financial benefits offered by Ha'avara were the exception that proved the dismal general rule.

the country's foreign reserves were constantly in jeopardy. According to the German Central Bank (Reichsbank), between January 1933 and June 1935 the Reich lost RM 124.8 million in currency reserves as a result of Jewish emigrants' conversion of their **Reichsmark** to foreign currencies. With total currency reserves in the summer of 1934 standing at only RM 100 million, transfer overseas at a rate of RM 6 million per month was seen as too high. As a result the Reich "flight tax," previously levied only on those with capital in excess of RM 200,000, was from May 1934 onwards extended to assets of RM 50,000 or more.[17] To gouge further value from Jewish assets, the tax was computed on the basis of the last officially estimated value of the property—regardless of the sale price received when the property was sold before emigration. Thus, the effective tax could be much higher than its nominal rate of 25 percent. What the emigrants could actually take with them was then further reduced by the punitive rate at which the Reichsbank converted foreign currency. Until the beginning of 1935, the German Central Bank paid just half the official market rate for currency conversions. Thereafter it reduced this to only 30 percent (and in later years the rate would fall much further).[18] Avraham Barkai concluded that "until 1938, a middle-class Jew with a certain amount of assets either had to have some money stashed away abroad or be possessed of a considerable degree of farsightedness in order to make the difficult decision to emigrate. Most had neither, so they stayed on—while the younger and less affluent, who had greater resultant mobility, chose to leave."[19]

According to the ZAHA's 1936 report, the "migration question" (*Wanderungsfrage*) had come to occupy center stage in Jewish social work. The report also noted a key difference from previous years: the "subjective question of the will to emigrate" had been pushed into the background by the daunting "objective question of emigration possibilities."[20] Individual initiative remained important. For emigration to the United States in particular, personal connections and the ability to find a U.S. citizen willing to provide an **affidavit** made all the difference. However, in many other cases communal negotiation of entry rights, shipping opportunities, and so forth was at least as important in facilitating Jewish migration as individual will. Some fifty-five hundred emigrants to destinations other than Palestine enjoyed the direct support of official bodies,

---

17. On the impact of Jewish emigration and the withdrawal of assets owned by Jews from the German economy, see Tooze, *Wages*, 73–75.

18. Avraham Barkai, *From Boycott to Annihilation: The Economic Struggle of German Jews, 1933–1943* (Hanover, NH: Brandeis University Press and University Press of New England, 1989), 99–100.

19. Barkai, *From Boycott*, 100.

20. "Arbeitsbericht des ZAHA 1936," 14.

but many more indirectly profited from the advice and other help that Jewish organizations provided.[21]

South Africa, for example, which like many of the British dominions had a fairly restrictive immigration policy, had over the course of 1933 to 1935 admitted more than one thousand German Jewish refugees. Jewish immigration there soared in 1936, with between twenty-five and twenty-six hundred German Jews entering the country, but domestic agitation against foreigners increased too.[22] As a result, the ruling United Party declared in September 1936 that, starting November 1, 1936, a new set of immigration regulations would be introduced. Above all, each immigrant would have to make a cash deposit of £100 instead of simply producing a guarantee for that amount—a formidable barrier for refugees who had been stripped of their assets at home. The Jewish authorities in Germany, above all the **Hilfsverein** responsible for non-Palestine emigration, scrambled to beat the deadline and managed to charter an entire ship to bring qualifying emigrants to South Africa before November 1.[23]

South America was another promising destination. As well as promoting individual emigration, German Jewish authorities also worked with an established network of organizations like the London-based Jewish Colonization Association (JCA), the Hebrew Immigrant Aid Society (HIAS) in New York, and their cooperative body **HICEM** to promote some Jewish settlements, emulating the **kibbutz** model on Argentine territory. For a while, Brazil proved willing to open its doors, and in 1936 the Hilfsverein assisted over one thousand German Jews in entering the country. Here, too, however, the domestic political scene changed abruptly. New, more rigid rules were introduced, and in 1937 Brazil accepted less than a third of 1936's intake.[24] Thus, behind the broad outlines of Jewish emigration lie a striking series of rapid changes and organized responses, as the Jewish authorities in Germany and their international counterparts in HICEM and JCA sought to open up new destinations, then had to respond when existing ones closed down.

One example of Jewish communal effort within German borders was the training school at Gross-Breesen. As even the non-Zionist organizations came

---

21. "Arbeitsbericht des ZAHA 1936," 43.

22. Louise London, *Whitehall and the Jews, 1933–1948: British Immigration Policy, Jewish Refugees and the Holocaust* (New York: Cambridge University Press, 2000), 44; *AJYB* 42 (1940–1941): 622.

23. See Linda Coetzee, Myra Osrin, and Millie Pimstone, eds., *Seeking Refuge: German Jewish Immigration to the Cape in the 1930s* (Cape Town: Cape Town Holocaust Centre, 2003).

24. "Arbeitsbericht der Reichsvertretung für das Jahr 1937," 29.

to devote more and more of their efforts to emigration, a particular focus of concern became children. In order to qualify them for emigration, the CV and other bodies saw it as vital to provide skills that were in demand in the receiving countries; that in turn required teachers, schools, and curricula.

In early 1936, more than forty leading representatives of several organizations within the Reichsvertretung—including **Leo Baeck, Otto Hirsch, Max Warburg**, and **Ottilie Schönewald**—met to discuss the creation of a training school for Jewish girls and boys in preparation for their emigration to countries other than Palestine. South America still looked promising, and the idea of a collective farming settlement there was particularly attractive to young Jews from assimilated families looking for ways to leave the Reich. At the time of the meeting, one hundred applications for the school had already been received from members of the **Bund Deutsch-Jüdischer Jugend** (BDJ, or Bund).

During the meeting, the willingness to address new challenges clashed visibly with traditional patterns of leadership and representation. Old gender imbalances were visible. On the eight person board (*Kuratorium*) elected to supervise the new school, there was only one woman; on the working committee (*Arbeitsausschuss*) with its nine male and two female members, Baeck promised Schönewald to increase the number of women; and in the work of the school, its director **Curt Bondy** expressed the need for *Mädchenarbeit*, or efforts to improve the chances for girls, as one priority area. The discussion also started off on a familiar Zionist versus non-Zionist note. Yet it was soon apparent that old antagonisms had eroded in the face of the massive tasks ahead.

DOCUMENT 8-7: File note by CV head office on a discussion "regarding the creation of a training school for Jewish émigrés," January 1936, USHMMA RG 11.001M.31, reel 98 (SAM 721-1-86, 120–26) (translated from German).

[. . .] Dr. Lubinski presents some thoughts debated among his circle of friends with regard to the emigration school. The opinion prevailing among them is that the composition of the committee, in which he is the only official Zionist member [*organisierte Zionist*], reflects an anti-Zionist bias. Furthermore, they believe that collective emigration is possible only to Palestine. The persons present here represent so many elements [within the Jewish community] that one must hope they will not confine themselves only to discussing the training school for Jewish emigrants. Finally, he asks that a special fund-raising effort not endanger the financing of the emigration and retraining enterprises that already exist. In closing he emphasizes his desire not to be misunderstood; he merely wants to point to some practical issues, not ideological aspects [*weltanschauliche Gesichtspunkte*].

Dr. Seligsohn, as chairman, responded immediately that none of Dr. Lubinski's stated concerns were substantiated. The school would be pleased to have staff members, including from Zionist circles, who joyfully offer their services. No competition with an established endeavor is desired; rather, the aim is to complement.

Dr. Hahn (Essen) is glad that establishing this institution does not call into question other Jewish work and promises cooperation; in particular he requests that the circle of participants be expanded as the work progresses.

Max M. Warburg (Hamburg), in the name of the Hilfsverein, of which he is the president, expresses his satisfaction with the establishment of the school. He indicates, however, that he regards this school as only a small beginning. There are thousands of young people who are willing to emigrate and must be prepared for it. Today he cannot understand ideological discussions about Jewish questions anymore. Incidentally, he believes that it is certainly possible to be able to influence the endeavor without sitting on a board of directors.

Justice Counselor [*Justizrat Julius*] Brodnitz abstains from commenting after Warburg's remarks.

Retired senior regional court judge [*Oberstlandesgerichtsrat i.R.*] Neumeyer (Munich) expresses his pleasure about the establishment of the school in the name of the South German Jewish communities association. He also emphasizes, however, that he does not understand inner-Jewish disputes. In southern Germany, one has been fully and completely Jewish for a long time, without regard to Jewish faction [*ohne jüdische Parteiunterstreichungen*].

Heinz Kellermann states, as the spokesperson for the youth first in line for being enrolled in the school, that the plan in its current form was not decided immediately when the school was initially discussed, but instead was developed in a roundabout way and after long discussions. Initially, a social question had arisen in the Bund [Deutsch-Jüdischer Jugend]: what will happen to the students affiliated with the Bund who had finished school and their vocational training? Next, a Jewish pedagogical problem emerged: how can one bring people imbued with a variety of sentiments about their Jewishness—from enthusiastic devotion to feelings of downright hatred—to a balanced and positive attitude toward Jewish identity? One should not establish a complete Jewish educational program but rather leave it to the lively work of the young people in the school as to how they would attain success under competent leadership.

Rabbi Dr. Levi-Mainz notes that when news of the plan reached the Hessian communities, a sigh of relief went through many circles. He would request that the financial foundation be secured quickly so that the Hessian communities could respond [to the financial plan]. He proceeds to make the following suggestions:

a. He requests that the Jewish youth from small and rural communities be given consideration when selecting students.

b. He requests that contacts be established with existing Jewish schools in order to exchange information.

c. He favors a very strong emphasis on the importance of intellectual and spiritual matters [*Bedeutung des Geistigen*] within the school curriculum.

Frau Schönewald (Bochum) for her part also emphasizes the importance of Jewish issues [*das Jüdische*] in regard to celebrations, as well as the daily routine of the school. She was thrilled to see a strong link through [the involvement of] Hanna [*sic*] Karminski, the secretary of the League of Jewish Women [Jüdischer Frauenbund]. [. . .]25

The discussions led to the creation later that year of an emigration training school (*Auswandererlehrgut*) under the leadership of Curt Bondy, located at Gross-Breesen in Lower Silesia, about twenty miles from the city of Breslau, on more than 560 acres of farmland. Gross-Breesen offered an alternative to the Zionist-led efforts for **Hachsharah** and **Aliyah** to Palestine, especially for those children who had been active in the BDJ or a similar mainstream youth organization. Demand far outstripped supply. From Mannheim, the local BDJ chairman urged **Heinz Kellermann**, the organization's leading figure, not to overlook the plight of those who seemed too old to be considered as Gross-Breesen students but too young to have been able to develop a perspective for life either in- or outside Germany.

---

25. Georg Lubinski (1902–1974), director of the Reichsvertretung's education department from 1933 to 1938, emigrated to Palestine in 1938. Hugo Hahn (1863–1967) was a rabbi in Essen and involved with *Der Morgen* and the *CV-Zeitung* until his emigration to the United States in 1939. Alfred Neumeyer (1867–1944) served as president of the association of Jewish communities in Bavaria (Verband Bayerischer Israelitischer Gemeinden) and on the CV board; he emigrated to Argentina in 1941. For information on Julius Brodnitz, Ottilie Schönewald, Heinz Kellermann, Max M. Warburg, and Curt Bondy, see the glossary.

DOCUMENT 8-8: **Letter by Erich Sonnemann, head of the Mannheim branch of the BDJ, to Heinz Kellermann, May 12, 1936, USHMMA RG 11.001M.48, reel 193 (SAM 1207-1-8, 82) (translated from German).**

[. . . ; after describing internal problems of the BDJ, Sonnemann writes,] Furthermore, we are greatly depressed by the decision of Bondy's emigration school to accept for the time being only persons up to 23 years of age. What should I now advise all my "old" comrades to do?? Truly, only two things remain: Move toward Zionism where one does not stop being a human being at age 23 or buy yourself a rope! No, seriously, Heinz, I have to tell you that this has unsettled the basis of the Bund very severely[;] what advice can you give me? If I want to be honest, I can conceive no future, none at all, for the majority of my friends here, insofar as they have not discovered an "Uncle in America." This is currently the biggest and most difficult problem for me, but it has to be solved. [. . .]²⁶

Groups like the BDJ did not see their activities merely as efforts to build a road, any road, to emigration; instead, they wanted to conserve and re-create essential elements of their distinct identity. Ironically, but not surprisingly, then, the Gross-Breesen project's kibbutz style showed that even the more assimilated German youth had been strongly influenced by Zionism. However, despite energetic efforts by the school's leaders and their supporters, neither the goal of closing the gender gap among the students nor that of communal settlement abroad could be reached; as it turned out, until 1938 only individuals or small groups found a way to leave Germany.²⁷

UNEVEN CHANCES, VARIED FATES

The Gross-Breesen school was merely one initiative among many designed to help young people into safer and more congenial environments. Organizations abroad tried to assist with visas and schooling and to find foster/guest parents;

26. This may have been Erich O. Sonnemann (b. 1910); see *Datenbank zur Liste der jüdischen Einwohner im Deutschen Reich, 1933–1945* (Berlin: Bundesarchiv, 2008). The authors have been unable to find further information about his fate.

27. On Gross-Breesen, see Werner T. Angress, *Between Fear and Hope: Jewish Youth in the Third Reich* (New York: Columbia University Press, 1988), which also includes photographs and letters from 1938 to 1943. Archival sources on the school can be found interspersed in the records of the CV (USHMMA RG 11.001M.31) and other USHMMA collections (Acc. 2000.227 Herbert Cohn collection; Acc. 2007.96 Kellermann collection).

yet, between 1934 and 1937 the number of unaccompanied children whom the Reichsvertretung's Children Emigration Section (Abteilung Kinderauswanderung) led by **Käthe Rosenheim** successfully managed to get out of Germany hovered around only one hundred per year, with most going to the United States.[28]

In the United States, the National Council of Jewish Women, aided from April 1934 by the German Jewish Children's Aid (GJCA), agreed to facilitate the emigration of 250 girls and boys under age sixteen. Yet, even for this small number, the application procedure was laborious, involving many bureaucratic hurdles both in Germany and the receiving country. Once all hurdles had been surmounted, groups of fifteen to twenty children accompanied by chaperones, mostly female teachers, made their way to the United States. In October 1936, thirteen-year-old Ruth Calmon from Berlin arrived in New York with a group led by Käthe Rosenheim. Although Ruth had the benefit of an aunt and uncle in the country who had helped greatly with the formalities at the U.S. end, her parents had not been able to accompany her and remained behind in Germany. Ruth's new guest parents took her to Cleveland, Ohio, where she wrote the thank-you letter presented in document 8-9.

DOCUMENT 8-9: Letter by Ruth Calmon, November 6, 1936, to German Jewish Children's Aid, New York, translated from Gudrun Maierhof, Chana Schütz, and Hermann Simon, eds., *Aus Kindern wurden Briefe: Die Rettung jüdischer Kinder aus Nazi-Deutschland* (Berlin: Metropol, 2004), 217.

Dear Committee,

Pardon me for not writing sooner, but everything is so new to me here that I haven't gotten around to writing much. I would like to thank you again so much for everything you've done for me.

It is, in a word, wonderful [English word in the original] here. I don't live right in the city, and that's really nice. The Thatchers [her guest parents] have a small single-family home and a garden/backyard [*Garten*]. The fact that they have a car here in America goes without saying. I go to the Junior High School [English words in the original], where everyone is very nice to me. The nicest thing, though, is that no distinction is made between Jews and Christians. Mrs. Thatcher is like a mother to me. On Saturday we went shopping in the city. I received a pair of leather shoes,

---

28. See statistics printed in Maierhof, Schütz, and Simon, eds., *Aus Kindern wurden Briefe*, 204.

tennis shoes, a hat, and a diary. At the moment, it's snowing here. Unfortunately, the snow doesn't stick. In closing, please give my regards to Miss Rosenheim and Miss Auerbach,[29] and to you, all my best.
Gratefully yours,
Ruth Calmon

In some cases, families had a chance to reunite, at least temporarily. In the spring of 1937, **Willy Cohn** and his wife Trudi from Breslau visited their son Ernst, who had emigrated to Palestine in 1935 and lived in Kibbutz Givat Brenner. In his diary, Willy Cohn gives a lengthy report of his wife's and his own impressions of life in *Erez Israel* from their arrival until their departure, mixed with reflections on their son's and their own future.

DOCUMENT 8-10: Willy Cohn, diary entries for late March to early May 1937, translated from Norbert Conrads, ed., *Kein Recht, Nirgends: Tagebuch vom Untergang des Breslauer Judentums, 1933–1941* (Cologne: Böhlau Verlag, 2007), 1:392–93, 397, 418, 425, 427, 430.

[. . . ; March 26, 1937; arrival in Haifa harbor: The revision of the passport took place on the boat without any problems. The commission worked very fast; disembarking, then a long wait in the custom's hall until everyone's luggage arrived. Commissioner, baggage carrier, altogether the landing costs us almost a pound. Finally we get out [of the custom's hall], a policeman searches even our most intimate body parts.

Outside, Ernst, he has turned into a grown man, hardly recognizable, tanned, just as one imagines a *Chaluz* [Hebrew: "pioneer"; in this context: young Jews settling in Palestine]. Very calm and even-keeled.

[. . .] Went with Ernst to the synagogue of Dr. Elk[30]—back in the days he had been a rabbi in Stettin—a big hall, halfway underground. Very overcrowded: First night of Pessach; a nice service, quite conservative. Communal singing! Emotions overwhelmed me: I was close to tears. Pessach in *Erez Israel.* Many acquaintances.

---

29. Affiliated with the Children Emigration Section of the welfare organization Zentralwohlfahrtsstelle der deutschen Juden, Eva Auerbach accompanied Ruth Calmon and more than a dozen other children as they set sail from Hamburg to New York in October 1936. Following a second trip in 1938, she remained in the United States. See Maierhof, Schütz, and Simon, eds. *Aus Kindern wurden Briefe*, 203, 212–14.

30. Max Elk (1898–1984) was a rabbi in the German city of Stettin until 1935, when he emigrated to Palestine. He founded the German Jewish community in Haifa (see Conrads, *Kein Recht*, 1:392).

While I was saying the Tau prayer [Sabbath prayer, Psalm 92:2], I thought about what kind of commitment it means to hold on to this prayer in the *Galuth* [Hebrew: exile outside the Promised Land] under completely different climatic circumstances. [. . .]

Those who prayed hardly spoke Hebrew with each other. Most of the time I also heard a German dialect. We have a great view across the sea! Cows are approaching; cars are standing around. A Jewish milieu. Today, the Arabs drive the garbage trucks. Other than that, the city is resting! [. . .]

[March 31, 1937, Givat Brenner:] The most beautiful thing here, you can get drunk on seeing it over and over again, are the young people, who have built up everything. We slept very well this night in the tent; it was even a little bit romantic. I have not slept that way since the war. [. . .]

[April 14, 1937; Jerusalem:] *Yerushalaim* [Hebrew: Jerusalem], the holy city, when will you reemerge in your old glory? While the others stayed on the roof of the synagogue, I sat in a cold room and talked to a *Yeshivah bocher* [Hebrew: student of the Talmud] from Warsaw. A lot of people here survive on what the Jews from abroad send them so that they can conduct their pious lifestyle. All *Minjanmen* positions [reference to the minimum of ten men needed for communal prayer] are already taken by *Baltlanim* [Hebrew for those living on donations from the community] so that there is no position left for me. And then we went to the Wailing Wall, [through] narrow, branching alleys, secured by the police. Again on Arab soil, past a police post. And what a memorable moment in my life, to stand in front of these cuboids for which uncountable tears have been shed. Certainly the surroundings with the beggars are not pleasant, but the stones speak about our history. We said *Tehilim* [psalms, prayers of thanks]. The psalm of the waters of Babel, and Golinski explained some of it very nicely. It was hard for me to say goodbye. [. . .]

After dinner, Professor Baer[31] came over. We talked first about academic questions (the origins of Jewish persecution during the Middle Ages) and then we discussed an eventual academic future here. For the moment he also does not see any opportunities, but he assured me in a very heartfelt way that he will keep paying attention if something comes up. He was visibly sorry for not being able to help; of course, I also did not expect that. [. . .]

[April 24, 1937, Haifa:] By accident we ended up in an Eastern synagogue. Trudi [Willy Cohn's wife] was the only woman. Polish Jews

---

31. Willy Cohn had been reading and reviewing the work of (Yitzhak) Fritz Baer (1888–1980) on Jews in medieval Spain for some time. See Conrads, *Kein Recht*, 1:88, 344–47, 416.

prayed with an *Ashkenazi* [German] accent. Very dignified figures. In these synagogues you have the impression that people are really praying, even though for us the background noise is disturbing. [. . .]

Hardly any connections could be established between Eastern and Western Jews [*Ostjuden und Westjuden*]; they live in completely separated circles. One can only hope that the next generation will find their way to one another. It is the only way we can become a unified people! The German Jews are fast losing the layer of European civilization here, without taking on Jewish values! Their mutual social support is also disappointing. They have not learned anything but forgotten a lot. For the Eastern Jews it is of course more difficult to reach a certain level of civilization, but they are sticking together, and they are extraordinarily modest, almost without any needs. I feel a certain love for the Eastern Jews since they are closer to Judaism than we are. If they position themselves against German Jews, it is because they have never been treated with much compassion by German Jewry. [. . .]

[April 28, 1937, Haifa:] The last day in *Erez Israel* begins! It is a melancholic feeling for a person who would like to stay. But there is nothing to be done about it. May G'd [God] grant that one is allowed to return. [. . .] The last days are among the most eventful of my life despite the enormous difficulties that had to be overcome. May G'd grant that I am allowed to return soon and able to participate in the construction [*Aufbau*]. [. . .]

[May 3, 1937, aboard ship off the island of Elba:] I feel very lonely. In many ways I have drifted apart from Trudi; of course, I cannot blame her that I have become someone else in many ways, someone who is certainly difficult to get along with. Like the ship, life slowly steers towards its destination. We let ourselves be carried along. The wave surges forward, swelling upward, but we are sinking![32] [. . .]

---

32. The German sentence (*"Es hielt die Welle, es trägt die Welle, und wir versinken!"*) is ambiguous in its connotations regarding the direction of the movement of the "wave" and those who are carried by it or are sinking.

DOCUMENT 8-II: Youth from Germany in Kibbutz Givat Brenner having a meal in the field, 1934–1936, USHMMPA WS# 69611.

This was the last time that Trudi and Willy Cohn were to see their son. Unsuccessful in their emigration attempts before the beginning of the war, they were deported to "the East" in the fall of 1941 and murdered on arrival in Kovno, Lithuania.

For those labeled, but not self-identifying, as Jews, emigration could seem just as appealing. There were fewer options in terms of destination but more regarding assistance from outside the country. While "non-**Aryan** Christians" discovered that even after frank and confidential conversations, many foreign visitors still had difficulty fully understanding the situation in the Reich, in George Bell they found one of their most indefatigable spokesmen.[33]

33. The visit by George Bell (1883–1958), bishop of Chichester since 1929, to Berlin in January 1937 led to the creation of an office (Büro Laura Livingstone) in Berlin that assisted Jews of Christian denomination. See Andrew Chandler, *Brethren in Adversity: Bishop George Bell, the Church of England and the Crisis of German Protestantism, 1933–1939* (Woodbridge, Suffolk: Boydell Press, 1997); Jana Leichsenring, *Die Katholische Kirche und 'ihre Juden': Das 'Hilfswerk beim Bischöflichen Ordinariat Berlin,' 1938–1945* (Berlin: Metropol Verlag, 2007), 30–50.

DOCUMENT 8-12: Letter by George Bell, bishop of Chichester, to David Glick, AJJDC, on Bell's visit to Berlin, January 1937, quoted from Ronald C. D. Jasper, *George Bell, Bishop of Chichester* (London: Oxford University Press, 1967), 138–39.

[. . .] I spent several hours with non-Aryan Christians' representatives. They were Dr. Spiero, who represents the Paulusbund,[34] and Miss Friedenthal, who is in charge of the department dealing with non-Aryan Christians under the Provisional Church Government at Dahlem. These were obviously the people who were most representative. They gave me an immense amount of information about the present situation, though I do not think their names ought to be mentioned as having given the information, for they were most anxious not to be overheard while in my room. But the position has got even worse, or at any rate their attitude to the position has become more pessimistic than it was in the autumn. There is no future for them in Germany, and they are absolutely clear about this; and it is for the growing generation that their chief concern exists. This problem is in two departments, (1) the education of the children, and (2) their employment afterwards. They were grateful for the steps that were being taken for them by the Inter-Aid Committee[35] in London, which has received some forty children for placing in English schools (they said they could send four hundred easily enough); but it is what the children are to do after they are educated that wrings their hearts. They want to go abroad

---

34. On Dr. Heinrich Spiero, the RVC, the Paulusbund, and their successor organizations, see Eberhard Röhm and Jörg Thierfelder, eds., *Juden-Christen-Deutsche* (Stuttgart: Calwer Verlag, 1990), 2:226–57. Charlotte Friedenthal (1892–1973) was the daughter of a Berlin bank director and trained as a social worker. Labeled a "non-Aryan Christian," she was a member of the Confessing Church (Bekennende Kirche), an opponent of the Nazi-regime-friendly German Christians (*Deutsche Christen*) within the German Protestant Church. Since the mid-1930s, she served in a number of positions in the Confessing Church before she left Germany for Switzerland in September 1942 as part of a clandestine rescue operation. See Victoria Barnett, *For the Soul of the People: Protestant Protest against Hitler* (New York: Oxford University Press, 1992), 130–31, 319n63.

35. The Children's Inter-Aid Committee was founded in March 1936 by agreement between the Council for German Jewry, the Save the Children Fund, and the American Friends Service Committee with the special task of looking after "non-Aryan" Christian children. The Inter-Aid Committee sought out children whose anti-Nazi parents had been arrested or were in danger of incarceration; by the end of 1938, the committee was able to allow approximately 450 children to attend schools in Britain. See Yehuda Bauer, *My Brother's Keeper: A History of the American Jewish Joint Distribution Committee, 1929–1939* (Philadelphia: Jewish Publication Society of America, 1974), 272; Kaplan, *Between Dignity*, 252n61; Werner E. Mosse, ed., *Second Chance: Two Centuries of German-Speaking Jews in the United Kingdom* (Tübingen: J. C. B. Mohr, 1991), 589–91.

to some new world—or rather to some of the large unpopulated territories which are to be found in the world. They said pathetically enough how happy they would be if they could only go to Australia or Canada and live with other Christians of different nationalities, and work out a new life. They were thinking especially of an agricultural or farming community as the kind they would like to build up.

It was really heart-breaking to listen to what they told me without any reserve, and I longed to be able to help them. [. . .] I think there probably are a good many non-Aryan Christians in Germany who are not associated with the Paulusbund, and I got the impression from the Quakers in London, and also from the Quakers in Berlin, that there were many non-Aryan Christians who felt that they must be very careful indeed as to their relations with foreigners and that they might be often embarrassed by being known to be talking with foreigners about their troubles. [. . .][36]

Overall, it is difficult to follow those historians who see the slight drop in overall emigration in 1937 as against 1936 as a sign that the community hoped that things might be improving. It may be true that few Jews at that stage perceived how imminently their very lives would be under threat, and there were always those who hoped that the Nazis would fail sooner or later. But the effort and energy invested in emigration was visible everywhere. The real problem was that so many of the best destinations in 1935 or 1936 had increased the hurdles to entry—notably Palestine, South Africa, and Brazil. The impact of these changes would have been even more disastrous had not 1937 seen a certain easing of policy by the United States, with the result that German Jewish emigration there almost doubled.[37] In December 1937, the Reichsvertretung created a new central office for Jewish emigration, above all to provide a single body that could keep the Jewish public informed.[38]

It is undoubtedly true that despite the pressures to leave, many of those involved in work for the Jewish community felt an obligation to stay despite all odds. In his diary note **Friedrich Brodnitz** called the day when he bid

---

36. In addition to the British Society of Friends, the American Friends Service Committee was a Quaker organization active in Nazi Germany, providing assistance especially for Jewish children. In the absence of a monograph study on the Quakers' work in Nazi Germany, see Friedlander and Milton, *Archives of the Holocaust*, vol. 2 (parts 1 and 2). For a personal account, see Leonard S. Kenworthy, *Another Dimension of the Holocaust: An American Quaker inside Nazi Germany* (Kennet Square, PA: World Affairs Material, 1982).

37. For the evolution of U.S. emigration policy, see Richard Breitman and Alan M. Kraut, *American Refugee Policy and European Jewry, 1933–1945* (Bloomington: Indiana University Press, 1987).

38. Adler-Rudel, *Jüdische Selbsthilfe*, 80.

farewell to his colleagues at the Reichsvertretung Berlin head office prior to his emigration in 1937 "the worst day"; he felt like a deserter (*fahnen-flüchtig*). "May God punish," he added en route to Amsterdam, "those who did this to us."[39]

JEWISH CULTURE AND LEISURE IN NAZI GERMANY

DOCUMENT 8-13: Jewish community (*Synagogengemeinde*) Bielefeld announcing a concert in support of the Jewish Winter Relief (Jüdische Winterhilfe) on January 30, 1937, in the Bielefeld synagogue, USHMMA Acc. 2008.282 Kronheim collection, box 3.

---

39. Friedrich Brodnitz, notebook entry for July 2, 1937 (written on the plane from Berlin to Amsterdam), USHMMA Acc. 2008.189.1 Brodnitz collection.

In the hostile environment of the Third Reich, German Jews, unsure of the possibility of escaping abroad, needed opportunities to escape within, even if only for brief periods. Cultural activities, broadly defined, offered a chance to elude the iron grip of a depressing reality. Yet, no cultural recipe worked for all; while some found solace in established traditions and rituals, others expected new approaches that would respond to German Jews' recent experiences and spiritual needs. In a letter to his son's family in Palestine, the former Social Democratic parliamentarian **Julius Moses** describes a religious service in Berlin he found less than appealing.

DOCUMENT 8-14: Letter by Julius Moses, Berlin, to Erwin Moses, Tel Aviv, December 20, 1935, translated from Dieter Fricke, *Jüdisches Leben in Berlin und Tel Aviv, 1933–1939: Der Briefwechsel des ehemaligen Reichstagsabgeordneten Dr. Julius Moses* (Hamburg: von Bockel, 1997), 413–35.

[. . .] After a long time, I went to my neighborhood temple again last Friday. I assumed that especially during these times, Jews would stream into the temple on such a Friday evening service. I went there early to secure a space: What a sight [*Tableau*]!! The gallery was closed. The head of the community knows what to expect from his *Kehillah* [Hebrew: "community"] members, and downstairs less than half of the seats were occupied. Maybe they had been quite deterred by the advance notification about Lewkowitz![40] Boy oh boy, the sermon he gave was a disgrace! In Berlin! And the service as a whole! I was really repelled, whereas a service at the Chassidic Schul in Grenadierstreet[41] on Yom Kippur shook me to the core. There Jewish tradition [*Volkstum*], here Protestant Reform Judaism. Not a single word of the sermon touched my soul, not a single song, not to mention the prayers. Emptiness inside and emptiness outside: despite Zionism and everything else. Is there anything here that is really connecting with our innermost Jewish, let's say Jewish-spiritual life [*jüdisch-seelische Leben*],

---

40. Albert Lewkowitz (1883–1954) was a rabbi at Berlin's Levetzowstrasse synagogue; he emigrated to the Netherlands and in 1943 was deported to Bergen-Belsen concentration camp, after the war, he served as a rabbi in Haifa. See Fred Skolnik and Michael Berenbaum, *Encyclopedia Judaica*, 2nd ed. (Detroit: Macmillan Reference USA in association with the Keter Publishing House, 2007), 12:771.

41. This refers to a small prayer room in Berlin-Spandau maintained by members of the Chassidic movement popular among Jews in Eastern Europe, which questioned the role of rabbis (Dieter Fricke, *Jüdisches Leben in Berlin und Tel Aviv, 1933–1939: Der Briefwechsel des ehemaligen Reichstagsabgeordneten Dr. Julius Moses* [Hamburg: von Bockel, 1997], 416–17n9f).

and with the transformation [*Umstellung*] of the Jews in Germany? I see very few signs of success! But we could talk endlessly about this; today, I will leave it at these few remarks. [. . .]

Nazi propaganda characterized art produced by Jews, as well as by many avantgarde or otherwise unconventional non-Jewish artists, as "un-German" and "degenerate," excluding from the mainstream public sphere all those stigmatized with these arbitrary categories. One advantage of being ghettoized into a Jewish sector, however, was that German Jews experienced relatively little direct interference in their cultural life. Yet, having the freedom to roam the ghetto also occasioned a lot of soul-searching about what artistic forms were appropriate to this new situation. Jewish art critics vacillated between measuring works according to pre-1933 terms of formal quality on the one hand and their psychological utility for the specific needs of their beleaguered audience on the other. Reviewing an exhibition by painter Lotte Laserstein, the *CV-Zeitung* applauded well-done images depicting Palestine but noted with satisfaction that "there are still other things for Jewish artists [to address] than just the Jewish question."[42]

42. "Kunstausstellungen," *CV-Zeitung*, December 12, 1935, 6. Lotte Laserstein (1898–1993) studied at the *Akademische Hochschule für die bildenden Künste* in Berlin. She graduated in 1927 and supported herself through her artwork. In 1937, she emigrated to Sweden, where she remained until her death. See Anna-Carola Krausse, *Lotte Laserstein, 1898–1993: Leben und Werk* (Berlin: Reimer, 2006).

DOCUMENT 8-15: "Self-portrait at the Easel," painting by Lotte Laserstein, ca. 1935, printed from Anna-Carola Krausse, *Lotte Laserstein: My Only Reality/Meine einzige Wirklichkeit* (Dresden: Philo Fine Arts, 2003), 203.

Art forms that depended on the use of language, rather than more abstract media like graphic art or music, raised the most questions. Given the enforced segregation from German *Kultur* and feeble links to Hebrew literature, what traditions remained to draw on? With so many creative Jewish writers leaving the country, was there enough substance to sustain an acceptable level of literary production? How Jewish and how innovative was the new poetry written by Jews in Nazi Germany? Was it inevitable that confinement in a social and linguistic ghetto would lead to work of inferior quality?[43] Poet Jakob Picard disagreed with this notion while recognizing

43. See, e.g., Julius Bab, "Neue jüdische Dichtung?" *Bayerische Israelitische Gemeindezeitung,* November 15, 1935, 486–88, who doubts that there could be any Jewish poetry, in the true sense of the word, written in German and quotes Leo Baeck's reference to the "educational narrowness" (*Bildungsenge*) to which German Jews were exposed.

that "even the most vicious anti-Jewish legislation cannot turn someone into a poet who wasn't one before."[44]

The two poems that appear in document 8-16 have been selected from a wealth of literary products by Jews in Germany because they seem to contain references to Nazi persecution.[45] At the same time, neither are these references specific enough to rule out other intentions on the part of the author—hardly surprising under the circumstances—nor can they be regarded as representative of the body of German Jewish writing during the Nazi era.[46]

---

44. Jakob Picard, "Unsere jüdische Dichtung in diesen Tagen," *Bayerische Israelitische Gemeindezeitung,* January 1, 1936, 4–6. Jakob Picard (1883–1967), lawyer, WWI veteran, and poet, was on the staff of the *CV-Zeitung* from 1922 to 1939. In 1936 he published *Der Gezeichnete* ("The Marked One"), with poems describing the lives of Jews in rural Germany. Shortly before the outbreak of World War II, he escaped from Germany and made it to the United States via Russia and Japan. He lived in the United States for eighteen years and in 1958 returned to Europe, where he remained until his death. See LBINY catalog.

45. German Jewish periodicals from the time contain many references to, and examples of, poetry during the Third Reich; see, e.g., Schalom Ben-Chorin, "Die drei Männer im Feuerofen," *Der Morgen,* 1937–1938 (January 1938), 426–27; F. A., "Gedichte?—Gedichte!!" *Der Morgen,* 1937–1938 (March 1938): 527–29.

46. The poet Manfred Sturmann (1903–1989) was born in Königsberg (East Prussia) and later lived in Munich, where he became active in local Zionist groups and the Kulturbund. He emigrated to Palestine in 1938 and continued to publish poetry and short stories in German. See Skolnik and Berenbaum, *Encyclopedia Judaica* 19:276; Hans Lamm, ed., *Vergangene Tage: Jüdische Kultur in München* (Munich: Langen Müller, 1982), 319–22, 518.

DOCUMENT 8-16: Poems by Manfred Sturmann and Jakob Picard, *Bayerische Israelitische Gemeindezeitung*, January 1, 1936, 4–6 (translated from German).

Was find wir anders?

Von Manfred Sturmann

Was find wir anders,
Die uns der Zufall treibt
Über die Falten der Erde,
Als Eintagsflug
Im leuchtenden Jahr.

Unter uns lauern
Die schwarzen Grüfte
Unserer Vermessenheit,
Und die lächelnde Wange
Streift der verborgene Tod,
Eh' fie es ahnt.

Einmal werden wir fallen
Wie Vögel vom tödlichen
Blei der Verfolger,
Ehe wir fagen können,
Was uns erhielt
Im gütigen Licht.

Aus dem Gedichtband „Wunder der Erde"
Hesse & Becker Verlag, Leipzig 1934

Und jeden Morgen . . .

Und jeden Morgen fchnürft du deine Schuh,
Gehft ftill dem Tagwerk zu.
Und Regen raufcht an deine Fenfterfcheiben,
Du bift nicht froh und weißt,
Vom Geftern wird nichts bleiben
Und nicht vom Morgen, das dir nun entgegenkreift.
Und Stund' um Stunde geht die Uhr,
Die Monde wechfeln ftumm in Gottes Namen;
Vielleicht wächft Neues einft aus deinem Samen,
Vielleicht läßt keiner deiner Schritte eine Spur.
Ein kleiner Wind fchon läßt dich tief erfchauern,
Ein wenig Regen läßt dich taglang trauern
Und jeden Abend bift du arbeitsmüd;
Nachtfalter find dir Einfamem Genoffen
Und eh du denkft ift alles dies verfloffen
Wie ein von irgendwo gefungenes Lied . .
Ob fei gelaffen im Gewölk und hab Geduld,
Fühl deine Gnade tiefer noch als deine Schuld,
Wie alle, die wie du berufen find
Zu horchen auf den grauen Schickfalswind,
Zu wachen, wenn aus dumpf befangenem Schlaf
Die anderen ftöhnen, weil ein Traum fie traf.

Jakob Picard

How Different Are We!

By Manfred Sturmann

How different are we,
We, who are driven by chance
Across the folds of the earth,
On our day of flight
In this brilliant year.

Below us lurk
The black tombs
Of our presumption.
And the smiling cheeks
Are stroked by hidden death
Before they sense its presence.

One day we will fall
Like birds struck down
By the lethal bullets of our persecutors
Before we can say
What kept us alive
In the kindly light.

And Each Morning . . .

By Jakob Picard

And each morning you bind your boots,
And quietly go about your daily tasks,
And rain rushes against your windowpane,
You are not joyous and you know
Nothing will be left of yesterday
And nothing of tomorrow now approaching you.
And hour by hour the clock moves on,
The moons change silent in God's name;
Perhaps one day your seed will bring forth new
    life,
Perhaps none of your steps will leave a trace
A small wind already makes you shiver,
A little rain casts you into daylong gloom
And every night you feel fatigued from work;
Your lonely companions are the moths
And before you know it all this has gone
Like a song sung somewhere. . . .
Oh stay calm in the clouds and be patient,
Feel your grace still deeper than your guilt,
As everyone who is called upon like you
To listen to the gray wind of fate,
To wake up, when from numb sleep
The others moan, struck by a dream.

If Jewish authors in Germany had limited means at their disposal to express
their thoughts and feelings in a published literary format, artists outside the
Reich faced the problem of how best to convey the German Jewish experience
to audiences not always tuned in or receptive to what was in any case a confusing and open-ended story.

DOCUMENT 8-17: "Play Portrays Berlin," *New York Times*, **February 10, 1937, 18.**

Albert Ganzert's "Borderline," a play set in the Berlin of today, was presented by Maurice Schwartz and the Yiddish Art Theatre Company at the
Forty-ninth Street Theatre last night. It describes the havoc wrought in a
substantial, happy family when certain persons discover that the grandfather of the head of the family (an eminent physician) was a Jew. At
this safe distance from concentration camps, one asks, So what? Even if
the consequences are such as can be confirmed in fact—a devoted wife
and mother (who happens to be Aryan) thinks of "arranging" to illegiti-
matize her son for the sake of his career; old friends are estranged, and
finally there are arrests, death from overstrain and suicide in rapid-fire
succession—the Nuremberg Laws ostracizing Jews remain incredible. Mr.
Ganzert, whose play is said to be having a successful run in Vienna, is not
imaginative enough to prove that they are not really a cruel fantasy.

Neither Mr. Schwartz, as Dr. Karl Leist, nor Eddie Friedlander, as his
son, Hans, elicit the full mental anguish of their roles. Berta Gersten is fairly
persuasive as Frau Leist, while Morris Silberkasten creates a full-blooded character as Karl's father, whom no laws will convince that he is not a German.

"Borderline" is intended for performance during the first part of the
week. The main attraction for the rest of the week continues to be that
slam-bang satire, "The Water Carrier."[47]

Back in Germany, though German Jewish performers were now very
restricted as to their audience, even in the mid-1930s Jews as consumers of culture and leisure were still not wholly restricted to an all-Jewish sphere. Indeed,
Jewish youth might well find itself forced back to the movie theater or ice-cream
parlor because the Jewish youth activity it would otherwise have taken advantage

47. Albert Ganzert (1881–1965), born Abraham Halberthal in Romania, aka Awrum
Halburt, emigrated from Germany to Switzerland in 1933. His writings, particularly his play
Die Grenze ("The Borderline"), gained traction not only in his newly adopted homeland but
throughout Europe and the United States as well. See Herbert A. Strauss and Werner Röder,
eds., *International Biographical Dictionary of Central European Émigrés, 1933–1945*, vol. 2,
The Arts, Sciences, and Literature (Munich: K. G. Saur, 1982), 452.

of had been shut down. Günther Friedländer's three-part article published in *Der Morgen* in late 1937 described the "devaluation of all values" and the demise of traditional forms of youth work. Triggered by the absence of a positive outlook for the future, young German Jews increasingly escaped into the private sphere. Having zero chances to build a future through work, Friedländer argued, these youths also placed no value on the creative use of leisuretime. Rebelling against the older generation offered no creative outlet for youthful energy either, given that parents for the most part saw no point in defending their defunct value system.

DOCUMENT 8-18: Günter Friedländer,[48] "The End of the Youth Leagues," *Der Morgen* 1937–1938 (October–December 1937): 278 (translated from German).

[. . .] Today's Jewish youth no longer has a world of its own [*Jugendland*]. The very absence of a youthful realm shows more clearly than ever that nothing is a substitute for youthful experience.

The experience of those who are young now has undergone fundamental change. If we were to capture this change in a single phrase, we could say that their experience has turned into something "second-hand." It is no longer original and unique, and thus it fails to have the great impact—producing and releasing tensions—that one's coming-of-age once offered. "Second-hand experiences" mean that most are only relived, not newly experienced. [. . .]

This lack of youthful experience reveals itself acutely and with as yet unclear consequences in the sexual realm. The ice-cream parlor and the cinema play a dominant role in the life of the young person who does not know what to do with his free time. Youth who are only thirteen or fourteen years old are confronted in the movie theater with problems not of their own making. But they see them and take them in and are drawn into them at far too early an age. Most young people have their first sexual experience at a time when they are not mature enough yet—and they would probably not seek it out, if they did not have so much idle time on their hands! Thus, puberty, rich in opportunity and rife with conflict, lands at a premature and inauthentic resolution, before it could really develop and flower. The forces that it [puberty] could unleash under more favorable circumstances and that can in most cases set one's future course are senselessly used up, exhausted. [. . .]

---

48. Presumably Günther Friedländer (b. 1914), a rabbi active in German Jewish youth work in the 1930s, emigrated to Bolivia in 1939 before settling in Chile in 1962. See Röder and Strauss, *Biographisches Handbuch*, 1:199–200.

Of course, Friedländer's piece, while undoubtedly responding to the particular challenges of the 1930s, also belonged to a long tradition of grown-ups worrying that young people were being exposed to the adult world too early. Children themselves saw things differently, and with fewer pre-Nazi memories of how things were "supposed" to be, they were often better at seizing the opportunities still available in a hostile environment.

DOCUMENT 8-19: Students from different Jewish schools in Berlin gather around their banners, 1936–1938, USHMMPA WS# 12854.

Among the students is a group from the Waldschule Kaliski, a well-known Jewish private school located in Berlin-Dahlem.

It is hard to find any authentic contemporary accounts of youthful sexual activity. If sexual experiences and acts of revolt against commonly accepted morality during the years of persecution are expressed explicitly at all, then they emerge in survivor memoirs written well after the Holocaust—although even here such references are sparse. At the time, references to sexual matters may well have appeared as too private or unacceptable.[49] Instead, most of the contemporaneous accounts of Jewish leisure activities describe organized or private sports and social activities and stay well within the bounds of what appeared proper. Perhaps even more than in normal times, sport was particularly important for young Jews and served as a release valve for physical energy, a source of personal self-esteem, and a means of communal bonding. Despite the disintegrative pressure Jews in Germany had been exposed to since 1933, the communal fabric woven from the many threads of organizational, religious, and private activities thus prevented basic structures and social values from crumbling.

DOCUMENT 8-20: Jewish teenagers attend a Purim party in Frankfurt am Main, 1933–1936, USHMMPA WS# 56413.

49. See, e.g., Gad Beck (written with Frank Heibert), *An Underground Life: The Memoir of a Gay Jew in Nazi Berlin* (Madison: University of Wisconsin Press, 1999). See also Kaplan, *Between Dignity*, 109–16.

CHAPTER 9

JEWISH QUESTIONS
AFTER NUREMBERG

RACISTS AND SCHOLARS

After 1933, Nazi policy rapidly swept Jewish scientists and scholars from their positions in German universities and research institutes and on editorial boards. Racial studies boomed as one discipline after another made the *völkisch*-biologistic turn. In a state dominated by antisemitic ideologues and opportunists, Jews found that disputing racial myths dressed up as science was turning from a futile into a dangerous pursuit. Even so, Jewish scholars continued to be allowed to publish in Jewish journals and Jewish presses, and Jewish students to complete dissertations at Jewish higher education institutions. Though many scholars had left the country, even in 1937 Jews produced most of the books and articles published in Germany on Jewish history.[1] For the most part, Jewish scholarship and German academia were now completely separate. Where the new nazified academic elite ventured onto the unfamiliar ground of what Jewish scholars termed "scholarship on Jewry" (*Wissenschaft vom Judentum*) and what for antisemites formed the "Jewish question,"[2] however, their anti-Jewish attacks might yet provoke Jewish scholars' opposition. Of course, the two sides were very unevenly matched in any dispute. What the

---

1. See Alan E. Steinweis, *Studying the Jew: Scholarly Antisemitism in Nazi Germany* (Cambridge, MA: Harvard University Press, 2006), 93.
2. Michael Brenner and Stefan Rohrbacher, eds., *Wissenschaft vom Judentum: Annäherungen nach dem Holocaust* (Göttingen: Vandenhoeck & Ruprecht, 2000).

Nazi academics lacked in soundness of approach, they compensated for in terms of superior material resources and political clout.

In 1934, Wilhelm Grau published a book titled *Antisemitism in the Middle Ages* based on his PhD thesis about the Jewish community in the Bavarian city of Regensburg. The work was accepted by Karl Alexander von Müller, a well-known history professor at the prestigious Munich University. The author was a Nazi Party member and about to become one of the leading figures conducting the academic "study of the Jewish question" under the auspices and for the political purposes of the regime.[3] Grau's claim to have produced an "objective" study hid an antisemitic agenda. It was also a poor reward for the many insights and sources that he had received from the Jewish medievalist Raphael Straus before the latter's emigration to Palestine. Yet this Nazi attempt at usurping and distorting an area of historical studies that Jewish scholarship had cultivated did not go unchallenged. Resistance came from those who had lost their positions at German universities and were now restricted to teaching at Jewish seminaries or to publishing in Jewish journals, if they had not been pushed out of the country altogether.[4] In refuting Grau's misrepresentation of medieval Jewish life, even émigrés like Raphael Straus had to gauge carefully how far they could go in their criticism. When Grau's book came out, Straus voiced his shock at the author's perfidy and conformism with current attitudes (*zeitgemässe Gesinnung*) manifest in Grau's reading racial motives into medieval Christian antisemitism.[5] Other reviewers with a solid background in *Wissenschaft vom Judentum* like Guido Kisch came to similar conclusions.

---

3. In 1936, Grau became the head of the Research Division Jewish Question (Forschungsabteilung Judenfrage) of the Nazi Reichsinstitut für Geschichte des neuen Deutschland under Walter Frank. See Steinweis, *Studying the Jew*, 100–1; Max Weinreich, *Hitler's Professors: The Part of Scholarship in Germany's Crimes against the Jewish People* (1946: rpt. New Haven, CT: Yale University Press, 1999), 48–54; Patricia von Papen-Bodek, "Anti-Jewish Research of the Institut zur Erforschung der Judenfrage in Frankfurt am Main between 1939 and 1945," in *Lessons and Legacies VII: New Currents in Holocaust Research*, ed. Jeffry M. Diefendorf (Evanston, IL: Northwestern University Press, 2004), 155–89.

4. For Jewish seminaries and *Lehranstalten* in Nazi Germany, see Jacob Boas, "Countering Nazi Defamation: German Jews and the Jewish Tradition, 1933–1938," *LBIYB* 34 (1989): 205–26.

5. Raphael Straus, Jerusalem, to Ludwig Feuchtwanger, August 6, 1934; LBINY Ludwig Feuchtwanger collection, MF 562, reel 3. In late 1934, a reviewer writing for the Bavarian Jewish community journal noted the "undeniable antisemitic tendency" of Grau's book (*Bayerische Israelitische Gemeindezeitung*, November 1, 1934, 438–40).

DOCUMENT 9-1: Letters by Guido Kisch,[6] Halle, to Ludwig Feuchtwanger, September 23, and December 16, 1934, LBINY MF 562, reel 3 (translated from German).

[September 23, 1934:] [. . .] Working on this book may be the most unpleasant thing I have ever experienced in my time as a critic. Sometimes I ask myself why I am still taking on the big, surely fruitless burden of checking, tracking, and exposing [Grau's book as wrong] since it will not teach the author or his supporters anything. And so I have to find the courage over and over again to conduct this time-consuming, unpleasant work. [. . .]

[December 16, 1934:] I have already invested a lot of, some may think way too much of, my time and effort [in writing the review]. In doing this I have been absolutely convinced of the author's antisemitic disposition. Everything flows from an ideological [*gesinnungsmässigen*] background. If he himself denies that, then he is the victim of a severe delusion. [. . .]

Although Kisch finished a long review of Grau's book, it was never published.[7] But other outspokenly negative German Jewish reactions to Grau's thesis did enter the public sphere. **Ismar Elbogen**, a scholar on the editorial board of the *Zeitschrift für die Geschichte der Juden in Deutschland*, reviewed the book for *Der Morgen*, stressing its misrepresentation of historical facts.[8] In the *Zeitschrift* itself, Raphael Straus, after consultations with the journal editors, criticized Grau for his lack of sensitivity, factual ignorance, and "grave blunders" (*schwere Entgleisungen*) in dealing with his subject.[9]

Any doubts Jewish scholars may have had about the potential danger of speaking out publicly against one of the exponents of the new school in German historiography disappeared when Grau anonymously published a nasty rebuke of Straus's review in the ***Völkischer Beobachter*** and demanded space to reply in the *Zeitschrift*, the flagship journal of the *Wissenschaft vom Judentum*. More so than Straus in Palestine, the Germany-based editors of the Jewish press

---

6. Guido Kisch (1889–1986), an expert on the history of the Jews in the Diaspora and a professor at different German universities until his dismissal in 1933, taught at the Jewish Theological Seminary in Breslau and emigrated to the United States in 1935.

7. The following reviews of Grau's book written by Jews were published: Hertha Lieber, *Bayerische Israelitische Gemeindezeitung*, November 1, 1934, 438–40; Itzchak Baer, *Kirjat Sefer* 12 (1935–1936): 461–67 (in Hebrew). See also Michael Brenner, *Propheten des Vergangenen: Jüdische Geschichtsschreibung im 19. und 20. Jahrhundert* (Munich: C. H. Beck, 2006), 199–200.

8. Ismar Elbogen, review of Wilhelm Grau, "Antisemitismus im Mittelalter," *Der Morgen* 4 (July 1935): 184–88.

9. Raphael Straus, *Zeitschrift für die Geschichte der Juden in Deutschland* 1 (1936): 17–24.

carrying reviews of his work had to consider the ramifications of their actions. In the **CV** head office, **Alfred Hirschberg** warned against the "nonsense of bickering with Dr. Grau about words and phrases" and urged others to dump the "bad old methods" of delaying the inevitable.[10] Grau did indeed get a chance to reply in the *Zeitschrift*, prefaced by an editorial note.

DOCUMENT 9-2: Preface by the editors of *Zeitschrift für die Geschichte der Juden in Deutschland* to Wilhelm Grau, "Antisemitismus im Mittelalter: Ein Wort contra Raphael Straus," *Zeitschrift für die Geschichte der Juden in Deutschland* 4 (1936): 186 (translated from German).

Dr. Wilhelm Grau feels exceptionally hurt in his scholarly honor by Dr. Straus's accusation of sloppy research [*ungründlicher Forschung*]. We regret this accusation which, according to Dr. Grau's elaborations, is unfounded and have granted him space in this journal to refute it.

While Grau had the last public word in the debate, Straus reacted with a "final word" in a letter to Ludwig Feuchtwanger.[11] Straus was not happy about the *Zeitschrift* giving room to his opponent and distancing itself in ever so careful words from his own criticism of Grau's book. More importantly, he tried to maintain his position despite the lopsidedness of an exchange in which scholarly substance and the urge to understand were poised against political power and racial hatred. Grau's comments, Straus wrote about his **"Aryan"** critic in an "open letter" that remained unpublished, had not convinced him; instead, the renewed polemic contained, in Straus's words, "a lot that is amazing, some that is mistaken, and sadly—nothing at all that is convincing." In terminating the "unpleasant exchange," Straus insisted that the "Jewish question" was "accessible to a 'mature judgment'" but could not be unlocked by Grau's "youthful foolishness."[12]

---

10. Letter by CV head office (Hirschberg) to Ludwig Feuchtwanger, February 21, 1936; USHMMA RG 11.001M.31, reel 141 (SAM 721-1-2982, 288–90).

11. A publisher with legal training and brother of the writer Lion Feuchtwanger, Ludwig Feuchtwanger (1885–1947) was the longtime director of the eminent Duncker & Humblot publishing house in Munich. Forced to leave his post in 1936, he took over the editorship of the *Bayerische Israelitische Gemeindezeitung*. After internment in Dachau concentration camp following the 1938 November pogrom, he emigrated to England in 1939. See Max Gruenewald, "Critic of German Jewry: Ludwig Feuchtwanger and His Gemeindezeitung," *LBIYB* 18 (1972): 75–92.

12. Letter by Raphael Straus, Jerusalem, to Ludwig Feuchtwanger, with attached "open letter" to Wilhelm Grau, October 10, 1936; LBINY MF 562, reel 11.

HOW TO BEHAVE AND THINK AS A JEW

Was there any way Jews could behave in the Germany of the **Nuremberg Laws** that would allow them to remain unmolested? In the hope of maintaining public peace, Jewish organizations and opinion makers felt obliged to prevent displays of Jewish behavior that corresponded with antisemitic clichés. What exactly qualified as such remained contested. One person's attempt to re-create the semblance of normal social interaction was seen by others as transgressing into the provocative or undignified. Despite being a fervent advocate of a return to a true sense of Jewish identity,[13] **Willy Cohn**, for example, complained a few days before the Nuremberg Laws' enactment that some Jews still had not learned to behave in public in a "simple and discreet" manner.[14]

But how to behave in such a manner, and what difference did it make in a social environment saturated with anti-Jewish sentiment? After Nuremberg, those Jews who invested any kind of hope in the regime's rhetoric about "normalized" relations were willing to do their part, especially where successes seemed still possible. From Pomerania, the CV regional office reported to Berlin that frequent visits by Jews to a popular restaurant in Bad Polzin had received unfavorable attention among locals. CV officials had no doubts that "this state of affairs" was "unacceptable" in a town where they could claim success in having had a sign displaying the slogan "Jews enter this town at their own risk" removed. To avoid precipitating further anti-Jewish agitation, Jews should give no cause for offence and behave unobtrusively (*zurückhaltende Benehmen*).[15] At the **Reichsvertretung, Cora Berliner** took up the case with the restaurant owner.

---

13. Willy Cohn, "Hat das Judentum in Deutschland eine wirkliche Umkehr vollzogen?" *Bayerische Israelitische Gemeindezeitung*, September 15, 1936, 385–86.
14. Willy Cohn, diary entry for September 9, 1935, in Conrads, *Kein Recht*, 1:272–73.
15. CV regional office Pomerania to CV head office, June 19, 1936; USHMMA RG 11.001M.31, reel 137 (SAM 721-1-2945, 161). For a similar case from West Germany, see CV regional office Rhineland-Westphalia to CV head office with copy of letter to Jewish community in Essen, June 30, 1937; USHMMA RG 11.001M.31, reel 134 (SAM 721-1-2914, 419–20).

DOCUMENT 9-3: CV copy of letter by Reichsvertretung (Berliner) to Hugo Moses,[16] Polzin, June 25, 1936, USHMMA RG 11.001M.31, reel 137 (SAM 721-1-2945, 155–56) (translated from German).

[. . .] A gathering of cars directly in front of the restaurant can easily lead to misunderstandings, in the same way as a congregation of larger groups and loud, lively conversations on the street. We ask you not to understand our communication to the effect that we expect you to lecture or even criticize your guests. But perhaps you will have opportunity to point out to your guests that our exhortations for special restraint merely serve their own self-interest and those of the whole of Jewry.

Even in big cities, the increased level of discrimination made Jews ever more uncertain about how to respond to Nazi greetings and declarations of allegiance. After Nuremberg, German courts had started to convict Jews for using the increasingly standard greeting "Heil Hitler"[17]; yet, many Jews remained unsure whether in their everyday interactions with fellow Germans they would be penalized for *not* giving this display of loyalty. A woman in Hirschberg, a town in Lower Silesia, whose husband had been taken to a concentration camp, speculated that the Gestapo had arrested him for refusing to salute the "German way" at the local labor office; the CV wrote back that this could not have been the case as Jews were prohibited from using "Heil Hitler."[18]

In the nazified public sphere, attempts at expressing common courtesy could thus easily be misunderstood—and misread as an illegal claim to belong to the "people's community." **Toni Lessler**, the former female director of a renowned Jewish school in Berlin-Grunewald writing after her emigration to the United States, conveys an example of a Jewish boy in the mid-1930s responding to a mistaken assumption of identity.

---

16. This may have been Hugo Moses (1889–1944), born in Bad Polzin in the Pomeranian region of Germany. Deported from Berlin to the Theresienstadt ghetto in April of 1943, he was sent to his death in Auschwitz in 1944. See www.bundesarchiv.de/gedenkbuch.

17. See CV head office (Reichmann) to regional offices, May 22, 1936; USHMMA RG 11.001M.31, reel 127 (SAM 721-1-2813, 86), on a case involving a Jew who used the "German greeting" and was sentenced to three months in jail for slander. The CV informed its staff functionaries but advised them not to pass this information on to members.

18. CV regional office Lower Silesia (Breitbarth) to CV head office, November 30, 1936; USHMMA RG 11.001M.31, reel 135 (SAM 721-1-2915, 423–25). At court, Jews were forbidden to use the "German salute" only in late 1937 (Walk, *Sonderrecht* 204, no. 371).

DOCUMENT 9-4: Toni Lessler on her work as director of the Lessler school in Berlin-Roseneck in the mid-1930s, LBINY ME 726, 27 (translated from German).

[. . .] I am very proud that our students did nothing to draw attention to themselves and behaved calmly and modestly especially in the tramcars the traffic association provided until the end. A ten-year-old boy, a blond nice little fellow, came up to me one day and said, "Today I made space for an elderly woman. She was patting me benevolently on the shoulders and said, 'That's right my dear boy, that is how a real *Hitlerjunge* [member of the Hitler Youth] is supposed to behave. That was good of you.' I replied, 'But I am not a *Hitlerjunge*, I am a Jewish boy,' and then I got off the tram." [. . .]

DOCUMENT 9-5: Group photos of activities by students of the Lessler school, Berlin-Grunewald, LBINY ALB-OS2 #1573066.

Upper left: "River cruise"; upper right: "Country School 1935[,] Lessler School"
Lower left: "Play during an outing"; lower right: "Coffee break"

Only when among themselves did Jews not worry about how to behave. But even when in purely Jewish company, being Jewish was not so simple. Many assimilated Jews faced the question of what they now believed in and what, if anything, remained of their former identities. Members of the older generation might hope to muddle through, but what kind of perspective could they offer the young? Assimilated, left-leaning Jews who—like seventeen-year-old **Ruth Maier**—had to leave public schools felt the prevailing sense of panic but had trouble embracing a new orientation.

DOCUMENT 9-6: **Ruth Maier, diary entry for October 2, 1938, translated from Ruth Maier, "Das Leben könnte gut sein": Tagebücher 1933 bis 1942, ed. Jan Erik Vold (Stuttgart: DVA, 2008), 134–36.**

[. . .] I was at the Chajes *Gymnasium* [Jewish high school in Vienna] today for the first time. The school is fervently nationalistic [*national bis zur Bewusstlosigkeit*]. This poses a considerable danger, and who knows, perhaps I'm not a Zionist just out of a feeling of opposition.

The principal gave a low-key, pleasant speech loaded with Jewish national consciousness. He is a small, worn-out man who tilts his head this way and then the other. He preached at us about our responsibility, about "bearing with dignity," and he expressed his conviction that we would all end up in Palestine. He hopes that the "baptized Jews and those without denomination [*Getauften und Konfessionslosen*]" will find their way to the Jewish community.

It was a strange feeling to sit there, all of us young people, guys and girls, everything around us hostile and revolting; only us, relying on ourselves, on . . .

Well, that's where the danger lies: "the Jewish community." First my community was humankind. Now, suddenly, Jewishness [*Judentum*] is supposed to replace humankind for me? "A path leads from humanity through nationality to bestiality." I don't know who first said these words, but they have proven to be entirely true.[19]

Today the principal said during a preparatory class, "It's possible to explain and excuse national socialism but still reject it."

I can certainly explain, excuse, and <u>understand</u> Zionism (which is clearly connected to nationalism), but I reject it. Precisely because, as Anny Schermann [a fellow student] today said quite correctly, I constantly and physically feel the consequences of nationalism.

---

19. Austrian poet Franz Grillparzer (1791–1872) coined the epigram "*Von Humanität/ Durch Nationalität/Zur Bestialität.*"

Yes, right now I'm convinced that nothing could be further removed from me than nationalic feelings [*Nationalbewusstsein*], etc. And yet, isn't it something completely negative and unhealthy to always long for "assimilation," for one's own disappearance [*Untergang*], the disappearance of one's uniqueness? And so, I can't help but fluctuate between socialism and—though I <u>dread</u> having to write this—nationalism.

And maybe it's this, precisely this fluctuating position of Jews that has become the hallmark of being Jewish.

But to finally wrap things up on this issue: it's a fact that 75 percent of Jewish intellectuals and Jewish youth are being pushed towards Zionism. [. . .]

The youth group closely associated with the CV, the **BDJ**, tried its best to offer a viable alternative to Zionism. In the wake of the Nuremberg Laws, and having been forced to drop the "German" from its name, it adopted the prefix "Der Ring" ("the circle") and stressed its Jewish orientation by calling itself Bund jüdischer Jugend. At the same time, the organization intensified its efforts to prepare young German Jews for emigration, especially via the emigration school in Gross-Breesen featured in document 11-1. By mid-1936, Gross-Breesen had received more than five hundred applications, mostly from fifteen- to sixteen-year-old boys of bourgeois background. Some of the teenagers who ended up attending were thrilled: one boy noted that a true community was growing, "completely naturally, clean, free, and yet disciplined" ("*echt ungezwungen, sauber, frei und doch diszipliniert*").[20] Yet there were also major sources of contention. Next to the "girls' question" (*Mädchenfrage*) caused by their underrepresentation within the student body, the issue of Jewish orientation created the most vehement internal discussions. In addition to the committed and the uncertain, Gross-Breesen was believed to house a third group of students referred to as "antisemites," young Jews who had tried to embrace Jewish identity but failed.[21] The school's leadership, held in high esteem by most students, commented on their struggle to define Jewish orientation.

---

20. See the compilation of reports and letters on Gross-Breesen in USHMMA RG 11.001M.31, reel 98 (SAM 721-1-88, 405–21); also see *Bayerische Israelitische Gemeindezeitung*, October 15, 1936, 429–32, with letters by youth attending the training school.

21. Letter "E. D." to "Titi," June 5, 1937; USHMMA Acc. 2007.96 Kellermann collection, box 3.

DOCUMENT 9-7: Unsigned memo (possibly Curt Bondy), June 6, 1937, USHMMA Acc. 2007.96 Kellermann collection, box 3 (translated from German).

This afternoon and right after supper, I had a discussion with Edda's group relating to its meeting with Dr. Seligsohn[22] and my speech last Friday evening. Gerd Pfingst had come to me asking that I speak with the group. Apart from him, Edda, Rolf Falkenstein, Mösch, and Hans Goldmann, Kurt Herrmann also attended the meeting.[23]

The question was, How can we achieve a clear position on Judaism [*zum Jüdischen*] and Gross-Breesen? Rolf Falkenstein has a good and positive attitude toward Judaism, and so I do not include him in these remarks. All others hold a more or less problematic attitude toward Judaism. In the meeting that followed we discussed

1. whether any "active antisemites" are involved. We came to the conclusion that this is actually not the case and that no one poses a threat to Gross-Breesen or the Gross-Breesen community since everyone is behaving loyally and decently.

2. whether some regret being Jewish and would escape their Jewishness [*dem Jüdischen entfliehen*] if they could. We asked ourselves whether it is not impossible for these people to live in a Jewish community under these circumstances. We did not reach a clear conclusion. Still, I would not favor forcing [these] people to violate their scruples or throwing them out [for their beliefs]. However, everyone should ask themselves whether they are truly ready to live in a Jewish community, or if it is impossible for them to remain at Gross-Breesen. Thus, the decision would not be made

---

22. Julius Seligsohn (1890–1941), a Berlin lawyer and World War I veteran, served as a board member of the Hilfsverein and a leading official of the Reichsvertretung. Arrested in late 1940 as a result of protests against the deportation of Jews from Southwest Germany, he died in the Dachau concentration camp in 1941. See Kulka, *Deutsches Judentum*, 529.

23. Gerd or Gerhard Pfingst (b. 1916), formerly of Berlin, managed to escape to a farm project in Kenya before the war began, along with fellow Gross-Breesener "Edda" (Max Ludwig Neumann, b. 1916 in Berlin). "Mösch" (Gerhard Braun, b. 1919 in Cologne) went to Kenya in early 1939, later volunteered for the Pioneer Corps in the Middle East, and became a sergeant and translator in the British army before he returned to Kenya. Rolf Falkenstein (b. 1917 in Recklinghausen) was able to leave Germany with his parents before the war and later joined the U.S. forces. Hans Goldmann (later Clyde Hastings) managed to leave Germany for Australia, where he married and ran a dairy farm during the war (USHMMA Acc. 2000.227 Herbert Cohn collection, folder 3). Kurt Herrmann (later Thomas K. Hermann, b. 1914) escaped to Brazil via England and ended up volunteering for the U.S. Army. See Peter W. Landé, "Jewish 'Training' Centers in Germany: A List of Jews Attempting to Emigrate from 1930s Nazi Germany," USHMMA 2002; USHMMA Acc. 2000.227 Herbert Cohn collection, folders 1–3.

by the Gross-Breesen group but by the individual, who needs to determine whether he is suited for a life in this community.

3. It seems to me, as shown particularly by the letter from Juwa's father, that even without the help of the Reichsvertretung, it is quite possible for someone to obtain a training place in Parana [Brazil], to travel there, and once there, to get on.[24]

Mösch's problematic attitude to Judaism apparently stems from his clash with his Jewish parents.

Gerd Pfingst may be undecided and may end up going in either direction.

Hans Goldmann has no understanding for any of it.

Kurt Hermann and Edda probably harbor the strongest resentment and therefore [word missing]. The question of whether to stay in Gross-Breesen will probably become most acute for these two, as well as for Hans Goldmann.

Beyond this, there are a few other people in Gross-Breesen who are questioning the whole endeavor but who probably have a much more positive attitude toward Judaism [*im Jüdischen*] than those I have named.

Intensifying Judaism [*Intensivierung des Jüdischen*] in Gross-Breesen, however, indeed now seems possible and promising. [. . .]

A letter sent from Berlin to **Heinz Kellermann,** himself safely overseas at that point, describes the mental roller coaster experienced by young assimilated Jews during the few days of a youth meeting.

DOCUMENT 9-8: **Letter by Helmut Krotoszyner,[25] Berlin, to Heinz Kellermann, January 3, 1938, USHMMA Acc. 2007.96 Kellermann collection, box 4 (translated from German).**

[. . .] In the months November to December [1937], community youth evenings took place again like the year before.

---

24. This refers to a planned communal settlement by Gross-Breesen students in Paraná, Brazil. See Angress, *Between Fear,* 59–60, and document 11-1. After brief internment in Buchenwald concentration camp in 1938, "Juwa" (Hans Rosenthal, b. 1919 in Wetzlar) was released and managed to obtain temporary refuge in the Netherlands with others from the farm. He arrived in Brazil in the spring of 1939 and spent the war there farming.

25. Helmut Krotoszyner (1917–?) lived with his parents, sister, and brother in the Tiergarten district of Berlin in the late 1930s. He was deported to the Minsk ghetto in November 1941 with his father and siblings and presumed killed. His mother may have been deported separately but is also known to have been killed in 1941. See *Datenbank zur Liste der jüdischen Einwohner im Deutschen Reich, 1933–1945* (Berlin: Bundesarchiv, 2008).

With a lecture by Maybaum,[26] the first evening's theme was return to believing, praying, and learning Judaism. M. said that in the thinking of so-called intellectual Jews, the Jewish idea of God has been replaced over time with another one. He referred to concepts like the Jewish nation or also the abstract idea of beauty. (He elaborated the latter through a poem that a Palestinian Jew recently wrote on the Greek god Apollo), and so forth. He referred to it as idolatry and regards it—and not athe-ism—as the actual enemy of Jewish religion. Atheism is according to his view unthinkable for occidental people.

On the following evening Swarsensky[27] described how such idolaters can be brought back to Judaism. All Jews had a common fate and a com-mon history and that is why nobody could disassociate himself from the Jewish community.

Additionally, the Jewish *Weltanschauung* typical for all Jews and, just as significantly, the Jewish ethos have to be communicated to those spiri-tual outsiders [*geistig Aussenstehenden*]. Finally his last and most interest-ing point was that they have to be brought back to Jewish faith [*jüdischen Glaubenshaltung*]. For most of the so-called Jews today, the word "God" or "revelation" or "messiah" does not mean anything more than mere words; hardly anyone (he spoke of "racial Jews" [*Rassejuden*] and "cash Jews" [*Kas-senjuden*]) is still capable today of believing in the same naive, literal way as our forefathers did. In my opinion Swarsensky included himself in this remark. I found this reckless openness very sympathetic since I have also severely lost faith in religion during the last years.

(It is questionable if I ever had faith.) In any case, that evening—you will laugh—I felt as a Jew since I felt that I now knew that I was not at all the only doubting Thomas.[28] Schoeps,[29] who was also present, stated repeatedly that everyone born as a Jew belongs by virtue of his birth to Judaism and could not "fall out" [*herausfallen*] of it by having a different spiritual attitude. Anni J. protested and strongly hampered my happiness

---

26. This is most likely Ignaz Maybaum (see Glossary).

27. This was probably Dr. Manfred E. Swarsensky (1906–1981), a liberal rabbi in Berlin during the 1930s who also served as director of the CV in Berlin from 1936 to 1938. During the November 1938 pogrom, he was detained in Sachsenhausen concentration camp but managed to emigrate to the United States in March 1939. See Röder and Strauss, *Biogra-phisches Handbuch*, 1:751–52.

28. This is a standard German-language expression for someone questioning religious beliefs based on John 20:29 (the apostle Thomas believed in Jesus's resurrection only after seeing him).

29. This is most likely Hans-Joachim Schoeps.

over my rediscovered Judaism: such inclusiveness [*Weitherzigkeit*], as suggested by Schoeps, would be exaggerated and not in accordance with the essence of being Jewish. Thus, I, at the very moment I wanted to feel Jewish again, was immediately excommunicated.

After a presentation by Jospe[30] the next evening, the same questions came up again: what and how should one believe? [. . .] It was decided to read a random part of the Bible, maybe the chapter of the week, for the following evening. We want to find out this way if we are personally "touched intuitively by the word of the bible" (Schoeps).

I am sure the acting and would-be rabbis present will succeed in reading into the text something general that concerns everybody, and thus prove that they nevertheless have a significant contingent of Jewish faith at their disposal

Dear Heinz, please don't take what I said the wrong way. Despite all the sarcasm and skepticism, I don't feel quite comfortable about my attitude. I am jealous of Gerda Loewenst. [Loewenstein?],[31] who, as she told me, does not comprehend at all the problems raised during the different evenings since she was raised with a totally different understanding of Judaism, much more taken for granted, and has therefore also more naturally lived it and thought about it. [. . .]

CONTENDING WITH CRISIS

In April 1935, the major institutions for providing social relief to German Jews (**ZAHA**, Zentralstelle für jüdische Wirtschaftshilfe) had been integrated into the Reichsvertretung. By dint of massive efforts, voluntary appeals such as the Jewish Winter Relief (Jüdische Winterhilfe) raised the same amount of money in 1936 as in the year before, an extraordinary achievement given the shrinking economic base. For the first time in the winter of 1936–1937, however, the funds collected through charitable appeals fell below those of previous years.[32] The impact would have been far more direr had not Jewry in Britain and the United States played an increasingly important role in subsidizing their German brethren. As early as 1934, 60 percent of Jewish welfare funds in Germany were raised abroad, above all from the **AJJDC** and the Central British Fund for German Jewry administered

---

30. This may have been the Berlin Reform rabbi Dr. Alfred Jospe (1909–1994), who was briefly detained in Sachsenhausen concentration camp before emigrating to the United States in 1939. See obituary, *New York Times*, November 24, 1994.

31. The authors have been unable to find further information on Gerda Loewenstein.

32. "Arbeitsbericht der Reichsvertretung für das Jahr 1937," 48.

by the Council for German Jewry.[33] It was not surprising that the opening statements of the welfare agencies' annual reports always contained profound acknowledgment of the significance of foreign aid.

Thus, if 1936 was the year in which German Jewish organizations felt that external constraints had become far more decisive than individuals' desire to leave in determining levels of emigration, 1937 was the year in which Jewish welfare organizations first declared themselves unable to meet the material demands placed on them at home. To exemplify the scale of the problem, the Reichsvertretung's welfare division offered in its annual report a few sample cases of deserving individuals whom they had been forced to deny funding.

DOCUMENT 9-9: Progress report (*Arbeitsbericht*) by the Reichsvertretung for the year 1937 (translated from German).

[. . .] 2. Social Service for risk cases [*Gefährdeten-Fürsorge*]

We exceeded the RM 12,000 budget available for the year under review by approximately RM 4,300, even while rejecting many requests for aid with almost unconscionable severity. We offer two illustrations here:

Kurt H. in East Prussia is a mentally retarded boy living in complete isolation as the only Jewish adolescent in a small East Prussian village. His widowed mother runs a little shop that can barely support them. The boy was provided with accommodations on a farm, where he must pay a monthly allowance of RM 45 for nursing care. A brother living in Berlin was willing to provide RM 10 and the provincial association [i.e., the relevant regional office of the Reichsvertretung] provided an additional RM 10. Therefore, the application was for RM 25 monthly. Although the boy is perfectly suited for the farm, and they have agreed to accommodate him, he has had to be rejected due to lack of funds.

Hildegard B., Kassel District, 13 years old. Following complete impoverishment, dissolution of the household so that the parents could take up jobs. The children, otherwise without supervision and care, were taken to an orphanage in Kassel so that their parents could accept positions. Of the RM 45 required monthly, RM 20 can be raised through the

---

33. The proportion is an estimate, based on the figures for the first half of the year in "Arbeitsbericht des ZAHA 1934," 99. See also David Kramer, "Jewish Welfare Work under the Impact of Pauperization," in Pauker, *The Jews in Nazi Germany*, 180; David Silberklang, "Jewish Politics and Rescue: The Founding of the Council for German Jewry," *H&GS* 7, no. 3 (1993): 333–71.

Kassel [Jewish] Welfare Agency [*Wohlfahrtsstelle*]; RM 10 [to be given] by family members. The request to the Social Service for risk cases of the Central Welfare Office [*Zentralwohlfahrtsstelle*] to share the remaining monthly cost of RM 15 had to be rejected because of a shortage in funding. [. . .]

We offer these examples, to which any number of others could be added, only to show what a disparity already exists between the most urgent needs and available resources. [. . .]

For individuals such as those described by the progress report, the mid-1930s were a period of acute misery and need. But even those many still getting by were increasingly prone to bouts of introspection and desperation.

DOCUMENT 9-10: **Kurt Rosenberg, diary entry for April 26, 1936, LBINY AR 25279 (translated from German).**

The sphere of activity open to Jews grows ever more constrained. One regulation follows another. Now the Jewish pharmacists and the veterinarians are affected. And tomorrow? And the day after tomorrow? And things that don't fall under law and regulations fall into the category of boycott. For weeks the Jews have been whispering into each others' ears that it will become even worse after the Olympics in August. A road without end. Long ago we lost the ability to take pleasure in small things and celebrations—because over everything hangs the eternal question, <u>Is it still worth it?</u> Followed by the other question, <u>Where are we headed?</u> [. . .]

In the absence of social ties, material means, and a sense of purpose, daily life became depressingly monotonous and bleak. Writing to loved ones provided little reprieve. What was there to write about when your day's work consisted of little more than getting out of bed and doing chores?

DOCUMENT 9-11: **Letter by Julius Moses, Berlin, to Erwin Moses, Tel Aviv, for the third week of June 1936, translated from Dieter Fricke, *Jüdisches Leben in Berlin und Tel Aviv, 1933–1939: Der Briefwechsel des ehemaligen Reichstagsabgeordneten Dr. Julius Moses* (Hamburg: von Bockel, 1997), 451–53.**

My Dearest! It is only 7:30 a.m. I have had a coffee by now, home brewed, after I had already gone down to pick up rolls and milk. I get up regularly at 6:00 a.m.; you know otherwise I would surely never get done with my work and my affairs!!! Though I am also going to bed early to recover from the "exhausting" work of the day. Right after I get up, just so you know exactly, I give the bedding a good airing—in the meantime coffee is made—after the room has been tidied up. Thorough cleaning once a week by a [cleaning] lady, then getting the couch in order again—and now I sit down at the coffee table in the tidied room, and I begin reading the morning news and first, of course, I look at the regular war reports from Palestine; then I read through the paper while I drink my coffee, but only the daily newspaper *Berliner Tageblatt*. Twice a week the *Jüdische Rundschau* and the *CV-Zeitung* arrive. I read these papers only after coffee since I look them over very thoroughly; I read almost every article while smoking one or two cigars. It usually takes me one or two hours to read them: the coffee cups have already been done. And just to be exact: shaving, etc., takes place later. Around 11:00 a.m. I walk sometimes to the Tiergarten, sometimes to the zoo, and roam until lunch around 12:30 p.m.; then I go home to take a nap. Sometimes, though, these house rules are interrupted. Early in the morning, I always ring [his non-Jewish partner from whom he had to separate after the enactment of the Nuremberg Laws] Frieda's doorbell and learn if she or the pug [his son Kurt] will be visiting me or if we will be meeting up somewhere—on average 2 to 3 times a week—so we can both plan ahead for the day. Kurt comes by from school a couple of times a week, so he leaves later on those days, after he has had a little snack.

Holidays will be starting already the day after tomorrow: it is very doubtful whether they [i.e., Frieda and Kurt] will have the opportunity to go somewhere for recreation because their means are hardly sufficient. Although it would be very nice for Frieda if she were granted a break for recovery since taking care of her grandmother has also really left her low.

So, now you know my exhausting daily tasks. "Exhausting" is not meant ironically. Since nothing exhausts body and mind more than being doomed to do nothing. I cannot think of any work that is as exhausting. When I get up at six my work is already done! Over!! The awareness of being in the world for nothing is devastating. Life has lost its meaning. Stop, stop, don't continue this train of thought. That is pointless. [. . .]

Religiously minded Jews tried to create a historical frame of reference for understanding and transcending current events. Yet, for them too, a year after the passage of the Nuremberg Laws, the frustrations of life had greatly increased.

DOCUMENT 9-12: **Mally Dienemann, diary entry for September 14, 1936, LBINY MM 18 (translated from German).**

Yesterday Max [her husband] held a service [*Weihestunde*] at the synagogue. He read a few *Selichot*.[34] I experienced them as if I had never heard them before, and they devastated me. It was a bond of calamity and misery surrounding us all, in which we listened to the pleading and lamenting together, a bond of moaning that nevertheless elevated through the commonality of feeling. All of a sudden the certainty swelled up (so it seemed to me) deep inside that things with Georg [alias she uses on occasion for Hitler] would go downhill. It was a certainty that struck me like lightening diminished again by the day. But it was so absolute that I am writing it down in order not to forget it. This week was the [Nazi] party convention, which gave us something to read. Why actually this identification of Bolshevism and Jewry [*Judentum*]?[35]

It seems to me, if we really made the effort to fight against all these errors, it would be like trying to clear away Mont Blanc [mountain in France] with a toy shovel. [. . .] Today during the speech of H [Hitler], I thought, if there is a war, it will start with the extinction [*Ausrottung*] of the Jews. One never knows if these fears are only conceits of the nerves or well-grounded observations. No matter what happens, we are tied, and we have to stay.

A year later, even this heartfelt reflection from 1936 seemed optimistic in retrospect. By the end of 1937, Mally Dienemann had reached a deeper level of despair. After she was separated from her daughter her thoughts moved between wondering whether it would be possible to bring her daughter home and whether she could or should leave the country. As Mally Dienemann's reflections from the end of 1937 show, among themselves, communal leaders admitted to one another a sense of bewilderment at how little influence they had over the situation.

---

34. Hebrew; prayers for days of fasting and atonement.

35. Against the background of the Spanish Civil War, which began in July 1936, Hitler, Goebbels, and other high-ranking party officials ranted against "Jewish bolshevism" during the Nazi Party convention in Nuremberg in early September. See Friedländer, *Nazi Germany*, 1:183–84.

DOCUMENT 9-13: **Mally Dienemann, diary entry for December 9, 1937, LBINY MM 18 (translated from German).**

Yesterday, we were in Wiesbaden at a Western German Rabbinic Convention. 1–10 [*sic*] rabbis attended. Everyone was very depressed, and I realized for the first time that staying here does not depend on our own will and that we might be forced to leave. Until now I was under the illusion that it is, in the end, a question of one's own will. Everyone was talking about the new rules that will make it harder to get a passport or about the complete impossibility for a Jew to get a passport at all, [about the prospect] that one would be completely separated then from one's children. It was terrible, and it seemed all of a sudden impossible that we would have Gabi [her daughter in Holland] here with us. When I think about her longing letters and then imagine that she might have to turn back at the border! No, then I return to believing that these are just scare stories and that everything will work out. [. . .]

Yesterday's was not the usual Jewish get together, in the sense of people helping each other with anecdotes, amusing or serious ones, to get over the heaviness of the situation. We were silent for seconds. What will happen if the community continues to dwindle?

In the summer of 1937, a foreign observer, AJJDC emissary David Glick, had a chance to see for himself how German Jews were coping and to get a sense of what they were up against. Document 9-14 presents his report after his return to the United States from a tour of the Württemberg and Hesse regions, "in a private capacity" as he calls it but really for the AJJDC, and having met with Jewish officials as well as Gestapo officers.

DOCUMENT 9-14: **Letter by David Glick to Paul Baerwald (AJJDC), New York, no date (ca. summer 1937),[36] USHMMA Acc. 2004.320.2.**

[. . .] The first big thought I would like to convey to you is that, in spite of the terror and the daily pressure under which the Jews are living, they are displaying a courage and a mentality that is absolutely magnificent. They have no illusions about their status in Germany, for almost from week to week new regulations restricting their business activities, are issued, and despite the new restrictions, and in the face of the certain fate that is

---

36. See also David Glick's memoir article, "Some Were Rescued," *Harvard Law School Bulletin* (December 1960): 6–9.

theirs, they refuse to go down as cowards or animals, but are maintaining to the last a spirit of brave and cultured men and women. [. . .]

[. . . ; Glick reports on hardships faced by Jews in Frankfurt as well as in Hessian and Bavarian towns and villages.] In Stuttgart one old woman, whose name I will not disclose, lost her son during the war and he is buried near Paris. He fell in the battle of the Marne [in 1914]. She did not get this information until ten years after the war. A few days ago she wanted to revisit the grave of her son, and when she went to the officials and gave this as a reason, the reply given to her was, "We are not issuing passports for a '*Lustreise*' ['pleasure trip']." I talked myself to this woman of good repute, and her husband, an important man in the city.

Ten percent of the deaths in Mannheim last year were suicides among the Jews.

[. . . ; Glick provides figures of Hessian village population from 1933 to 1936.]

We must make no mistake about the German Government. The Nazi Party is the government in absolute fashion. The will of the party is maintained by the Gestapo. In each city that I visited the Chief of the Secret Police, I found him to be a young man around 30. It is a government of young men who mean to hold on to their power and jobs at all costs. The Nazis played for high stakes and won—and it will require a terrific revolution to unseat them.

It is impossible for me to give you an estimate of the heroic courage that is being displayed by all the Jews even in the villages. I did not see or hear any whining. They know that they are trapped and doomed, but by the gods they are going down like soldiers who care nothing for their lives, but while alive are taking it like men and women of heroic legends.

The increasingly hostile external environment made many former divisions within the Jewish community seem irrelevant. However, internal tensions did not entirely disappear. Zionists on both the Left and Right continued to feel that they had not been accorded the leading role in the Jewish community that the new situation warranted. The leadership of the weighty Berlin community, whose significance within German Jewry had grown as a result of the migrations from smaller towns, continued to claim greater influence in central decision making. Both these strands came to a head in a most bitter dispute in mid-1937. A small faction around **Georg Kareski**, the head of German Zionism's right wing (Staatszionistische Organisation) and board member of the Berlin Jewish community, demanded that the leadership of German Jewry be significantly restructured. The existing Jewish leadership was alienated not just by

Kareski's brusque challenge but also by his attempts to utilize the fact that the **Gestapo** and SD were better disposed to the Zionists than to the assimilationists and to enlist the Gestapo's help in gaining greater power. Kareski's aim was, on the one hand, to transform the Reichsvertretung from an umbrella organization, representing a host of established organizations, into a more authoritarian, top-down body capable of making decisions vis-à-vis the emerging center of Nazi anti-Jewish policy—**Heydrich**'s Gestapo and SD. On the other hand, Kareski and his followers hoped to use this power to achieve what they called the "liquidation" of German Jewry: its emigration to Palestine.[37]

The report in document 9-15, most likely written by a high-ranking German Jewish official involved in the Reichsvertretung while on a visit abroad, describes in unusually frank terms the challenges posed by Kareski's maneuvers to assert the Berlin community's dominance and revamp the Reichsvertretung. The report starts with a description of events in Germany stretching from the dissolution of the Jewish lodges in April 1937[38] via the brief arrest of leading Reichsvertretung figures, including **Leo Baeck**, to a meeting of top German Jewish leaders called by the Berlin Gestapo to force them to accept Kareski and his ideas. Baeck rejected this demand by pointing out that Britain's willingness to accept German Jewish immigrants to Palestine would hardly increase if a man like Kareski, with his outspoken anti-British agenda, took over the Reichsvertretung leadership. Baeck received strong outside support in the form of a letter from the chairman of the Council for German Jewry in Great Britain and former British high commissioner of Palestine, Sir Herbert Samuel, who threatened that his organization as well as others, including the AJJDC, "might be unable to maintain on the present lines their assistance to the programmes on behalf of German Jewry" should the position of the current Reichsvertretung leadership be undermined.[39] Given organized German Jewry's dependence on foreign funding, Samuel's message could not but scare those struggling over the shape of the Reichsvertretung. Making use of its council (*Rat*) established in mid-1936, roughly two dozen of the leading German Jewish functionaries came together on June 15, 1937, to discuss under the watchful eyes of the Gestapo how to resolve the situation. (It is noteworthy that the other reports on this meeting, reports produced in Germany, did not mention the presence of the

---

37. See Michael Wildt, *Die Judenpolitik des SD 1935 bis 1938: Eine Dokumentation* (Munich: Oldenbourg, 1995). On the use of the term *liquidation* by the *Staatszionistische Organisation*, see Kulka, *Deutsches Judentum*, 336–37n56.

38. See Karin Voelker, "The B'nai B'rith Order (U.O.B.B.) in the Third Reich," *LBIYB* 32 (1987): 269–95.

39. Letter by Council for German Jewry (Samuel), June 11, 1937, to Leo Baeck; cited in Kulka, *Deutsches Judentum*, 335.

Gestapo representatives, a sign of how often one has to read between the lines to understand the atmosphere in which Jewish business was conducted.)

DOCUMENT 9-15: Confidential anonymous report on a meeting of the Reichsvertretung Council, July 6, 1937, LBINY AR A 1579/4851 (translated from German).[40]

[. . .] The meeting of the council was well attended (with the exception of Max Warburg, who was being treated in a Karlsbad health resort) with 4 Stapo and Gestapo officers present, among them Mr. Kuchmann.[41] The general mood was excellent. Our friends from all over Germany expressed a greater unanimity of spirit in support for the Reichsvertretung than ever before. Seligsohn gave an excellent presentation and a summary of the Samuel letter, which was later distributed in copied form together with statements of confidence from throughout the Reich.[42] The negotiations were conducted in an astonishingly courageous manner. [. . .] In his final word, Seligsohn reminded everyone that the Torah passage for the previous Sabbath had been the story of the *Rotte Korah* (not a gang, as falsely translated by [Martin] Luther but noble and eminent members of the community as scripture has it).[43] Samuel's letter, which did not come up in the discussion, had visibly left a very strong impression. In a propagandistically skilled, but in terms of argument astonishingly poor, speech, Kareski tried to diffuse this impression by saying how easy it is to arrange for declarations of support. At the end of the meeting, an expression of trust [in the Reichsvertretung] was approved, with 7 of the 8 delegates from the Prussian regional association [dominated by the Berlin Jewish community] abstaining. [. . .]

Overall, our impression is that the Gestapo is really inclined to avoid coercive measures [*Zwangsmassnahmen*]. By applying moral pressure, Herr Flesch has tried again and again to nudge the Jews to "voluntarily" make the decisions he favors; however, he has repeatedly stated that he has no inclination to intervene directly. This applies especially to the Kareski question. In essence, the entire matter comes down to the question whether

---

40. Printed in Kulka, *Deutsches Judentum*, 322–27.

41. Kuchmann and Flesch were officers of the "Jewish desk" at the Berlin Gestapo office. See Wildt, *Die Judenpolitik*, 37–39; Klaus Drobisch, "Die Judenreferate des Geheimen Staatspolizeiamtes und des Sicherheitsdienstes der SS 1933 bis 1939," *Jahrbuch für Antisemitismusforschung* 2 (1992): 230–54.

42. On Julius Seligsohn, see note 22; on the letter by Herbert Samuel, see note 39.

43. Moses 4:16ff, referring to a conspiracy against Moses and Aharon with terrible consequences for the conspirators as well as the people of Israel at large.

one can keep one's nerves [*eine Frage des Nervenbehaltens*]. If Hirsch and Baeck stay firm, it is certainly possible that the Reichsvertretung will be strengthened by this crisis, at least for the immediate future. [. . .]

The report was right: Kareski, unable to get a foothold in the Reichsvertretung's leadership, left Germany for Palestine in September 1937, and the circle of leaders around **Otto Hirsch** and Baeck faced no further significant internal opposition. The affair showed that German Jewry's bargaining ability was now, above all, dependent on foreign influence. The less the Nazis took account of attitudes abroad, be they Jewish or non-Jewish, the more vulnerable German Jewry would become.

From late 1937, ominous portents were gathering of a new radicalism in Nazi foreign policy and with it a new intensification of Nazi persecution. Those in the know, that is to say, activists who had been working for German Jewish organization for a long time, were much better equipped than ordinary Jews to read the signs of the time. During the Nazi Party convention held in Nuremberg in September 1937, Hitler had further developed his theme of "Jewish world bolshevism" that he claimed threatened other peoples with extinction; Goebbels and party ideologue Alfred Rosenberg had tooted the same horn. In late 1937, leading CV official **Hans Reichmann** passed by a newsstand in the city of Freiburg and, according to recollections written down in the summer of 1939, was stunned by what he saw.

DOCUMENT 9-16: Autobiographical letter by Hans Reichmann, July to September 1939, translated from Hans Reichmann, *Deutscher Bürger und verfolgter Jude: Novemberpogrom und KZ Sachsenhausen 1937 bis 1939*, ed. Michael Wildt (Munich: R. Oldenbourg Verlag and Institut für Zeitgeschichte, 1998), 51.

[. . .] An unusually thick pile, about 200 copies, of the [SS journal] *Das Schwarze Korps* dated October 14, 1937. One cannot fail to notice the headline: "The Jews Will Get Help" [*Den Juden wird geholfen*].

Anxious and full of foreboding, I sit down on a bench and hastily glance through the article. It paints the economic situation of the Jews in shamelessly cynical colors. While the German businessman [*Kaufmann*] is working as part of the *Volk* for the benefit of the *Volk*, the Jew—lacking any sense of responsibility and purely for his own benefit—is skimming the cream off the economic upturn that occurred under national socialism. This cannot continue [according to *Das Schwarze Korps*]. And now a program of systematic interventions in the economic activities of Jews follows: no more freedom to participate in business or trade [*Gewerbe-freiheit*], no equal access to raw materials and goods rationed by the state, and—it goes without saying—an all-out boycott. Suddenly I realize this is no wishful thinking [*Wunschvorstellungen*]. This is an appalling program. So this was the purpose of that strident speech by the Führer![44] Now the goal is to cut to the quick of Jewish existence, targeting the economic body [*Wirtschaftstorso*] still left us after four and a half years of national socialism. The evening bells have begun to toll. [. . .]

Perhaps even Reichmann could not have predicted in late 1937 the dramatic deterioration in the lives of German Jews that would take place the following year. A cascade of punitive measures in 1938 culminated in what before 1933 would have appeared simply as an unrealistic nightmare: the state-sponsored pogrom of November 1938. Worse, the speeches and policies from late 1937 onward were also setting the stage for even further persecution, in the increasingly likely event of war.

---

44. During the annual Nazi Party rally in Nuremberg, Hitler had again committed the regime to the fight against "Jewish bolshevism," claiming that 98 percent of the Soviet leadership was Jewish and that its goal was a "Bolshevist world revolution." See Jeffrey Herf, *The Jewish Enemy: Nazi Propaganda during World War II and the Holocaust* (Cambridge, MA: Belknap Press of Harvard University Press, 2006), 42–43.

PART IV

DISPOSSESSION AND DISAPPEARANCE: 1938

WHEN DID LIFE in Nazi Germany become unlivable for Jews? The key steps in Nazi Jewish policy can be identified relatively easily, but specifying a clear chronology from the victims' perspective is more difficult. Jews' experience varied widely across regions, occupations, and generations, between one Nazi *Gau* (as the Nazis called the regional units of party organization) and the next, and between town and country. For one individual, the moment of truth might come in 1933 when, say, an **SA** man burst into the family home brandishing a weapon, and the frightened householder discovered that a call to the police found no one willing to assist and uphold the law. If one survived such an experience, it was easy to conclude, even in the first months of Nazi rule, that Jews had to get out of the country as soon as possible. But a couple of blocks away, on a street where no storm troopers made a particular nuisance of themselves, a Jewish businessman who was managing to make ends meet might come to this same conclusion only in 1937 or early 1938.

True, we have identified some common turning points. The violence in the spring and summer of 1935 unsettled many, and most community leaders recognized by the time of the **Nuremberg Laws** that Jewish children could have little future in Germany. Despite cosmetic easing of some facets of Nazi policy in the run-up to the Olympic Games, a steady narrowing of Jews' prospects continued. But while many more people seriously contemplated leaving Germany than the modest emigration figures might imply, it did still take time for the majority of German Jews to realize that soon they might not even be able to scrape by. In the course of 1937, however, this became ever more obvious. Those in a position to look beyond the narrow confines of their everyday life and assess the regime's words and deeds were particularly concerned. By October 1937, when **Hans Reichmann** caught sight of *Das Schwarze Korps* sardonic headline, "The Jews Will Get Help" (see document 9-15), many perceptive minds saw omens presaging the wholesale removal of Jews from the German economy. Yet, even then, while destitution appeared to beckon, probably few Jews believed that life and limb were also in danger.

In this respect, the year 1938 brought about a decisive transformation. Whatever uncertainties we have about Jewish perceptions in earlier years, there is no doubt about the lesson Jews learned from their experience in 1938: get out, if you can. For one thing, there was the unparalleled pillaging of Jewish assets. By the end of the year, virtually no Jewish businesses remained intact, all Jewish bank accounts were under official control, and a significant fraction of Jewish wealth had been, or was about to be, appropriated by the state. At the same time, there was a series of violent assaults on life and physical property. Early in the year Jews with Soviet citizenship were threatened with deportation and interned when they could not leave.[1] Romanian Jews in the Reich faced a similar fate in May, and in October tens of thousands of Polish Jews were subject to the crudest, most violent deportation then imaginable. In the meantime, the *Anschluss* with Austria was accompanied by a frenzied assault on Vienna's Jews and the brutal pushing of Jews over the border. Over the following months, arbitrary **Gestapo** deportations to concentration camps were syncopated with a growing series of violent incidents on the streets of Vienna, Berlin, and other German cities and towns. Casting everything else in the shade, "*Kristallnacht*" brought two days of terror that reached into every Jewish home, unleashing an experience that those who survived it would never forget.

Why should 1938 have proven such a fateful year for Germany's Jews? The same pressures and forces that had been at work in previous years continued to turn the grinder. Yet, in 1938, these forces had accumulated in intensity while many obstacles to radicalization had evaporated. With the hugely ambitious armaments program absorbing all available resources, there were no longer fears of unemployment to restrain assaults on Jewish businesses. Moreover, the Nazis were looking to any available reserve to help finance rearmament. As early as the fall of 1936, Hitler had proposed a law making the whole of Jewry liable for all

---

1. On the expulsion of Soviet and Romanian Jews, see Saul Friedländer, *Nazi Germany and the Jews*, vol. 1, *The Years of Persecution, 1933–1939* (New York: HarperCollins 1997, 2007), 263.

"damage" individual Jewish "criminals" had inflicted on the German economy.[2] This proposal evolved along a rather convoluted bureaucratic path over coming months, but the idea of assessing and penalizing Jewish wealth took concrete legislative shape in 1938. **Hjalmar Schacht's** resignation as Reich economics minister in November 1937 removed the last barrier to wholesale "**Aryanization**." From the fall of 1937, the grab for Jewish assets was on. Whereas in the past at least bigger Jewish companies had been acquired at something like their value, such niceties were no longer observed.[3] With the continued acute shortage of foreign currency reserves, the Nazis were also particularly sensitive to the potential costs of Jewish emigration. In April 1938 the Reichsbank concluded that to transfer German Jewish wealth abroad along the lines of the **Ha'avara Agreement** would cost between RM 2.2 and RM 5.15 billion, a sum many times Germany's currency reserves.[4] This was yet another reason for stripping emigrants of all their assets before they could leave.

The unprecedented push for rearmament was accompanied by increasing international tension—a sign of the regime's new willingness to flex its diplomatic and military muscles. The year 1938 would be dominated by a series of manipulated international crises, resulting in the absorption of Austria in March and the acquisition of the Sudetenland from Czechoslovakia in October.[5] With an eye to foreign opinion, Hitler remained careful that he should not be linked publicly too closely with new measures against Jews. Yet the more he was willing to risk war, the less foreign opinion really mattered. At the same time, the German top leadership perceived Jews as hostages and pawns in its diplomatic gambles. Particularly in moments of acute foreign crisis, most notably in the prelude to the Czech confrontation—and then in the aftermath, when radicals found they had not got their war after all—Jews would be the target of Nazi activists' wrath.

As intimated in Part III, the fiscal and economic risks associated with rearmament, as well as the fact that Hitler's foreign policy was clearly in danger of unleashing a European war, caused a number of conservatives to balk but did not lead to a crisis threatening the regime's legitimacy among Germans. With conservative influence curtailed, competing Nazi bigwigs applied pressure for more action against the Jews.

For **Heinrich Himmler**, Jews were only part of an even larger racial agenda as his attention shifted from clamping down on political opponents to purging

2. J. Adam Tooze, *The Wages of Destruction: The Making and Breaking of the Nazi Economy* (London: Allen Lane, 2006), 221.

3. Friedländer, *Nazi Germany*, 1:247.

4. Tooze, *Wages*, 275.

5. Ian Kershaw, *Hitler, 1936–1945: Nemesis* (New York: W. W. Norton, 2000), 46–50.

society of racial undesirables. The 1937–1938 winter in particular saw some fundamental decrees in this direction. Himmler aspired to create a rapidly expanding concentration camp system that would provide slave labor for ambitious construction projects.[6] At the beginning of November 1938, the concentration camp population was five times the size it had been in November 1936. Temporarily, following the November pogrom, it would more than double again.[7] As Himmler's star rose, so did that of his deputy, **Reinhard Heydrich**, whose bright young men in the **SS** think tank and intelligence organization, the SD, were evolving new plans to expel Jews as efficiently as possible. While the SD was often critical of uncontrolled street violence, one of those young men, **Adolf Eichmann**, had already noted in January 1937 that a pogrom would "help" uproot Germany's Jews.[8]

The SS continued to face considerable competition in Jewish questions from party circles. In 1938, it was Propaganda Minister and **Gauleiter** of Berlin **Joseph Goebbels** who often set the pace. Particularly in the wake of the *Anschluss*, Goebbels was eager to ramp up the anti-Jewish machine in Berlin. Nothing expressed more clearly the naked lawlessness of the new climate than his speech to a group of policemen whom Goebbels told in June 1938, "Our watchword is not 'the law' but 'chicanery.'"[9]

6. Karin Orth, *Das System der nationalsozialistischen Konzentrationslager: Eine politische Organisationsgeschichte* (Hamburg: Hamburger Edition, 1999), 46–50.

7. Orth, *Das System*, 51.

8. See Michael Wildt, *Generation of the Unbound: The Leadership Corps of the Reich Security Main Office* (Jerusalem: Yad Vashem, 2002), based on his groundbreaking study *Generation des Unbedingten: Das Führerkorps des Reichssicherheitshauptamtes* (Hamburg: Hamburger Edition, 2000). For the earlier role of the SD, see Michael Wildt, *Die Judenpolitik des SD 1935 bis 1938: Eine Dokumentation* (Munich: Oldenbourg, 1995).

9. Elke Fröhlich, ed., *Die Tagebücher von Joseph Goebbels*, Teil I, Bd. 5, *Dezember 1937–Juli 1938* (Munich: Saur, 2000), 340 ("*Nicht Gesetz ist die Parole, sondern Schikane*"; see also Friedländer, *Nazi Germany*, 1:260.

CHAPTER 10

"MODEL AUSTRIA" AND ITS RAMIFICATIONS

ANSCHLUSS AND THE JEWS

Probably no single event in 1938 did more to unleash the new onslaught against Jews than the annexation of Austria in March. Nazi propaganda euphemistically dubbed it a "joining" (*Anschluss*) of territories, a consensual term that belied the military invasion that preceded it but accurately reflected the massive German and Austrian popular support for the move. Be it coerced or consensual, the takeover marked a new phase in the Reich's expansion and its preparation for future war. For at least one group, however, it was most certainly not welcome and was indeed disastrous: Austria's approximately 200,000 Jews, most of them (roughly 175,000) in Vienna.[1] They immediately found themselves subjected to German racial policies, although the **Nuremberg Laws** officially took effect in the former Austria only in late May. Even before German troops crossed the border on March 12, anti-Jewish incidents started to occur and the days and weeks after the invasion saw an unprecedented wave of violent abuse and plunder. In the course of 1938, this would

---

1. The total figure of two hundred thousand Jews includes an estimated twenty-five thousand persons labeled Jewish due to the clauses of the Nuremberg Laws; figures are found in "Report of the Vienna Jewish Community" produced by the Jewish community (Israelitische Kultusgemeinde, or IKG) Vienna in January 1940. On the IKG Vienna, see Doron Rabinovici, *Instanzen der Ohnmacht: Wien 1938 bis 1945. Der Weg zum Judenrat* (Frankfurt am Main: Jüdischer Verlag, 2000). The USHMMA holds copies of the IKG archive comprised of collections from the IKG Vienna, the CAHJP in Jerusalem, and the SAM.

have brutal repercussions elsewhere as Jews throughout the enlarged German Reich harvested the fruits of the Austrian experiment.[2]

Though distressing scenes from Vienna were indeed reported in the foreign press, observers in other countries and even other parts of Germany had for the most part no inkling of the scale of the post-*Anschluss* violence. Early hopes that German Jewish organizations might be able to help their brethren across the former border were rapidly quashed.[3] The **Gestapo** radically redirected the activities of the Viennese Jewish community, with everything now focused on the goal of forcing as many Jews as possible to leave for other countries. A Central Office for Jewish Emigration (Zentralstelle für jüdische Auswanderung) set up in Vienna by **Adolf Eichmann** established a new standard in German anti-Jewish policy by ensuring a mass exodus of Jews after stripping them of all of their assets. The Viennese Jewish community thus became a laboratory for what German policy planners saw as a promising model of violent and enforced emigration that could then be extended elsewhere in the Reich.[4]

Elisabeth Block, the Jewish girl whose diary was quoted in document 5-18, witnessed the dramatic events of March 11 and 12, 1938, unfolding in her Bavarian hometown close to the Austrian border. With her customary obliviousness to her own situation, she noted the "happy excitement: Austria belongs to Germany, troops had entered Austria" while "swarms of planes were humming through the blue spring air."[5] Further away in Breslau, **Willy Cohn** saw the display of national fervor with a mixture of admiration and concern.

DOCUMENT 10-1: Willy Cohn, diary entry for March 14, 1938, translated from Norbert Conrads, ed., Kein *Recht, Nirgends: Tagebuch vom Untergang des Breslauer Judentums*, 1933–1941 (Cologne: Böhlau Verlag, 2007), 1:524.

[. . .] Bought the newspaper on the way home. Germany's annexation [*Anschluss*] of Austria will not undermine the peace! You have to admire the forceful way all this was accomplished. It is going to be difficult for the Jews

---

2. See Hans Safrian, "Expediting Expropriation and Expulsion: The Impact of the 'Vienna Model' on Anti-Jewish Policies in Nazi Germany, 1939," *H&GS* 14, no. 3 (2000): 390–414.

3. See Hans Reichmann, letter to "Trude" and "Paul," London, July 1939, in *Deutscher Bürger und verfolgter Jude: Novemberpogrom und KZ Sachsenhausen 1937 bis 1939*, ed. Michael Wildt (Munich: R. Oldenbourg Verlag and Institut für Zeitgeschichte, 1998), 60.

4. See Hans Safrian, *Die Eichmann-Männer* (Vienna: Europaverlag, 1993); Rabinovici, *Instanzen*.

5. *Erinnerungszeichen: Die Tagebücher der Elisabeth Block*, ed. Haus der Bayerischen Geschichte (Rosenheim: Bayerische Staatskanzlei, 1993), 146–47.

heavily concentrated in Vienna who were—as so many times—betting on the wrong horse and believed that a union with the clerics' party [*Klerikalen*] would bring them salvation. The Viennese Jews may have not been very passionate about *Chaluziut*;[6] maybe the Zionist impulse is taking root now. Perhaps we Jews in Germany should not join in this welling up of national emotion, but one does so nevertheless, and anyone with some feelings for his country can relate to this! We Jews should be just as unified.

Friedrich Brodnitz had left Germany for the United States in 1937. In early April 1938, a friend wrote to him about her sense of terror and suicidal thoughts caused by the "Austrian catastrophe" (*Österreichkatastrophe*), prompting Brodnitz to include a rare expression of emotional outrage in his diary: "What these swine have done."[7] Later that month, he received a letter written by **Leo Baeck** during a stay in a Czechoslovakian spa town. Despite the unprecedented nature of recent developments, Baeck tried to take a longer view and to see in them some familiar historical patterns. Without saying so directly, Baeck echoed a widely shared view that the Nazi movement's character and appeal revealed the dangers of modern, plebian mass society.

DOCUMENT 10-2: Letter by Leo Baeck, Johannisbad (Czech: Jánské Lázn) to Friedrich Brodnitz, New York, April 29, 1938, USHMMA Acc. 2008.189.1 Brodnitz collection (translated from German).

[. . .] I think sometimes that democracy will begin only after a century of experimentation. The Middle Ages also had such an experimental saeculum before it really began. I long held the belief that democracy cannot be based on the masses but only on an aristocracy. To come back to the experiment: we Jews, ever since our dispersal among other peoples, have always been the actual experimental objects in such world-historical trials. That is how the Middle Ages began, that is what the first stage of absolutism was like, and that is how it has been over the last century. We Jews in Germany carry the burden for all other Jews. And this year will be a difficult year; the wheel is turning faster and faster. It will really test our nerves

---

6. Hebrew: Jewish pioneer project in Palestine. "Clerical party" refers to the pre-*Anschluss* attempts by Austrian chancellor Kurt Schuschnigg to forge an anti-Nazi alliance by appealing to Catholic circles.

7. Diary note by Friedrich Brodnitz, April 5, 1938, USHMMA Acc. 2008.189.1 Brodnitz collection. On anti-Jewish violence in 1938 Vienna, see Hans Witek and Hans Safrian, *Und keiner war dabei: Dokumente des alltäglichen Antisemitismus in Wien 1938* (Vienna: Picus, 1988).

and our capacity for careful thought. I often think of Kipling's "Recession" [*sic*; "Recessional," a well-known poem by Rudyard Kipling; the following is in English in the original]: Lord, God of Hosts, be with us yet, lest we forget, lest we forget. [. . .]

While most outside observers found it difficult to fathom the depth of the changes taking place in Vienna and other parts of Austria, a representative of the **World Jewish Congress**, writing from the nearby vantage point of Trieste, Italy, did gain a clear sense of what was underway. Viennese Jews were "constantly taken out of their homes and forced to clean and scrape the slogans from the walls and sidewalks painted in connection with the Schuschnigg plebiscite" (the event planned by the Austrian government of Kurt Schuschnigg that Germany had used as subterfuge for invasion). The number of Jewish funerals had risen from an average of 3 or 4 to 140 a day; among them "suicides and heart failures are the majority."[8]

DOCUMENT 10-3: **Jewish refugees crossing the Austrian-Swiss border being searched by Swiss border police, August 20, 1938, USHMMPA WS# 66047.**

---

8. Baruch Zuckerman, WJC, Trieste, to Nahum Goldmann, April 5, 1938; facsimile reprint in Henry Friedlander and Sybil Milton, eds., *Archives of the Holocaust: An International Collection of Selected Documents* (New York: Garland Publishing, 1990ff.), doc. 11, 8:24–27.

For Jews in Austria, there was little time during the *Anschluss* to reflect. Writing in 1940 from their places of exile as part of an essay contest solicited by Harvard University on the topic "My Life in Germany before and after January 1933," Philipp Flesch and Margarete Neff-Jerome describe some of their experiences during these months.

DOCUMENT 10-4: Philipp Flesch,[9] "My Life in Germany before and after January 30, 1933," LBINY MM 22/ME 132, 10–17 (translated from German).

[. . .] Vienna covered itself in swastikas. Since not enough badges were for sale, people wore badges they had made themselves from sheet metal, tin foil, and other material. There were also not enough flags so that the red-and-white flags of the Schuschnigg era had to be waved again. Houses owned by Jews also had to be decorated with flags, contrary to the laws in Germany proper [*Altreich*].

Day and night, the SA took Jews and known Schuschnigg supporters out of their apartments. Mostly they had to clean the floors of party halls [*Parteilokale*]. On the streets, Jewish passers-by were stopped and forced to clean up Schuschnigg's campaign slogans.

[. . . ; on the first day after the reopening of the school at which Flesch had been teaching for 12 years and formerly had been a pupil:] Colleagues stood around in the teacher's room adorned with the badges they had so long been prohibited from showing off publicly. About half of them wore the symbols of the "illegals" [i.e., the Nazi Party previously outlawed in Austria], which demonstrated that they had already worked secretly for the "party" under the old regime [i.e., Austrian chancellor Schuschnigg]. [. . .] Nobody showed sneering satisfaction; everybody was uncomfortable when they saw me and the other "defeated" entering. Some of them even shook hands with us; everybody felt awkward. I felt quite dizzy, put my desk in order and emptied it, suppressed the swelling tears, and went with my companions in fate into the principal's office. There, instead of the "black" [i.e., Austro-conservative] principal who had succeeded the "red" [Socialist] one, we now found the "brown" [Nazi] one: a young man who—as I heard later—came directly from Stein, a well-known prison, where he had been incarcerated for violent Nazi propaganda. Just like the other longtime

---

9. Philipp Flesch (1896–?) was a World War I veteran and scholar specializing in German philology. He taught at a public school for over a decade in his home city, Vienna, and was detained after the November pogrom before emigrating to the United States via the Netherlands in 1939. See LBINY catalog.

"illegals," he was certainly friendly and announced to us simply that the municipal school administrator [*Stadtschulrat*] had ordered our dismissal. And so we went home. The female colleagues cried, and we, the men, did not feel any better since there is probably not a teacher who is not connected with his job on a deep emotional level [*seelisch verwurzelt*]. [. . .]

In May [1938] or thereabouts, hundreds upon hundreds of Jews were arrested. Nobody knew why, and nobody could believe it, even when it was already clear that these people had been randomly sent to Dachau [concentration camp]. Only when the first urns with ashes arrived, mostly of physically fit young people who had only recently been seen walking around healthy and happy, the terrible truth became obvious. "Your Jew is dead. Pick up the urn," was often the literal wording of the notification. I continued my life as usual, except that I always carried all my papers with me, three kerchiefs, ersatz glasses, and in my wallet a well-hidden razor blade—just in case. But I was not arrested. [. . .]

Margarete Neff-Jerome, an actress born in Vienna in 1892, starts her account of the *Anschluss* by noting how much it felt like a repetition of the Nazi takeover in Germany in 1933.

DOCUMENT 10-5: Margarete Neff-Jerome,[10] "My Life in Germany before and after January 30, 1933," LBINY MM II 42/ME 1225, 67–68 (translated from German).

[. . .] Many of the finest who were not as blind as the rest committed suicide. Some men who had been frontline soldiers during the war assumed that this fact would protect them as it had been the case so far in Germany proper [*Altreich*]. It was difficult, actually almost impossible, to make a decent, impeccable, and apolitical person realize that since March 12, 1938, he had been outlawed in the very country he considered his home and had fought for. These naïve people put on their war medals when they left their home in order to protect themselves from harassment and mistreatment. If these people happened to be spared from cleaning the streets or insults, they deluded themselves by thinking it was the little ribbon in their buttonhole that had saved them. I pleaded urgently to my husband to prepare for our emigration, but he was so attached to this country that

10. Margarete Neff-Jerome (alias Franziska Schubert, b. 1892) was a stage actress first in Weimar and, after her emigration in 1935, in Vienna; she and her husband (who had been arrested after "*Kristallnacht*") managed to escape to Switzerland in March 1939. See *Datenbank zur Liste der jüdischen Einwohner im Deutschen Reich, 1933–1945* (Berlin: Bundesarchiv, 2008); LBINY catalog.

he could not go through with it. His mother created the most difficulties. She refused to hear and see what was going on around her and was convinced that she and her family would doubtless be spared. So all my pleading was in vain. [. . .]

Protected by foreign passports, tourists and foreign visitors who happened to be in Vienna in these tumultuous days could often speak more openly than their Jewish counterparts. Among them were the Bakers, a Christian family from New York City, who had spent several months in what was then still autonomous Austria before they got caught in the *Anschluss* on their way back to the United States. From Venice, Helen Baker wrote to her son Phil in the United States about what they had witnessed in the former Austrian capital.

DOCUMENT 10-6: Letter by Helen Baker, Venice, to Phil Baker, May 1, 1938, USHMMA Acc 2006.265 Baker collection.

[. . .] Boy-oh boy! Were we glad to shake the dust of Vienna from our feet! It was awfully interesting and exciting while the bloodless revolution was actually in progress of revolving, but after the election [plebiscite held on April 10 regarding the *Anschluss*] things began to tighten up and we became more and more uncomfortable until we could hardly wait to get out.

Before the election the drive against the Jews was bad, but as soon as the vote was in,[11] they really began to put the screws on. On the last Saturday that we were there, a Nazi was stationed in front of every Jewish store to prevent Aryans from going in. We ran several experiments knowing that, as Americans, we could go wherever we chose. They stopped us, asked if we were Aryan, and then informed us that it was a Jewish store. With one exception, it was sufficient to say that we were *"Ausländer"* ["foreigners"], but this man was downright mean and threatened to arrest me if I went in. It was too close to our departure to take any chances, but I certainly was tempted to call his bluff, for of course he had no right to stop me. As there were all sorts of unreasonable arrests, I probably would have been taken and no telling how long it would have been before my case came up. [. . .]

Jewish restaurants were raided by Nazis, and everyone had to show his pass to prove that he was Jewish. An Aryan caught buying in a Jewish

---

11. The plebiscite ended with an approval rate aimed at by all dictatorships: according to the official result, 99.5 percent of eligible voters in Austria and the Reich cast their ballot, with 99.73 percent (Austria) and 99.02 percent (Reich) agreeing to the *Anschluss* and a total of about 440,000 persons voting against it.

store was often made to walk the streets wearing a large placard [saying,] *"Ich bin ein deutsches Schwein und kauf' bei Juden ein"* ["I am a German swine and buy at Jewish shops"]. They even branded some on the forehead with indelible ink, with this same rhyme.

We met a very nice Jewish couple at the [U.S.] mission. He was an electrical engineer in Germany, making an excellent living until driven out. They came to Vienna and had—or have a few roomers. The Nazis first took his license plates and then came back and took his car. He was also one of hundreds who were compelled to scrub the streets on their hands and knees to remove the Schuschnigg propaganda signs. [. . .]

Of course the suicides among the Jews and the active members of the Vaterländische Front (Schuschnigg's organization) reached appalling numbers. One doctor that we know of was called for sixty [suicides] in one day, and there were probably about two hundred daily for the first week or two.

Father saw a store owner being made to paint his own window with a huge *JUDE* [Jew]—that was just before we left. They [shops owned by Jews] all were so designated. [. . .]

The extract in document 10-7 is from a long litany of discriminatory measures reported to the Jewish Telegraph Agency in Paris by an anonymous correspondent. It adds further detail to the picture in what had once been Austria and also offers a clear indication that in the wake of the *Anschluss*, anti-Jewish policy was heating up elsewhere in Germany too.

DOCUMENT 10-7: **Report by anonymous author on the persecution of Jews in Central European countries in the first half of June 1938, USHMMA RG 11.001M.25, reel 106 (SAM 674-1-109, 114–22) (translated from German).**

Germany.

[. . .] Property must be registered by June 30. The forms and ordinances concerning implementation were issued during the first week of June.

The banking firm of M. Warburg & Co. in Hamburg has been made Jew-free.[12]

---

12. See A. J. Sherman, "A Jewish Bank during the Schacht Era: M. M. Warburg & Co., 1933–1938," in *Juden im nationalsozialistischen Deutschland: The Jews in Nazi Germany, 1933–1945,* ed. Arnold Paucker (Tübingen: J. C. B. Mohr, 1986), 125–52.

Aryanization in Germany has proceeded at an increased pace. [. . .]

The Gestapo informed the Jewish community in Saarbrücken that Saarbrücken must be free of Jews within three years. [. . .]

Hitler has ordered that the big synagogue in Munich be torn down to make room for a parking lot. Demolition began immediately, and only with considerable effort were the community's religious functionaries able to save the holy Torah scrolls and other religious articles.[13]

Nazi officials have ordered immediate razing of the synagogue in Nuremberg in the middle of the city, a large structure built in the Moorish style. [. . .]

Austria

The suffering of Jews in Austria continues to increase. The persecution has no end. On the contrary: it becomes ever more vicious. [. . .]

One day SA men mounted a *Stürmer* poster on the gates of the Rothschild Hospital. Despite entreaties from hospital administrators to show some consideration for the patients, the poster remained up. The administration was even obliged to hire officers from a private security company [*Wach- und Schliessgesellschaft*] for two nights and pay them out of their own funds to protect the poster as it was assumed that Nazi provocateurs would tear down the poster and that the hospital administration would then face extremely harsh reprisals. [. . .]

Dr. David Schapira of 3 [Vienna's 3rd district] Hohlweggasse 12, a veteran frontline officer and blind from his war injuries, owned a law office and a tobacco and newspaper shop. The law firm had of course lost its clientele, and despite the assurances of some high Nazi officials, the shop was also taken away from him after the boycott. Guided by his wife, he then went to the ministry to hand in a petition, and he took all of his war decorations and medals for bravery along. He was nonetheless dismissed by a Nazi functionary with the following words: "Jewish scoundrel [*Lump*], you can shove that Habsburg stuff [*Habsburgerstand*] up your ass.

---

13. On the destruction of the Munich synagogue, see the memoir by Alfred Neumeyer, longtime president of the Munich Jewish community and board member of the Reichsvertretung, LBINY MM 59, 212–13. Neumeyer states that the Jewish community leaders voiced a "suppressed protest" (*verhaltenen Protest*) against the demolition order by the Bavarian state secretary of the interior; on June 8, 1938, after the last service, the Torah scrolls were taken "in a solemn procession" to the community administration. The next day the demolition started; the nearly new organ was taken by the Catholic archbishop for use in a church.

Shove off, and don't come back, or I'll throw you down the stairs—maybe then you'll be able to see again."[14] [. . .]

At the beginning of June, park benches for Jews [*Judenbänke*] appeared for the first time, namely, in the 9th district on the Elisabeth Promenade. Every fourth bench had white block letters written on it with the words, "Jews Only" [*Nur für Juden*]. These benches were not painted yellow but brown [like the benches for non-Jews]. Needless to say, no one dares to sit on these benches out of fear of being accosted [compare document 10-8 below]. Soon these Jewish benches, whose introduction was announced in advance some time ago, will be found in all the parks.

During the first days of June, around 10,000 Jewish prisoners from Vienna were taken to Dachau concentration camp.

An estimated 6,000 Jews were arrested in Austria during the Pentecost week. [. . .]

A series of deaths have been reported from Dachau.

All Jewish lawyers have been forbidden from practicing their profession. They must wind up their business affairs within the next three weeks.

In the Burgenland the SA again violently dragged 40 Jews to the border [*an die Grenze*]. We have not been able to learn what happened to them since then. The Jews in the Burgenland are in a state of panic.[15]

Aryan lawyers in Vienna are not allowed to represent Jews.

Countless young Jewish academics have been sent to perform forced labor on the floodplain [*Überschwemmungsgebiet*] of Styria [Steiermark]. [. . .]

An antisemitic newspaper is calling on the streetcar authority to institute special compartments for Jews, similar to the "Jim Crow" (Negro compartment in America).

---

14. This may have been Dr. David Schapira (b. 1897), who was deported to the Theresienstadt ghetto in the autumn of 1942 but survived the war and returned to Vienna at least for a time. See Hubert Steiner and Christian Kucsera, *Recht als Unrecht: Quellen zur wirtschaftlichen Entrechtung der Wiener Juden durch die NS-Vermögensverkehrsstelle* (Vienna: Österreichisches Staatsarchiv, 1993), 249; *USHMM ITS Collection Data Base Central Name Index*.

15. In 1934, roughly thirty-six hundred Jews lived in Burgenland, an eastern Austrian province. Immediately following the *Anschluss*, Nazi police agencies implemented a policy of expulsion across the border into Hungary. By the end of 1938, some 1,286 Jews had either emigrated or been expelled from the province. See Wolfgang Neugebauer and Herbert Steiner, *Widerstand und Verfolgung im Burgenland, 1934–1945: Eine Dokumentation,* (Vienna: Österreichischer Bundesverlag, 1983), 319–20; Gert Tschögl, Barbara Tobler, and Alfred Lang, *Vertrieben: Erinnerungen burgenländischer Juden und Jüdinnen* (Vienna: Mandelbaum, 2004), 505. On the expulsion of Jews, including citizens of Czechoslovakia, from annexed Austria later in 1938, see Friedländer, *Nazi Germany*, 1:265–66.

Well-informed circles are saying that the number of Jews who have been driven to suicide now exceeds 6,800 [in Austria]. A furniture dealer in the 2nd district [in Vienna] killed himself along with his spouse, son, daughter-in-law, and 5-year-old grandchild. The next day the SA affixed a poster to his shuttered business reading, "We strongly urge others to follow his example" [*"Zur Nachahmung dringend empfohlen"*].

DOCUMENT 10-8: **Racially segregated park benches, 1938, USHMMPA WS# 33983 and 11195.**

Lizi Rosenfeld, a Jewish woman, sits on a park bench marked "Only for Aryans," Vienna, August 30, 1938, USHMMPA WS# 33983

A woman who is concealing her face sits on a park bench marked "Only for Jews," unspecified date (March 1938?) and locality, USHMMPA WS# 11195

INTENSIFYING RACIAL SEGREGATION

Indeed, the wave of persecution in Austria swept not only back to Germany but out to other countries in Central Europe, providing stimulus to a large but disparate group of anti-Jewish activists. Though rooted in different traditions, driven by different interests, and manifesting themselves in different forms, antisemitic incidents spread from Romania to France, from Poland to Hungary. Together they conveyed one message: life for Jews in Europe, particularly in Central Europe, was becoming more and more difficult. Few sources capture the contemporary Jewish sense of a pan-European threat more clearly than a series of reports compiled by the Jewish Telegraph Agency in Paris from which we present a selection.

DOCUMENT 10-9: "Overview of the Persecution of Jews in Central European Countries" for the period April 25 to May 3, 1938, USHMMA RG 11.001M.25, reel 106 (SAM 674-1-109, 1–5) (translated from German).

[. . . ; regarding the intensified expulsion of Jews from the German economy:] The law on the disclosure of Jewish assets already applies to foreign Jews. The drift of anti-Jewish persecution in Germany points to the future inclusion of foreign Jews in Nazi legislation. The German Nazis are beginning to extend anti-Jewish laws to citizens of allied states too small to fight back. For instance, Jews from Hungary are no longer able to obtain visas. These actions represent attempts to discriminate against foreign Jews in the same manner as against the German Jews. [. . .]

[Austria:] The president of the community, Dr. Desider Friedmann, was detained in Dachau [concentration camp].[16] He was released and held office in Vienna for two days only to be arrested by the Gestapo again. His current whereabouts in prison are unknown.

The number of suicides since Hitler took over Austria is estimated to be 2,000; the number of Jews arrested is estimated to be 12,000; the number of Jewish workers and employees laid off without notice or further payment amounts to 8,000.

The Jewish section of the central cemetery [*Zentralfriedhof*] in Vienna receives dead bodies in closed caskets from the Nazis on a daily basis. They

16. Desider Friedmann (1880–1944) was a lawyer and from 1933 the president of the Jewish community in Vienna. After incarceration in the Dachau concentration camp from April 1938 to the spring of 1939, he was deported to Theresienstadt in September 1942; he and his wife, Ella, died after being deported to Auschwitz in October 1944. See Rabinovici, *Instanzen*.

are ordered to bury them immediately. Opening the caskets is severely punished. [. . .]

The inmates of the Jewish orphanage at [street address:] Türkenschanz Place—there are 70 orphans between the ages of 6 months and 14 years—have been evicted. The orphanage was seized. Even the clothes supplied by the orphanage were taken away from the children.

The Gestapo demands that 25,000 Jews emigrate by the end of 1938. Raids of Jewish homes continue. Above all, money, jewelry, silver dishes, and rugs are taken.

Every Jew wanting to emigrate from Austria has to provide a confirmation that all taxes have been paid and that he will never return to Austria or Germany, respectively. They are also forbidden from taking cash with them.

The treatment of the Austrian Jews and the expulsion from Austria is comparable to only one historic incident: the Armenian expulsion from Asia Minor by the Turks.[17] [. . .]

DOCUMENT 10-10: "Overview of the Persecution of Jews in Central European Countries" for the period May 11 to 17, 1938, USHMMA RG 11.001M.25, reel 106 (SAM 674-1-109, 26–39) (translated from German).

[. . . ; Germany:] A debate ensued in the German newspapers about whether a German can be forced to share a house with Jews. Through this debate the Nazis want above all to devalue Jewish-owned houses. [. . .] The effective outcome of the whole thing will be the creation of a Jewish ghetto [. . .]

[Austria:] The Austrian provinces in Upper and Lower Austria and Styria treat the Jews especially inhumanely. Jews are put on trucks, prohibited from taking any of their possessions, and then taken either to some border or to Vienna, where they are dumped in front of the Rothschild Hospital or else before the Jewish nursing home. No office cares what happens to them. Those who dare to go back to their hometowns are arrested. [. . .]

Schools: A letter from a student of a middle school [*Realschule*] in Glasergasse, Vienna's 9th district: "All Jewish children had to leave the school, since they are to be concentrated in purely Jewish schools. However, most of them are leaving school altogether. So am I." [. . .]

---

17. For the persecution of Armenians and the Armenian genocide during World War I, see Donald Bloxham, *Genocide, the World Wars and the Unweaving of Europe* (London: Vallentine Mitchell, 2008), 19–98.

[Belgium:] Because of the coming communal elections in Belgium, followers of the Rexist leader Degrelle organized a particularly antisemitic demonstration: "Jews out!" "Down with the Jews!" "Let us do the same as in Germany and Austria!" Those were the slogans protesters carried through the streets.[18]

[France:] In France the number of anti-Jewish pamphlets sold very cheaply at kiosks or on the street is increasing daily. It is likely that most of these pamphlets are paid for with German money.[19] [. . .]

DOCUMENT 10-11: "Overview of the Persecution of Jews in Central European Countries" for the period May 18 to 24, 1938, USHMMA RG 11.001M.25, reel 106 (SAM 674-1-109, 55–65) (translated from German).

[. . . ; Austria:] In Kobersdorf (Burgenland) a pack of SA men attacked the 30-year-old rabbi, a Hungarian citizen named Goldberger.[20] His entire property, everything that could be sold quickly, was confiscated. Later, the rabbi, his wife who had recently given birth, and three children— aged three weeks, a year and a half, and three years—were put on a truck together with the furniture left by the German robbers. They were brought close to the Hungarian village Harko. Three hundred steps away from the Hungarian customs official, yet still on Austrian soil, the SA men threw humans and furniture onto the street in the crudest way. The rabbi wanted to cross the border; yet, the Hungarian border control had to explain to him that according to new regulations, he was allowed to cross the border only with the permission of the Hungarian consulate in Vienna. Rabbi Goldberger had to shelter himself and his family from the icy cold and the raging snowstorm in a small hut. This hut did not have a door but simply an opening in the wooden wall. He had to sleep the night on the muddy floor. People from the close-by border town of Szopozn [correct (Hungarian): Sopron] (Oedenburg) who had heard of the incident came to the border station with pillows and food. Yet, they were not allowed to

---

18. Léon Degrelle (1906–1994) founded the extreme right-wing Rexist Party in Leuwen (Louvain, Belgium) in 1930, collaborated with the Germans during the occupation of Belgium, and commanded a Walloon/Flemish military unit.

19. See Michael R. Marrus, "Vichy before Vichy: Antisemitic Currents in France during the 1930s," *WL Bulletin* 33 (1980): 13–19; Renée Poznanski, *Jews in France during World War II* (Waltham, MA: Brandeis University Press in association with the USHMM, 2001), 1–17.

20. The authors have not been able to find further information on this family or its fate.

see the rabbi, who was still located on Austrian soil. Again and again they were scared away across the border by the SA men.

After a few hours, three armed SA men ejected the rabbi from the hut with the words, "Get up, Jewish pig [*Saujud*]. Take your stuff on your crooked back and get out immediately." The three SA men hit the rabbi with rifle butts. He suffered a broken rib, lying in his own blood. Meantime, the other SA men took away the blanket the children were lying on, saying, "Jew children should lie on the floor." The rabbi hauled himself in the direction of the Hungarian border police, even though the Nazis continued beating him. He succeeded in reaching the border. Now the Hungarian border police had mercy and called for medical help from Szoporn [Sopron]. Rabbi Goldberger has suffered severe injuries. The children's fingers and feet were frozen. At the moment the family is in Oedenburg. [. . .]

[Poland:]: At the main council meeting of the OZON (the ruling party),[21] 15 items regarding the Jewish question were decided. The Jews were treated as an alien, even hostile element of the state. The main task of the Polish state in the future is to reduce the number of Jews through emigration. On the basis of special laws, the Jews will be removed from those branches of public life in which they still play a role. [. . .]

DOCUMENT 10-12: "Overview of the Persecution of Jews in Central European Countries" for the period May 25 to 31, 1938, USHMMA RG 11.001M.25, reel 106 (SAM 674-1-109, 66–74) (translated from German).

[. . . ; Austria:] The wave of suicides in Austria will not end. [. . .] Several Jewish people who escaped from Austria and wanted to swim across the March River on the border were shot and subsequently drowned. [. . .]

The introduction of the Nuremberg Laws [in former Austria on May 20, 1938] was followed by a Gestapo action in the course of which hundreds of Jews were taken to prison. October 1, 1935, is supposed to be the cutoff date. The police are forced to intervene in any case of race defilement [*"Rassenschande"*] that has occurred since then. Denunciation flourishes. [. . .]

[Poland:] Following the example of the Jewish factory owners in Łódź, Warsaw businessmen, wholesale dealers, and salesmen decided to

---

21. OZON is short for Obóz Zjednoczenia Narodowego (Camp of National Unity), a Polish political party founded in 1937 with an antisemitic agenda.

boycott Nazi merchants from Danzig, who have put up signs on their stores: "Jews are not wanted here." [. . .] The association of Christian retailers handed over a memorandum to the minister of trade, demanding the establishment of ghetto markets especially for Jewish traders "to calm the situation."

DOCUMENT 10-13: **"Overview of the Persecution of Jews in Central European Countries" for the period June 1 to 6, 1938, USHMMA RG 11.001M.25, reel 106 (SAM 674-1-109, 98–103) (translated from German).**

[. . . ; Austria:] A lot of nervous breakdowns and screaming fits occur in front of the Viennese registrar's offices when persons unexpectedly find out about their non-Aryan descent. Students who have finished their studies and have to pass their last exam have to file as Jews for admission. These petitions have been denied without exception.

Members of the Hakoah swimming club were taken from their apartments by their competitors, the First Viennese Swimming Club. They had to scrub the streets with a hot acid. Following this treatment, it was impossible for the swimmers to practice. That way the Nazi swimmers got rid of their competitors. [. . .]

[Danzig:] Due to the five-year celebration of the Nazis' rise to power in Danzig, the Nuremberg Laws are expected to be announced on June 19, and thus a state of affairs will become official that has in practical terms long been in effect.[22] [. . .]

REVERBERATIONS IN THE REICH

Although "*Kristallnacht*" has justifiably been seen as a major turning point, many of the documents above make clear that the marked deterioration in the position of German Jews in 1938 began well before November. As Frank Stern has pointed out in relation to the postwar memories of non-Jewish Germans, many observers tended in retrospect to telescope onto November 9 events that in fact occurred over a much longer period.[23] After the *Anschluss*, German *Juden-*

---

22. Despite a Nazi Party majority in the city's parliament, Danzig remained a "free city" under the League of Nations until its occupation by German troops at the onset of the war against Poland in September 1939. See Carl Jacob Burckhardt, *Meine Danziger Mission, 1937–1939* (Munich: Callwey, 1980).

23. Frank Stern, *The Whitewashing of the Yellow Badge: Antisemitism and Philosemitism in Postwar Germany* (Oxford: Pergamon Press 1992).

politik went into overdrive, accelerating earlier trends and preparing the ground for the November pogroms. The two most important components of this assault were a massive push for Jewish emigration, coordinated by **Heydrich**'s burgeoning security police and SD apparatus, and the equally overwhelming grab for Jews' remaining assets. The latter was presaged by the compulsory registration of Jewish property.

DOCUMENT 10-14: **Luise Solmitz, diary entry for April 27, 1938, FZGH 11 S 12 (translated from German).**

April 27, 1938

"Compulsory registration of Jewish property with a value exceeding RM 5,000." "The Plenipotentiary for the Four-Year Plan [Hermann Göring] may implement the measures necessary to secure use of the compulsorily registered property in the interests of the German economy."[24] This means: expropriation. Date fixed for registration: June 30. Registration is also compulsory for non-Jewish spouses. "Property does not include: movable goods that are intended exclusively for the personal use of the person obliged to register property & household goods, to the extent that they are not luxury items."

And so our house is "property." Our mortgage, in the trusty hands of Frau W., will be invested as one thinks best.

We don't want to whine. What use would it be? We all go our own way. When I think back on how I used to imagine my life, I could never have anticipated such troubles. [The following two words are in English in the original:] Outcast, outlaw . . . that's the only fate left to the two of us, the realm that will remain for us.

Referring to his distinguished military service during World War I and his "mixed marriage," **Luise Solmitz**'s Jewish husband, Fredy, appealed the property decision. Despite increased overall dispossession after "*Kristallnacht*," in the spring of 1939 his appeal was granted—according to his wife's diary, it was the only exemption the authorities allowed for the entire Hamburg area.

Once the authorities had stripped them of their belongings, Jews became a liability, dependent on outside support and not one that German government

---

24. "Verordnung über die Anmeldung des Vermögens von Juden," issued on April 26, 1938, by Göring (Beauftragter für den Vierjahresplan); see Joseph Walk, ed., *Das Sonderrecht für die Juden im NS-Staat: Eine Sammlung der gesetzlichen Maßnahmen und Richtlinien—Inhalt und Bedeutung* (Heidelberg: UTB, 1996), 223, no. 457.

agencies were eager to shoulder. On the contrary, with the German economy gearing up for war in the interest of "**Aryans**" only, social welfare and other benefits for Jews, even where still guaranteed under existing law, appeared as outdated aberrations. If anyone was to pay for Jews remaining in Germany, it should be the Jews. In this climate, eager bureaucrats practiced piecemeal discrimination until new, more sweeping regulations came into force. As early as the spring of 1938, to take one example, Jews who had lost all their assets and were forced to apply for public welfare found themselves drafted for forced labor. As document 10-15 shows, state-sponsored robbery of the Jews went hand in hand with humiliating them.

DOCUMENT 10-15: Correspondence between CV regional office East Prussia (Angerthal)[25] and CV head office Berlin, March 31/April 1, 1938, USHMMA RG 11.001M.31, reel 146 (SAM 721-1-3030, 23–24) (translated from German).

[Letter by Max Angerthal, March 31, 1938, regarding welfare recipients (*Wohlfahrtsempfänger*) in Marienburg:]

Three welfare recipients, including two longtime residents and former business owners, were, as part of their weekly duty work [*Pflichtarbeit*] of two days, assigned to sweeping the streets in front of the new and old town hall as well as the "Lauben" (the main business street).

Though we understand that they are severely depressed, we are not of the opinion that we can advise them not to do the work. We would be grateful for an immediate response and instructions.

[Response letter by the CV head office, April 1, 1938:]

The relevant instructions are to be found in § 19 of the [Prussian] Welfare Regulation [*Verordnung über die Fürsorgepflicht*] dated February 13, 1924. It is stated there:

["]The support for those capable of work can be supplied in suitable cases by requiring appropriate work for the communal benefit or made dependant on such work, except where this would result in obvious hardship or where a law rules out such work.["] In our experience, the concept of "appropriate work" is in practice very broadly defined, while "obvious hardship" is very narrowly defined. We thus cannot recommend declining the work. [. . .]

---

25. For information concerning Dr. Max Angerthal (b. 1906 in Stettin) see page 106, note 11.

DOCUMENT 10-16: **Two Jewish men on their way to forced labor, Berlin, March 1938, printed from Barbara Schieb, *Nachricht von Chotzen* (Berlin: Edition Hentrich, 2000), 86.**

Fifty-four-year-old Josef Chotzen (right) with his colleague Buxbaum on their way to forced labor, Berlin, in March 1938.

This was just the beginning; far worse, in fact deadly, forms of exploitation by labor followed during the war.[26]

Another example of bureaucratic initiative from 1938 can be seen in the efforts to drive Jews out of their often long-held places of residence, even though such internal displacement had no basis in German law. In the cities, as the author of the report quoted in document 10-10 states, the pressure to segregate Jewish from non-Jewish tenants raised the real danger of "the creation of a Jewish ghetto."[27] Outside the urban centers, eager local Nazi activists agitated to remove the Jews completely from their villages and small towns.

Jewish relief and self-help agencies had had to contend for some time with the issue of migration from rural areas to the cities. On occasion, the Jewish

---

26. See Wolf Gruner, *Jewish Forced Labor under the Nazis: Economic Needs and Racial Aims, 1938–1944* (New York: Cambridge University Press in association with the USHMM, 2006).

27. See document 10-10.

bodies were able to coordinate their activities with the state agencies. In Bavaria, for example, the Munich-based Association of Bavarian Jewish Communities (Verband Bayerischer Israelitischer Gemeinden) managed the exodus from the rural communities and worked out a schedule with the authorities. In the spring of 1938, however, the few remaining Jews in the village of Schopfloch in Bavaria received an unexpected "expulsion order" (*Ausweisungsbefehl*) from the local Nazi Party leader. In a letter to the Jewish community in Schopfloch, the Association of Bavarian Jewish Communities stated that the order must have been a "misunderstanding" as "the entire relocation planning [*Wanderungsplanung*] can be determined and executed only in conjunction with the Reich leadership and thus the party." The community, according to the advice from Jewish leaders in Munich, should check with the local Nazi Party leader, while Jewish World War I veterans, "who as is generally known enjoy special status, according to the will of the Führer," should try to calm down community members.[28]

This letter did little to allay the fears of the Schopfloch community. As the **CV** had been disallowed in Bavaria in 1933, one of its local branches in the neighboring state of Württemberg took up the Schopfloch case with the Berlin head office, which in turn tried to remove the "relocation" threat via the Bavarian Association and the **Hilfsverein**. The CV regional branch Württemberg office noted in early June 1938 that the issue had not been resolved satisfactorily and attached the letter presented in document 10-17, written by a Jewish resident in Schopfloch, for it to be passed on via the CV head office to the **Reichsvertretung**.

---

28. Letter by Verband Bayerischer Israelitischer Gemeinden (Dr. Weiler), Munich, to the head of the Jewish community Schopfloch, April 10, 1938; USHMMA RG 11.001M.31, reel 101 (SAM 721-1-2317, 340).

DOCUMENT 10-17: Letter by CV regional office Württemberg, Stuttgart, to CV head office Berlin, June 1, 1938, with attached copy of a letter by an anonymous Jewish resident ("Alfred")[29] in Schopfloch, Bavaria, May 30, 1938, USHMMA RG-11.001M.01, reel 101 (SAM 721-1-2317, 336–37) (translated from German).

[Letter by "Alfred" from Schopfloch:]

Dear ones,

I was in Munich at the offices of the Bavarian Jewish communities concerning our move away from here. I discussed everything in detail with Justice Councillor [*Justizrat*] Österreicher, deputy chairman of the association [Association of Bavarian Jewish Communities].[30] However, the gentlemen are completely powerless and thus cannot intervene.

Since then our situation has deteriorated because on Friday we received the so-called expulsion order. The local head of the Nazi Party [*Ortsgruppenleiter*] literally said, "If you Jews don't disappear soon, we'll make an awful mess [*dann machen wir einen Saustall*], even bigger than the one in Feuchtwangen."[31]

We are placing all our hopes on the sale of our house and on leaving Schopfloch as quickly as possible. Frankfurt is probably an option. We are

---

29. Perhaps this is Alfred Cahn (1893–?), a longtime resident of Schopfloch who later moved to Frankfurt am Main. In October 1941 he was deported to the Łódź ghetto, where he died. See www.alemannia-judaica.de/schopfloch_synagoge.htm#Zur%20Geschichte%20d er%20jüdischen%20Gemeinde (accessed November 24, 2008). Other Jews from Schopfloch relocated to Nuremberg, Würzburg, or Stuttgart, from where they were deported to their death in Kovno and Riga (see Wolfgang Scheffler and Diana Schulle, eds., *Buch der Erinnerung: Die ins Baltikum deportierten deutschen, österreichischen und tschechoslowakischen Juden*, 2 vols. (Munich: K. G. Saur, 2003).

30. This may have been Carl Österreich (1877–1961), a longtime Munich lawyer who served as a leader in the Jewish community in Munich and was active in Bavarian Jewish organizations. Interned in Dachau in 1938, he managed to emigrate to London in 1939, where he died in 1961. See Hans Lamm, ed., *Vergangene Tage: Jüdische Kultur in München* (Munich: Langen Müller, 1982), 447–48, 515; Werner Röder and Herbert A. Strauss, eds. *Biographisches Handbuch der deutschsprachigen Emigration nach 1933*, Bd. 1, *Politik, Wirtschaft, Öffentliches Leben* (Munich: K. G. Saur, 1980), 538; *Datenbank zur Liste der jüdischen Einwohner im Deutschen Reich, 1933–1945*.

31. In December 1937, Nazi Party members agitated for the expulsion of Jews from Feuchtwangen, Bavaria. Over the next several months, the majority of Feuchtwangen's Jewish population relocated, making the community *judenfrei* as early as March of the following year. See Dietrich Weiss, Erich Binder, and Fritz Wunschenmeyer, *Aus der Geschichte der jüdischen Gemeinde von Feuchtwangen, 1274–1938* (Feuchtwangen: Arbeitsgemeinschaft für Heimatsgeschichte, 1991), 48–66.

hoping that everything proceeds smoothly, and we only wish that it were all over already. In case I hear from the Hilfsverein, I will let you know. We do not know yet how we shall support ourselves since we cannot take the children. Everything is very difficult, although we should be glad to have a little peace for a change.

It is not clear whether the Jews of Schopfloch left because they were forcibly relocated or because the threat of the "eviction order" was sufficient to make them flee their homes with whatever assets they could liquidate. Whatever the cause, the outcome is clear. Even before the November pogrom, a number of Bavarian communities had managed to become—as a report by the regional government in Franconia noted—"entirely free of Jews" (*völlig judenfrei*).[32]

As in earlier phases, some changes in the regulations applying to Jews were small and barely visible for those not directly affected; others represented more significant policy changes—almost exclusively for the worse. In the context of such a downward spiral, even those few newly implemented measures that might have some temporary or marginally positive side effect often appeared in a negative light. One of these measures was a change in German family law on April 12, 1938, that became part of the German civil code and affected the way in which German authorities determined who was a Jew. Triggered by earlier discussions among state jurists in Germany rather than by the *Anschluss*, the revision enabled prosecutors to open cases for the purpose of determining the paternity of a person whose racial ancestry was unclear. In essence, the new law charged prosecutors with establishing whether that person's father was the mother's husband—the father of record—or another man—the biological father. When the amendment to the family law was being introduced, the World Jewish Congress office in Paris saw the change as just one of many discriminatory measures enacted in early 1938 that further eroded the status of Jews in Germany.[33] They were right insofar as the regime now had the legal tools to redefine a person's racial status. Yet, the more the situation in the Reich worsened, the more Jews grasped this unlikely opportunity to escape the trap of the Nuremberg Laws either for themselves or their descendents.

32. Report by Regierungspräsident Ober- und Mittelfranken for September 1938, quoted in Michael Wildt, *Volksgemeinschaft als Selbstermächtigung: Gewalt gegen Juden in der deutschen Provinz, 1919–1939* (Hamburg: Hamburger Edition, 2007), 316.

33. See "Übersicht über die Verfolgungen gegen die Juden in den zentraleuropäischen Ländern (18.–24. Mai 1938)," World Jewish Congress Office Paris; USHMMA RG 11.001M.36, reel 106 (SAM 674-1-109).

Approaching a state prosecutor with the request to open a paternity case required evidence to the effect that the father of record was in fact not the biological father and that the child had been conceived in an adulterous affair. Even in cases where it was true, this argument went against the most basic tenets of conventional morality and filial loyalty, especially when the parents were still alive. It also required each applicant to agree to (and pay for) a full-scale genealogical and racial investigation by court-appointed experts. Numerically speaking, only a fraction of those labeled as Jews or *"Mischlinge"* could and did challenge the application of the Nuremberg race code by seeking to change the state's definition; as part of the spectrum of Jewish reactions, however, the hundreds, if not thousands, of cases brought before German prosecutors by Jewish applicants from 1938 and especially after the beginning of deportations to "the East" in the fall of 1941 are important.[34] Document 10-18, written by a *"Mischling"* and retired captain in the German army on behalf of his eight-year-old son, offers an example of an early case.

DOCUMENT 10-18: Letter by Hellmut S., Berlin, to Berlin Public Prosecutor's Office (*Staatsanwaltschaft*), September 13, 1938, USHMMA RG 14.070M, reel 1493, frames 136–38 (LAB A Rep. 358-02, #55243, 1–2)[35] (translated from German).

Re: Paternity suit (*Anfechtungsklage*) on behalf of Leo Günther S.
To the Berlin Public Prosecutor's Office:
As legal custodian and father of record of Leo Günther S., I dutifully report the following facts to the Berlin Public Prosecutor's Office:
On May 21, 1926, I married Miss Dorothea N. of Kolberg in Kolberg.
Evidence: book of authenticated family documents [*Familienbuch*], 4–5: Appendix 1 [This and the following appendices not reprinted here.]
(I request return of this book.)
On April 26, 1930, a boy who was given the name Leo Günther was born in wedlock in the city of Stuttgart. The birth was entered in the registry of births in Stuttgart as number 1961 for the year 1930.
Evidence: book of authenticated family document, 6: Appendix 1
Three years into the marriage, I determined that the boy's father was not myself but rather a Mr. Alfred B. from Mariatal bei Glatz in Silesia.

---

34. See Jürgen Matthäus, "Evading Persecution: German-Jewish Behavior Patterns after 1933," in *Jewish Life in Nazi Germany*, ed. Francis R. Nicosia (New York: Berghahn, 2010).

35. The authors have rendered the surnames mentioned in this document anonymous. The later fate of Hellmut S., born in Silesia in 1896 and residing in Berlin by the mid-1930s, is not clear.

No objection to [the boy's] in-wedlock status [*Einspruch gegen die Ehelichkeit*] was lodged at that time because it would not have been possible under the German Civil Code.

The Berlin regional court [*Landgericht*] granted a divorce [to us], ruling that both partners shared guilt. The verdict took effect on February 13, 1934, under the number 289R.10293.33.

Evidence: excerpts copied from the divorce decree: Appendix 2

In the spring of 1938, I learned that my father, also the grandfather of Leo Günther S., according to the current register entry, was a full Jew [*Volljude*] by birth.[36]

Evidence: birth certificate of the Counselor of Medicine [*Sanitätsrat*] Dr. Kurt S., grandfather of the child: Appendix 3

birth certificate of Hellmut S., up to now [recorded as] father of the child: Appendix 4

marriage certificate for med. coun. Dr. S.: Appendix 5

(I request return of these 3 [documents].)

The child [Leo Günther S.] would thus currently be deemed a *Mischling*.

However, due to the fact that the real father, Alfred B., currently armorer [*Waffenmeister*] with the border command station [*Grenzkommandantur*] Trier, fully and legally acknowledges his paternity, the child is—like his real father and the child's mother—purely Aryan since both the parents of B. and the parents of my former wife were Aryan. My former wife currently works as midwife in Berlin-Müggelsee, Krampenburgerweg 59.

Both now and in the future, the child is facing completely unwarranted and grave disadvantages. As a result, none of those involved wish to perpetuate this situation.

Consequently, I ask the Berlin Public Prosecutor's Office to open a paternity suit in the interest of the child in accordance with the law of April 12, 1938.

Since the divorce, the child has been educated by my brother-in-law, Lieutenant Colonel in the War Ministry N., Berlin Zehlendorf-Mitte, Schützallee 9. Due to his imminent transfer to another position, N. has requested that the case be speedily dispatched. I have thus already initiated the following:

---

36. According to the Nuremberg Laws, *Volljude* denotes a person who, irrespective of her or his religious denomination, has three or more Jewish grandparents.

The father of the child, the armorer B., has today received a copy of this letter with a request to send the relevant declaration [accepting his paternity] to the Public Prosecutor's Office directly and immediately and, furthermore, to document his Aryan ancestry in connection with the new grandparents of the child for the Public Prosecutor's Office.

I have asked Lieutenant Colonel N., who has also received a copy of this letter, to supply the Prosecutor's Office with documentation of the Aryan ancestry of the child's grandparents.

With German greeting [*mit deutschem Gruss*]

[signed:] S.

For the claimants, especially those, like Hellmut S., who wanted to protect their children or grandchildren, these paternity cases took stamina, determination, and patience—with success anything but guaranteed. In Leo S.'s case, as in most others, racial evaluators delivered an ambiguous expert opinion as to who was the likely biological father; however, the unequivocal testimonies by his father of record, his biological father, and his mother helped him. In 1940, the Berlin court decided that Leo was indeed fathered by an "Aryan" man and racially "upgraded" the child from "*Mischling* second degree" to "German blooded" (*deutschblütig*).

Confronted with so many new threats, German Jews, whenever they could get their breath back, wondered what could possibly lie ahead. The elderly might resign themselves to the thought that their life lay behind them. Even so, the prospects were alarming. Alone in his small Berlin apartment on his seventieth birthday, **Julius Moses** wrote to his son in Tel Aviv about how much he would like to be able to see the outcome of the whirlwind into which the world would surely be tossed soon, "sweeping away so much, the good, the bad, and the evil."[37] And what could possibly be on offer for Jewish youth?

Beyond the challenge of finding economic and physical security, there loomed the more philosophical question of how to make sense of events that seemed unprecedented and yet, at the same time, reminiscent of earlier epochs in Jewish history. Document 10-19 illustrates how, in the spring of 1938, Rabbi **Ignaz Maybaum** addressed this question.

---

37. Julius Moses, Berlin, to Erwin Moses, Tel Aviv, June 1938, in Dieter Fricke, *Jüdisches Leben in Berlin und Tel Aviv, 1933–1939: Der Briefwechsel des ehemaligen Reichstagsabgeordneten Dr. Julius Moses* (Hamburg: von Bockel, 1997), 530–32.

DOCUMENT 10-19: **Ignaz Maybaum, Berlin, "The Priestly Way: Jewish Wanderings in the Light of Jewish Faith,"** *Youth Magazine of the World Union for Progressive Judaism* **1 (April 1938): 22–26, USHMMA Acc. 2007.96 Kellermann collection, box 3.**[38]

World history is the history of the wanderings of the nations. The driving forces of those wanderings are political and economic causes. Jewish wanderings as a phenomenon of world history will primarily also have to be explained on such materialistic grounds. But Jewish wanderings are also a fact which is correlated to the history of revelation. Revelation goes on its way across the earth. With this way that of the Jews is interwoven. Who sends the Jew on his wanderings through the world? We give this answer: It is not a sinister destiny. Were it that, it would be a destiny with which we could not cope. But however much wanderings mean suffering, Jewish wanderings are the destiny of the chosen. The mysterious but ever merciful will of God sends us out into the world. We are to be God's witnesses over all the world and throughout all time. . . .

We are living in the dispersion, in the Diaspora, in the *galuth*.[39] We do not realize this to-day for the first time. But we have every reason to discuss anew this old fact of our destiny, the Diaspora. For a diaspora is taking place before our eyes. Jewry in Germany was a community which was held together by a powerful network of groups of every kind, from the various youth societies to a society of the type of the *Chevra Kadisha*,[40] from literary societies to the actual religious community, from the various social societies to the Centralverein and the Zionistische Vereinigung. It was an organization knitting the community together with numerous links, and here we can see clearly that organization need imply nothing dead, nothing bureaucratic, but can be the living will of the human heart, seeking its way to its brother and maintaining community with him. This community of Jewry in Germany is now dispersed in all parts of the world. We now know what it means, dispersion, diaspora. [. . .]

Whether the Jew's holy way through the world is looked upon only as the way of suffering, or whether it is regarded as the way of the chosen,

---

38. Within its eleven pages, the April 1938 issue of the World Union for Progressive Judaism news bulletin contained under the heading "Germany" only a four-line "reverent appreciation of the activities of the German Rabbis in leading their various Congregations to realize more and more the value and stimulating influence of Progressive Judaism."

39. Both terms denote Jewish life outside the Promised Land.

40. This is a brotherhood conducting the burial of Jews.

wherein a lofty happiness is the dominating factor in spite of every suffering, is only a matter of opinion. And it is also a matter of opinion whether the priest is looked on as a parasite or as a bringer of blessing. To be a bringer of blessing to the peoples among whom the Jewish people is scattered, that is the Jew's concern in the world. Out of it there arises a destiny, a priestly destiny. When Jews from Central and Eastern Europe now emigrate to all parts of the world, it is a cruel destiny that we again must bear on our shoulders. The peoples to whom we come look at us from the security of their residence and the pride of their residence, and they ask, Who is this coming to us? Are they to regard us simply as those whom the overpopulated European continent has sent beyond its borders, because the Jew, the man without power, is always the point of least resistance when historical upheavals are taking place? Or shall they look upon us as men whose dominating characteristic is that their faith has become their destiny? Even to the most radical revolutionary the picture of a dethroned prince is a picture of horror. And in that horror he is being impressed by the sanctity of a lofty destiny.

The Jew holds the view that, without seizing political power, he can realize the power of truth and good. Thus we pass on our way through the world: despite all suffering, in the lofty happiness of the chosen. It depends on us whether the world looks upon us as emigrants or as Jews, as men uprooted or as priests, whose destiny it is, not to be uprooted out of the earth, but to be scattered over the earth, and that because of the will of God. God sent us out into the world to believe in Him, to serve mankind and to fulfill the commandment which was give[n] to Abraham to take with him on his wanderings: Thou shalt be a blessing!

One way to make sense of suffering was, as Maybaum showed, by reference to Jews' destiny in the Diaspora and by seeking to emphasize the positive values of one's Jewishness, irrespective of national affiliation. But many still hoped that something would survive of their once proud German Jewish identity. The question of what would be remembered presented itself in particularly poignant and personal form for those Jews in mixed marriages whose non-Jewish relatives and part-Jewish descendants were doing all they could to distance themselves from the "non-Aryan" members of the family. The unsent letter featured in document 10-20, kept in the family of Max Mayer until after the war, presents a Jewish grandfather's attempt to sensitize the younger generation to their virtuous ancestry at a time when any positive reference to being Jewish was drowned out by state-sponsored slogans of race hatred.

DOCUMENT 10-20: Unsent letter by Max Mayer, Freiburg, to his grandchild, Peter Paepcke,[41] May 9, 1938, printed from Martin Doerry, *My Wounded Heart: The Life of Lilli Jahn, 1900–1944* (London: Bloomsbury, 2004), 76–82.

My dear grandson Peter! [. . .]

Yesterday, 8 May 1938, you were baptized in the chapel of the Lutheran Church in Stadtstrasse, Freiburg. Your parents had informed us of their intention in advance. It came as a shock to me in my Jewishness, because the latter—previously no more than an accident of birth which I never denied but made light of—has become my stronghold during these last few years of persecution. I saw you going off to be christened from their balcony. But I promptly came to the conclusion that your father's motives were apt, not to say compelling. At present, in this German era of the mass man, a standard is demanded of every German. He requires a number, a pigeonhole, a category, an identifying mark; he must have some subcommunity into which he can fit. I have no desire to analyze the type of person which this modern, standardized German becomes. I shall also refrain from pointing out the route opened up for you by baptism and, therefore, inclusion. In any case, a young person cannot be guided by his grandfather in questions to be posed and answered by a new generation. But there is one matter on which you must listen to my voice, and on which I desire to be heard. Listen to me, my grandson Peter! For five years now, Jews in Germany have been subjected to a relentless process of expulsion from the body politic [*Volkskörper*]. After years of preparatory agitation by the party that sustains it, the government of the Third Reich has postulated—and invested that postulate with the force of law—that the Jews constitute a foreign body within the nation [*Volk*], and one that is inhibiting the German nation [*Volk*] from legitimately affirming its status as a chosen people. This people, it is said, needs to be cleansed and liberated from Jewish members and elements.

In fulfillment of this theory [*Weltanschauung*], which is dressed up as an "ideology," an orgy of racial hatred has been instituted, together with a process whereby Jewish persons are subjected to total and systematic disqualification. The entire Party machine, the press, vocational training, broadcasting, official propaganda, the political education of the young,

---

41. Peter Paepcke (1935–1995), son of Dr. Ernst and Lotte Paepcke (née Mayer), later became a lawyer in Karlsruhe. Lotte Paepcke survived the war and described her experiences in a memoir, *Ich wurde vergessen: Bericht einer Jüdin, die das Dritte Reich überlebte* (1952; rpt. Freiburg im Breisgau: Herder, 1979).

the whole of national life—all have been harnessed to the task of stripping Jews of their good name and social acceptability, regardless of personal standing. They are being ousted from their homes and livelihoods and compelled to emigrate destitute of means, and the belief in their human inferiority is being duly incorporated in the Aryan world of ideas. [. . .]

As things stand now, you are unavoidably subject to the new German legislation that brands you a *Mischling* because your mother is of Jewish blood. This puts you half a rung above your mother, and your mother is classified as inferior to you in terms of human merit. You are legally subject to these regulations. It is up to you whether you acknowledge this classification and order of precedence. I venture to assume that you will stand by your mother from a sense of filial duty. But you should not base your attitude on the law of nature alone, whereas your Aryan fellow Germans, with their family trees, infer the merits of their parents from the number, merits, and names of their Aryan forebears. [. . .]

"Jewish grandmother" is the catch phrase, both humorous and serious, of the present time. That is why I consider it important, my dear Peter, to introduce your Jewish grandmother to you.

Your grandmother Olga is a woman of exemplary character, opposed to all that is technically and objectively false. Although devoid of social pretensions, she is distinguished by her exceptional dependability, her sense of duty, her trustworthiness in matters great and small, and her simple, steadfast way of life.

Your grandmother Olga is self-sacrificing, fair, and lenient in her judgment of others, and conciliatory toward all human weaknesses, provided they do not run counter to her own conception of loyal and upright conduct. She confronts life's difficulties with courage, but Germany's persecution of the Jews is gnawing at her heart. Your grandmother Olga dispenses love from the clear and abundant wellsprings of her profound and genuine goodness—but she is utterly unsentimental and uncomplicated, candid and transparent, pure and fine in the extreme. She has an unclouded mind, and is severely critical of herself. Although naturally selfish in her maternal solicitude for her children and family, she has always maintained a lively and genuine relationship with the interests of the nation as a whole, whose ideologies—when they did not compel her to discard her own, independent views—she has sincerely shared. She looked upon the world war of 1914–18 as a matter of national concern, and her conduct throughout could not have been bettered.

In every country in the world, a woman endowed with these qualities would be called a truly moral person. In Germany, pretentiously, she is termed "a genuinely German woman." The former description is sufficient, dear Peter. You can be proud of your Jewish grandmother, and have no need to feel that she is the weak spot of your certificate of descent. You may regard her inclusion with total confidence; no nobler grandmother is inscribed in any Aryan certificate. She herself would reject this description in a resolutely self-critical manner, or accept it only with the reservation that there are millions like her in every class of society. True enough, and this equivalence is precisely what I wished to affirm. Greetings, my grandson Peter,

> Your grandfather, Max Mayer

During the November pogrom of 1938, the sixty-five-year-old Max Mayer was arrested, together with thousands of other Jewish men, and taken to the Dachau concentration camp. Released after a month, he and his wife, Olga Mayer, managed to cross the border to Switzerland on September 1, 1939, the day the war began.[42]

---

42. Martin Doerry, *My Wounded Heart: The Life of Lilli Jahn, 1900–1944* (New York: Bloomsbury, 2004), 83.

CHAPTER 11

ÉVIAN AND THE
EMIGRATION IMPASSE

ESCAPE PLANS AND REALITIES

The *Anschluss* had profound but contradictory implications for German Jew-ish emigration. As before, Jews found themselves tossed back and forth, caught between growing pressures to leave the country and increasingly insuperable obstacles to getting out. On the one hand, the pressures forced more lucky individuals through the cracks, enabling them to escape the land of their per-secution, even if often stripped of everything but the clothes on their backs. On the other hand, the obstacles held back a huddle of increasingly vulnerable, impoverished, and frightened people for whom the possibility of emigration seemed ever more remote.

The pressures resulted from energies generated by different power sources. Even more strongly than before the *Anschluss,* the German security police and SD now stepped up the pace of forced emigration. **Reinhard Heydrich**'s staff had for some time been developing new procedures to dispatch Jews from Ger-man soil more efficiently. In Vienna, **Adolf Eichmann** had the chance to put these ideas into practice, cajoling and enticing other authorities to streamline the process of expropriation and emigration. For Heydrich and his staff, their "success" in Vienna raised the possibility of achieving the utopian aim of a Germany "free of Jews" and strengthened their arm in tussles with other bodies. In Berlin, recalcitrant authorities such as local tax offices, who did not see why they should give Jewish matters any priority, would soon find themselves facing

Gestapo expectations to stamp the necessary papers, rob the victims, and send them on their way.

The explosion of violence in Vienna made Austrian Jews ready to leave at any price and helped to galvanize their search for even the most distant relative in the United States to provide an **affidavit**. Any existence abroad had to be better than exposure to this. Simultaneously, triggered by relief agencies and committed politicians such as former **League of Nations** high commissioner James McDonald, concerns grew in the capitals of major countries over the fate of refugees and the longer-term impact of German *Judenpolitik*. Despite a common legacy of antisemitism and the gloomy economic outlook with which all countries had to struggle, the international implications of what happened to Jews in Germany and Austria called for coordinated attempts at resolving at least the most pressing aspects of the crisis.

But the counterforces against lowering immigration hurdles in the wake of the *Anschluss* were equally serious. For one thing, by dint of the incorporation of Austria, the growth in the number of Jews living under German rule was far larger than any increase in the willingness of foreign governments to open their gates. For another, the push for emigration was accompanied by ever more brutal economic expropriation and growing bureaucratic hurdles. If the recipient countries were concerned about Jewish immigration under the best of circumstances, they were most certainly alarmed about the prospect of Jews without assets knocking at their doors. In the case of Britain, the swelling numbers of would-be refugees overwhelmed Anglo-Jewry's ability to help, prompting their leaders to inform the British government that they could no longer guarantee that incoming refugees would not burden the taxpayer. The British government responded by reintroducing visa requirements as well as strict new criteria before a visa would be issued. The question was, therefore, whether the international community's new awareness of the severity of the German Jewish refugee problem would lead to any positive measures or merely to further raising of the drawbridge.

For German Jewish organizations, the new international atmosphere endangered years of arduous and painstaking work at facilitating emigration. Especially affected were those efforts aimed at channeling young Jews in large numbers or as groups to countries other than Palestine, not least because the Nazis were undermining the infrastructure within Germany necessary to prepare for such a collective enterprise. Unlike in the case of emigration to Palestine, one could not rely on established structures in the receiving countries to bear the brunt of the administrative burden. We have seen earlier how the **CV**-sponsored farm at Gross-Breesen in Silesia had tried to cater to those young Jews who sought a communal Jewish settlement but did not want to go to Palestine. In early 1938, when the farm's programs started to bear fruit, teachers and students looked all around the globe for suitable places of refuge.

DOCUMENT 11-1: Protocol of the Jewish émigré training farm Gross-Breesen board meeting held on April 28, 1938, USHMMA RG 11.001M.31, reel 99 (SAM 721-1-110, 2–12)[1] (translated from German).

Dr. Hirschberg opened the meeting. The entire working group [*Arbeitsausschuss*] has assembled again after a long interval. As you will see from the reports, the work has gone on despite a break in [our] meeting schedule. We did not wish to burden all of our friends with the uncertainty that arose during individual stages of our plan, but instead wished to appear before you with some fairly certain results in hand. Today's *CV-Zeitung* has partially printed the report that Prof. Bondy will now present.[2] What we will hear in this setting, however, are precisely those details that did not appear in the article: an account of the whole atmosphere and details of the plan, the future direction of the project. [. . .]

Prof. Bondy addressed point 1 of the agenda, business report and report on his trip to America.

I will keep my comments to a minimum and whatever I leave out can be taken up later [illegible] in the question and answer period. Herr Borchardt proposed to a man named Thalheimer from Richmond in Virginia, owner of a large department store there, that he buy a piece of land where young Jews from Germany can settle.[3] We drove to Richmond to speak with the people. Four men are involved, and Herr Thalheimer in particular is in

---

1. During this meeting of the Gross-Breesen board, twelve members were present, among them Gross-Breesen director Curt Bondy, *CV-Zeitung* editor Alfred Hirschberg, and Hannah Karminski, the only woman. In line with the obligation of Jewish organizations, the report was sent to the Berlin Gestapo, and we can assume that Gestapo officers also attended the meeting.

2. See *CV-Zeitung,* April 28, 1938, 3.

3. On Hyde Farmland in Burkeville, Virginia, its sponsor William B. Thalheimer, and the fate of thirty-six immigrants from Gross-Breesen, see the exhibition "A Survival Story" at the Virginia Holocaust Museum; www.richmond.com/museums-galleries/25200 (accessed October 19, 2008). Frederick (Fritz) W. Borchardt (1901–1956) was a German-born businessman active in Jewish aid organizations both before he left Germany and after he emigrated to the United States in 1937. Some members of the Gross-Breesen community sought support from men such as Borchardt and the organizations they worked for in the United States. See Werner T. Angress, *Between Fear and Hope: Jewish Youth in the Third Reich* (New York: Columbia University Press, 1988), 88, 91, 106, 168n; Röder and Strauss, *Biographisches Handbuch,* 1:80.

a great hurry to get this project going. A Mr. Schwarzschild, who curiously enough is dealing with the finances,[4] and two other gentlemen also want to provide financial support. In the meantime they have already bought a farm and made money available to purchase the necessary equipment, including livestock. They are assuming that after a year it may be possible for the farm [*Gut*] to be self-supporting. The question of affidavits appears to be solved, mainly through the efforts of Ingrid Warburg.[5] Out of the approximately 30 affidavits that we will be getting, only 6 or 7 will go to people with relatives already there [*Verwandtenaffidavits*]. We hope to have the affidavits in our hands by the end of the month. There is also talk of setting up a further enterprise of this sort in North Carolina, and people in New York [not specified] have similar plans. There is thus some possibility of setting up Gross-Breesen settlements on a larger scale.

The farm lies about 70 miles from Richmond, a parcel of 2,000 acres. It is situated in a pretty area that includes forestland, some quite good, with pine and oak trees. Around 500 acres are under cultivation. Crops will include all the things we plant here, but also tobacco, peaches, and other fruit. [. . .]

At the conclusion of the presentation, Dr. Hirschberg asked about the composition of the group that will be going to Virginia.

<u>Bondy</u>: We have chosen 25 people from Gross-Breesen, almost entirely young people, four of them over age 20, and all are single. Most are between 17 and 20 years old, and there are 6 girls in the group. In part the people come from economically more privileged circles. Around 15 of the 25 can carry the cost of what they will need to outfit themselves and for their passages. [. . .]

[A discussion follows about how to ensure that the people will stay on the land, how to prevent "flight from the land," and about the contract that should be drafted to commit settlers to stay.]

<u>Schwarzschild</u> turned to <u>point 2</u> on the agenda, <u>business reports of the head of finances on the board of trustees [*Kuratorium*], and reported on plans concerning South America.</u>

---

4. The reference to the "oddity" of a Mr. Schwarzschild's taking care of financing the Virginia project was most likely meant as a joke due to the fact that a man with the same last name was also in charge of finance matters in the Gross-Breesen *Arbeitsausschuss*.

5. Ingrid Warburg (later Spinelli; 1910–2000) was born in Hamburg to Fritz and Anna Warburg, her father a partner in the Warburg banking concern and her mother active in youth work. After attending university in Germany and England in the early 1930s, she emigrated to New York in 1935, where she engaged in refugee aid work. See Ron Chernow, *The Warburgs* (New York: Random House, 1993), 425–28, 493–99.

The JCA is prepared to help six groups of five individuals each from Gross-Breesen to resettle under the condition that they agree to stay together for 5 years. If before that point some individuals are able to help family members follow them, or if they marry, the JCA wants them to settle on their own plots, although it is envisaged that the settler couples remaining in the original settlement would be obligated to guarantee the departing settlers a certain sum of money or rights. The JCA offer came to us when the Richmond plan had already proven feasible. Suddenly it proved difficult to find 30 people [for the JCA plan]. Herr Oungre of Paris then agreed that qualified trainees from other training programs could be brought together to make up the groups so that virtually none of the places connected with this special offer would be lost. Oungre emphasized that this one-time JCA offer should not be regarded as a precedent but rather as an exception made for Gross-Breesen.[6]

Beyond this, the JCA has agreed to find suitable families in Buenos Aires for two girls; perhaps families that already have some daughters can be selected.

Our Brazilian projects, which are now being processed by the JCA, remain in a preliminary stage, given that the emigration question has not yet been solved. All the optimism around the Brazil question has proven premature. However, I feel that the Parana [*sic*] project shows special promise.[7]

Hirschberg: Let me add that two people from Gross-Breesen are on their way to Kenya. In addition, two other married couples along with one helper from the JCA each are settling on their own plots [*Siedlerstellen*]. Altogether then: 30 people in North America, 15 people on a collective settlement [*Gemeinschaftssiedlung*] in Argentina, 6 people (including 2 married couples) in JCA territories, and 2 people in Kenya. Beyond this, a number of individuals have already emigrated on their own. In other words, the first and second generations of Gross-Breesen people have all secured a place in their chosen occupation. I believe that we can express a certain satisfaction after the task force's long series of meetings at which so many concerns arose. [. . .]

---

6. Dr. Louis Oungre was the JCA's head; see Richard Breitman, Barbara McDonald Stewart, and Severin Hochberg, eds., *Advocate for the Doomed: The Diaries and Papers of James G. McDonald, 1932–1935* (Bloomington: Indiana University Press in association with the USHMM, 2007), 133, 158.

7. On the communal settlement project in the Brazilian province of Paraná, see Angress, *Between Fear*, 59–60. See also Jeffrey Lesser, *Welcoming the Undesirables: Brazil and the Jewish Question* (Berkeley: University of California Press, 1995).

[A discussion follows of budget, planning and staffing for 1938–1939; Hirschberg:]

I hope that the 45 people who will shortly be leaving Gross-Breesen—almost all at the same time—will still have time for a [final] ceremony [*Feierstunde*]. The working group, as well as members of the board of trustees, will be invited. After two years of the most taxing work imaginable, it seems proper to have a special ceremony, a gathering that also pays tribute to [the] contributions of our departing member, Schwarzschild. I must ask all of you not only to continue your work on the Gross-Breesen project in the future but to work even harder and also to make suggestions to me in the coming period about who we might add to our task force. Only then will we be able to fill the gaps in our working group again.

Dr. Rosenberg thanked Hirschberg for serving as working group chairman and suggested that it receive reports and meet with greater frequency.

Hirschberg concurred. The budget passed will be presented to the board of directors for approval as laid down in the bylaws.

Hirschberg took up point 5, miscellaneous matters.

Hirschberg addressed the question of replenishing the ranks of students at Gross-Breesen and the necessity of propaganda to this end. Four hundred copies of Bondy's article in the *CV-Zeitung* will be reprinted and distributed in appropriate settings as propaganda.

Rosenberg pointed to the need for improving and expanding English lessons.

Hannah Karminski underlined the importance of setting up a vocational training site for girls who are not going into domestic service but are planning to emigrate later. A great need exists for this kind of training. We must get the communities where necessary to provide subsidies for the cost of training.

Hirschberg agreed that this question deserved attention and adjourned the meeting.

Despite mounting problems, between April 1933 and April 1938 more than 18,400 young Jews who had received training in the many training facilities managed to leave Germany.[8] But in 1938, the regime's new anti-Jewish measures threatened the future of such undertakings. Following a law enacted on March 28, 1938, the Jewish communities lost their long-held status as religious bodies, with all the attendant financial and other privileges (*Körperschaften*

---

8. Angress, *Between Fear*, 36.

des öffentlichen Rechts). Their relegation to the legal status of registered societies (*eingetragene Vereine*) created an avalanche of problems for the entire German Jewish organizational structure and called into question its ability to provide its members with even basic services. Berlin-based CV functionary **Alfred Hirschberg** had formerly been one of the CV's staunchest believers in the continuing viability of German Jewry. But now, as he put it in a speech to CV members in the city of Mannheim, the only task at hand was *Existenzabwicklung*, a term with many connotations ranging from "disposing of one's business" to "providing closure to one's life." We do not know whether the Gestapo were present at the Mannheim meeting and thus whether Hirschberg's report on his speech accurately reflected his verbal remarks. But even if he used the same language as the written text, his audience may well have understood his closing appeal—that they should take precautions to retain "unbreakable ties" to their Judaism even after emigration—as a coded reference not just to Judaism per se but to a German Jewish identity that could no longer be openly advocated even as a legacy for a future Diaspora.

DOCUMENT 11-2: **Report on a speech by Alfred Hirschberg, CV head office Berlin, at CV local branch Mannheim about "Our Place in the Work of the Jewish Community," late May/early June 1938, USHMMA RG 11.001M.31, reel 190 (SAM 721-1-950, 4-8)**[9] **(translated from German).**

[. . .] Dr. Alfred Hirschberg, who gave a presentation on the theme of "our place in the work of the Jewish community," began by recalling that he had last spoken here two years ago. In the meantime, the question has often come up whether such lectures serve any function. However, so often in recent times we have seen the positive effect on morale when Jews come together for even an hour of information, review, and reflection. This observation is itself relevant to our topic because such events can inform the individual about his place in work for the Jewish community. If there is no confidence in the leadership, then any work that makes demands on the group and requires sacrifices will be unsuccessful. Fruitful labor is possible only when there is good contact between the leadership and ordinary members. The speaker then developed his theme under the following headings: first, our place in the work within the borders [of Germany], in terms of both organizational and practical activities; next, the CV's stance within Germany as well as the effects of

---

9. The report was written by Hirschberg himself for publication in the newsletter of the Mannheim Jewish community.

its stance abroad on those who can influence Jewish circles ideologically related to the CV.

Turning to organizational matters, the speaker briefly recalled the story of the Reichsvertretung's establishment, in which the late chairman of the CV, Counselor of Justice [*Justizrat* Julius] Brodnitz was a leading participant. At that time there had been much infighting in the Reichsvertretung. Today, one cannot imagine Jewish work in Germany without its existence. Currently a change in the structure of the Reichsvertretung is to be expected as part of the reorganization of the Jewish communities' legal status. The speaker noted specific problems and came to the conclusion that the following would need to happen: first, all Jews living within the Reich's borders would need to be brought into a unified Reichsverband with subgroups,[10] and second, not only would all [Jewish] communities, but also those organizations that were already practically or ideologically aligned with the Reichsvertretung, need to be integrated.

The practical work of the CV, continued the speaker, is determined by the legal and regulatory requirements that have developed over the course of the last five years. Performance and success can be fairly assessed only when the legal situation is taken into account. If for years the main task was to work for our survival here, a task in full compliance with the then existing legal situation, today the problems of winding up our affairs and preparing for emigration dominate our field of vision. Here, too, those seeking advice benefit from the expertise of CV staff who approach their tasks equipped with a sense of the overall situation, in-depth expertise, and a profound sense of connection with their fellow man. From a purely quantitative point of view, this conclusion is confirmed not only by the continuous stream of visitors to the CV's advice bureaus [*Beratungsstellen*] but also by the development of the organization's membership.[11]

The audience paid special attention to the speaker's remarks about a number of special emigration projects that are to be completed by the CV, above all the plans for Gross-Breesen and the so-called Riegner

---

10. The term Reichsverband describes here a reorganized Reichsvertretung as planned at that time by Jewish leaders. Except for some public pronouncements (see document 11-11), the Reichsverband remained a rump body subordinated to the Reichsvertretung and without comparable functions in the Jewish sector.

11. For the decline in CV membership after 1935, see Avraham Barkai, *"Wehr Dich!" Der Centralverein deutscher Staatsbürger jüdischen Glaubens (C.V.), 1893–1938* (Munich: C. H. Beck, 2002), 354.

Group.[12] Both issues served to prove that, while some describe these plans as a superfluous and costly attempt to sustain emigration numbers, they ultimately proved to be the best means of capital investment. The better the reputation an emigrant community enjoys, the easier it will be for its members to get a start in a new world.

With this Dr. Hirschberg had laid the foundation for the final part of his speech, which dealt with our spiritual and ideological stance [*geistige Position*]. He justified the practical necessity of a planned Diaspora policy primarily in the light of the numerical growth of migration in recent times [to destinations other than Palestine]. Everyone hopes and wishes for a quick and favorable resolution of the questions regarding Palestine [*Regelung der Palästinafragen*]. But whatever the outcome, the issue of overseas migration is and remains an urgent problem. The Diaspora's center of gravity is moving, and we must make sure that outside of Palestine, too, people come to their new countries with a positive Jewish attitude and that they find a reliable Jewish environment [*eine zuverlässig jüdische Situation*] there or have the opportunity to develop one.

Related to this, the speech touched upon problems connected with the Évian conference and emphasized that, besides efforts to open up other countries for emigration, we must wage a moral propaganda campaign [*moralische Propaganda*] there, stressing the value of immigrants. A wholly factual account of Jewish involvement in the areas of culture, science, and economics [should be presented] so that those countries receiving immigrants know that they are reliable, constructive elements. The speaker concluded that we do not want our people to take their ghetto with them out of the country, as it were, but rather we want them to become citizens of their new countries and at the same time preserve unbreakable ties to their Judaism.

Sustained applause followed this compelling and instructive speech, for which the chairman [of the CV local branch], *Justizrat* Appel, expressed warm gratitude and, in so doing, drew attention to the CV's local advice bureau.

Despite the gloomy general outlook, Hirschberg was not alone among Jewish activists in hoping that the international conference to be held from July 6

---

12. This relates to a group of twenty-four people who managed to leave Germany with the help of the CV head office on October 27, 1938, for Argentina via Trieste; see Jüdischer CV (Hirschberg) to Stapostelle Berlin, November 4, 1938; USHMMA RG 11.001M.31, reel 99 (SAM 721-1-101, 3).

to 14, 1938, in the French spa town of Évian would bring a breakthrough in the immigration impasse. On the face of it, the prospects for the conference looked promising: following a suggestion by U.S. President Franklin D. Roosevelt that governments discuss the fate of "political refugees" from Germany and Austria, thirty-two nations from around the globe had sent representatives. Yet, the invitation's lack of explicit reference to Jews, combined with the assurance that none of the nations present would be asked "to receive a greater number of emigrants than is permitted by existing legislation," gave the conference an unreal air before it had even started.[13]

Under the circumstances, German Jewish leaders could do little more than pray for at least some positive material outcome. Among the proposals for discussion submitted by over twenty nongovernmental organizations, Jewish and non-Jewish, was a memorandum by the **Reichsvertretung** declaring the determination of German Jews to "use all means at their disposal for the purpose of putting its organizations and financial energy to the task of implementing an ambitious plan for emigration."[14] Unconstrained by the shackles of censorship and oriented toward the broader issues involved, **World Jewish Congress** leader Rabbi **Stephen Wise** called for more far-reaching action. His seemingly forthright call was noteworthy, however, for its frank statement early on that unless Germany improved the financial conditions it imposed on its emigrants, they had no chance of finding shelter abroad. Wise also acknowledged an issue that troubled many governments: German and Austrian Jews were not the only Jews in distress. Any particular concession to them was likely to lead to powerful calls for similar dispensation to their impoverished and persecuted Eastern European brethren.

DOCUMENT 11-3: Memorandum by the WJC to the delegates of the Évian conference, July 6, 1938, USHMMA RG 11.001 M.36, reel 106 (SAM 1190-1-257).

[. . .] The Conference is the only hope of hundreds of thousands of Jews who are today barbarously persecuted and evicted from positions which they had held for centuries. At a time when policies of brutal force and oppression of political, racial and religious minorities disgrace our century, the initiative of President Roosevelt has been a ray of hope; may it permit us to save a part at least of the victims and give them new opportunities.

13. On the Évian conference, see Friedländer, *Nazi Germany*, 1:248–50.
14. "Denkschrift der Reichsvertretung an die Eviankonferenz," June 1938, quoted in Otto Dov Kulka, ed., *Deutsches Judentum unter dem Nationalsozialismus*, vol. 1, *Dokumente zur Geschichte der Reichsvertretung der Juden, 1933–1939* (Tübingen: Mohr Siebeck, 1997), 403.

II. Naturally, the attention of the Conference will focus on the situation of the Jews in Germany. It is not necessary to enumerate all the iniquitous measures and barbarous persecutions visited upon the Jews since the advent of the Third Reich and which, since the annexation of Austria, have turned into a veritable orgy of bestial wantonness. While during the first years of the National Socialist regime, Jewish citizens of the Reich, although deprived of their rights, still had certain possibilities of leaving the country and lawfully taking away part of their property, today German authorities resort to arrests which run in thousands, and other arbitrary cruelties designed to terrorise German Jews, whom special fiscal provisions and expropriations deprive of any possibility of taking abroad the least fraction of their property. Germany is endeavouring to compel them to leave the country in a state of complete destitution. The Conference of Évian should fail in its duty if it did not raise a firm protest against this shocking system which tramples underfoot the fundamental principles of justice and humanity.

The governments represented at Évian owe it to themselves to condemn in unequivocal terms the persecution of men, woman, and children whose only crime is to belong to a people that gave the world the Ten Commandments and whose creed inspired the world's greatest religions.

Apart from the ethical aspect of the problem, it will be practically impossible to provide shelter and the possibility of making a new start to hundreds of thousands of German Jews if they are driven out of Germany in a state of complete destitution. It is contrary to fundamental principles of justice and international law that a nation should arrogate to itself the right of despoiling and expelling part of its citizens, compelling other nations to provide for destitute paupers. In the last five years, humanity has witnessed untold iniquities. It is time to ascribe limits to barbary [sic].

We beg to entreat the Conference to do everything in its power to bring the German government to modify their methods, and to obtain at least that Jews emigrating from Germany be allowed to take part of their property abroad. Surely, even under the German currency legislation, ways and means may be found to organise a system under which Jewish property might lawfully be transferred abroad, provided there is a minimum of goodwill on the part of the German government. If this is not achieved, it will hardly be possible to organise a large-scale emigration of the Jews from Germany, however eager and self-sacrificing the cooperation of the private organisations and however generous the contributions in favour of Jewish refugees from Germany, since the task to be tackled will be nothing less than to find new homes for at least 200,000 to 300,000 Jews from Germany and Austria within the next few years.

III. It is desirable that the Évian Conference should not confine itself to consider the case of German Jews, which, although the most painful, is but one of the aspects of the refugee problem. Following the nefarious example set by Germany, several European states have, for some time, been enacting legal and administrative measures designed to evict [the] Jewish population from employment and professions, to deprive Jews of their nationality and to force them to emigrate. In so doing, these states are violating their constitutions which guarantee to Jews equality of rights, and disregard the rights pledged to Jewish minorities by the peace treaties [following World War I]. We venture to think that one of the most urgent tasks incumbent upon the Évian Conference is to reaffirm the principles of equality of rights of the Jews in all countries, and to remind the States of Eastern Europe that they have no right to create new masses of refugees through driving out of their boundaries their Jewish citizens. [. . .]

The situation of these Jewish citizens of east European countries, difficult as it was before the war, has deteriorated to an alarming extent especially during the last few years. The growing jingoism which of late has become rampant in many nations has led to an increasingly grim struggle of the majority against the minority populations, depriving growing numbers of Jews of any possibility of earning their livelihood. In Poland, 38% of the Jews are supported by public charity, while the standard of living of 40% of the Jewish masses of Eastern Europe is far below what is regarded as the barest minimum. [. . .]

IV. The Jewish refugee problem cannot be discussed without taking into account the immense possibilities of Palestine as an outlet for Jewish immigration. The majority of the Jewish people has recognised a long time ago that nothing short of creating a Jewish State can restore the normal structure of the dispersed Jewish community. [. . .]

V. The Jewish people are unable to solve their refugee problem single-handed. They need the political and financial help of non-Jews in organising and financing a vast migration movement. Jewish emigration has not the support of a government. It is an irrepressible movement of a people, an overwhelming majority of whom are now destitute and whose well-to-do elements are unorganised and dispersed throughout the world, while central Jewish organisations have no power to tax them. It would not be the first time that an international problem of the scope of Jewish emigration should be solved through international cooperation and financial assistance. Let us refer to the precedent of international financial assistance in effecting the transfer of 1,400,000 Greeks from Turkey to Greece under the auspices of the League of Nations. In the course of four years (1920–1924) 300,000 Greek families were transplanted from Asia Minor to Greece. It is not without interest to note that most of these 300,000 families were composed of old people, women and children, many of the young men having perished in the war.[15]

The occupational structure of the Greek emigrants was not particularly favorable, and it was certainly not better than that of the Jewish emigrants today. The Greek emigrants included a high rate of city-dwellers such as traders, shop-keepers, etc., and very few young men, while the would-be Jewish emigration includes over one million young people aged from 20 to 25 years.

The Greek migration had proved possible because the League of Nations had guaranteed an international loan of over 12,000,000 pound[s] sterling, while private American organisations had contributed large sums of money. We realize the difference between the Jewish would-be emigrants and the Greeks who had behind them their own country and government. The Jewish people have no country of their own, but their achievement in Palestine has shown the Jewish people can provide immense means for a truly constructive solution of the Jewish problem. It is clear, however, that Jewish funds alone would not suffice for the requirements of Jewish migration. Only through international funding, and in the first place through an international loan, may it prove possible to mobilise the funds necessary to build up a Jewish National Home in Palestine and organise soundly a large-scale Jewish emigration to countries overseas.

Such an international financial transaction could be based upon two elements: in the first place, the property left behind by Jewish refugees in their country of origin, provided agreements are concluded with the governments of the countries concerned permitting the liquidation of such assets; and secondly, the assets to be created by Jewish emigrants in the immigration countries. A system of credits could be organized upon this two-fold basis. [. . .]

In closing, we wish to renew the expression of our gratitude to all the delegates to the Évian Conference. Jewish community the world over has

---

15. See Carole Fink, *Defending the Rights of Others: The Great Powers, the Jews and International Minority Protection, 1878–1938* (Cambridge: Cambridge University Press, 2004); Donald Bloxham, *The Great Game of Genocide: Imperialism, Nationalism, and the Destruction of the Ottoman Armenians* (Oxford: Oxford University Press, 2005), 170–73.

placed great hopes in the Conference. We fervently hope that the Conference may succeed in restoring to active life hundreds of thousands of distressed refugees, among whom there are so many young men and women, enthusiastic, self-denying and eager to work. In justifying the hopes of so many unfortunate people, the Conference shall have fulfilled a historic mission.

> Geneva, July 6, 1938.
> Stephen S. Wise
> President of the Executive Committee of the World Jewish Congress

However forcefully Jewish organizations tried to make the case for their brethren in Central and Eastern Europe, their voice found little resonance. Politicians and public opinion almost everywhere were preoccupied with their own domestic crises. Some were indeed inclined to view the Nazi way of dealing with the Jewish question as a model rather than a scandal. The often-quoted statement by the Australian representative to the effect that Australia had neither a "racial problem" nor the intention of importing one exemplifies the prevailing dominance of racial stereotypes over human concern.[16] Pushing unwanted ethnic groups out had been a familiar phenomenon accompanying the rise of the nation-state. While the suffering of those affected might lead to expressions of concern or diplomatic interventions by other countries, no one in the seats of power questioned the right of national governments to treat their own citizens as they pleased.[17] The only faint light on the horizon appeared the prospect of negotiating a plan—as the WJC memorandum put it, "an international financial transaction"—not unlike the **Ha'avara Agreement** concluded in 1933. Indeed, Évian led to the creation of an Intergovernmental Committee for Refugees as a basis for negotiations with the Reich. Still, it remained unclear whether such a plan could really address a refugee crisis that had grown massively since the days when the Ha'avara Agreement had been negotiated in 1933 and whether it could find a negotiating partner when German interest in such a financial deal had ebbed.[18]

---

16. See Paul Bartrop, *Australia and the Holocaust* (Melbourne: Australian Scholarly Publishing, 1994), 71; Michael Blakeney, "Australia and the Jewish Refugees from Central Europe—Government Policy, 1933–1939," *LBIYB* 29 (1984): 103–33; in general, see Michael R. Marrus, *The Unwanted: European Refugees in the Twentieth Century* (New York: Oxford University Press, 1985).

17. For an in-depth comparative analysis of the destructive elements in modern societies, see Mark Levene, *Genocide in the Age of the Nation State*, 2 vols. (London: Tauris, 2005).

18. On negotiations orchestrated by the Intergovernmental Committee in late 1938 and early 1939, see Friedländer, *Nazi Germany*, 1: 248–49, 315–16.

If leading diplomats did not know how to address the crisis, Jews in Germany and Austria felt like pawns in a game of chess played by others. Jewish officials in Germany were deeply concerned not only about domestic conditions but also their increasingly constrained ability to communicate openly with the outside world. Even fellow Jewish organizations seemed disconnected from what was happening in the Reich: in a letter to the **Jewish Agency for Palestine**, the **ZVfD** leadership in Berlin lamented the agency's failure to consult with Jews in Germany prior to submitting its memorandum to the Évian conference; in fact, at the time the ZVfD wrote its letter, none of the relevant German Jewish bodies had yet seen the memorandum.[19]

Despite the disconnect between Germany and the outside world, correspondence between Jews who had managed to escape the Reich and those left behind remained a lifeline for both sides. For members of youth groups still in Germany, the precious post from abroad was often passed around in multiple copies; letters of a more private nature were handed from one family member to another. Quite apart from the thrill of hearing about loved ones or the whiff of freedom that one could almost sniff on the thin airmail paper, news about life outside German borders always seemed more trustworthy when conveyed by a friend. Not all the news was encouraging, of course. From Argentina, one correspondent criticized the "politics of illusion [*Illusionspolitik*] often adopted in questions of Jewish emigration" and warned his friends in Germany that life in his new country of residence was a constant struggle.[20] For those about to leave for Argentina, the youth office of the CV struck a similar note in dampening unrealistic expectations: "You aren't bringing anything new to the country; you are a competitor and have to integrate yourself with humility; otherwise you won't achieve anything over there."[21] But others had more positive things to report, conveying with their experiences that it was possible to earn a living abroad and that the barriers to integration could be overcome. One such letter reached the CV head office from **Friedrich Brodnitz**, who, having just finished his medical exams, now had a temporary job as doctor in a summer camp for young American Jews in Maine.

19. ZVfD (Franz Meyer) Berlin, to the Jewish Agency for Palestine executive office in London, July 13, 1938; facsimile printed in Friedlander and Milton, *Archives of the Holocaust*, doc. 39, 3:179.

20. "KJR Sammelbriefe 11–13," April/May 1938; USHMMA RG 11.001M.31, reel 99 (SAM 721-1-93, 135).

21. "Ausrüstungsbrief" for émigrés to Argentina by CV youth office (G. Friedländer), June 1938; USHMMA RG 11.001M.31, reel 99 (SAM 721-1-93, 149).

DOCUMENT 11-4: **Letter by Friedrich Brodnitz, Naples (Maine), to CV head office, July 17, 1938, USHMMA RG 11.001M.31, reel 99 (SAM 721-1-93, 112–15) (translated from German).**

Dear friends,

It's high time you heard from me again. The long silence isn't my fault. Only someone who has gone through the hell of an American state exam knows what I've been feeling. It was a nightmare. It may have been the most intense experience I've ever had in terms of exertion, stress, and pure hard work. [. . .] When the exam was over, I had all of one day to go shopping for basic supplies and then drove immediately to the camp, where I've been serving as camp doctor.

[Underlined words in this and the following paragraphs are in English in the original.] We have approximately 85 girls in the camp, all between 12 and 16 years old and almost all from more or less wealthy Jewish families. Some have fathers who are lawyers in Manhattan. Others are salesmen in Brooklyn and even oil magnates in Texas. They cover just about the whole spectrum. A staff of over 20 people is at hand to take care of the girls. There's a director and an assistant director, a head councillor [sic], doctor, nurse, dietitian [sic], and office staff. We have three female teachers for the summer school, a music teacher, voice teacher, riding teacher, swimming teacher with two assistants, a tennis coach, plus a bunch of councillors [sic] who organize various other activities. There's always something going on, and the girls are kept busy from early in the morning until late in the day, very necessary so that they don't get into serious mischief. It's interesting to compare many features of this setup with the youth movement over there [drüben; i.e., in Germany]. [. . .]

The intellectual level of camp activities—plays, dances, etc.—is for the most part much lower than what we managed to do with far, far fewer resources. It's interesting that they're trying to give group activities a kind of ceremonial character. Every week there's a gathering around a campfire in a clearing that is decorated with an Indian totem pole and includes a ceremony borrowed from Indian customs. Very impressive and cleverly done and extremely good for these youth, who are growing up without any formal framework [die in einer völligen Formlosigkeit heranwächst]. A good deed for all those present if only for the fact that they are forced to keep quiet for an hour, but also very educational. Every Sunday morning a kind of service is held, also fairly well orchestrated, with some music, singing, and a speech [*Ansprache*]. It is truly moving to hear familiar texts from the Psalms for the first time in old English. "Thou preparest a table in the face of mine enemies." What do these girls understand of such words? [. . .]

[Descriptions of daily camp life follow.] All in all, this is proving to be a very interesting stay, and I'm learning a lot. And it's not a bad thing to be living in an environment for a change that is almost totally devoid of the conditions I brought with me. Of course, one has to figure out a way to adjust to such a totally different environment. And if you figure out how to do that, life here isn't bad. You don't change in the process in any fundamental way. But you sometimes ask yourself whether, under [our] special conditions, [back in Germany] we haven't paid a little too much attention to group-related aspects and too little to factors defining the individual, his or her qualities, temperament, and personality. [. . .]

Links with former relatives and friends provided a lifeline not only for Jews still in the Reich but also for the refugees themselves. Particularly those who had gone through some shared experience, such as a former youth group or a preparatory course for emigration (like the boys and girls attending the Gross-Breesen *Auswandererlehrgut* who hoped to settle together), maintained a close communication network for years—if Nazi Germany did not catch up with them later in their country of refuge.[22] Creating and cultivating such transnational connections helped them get through the rigors of the adjustment process and was often useful in the attempt to get remaining friends and family members out of Germany.

While the emigrants contended with the challenges and opportunities of their new places of refuge, those still in Germany were left to cope mentally with their situation. In New York, **Heinz Kellermann** received a letter from an old friend that cast light not only on German Jews' psychological predicament but also on the careful "diplomacy" that increasingly characterized letters sent abroad. Those left behind did not want to alienate potential helpers through importuning or whining. At the same time, every possible connection had to be mobilized if one were to have a chance to escape and if recipients were to be made to realize the seriousness of the current situation.

---

22. See Angress, *Between Fear*, 72–76.

DOCUMENT 11-5: **Letter by Gerhard Kann,[23] Berlin, to Heinz Kellermann, New York, October 24, 1938, USHMMA Acc. 2007.96 Kellermann collection, box 4 (translated from German).**

My dear Heinz!

Your letter was simultaneously an expression of encouragement, hope, and resignation for us. Kind words that are a balm for this feeling of abandonment [*Verlassenheit*], of resigning oneself to an unavoidable fate.

It is truly very difficult to avoid being overwhelmed by a feeling of unending passivity.

Each day we see the walls around us grow higher, and each week brings new obstacles to leaving the country. Hopes and plans are buried, and the number of fellow sufferers [*Schicksalsgefährten*] in Central Europe grows ever greater.

Germany, Italy, Czecho-Slovakia [*sic*] . . . the problems are becoming ever more daunting, and the need for an overall solution [*Allgemeinlösung*] has continued to grow. The fate of individuals has become unimportant, trivial. And one can only hope that the growth of the masses of people who are uprooted will make the world recognize the Jewish problem as one that it cannot ignore and not just a question that it can gloss over with a few conferences and speeches.

You on the outside don't of course see it with our eyes or hear what's going on with our ears; we don't share the same perspective. And that is a good thing. Human nature forces us to put ourselves and our own fate at the center of our concerns; only now and again does one realize that in the end a few hundred thousand Jews really don't play a very important role in the world.

And yet, as young, strong people we rise up against such feelings of resignation. And in this disintegration process affecting Jewry in Germany, we search for a meaningful position for as long as we are still here.

In the end, nothing is worse than being forced to sit around vegetating and waiting.

Regardless of all the energy I put into this serious, dogged search for a way to emigrate, I count myself lucky to be among the few people who

23. Born in 1910 in Berlin and a medical doctor by training, Gerhard Kann was interned in Dachau for over a month after the November pogrom. He managed to leave Europe before the war, landing in Palestine and eventually Bolivia, where he spent time working as a doctor in the rainforest. See *USHMM ITS Collection Data Base Central Name Index*; USHMMA Acc. 2000.227 Herbert Cohn collection, folders 2–3. The authors have been unable to find information about the further fate of Gerhard Kann's wife, Selma.

still have a job and one that even involves work and responsibilities in our sector.

I know that there is still a need for my work [as a doctor treating Jewish patients] and that I can and must help others. And I derive some sense of satisfaction from the fact that I have been equal to the demands of this work.

Perhaps I am deluding myself; perhaps I am creating an ethical justification for my work so that I have any chance of carrying on. Yet I believe that were I working as a sales clerk—discounting any external factors—I would have a much harder time standing my ground.

Do you understand what I'm trying to say? It's also a form of spiritual self-protection that I have drawn upon.

What I have derived from this just in the past few weeks is trust in myself, a feeling of security in the face of others and events, a feeling that will hopefully continue to serve me.

As for day-to-day reality! I'm continuing to work, day and night, more demands on me than ever. Selma is working in a private clinic, and we see each other for one or two hours at night and have a little private time. We are there for each other, help one another face the troubles, and hope that we can begin a life together somewhere else.

We do not know how long we will still be allowed to work. My livelihood is particularly uncertain. We are doing our work as best we can, as long as we can.

Our plans and hopes have more or less all come to naught. Despite registering at the consulate here, America seems like a very remote [*ungewiss*] possibility, something you have said. There now appears to be some chance of going to Peru.

In any event, entering the country would cost 4,000 French francs[24] per person, which would need to be raised for us abroad. Then we could get visas. I still have no idea how I could pull this off.

Is there some chance that you might look into this?

Perhaps there are some organizations or important people who could provide some assistance?

You are right when you say that I have dragged my feet a bit. But I believe that every person who is still here at some point failed to take advantage of an opportunity. *Kismet!* Islamic teaching says that everything is mapped out in the book of life.

---

24. In October 1938, four thousand French francs equaled roughly $100 (*New York Times*, October 25, 1938, 39).

Last Friday I visited your mother. Selma and I visit her as often as possible, and I believe that she enjoys our company a bit. The story with her eyes is a real problem and drags on but is apparently not dangerous. It would be good if she took better care of herself. For this reason it would be good if she spent a few days at a clinic.

Heinz, your mother is not lonely. She is the center of our circle. A kind person, who gives more in just a few words and gestures than anyone else.

And something else on a personal note. Your letters have never mentioned your personal life. I do not want to impose on you in these few short lines.

In our last one-on-one conversation, Aunt Emmi mentioned that you had gotten married, and I was truly happy for you. I know how important it is not to have to be alone.

I know that, particularly when outside pressure is growing, [it's good that] someone is standing by, ready to lend support.

And finally, Heinz, I can feel the cares and worries and also the relieving bliss that comes when the bond between a husband and wife reaches its most precious natural expression through the arrival of a new family member [*durch das gemeinsame Dritte*].

If for no other reason than this, I congratulate you and your wife and send all best wishes to both of you and your child.

Last night Selma and I talked about you with great pleasure. She sends warm wishes and thanks for your letter.

Take care of yourself, Heinz.

With warmest wishes to you and all friends over there,

Your Gerhard

DEFENSE WITHOUT WEAPONS

Such hopes for international resolution as the Évian conference may have triggered among Germany's Jews were soon drowned out by the continuing bad news from within the Reich. One anti-Jewish measure followed another, many with massive material, social, or psychological ramifications. A telling sign of the new climate was that until the spring of 1938, organized German Jewry had continued to elicit at least some positive responses from a few helpful government officials; now, all that was over. Within this unfolding process, mass arrests in June 1938 marked a new stage in German *Judenpolitik*. As part of **Himmler**'s new emphasis on preventive custody of groups seen as racially incompatible with the *Volksgemeinschaft*, the police incarcerated roughly ten thousand "asocials" or "work-shy." These were mostly men with some kind of criminal record (which might include the most trivial violations of laws or regulations), among them approximately fifteen hundred Jews and several hundred "Gypsies." Together they were sent to the Buchenwald, Sachsenhausen, and Dachau concentration camps, where they joined the almost two thousand Austrian Jews who had been incarcerated in the aftermath of the *Anschluss*.[25] German Jewish organizations did their utmost to free the arrested Jews, knowing full well that falling prey to the camp **SS** would mean death for many. Since 1933, **Hans Reichmann** had fought as one of the leading Berlin CV officials for Jews' release from concentration camps. From his English exile in the summer of 1939, he recalled the case that had crushed all his hopes of making a difference. He had tried everything to rescue sixty-three-year-old Görlitz businessman Ludwig Cohn from a concentration camp to no avail; Cohn died there in mid-July.

DOCUMENT 11-6: Autobiographical letter by Hans Reichmann on the effect of the mass arrests in June 1938, July–September 1939, translated from Hans Reichmann, *Deutscher Bürger und verfolgter Jude: Novemberpogrom und KZ Sachsenhausen 1937 bis 1939*, ed. Michael Wildt (Munich: R. Oldenbourg Verlag and Institut für Zeitgeschichte, 1998), 92–93.

[. . .] Since that day my strength was broken. I think I can say about myself that I had survived the Hitler era with its thousands of attacks on my nerves well enough; neither my humor nor my joy about the good things in life diminished. I believe that I helped many people, that for some I saved their health, freedom, and perhaps even their lives. I saw hundreds who were in despair and was happy when I could give them new strength. When in 1935 the Nuremberg Laws were prepared through a similar, but hardly as terrible, campaign, I drove my colleagues into the line of fire, encouraged them, and dispelled their concerns. And we all stuck it out. Never before had a man died under my care. [. . .]

It was all over. It required no such devastating documentation of my, of our impotence to make clear to me that the fate of German Jews had come to an end. I had known it for a long time, but only now did I feel that my ability to fight back [*Kampffähigkeit*] was gone.

---

25. See Friedländer, *Nazi Germany*, 1:257–61.

In late April 1938, Reichmann took the precaution of burning the list he had compiled of Jews murdered since 1933.[26] Still, he stayed on in his post until *"Kristallnacht."*

Before his emigration, Joseph Levy had worked for the Jewish community of Frankfurt am Main by providing assistance to arrestees' families, including helping arrange burials of those who had died in custody. Writing in 1940 from his place of exile about his experiences in Germany, he was sure the sole purpose of the "June action" against "asocials" had been to strike fear and terror in the heart of innocent Jews, "to wear them down and in this way make them leave the country."[27]

But where could the Jews go? And if they stayed, where would the next blow come from? The anonymous report in document 11-7, which reached the Paris office of the Jewish Telegraph Agency, tried to sum up the situation in the summer of 1938.

DOCUMENT 11-7: **"Report about a Trip through Germany, Czechoslovakia, and Austria from July 23 to August 4, 1938" by an anonymous author from the files of the Jewish Telegraph Agency office Paris, August 8, 1938, USHMMA RG 11.001M.25, reel 106 (SAM 674-1-109A) (translated from German).**

A) Germany

In the past few years, I paid annual visits to Germany. The current situation in no way resembles the way it still was last year or two years ago. [. . . ; a description of the earlier situation follows.]

The situation today is completely different! One gets the impression that people from every segment of German Jewry, both in Berlin and in the provinces, are in a mood of panic. A feeling of complete disorientation has set in, and in response, people in many places have resorted to illegal flight over the border, completely unprepared, leaving behind everything they own. There is only one topic of conversation now: to which country should one go, what doors are still open to the outside world, and whether and in what form an individual can get assistance. [. . . ; a description of reasons and an arrest wave in Berlin and other cities follows.]

Jews who cross the street against a red light—or even give the appearance of wanting to do so—have been, and still are, subject to

---

26. Reichmann, *Deutscher Bürger*, 63–64.

27. Joseph B. Levy (before his emigration, a teacher and cantor in Frankfurt am Main), "Mein Leben in Deutschland vor und nach dem 30. Januar 1933," LBINY MM 47/ME 483.

arrest. Anyone who drives a car and has license plates that are allegedly not clean enough also faces arrest. Those who have been arrested are either kept in police arrest [*Polizeihaft*] for a few weeks, or they are sent to concentration camps, a decision left entirely in the hands of the police official in charge. To this end two new concentration camps have been built in the vicinity of stone quarries, one in Buchenwald by Weimar and the second in Sachsenhausen near Frankfurt.[28] Reliable sources estimate that some 3,000–4,000 Jews have been sent to these camps in the last five to six weeks. The treatment accorded these people is extremely brutal, regardless of whether they are young people or older, aged 60 or so. In the last three weeks, notification has been issued of around 200 deaths of Jews. Their relatives either suddenly receive an urn or a short message that the person in question has died from a heart attack. [. . . ; a description follows of panic among Jews, further anti-Jewish measures, and their effects.]

A few years ago the Reichsvertretung could still justifiably gear its work to the longer term and could, for instance, pursue on a grand scale a policy of building up [separate] Jewish schools and cultural projects. But today such work has to be seen largely as useless and as a waste of Jewish communal energies [*eine Zersplitterung der zentralen Kräfte der jüdischen Gemeinschaft*]. One cannot escape the impression that only two tasks remain: on the one hand, emigration and preparations for emigration for those groups for whom leaving Germany seems possible, and on the other, securing even the most primitive provision for those people who are unlikely to be able to emigrate. I am convinced that time is running out— perhaps already past—for going through the process of emigrating. The social situation of the vast majority of German Jews has indeed become desperate through expropriation measures and the loss of any means to earn a living for tens of thousands of people. The ever-intensifying preparations for war, the mobilizing of a broad section of the German people for compulsory labor service, for the construction of border forts, etc., and the fact that the legal path has been cleared for drafting of Jews for this purpose [i.e., for forced labor] have created an atmosphere in which everyone, rightly or wrongly, now assumes that the time remaining for Germany Jews to leave this country by some means is growing very short. Everyone is waiting for the results of Évian; no foreign place name has been mentioned so often in the past months. [. . .]

---

28. See the entries on Buchenwald and Sachsenhausen in *USHMM Encyclopedia of Camps and Ghettos*, vol. 1 (Bloomington: Indiana University Press, 2009).

C) Austria

The situation in Austria today resembles that in Germany after five years of National Socialist rule. The mood among the Jewish population is perhaps even more panicked, a fact that can be explained by the extreme shock at the suddenness with which Nazism fell upon Austria. [. . . ; descriptions follow of mass expropriation, abuse, pervasive feelings of misery, and the urge to emigrate among Jews.]

Thousands of people applying for emigration besiege the offices of the Jewish community; all the consulates are overrun, even those of the smallest countries. Because people are seizing every opportunity to get hold of a visa from some consulate without any goal or plan, the consulates will soon be locking their doors to avoid the countries they represent being overrun by the Jewish masses. [. . . ; a description follows of relief and emigration efforts by the Jewish community of Vienna.]

One cannot escape the impression that the work of the Jewish community would benefit from more systematic procedures. The community needs to plan for a longer time period since it is completely impossible to liquidate the question of Austrian Jewry [*die Frage der österreichischen Judenheit zur Liquidation gebracht werden kann*] in just a few months. The efforts of foreign aid organizations must, as their first order of business, focus their efforts so that the Jewish organizations in Austria have a chance to pursue [such planning]. They will have no chance to do so if, for example—as was the case in Vienna today—hundreds of Jews were given notice to vacate their apartments overnight (even officials of the Jewish community), and these Jews have absolutely no chance of finding a place to live. And there will be no chance if Jews are suddenly at short notice expelled [*ausgewiesen*] from entire areas, as occurred, for example in the Burgenland or just now in the Salzburg district.

Many of the measures aimed at forcing Jews out also served the purpose of preparing the ground for more severe persecution within the Reich. Among the regulations enacted in the summer of 1938, two were especially painful: on July 23, it was announced that Jews were required by law to apply for a special ID card (*Kennkarte*) by the end of the year so they could henceforth always be recognized as Jews when dealing with the authorities. On August 17, another regulation forced Jews who did not have "Jewish first names"—a demeaning list of which was later issued by the Reich Interior Ministry—to adopt "Sara" (for women) and "Israel" (for men). **Luise Solmitz** recorded her reaction and that of her Jewish husband, Fredy.

DOCUMENT 11-8: Luise Solmitz, diary entry for August 24/25, 1938, FZGH 11 S 12 (translated from German).

August 24, 1938

Phone call . . . "And how are you?" It's such a bitter pill, having to answer, "Thanks, fine!"—even if you're fighting for your bare life and are regarded as no different than a jailbird.

That evening the next new blow we were expecting struck. Fr. [Fredy, her Jewish husband], looking very pale and quiet, gave me the news.

Germans [are supposed to have] only German first names, including a few adapted from foreign languages [*eingebürgerte*]. But Jews [get] Jewish names. I had said earlier, "Mark my words, they will rule which ones!" And that is just what happened. Not Jonas, Josua, Benjamin, names that are tolerable, but the most awful, totally obscure, and in part insulting names. And in Fr.'s case, anyone who has other first names must add "Israel" to their names in the case of men and "Sara" in the case of women. What can one say? Every official signature must reflect this change; this is how names will appear in the telephone book, in printed address books, on bank accounts.

Fr. immediately wrote to Interior Minister Frick, asking to be exempted and giving the reasons. Who knows whether that won't be regarded as some sort of rebellious act? [. . .]

August 25, 1938

. . . This is a war with too many fronts and one's soul longs for some light, even a glimmer, though it is of course just a form of running away from oneself, a numbing. There is nothing worse than being homeless in one's own home [*heimatlos in der eigenen Heimat*], having no rights in a country. [. . . ; she describes the consequences for her husband, Fredy, despite his multiple military awards and war injuries.] And what will be next, after "Israel" and the identification card [*Kennkarte*]. No more trips, no more hotels, no more meals in restaurants. [. . .] One could hardly describe Fr. as a fearful man: despite all his buddies' warnings, he flew in Fokker's wooden planes[29] held together with packing string. He spent four years of the war fighting in the front lines and before that worked in the wiretapping service [*im Abhördienst*]. He could sleep right through when

---

29. The Fokker aircraft company built planes used by the German army during World War I.

bombs were falling all around him. But on the morning after we got the first news about Jewish first names from Strasbourg [radio station], he said, "I woke up bathed in sweat; it was nothing but a very ordinary, very nasty attack of fear." It's a kind of war, and we find ourselves in it without any defenses, without weapons, without the remotest possibility of defending ourselves by legal means or protests. [. . .]

A month later, Fredy Solmitz was informed by the Hamburg police that his plea to Reich Interior Minister **Wilhelm Frick** had been rejected; the new law allowed no exceptions. The former officer and staunch German nationalist was also reminded that Jews were prohibited from using the phrase "Heil Hitler" in their correspondence with government agencies. The only privilege granted to him and other veterans related to the new ID card. Like other Jews, veterans would have to obtain such a card, paying a fee of RM 3 by the end of the year. But instead of four passport photographs for the application, former soldiers needed only three.[30]

While the barrage of anti-Jewish regulations swept through the Reich, the regime geared up for further territorial expansion. The call to protect and "bring home" Germans living abroad—the so-called *Volksdeutsche* or ethnic Germans—provided a welcome subterfuge for the Nazi aim of liquidating the borders stipulated by the **Versailles Treaty**.[31] In September 1938, the European crisis created by the German government's demands against Czechoslovakia reached its peak and raised the prospect of imminent war. As part of Germany's grab for the Sudetenland with its sizable German population, synagogues were burned down in two of the region's towns. The Munich agreement concluded on September 27 brought what turned out to be a temporary reprieve from the danger of war but led to the annexation of the Sudetenland to the Reich and, in a few months, to Czechoslovakia's complete destruction. At the same time it added yet more Jews to the German sphere of influence, aggravating the emigration crisis still further.

Jews and their families shared the relief felt throughout Europe at having avoided war by diplomatic agreement, but only to a degree. Those around her returned to the tranquility of their daily affairs, Luise Solmitz noted in her diary, "but we—after having shared the torturing days before 'the outbreak of war' with all others—go back to our misery."[32] Writing in 1940 from a safe distance, Siegfried Neumann, until his emigration a lawyer in a town near Berlin,

30. Luise Solmitz, diary entries for September 24 and October 1, 1938; FZH 11 S 12.

31. See Doris L. Bergen, *War and Genocide: A Concise History of the Holocaust* (Lanham, MD: Rowman & Littlefield, 2003), 85–86.

32. Luise Solmitz, diary entry for October 1, 1938; FZH 11 S 12.

remembers feeling nausea for three days after the signing of the Munich agreement, "as if I foresaw what we Jews would have to face. Now that the world had given in to him, the Führer didn't have to listen to anyone anymore."[33]

Indeed, the accord over the Sudeten region soon fell victim to further German aggression, though for the time being still without causing war. In the meantime, roughly two hundred thousand people escaped from the newly annexed Sudeten or were pushed out, among them the vast majority of the Jewish population. While more displaced and desperate people struggled to leave, the possibilities for slipping over the German border were further curtailed. In early October, the Swiss government, fearing the country would be flooded with Jewish refugees from the Reich, reached an agreement with Germany that called for the passports of German Jews to be stamped with the letter *J*. Their bearers could now be easily identified and turned back when trying to cross the border.[34] More often than not, those who had the chance to escape to some far-away place of abode took it, despite the uncertainties awaiting them.

REFUGE AND REFLECTION

Sometimes, making sense of Nazi persecution required distance as well as time to get ones breath back and reflect. The testimony of Siegfried Neumann above and of some others quoted earlier was solicited in 1940 as part of an essay contest advertised by Harvard University on the topic "My Life in Germany before and after January 30, 1933." The contest yielded more than two hundred submissions and served as the basis for research by a group of Harvard professors around Gordon Allport. Though written in safety and thus somewhat removed from the events they describe, the texts are not subject to the transforming hindsight that necessarily shaped postwar memoirs. Not directed to Jewish émigrés exclusively, the contest asked for nonfictional autobiographical texts for the

---

33. Siegfried Neumann, "Mein Leben in Deutschland vor und unter Hitler," LBINY MM 59/ME 468, 64; published in German as *Nacht über Deutschland: Vom Leben und Sterben einer Republik* (Munich: List Verlag, 1978). Siegfried Neumann, born in 1895 in East Prussia, served during World War I. He practiced law with increasing difficulty until 1938 in the region that surrounds Berlin. Sent to a concentration camp following the November 1938 pogrom, he and his family fled to Shanghai in 1939. See Margarete Limberg and Hubert Rübsaat, *Germans No More: Accounts of Jewish Everyday Life, 1933–1938* (New York: Berghahn Books, 2006), 187.

34. Friedländer, *Nazi Germany*, 1:263–65. On the fate of Jewish refugees in or from the Sudeten, Slovakia, and the Czech lands and those expelled under the Munich agreement, see the facsimile copies of memoranda and newspaper reports printed in Friedlander and Milton, *Archives of the Holocaust*, doc. 105, 10:475–88.

study of "the social and psychological effects of National Socialism on German society and on the German people" to be submitted by April 1, 1940. In September 1941, psychologist Allport and his colleagues published their findings in an article titled "Personality under Social Catastrophe: Ninety Life-histories of the Nazi Revolution." The project was not designed as a historical study; nor was its focus on Jewish behavior. Nevertheless, the high percentage of Jews among the authors—sixty-one out of the ninety used for the article identified themselves as being of Jewish religious affiliation—make this an insightful source not only for Jewish reactions after 1933 but also for how the experiences of those who made it out of Germany were interpreted at the time by others who lacked that experience.[35]

As one of the main psychological mechanisms for coping with the impact of the Nazi takeover, the authors of the study identified the fact "that our subjects actively resisted recognition of the seriousness of the situation, or in the cases where the seriousness was realized, failed at first to make a realistic adjustment to it." Delay in clearly recognizing "the menace that National Socialism might contain for their own personal lives" left many reluctant to consider "emigration as an adjustment to the situation." Among the reasons Allport and his colleagues identified for this delayed recognition were the absence of what they called the "intensity of shock required to bring realization of catastrophe" and the "lure of the familiar" that made people prefer staying in Germany over "the disagreeable uncertainties awaiting them in an unknown land," both strong factors until 1938. Overall, the study addressed less the concrete conditions in Germany or the hurdles would-be émigrés had to overcome than more subjective factors and general behavior patterns discernible in the submitted texts. In so doing they helped give rise to an emphasis on complacency and self-delusion that until recently were dominant themes in the literature. Here are some of the team's findings from the chapter

---

35. G. W. Allport, J. S. Bruner, and E. M. Jandorf (Harvard University), "Personality under Social Catastrophe: Ninety Life-Histories of the Nazi Revolution," *Character and Personality* 10, no. 1 (September 1941): 1–22. Gordon Willard Allport (1897–1967) was a noted American psychologist long affiliated with Harvard University; see obituary, *New York Times*, October 10, 1967, 47. Jerome Seymour Bruner (b. 1915), an American psychologist instrumental in establishing modern cognitive psychology in the United States, served as a U.S. Army intelligence officer during World War II after receiving his doctorate from Harvard in 1941; see Fred Skolnik and Michael Berenbaum, *Encyclopaedia Judaica*, new edition (Detroit, MI: Macmillan Reference USA in association with the Keter Publishing House, 2007), 4:222–23. Ernst Jandorf may actually have been Ernst Jahndorf, who originally submitted an entry in the "My Life in Germany" essay contest. The authors have been unable to find information about his further career. For extracts from select essays based on the Harvard collection, see Limberg and Rübsaat, *Germans No More*.

headed "Frustration and Its Consequences" with quotes from unidentified contributors to the essay contest.

DOCUMENT 11-9: **G. W. Allport, J. S. Bruner, and E. M. Jandorf, "Personality under Social Catastrophe: Ninety Life-histories of the Nazi Revolution,"** *Character and Personality: A Quarterly for Psychodiagnostics and Allied Studies* **10, no. 1 (September 1941): 12–17.**

[. . .] The two hundred life-histories submitted to our competition unexpectedly provided a test of reliability for many statements of Nazi barbarity. In several cases it so happened that more than one of our contributors had been prisoners in the same concentration camp (photostats of releases from the camp sometimes being included with the life-histories). Although entirely unacquainted with each other, the separate writers many times reported events, sometimes of a routine order and sometimes bizarre, which agreed fully with each other. The following excerpts from three separate ex-prisoners at one concentration camp [most likely Sachsenhausen] illustrate the point.

> The hands are bound together on your back with a chain which is then fastened to a hook in a tree, so that the tips of your toes don't touch the ground. . . .

> His hands were bound together on his back, and he was hung from the tree by a chain. . . .

> I was bound to a tree and had to hang there for two hours. . . . The arms are bound together on the back by the wrists with a chain. Then one is hung from the hook so that, at the most, you touch the ground with the tips of your toes. The whole body weight hangs on the drawn-back arms. The pain is excruciating. [. . .]

[The authors then move on from the issue of reliability to considering the accounts more generally.] So diverse were these responses that they fail to fit the three categories provided by the Yale hypothesis [described earlier in the article]: aggression, displaced aggression, substitute activity. The responses we find demand rather a ninefold classification.

1. Resignation and other defeat reactions. One of the possible responses to frustration not mentioned by the Yale authors is resignation.

Not infrequently our writers reported giving up in their struggles to resist Nazi intrusions into their lives. With a minimum of action and no aggression whatsoever, they seemed to surrender to the irresistible tide. [. . .]

2. Adoption of temporary frames of security. Another common response to the insecurity engendered by frustration is the adoption of temporary islands of security. Table 7 lists some of their forms.

Table 7 Percentage of Cases Adopting Various Temporary Frames of Security (percentage of cases reporting temporary frames of security = 74)

Frame of Security	Percentage of Cases
Faith in underground movement	23
Hope for emigration	75
Official conformity	26
Occupational continuity	47
Continuation of routine activities	32

Some women found a sense of safety in the routine of housework, some men in continuing day by day in occupational activities; many in thinking of the day when they might escape. Others show in their accounts how they shopped around for islands of security, sampling in turn political Zionism, rumors of underground movements, religious activities—anything, in short, that would provide distraction and hope. [. . .]

3. Heightened in-group feelings. Another response to frustration, possibly an instance of substitute satisfaction for thwarted desires, was the strengthening of ties within already established groups. Most dramatic are the many instances of return to the healing intimacy of the family after bitter experiences of persecution on the street, in the office, or in prison. Others turned with new zest to their remaining friends as a means of alleviating frustration, still others to clubs or religious groups. [. . .]

4. Shifts in the level of aspiration. Still another consequence of frustration was a marked lowering of ambitions. For the 44 subjects on whom relevant data are available, appreciable diminishing of the level of aspiration is found in respect to occupational status (29 cases), community status (13 cases).

5. Regression and fantasy. [. . .] Some of the cases of heightened in-group feeling within the family might safely be classified likewise as instances of regression, possibly too some of the cases of return to religion.

Twenty-five per cent of the cases on whom there were data respecting change in higher mental processes reported an increase in the amount of daydreaming, and none a decrease. Twelve per cent reported experiencing suicide fantasies. In only two cases had there been a mental breakdown. As compared with later evidence on the increasingly realistic character of thought and planning under conditions of frustration, these figures respecting fantasy life are notably low.

6. Conformity to the regime. That a severe frustrating situation will not gain the voluntary assent of the sufferer is obvious; and yet a kind of segmentalized conformity to the demands of the situation serves as a means of avoiding punishment and further frustration. Evidence of such partial conformity is found frequently in our manuscripts. The writers' stories seem an endless procession of petty conformities to the harrowing demands of the Nazi persecutors. As for conformity-behavior, virtually all the cases for whom we have data justified themselves in terms of the avoidance of punishment. A few gave as their reasons the safeguarding of emigration plans or of schemes to bore from within.

7. Changes in philosophy of life. As the months of persecution went on, 42 per cent of the cases for whom data are available betrayed an increased fatalism in outlook. [. . .] In none of these instances was the change revolutionary; rather, it took the form of an accentuation of the dominant pre-existing philosophical tendency. Such alterations as occurred are seen to best advantage in a qualitative analysis of the documents. In some cases, for example, moral standards were disturbed.

> Do we know what the next day will bring? A girl whom I begged to give herself to me and who had consistently said no, now said: "Perhaps soon." Esther, whom I was still in love with, had left without my being able to see her. Would I ever see her again? What of principles! Principles? What for.

In other cases, hedonic scales of valuation were markedly shifted. "Since we have expected the worst and most dreadful at all times, things struck us Jews as pleasant which among people of culture are taken for granted and do not command particular attention." On the whole, however, our evidence does not uncover drastic alterations in the philosophy of life, but rather a modulation here and an intensification there.

8. Planning and direct action. Intelligent planning and action to overcome obstacles are also stimulated by frustration. [. . .] Problems of adaptation arising from severe personal frustration beset our subjects, calling for realistic ingenuity. That ingenious solutions occurred, culminating in emigration, is clear proof of one primary psychological consequence of frustration: nonaggressive planning.

9. Aggression and displaced aggression. With the threat of punishment immediate and severe, there was, naturally, little evidence of direct aggression against Nazi persecutors. Only three physical attacks against Nazis are reported. Antagonism toward the regime, to be sure, was expressed by a majority of the cases among friends in secret. In 45 per cent of the cases for whom there are adequate data on fantasy-life, aggression against the regime played a prominent part in the content of dream and fantasy. Occasional clear instances of displaced aggression were recorded. "Hatred rose within me. Hatred for this symbol, swastika: hatred for this flag and everything connected with it. I could not look at it without becoming furious. I became incensed and would take it out even upon my poor mother in rudeness."

Mentions of desire for revenge against Hitler occurred in 14 per cent of the total sample, against the Nazis in general in 22 per cent. Two or three of the authors report at the time of writing that revenge is now their sole motive in living. [. . .]

Back in the Germany of late 1938, Jews struggled on, and German Jewish organizations continued to provide what help and comfort they could. During the Jewish high holidays in 1938, there was little cause for celebration. As in previous years, the CV, though now in merger negotiations with the **Hilfsverein**,[36] issued a calendar for the New Year 5699 with useful information on its work, its thirteen regional branches, and the services offered by other Jewish organizations. The calendar's editors could offer their readers precious little by way of consoling messages, though the CV's loyal members will have understood the references to the "communal Jewish heritage" as reminding them of a shared German Jewish heritage that could no longer be named.

DOCUMENT 11-10: CV calendar for the year 1938–1939/5699, September 1938, LBIJMB MF 323 (translated from German).

To our Friends!

A year comes to an end and a new one begins—this is not just the shapeless, uniform passage of time, but rather the religious law of the Jews, for whom the turn of the year is a milestone surrounded by a particular sanctity. Never in the experience of the living has the passage of time [*Zeitablauf*] been so identical with flow of our fate [*Schicksalsablauf*] as in recent years. The beginning of solemn religious celebrations of the new

---

36. See Barkai, *"Wehr Dich!,"* 354–55.

Jewish year has thus never converged so closely with our innermost needs as it does now.

With this calendar the CV offers its Jewish friends heartfelt wishes. It [the CV] stands in the center of life in the Jewish community of Germany and is a stranger neither to the depth nor the diversity of feelings that today are associated with such New Year's wishes. It knows both the worries and the hopes of the Jewish people in Germany, and it does its part to make these worries bearable and to fulfill such hopes. It knows that these hopes have to rest almost exclusively on building a future in distant countries and that many of those who receive this calendar will look through its back pages[37] as they use their entire strength to prepare a new home far from their place of origin.

May this little blue booklet accompany people, especially those facing emigration in the future, as a symbol of support. Not as a symbol of an irreplaceable past, grieving for which would require all one's strength, but rather as a symbol of being indebted and belonging to a community that is not lost even as it is scattered across the world. Whoever receives this calendar from the CV carries with him the spirit of his homeland. He should and will integrate into his new environment while making changes to his new residence to the extent necessary. But he would condemn himself to rootlessness if he abandoned his communal Jewish heritage [*jüdisches Gemeinschaftserbe*], which has proved its value in both good times and bad. This calendar is only for one short year and then will be old and no longer of any use. Yet to those who can see in it what it is meant to be—a testimony of loyalty to the CV and to the message [*Lehre*] it wishes to offer those departing—it will become an enduring symbol.

The dwindling of major Jewish communities in Germany and the disappearance of smaller ones signified the end of an era: not only the era of the Enlightenment with its underlying hopes for tolerance and coexistence but the entire chapter of organized Jewish life in Germany. What few had predicted already in 1933 had become a reality five years later. True, the Reichsvertretung and the organizations associated with it soldiered on. In the fall of 1938, it was in fact on the brink of a major reorganization that would streamline the process of emigration and replace the domestic infrastructure previously offered by the individual communities.[38] But the Reichsvertretung's

---

37. The calendar's back pages contained information on emigration. The popular *Philo-Atlas: Handbuch für die jüdische Auswanderung* (Berlin: Philo, Jüdischer Buchverlag, 1938) offered even more information for would-be emigrants.

38. See Kulka, *Deutsches Judentum*, 24–27.

leaders were clear that they were merely the caretakers of the last phases of German Jewry's demise.

Beyond the more tangible aspects of its work, the Reichsvertretung was getting ready to partake in a highly symbolic act. In the spring of 1938, Joseph Weiss, the Berlin representative of the Jewish National Fund for Germany (Keren Kajemeth Lejisrael) floated the idea of creating a memorial book to document the history of German Jewry and preserve its memory. Such memorial books (German: *Erinnerungsbuch*; Yiddish: *Yiskor* books; Hebrew: *sefer zikaron*) had a long tradition in Jewish history. Weiss hoped that every German Jew would register his or her name and that every Jewish community, institution, and organization would create its own text, complete with a short history and photographs. At the same time, the project collected contributions for a fund that would help establish a new settlement in Palestine named Kfar (or Tel) Sikaron.[39] While the CV declined to participate in the project, pointing to the "nonindependent" (*unselbständigen*) character of its local branches,[40] the German Jewish umbrella organization approved the plan in September and approached the remaining communities with the call presented in document 11-11.

DOCUMENT 11-11: Circular by Reichsverband der Juden in Deutschland, late September 1938, *Gemeindeblatt der Israelitischen Religionsgemeinde Dresden* (September 23, 1938): 3 (translated from German).

To the Jews in Germany!
    Tens of thousands of Jews are leaving the country. Many Jewish communities in Germany are being dissolved. But they should not be forgotten: we wish to preserve for coming generations the memory of this long and eventful [*ereignisschwere*] epoch in the development of the Jews and also the memory of the last ones who brought it to a close [*die Letzten, die sie abschlossen*]. On the eve of a new Jewish year, Keren Kajemeth Lejisrael calls upon us to partake in a beautiful and great work: the Jews of Germany and their communities should enter their names into a
    "Book of Remembrance"—*Sefer Sikaron*
    and at the same time use this work to generate the resources for the acquisition of land where a new settlement of Jews from Germany can take root in *Erez Israel*. It will carry the name

---

39. See Kurt J. Ball-Kaduri, *Vor der Katastrophe: Juden in Deutschland, 1934–1939* (Jerusalem: Olamenu, 1967), 139–41.
    40. See CV head office Berlin to branch offices, October 3, 1938; USHMMA RG 11.001M.31, reel 99 (SAM 721-1-93, 52).

Tel Sikaron—"Settlement of Remembrance" [*Siedlung des Gedenkens*]
Tel Sikaron—Settlement of Remembrance—shall be the expression
of a communal effort by which both the past is preserved and something
is created that points to the future. We gladly join in the effort to realize
this plan, which has a worthy and powerful goal, and embrace the call
that Keren Kajemeth Lejisrael has issued to the Jews of Germany on this
occasion.
   Reichsverband der Juden in Deutschland
   Dr. Leo Baeck   Dr. Otto Hirsch
   Board of directors of the Dresden Jewish Community
   Zionistische Vereinigung für Deutschland
   Subscription list available in the community office. At the conclusion
a clean copy will be entered into the "Sefer Sikaron" of the Dresden Community that can be viewed at the community office.

Some communities transmitted this call for the memorial book to their
members.[41] In the following weeks, however, new, even more dramatic events
not only shattered all hopes for the project and for organized German Jewry
but for the first time raised dramatic questions about the physical survival of
German Jews as individuals.

---

41. See circular letter by Keren Kajemeth Lejisrael in Berlin, Rosh Hashanah 5699/1938,
September 26, 1938; USHMMPA WS# 59068.

CHAPTER 12

"*KRISTALLNACHT*" AND ITS CONSEQUENCES

SOLIDARITY WITH THE DEPORTED

As part of the murderous Austrian onslaught, a new element of anti-Jewish policy emerged when unwanted Jews, particularly in the Burgenland bordering on Hungary, were forced over the frontier. After the Nazi annexation of the Sudeten region in October 1938, the pattern of forceful removal was repeated, with Sudeten Jews expelled into what remained of the Czech Republic. In late October of that year, the Nazis found a new target for deportation: Polish citizens living in Germany, many of whom had been there for decades. The brutality of the enterprise was all the Nazis' own, but the background to the deportation was a Polish effort to rid itself of responsibility for Polish citizens living abroad. Eyeing the growing ruthlessness of Nazi antisemitic measures, the Polish government had become increasingly anxious that the tens of thousands of Polish Jews living on German soil might seek to return to their home country. The Polish government set a deadline for these Jews to reregister as Polish citizens or forfeit their right to return. Preempting that deadline, the German authorities struck against this minority within the Jewish community in a surprise move on October 28, 1938. Roughly seventeen thousand men, women, and children were arrested, transported to the border, and forced on to Polish territory. As Poland pushed them back, many of the hapless deportees sought shelter in makeshift camps along the border. They were among the first to share a fate common to many victims of interstate rivalry in the twentieth century.[1]

For decades, *Ostjuden* had been prime targets of German antisemitism and, for many assimilated German Jews, either the cause of consternation or sometimes a stimulus for rethinking Jewish identity.[2] As we have seen, the Nazi assault had first triggered demonstrative dissociation from *Ostjuden* by those German Jews on the right fringe who thought they could convince the new authorities of their unflinching loyalty. For the most part, however, organized efforts to assist those in need of help were extended to Eastern Jews, many of whom proved particularly vulnerable to Nazi economic discrimination.

Whatever tensions between the two groups may still have existed, the deportation of Polish Jews saw an amazing response from those Jews not yet subject to Nazi expulsion orders as well as from Jews abroad. Despite the destruction of established communal structures, an array of Jewish organizations and communities joined informal networks of neighbors and friends in doing what they could to help.[3] Their efforts were geared primarily toward helping deportees and returnees (because many of those expelled were rapidly allowed back) and their families. At the same time, however, such engagement served as a release valve for excess energy and a hitherto largely frustrated desire to act and make a difference. Perhaps more strongly than preceding events, this dramatic, enforced exodus summoned up resonances from Jewish history. In a letter to his son, Benjamin Perlman, an orthodox Jew living in Hamburg, broke with his

---

1. On the October deportations, see Sybil Milton, "The Expulsion of Polish Jews from Germany, October 1938 to July 1939: A Documentation," *LBIYB* 29 (1984): 169–99; Trude Maurer, "The Background for *Kristallnacht*: The Expulsion of Polish Jews,'" in *November 1938: From "Reichskristallnacht" to Genocide*, ed. Walter H. Pehle (New York: Berg, 1991), 44–72. For expulsions of ethnic minorities in a broader context, see Donald Bloxham, *Genocide, the World Wars and the Unweaving of Europe* (London: Vallentine Mitchell, 2008); Marrus, *The Unwanted*.

2. See Stephen E. Aschheim, *Brothers and Strangers: The East European Jew in German and German-Jewish Consciousness, 1800–1923* (Madison: University of Wisconsin Press, 1982).

3. See reports on relief efforts for the Polish deportees in a letter from CV regional office Central Germany (Sabatzky) to CV head office, November 2, 1938, USHMMA RG 11.001M.31, reel 99 (SAM 721-1-101, 75–80). Kurt Sabatzky, a lawyer and CV functionary in Königsberg, later in Leipzig (a city with a heavy Polish Jewish minority of which one thousand were deported in October 1938), recalls this event in his memoirs written after his emigration to England in late August 1939: "Meine Erinnerungen an den NS," n.d. (ca. 1944/1945); LBINY MM 65, 36. On the October deportations, see also Max Eschelbacher, "Der achtundzwanzigste Oktober 1938," written ca. 1939, in Max Eschelbacher, *Der zehnte November 1938* (Essen: Klartext, 1998), 34–39; Reichmann, *Deutscher Bürger*, 106–8; Norbert Conrads, ed., *Kein Recht, Nirgends: Tagebuch vom Untergang des Breslauer Judentums, 1933–1941* (Cologne: Böhlau Verlag, 2007), 1:529–31.

usual practice of ignoring political events in his correspondence and invoked Genesis 12:2, noting also that he was reminded of the expulsion from Spain.[4] As bitter as the fate of those affected was, the mobilization of solidarity for the deportees at least had the positive effect of reminding Jews that, within certain limits, they were not powerless to affect their situation (an insight that would be sorely tested just a couple of weeks later). In document 12-1 **Mally Dienemann** describes how she and her friends quickly established a self-help network in the Hessian city of Offenbach after the news of the deportation had spread on the morning of October 26. As Dienemann's letter makes clear, a significant number of the deportees returned rapidly to their homes. But even if the experience for many was short-lived, the brutal circumstances of the deportation were, perhaps even more than the spectacular violence of *"Kristallnacht,"* a harbinger of the mass transports to ghettos and extermination camps that were to come during the war.

DOCUMENT 12-1: **Mally Dienemann, diary entry for November 1, 1938, LBINY MM 18[5] (translated from German).**

[. . .] We rang several different Jewish families from the East, but the police had picked them all up. The next day those who had been left behind, women or mothers, came by. They had absolutely no clue about why everyone had been arrested and wanted to ask us whether we knew the reason. Gradually we learned that it was a measure undertaken against Poland, which wants to strip its nationals of their citizenship if they have not been in Poland in the last 5 years and have thus not demonstrated an interest in their native country. The people who had managed to avoid being arrested went to the Polish consul, who informed them that negotiations with Poland would be taking place to ensure that the Poles who then became stateless would not become a burden on Germany. As the day wore on, we learned that the negotiations had come to nothing and that the Polish Jews—about 50 to 60 such families live in Offenbach—would be transported away that evening. Those left behind were all deported—children, invalids, old people, pregnant women—with very few exceptions, the people who had not been at home. Local policemen [*Schutzmann*] (the great majority of whom were humane) brought some of

---

4. Letter by Benjamin J. Perlman, Hamburg, to Michael Perlmann, October 10, 1938, in *Verfolgung und Gottvertrauen: Briefe einer Hamburger jüdisch-orthodoxen Familie im "Dritten Reich,"* ed. Ina Lorenz (Hamburg: Dölling und Galitz Verlag, 1998), 139–40.

5. The typed diary text contains two slightly different versions; the quoted passage is from p. 24 in the diary.

the people to their homes toward evening and gave them about 15 minutes to collect the bare essentials.[6] But apart from that they had to leave their apartments without being able to make any arrangements. Some were taken from the street, escorted to their homes, and given some 15 minutes to pack. They were brought to Beuthen [city in Upper Silesia; Polish: Bytom], and after spending some 6 to 10 hours in Beuthen, they returned because the Poles had evidently issued similar measures (although I don't know this for a fact). Our people [i.e., the Jews deported from Offenbach] came back on Sunday around ten o'clock, received a meal in the synagogue, and then returned to their apartments. [. . .]

Leipzig and Dresden were exemplary in providing shelter for the people, offering them warm meals, sending dispatches to their family members, distributing linens. In short, they provided everything a person might need and even more. Today I made more rounds and visited the Schnitzers, wondering how this very high-strung wife had coped up to now. Because she and her husband only had one passport between them, she had been left behind during the arrests on Thursday evening. But on Friday, as she was on her way home, she ran into her children on the street accompanied by a policeman (the children are 7 and 10 years old); they returned home, and she was still able to pack a few things. We then visited [the family] Waldmann; there's a rather deaf daughter who has never been normal, and she was completely disturbed. She's afraid of everyone, refuses to eat or speak, is utterly confused. The mother is completely beside herself and says, ["]There must be a limit to how much misfortune one is forced to endure. Isn't there a limit? Tell me, isn't there a limit?["] [. . .][7]

---

6. The Schutzpolizei was part of the Order Police (Ordnungspolizei) and the closest equivalent to the local bobby on the beat in the United Kingdom or the local precinct policeman in the United States. In mid-1936 they had been integrated into Himmler's police apparatus, and increasingly their regular police duties were coordinated with the Security Police and SD. With the beginning of World War II, order policemen became a key tool for "pacifying" and controlling occupied territories, especially in Eastern Europe, where the Order Police participated massively in the killing of Jewish men, women, and children. See Christopher R. Browning, *Ordinary Men: Reserve Battalion 101 and the Final Solution in Poland* (New York: HarperCollins, 1992).

7. This may have been Jakob (Chaim) Waldmann, born in Lvov (Lemberg) in 1879, his wife Fradel, also born in Lvov in 1879, and daughter Ottilie, born in Leipzig in 1907. The father was sent to Buchenwald in 1939, where he died the following year, while mother and daughter were most likely deported to Treblinka in 1942 and murdered. See www.bundesarchiv .de/gedenkbuch; *USHMM ITS Collection Data Base Central Name Index*; Klaus Werner, *Zur Geschichte der Juden in Offenbach am Main* (Offenbach am Main: Magistrat der Stadt, 1988), 1:191. The authors could not trace any information on the other friends of the Dienemanns mentioned in the document.

Those who had been forced across the German border into Poland and failed to make it back confronted in many cases an impossible situation. Even so, some found the time to tell relatives about their experiences. In broken German, Josef Broniatowski wrote his sons in the United States how he and the rest of his family were deported from the city of Plauen in Saxony, abused by Germans, and taken care of by Jews and non-Jews in Poland.

DOCUMENT 12-2: Letter by Josef Broniatowski,[8] Częstochowa (Poland), no date (most likely early November 1938), USHMMA Acc. 2000.30 (translated from German).

My dear boys! We sent you a telegram from Kattowitz [Polish: Katowice] to say that the German barbarians had thrown us out and that we ended up in Czenstochau [Polish: Częstochowa], now I want to tell you what happened: on Thursday, October 28, at <u>one o'clock in the morning</u> a regular policeman [*Schutzmann*] rang our bell and told us to open up, when he came into the apartment, he gave us a letter saying we were all being deported out of Germany and that very night had to get into the paddy wagon and go to the police station [*Polizeihaus*]. We took <u>nothing</u> with us, and we found that all of the Polish Jews in Plauen were already there, about 75 souls, old people, and little children aged 1 year, and also Grandpa, Grandma, and Uncle Moritz with his kids and Uncle Markus. We sat in the station the whole night and were then brought to <u>Chemnitz</u> in a bus; there they forced us on a special train where we found all the Jews from Zwickau and Chemnitz, and we couldn't buy <u>even a glass of water</u>, even though the little ones had been pulled out of bed and hadn't eaten all night! The train went to Dresden, where two trains with Jews from Leipzig were already waiting, and after a <u>12</u>-hour trip that was guarded by Nazi bandits, they arrived at <u>Beuthen</u> [in Upper Silesia] on the Polish border. Here the <u>worst crimes</u> began since the world war, when the German barbarians went on a murder spree that has no equal: more than <u>8,000</u> people, only <u>Jews</u>, people ranging from 80 years old on down to children who were <u>14</u> days old were driven out of the cars <u>in the night</u> at eleven o'clock onto an open field, and on both sides there were thousands of SS bandits, and all were forced to march over meadows in the dark of night, after marching for 3 kilometers we heard

---

8. Sascha (or Sascha-Doff) Broniatowski was born in 1930 in Leipzig, and the child's fate is unknown. "Mammi" may have been Josef's wife, Sara (née Krzepicki or Klein), born in Sdunska (Poland) in 1902. The authors have been unable to find further information on the other family members and friends mentioned in this letter. See *USHMM ITS Collection Data Base Central Name Index*; *Datenbank zur Liste der jüdischen Einwohner im Deutschen Reich, 1933–1945*.

the pitiful cries of people who were being murdered, we were led to a spot where there is a water-filled ditch four meters wide and up to a meter high, the border between Poland & Germany, people were thrown into the water there so that they would go over to the Polish side. Many people died during this, the bandits stole everything that people had quickly packed into their suitcases. I jumped into the water and Mammi threw Sascha to me and I threw Sascha over the water onto the meadow, then Mammi threw herself on me and I took her across, afterwards Mammi pulled me out of the muck with her bare hands and that's how it was for everyone, Uncle Moritz got Donald and Achim across and Grandma sprained her leg. The Nazi bandits screamed drown the Jewish brood while this was happening. Thousands of Jews ended up on the meadow and marched soaked up to their waists across the fields. As we were getting close to a Polish village, some Polish soldiers came and chased us back to the German border, all the while hitting people and shooting. The Poles said that the German barbarians should take us to the legal border, not the smugglers' border: and so thousands were pushed back and forth between the borders the whole night, during which many old people and little children died. Early in the morning we were on the German side again and were driven about 8 kilometers to the legal border crossing, where a Pole let us through. There the Jews from Kattowitz already knew what had happened and quickly brought milk and bread to the children and old people and brought them to a shelter [Lager], where they could dry their wet clothes. The suffering was terrible, in the village to which they chased us the miners, who are Catholics, started crying when they saw all this suffering and misery. The next day we took a special train to Kattowitz and then traveled as far as Czenstochau. We took nothing with us, only the clothes on our backs, everything was left behind in Plauen. We are here at our parents' place, Grandpa, Grandma, Uncle Moritz, Aunt Loni, Sascha, Achim, and Donald. They are bargaining with the barbarians to let us go back to Plauen to fetch our furniture and clothes. My children, we will never forget this, and the Jewish people will know for eternity what the German culture of thieves [Räuber-Kultur] has done. For the time being write to us at this address:

Ch. Broniatowski, Częstochowa (Poland) ul. farbyczna 22

Give this letter to Rabbi Miller to read and also our other friends. You can also let the newspapers know but don't give our names because there are also German informers around here. We are happy that none of us was hurt because we all could have gotten sick after wandering around all night in wet clothes. Even little Donald had to join this funeral march. We hope that Mr. Kirschmann already sent the tax certificate [*Steuerzettel*] so that we can get the visa from the American consul in Warsaw as quickly as possible.

I send loving greetings and kisses, Your Papa.

DOCUMENT 12-3: **Deportees at Zbaszyn, October/November 1938, USHMMPA WS# 95551.**

Jewish refugees, who have been expelled from their homes in Germany, peel potatoes at the Zbaszyn refugee camp.

Negotiations between the two governments brought a reprieve for Polish citizens in Germany. Nevertheless, international Jewish relief organizations continued to confront the problem of how to help the deportees left in limbo. Within a year, tens of thousands more Jews would be uprooted by the further expansion of the Reich's realm of influence into Eastern Europe. As document 12-4, a report by the AJJDC, shows, even before the war massive hurdles had to be overcome before any relief could reach the displaced.

DOCUMENT 12-4: "Eyewitness Report of Rescue Activities of JDC at Polish-German Border," November 18, 1938, AJJDC Archive AR 3344/878.[9]

The instantaneous and life-giving assistance rendered by the Joint Distribution Committee [AJJDC] to 15,000 Polish Jews who were expelled from Germany over the German-Polish border three weeks ago is described in an eye-witness report just received by the JDC office in New York. Additional funds are needed at once, the JDC has been advised by cable from its European director, to meet the daily requirements of food and medical supplies which are being provided by the Joint Distribution Committee, the Polish Red Cross and the local Jewish organizations at a cost in some communities of $2,000 a day.

The eye-witness report, dated November 10, describes a visit to one border town, Zbaszyn, which harbors from 6,000–7,000 of the deportees. It reads in part:

"Zbaszyn is a village of 5,000 people of which there are seven Jewish families. When the director of the Warsaw office of the Joint Distribution Committee came to Zbaszyn he saw thousands of the deportees lying on the streets. The first problem was what should be done with these people. The Polish Government put at their disposal a stable formerly used by the Polish army. After the stable had been lined with straw, it was able to harbor from 1,500 to 2,000 people. Another 2,000–2,500 refugees were cared for in private homes. Small barracks formerly used for prisoners were made available, each housing from 15 to 20 people. A clubhouse belonging to the Rifle Corps, and a building which had housed a Jewish mill, were also occupied by refugees. In this manner some form of shelter was provided for these luckless people who were out on the street in a torrential autumn rain.

The Joint Distribution Committee instantly opened an office where every one of the refugees was required to register. The office contains a bureau for the distribution of clothes and another where food is parceled out. It is amazing how quickly all of this was organized and made to function. A hospital was established where 100 sick people are being cared for.

---

9. Printed in Friedlander and Milton, *Archives of the Holocaust*, doc. 106, 10:489–90. The author of the report quoted in this document might have been Emanuel Ringelblum, who was working at that time in Zbaszyn on behalf of the AJJDC Warsaw office and during the war founded the *Oyneg Shabes* underground documentation group in the Warsaw ghetto; see Samuel D. Kassow, *Who Will Write Our History? Emanuel Ringelblum, the Warsaw Ghetto, and the Oyneg Shabes Archive* (Bloomington: Indiana University Press, 2007), 90–92, and the forthcoming second volume in *Jewish Responses to Persecution*. For later accounts on the fate of Polish Jews deported in October, see *Archives of the Holocaust*, docs. 105–13, 10:491–529.

Among them are from 25 to 30 critically ill persons, some of them with serious heart conditions and other major diseases. It is heart-rending to see these sick people lying there. Naturally, there is an acute shortage of equipment, pillows and bed-linens. Doctors were called and nurses were found. Despite the fact that these sick people find themselves in most primitive conditions, they nevertheless regard their present state as a paradise compared to what they had lived through. There are several old men over 80 years of age and a separate division for women.

Another accomplishment of the Joint Distribution Committee was the establishment of a nursery in what was formerly a gymnasium. This is really a remarkable thing. From 300–500 children are cared for, kept clean and nourished. They sing and play and forget the misery they have just gone through and in which, in fact, they still find themselves.

All this is due to the remarkably rapid action taken by the Joint.

The Polish-Jewish community cooperated splendidly. As soon as they heard of the tragedy they sent trucks from Posen and from other cities, such as Łódź, Kraków, etc., bearing food and warm clothing. However, there is a serious lack of money. Polish Jews furnished from 25,000 to 30,000 zlotys[10] but this represents only one-third of the total funds expended. The balance was supplied by the Joint. The JDC also organized a corps of 300 young people from the refugees themselves who are assisting in the work of caring for their fellow-sufferers.

Between Zbaszyn, which is in Poland, and New Zbaszyn, which is across the border in Germany, there are still about 50 people in a sort of No-Man's Land. No one is allowed to go to them and no one knows what is to become of them.

There are a number of dangers inherent in the situation. Should an epidemic break out, the results are unthinkable, because all of these thousands are crowded together and it would be impossible to isolate the sick in sufficient time to stop the epidemic. Should a fire occur in the mill, for instance, the inhabitants would be lost; rescue would be impossible as there is only one small exit."

EXPERIENCING THE POGROM

The deportations of Polish Jews from Germany can be seen as the indirect trigger of *"Kristallnacht,"* the Germany-wide pogrom of November 1938. Among

---

10. In 1938, this amounted to less than $6,000; see Joseph Marcus, *Social and Political History of the Jews in Poland, 1919–1939* (Berlin: Mouton, 1983), 256.

the deported Polish Jews were the parents of seventeen-year-old Hershel Grynszpan. On November 7, the distraught Grynszpan shot German diplomat Ernst vom Rath at the German embassy in Paris, in turn providing the background to what Nazi propaganda presented as "spontaneous outbreaks of public outrage" against "the Jews."

But the timber that Grynszpan's spark ignited had in reality been ready to erupt in flames since the summer. How radically the situation in the Reich had changed since the last violent attack by a Jew on a higher-ranking Nazi official, the NSDAP chief in Switzerland, Wilhelm Gustloff, in 1936![11] Then, concerns about undermining the positive diplomatic repercussions of Germany's hosting the winter Olympics had suppressed all negative reaction. Now that Germany had started on a path of aggressive expansion, diplomatic considerations weighed far less heavily. Moreover, ever since the summer, **Goebbels** had been heating up the public mood against the Jews. The tense atmosphere surrounding the Czechoslovakian crisis, followed by the diffusion of the warlike mood, had left party radicals spoiling for a fight—and there was always one target ready on which aggression could be unleashed with virtually no risk.

As we have seen, mass arrests of Jews and demolition of synagogues, two of the defining features of the November pogrom, had already started in the summer of 1938, though on a limited scale. Even before Grynszpan's assassination attempt, local Nazis were eager to move ahead: in Kassel on November 5 and 6, members of the Hitler Youth and other Nazi sympathizers damaged the synagogue and Jewish community building.[12] While trying to prevent further escalation, German Jewish leaders knew they had no influence over the course of events in the Reich. After vom Rath died on the afternoon of Wednesday, November 9, the Berlin leaders of the **Reichsvertretung** decided to send a telegram to Hitler with their condolences based on what CV functionary **Hans Reichmann** later called the faint hope "that such a declaration, published in the foreign press, would make things more difficult for our ruthless enemy."[13] It took only a hate speech by Propaganda Minister Goebbels in front of leading Nazi officials in Munich on the same day, Hitler's nod of approval a little

---

11. Wilhelm Gustloff, Nazi Party leader (*NSDAP-Landesgruppenführer*) in Switzerland, was killed in February 1936 by the Jewish student David Frankfurter. German propaganda used the case as confirmation of the existence of a "Jewish conspiracy" against Nazi Germany; however, in view of the 1936 Olympic Games and fearful of Germany's image abroad, the regime refrained from initiating a massive anti-Jewish campaign. See Friedländer, *Nazi Germany*, 1:181–82.

12. See Reichmann, *Deutscher Bürger*, 109–11. Similar events were reported from Rotenburg/Fulda, Bebra, and Dessau in Saxony (Friedländer, *Nazi Germany*, 1:270–71).

13. Reichmann, *Deutscher Bürger*, 111.

later that evening toward "spontaneous" anti-Jewish actions, and a flurry of late-evening phone calls from regional party leaders assembled in Munich to get party activists all over the Reich out on the streets for an orgy of violence, first on the night of November 9 and then on the morning of November 10, in full sight of the German public.[14]

Across the Reich, Jews and Jewish property became targets of Nazi aggression in what often initially appeared to their victims to be isolated assaults. From diary entries and letters written clandestinely or in exile through to the reporting by relief agencies, diplomats, and the international media—the process of documenting the outrages of those days started almost immediately.[15] Once it became clear that the pogrom was national in scope, it was almost universally seen as a watershed event, irrespective of what Jews and their families had experienced individually. The following documents 12-5 to 12-12 represent but a fraction of the numerous accounts created at the time or shortly thereafter.

DOCUMENT 12-5: Rudolf Bing, "My Life in Germany before and after January 30, 1933," written 1940, LBINY, MM 10/ME 267, 42–43 (translated from German).

[. . . ; Nuremberg, November 10, 1938:] We, my wife and I, were rudely awakened around three in the morning. We heard a frightening racket in front of the door of the building and saw a crowd of people standing outside in the dark. They were ringing all the bells and we heard voices screaming, "Open up! Open up right now!"

I immediately phoned police headquarters and after giving my name told them, "A mob is trying to push its way into my building."

"Are you Aryan?" asked a female voice.

"No," I answered, whereupon she broke off the connection without further comment. . . . ; an account of mob assaults on the tenants of the house Bing and his wife lived in follows.]

We heard pitiful cries on the steps; a Jewish neighbor—we recognized his voice—was evidently being beaten up. "We wanted to avoid falling into their hands at all cost." My wife came to this conclusion first. As a kind of game we had sometimes in the past tried to figure out how we

14. For a concise account of *"Kristallnacht"* and its context, see Friedländer, *Nazi Germany*, vol. 1, ch. 9; Pehle, *November 1938*.

15. See, e.g., Angress, *Between Fear*, 80–116; Wolfgang Benz, ed., *Die Juden in Deutschland, 1933–1945: Leben unter nationalsozialistischer Herrschaft* (Munich: C. H. Beck, 1989), 505–34. For accounts published at the time, see the daily press coverage as well as Gustav Warburg, *Six Years of Hitler: The Jews under the Nazi Regime* (London: Allan & Unwin, 1939).

could escape our apartment should we ever face the possibility of being arrested. Now we acted accordingly. We locked the door to the apartment, then the door of our bedroom, which has an adjoining dressing room, tied linen sheets together, and fastened them to the crossbars of the window frame. I expressed some doubts about whether these could carry our weight. We could already hear them breaking down our apartment door. The window of the dressing room overlooks a narrow alley, with storage rooms for hops on the other side. Across from the window and in front of the warehouse was a front section of roof, somewhat lower than the rest, which left an opening in the alley of around two and half meters between the warehouse and the window. In an instant I decided to throw a mattress down on the ground and jumped down. Above, people were pushing their way into the apartment. My wife decided that the window frame and linen sheets would not hold her weight. Suddenly she was hanging by her fingertips from the window ledge, let go, and fortunately fell into my arms, for I had been standing right under her on the mattress that I had thrown down.

Of course I fell down in the process, but the mattress broke our fall. We were saved. [. . .]

Rudolf Bing and his wife spent the night hiding in a shed with Christmas trees; they managed to emigrate but lost all their money (ca. RM 125,000), which they had to leave behind in Germany.[16] In Hamburg that night, Fredy Solmitz and his family remained unmolested and only found out the next day what was going on.

DOCUMENT 12-6: Luise Solmitz, diary entries for November 10 and 12, 1938, FZGH 11 S 12 (translated from German) (stray punctuation in the original).

November 10, 1938

A terrible, terrible day. Fredy heard it first at Gruenmann's [grocery store]: Jewish businesses had been wrecked and were closed. We went into the city, did some shopping. . . . Everyone incredibly busy, occupied with things, groups, masses of people clustered together, areas blocked off, all the big Jewish stores closed, all the windows were broken in [at] Robinsohn's place and Hirschfeld's. An incessant rattling and clinking from the splintered windowpanes on which glaziers were working. I've never heard such a clattering in all my life. [. . .]

---

16. Rudolf Bing (b. 1876), a World War I veteran and lawyer from Nuremberg, fled to Palestine with his wife, Gertrud (née Tuchmann, b. 1895), in the late 1930s; see LBINY catalog.

On the radio around 6:00 p.m.: demonstrations and actions [*Aktionen*] against Jews must end immediately. The Führer will order regulations regarding the murder of Herr vom Rath—Goebbels has issued this message. This means that our fate is relentlessly approaching doom [*läuft unaufhaltsam dem Untergang zu*]. [. . .] I always thought, now we have reached the worst point. But now I see it was always just a prelude to the next thing. Now the end is near.

November 12, 1938

[. . . ; Solmitz describes a Gestapo visit to their house:] Two men in civilian clothing. Fredy says, "Luise, the men are from the Gestapo." "Yes, what can I do for you?" I said in the same calm voice and in fact felt calm. As I joined them in the room, one of the officials said to Fredy, "Can I speak to you alone?"

I left the room. Still heard, as he said, "Do you have any medals?"

"War decorations? Yes, quite a few."

"Show me the certificates [for the medals]"—"You were a pilot?"

"Yes, one of [Germany's] first pilot officers [*Fliegeroffiziere*] and because of that 50 percent disabled." The motto for all occasions: please, keep it brief. Fredy said, "We were just at the Gestapo [offices] about turning in weapons."

"You have weapons?!"

"Heaps of them since I'm an old frontline officer."

"Oh, then turn them all in."

That goes without saying, Fredy said again, and is certainly the case. "May I inquire about the reason for your visit?"

"From the fact that we will leave you like this, you can see that everything is in order." Would they have taken Fr. along if he had not had his decorations or ordered him to show up somewhere at a given place and time? He made it through a bad quarter of an hour. [. . .]

And that evening the blow fell. I was so frightened I didn't hear it. [Radio] Paris announced, Jews would have to pay a billion Reichsmark for the murder in Paris. And also complete exclusion from economic life. And now Fredy also admitted it: we are destroyed.[17]

---

17. As part of a flurry of decrees enacted immediately after the pogrom, Jews were prohibited from owning or carrying arms (November 11) and from owning and directing most businesses, while they were forced to pay a "compensation" (*Sühneleistung*) of one billion Reichsmarks (November 12, 1938), later renamed *Judenvermögensabgabe*, which amounted to 20 percent of all individual property (November 21, 1938); after October 1939, this number rose to 25 percent (see Friedländer, *Nazi Germany*, 1:281–83).

Even those who were not directly targeted by the organized mob could hardly sustain a sense of normalcy. As what had once been reasonably sheltered spaces within the Jewish sector now came under attack, many saw the family as the only place of refuge. **Toni Lessler**, the female principal of a well-known Jewish school in southwestern Berlin, shares what she later remembered.

DOCUMENT 12-7: Toni Lessler memoir, November/December 1938, LBINY ME 726, 31–32 (translated from German).

[. . .] A grey, foggy November morning dawns; outside in the Grunewald [forest in southwest Berlin], no one had an inkling as yet of the sad things that were at that moment unfolding in the city—in fact, all over the German Reich. The first streetcar, which takes some sixty children from the area around Kurfürstendamm to school, arrives. Trembling, so upset they can barely speak, the children are whispering as they enter the school: "The synagogue on Fasanenstrasse is burning." Keep quiet, I warn them. "Don't repeat that until I've telephoned my friends who live on Fasanenstrasse and gotten confirmation." Then the second car arrives, bringing the children who live in the Bayrischer district out to the school. The students' faces reveal the same terror, the same alarm.

"The synagogue in the Prinzregentenstrasse is burning," and at the same moment the children from the Grunewald [district] who walk to school show up. They confirm that our dear little temple in Grunewald is burning and that the firefighters are standing around without intervening. The older students claim to have heard the remark, "Ordinarily we have to help put out fires, but today we're not allowed to help." Now I clearly no longer needed to telephone around—children were arriving from all over Berlin and reporting that the temple in their neighborhood had been set on fire.

After thinking it over briefly, I sent the children back to their various parts of the city in the company of a teacher so that the parents at least had their children close by. Of course no one knew what would still happen. And it was good that I had immediately sent the children home. The Jewish schools had to stay closed for 10 days until the "excitement" of the populace had died down. There were constant references to "the rage of the *Volk*" [*Volkwut*], which had demanded the destruction of the houses of worship, but everyone knew full well how this "rage" had been stoked up.

After a break of 10 days, we began to teach again, but many children were missing. Those who could manage to leave in some way with their families disappeared in both ordinary and seemingly impossible ways; according to the exact figures, it turned out that 92 of our students' fathers were in concentration camps. [. . .]

During the pogrom, the mob murdered several hundred Jews, including women; among those who narrowly escaped was Hedwig Marcus in Düsseldorf. Her husband had been killed by SS men in front of her eyes; she had been beaten up severely and later took a bullet to the stomach.[18] Tens of thousands of Jewish men got arrested on or after *"Kristallnacht."* From a safe distance and as part of his contribution to the Harvard essay contest, Philipp Flesch reflected on his experiences in a Viennese prison.

DOCUMENT 12-8: Philipp Flesch, "My Experiences on November 10, 1938, in Vienna" (translation by the author from a German text submitted as part of his essay on "My Life in Germany before and after January 30, 1933"), LBINY MM 22/ME 132, 3–6 (tense shifts in the original).

[. . .] The cellar is full of people and the odor of sweat. For two hours two thousand captives had been forced to exercise in their coats and hats. Now it is quiet. I lay my dirty coat on the ground and lie down on it and cry for the deep disgrace of humanity.[19] This was worse than anything that I had seen during the world war. How could I ever become a teacher again since I had lost all confidence in mankind?

The others were quiet. Jews are accustomed to suffering. [. . . ; a description follows of the release of select prisoners by police, SS ("black"), and SA ("brown") officers.] Several [prisoners] announce themselves, show their papers and their hands. "You can go home." In one case the police contradict: "We know him. He is a Communist." The members of the former [Austrian] Jewish Frontline Soldiers ask to be released. "You? Never! You were a Dollfuss organization [i.e., a member of the party supporting

---

18. Undated memoir by Hedwig Marcus, in Barbara Suchy, *Düsseldorf, Donnerstag, den 10. November 1938: Texte, Berichte, Dokumente* (Düsseldorf: Mahn- und Gedenkstätte/Stadtarchiv, 1989), 91–93.

19. Flesch's English and German texts differ slightly. Here, the German text adds two sentences to the effect that all the others in the cell retained their composure as a result of two millennia of Jewish suffering (*"Die anderen bewahren ausgezeichnete Haltung. Tausendjähriges Leidenstraining der Juden"*) (Suchy, *Düsseldorf,* 18).

Austrian chancellor Dollfuss murdered by Nazis in 1934]." My neighbor, my pupil's father, takes out of his pocket [note]book the document which entitles him to wear a war medal. I whisper, "Don't show it!" but he does. He is released. Now I follow his example. "You can go too." Then I say to the dismay of the envious, unhappy remaining ones: "Before I leave I'd like my hat back that they took from me." The black officer orders a brown soldier to go with me to look for my hat. The brown soldier hands me to an army soldier. He leads me to a huge pile of hats. I take the first one that came to hand. [. . .] I was dismissed. The street! Frightened women ask me about their husbands. I see strange circles and flashes, the consequence of a slap in the face. I take the street car. A stranger pays my fare. I go home. Everything [is] unchanged—the curtains waft in the draft—while I was in hell. [. . .]

When I met my friends again, I could see the whole tragedy which had occurred: wrecked furniture, women's faces deformed [*sic*] by slaps. I was told that one of my colleagues had lost an eye, and his skull had been fractured. Many of my friends were in Dachau [concentration camp]. Immediate efforts to liberate them were started. The Jewish community opened its doors again to the suffering crowd. Germany had drawn a strong line of demarcation between itself and civilization.

For organized German Jewry, its press, and any self-directed initiatives within the Jewish sector, "*Kristallnacht*" marked the end. Many of the Reichs-vertretung's functionaries, including **Otto Hirsch**, were arrested, its top leaders unable to intervene with the authorities. With the offices of most other orga-nizations closed, their staff under arrest and their files confiscated, the Reichs-vertretung remained the only institution permitted to function, though on an extremely reduced level.[20] After forty-five years, the **CV** ceased to exist. In the summer of 1939, Hans Reichmann recalled having witnessed the last day in the CV's history, November 10, 1938, from the vantage point of the Berlin head office.

---

20. The regime's interest in retaining the Reichsvertretung was to ensure an increased emi-gration rate, which in 1939 led to the creation of the Reichsvereinigung as a fully Gestapo-controlled successor organization. The Reichsvertretung head office opened its doors again on November 29, 1938. See Kulka, *Deutsches Judentum*, 431–35.

DOCUMENT 12-9: Autobiographical letter written in July–September 1939 by Hans Reichmann describing the closing of the CV head office on November 10, 1938, translated from Hans Reichmann, *Deutscher Bürger und verfolgter Jude: Novemberpogrom und KZ Sachsenhausen 1937 bis 1939*, ed. Michael Wildt (Munich: R. Oldenbourg Verlag and Institut für Zeitgeschichte, 1998), 114–15 (tense shifts in the original).

[. . .] Around 1:30 [p.m.] my door was kicked open. Criminal police inspector [*Kriminalsekretär*] [Franz] Prüfer, from the Berlin headquarters of the Gestapo, pushed his way into my room, followed by five of the new-style detectives, real Gestapo types [*Gestapisten*].

"You [Reichmann] are the boss here. Take your coat and get out of here! Sit down in the hallway! The joint [*Bude*] is being closed. All fire hazards should be shut off."

Never in my nearly six years of confrontations with Gestapo types have I remained so calm. Usually when I encountered these hatchet men [*Schergen*], I always felt helpless in the face of their arbitrariness and malice [*Bosheit*], and this left me feeling insecure. Now there is nothing left to bargain for, and so I can remain calm. My colleagues are thrown out of their offices in a similar manner. A couple of visitors are standing in the hall and ask the officials for permission to leave the office. They are questioned and then allowed to leave.

I stand up and attempt to return to my office.

"What business do you have going in there?"

"My cigar is still lit and I want to stub it out." Günther Friedländer laughs.[21]

"So you think that's funny. You'll stop laughing soon enough," Prüfer, the hard-working criminal inspector, offers in return.

He has a "very big" job today: he is "closing down" the Jewish organizations. Perhaps that will help toward a promotion.

Each of us is called in turn. And each received the same speech: "The joint is closed; operations have been shut down. I do not know if this is only temporary. The head of your office will let you know. Make yourself scarce!" It became apparent they had no interest in the office workers; I had expected as much. They will of course take me with them straightaway. And finally I am the last to be summoned. Herr Prüfer confers the special honor of searching me physically [*Leibesvisitationen*] and, to my great surprise, releases me. I go out the door and slowly descend the steps.

---

21. This might be Günther Friedländer, the author of document 8-18.

In a last glimpse I catch sight of our black nameplate. I have taken leave of the CV! [*Abschied vom Centralverein!*] [. . .]

Reichmann was not free for long; on the evening of the same day, he was arrested and brought with thousands of other Jewish men to Sachsenhausen concentration camp near Berlin. Others experienced the peak of violence early on and were arrested without being dragged to a concentration camp. During the pogrom in Düsseldorf, Rabbi Max Eschelbacher was attacked by the mob and spent almost two weeks in one of the city's prisons. Between his release and his emigration, he learned about many cases of murder and suicide among Jews in and around Düsseldorf; in prison he witnessed the impact of his own reactions on others.

DOCUMENT 12-10: Max Eschelbacher, "November 10, 1938," written in spring/early summer 1939, translated from Max Eschelbacher, *Der zehnte November 1938* (Essen: Klartext, 1998), 41–54.

[. . . ; he describes how he is assaulted and arrested during *"Kristallnacht"*:] These fellows [*Kerle*] descended on me with clenched fists. One grabbed me and shouted at me that I should go downstairs. I was convinced that I would be beaten to death, went into the bedroom, took off my watch, put down my wallet and keys, and said good-bye to Berta [his wife]. All she said was, "Chasak!" [Hebrew: "Be strong!"].

[. . . ; a description of his arrest and imprisonment follows.] Only one experience was positive in the twelve days that I was a prisoner. On Saturday, November 19, a warder appeared at the cell door. He pulled a long object wrapped in white paper out of his pocket and handed it to me with these words: "Your fellow sufferers are sending you this together with their greetings." At least 52 of us were being held in one large room down in the basement. Now they had sent me a huge meat sausage [*Mettwurst*] as a greeting. I thanked the jailer but told him I could not eat it and asked him to return it with my warmest thanks. He thought that the others might also want to eat it, whereupon I told him we had [our] dietary laws and each of us would have it on his conscience.

A legend grew out of this story, and it apparently left quite an impression at the jail. The story got around among the warders that my jailer [*Kerkermeister*] had said, "But no one will see it," and that I had responded, "God will see it!" In this version the story appears to have really affected people. [. . .]

The roughly thirty-six thousand Jewish men dragged to the Buchenwald, Dachau, and Sachsenhausen concentration camps joined the ranks of the "asocials" already arrested en masse in the summer of 1938. On the transport, abuse and terror claimed the first victims; in the weeks and months to come, hundreds more were killed by their SS guards or succumbed to the impossible conditions in the camps. The official Sachsenhausen camp statistics recorded fifty Jewish dead for the period November 10 to December 31, 1938. Hans Reichmann ended up in Sachsenhausen as prisoner number 7687; among his fellow prisoners were his colleagues **Alfred Hirschberg** and Fritz Goldschmidt from the CV head office. For them and others who had dealt with the regime for the past five years, being in the heart of the Nazi terror system almost made sense. Reichmann said half-jokingly to Goldschmidt while both were dragging a heavy load under the eyes of the SS, "Finally we are at the place where we belong. The clueless others should not be here."[22] Prior to his arrest, Reichmann had been heavily involved in the CV's efforts to get Jews released from concentration camps; now he found himself on the other side of the fence. Document 12-11 presents extracts from Reichmann's account about his seven-week incarceration.

DOCUMENT 12-11: Autobiographical letter by Hans Reichmann on his time in Sachsenhausen concentration camp, written July–September 1939, translated from Hans Reichmann, *Deutscher Bürger und verfolgter Jude: Novemberpogrom und KZ Sachsenhausen 1937 bis 1939*, ed. Michael Wildt (Munich: R. Oldenbourg Verlag and Institut für Zeitgeschichte, 1998), 131, 171, 173–74, 228 (tense shifts in the original).

[. . . ; following a detailed description of his arrival in Sachenhausen, the brutal abuse by the SS guards, and expressions of solidarity from veteran inmates, among them "old Jews," i.e., those Jews arrested in June 1938:] Despite everything the day brought, despite our encounter with this bestial behavior, despite the horror—the agonizing tension has left me. I feel more relaxed than I was this morning. I no longer need to ask whether they are coming or when they are coming. I will no longer strain to hear in the early hours of the morning, as I have every day this summer, whether their stooges are coming for me. They did come; the path has come to its predestined end.

---

22. F. Goldschmidt, "Nachruf," in *Zum Gedenken an Hans Reichmann,* ed. Council of Jews from Germany (London: Council of Jews from Germany, 1964), 20.

Our little head teacher [*Oberlehrer*] Kober once spoke to us about the elation, the feeling of complete freedom, that used to come over him [during World War I] in the hours before every assault began. Thinking his life had come to a close, he had reached a point where he had elevated himself above the death he felt sure to be near. Life—or what he still felt of it—was a precious gift that he had received by chance. Thus, he savored these minutes of total freedom, completely relaxed and calm. As a boy I tried to replicate this feeling. For us boy soldiers, these ideas seemed natural.[23] But only now, in a concentration camp, did I begin to understand Kober for the first time. (Incidentally, his brother, a well-respected lawyer in Breslau, did not understand him. When his arrest was imminent on November 10, [1938,] he took his own life.) This feeling of inner release [*Gelöstsein*], this tranquility [*Entspannung*], became part of me during the first weeks I spent in the camp. They evaporated only when some hope began to emerge that we might again know freedom. In this instant the will to live [*Lebensdrang*] awakened anew—and with it, fear for one's life [*Lebensangst*].

[. . . ; descriptions follow of the prisoner hierarchy and society in the camp and aid received, especially from political and "criminal" prisoners.] One evening the Jewish foreman I. L. [name rendered anonymous by Reichmann] sat down at the table with us, four lawyers and a doctor. L. is a driver and had a criminal record for traffic violations, for which the man from Breslau was sent to the camp in June. One would say he's a "big fellow," accustomed to heavy physical labor, and he had been appointed foreman for his good work performance. [L. tells the five men around the table,] "You won't believe what happened to me today! Bugdalle[24] comes up to me in the Klinker and brings me an asocial and a Jew[25]: 'You need

---

23. German: "*Uns Kinder-Soldaten haben sich ja solche Gedanken aufgedrängt.*" This refers to the generational experience of men like Reichmann (born 1900) who experienced their adolescence during World War I. See Wildt, *Generation.*

24. Richard Bugdalle (Reichmann misspelled his name "Bogalle") was one of the SS guards in charge of prisoners at the notorious brick factory (*Klinker* or *Klinkerwerk*) attached to the Sachsenhausen camp. See Christel Trouvé, "Richard Bugdalle, SS-Blockführer im Konzentrationslager Sachsenhausen: Stationen einer Karriere," in *Tatort KZ: Neue Beiträge zur Geschichte der Konzentrationslager,* ed. Ulrich Fritz, Silvija Kavčič, and Nicole Warmbold (Ulm: Klemm & Oelschläger, 2003), 20–56.

25. "Asocial" and "Jew" refer to prisoner categories used in German concentration camps. See David A. Hackett, ed., *The Buchenwald Report* (Boulder, CO: Westview Press, 1995); Wolfgang Sofsky, *The Order of Terror: The Concentration Camp* (Princeton, NJ: Princeton University Press, 1997).

to give it to these two' [*'Die zwei musst du mir fertigmachen'*]. So I give the asocial a kick and punch the Jew and then yell at both of them. Bugdalle doesn't move an inch. 'Didn't you hear me? You're supposed to take care of them for me. So that I see some clear results!' [*'dass ich was laufen sehe!'*] What was I supposed to do? The order was pretty clear: I was supposed to beat them so blood would flow. So I slug each of them in the jaw and chase them. Finally Bugdalle leaves. The Jew is lying on the ground; he was a weak guy. I go over to him, apologize, and move him so that he can catch his breath. What would you have done in my place?" I. L. has turned red. He has a bad conscience. He feels bad and wants to unburden himself. Four lawyers and a doctor shrug their shoulders. Embarrassed, we don't say a word. Truly, what would we have done in his place? It's a bitter lot to be a victim of brutality, monstrous to be turned into its tool! [*"Bitter, ein Opfer der Brutalität, ungeheuerlich ihr Werkzeug zu werden!"*] [. . .; further descriptions of camp life follow.]

What we experienced today [the first day in Sachsenhausen concentration camp] is apparently going to happen every day. How is such a thing to be borne! Outside our wives will be fighting to free us, but will they be able to do it on their own? The lawyers [who prior to their arrest were involved in the struggle to free concentration camp inmates] are here with us, and our organizations could [even] be holding their consultation hours here. Five months ago, as we were fighting on behalf of Ludwig Cohn, I and a lawyerly friend were not able to solve the dilemma in which each of us felt tragically entangled: as a lawyer, can one in good conscience and responsibly take on a "concentration camp case," which is a race against death, for which one must constantly fight against the self-recrimination that one is not doing enough, that one is not working quickly enough, that one is losing precious hours. The alternative argument is clear, and yet I felt this conflict more deeply after my first day as a prisoner at the Klinker works than I did when I was free. Someone quietly says what many are feeling: the world must learn what is happening to us. Many countries would perhaps then open their doors, and if they could not do that—for legal reasons or out of political considerations—then our family members on the outside must do something extraordinary, something that shocks the world into recognizing the depths of our own distress. We should go down on our knees before Roosevelt, someone says, and as much as I feel disgusted by this image of degradation in front of my eyes, I understand the mood among my comrades.

[. . . ; a description follows of further abuse by SS guards and rumors about their release:] It is Hanukkah time. In the afternoon after roll call has ended one can hear the quiet humming of the *Moaus Zur*[26] throughout the Jewish barracks. Shortly before lights out Karl Fichtmann comes in with sparkling eyes: "I was just with the children. I collected some things and made a plate of treats for the boys. The children were so pleased! They also send their best thanks." It hadn't occurred to any of us [older Jewish prisoners] to bring the "children" in the "youth barracks" a little happiness. Karl Fichtmann, a vagabond [*Landstreicher*] from Elbing living on the streets for the past 15 years, "pals with the Jews" [*bei die Juden gehend*], bought some spice cookies and candies and brought Hanukkah to the "children" in their Spartan barracks.[27]

By seven o'clock we are lying on our straw sacks. "Quiet, Adi wants to sing!" And now Adolf Burg begins, very quietly and expressively, to sing the *Berochaus* for the lighting of the candles with a sweet voice, just as he may have heard it sung in the Offenbach synagogue.[28] Then he begins with the old song *Moaus Zur*, and the men in the barracks hum along. Next to me tears fill Arthur Frankberg's eyes: "I have to think of home. I have a child that I haven't seen yet, born in July."[29] The song comes to an end, and without being asked, a farmer from Hesse begins to speak, one of the roughest [*ungeschliffensten*] old Jews. He recites a Bar Mitzvah speech that the village teacher sketched out for him 45 years ago. He rattles it off with the same false intonations as he did when he was thirteen. It is apparently the only formal speech that he learned to deliver in his whole life. "Give it a rest!" [*"Schon genug!"*], someone yells. "Leave the old man alone!"

Some baptized Jews also share our barracks [Block 16]; but along with all of us, they are thankful for the Hanukkah atmosphere, of which we get a glow each evening during this week when Adi sings a sweet *Moaus Zur* before lights out. Adi doesn't allow the atmosphere of religiosity [*Stim-*

---

26. Reichmann means *Ma'oz tzur*, a song sung at Hanukkah that translates as "Rock of Ages." *Berochaus* refers to *brachahs*, meaning "blessing."

27. Karl Fichtmann (1886–1940) had worked as a barber at some point before he was incarcerated in Sachsenhausen. He died in the camp in 1940. See *USHMM ITS Collection Data Base Central Name Index.*

28. This may have been Adolf Bernhard Burg (b. 1913) of Offenbach am Main, who was incarcerated for several months in Sachsenhausen during 1938 and 1939 before fleeing to Shanghai with his wife, Margarete (b. 1914). See *USHMM ITS Collection Data Base Central Name Index.*

29. This was probably Arthur Frankenberg, born in Berlin in 1898, who was a Sachsenhausen prisoner for a time but managed to escape to Shanghai, where he spent the latter years of the war. See *USHMM ITS Collection Data Base Central Name Index.*

mung religiöser Erinnerung] to last for too long; a popular song comes on the tails of *Moaus Zur*, which he croons in a languishing voice like a tenor in some film: "A ship sails to Shanghai, never to return." [. . .]

Of the Jews arrested in the wake of the pogrom, 6,400 were brought to Sachsenhausen; by the end of December, 1,064 were still there.[30] Like many other of the Jewish *"Kristallnacht"* prisoners, Hans Reichmann owed his release from the concentration camp to his wife's tireless efforts in overcoming the many hurdles administered by malevolent authorities. Herself briefly arrested on November 10, **Eva Reichmann** managed to convince the police that her husband was needed in the effort by German Jewish leaders to organize the exodus from the Reich. Other Jewish women ran the gauntlet of endless offices and managed to get emigration papers required for their husbands', fiancés', or brothers' release; not all were successful.[31] In April 1939, the Reichmanns emigrated to England; by that time most leaders of Jewish organizations and communities had already fled the Reich.

In her memoir written about a year after *"Kristallnacht,"* Mally Dienemann offers a glimpse at what it meant to arrange simultaneously both her husband's release and their emigration with state officials, few of them helpful, fewer sympathetic to her cause. With her children safely settled in Palestine and Britain and herself well connected to the upper middle class in her hometown of Offenbach, Mally was in a better position than many Jewish women whose husbands had been dragged away to concentration camps. However, she had even more reason to worry deeply as her sixty-three-year-old husband's health had been bad, aggravated by his detainment five years earlier in the Osthofen concentration camp. Her account starts after Max Dienemann was taken into police custody on November 10, 1938.

DOCUMENT 12-12: Mally Dienemann, diary entries, late 1938/early 1939, LBINY MM 18, 30, 32, 34–35 (translated from German) (tense shifts in the original).

[. . .] What do you do to get your husband released from prison? He [Max Dienemann] had been to the doctor in the days [leading up to his arrest]; he was suffering from severe foot pain and perhaps a certificate from his doctor, Dr. Hohmann, professor for orthopedics at the Frankfurt University Clinic, could secure his release. I received a friendly answer when I phoned to inquire. Of course my husband was not fit for prison. A certificate was issued for me. At four o'clock [4:00 p.m. on November 10] I

---

30. Michael Wildt, introduction to Reichmann, *Deutscher Bürger*, 31.
31. For two well-documented cases, see Suchy, *Düsseldorf,* 140–205.

went to the police [the German Order Police as opposed to the Gestapo]. After a short wait I was brought before Superintendent [*Kommissar*] Richmann, who was not impolite. I handed over the certificate and received a promise that it would be passed on. However, I needed to go back to the Gestapo. I asked for permission to speak briefly with my husband and to give him some food. This was permitted, and we were able to talk for a few minutes. He looked terribly ill, was resigned and brave, told me that he shared a room with 11 men, that they had just prayed together, that they were in good spirits. He did not mention any interrogation. I had to take my leave and again went to the Gestapo. Tress, their man in charge, has a bulldog face (he at one time had many connections to the Jewish community) but was not unfriendly and promised to help get the medical certificate accepted [so that Max Dienemann would be released]. I departed. In the street one could see shattered glass in front of Jewish firms and shops. Display windows were broken. Remnants of wares lay on the ground. Along the way I encountered women weeping; their husbands had been picked up in the course of the day. I heard a whole string of frightful stories. Almost all Jewish men had been arrested; almost all Jewish apartments had been vandalized [*zerstört*]. Because the "rage of the *Volk*" was not allowed to extend into the evening, they had not quite finished and thus some Jewish houses had not been touched. It was only that evening that we Offenbachers learned from the radio that this day had been a misfortune not only for our city, that not only the Offenbach synagogue had been set on fire but a whole wave of misfortunes had spread over all the Jewish communities in Germany. Not even the smallest village community had been spared.[32] I lay down that night, beaten down [*zerschlagen*], dead tired. But sleep did not come. At five o'clock [5:00 a.m. on November 11] friends telephoned to say that the prisoners from Offenbach were supposed to be sent away. The car that would take them was leaving at six o'clock. Perhaps there was a chance that I could say good-bye at the police station beforehand and deliver some food [to her husband]. My girlfriend filled a basket with groceries, we went to the police, and when we arrived the driver was just starting the engine. We managed to get a brief glimpse inside a bus that was packed full with friends who were sitting and standing. We waved, and the bus drove away. We asked the policemen standing

---

32. For a listing of synagogues destroyed in and around Offenbach, see Wolf-Arno Kropat, *"Reichskristallnacht": Der Judenpogrom vom 7. bis 10. November 1938—Urheber, Täter, Hintergründe* (Wiesbaden: Kommission für die Geschichte der Juden in Hessen, 1997), 223–25. As we saw earlier, many small Jewish communities had already been disbanded well ahead of the November pogrom.

in front of the building, "Where are the men being taken?" They answered gruffly, ["]We don't know a thing.["]

At eight o'clock I again went to Superintendent Richmann, who told me correctly that the men were being taken to Buchenwalde [*sic*] (concentration camp near Weimar). I mentioned my husband's illness, his age (63 years), his need for medical attention, and the certificate issued by the university professor stating that he was unfit for prison. "Don't worry," Kommissar Richmann told me, "there will be medical services available. The prisoners are getting some firm Prussian treatment [*hart und preussisch angepackt*], but nothing will happen to them. At most they will lose a few extra pounds."

I was so gullible that this provided some comfort on my way home. We had to wait and in the meantime pay visits to the police and Gestapo. [. . .]

[Firsthand descriptions of the fate of the prisoners in Buchenwald follow. Jews remaining in Offenbach were in the meantime being cut off from basic provisions.] On Saturday, November 12, we heard that the Jewish prisoners were being released if they could prove that they had a visa for some foreign country or a Palestine Certificate and that their departure was imminent. I sent a telegraph message on Saturday to my children in Palestine asking them to acquire a Palestine Certificate as quickly as possible. [. . .]

[A description of postpogrom anti-Jewish measures in and around Offenbach follows.] On November 17, I received a telegram from my married daughter in London, Frau Jakoby, saying that an entrance visa for both of us to go to England had been secured. I should go to the consulate immediately and pick it up. Owing to an error, I did not receive it right away, but the consulate sent it to me on Sunday [November 20]. And now I had the paper in my hands that I needed to free my husband.

I could prove to the Gestapo that nothing should interfere with our expedited departure. First I went to the passport office, to this [Mr.] German in order to apply for passports. It appeared that I would be able to obtain it [*sic*] right away. There were still further issues to take care of and just when I believed I would be getting it on the spot, after being sent all morning from one office to the other, German said to me—this was a man who had known us for many years—"Well, you need to show me evidence first that your husband has a doctoral degree. How do you intend to prove that to me?" I ran home and brought back his doctoral diploma, something about which he [Mr. German] had no comprehension. He then said, ["]Fine, in eight days you can pick up the passport.["]

And now another series of offices awaited me. The official emigration office in Frankfurt, the Gestapo, the police, the finance office [*Finanzamt*], a petition to Buchenwald, a petition to the Gestapo in Darmstadt, and it still took until Tuesday of the third week [November 29] before my husband returned. On Tuesday at midday I was back at the official emigration advice bureau in Frankfurt. The director was very friendly, promised to do everything in his power, for he understood that every extra day presented a life-threatening situation for a 63-year-old man. When I returned home from making these rounds, I ran into some acquaintances who called to me, "Frau Doktor, your husband is coming today. He is being released today. Make sure you have a great deal to drink on hand because he is terribly thirsty." I dared not believe it, but at two o'clock a telegram arrived from Weimar giving his arrival time. I picked my husband up from the train station. This was not like picking him up when he was released from Osthofen [concentration camp in late 1933]; this was not a man who had returned with his old familiar sense of humor intact. We greeted each other, and he said very gravely, "If I go through this again, Mally, I will not survive." We went home. But this deadly earnestness did not leave him. I was happy, but how could one remain happy for long? The husband of my daughter was still in a camp, and many a friend languished there as well. [. . .]

While the Dienemanns and so many others made arrangements to leave, a few of German Jewry's leaders, among them **Leo Baeck**, **Hannah Karminski**, Otto Hirsch, and Cora Berliner, stayed behind with the remnant of German Jewry. With all other Jewish organizations disbanded, the Gestapo reopened the Reichsvertretung, the **Hilfsverein**, and the **Kulturbund** in late November 1938 for the purposes of organizing the exodus of those able to find refuge abroad and caring for those who remained in Germany. In early 1939, the authorities reorganized the Reichsvertretung, the German Jewish umbrella organization formed in September 1933 under the auspices of Leo Baeck and other widely acknowledged Jewish leaders, to become the **Reichsvereinigung der Juden in Deutschland** for purposes diametrically opposed to those Baeck and his colleagues had wanted to achieve. With the onset of large-scale deportations during the war, the Reichsvereinigung became a tool for the purpose of administering the envisioned "final solution of the Jewish question."[33]

---

33. For an assessment of the role of the Reichsvereinigung, see Beate Meyer, "The Inevitable Dilemma: The Reich Association (*Reichsvereinigung*) of Jews in Germany, the Deportations, and the Jews Who Went Underground," in *On Germans and Jews under the Nazi Regime*, ed. Moshe Zimmermann (Jerusalem: Hebrew University Magnes Press, 2006), 297–312. On the post-"*Kristallnacht*" period, see Konrad Kwiet, "To Leave or Not to Leave: The German Jews at the Crossroads," in Pehle, *November 1938*, 139–53.

DOCUMENT 12-13: Letter by Hilfsverein regarding the release of prisoner Simon Zweig from Dachau concentration camp for emigration to Paraguay, November 29, 1938, USHMMPA WS# 07501.

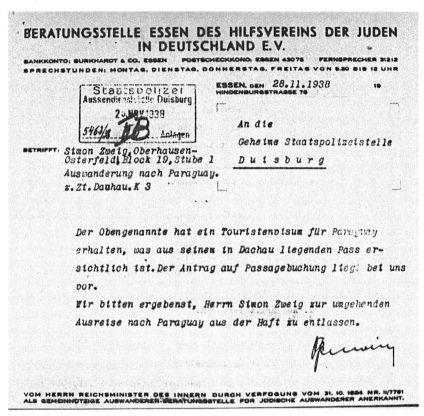

Letter sent by the Essen branch office of the Hilfsverein to the Gestapo in Duisburg, informing them that Simon Zweig, who was being detained in Dachau, had received a tourist visa for Paraguay and requesting that he be released and allowed to emigrate. Simon Zweig, born in 1908 in Poland (stateless or of Polish citizenship), was arrested in 1938 in the German city of Oberhausen, where he lived, and sent to Dachau concentration camp. It is unclear whether he was released and managed to escape the Reich. See *Datenbank zur Liste der jüdischen Einwohner im Deutschen Reich, 1933–1945* (Berlin: Bundesarchiv, 2008); *USHMM ITS Collection Data Base Central Name Index.*

WHAT NEXT?

Once the fury of the pogrom had ebbed and those arrested started coming back to their families, a semblance of normalcy returned to Jewish homes despite the flurry of fierce regulations and the grim prospects for the future. Fifteen-year old **Elisabeth Block**, in her diary entries usually upbeat about life in idyllic Bavaria and oblivious to the tightening of the net that was to engulf herself and her family, bemoaned the death of an uncle killed during the pogrom and the fact that she had to leave her beloved school as a result of the prohibition on Jews attending non-Jewish German schools.[34] In Hamburg, Luise Solmitz maintained her chronicle, now noting the first moves toward concentrating Jews in special houses and the utterances of leading Nazis on the solution of the "Jewish question," utterances that prompted her Jewish husband to comment, "That's alright; at least that way we don't maintain false hopes, like in the past."[35] In Vienna, **Ruth Maier** wrote an imaginary letter addressed to the famous Jewish actor Ernst Deutsch in her diary. She expressed her joy that he had escaped to the United States in time, was spared the misery and pain of persecution, and could again make audiences elsewhere "laugh and cry."[36] Where communal life still existed, its reduction to its basic elements could occasionally be seen in a positive light. In Düsseldorf after the destruction, staple items in the services of German Reform Jewry—the organ, choir, and pulpit in the synagogue and the priestlike black gown (*Talar*) of the rabbi, as well as use of the German language—were gone; instead, Rabbi Max Eschelbacher conducted services he described in 1939 as "very simple, but full of dignity and in a way even full of beauty."[37]

Many had lost all hope; suicides abounded among the elderly, impoverished, and disillusioned remnant community. They departed for the most part quietly, making all necessary arrangements so that the remaining family members would not have to bother about dealing with inquisitive policemen or

34. Diary entries of Elisabeth Block for November 16 and 17, 1938, in *Erinnerungszeichen: Die Tagebücher der Elisabeth Block*, ed. Haus der Bayerischen Geschichte (Rosenheim: Bayerische Staatskanzlei, 1993), 162–63.

35. Luise Solmitz, diary entries for December 3 and 5, 1938; January 30 and February 8, 1939; FZGH 11 S 12.

36. Ruth Maier, diary entry for November 26, 1938, translated from Ruth Maier, *"Das Leben könnte gut sein": Tagebücher 1933 bis 1942*, ed. Jan Erik Vold (Stuttgart: DVA, 2008), 150.

37. Max Eschelbacher, "Die Zeit nach dem 10. November," written ca. 1939, published in Max Eschelbacher *Der zehnte November 1938* (Essen: Klartext, 1998), 66–67. An expert in Jewish law, Max Eschelbacher (1880–1964) served as a rabbi in Bruchsal beginning in 1906 and later in Düsseldorf from 1913 until he left Germany. He spent nearly two weeks in prison after being attacked during the November 1938 pogrom and in 1939 managed to emigrate with his wife, Berta, to England, which became their permanent home. See Falk Wiesemann, "Einleitung," in Eschelbacher, *Der zehnte November*; Röder and Strauss, *Biographisches Handbuch*, 1:161–62.

unpaid bills. Some saw their suicide as an act of revolt. Before the forced introduction of "Jewish names" came into effect, seventy-six-year-old Hedwig Jastrow from Berlin took her life, leaving behind the note presented in document 12-14.

DOCUMENT 12-14: Suicide note by Hedwig Jastrow,[38] Berlin, November 29, 1938; LAB APr.B Rep. 030, tit.198B, # 1943, quoted in translation from Christian Goeschel, "Suicides of German Jews in the Third Reich," German History 25 (2007): 29.

Nobody should attempt to save the life of someone who does not want to live!

This is not an accident or an attack of depression.

I am leaving life as someone whose family has had German citizenship for over 100 years and has always remained loyal to Germany. I have taught German children for 43 years and have helped them through all their trials and tribulations. I have done charity work for the German *Volk* for even longer, both in times of war and times of peace. I don't want to live without a Fatherland, without a homeland, without an apartment, without citizenship rights, ostracized and reviled. And I want to be buried with the name my parents both gave me and passed on to me, which is untainted. I do not want to wait until it gets defamed. Every convict, every murderer keeps his name. It cries to heaven!

Those who remained had to deal with the shrinking Jewish sphere—if there was still one worth speaking of after authorities had ordered select institutions like the Kulturbund to resume their activities as best they could. What little solace this sphere might have offered stood in no comparison to the denigration Jews experienced on a daily basis. Even if the public pogrom and the senseless destruction of property found few supporters within the German population at large, Jews could not express their feelings openly in a non-Jewish environment without running the risk of arrest or worse. In document 12-15, Heinrich Mugdan describes his encounter with the "people's community" in the town of Heidelberg after *"Kristallnacht."*[39]

---

38. Hedwig Jastrow (1862–1938), born in Nakel, lived in Berlin at the time of her death.

39. Heinrich Mugdan was born in 1916 in Neckargemünd to a Jewish father and non-Jewish mother. His grandmother committed suicide to escape deportation. See LBINY catalog.

DOCUMENT 12-15: Heinrich Mugdan, diary entry for November 20, 1938, LBINY MM 58/ME 457, 3 (translated from German).

[. . .] Four people are sitting in the train compartment discussing it [the pogrom]: a mail carrier, who holds back; a worker, who "would have liked to have been there"; a disgusting petit bourgeois female, the most talkative of them all; and a nondescript, grayish Nazi Party member who boarded the train at Karlstor. At some point I pick up my coat and move into the next compartment. But it is dark and quiet there, too quiet, and I get more and more unsettled hearing the words from the other compartment. My heart begins to beat violently. Finally I can no longer bear it, and shortly before we reach Neckargemünd, I go back over, wait until their laughter pushes my anger to its boiling point, and say, "Do you really find that so funny?" The party member opens his mouth: "What—how can you—" The woman [*Weib*] jumps up. [Mugdan says,] "I in any case think it is barbaric!" To which the woman retorts, "He's also one of them, in case you're feeling sympathy—" "I'm no Jew, but you can also ask good National Socialists [Nazis] all about it!" "My husband ought to be here— he'd give it to him good! Where's he getting out, the crook [*Schlawiner*]?" She need not wait long for her answer. Just then the train stops, and I climb out as calmly as possible. "Isn't anyone around, who knows 'im, that crook, could get 'im arrested?" Bang—I shut the compartment door in her face and disappear into the darkness. A short time later I am riding home alongside the grayish Nazi. He sits next to me in the tram, and I am already picturing how I would drag him from the stop at Kaiserhof into the woods. "Unfortunately," however, he does not recognize me or want to recognize me.

Thus the things Jews in Germany would have liked to do or say remained, to a large degree, undone and unsaid. Given the physical threat, any response to the massive onslaught would have to be extremely subtle. Compared to the heavy coverage of "*Kristallnacht*" in foreign media as well as in private diaries and memoirs, any kind of public German Jewish acknowledgment of the reality at the time is extremely rare. Yet, in what was left of the Jewish press—mostly periodicals designed to announce new regulations and ensure compliance—and Jewish cultural institutions, one can find oblique references to what was going on. Document 12-16, a review of a film that the Kulturbund chose as the season premiere of its movie program (*Filmbühne*), serves as an example.

DOCUMENT 12-16: "The Opening of the *Filmbühne,*" *Jüdisches Nachrichtenblatt Berlin,* December 30, 1938, 3 (translated from German).

[. . .] Chicago

A city is burning, and the fire department stands idly by. All fire hoses are at the ready, the ladders are in position, the nozzles are in place, but no one makes a move. The men obey orders, but no order comes. Only when the city, which stretches out over 500 acres, has burned to the ground, reduced to rubble and ashes, does the order come. The fire brigade returns to the station.

Malicious rumor? An ugly fairy tale? No, the truth. And it took place in Hollywood.

Now we are asked to experience that period between 1850 and 1871 again. Not in books and thus only in our imaginations, but as witnesses who see and hear all of it. Henry King, working under the artistic direction of Darryl F. Zanuck, has conjured up these two decades on the silver screen. [. . .]

For many readers, the article's reference to the second half of the nineteenth century likely evoked images or memories of a relatively harmonious period in German Jewish history; few would have much idea what this period meant for the U.S. history featured in the movie. All would think instantly, however, of very recent events in the Reich when reading about burning buildings and idle firefighters. On the print page, the film review, framed by a graphic ad depicting burning city buildings, was followed by an announcement for a stage production of Mendele Mocher Sforim's *Benjamin, Whither?*[40]

In Western countries, uncensored news about Germany's relapse into barbarism shocked many, but this did not significantly increase foreign governments' readiness to open their gates—a notable exception being the organized transports of Jewish children, so-called *Kindertransporte,* after November 1938. These brought up to ten thousand children to England and about one-third of

---

40. Mendele Mocher Sforim was the pseudonym of Sholem Yankev Abramovitsh (1835?–1917), a writer highly influential in laying the foundation of modern Yiddish and Hebrew literature. See Ken Frieden, *Classic Yiddish Fiction: Abramovitsh, Sholem Aleichem, and Peretz* (Albany: SUNY Press, 1995), 12–15; Skolnik and Berenbaum, *Encyclopaedia Judaica,* 1:318–22.

that number to Palestine, building on already existing *Aliyah* projects.[41] One night in mid-December, Ruth Maier accompanied her mother to the Vienna train station to say farewell to her sixteen-year-old sister, Judith, bound for England.

DOCUMENT 12-17: Ruth Maier, diary entry for December 11, 1938, translated from Ruth Maier, *"Das Leben könnte gut sein": Tagebücher 1933 bis 1942*, ed. Jan Erik Vold (Stuttgart: DVA, 2008), 158.

[. . .] The Jewish orderlies lit the scene with flashlights. And children up to 17 years of age, boys and girls with rucksacks and little suitcases. One more kiss and another and one last one. Next to me a woman was crying, not quietly to herself; instead, she whimpered and moaned. [. . .] As I was watching Jews, only Jews, whose children are dragged away before they have finished kissing [good-bye], I think to myself: isn't there something special about Jews? They have so much pain to bear. So much pain! Because they are Jews! That's why. It has such a charming ring to it: "We witnessed many a heartbreaking farewell." No, hearts don't break that quickly. Mama says: "If one of all those people had screamed, just one, all would have started." No, no one screamed, no one cursed. They only cried. Only tears, I saw nothing but tears. [. . .]

Those refugees who did make it out fought for a better life for themselves and their children and tried to spread the word about their experiences to those who would listen. Yet, apart from themselves, few outside Germany had a clear idea of the obstacles refugees faced, much less of the situation of those remaining in Germany. Reasonably well-informed Jewish experts painted a bleak picture; in view of the ever-expanding scope of the refugee crisis in Europe, some even resigned themselves to the idea "that all the 112,500 Jews over 60 years old in Germany and Austria should be left there and allowed to die out, as well as many of those between 45 and 60."[42] At the end of November, the SS journal *Das Schwarze Korps* published an article under the heading "Jews, What Now?" (*Juden, was nun?*), predicting the rapid impoverishment of the remaining Jews

41. See Mark J. Harris and Deborah Oppenheimer, *Into the Arms of Strangers: Stories of the Kindertransport* (New York: Bloomsbury, 2000); Claudia Curio, *Verfolgung, Flucht, Rettung: Die Kindertransporte 1938/39 nach Großbritannien* (Berlin: Metropol, 2006).
42. "Note on conditions of Jews in Germany and Austria made by a recent visitor from Palestine," anonymous, no date (ca. late 1938); facsimile printed in *Archives of the Holocaust*, doc. 15, 3:84.

and proclaiming "the iron necessity of exterminating the Jewish underworld [. . .] with fire and sword" (*"harten Notwendigkeit, die jüdische Unterwelt genau so auszurotten, wie wir in unserem Ordnungsstaat Verbrecher eben auszurotten pflegen: mit Feuer und Schwert"*). While at the time outside observers found such rhetoric too wild to take seriously, many German Jewish officials thought otherwise.[43]

DOCUMENT 12-18: Letter by Georg Landauer, Central Bureau for the Settlement of German Jews in Palestine, Jerusalem, to Henry Montor,[44] United Palestine Appeal, New York, December 2, 1938 ("strictly confidential"); CZA RG S25/9703.

[. . .] German Jewry is panic-stricken. They [*sic*] know they are lost. They fear they have no help, and what they think is that the Nazis are preparing a similar plot in America, presumably in the States.[45] They, i.e., the Nazis, cannot continue feeding tens of thousands of Jews in the camps inside Germany. Although the persons in the concentration camps have to pay for their nutrition, according to the Nazi conception, they are paying with German money because all Jewish money belongs to the German State. They are not sure that other countries will take them out of Germany, and so far, they are not yet convinced that world Jewry will nourish them in Germany or pay the ransom hoped for by the German Government. Therefore, there are Jews in Germany who think that the intention is to arrange for a second plot and then to make short work of the Jews in Germany, or a considerable part of them. [. . .]

Assimilated Jewish families like Ruth Maier's often celebrated Christmas, the joyful Christian holiday; after "*Kristallnacht*," it did nothing to alleviate the feeling of pain and anxiety.

---

43. See the account by E. Hoofien on the situation in Berlin, November 11, 1938, and the 1945 memoir by the last CV president, Ernst Herzfeld, on his reading of this article in *Das Schwarze Korps*, both printed in Kulka, *Deutsches Judentum*, 436–41.

44. Georg Landauer (1895–1954), a German-born Zionist activist, became director of the Berlin Palästina-Amt and the ZVfD in the 1920s. After resettling in Palestine in 1934, he worked to help German Jews resettle there and was instrumental in organizing the Youth Aliyah movement. See obituary, *New York Times*, February 6, 1954. Henry Montor (1905–1982), active in Zionist affairs since his youth in the United States, became a major fundraiser for the United Palestine Appeal in the 1930s and one of the founders of the United Jewish Appeal. See obituary, *New York Times*, April 16, 1982.

45. This refers to rumors circulating among Jews about attempts by antisemites to stage "*Kristallnacht*"-like pogroms outside Germany, in this case in the United States.

DOCUMENT 12-19: Ruth Maier, diary entry for December 24, 1938, translated from Ruth Maier, *"Das Leben könnte gut sein": Tagebücher 1933 bis 1942*, ed. Jan Erik Vold (Stuttgart: DVA, 2008), 164–65.

Saturday, December 24, 1938, Vienna
   Ten thirty at night.
   So it's Christmas. Walked the streets [of Vienna] . . . Snow . . . empty streets . . . Christmas carols blare from the radio; achingly sweet. One catches a glimmer of the smashed-in windows of a Jewish shop, marked with Hebrew letters, on the other side of the street. The world is so hypocritical, so very hypocritical. . . . A car tire explodes . . . couldn't that have been a gunshot? . . . a gunshot on Christmas Eve . . . the sound of a bell cuts through the air. . . . "Jew" has been daubed on the shop, nothing else. On another . . . "Off to Dachau you go, Satan." . . . Christmas candles glow in the window above . . . Christmas in Hitler's Germany. I had to kiss this smeared-on "Jew." Yes, indeed, kiss it. How painful to be a Jew, how sad. And yet . . .

Irrespective of their expectations about a future in the Reich, many German Jews faced the gloomy reality of not being able to escape the country. Even those who managed to overcome all the formal hurdles for emigration still could not be sure until the very last minute that they would make it safely across the border. After Mally Dienemann had managed to get her husband, Max, out of Buchenwald concentration camp, the couple prepared for their departure, a process that, as for all other Jews escaping from Germany, involved handing over most of their possessions to the Reich. On the verge of the couple's escape from the Reich, the guardians of the racial state still separated Mally and Max Dienemann from a new future abroad.

DOCUMENT 12-20: Mally Dienemann, diary entry on her and her husband's escape from Germany on December 30/31, 1938, written ca. 1939, LBINY MM 18, 38–40 (translated from German).

[. . .] Our trip went smoothly until we got to Emmerich, the city before the Dutch border. In Emmerich two young SS men came into our compartment wearing their tight black uniforms, perhaps 20 or 22 years old. They inspected our passports and asked gruffly, "Are you Jews?" We answered in the affirmative. ["]Where is the *J* in your passport? What? I'm sure you'd like that, traveling through the world without having a *J* in your passport.[46] You need to get off the train and return to Offenbach, and above all, give us your passports. Come to the platform tomorrow morning and pick up your passports for the trip back." We answered, "We were never again going to return to Germany[,"] and that it must be all the same to him whether Jews who were emigrating and no longer living in Germany had the *J* or not. It was to no avail. We had to get off the train. We began to look for a hotel where we could spend the night. At two hotels we were told, ["]We do not allow Jews to stay here.["] We went to the Christian travelers' aid office at the train station [*Bahnhofsmission*]. I could have spent the night there, but not my husband. Naturally I would not be separated from my husband. In the fourth hotel no one enquired, and we were finally able to put our things down. The weather was terrible, and we were dead tired after all this excitement. First we had to make a call to Holland, where we had been expected that evening. It took a long time before we got through to The Hague. We then lay down in bed—but we did not sleep that night. Early on a gloomy December morning, it was raining and snowing, we went to the train platform to face our tormentors. They appeared around eight o'clock and after drawn-out pleas gave us back our passports. After repeated requests they gave their consent for us to go to the police in Emmerich to have the *J* stamped into our passports. A long distance from the train station in Emmerich through the city to the police station. There we again had to wait before it was our turn. Our hearts beating anxiously: would they provide it or not? The police official condescended to apply the *J* stamps. We were able to pick up our luggage and go to the train station and take the next express train heading for The Hague. A terrible hour still spent at the train station, for the train had been delayed by 40 minutes, and the two SS men constantly went up and down the platform and into the waiting room. Finally we could board the train, finally the train left. All of a sudden these young men clad in black, lads who felt all-powerful, examined our passports—but there were no questions about our luggage, no questions about what currency we were carrying. Perhaps they saw in our faces what this night in Emmerich had done to us. We arrived at the Dutch border, and our bitterness about everything that had been done to us was much greater than our feeling of happiness about being out of this land of anguish and ignominy. But as we then changed over into the train

---

46. It was mandatory that the letter *J* be stamped into the passport of German Jews after early October 1938. See Walk, *Sonderrecht* 244, nos. 556, 557.

to The Hague and saw the friendly, well-fed people, as we again heard a polite please and thank you (something one no longer hears in Germany), a true and intense feeling of gratitude and happiness arose within us. We gave a prayer of thanks for our liberation and a prayer of supplication for all those who still remained in Germany.

[. . . ; she describes her and her husband's brief stay in Holland and England and their struggle to get their remaining possessions out of Germany.] After a two-month stay in England, we left for Palestine on March 15. We landed in Tel Aviv on March 21, 1939. Two weeks after we arrived, my husband became ill with a mild attack of pleurisy. The pain in his legs became very intense. The pain was attributed to all the standing he had to do and the exertion of being in a concentration camp. On April 10 he got up for the first time again. We were sitting in the sun in the garden that morning for an hour; in the afternoon a heart attack ended his life.

And now I'm sitting here in Palestine on Mount Canaan without my beloved life partner, without my circle of friends, without having saved even a fraction of our property. Because of the war we have lost any hope that the transfer payment [for moving funds from Germany to Palestine] can be made. I am truly "Gone with the wind" [English in the original] here. "Gone with the wind ["]? And yet, despite the many hours of despair, despite the many hours of the most bitter attacks and the loss of faith, somewhere in the depths of my soul an absolutely unshakeable faith remains, impervious to all the terrible things that have happened to people: though we cannot see it with our eyes, this must, must all have a meaning.

For Jews, historian Marion Kaplan writes, predictability and normalcy "came to a standstill on November 9, 1938." After the pogrom, "daily life consisted of the unexpected."[47] More so than any other event, *"Kristallnacht"* marked German Jewry's "social death" by excluding it from the "legitimate social or moral community."[48] At the same time, paradoxically, Jews' importance in the eyes of Germans, most visibly as objects of antisemitic propaganda, had increased massively compared to before 1933. Jewish fears that they were constantly in the limelight of German attention were not the fantasies of a beleaguered, segregated, and claustrophobic group.

---

47. Marion A. Kaplan, *Between Dignity and Despair: Jewish Life in Nazi Germany* (New York: Oxford University Press, 1998), 10.

48. Kaplan, *Between Dignity*, 5, quoting Orlando Patterson, *Slavery and Social Death* (Cambridge, MA: Harvard University Press, 1982); Orlando Patterson, *Freedom*, vol. 1, *Freedom in the Making of Western Culture* (New York: Basic Books, 1991).

Instead, it was the regime that was obsessed with fantasies about the Jewish enemy, and it was the German general public that grew increasingly accepting of such antisemitic images. Despite German Jewry's decline into an ageing and impoverished fringe group (by the beginning of the war in September 1939, about half of the roughly 525,000 Jews living in the Reich in January 1933 had left the country), the Jewish "world enemy number one" figured ever larger in Nazi propaganda. The closer the regime moved to realizing its plans for territorial expansion, the more it invoked the Jewish enemy as a prop to prepare the nation psychologically for war. Nowhere did the negative integration of "the Jew" into Nazi policy making become more obvious than in Hitler's speech of January 30, 1939, in which he threatened that a new world war would bring about the destruction of the Jewish "race" in Europe.[49]

At the time Hitler delivered his speech, the regime still sought to solve the "Jewish question" through emigration. But the more Germany strove to expand its borders, the larger became the number of Jews within its realm of influence and the smaller their chances of escaping. In March 1939, Germany invaded the western parts of Czechoslovakia and annexed the Memel area on the border with Lithuania. In September 1939, with the attack on Poland, the war, and with it a new phase in German anti-Jewish policy, started. In the subsequent volumes of this series, we will follow the catastrophic consequences of this trajectory for the Jewish populations of Europe.

In the introduction to this volume, we pointed to the discrepancy in perspectives created by the openness and unpredictability of the situation as experienced by Jews at the time, on the one hand, and a postwar world familiar with the Holocaust, on the other. Rarely in human history has there been such a gulf between what it was to be an uncertain contemporary and what it is to be armed with hindsight. Shedding light on that difference to illuminate the murky atmosphere within which Jews in Nazi Germany were forced to make their choices has been a principal aim of this volume. Yet, at the same time, we have seen much that was prescient and little that was complacent in contemporary German Jewish responses. The leading organizations recognized strikingly early on that there was no future in Germany for Jewish youth, even if they could not have predicted the violence and murder that would follow. But could they, should they, have done more?

That question was a particularly troubling and poignant one after the war for those contemporaries who had played active roles in communal leadership in the 1930s and later learned of the full scope of the "final solution." Were

---

49. See Kershaw, *Hitler: Nemesis*, 152–53; Hans Mommsen, "Hitler's Reichstag Speech of 30 January 1939," *History & Memory* 9, nos. 1/2 (1997): 147–61.

their relief attempts for people in need in fact misplaced efforts to create optimism when they should have urged immediate escape? Looking back after the war, **Robert Weltsch** felt that his call published in the *Jüdische Rundschau* in conjunction with the Nazi boycott of April 1, 1933, under the title "Wear the Yellow Badge with Pride" (*Tragt ihn mit Stolz, den gelben Fleck*) had been based on a tragic misapprehension and represented a failure to provide proper leadership. Commenting on Weltsch's postwar distancing from this 1933 article, **Friedrich Brodnitz** remembered in the 1980s that Weltsch "felt he should instead have written: All is lost. Get out as fast as possible."[50] Yet, if such a view was more than understandable, perhaps Weltsch, too, was now blinded by hindsight. If nothing else, the documents in this volume have shown Jewish women and men, as individuals and group members, trying to make sense of an unpredictable process driven by outside forces. At least until the late 1930s, the scale of the evil that was about to be unleashed upon the world remained unimaginable.

---

50. Friedrich S. Brodnitz, "Memories of the Reichsvertretung: A Personal Report," *LBIYB* 31 (1986): 276–77. Brodnitz made the same point in his contribution to the discussion during a 1985 Berlin conference; see Paucker, *The Jews in Nazi Germany*, 398.

LIST OF DOCUMENTS

PART I: THE BATTLES OF 1933

1 Confronting the Nazi Revolution

Early Weeks

Document 1-1: "The New Situation," *Der Israelit*, February 2, 1933, 1–2 (translated from German).

Document 1-2: "Inner Security," *Jüdische Rundschau*, February 3, 1933, 45–46 (translated from German).

Document 1-3: Letter by Hans Kronheim, Bielefeld, to Senta Wallach, Hannover, March 21, 1933, USHMMA Acc. 2008.292 box 3 (translated from German).

Document 1-4: Jewish war veterans march in protest against the Nazi persecution of German Jews, New York City, March 23, 1933, USHMMPA WS# 11152.

Document 1-5: CV press release dated March 24, 1933, *CV-Zeitung*, March 30, 1933, 2 (translated from German).

Document 1-6: Letter by Enni Hilzenrad, Berlin, to CV head office Berlin, March 25, 1933, USHMMA RG 11.001M.31, reel 100 (SAM 721-1-2292, 316–17) (translated from German).

Boycott

Document 1-7: Letter by CV regional office Rhineland-Westphalia (Ernst Plaut) to CV head office Berlin, March 20, 1933, USHMMA RG 11.001M.31, reel 101 (SAM 721-1-2321, 67) (translated from German).

379

Document 1-8: Antiboycott flyer by H. and E. Leyens, USHMMA RG 11.001M.31, reel 101 (SAM 721-1-2321).

Document 1-9: Willy Cohn, diary entries for March 31 and April 1, 1933, translated from Norbert Conrads, ed., *Kein Recht, Nirgends: Tagebuch vom Untergang des Breslauer Judentums, 1933–1941* (Cologne: Böhlau Verlag, 2007), 1:24.

Document 1-10: Poster from *Der Gelbe Fleck: Die Ausrottung von 500.000 deutschen Juden* (Paris: Editions du Carrefour, 1936), 29.

Document 1-11: Mally Dienemann, diary entry for April 3, 1933, LBINY MM 18, 11a (translated from German).

Document 1-12: Letter by Jüdischer Frauenbund to the Bund Deutscher Frauenvereine, May 10, 1933, *Blätter des JFB*, May 1933, 12 (translated from German).

Physical Threats

Document 1-13: Else R. Behrend-Rosenfeld, diary entry for September 2, 1939, reflecting on events up to October 1933, translated from Else R. Behrend-Rosenfeld, *Ich stand nicht allein: Leben einer Jüdin in Deutschland, 1933–1944* (Munich: C. H. Beck, 1988), 23–24.

Document 1-14: Max Abraham on his incarceration in the Papenburg concentration camp, fall 1933, first printed in Max Abraham, *Juda verrecke: Ein Rabbiner im Konzentrationslager* (Templitz-Schönau: Druck- und Verlagsanstalt, 1934) (translated from German).

Document 1-15: Final letter by Fritz Rosenfelder to his friends, April 1933 (translated from German).

Document 1-16: "Personal Tragedy," *Jüdische Rundschau*, April 25, 1933 (translated from German).

2 Exclusion and Introspection

Embattled Identities

Document 2-1: Luise Solmitz, diary entries, late May 1933, FZGH 11 S 11 (translated from German).

Document 2-2: Kurt Rosenberg, diary entries for August 20 and 31, 1933, LBINY AR 25279 (translated from German).

Document 2-3: Theodor Lessing, "Germany and Its Jews," 1933, translated from Jörg Wollenberg, ed., *"Wir machen nicht mit!" Schriften gegen den Nationalismus und zur Judenfrage* (Bremen: Donat Verlag, 1997), 225, 239–40.

Document 2-4: Letter by Richard O., Berlin-Lichtenberg, to Protestant bishop (*Reichsbischof*) Friedrich von Bodelschwingh, May 29, 1933, translated from Eberhard Röhm and Jörg Thierfelder, eds., *Juden-Christen-Deutsche*, vol. 1, *1933–1935* (Stuttgart: Calwer Verlag, 1990), 256.

Document 2-5: Letter by Alex Lewin, Hoppstädten (Southwest Germany), to Ismar Elbogen, April 25, 1933, LBINY MF 515, reel 1 (translated from German).

Document 2-6: "Beacon and Reflection," *Jüdische Rundschau*, May 12, 1933 (translated from German).

Document 2-7: Anonymous report on the situation of German Jews sent to the Office of the Executive Committee of the World Jewish Congress in Paris, n.d., ca. June 1933, USHMMA RG 11.001M.36, reel 193 (SAM 1190-3-7, 172–78) (translated from German).

Document 2-8: Willy Cohn, diary entry for August 30, 1933, translated from Norbert Conrads, ed., *Kein Recht, Nirgends: Tagebuch vom Untergang des Breslauer Judentums, 1933–1941* (Cologne: Böhlau Verlag, 2007), 1:72.

Jewish Leadership and the "Jewish Sector"

Document 2-9: Circular issued by the board and representatives of the Jewish community of Görlitz, May 28, 1933, USHMMA RG 11.001M.31, reel 191 (SAM 721-1-1989, 1–2) (translated from German).

Document 2-10: Kurt Rosenberg, diary entry for June 1, 1933, LBINY AR 25279, folder 6 (translated from German).

Document 2-11: Report sent to the CV head office on the inaugural meeting of the New Front of German Jews held June 13, 1933, in Berlin, USHMMA RG 11.001M.31, reel 191 (SAM 721-1-1985, 1–8) (translated from German).

Document 2-12: Ignaz Maybaum, "Rejection of the RjF," *Jüdische Rundschau*, June 16, 1933 (translated from German).

Document 2-13: Appeal at the inauguration of the Reichsvertretung, *Bayerische Israelitische Gemeindezeitung*, October 1, 1933 (translated from German).

Document 2-14: Letter by the Free Association for the Interests of Orthodox Jewry to Hitler, October 4, 1933, quoted in translation from Marc B. Shapiro, *Between the Jeshiva World and Modern Orthodoxy: The Life and Works of Rabbi Jehiel Jacob Weinberg, 1884–1966* (Portland, OR: Littman Library of Jewish Civilization, 1999), 225–33.

Document 2-15: "Führerausweis" Heinz Kellermann; USHMMA Acc. 2007.96 Kellermann collection, box 2.

Document 2-16: Speech by Kurt Singer on the opening night of the Kulturbund production of *Nathan the Wise*, October 1, 1933, translated from Herbert Freeden, *Jüdisches Theater in Nazideutschland* (Tübingen: Niemeyer Verlag, 1964), 28.

3 Strategies for Survival

Emigration, Hopes, and Realities

Document 3-1: Willy Cohn, diary entry for June 27, 1933, translated from Norbert Conrads, ed., *Kein Recht, Nirgends: Tagebuch vom Untergang des Breslauer Judentums, 1933–1941* (Cologne: Böhlau Verlag, 2007), 1:56.

Document 3-2: Letter by Erwin Moses, Tel Aviv, to Julius Moses, Berlin, November 5, 1933, translated from Dieter Fricke, *Jüdisches Leben in Berlin und Tel Aviv, 1933–1939: Der Briefwechsel des ehemaligen Reichstagsabgeordneten Dr. Julius Moses* (Hamburg: von Bockel, 1997), 115–19.

Document 3-3: Beate Berger and youth from the Beith Ahawah Children's Home on an excursion near Berlin, 1934, USHMMPA WS# 48874.

Document 3-4: Siddy Wronsky, published diary entries, Haifa, September 1933 and January 1934; *Blätter des JFB*, December 1933, January 1934 (translated from German).

Document 3-5: List of youth from the Beith Ahawah Children's Home in Berlin emigrating to Palestine, 1934, USHMMPA WS# 48876.

Document 3-6: Letter by Lea Folk, Amsterdam, November 30, 1933, to the Jewish Refugee Committee in Amsterdam, WL 049-EA-0623, 2–4 (translated from German).

Targets of the "People's Community"

Document 3-7: CV report on a search by SA and police in the Wolzig Youth and Training Home, June 1933, USHMMA RG 11.001M.31, reel 151 (SAM 721-1-3071, 370–72) (translated from German).

Document 3-8: Max Abraham, "The Jewish Company," first printed in *Juda verrecke: Ein Rabbiner im Konzentrationslager* (Templitz-Schönau: Druck- und Verlagsanstalt, 1934) (translated from German).

Document 3-9: Letter by Dr. Rudolf Löwenstein, Soest (Westphalia), to CV head office, October 20, 1933, USHMMA RG 11.001M.31, reel 137 (SAM 721-1-2942, 138) (translated from German).

Document 3-10: Letter by Willy Rosenfeld, Konstanz, to CV head office, November 6, 1933, USHMMA RG 11.001M.31, reel 137 (SAM 721-1-2942, 86–87) (translated from German).

Document 3-11: Kurt Rosenberg, diary entry for November 11, 1933, LBINY AR 25279 (translated from German).

Taking Stock after One Year

Document 3-12: Margarete Susman, "On the Edge," *Blätter des JFB*, April 1934, 1–2 (translated from German).

Document 3-13: Letter by Julius Moses, Berlin, to Erwin Moses, Tel Aviv, December 23, 1933, translated from Dieter Fricke, *Jüdisches Leben in Berlin und Tel Aviv, 1933–1939: Der Briefwechsel des ehemaligen Reichstagsabgeordneten Dr. Julius Moses* (Hamburg: von Bockel, 1997), 133–34.

Document 3-14: H. Rn. [Hans Reichmann], "After One Year," *Der Morgen*, 1934–1935 (April 1934): 1–3 (translated from German).

PART II: FEELING ONE'S WAY: JANUARY 1934 TO AUGUST 1935

4 Stretching the Limits of Influence

Central and Regional Perspectives

Constrained Communications

Document 4-9: Letter by Julius Moses, Berlin, to Erwin Moses, Tel Aviv, March 24, 1934, translated from Dieter Fricke, *Jüdisches Leben in Berlin und Tel Aviv, 1933–1939: Der Briefwechsel des ehemaligen Reichstagsabgeordneten Dr. Julius Moses* (Hamburg: von Bockel, 1997), 138–39.

Document 4-10: Letter by Adolf Adler, Sandersleben, to CV head office, July 9, 1934, USHMMA RG 11.001M.31, reel 102 (SAM 721-1-2397, 104–5) (translated from German).

Document 4-11: "Wanted" ad published by Jewish community Sandersleben, July 1934, USHMMA RG 11.001M.31, reel 102 (SAM 721-1-2397).

5 Everyday Life in an Era of Uncertainty

Bread on the Table

Document 5-1: "Interesting Judgment of a Labor Court," *Jüdische Rundschau*, March 15, 1935, 4 (translated from German).

Document 5-2: Letter by Karl Cohn-Biedermann, Berlin, to Alfred Hirschberg, CV head office, May 9, 1935, USHMMA RG 11.001M.31, reel 190 (SAM 721-1-1592, 2–3) (translated from German).

Document 5-3: Response letter by Alfred Hirschberg to Karl Cohn-Biedermann, May 13, 1935, USHMMA RG 11.001M.31, reel 190 (SAM 721-1-1592, 5–7) (translated from German).

Negotiating Public Spaces

Document 5-4: Letter by Julius Moses, Berlin, to Erwin Moses, Tel Aviv, for the week of January 28 to February 3, 1935, translated from Dieter Fricke, *Jüdisches Leben in Berlin und Tel Aviv, 1933–1939: Der Briefwechsel des ehemaligen Reichstagsabgeordneten Dr. Julius Moses* (Hamburg: von Bockel, 1997), 288.

Document 5-5: Letter by Helmuth Bernhard, Berlin, to editors of *CV-Zeitung*, February 7, 1934, USHMMA RG 11.001M.31, reel 113 (SAM 721-1-2553, 6) (translated from German).

Document 5-6: Letter by Friedrich Eppstein, Mannheim, to CV head office, March 9, 1934, USHMMA RG 11.001M.31, reel 128 (SAM 721-1-2813, 154) (translated from German).

Document 5-7: Kurt Rosenberg, diary entry for May 13, 1934, LBINY AR 25279 (translated from German).

Document 5-8: Letter by CV regional association Rhineland (left bank) to CV head office, November 3, 1934, USHMMA RG 11.001M.31, reel 100 (SAM 721-1-2303, 118) (translated from German).

Document 5-9: Letter by Bernhard Taitza, Merseburg, to Alfred Hirschberg, CV head office, August 22, 1934, USHMMA RG 11.001M.31, reel 112 (SAM 721-1-2499, 77) (translated from German).

Document 5-10: Letter by CV regional association Rhineland (left bank), Cologne, to CV head office, October 22, 1934, with copy of letter by the chairman of the CV local branch Meckenheim, Benny Juhl, October 14, 1934, USHMMA RG 11.001M.31, reel 150 (SAM 721-1-3070, 254–55) (translated from German).

Document 5-11: Letter by N. Michelsohn, Minden, to CV regional office East Westphalia, November 27, 1934, USHMMA RG 11.001M.31, reel 112 (SAM 721-1-2499, 37) (translated from German).

Document 5-12: Letter by CV regional association Central Germany to CV head office, March 11, 1935, USHMMA RG 11.001M.31, reel 112 (SAM 721-1-2499, 24) (translated from German).

Document 5-13: CV memorandum for Hans Reichmann and Alfred Hirschberg, March 14, 1935, USHMMA RG 11.001M.31, reel 112 (SAM 721-1-2499, 23) (translated from German).

Jewish Children in the Schools of the "People's Community"

Document 5-14: CV copy of a letter by the executive of the Jewish community Sterbfritz to the county school officer in Schlüchtern, Kassel region, November 14, 1934, USHMMA RG 11.001M.31, reel 119 (SAM 721-1-2667, 378–79) (translated from German).

Document 5-15: Group portrait of German school girls, 1935, USHMMPA WS# 97273.

Document 5-16: Letter by Alex Blumenau, Wuppertal-Elberfeld, to CV head office, April 14, 1935, with attachment, USHMMA RG 11.001M.31, reel 119 (SAM 721-1-2667, 36, 42) (translated from German).

Document 5-17: Letter by CV head office to Alex Blumenau, May 2, 1935, USHMMA RG 11.001M.31, reel 119 (SAM 721-1-2667, 33–35) (translated from German).

Document 5-18: Elisabeth Block, diary entry for March 28, 1934, translated from *Erinnerungszeichen: Die Tagebücher der Elisabeth Block*, ed. Haus der Bayerischen Geschichte (Rosenheim: Bayerische Staatskanzlei, 1993), 66–67.

Document 5-19: Betty Schleifer, "School Kids Today," *Frankfurter Israelitisches Gemeindeblatt* (September 1935): 508 ("women's page") (translated from German).

Document 5-20: Letter by Erna Rehberg, Malchow, to CV head office, August 13, 1934, USHMMA RG 11.001M.31, reel 144 (SAM 721-1-3012, 116) (translated from German).

Document 5-21: Response letter by CV head office to Erna Rehberg, Malchow, August 17, 1934, USHMMA RG 11.001M.31, reel 144 (SAM 721-1-3012, 114–15) (translated from German).

6 Segregation and Exclusion: Spring and Summer 1935

Reacting to Exclusion in the Spring of 1935

Document 6-1: CV copy of a letter by Gebr. Alsberg & Georg Blank Company, Witten, to Reich Economics Ministry, January 19, 1935, USHMMA RG 11.001M.31, reel 141 (SAM 721-1-2980, 311–12) (translated from German).

Document 6-2: Information sheet no. 3 for the members of the CV regional association Central Germany, November 2, 1934, USHMMA RG 11.001M.31, reel 223 (SAM 721-1-20, 36–41) (translated from German).

Document 6-3: Honor Cross certificate issued "in the name of the Führer and Reich chancellor" to David Schwab, Lörrach, 1935, USHMMPA WS# 01234.

Document 6-4: Willy Cohn, diary entry for February 5, 1935, translated from Norbert Conrads, ed., *Kein Recht, Nirgends: Tagebuch vom Untergang des Breslauer Judentums, 1933–1941* (Cologne: Böhlau Verlag, 2007), 1:208.

Document 6-5: CV copy of a letter by CV regional association Pomerania to the Stettin chief of police, March 20, 1935, USHMMA RG 11.001M.31, reel 145 (SAM 721-1-3019, 220–21) (translated from German).

Document 6-6: Letter by German Vanguard, German Jewish Followers (Der Deutsche Vortrupp, Gefolgschaft Deutscher Juden) to CV head office Berlin, March 22, 1935, USHMMA RG 11.001M.31, reel 181 (SAM 721-1-3221, 253) (translated from German).

Document 6-7: Luise Solmitz, diary entry for August 13, 1935, FZGH 11 S 11 (translated from German).

Document 6-8: Letter by CV head office (Hirschberg) to CV regional association Baden, March 29, 1935, USHMMA RG 11.001M.31, reel 147 (SAM 721-1-3032, 96–98) (translated from German).

Mounting Pressure, Changing Perspectives

Document 6-9: Letter by Julius Moses, Berlin, to Erwin Moses, Tel Aviv, for the second week of March 1935, translated from Dieter Fricke, *Jüdisches Leben in Berlin und Tel Aviv, 1933–1939: Der Briefwechsel des ehemaligen Reichstagsabgeordneten Dr. Julius Moses* (Hamburg: von Bockel, 1997), 302–4.

Document 6-10: Bar Mitzvah note by Max Rosenthal to his grandson, Hans Rosenthal, USHMMPA WS# 28738.

Document 6-11: "The Spirit of Work," *Jüdische Rundschau*, May 10, 1935, 1–2 (translated from German).

Document 6-12: Local branch circular (*Ortsgruppenrundbrief*) no. 4 by CV head office "only for personal information of board members and CV persons of trust. Publication, also of extracts, prohibited," April 15, 1935, USHMMA RG 11.001M.31, reel 97 (SAM 721-1-67, 1–10) (translated from German).

Document 6-13: Confidential letter (to supporters) by CV head office (Hirschberg), May 31, 1935, USHMMA RG 11.001M.31, reel 97 (SAM 721-1-69, 338–41) (translated from German).

The Onslaught of the "People's Community"

Document 6-14: Memorandum by CV head office Berlin, July 16, 1935, USHMMA RG 11.001M.31, reel 102 (SAM 721-1-2345, 4–6) (translated from German).

Document 6-15: CV copy of letter by Reichsvertretung (Berliner) to Reich and Prussian Interior Ministry, July 2, 1935, USHMMA RG 11.001M.31, reel 113 (SAM 721-1-2555, 155–58) (translated from German).

Document 6-16: CV copy of letter by CV regional association Central Germany (Sabatzky) to regional government head (*Regierungspräsident*) in Magdeburg, March 15, 1935, USHMMA RG 11.001M.31, reel 130 (SAM 721-1-2845, 56–57) (translated from German).

Document 6-17: Letter by CV local branch Aachen (Löwenstein) to CV head office, April 30, 1935, USHMMA RG 11.001M.31, reel 113 (SAM 721-1-2555, 131–32) (translated from German).

Document 6-18: "Report on a Trip to the Jewish Communities of Schlüchtern and Gelnhausen on August 19, 1935" by Hilde Meyerowitz and Curt Bondy, USHMMA RG 11.001M.31, reel 99 (SAM 721-1-98, 1–6) (translated from German; appendices not attached).

Document 6-19: Memorandum by CV head office (possibly Hans Reichmann), August 28, 1935, USHMMA RG 11.001M.31, reel 117 (SAM 721-1-2605, 509) (translated from German).

PART III: SUBJECTS UNDER SIEGE: SEPTEMBER 1935 TO DECEMBER 1937

7 The Nuremberg Laws and Their Impact

Immediate Reactions after Nuremberg

Document 7-1: Luise Solmitz, diary entry for September 15, 1935, FZGH 11 S 11 (translated from German).

Document 7-2: Willy Cohn, diary entries for September 1935, translated from Norbert Conrads, ed., *Kein Recht, Nirgends: Tagebuch vom Untergang des Breslauer Judentums, 1933–1941* (Cologne: Böhlau Verlag, 2007), 1:275–78.

Document 7-3: Letter by Julius Moses, Berlin, to Erwin Moses, Tel Aviv, September 1935, translated from Dieter Fricke, *Jüdisches Leben in Berlin und Tel Aviv, 1933–1939: Der Briefwechsel des ehemaligen Reichstagsabgeordneten Dr. Julius Moses* (Hamburg: von Bockel, 1997), 370–71.

Document 7-4: Jewish schools in Germany; ZAHA calendar for 5696 (1935–1936), issued September 1935.

Document 7-5: Letter by CV president Julius Brodnitz to the members of the CV central executive (*Hauptvorstand*) with a copy of an application regarding changes to the CV bylaws for submission to the Berlin district court, September 16, 1935, USHMMA RG 11.001M.31, reel 97 (SAM 721-1-69, 23–24) (translated from German).

Document 7-6: Luise Solmitz, diary entry for November 15, 1935, FZGH 11 S 11 (translated from German).

Document 7-7: Report sent to the WJC Paris office on "The Situation of the Jews in Germany (January 1936)," USHMMA RG 11.001M.36, reel 193 (SAM 1190-3-7, 140–58) (translated from German).

Could One Live in the New Germany?

Document 7-8: Letter by Rabbi Dr. Karl Rosenthal, Berlin, to CV head office, quoting anonymous letter from Preussisch-Holland, East Prussia, September 26, 1935, USHMMA RG 11.001M.31, reel 183 (SAM 721-2-172, 35) (translated from German).

Document 7-9: Flyer handed out by Jewish community Bielefeld, November 7, 1935, USHMMA Acc. 2008.292 Kronheim collection, box 2.

Document 7-10: File note by CV head office Berlin for department heads (*Dezernenten*), November 6, 1935, USHMMA RG 11.001M.31, reel 127 (SAM 721-1-2807, 7) (translated from German).

Document 7-11: Letter by CV head office Berlin to CV regional offices and officials with a copy of a petition to the Reich Economics Ministry, October 30, 1935, USHMMA RG 11.001M.31, reel 135 (SAM 721-1-2915, 567–72) (translated from German).

Document 7-12: Letter by Georg Rosenberg, Frankfurt am Main, to Kurt Rosenberg, Wetzlar (Hesse), March 2, 1937, translated from Oliver Doetzer, *"Aus Menschen werden Briefe": Die Korrespondenz einer jüdischen Familie zwischen Verfolgung und Emigration, 1933–1947* (Cologne: Böhlau Verlag, 2002), 36–37.

Document 7-13: Gestapo interrogation protocol of Hanny R., Berlin, January 24, 1939, regarding her abortion performed by an "Aryan" midwife in the spring of 1936, USHMMA RG 14.070M, reel 416 (LAB A Rep. 358.02), case 22666, frames 816–17 (translated from German).

Document 7-14: Dr. Rudolf Stahl, Frankfurt am Main, "Job Wishes of the Youth," *Jüdische Wohlfahrtspflege und Sozialpolitik* 5 (1935): 185–89 (translated from German).

8 Bonds and Breaks with Germany

Emigration Revisited

Document 8-1: ZAHA progress report for 1936, 10; source: http://deposit.d-nb.de/online/jued/jued.htm (translated from German).

Document 8-2: Confidential report by Bernhard Kahn, AJJDC, European Executive Council, Geneva, titled "Jewish Conditions in Germany," November 29, 1935; ADJJC Archive AR 3344/629.

Document 8-3: Internal CV head office note for Alfred Hirschberg, June 20, 1936, USHMMA RG 11.001M.31, reel 99 (SAM 721-1-113, 53–54) (translated from German).

Document 8-4: Letter by CV regional association Lower Silesia (Breitbarth) to CV head office, September 14, 1936, USHMMA RG 11.001M.31, reel 99 (SAM 721-1-113, 18–20) (translated from German).

Document 8-5: Marriage ad in *Jüdische Rundschau*, September 24, 1935, 16.

Document 8-6: Letter by CV regional association Central Germany to CV head office, August 14, 1936, USHMMA RG 11.001M.31, reel 102 (SAM 721-1-2397, 243) (translated from German).

Document 8-7: File note by CV head office on a discussion "regarding the creation of a training school for Jewish émigrés," January 1936, USHMMA RG 11.001M.31, reel 98 (SAM 721-1-86, 120–26) (translated from German).

Document 8-8: Letter by Erich Sonnemann, head of the Mannheim branch of the BDJ, to Heinz Kellermann, May 12, 1936, USHMMA RG 11.001M.48, reel 193 (SAM 1207-1-8, 82) (translated from German).

Uneven Chances, Varied Fates

Document 8-9: Letter by Ruth Calmon, November 6, 1936, to German Jewish Children's Aid, New York, translated from Gudrun Maierhof, Chana Schütz, and Hermann Simon, eds., *Aus Kindern wurden Briefe: Die Rettung jüdischer Kinder aus Nazi-Deutschland* (Berlin: Metropol, 2004), 217.

Document 8-10: Willy Cohn, diary entries for late March to early May 1937, translated from Norbert Conrads, ed., *Kein Recht, Nirgends: Tagebuch vom Untergang des Breslauer Judentums, 1933–1941* (Cologne: Böhlau Verlag, 2007), 1:392–93, 397, 418, 425, 427, 430.

Document 8-11: Youth from Germany in Kibbutz Givat Brenner having a meal in the field, 1934–1936, USHMMPA WS# 69611.

Document 8-12: Letter by George Bell, bishop of Chichester, to David Glick, AJJDC, on Bell's visit to Berlin, January 1937, quoted from Ronald C. D. Jasper, *George Bell, Bishop of Chichester* (London: Oxford University Press, 1967), 138–39.

Jewish Culture and Leisure in Nazi Germany

Document 8-13: Jewish community (*Synagogengemeinde*) Bielefeld announcing a concert in support of the Jewish Winter Relief (Jüdische Winterhilfe) on January 30, 1937, in the Bielefeld synagogue, USHMMA Acc. 2008.282 Kronheim collection, box 3.

Document 8-14: Letter by Julius Moses, Berlin, to Erwin Moses, Tel Aviv, December 20, 1935, translated from Dieter Fricke, *Jüdisches Leben in Berlin und Tel Aviv, 1933–1939: Der*

Briefwechsel des ehemaligen Reichstagsabgeordneten Dr. Julius Moses (Hamburg: von Bockel, 1997), 413–35.

Document 8-15: "Self-portrait at the Easel," painting by Lotte Laserstein, ca. 1935, printed from Anna-Carola Krausse, *Lotte Laserstein: My Only Reality/Meine einzige Wirklichkeit* (Dresden: Philo Fine Arts, 2003), 203.

Document 8-16: Poems by Manfred Sturmann and Jakob Picard, *Bayerische Israelitische Gemeindezeitung*, January 1, 1936, 4–6 (translated from German).

Document 8-17: "Play Portrays Berlin," *New York Times,* February 10, 1937, 18.

Document 8-18: Günter Friedländer, "The End of the Youth Leagues," *Der Morgen,* 1937–1938 (October–December 1937): 278 (translated from German).

Document 8-19: Students from different Jewish schools in Berlin gather around their banners, 1936–1938, USHMMPA WS# 12854.

Document 8-20: Jewish teenagers attend a Purim party in Frankfurt am Main, 1933–1936, USHMMPA WS# 56413.

9 Jewish Questions after Nuremberg

Racists and Scholars

Document 9-1: Letters by Guido Kisch, Halle, to Ludwig Feuchtwanger, September 23 and December 16, 1934, LBINY MF 562, reel 3 (translated from German).

Document 9-2: Preface by the editors of *Zeitschrift für die Geschichte der Juden in Deutschland* to Wilhelm Grau, "Antisemitismus im Mittelalter: Ein Wort contra Raphael Straus," *Zeitschrift für die Geschichte der Juden in Deutschland* 4 (1936): 186 (translated from German).

How to Behave and Think as a Jew

Document 9-3: CV copy of letter by Reichsvertretung (Berliner) to Hugo Moses, Polzin, June 25, 1936, USHMMA RG 11.001M.31, reel 137 (SAM 721-1-2945, 155–56) (translated from German).

Document 9-4: Toni Lessler on her work as director of the Lessler school in Berlin-Roseneck in the mid-1930s, LBINY ME 726, 27 (translated from German).

Document 9-5: Group photos of activities by students of the Lessler school, Berlin-Grunewald, LBINY ALB-OS2 #1573066.

Document 9-6: Ruth Maier, diary entry for October 2, 1938, translated from Ruth Maier, *"Das Leben könnte gut sein": Tagebücher 1933 bis 1942,* ed. Jan Erik Vold (Stuttgart: DVA, 2008), 134–36.

Document 9-7: Unsigned memo (possibly Curt Bondy?), June 6, 1937, USHMMA Acc. 2007.96 Kellermann collection, box 3 (translated from German).

PART IV: DISPOSSESSION AND DISAPPEARANCE

10 "Model Austria" and Its Ramifications

Anschluss and the Jews

Document 10-4: Philipp Flesch, "My Life in Germany before and after January 30, 1933," LBINY MM 22/ME 132, 10–17 (translated from German).

Document 10-5: Margarete Neff-Jerome, "My Life in Germany before and after January 30, 1933," LBINY MM II 42/ME 1225, 67–68 (translated from German).

Document 10-6: Letter by Helen Baker, Venice, to Phil Baker, May 1, 1938, USHMMA Acc 2006.265 Baker collection.

Document 10-7: Report by anonymous author on the persecution of Jews in Central European countries in the first half of June 1938, USHMMA RG 11.001M.25, reel 106 (SAM 674-1-109, 114–22) (translated from German).

Document 10-8: Racially segregated park benches, 1938, USHMMPA WS# 33983 and 11195.

Intensifying Racial Segregation

Document 10-9: "Overview of the Persecution of Jews in Central European Countries" for the period April 25 to May 3, 1938, USHMMA RG 11.001M.25, reel 106 (SAM 674-1-109, 1–5) (translated from German).

Document 10-10: "Overview of the Persecution of Jews in Central European Countries" for the period May 11 to 17, 1938, USHMMA RG 11.001M.25, reel 106 (SAM 674-1-109, 26–39) (translated from German).

Document 10-11: "Overview of the Persecution of Jews in Central European Countries" for the period May 18 to 24, 1938, USHMMA RG 11.001M.25, reel 106 (SAM 674-1-109, 55–65) (translated from German).

Document 10-12: "Overview of the Persecution of Jews in Central European Countries" for the period May 25 to 31, 1938, USHMMA RG 11.001M.25, reel 106 (SAM 674-1-109, 66–74) (translated from German).

Document 10-13: "Overview of the Persecution of Jews in Central European Countries" for the period June 1 to 6, 1938, USHMMA RG 11.001M.25, reel 106 (SAM 674-1-109, 98–103) (translated from German).

Reverberations in the Reich

Document 10-14: Luise Solmitz, diary entry for April 27, 1938, FZGH 11 S 12 (translated from German).

Document 10-15: Correspondence between CV regional office East Prussia (Angerthal) and CV head office Berlin, March 31/April 1, 1938, USHMMA RG 11.001M.31, reel 146 (SAM 721-1-3030, 23–24) (translated from German).

Document 10-16: Two Jewish men on their way to forced labor, Berlin, March 1938, printed from Barbara Schieb, *Nachricht von Chotzen* (Berlin: Edition Hentrich, 2000), 86.

Document 10-17: Letter by CV regional office Württemberg, Stuttgart, to CV head office Berlin, June 1, 1938, with attached copy of a letter by an anonymous Jewish resident ("Alfred") in Schopfloch, Bavaria, May 30, 1938, USHMMA RG-11.001M.01, reel 101 (SAM 721-1-2317, 336–37) (translated from German).

Document 10-18: Letter by Hellmut S., Berlin, to Berlin Public Prosecutor's Office (*Staatsanwaltschaft*), September 13, 1938, USHMMA RG 14.070M, reel 1493, frames 136–38 (LAB A Rep. 358-02, #55243, 1–2) (translated from German).

Document 10-19: Ignaz Maybaum, Berlin, "The Priestly Way: Jewish Wanderings in the Light of Jewish Faith," *Youth Magazine of the World Union for Progressive Judaism* 1 (April 1938): 22–26, USHMMA Acc. 2007.96 Kellermann collection, box 3.

Document 10-20: Unsent letter by Max Mayer, Freiburg, to his grandchild, Peter Paepcke, May 9, 1938, printed from Martin Doerry, *My Wounded Heart: The Life of Lilli Jahn, 1900–1944* (London: Bloomsbury, 2004), 76–82.

11 Évian and the Emigration Impasse

Escape Plans and Realities

Document 11-1: Protocol of the Jewish émigré training farm Gross-Breesen board meeting held on April 28, 1938, USHMMA RG 11.001M.31, reel 99 (SAM 721-1-110, 2–12) (translated from German).

Document 11-2: Report on a speech by Alfred Hirschberg, CV head office Berlin, at CV local branch Mannheim about "Our Place in the Work of the Jewish Community," late May/ early June 1938, USHMMA RG 11.001M.31, reel 190 (SAM 721-1-950, 4–8) (translated from German).

Document 11-3: Memorandum by the WJC to the delegates of the Évian conference, July 6, 1938, USHMMA RG 11.001 M.36, reel 106 (SAM 1190-1-257).

Document 11-4: Letter by Friedrich Brodnitz, Naples (Maine), to CV head office, July 17, 1938, USHMMA RG 11.001M.31, reel 99 (SAM 721-1-93, 112–15) (translated from German).

Document 11-5: Letter by Gerhard Kann, Berlin, to Heinz Kellermann, New York, October 24, 1938, USHMMA Acc. 2007.96 Kellermann collection, box 4 (translated from German).

Defense without Weapons

Document 11-6: Autobiographical letter by Hans Reichmann on the effect of the mass arrests in June 1938, July–September 1939, translated from Hans Reichmann, *Deutscher Bürger und verfolgter Jude: Novemberpogrom und KZ Sachsenhausen 1937 bis 1939*, ed. Michael Wildt (Munich: R. Oldenbourg Verlag and Institut für Zeitgeschichte, 1998), 92–93.

Document 11-7: "Report about a Trip through Germany, Czechoslovakia, and Austria from July 23 to August 4, 1938" by an anonymous author from the files of the Jewish Telegraph Agency office Paris, August 8, 1938, USHMMA RG 11.001M.25, reel 106 (SAM 674-1-109A) (translated from German).

Document 11-8: Luise Solmitz, diary entry for August 24/25, 1938, FZGH 11 S 12 (translated from German).

Refuge and Reflection

Document 11-9: G. W. Allport, J. S. Bruner, and E. M. Jandorf, "Personality under Social Catastrophe: Ninety Life-histories of the Nazi Revolution," *Character and Personality: A Quarterly for Psychodiagnostics and Allied Studies* 10, no. 1 (September 1941): 12–17.

Document 11-10: CV calendar for the year 1938–1939/5699, September 1938, LBIJMB MF 323 (translated from German).

Document 11-11: Circular by Reichsverband der Juden in Deutschland, late September 1938, *Gemeindeblatt der Israelitischen Religionsgemeinde Dresden* (September 23, 1938): 3 (translated from German).

12 "*Kristallnacht*" and Its Consequences

Solidarity with the Deported

Document 12-1: Mally Dienemann, diary entry for November 1, 1938, LBINY MM 18 (translated from German).

Document 12-2: Letter by Josef Broniatowski, Częstochowa (Poland), no date (most likely early November 1938), USHMMA Acc. 2000.30 (translated from German).

Document 12-3: Deportees at Zbaszyn, October/November 1938, USHMMPA WS# 95551.

Document 12-4: "Eyewitness Report of Rescue Activities of JDC at Polish-German Border," November 18, 1938, AJJDC Archive AR 3344/878.

Experiencing the Pogrom

Document 12-5: Rudolf Bing, "My Life in Germany before and after January 30, 1933," written 1940, LBINY MM 10/ME 267, 42–43 (translated from German).

Document 12-6: Luise Solmitz, diary entries for November 10 and 12, 1938, FZGH 11 S 12 (translated from German).

Document 12-7: Toni Lessler memoir, November/December 1938, LBINY ME 726, 31–32 (translated from German).

Document 12-8: Philipp Flesch, "My Experiences on November 10, 1938, in Vienna" (translation by the author from a German text submitted as part of his essay on "My Life in Germany before and after January 30, 1933"), LBINY MM 22/ME 132, 3–6.

Document 12-9: Autobiographical letter written in July–September 1939 by Hans Reichmann describing the closing of the CV head office on November 10, 1938, translated from Hans Reichmann, *Deutscher Bürger und verfolgter Jude: Novemberpogrom und KZ Sachsenhausen 1937 bis 1939*, ed. Michael Wildt. (Munich: R. Oldenbourg Verlag and Institut für Zeitgeschichte, 1998), 114–15.

Document 12-10: Max Eschelbacher, "November 10, 1938," written in spring/early summer 1939, translated from Max Eschelbacher, *Der zehnte November 1938* (Essen: Klartext, 1998), 41–54.

Document 12-11: Autobiographical letter by Hans Reichmann on his time in Sachsenhausen concentration camp, written July–September 1939, translated from Hans Reichmann, *Deutscher Bürger und verfolgter Jude: Novemberpogrom und KZ Sachsenhausen 1937 bis 1939*, ed. Michael Wildt (Munich: R. Oldenbourg Verlag and Institut für Zeitgeschichte, 1998), 131, 171, 173–74, 228.

Document 12-12: Mally Dienemann, diary entries, late 1938/early 1939, LBINY MM 18, 30, 32, 34–35 (translated from German).

Document 12-13: Letter by Hilfsverein regarding the release of prisoner Simon Zweig from Dachau concentration camp for emigration to Paraguay, November 29, 1938, USHMMPA WS# 07501.

What Next?

Document 12-14: Suicide note by Hedwig Jastrow, Berlin, November 29, 1938; LAB APr.B Rep. 030, tit.198B, # 1943; translation quoted from Christian Goeschel, "Suicides of German Jews in the Third Reich," *German History* 25 (2007): 29.

Document 12-15: Heinrich Mugdan, diary entry for November 20, 1938, LBINY MM 58/ME 457, 3 (translated from German).

Document 12-16: "The Opening of the *Filmbühne*," *Jüdisches Nachrichtenblatt Berlin*, December 30, 1938, 3 (translated from German).

Document 12-17: Ruth Maier, diary entry for December 11, 1938, translated from Ruth Maier, *"Das Leben könnte gut sein": Tagebücher 1933 bis 1942*, ed. Jan Erik Vold (Stuttgart: DVA, 2008), 158.

Document 12-18: Letter by Georg Landauer, Central Bureau for the Settlement of German Jews in Palestine, Jerusalem, to Henry Montor, United Palestine Appeal, New York, December 2, 1938 ("strictly confidential"); CZA RG S25/9703.

Document 12-19: Ruth Maier, diary entry for December 24, 1938, translated from Ruth Maier, *"Das Leben könnte gut sein": Tagebücher 1933 bis 1942*, ed. Jan Erik Vold (Stuttgart: DVA, 2008), 164–65.

Document 12-20: Mally Dienemann, diary entry on her and her husband's escape from Germany on December 30/31, 1938, written ca. 1939, LBINY MM 18, 38–40 (translated from German).

BIBLIOGRAPHY

THIS SELECTION from a vast and continuously growing number of pub-lications is designed to serve as orientation for further study. We could not include here all relevant publications, such as those of the Leo Baeck Institute—especially the articles in its yearbook (*LBIYB*) published since 1956—postwar memoirs by survivors, and local studies on the history of Jewish communities in Germany and Austria.

MEMORIAL BOOKS AND LISTINGS OF HOLOCAUST VICTIMS AND SURVIVORS

Datenbank zur Liste der jüdischen Einwohner im Deutschen Reich, 1933–1945. Berlin: Bundes-archiv, 2008.

Gedenkbuch. Bundesarchiv memorial book of victims. Available online at www.bundesarchiv.de/gedenkbuch.

Pinkas ha-kehilot Germanyah: Entsiklopedyah shel ha-yishuvim ha-Yehudim le-min hivasdam ve-'ad le-ahar Sho'at Milhemet ha-'olam hasheniyah. 4 vols. Jerusalem: Yad Vashem, 1972–2007. (In Hebrew; for English-language summary translations, see www.jewishgen.org/Yizkor/pinkas germany.)

Röder, Werner, and Herbert A. Strauss, eds. *Biographisches Handbuch der deutschsprachigen Emigration nach 1933,* Bd. 1, *Politik, Wirtschaft, Öffentliches Leben.* Munich: K. G. Saur, 1980.

Scheffler, Wolfgang, and Diana Schulle, eds. *Buch der Erinnerung: Die ins Baltikum deporti-erten deutschen, österreichischen und tschechoslowakischen Juden.* 2 vols. Munich: K. G. Saur, 2003.

Strauss, Herbert A., and Werner Röder, eds. *International Biographical Dictionary of Central European Émigrés, 1933–1945*. Vol. 2, *The Arts, Sciences, and Literature*. Munich: K. G. Saur, 1982.

USHMM ITS Collection Data Base Central Name Index.

PUBLISHED SOURCES

American Jewish Joint Distribution Committee. *Jewish Constructive Work in Germany during 1936: Summary of the Report of the Zentralausschuss für Hilfe und Aufbau*. Paris: American Jewish Joint Distribution Committee, 1937.

Arad, Yitzhak, Yisrael Gutman, and Abraham Margaliot, eds. *Documents on the Holocaust: Selected Sources on the Destruction of the Jews of Germany and Austria, Poland, and the Soviet Union*. Jerusalem: Yad Vashem, 1981.

Arbeitsberichte der Reichsvertretung der Juden in Deutschland, 1933–1938. Partly available online at http://deposit.d-nb.de/online/jued/jued.htm.

Arbeitsberichte des Zentralausschusses der deutschen Juden für Hilfe und Aufbau (bei der Reichsvertretung der Juden in Deutschland), 1933–1938. Partly available online at http://deposit.d-nb.de/online/jued/jued.htm.

Aufbau: Nachrichtenblatt des German-Jewish Club. New York, 1934ff.

Ball-Kaduri, Kurt Jakob. *Das Leben der Juden in Deutschland im Jahre 1933*. Frankfurt am Main: EVA, 1963.

———. "Testimonies and Recollections about Activities Organized by German Jewry during the years 1933–1945: Catalogue of Manuscripts in the Yad Vashem Archives." *YVS* 4 (1960): 317–40.

———. *Vor der Katastrophe: Juden in Deutschland, 1934–1939*. Tel Aviv: Olamenu, 1967.

Barkow, Ben, ed. *Testaments to the Holocaust*, Series 1, *Archive of the Wiener Library* (document collection on 76 microfilms). Woodbridge, NY: Primary Source Media, 1998.

Benz, Wolfgang, ed. *Das Tagebuch der Hertha Nathorff: Berlin–New York: Aufzeichnungen 1933 bis 1945*. Frankfurt am Main: Fischer Taschenbuch, 1988.

Blätter des Jüdischen Frauenbundes: Für Frauenarbeit und Frauenbewegung. Berlin, 1924–1938.

Blau, Bruno. *Das Ausnahmerecht für die Juden in den europäischen Ländern, 1933–1945*, I. Teil, *Deutschland*. New York: B. Blau, 1952.

Boberach, Heinz, ed. *Meldungen aus dem Reich: Die geheimen Lageberichte des Sicherheitsdienstes der SS, 1938–1945*. Herrsching: Pawlak Verlag, 1984.

Bohrmann, Hans, and Gabriele Toepser-Ziegert, eds. *NS-Presseanweisungen der Vorkriegszeit: Edition und Dokumentation, 1933–1939*. Munich: K. G. Saur, 1984–2001.

Breitman, Richard, Barbara McDonald Stewart, and Severin Hochberg, eds. *Advocate for the Doomed: The Diaries and Papers of James G. McDonald*, vol. 1, *1932–1935*. Bloomington: Indiana University Press in association with the USHMM, 2007.

Bundesarchiv, Institut für Zeitgeschichte, and Lehrstuhl für Neuere und Neueste Geschichte an der Albert-Ludwigs-Universität Freiburg, eds. *Die Verfolgung und Ermordung der europäischen Juden durch das nationalsozialistische Deutschland, 1933–1945*. Vol. 1, *1933–1937*. Munich: R. Oldenbourg Verlag, 2008.

Central-Verein-Zeitung: Blätter für Deutschtum und Judentum, Allgemeine Zeitung des Judentums. Berlin, 1922–1938. Available online at www.compactmemory.de.

Centralverein deutscher Staatsbürger jüdischen Glaubens, ed. *Anti-Anti: Tatsachen zur Juden- frage.* Berlin: Philo Verlag, 1932.

Comité des Délégation Juives, ed. *Das Schwarzbuch: Tatsachen und Dokumente: Die Lage der Juden in Deutschland 1933.* Paris: Imprimerie "Pascal," 1934 (reprint edition 1983).

Conrads, Norbert, ed. *Kein Recht, Nirgends: Tagebuch vom Untergang des Breslauer Judentums, 1933–1941,* vol. 1. Cologne: Böhlau Verlag, 2007.

Deutschland-Berichte der Sozialdemokratischen Partei Deutschlands (Sopade). 7 vols. Frankfurt am Main: Nettelbeck, 1980.

Doerry, Martin. *"Mein verwundetes Herz": Das Leben der Lilli Jahn, 1900–1944.* Munich: DVA, 2002; English edition: *My Wounded Heart: The Life of Lilli Jahn, 1900–1944.* London: Bloomsbury, 2004.

Doetzer, Oliver. *"Aus Menschen werden Briefe": Die Korrespondenz einer jüdischen Familie zwischen Verfolgung und Emigration, 1933–1947.* Cologne: Böhlau Verlag, 2002.

Evangelische Hilfsstelle für ehemals Rasseverfolgte in Berlin, ed. *An der Stechbahn: Erlebnisse und Berichte aus dem Büro Grüber in den Jahren der Verfolgung.* Berlin: EVA, 1957.

Freier, Recha. *Let the Children Come: The Early History of Youth Aliyah.* London: Weidenfeld and Nicholson, 1961.

Fricke, Dieter. *Jüdisches Leben in Berlin und Tel Aviv, 1933–1939: Der Briefwechsel des ehema- ligen Reichstagsabgeordneten Dr. Julius Moses.* Hamburg: von Bockel, 1997.

Friedlander, Henry, and Sybil Milton, eds. *Archives of the Holocaust: An International Collec- tion of Selected Documents.* 21 vols. New York: Garland Publishing, 1990–1995.

Guide to the Oral History Collection, Research Foundation for Jewish Immigration. New York, Munich: K. G. Saur, 1982.

Gyßling, Walter. *Mein Leben in Deutschland vor und nach 1933 und Der Anti-Nazi: Handbuch im Kampf gegen die NSDAP.* Edited by Leonidas E. Hill. Bremen: Donat Verlag, 2003.

Haus der Bayerischen Geschichte, ed. *Erinnerungszeichen: Die Tagebücher der Elisabeth Block.* Rosenheim: Bayerische Staatskanzlei, 1993.

Herrmann, Klaus J. *Das Dritte Reich und die deutsch-jüdischen Organisationen, 1933–1934.* Cologne: Karl Heymanns Verlag, 1969.

Hilberg, Raul. *Documents of Destruction: Germany and Jewry, 1933–1945.* Chicago: Quad- rangle, 1971.

Hitachdut Olej Germania, ed. *Die deutsche Alijah in Palästina—Bericht der Hitachdut Olej Germania für die Jahre 1936/1937.* Tel Aviv: Palestine Publishing Co., 1937.

Ja-Sagen zum Judentum: Eine Aufsatzreihe der "Jüdischen Rundschau" zur Lage der deutschen Juden. Berlin: Verlag der "Jüdischen Rundschau," 1933.

The Jews in Nazi Germany: The Factual Record of Their Persecution by the National Socialists. New York: American Jewish Committee, 1933.

Jüdische Wohlfahrtspflege und Sozialpolitik: Zeitschrift der Zentralwohlfahrtsstelle der deutschen Juden und der Hauptstelle für Jüdische Wanderfürsorge und Arbeitsnachweise. Berlin, 1930–1938. Available online at www.compactmemory.de.

Klein, Thomas, ed. *Die Lageberichte der Geheimen Staatspolizei über die Provinz Hessen- Nassau, 1933–1936.* Cologne: Böhlau Verlag, 1986.

Klemperer, Victor. *I Will Bear Witness: A Diary of the Nazi Years.* New York: Random House, 1998.

Kommission zur Erforschung der Geschichte der Frankfurter Juden, ed. *Dokumente zur Geschichte der Frankfurter Juden 1933 bis 1945.* Frankfurt am Main: Kramer, 1963.

Kropat, Wolf-Arno. *Kristallnacht in Hessen: Der Judenpogrom vom November 1938. Eine Dokumentation.* Wiesbaden: Kommission für die Geschichte der Juden in Hessen, 1988.

Kulka, Otto Dov, ed. *Deutsches Judentum unter dem Nationalsozialismus,* Bd. 1, *Dokumente zur Geschichte der Reichsvertretung der Juden, 1933–1939.* Tübingen: Mohr Siebeck, 1997.

Kulka, Otto Dov, and Eberhard Jäckel, eds. *Die Juden in den geheimen NS-Stimmungsberichten, 1933–1945.* Düsseldorf: Droste, 2004 (incl. CD-ROM with 3,744 documents, a glossary, a chronology, etc.).

Limberg, Margarete, and Hubert Rübsaat, eds. *Germans No More: Accounts of Jewish Everyday Life, 1933–1938.* New York: Berghahn Books, 2006.

Longerich, Peter, and Dieter Pohl, eds., *Die Ermordung der Europäischen Juden: Eine umfassende Dokumentation des Holocaust, 1941–1945.* Munich: Piper, 1989.

Löwith, Karl. *My Life in Germany before and after 1933: A Report.* Urbana: University of Illinois Press, 1994.

Maier, Ruth. *"Das Leben könnte gut sein": Tagebücher 1933 bis 1942.* Edited by Jan Erik Vold. Stuttgart: DVA, 2008.

Marcus, Jacob R. *The Rise and Destiny of the German Jew.* Cincinnati, OH: Union of American Hebrew Congregations, 1934.

Palästina-Amt der Jewish Agency for Palestine. *Alijah: Informationen für Palästina-Auswanderer.* Berlin: Palästina-Amt der Jewish Agency for Palestine, 1934–1936.

Prinz, Joachim. *Wir Juden.* Berlin: Erich Reiss, 1934.

Reichmann, Hans. *Deutscher Bürger und verfolgter Jude: Novemberpogrom und KZ Sachsenhausen 1937 bis 1939.* Edited by Michael Wildt. Munich: R. Oldenbourg Verlag and Institut für Zeitgeschichte, 1998.

Rosenthal, Erich. "Jewish Population in Germany, 1910–1939." *Jewish Social Studies* 6 (1944): 233–73.

Rupeiper, Hermann-Josef, and Alexander Sperk, eds. *Die Lageberichte der Geheimen Staatspolizei zur Provinz Sachsen 1933 bis 1936.* Halle: Mitteldeutscher Verlag, 2003.

Schieb, Barbara, ed. *Nachricht von Chotzen: "Wer immer hofft, stirbt singend."* Berlin: Edition Hentrich, 2000.

Schleunes, Karl A., ed. *Legislating the Holocaust: The Bernhard Loesener Memoirs and Supporting Documents.* Boulder, CO: Westview Press, 2001.

Stahl, Rudolph. "Vocational Retraining of Jews in Nazi Germany, 1933–1938." *Jewish Social Studies* 2 (1939): 169–94.

Tausk, Walter. *Breslauer Tagebuch, 1933–1940.* Edited by Ryszard Kincel. Berlin: Aufbau Taschenbuch Verlag, 2000.

Trunk, Isaiah. *Jewish Responses to Nazi Persecution: Collective and Individual Behavior in Extremis.* New York: Stein & Day, 1979.

Walk, Joseph, ed., *Das Sonderrecht für die Juden im NS-Staat: Eine Sammlung der gesetzlichen Maßnahmen und Richtlinien—Inhalt und Bedeutung.* Heidelberg: UTB, 1996.

Warburg, Gustav. *Six Years of Hitler: The Jews under the Nazi Regime.* London: Allan & Unwin, 1939.

Weidenhaupt, Hugo, ed., *Ein nichtarischer Deutscher: Die Tagebücher des Albert Herzfeld, 1935–1939.* Düsseldorf: Triltsch Verlag, 1982.

Wildt, Michael, ed. *Die Judenpolitik des SD 1935 bis 1938: Eine Dokumentation.* Munich: R. Oldenbourg Verlag, 1995.

Witek, Hans, and Hans Safrian, *Und keiner war dabei: Dokumente des alltäglichen Antisemitismus in Wien 1938*. Vienna: Picus, 1988.

Zentralwohlfahrtsstelle der deutschen Juden, *Informationsblätter im Auftrage des Zentralausschusses der deutschen Juden für Hilfe und Aufbau*. Berlin: no publisher, 1933–1935.

MEMOIRS

Angress, Werner T. *Between Fear and Hope: Jewish Youth in the Third Reich*. New York: Columbia University Press, 1988.

Behrend-Rosenfeld, Else R. *Ich stand nicht allein: Leben einer Jüdin in Deutschland, 1933–1944*. Munich: C. H. Beck 1988.

Brodnitz, Friedrich S. "Memories of the Reichsvertretung: A Personal Report." *LBIYB* 31 (1986): 267–77.

Crane, Peter. *"Wir leben nun mal auf einem Vulkan."* Bonn: Weidle Verlag, 2005.

Deutschkron, Inge. *Ich trug den gelben Stern*. Munich: DTV, 1994.

Gay, Peter. *My German Question: Growing Up in Nazi Berlin*. New Haven, CT: Yale University Press, 1998.

Herzberg, Arno. "The Jewish Press under the Nazi Regime: Its Mission, Suppression and Defiance. A Memoir." *LBIYB* 36 (1991): 367–88.

Kellermann, Henry J. "From Imperial to National-Socialist Germany: Recollections of a German-Jewish Youth Leader." *LBIYB* 34 (1994): 305–30.

Koehn, Ilse. *Mischling, Second Degree: My Childhood in Nazi Germany*. New York: Greenwillow Books, 1977.

Krüger, Helmut. *Der halbe Stern: Leben als deutsch-jüdischer "Mischling" im Dritten Reich*. Berlin: Metropol, 1993.

Lasker-Wallfisch, Anita. *Ihr sollt die Wahrheit erben: Breslau, Auschwitz, Bergen-Belsen*. Bonn: Weidle Verlag, 1997.

Strauss, Herbert A. *In the Eye of the Storm: Growing Up Jewish in Germany, 1918–1943*. New York: Fordham University Press, 1999.

Walb, Lore. *Ich, die Alte—ich, die Junge: Konfrontation mit meinen Tagebüchern, 1933–1945*. Berlin: Aufbau Verlag, 1997.

MONOGRAPH STUDIES, EDITED VOLUMES, AND ARTICLES

Adam, Uwe Dietrich. *Judenpolitik im Dritten Reich*. Düsseldorf: Droste, 1972.

Adler-Rudel, Salomon. *Jüdische Selbsthilfe unter dem Naziregime 1933–1939 im Spiegel der Berichte der Reichsvertretung der Juden in Deutschland*. Tübingen: J. C. B. Mohr, 1974.

Akademie der Künste, ed. *Geschlossene Veranstaltung: Der Jüdische Kulturbund in Deutschland, 1933–1941*. Berlin: Akademie Verlag, 1992.

Amkraut, Brian. *Between Home and Homeland: Youth Aliyah from Nazi Germany*. Tuscaloosa: University of Alabama Press, 2006.

Bajohr, Frank. *"Aryanization" in Hamburg: The Economic Exclusion of Jews and the Confiscation of Their Property in Nazi Germany, 1933–1945*. New York: Berghahn Books, 2002.

————. "The Beneficiaries of 'Aryanization': Hamburg as a Case Study." *YVS* 26 (1998): 173–201.

————. *"Unser Hotel ist judenfrei": Bäder-Antisemitismus im 19. und 20. Jahrhundert.* Frankfurt am Main: Fischer TB, 2003.

Ball-Kaduri, Kurt Jakob. "The Central Jewish Organization in Berlin during the Pogrom of November 1938." *YVS* 3 (1959): 261–81.

————. "The National Representation of Jews in Germany—Obstacles and Accomplishments at Its Establishment." *YVS* 2 (1958): 159–78.

Bankier, David. "German Interests in the Ha'avara-Transfer Agreement, 1933–1939." *LBIYB* 35 (1990): 245–66.

————. *The Germans and the Final Solution: Public Opinion under Nazism.* Oxford: Blackwell Publishers, 1992.

————, ed. *Probing the Depths of German Anti-Semitism: German Society and the Persecution of the Jews, 1933–1941.* New York: Berghahn, 2000.

Barkai, Avraham. "Between *Deutschtum* and *Judentum*: Ideological Controversies inside the Centralverein." In *In Search of Jewish Community: Jewish Identities in Germany and Austria, 1918–1933,* edited by Michael Brenner and Derek J. Penslar, 74–91. Bloomington: Indiana University Press, 1998.

————. "The C.V. and Its Archives: A Reassessment." *LBIYB* 45 (2000): 173–82.

————. *From Boycott to Annihilation: The Economic Struggle of German Jews, 1933–1943.* Hanover, NH: University of New England Press, 1989.

————. *"Wehr Dich!" Der Centralverein deutscher Staatsbürger jüdischen Glaubens (C.V.), 1893–1938.* Munich: C. H. Beck, 2002.

Barkai, Avraham, Paul Mendes-Flohr, and Steven Lowenstein. *Aufbruch und Zerstörung, 1918–1945.* Vol. 4, *Deutsch-Jüdische Geschichte der Neuzeit.* Munich: C. H. Beck, 1997.

Bauer, Yehuda. *My Brother's Keeper: A History of the American Jewish Joint Distribution Committee, 1929–1939.* Philadelphia: Jewish Publication Society of America, 1974.

Benz, Wolfgang, ed. *Das Exil der kleinen Leute: Alltagserfahrungen deutscher Juden in der Emigration.* Munich: C. H. Beck, 1991.

————, ed. *Die Juden in Deutschland, 1933–1945: Leben unter nationalsozialistischer Herrschaft.* Munich: C. H. Beck, 1989.

————. *Patriot und Paria: Das Leben des Erwin Goldmann zwischen Judentum und Nationalsozialismus.* Berlin: Metropol, 1997.

Bergemann, Hans, and Simone Ladwig-Winters, *Richter und Staatsanwälte jüdischer Herkunft in Preußen im Nationalsozialismus: Eine Dokumentation.* Cologne: Bundesanzeiger Verlag, 2004.

Bergen, Doris L. *Twisted Cross: The German Christian Movement in the Third Reich.* Chapel Hill: University of North Carolina Press, 1996.

————. *War and Genocide: A Concise History of the Holocaust.* Lanham, MD: Rowman & Littlefield, 2003.

Boas, Jacob. "Countering Nazi Defamation: German Jews and the Jewish Tradition, 1933–1938." *LBIYB* 34 (1989): 205–26.

————. "German-Jewish Internal Politics under Hitler, 1933–1938." *LBIYB* 29 (1984): 3–25.

————. "Germany or Diaspora? German Jewry's Shifting Perceptions in the Nazi Era (1933–1938)." *LBIYB* 27 (1982): 109–26.

————. "The Shrinking World of German Jewry, 1933–1938." *LBIYB* 31 (1986): 241–66.

Bock, Gisela. "Ordinary Women in Nazi Germany: Perpetrators, Victims, Followers, and Bystanders." In *Women and the Holocaust,* edited by Dalia Ofer and Lenore J. Weitzman, 85–100. New Haven, CT: Yale University Press, 1998.

Breitman, Richard. *The Architect of Genocide: Himmler and the Final Solution.* New York: Alfred A. Knopf, 1991.

Breitman, Richard, and Alan M. Kraut. *American Refugee Policy and European Jewry, 1933–1945.* Bloomington: Indiana University Press, 1987.

Brenner, Michael, and Derek J. Penslar, eds. *In Search of Jewish Community: Jewish Identities in Germany and Austria, 1918–1933.* Bloomington: Indiana University Press, 1998.

Burleigh, Michael. *The Third Reich: A New History.* New York: Hill and Wang, 2000.

Burleigh, Michael, and Wolfgang Wippermann. *The Racial State: Germany, 1933–1945.* Cambridge: Cambridge University Press, 1991.

Caron, Vicky. "Loyalties in Conflict: French Jewry and the Refugee Crisis, 1933–1935." *LBIYB* 36 (1991): 305–38.

Childers, Thomas. *The Nazi Voter: The Social Formations of Fascism in Germany, 1919–1933.* Chapel Hill: University of North Carolina Press, 1983.

Cochavi, Yehoyakim. "Arming for Survival: Martin Buber and Jewish Adult Education in Nazi Germany." *LBIYB* 34 (1989): 205–26.

Cohn, Werner. "Bearers of a Common Fate? The 'Non-Aryan' Christian 'Fate-Comrades' of the Paulus-Bund, 1933–1939." *LBIYB* 32 (1988): 327–66.

Crane, Cynthia. *Divided Lives: The Untold Stories of Jewish-Christian Women in Nazi Germany.* New York: St. Martin's Press, 2000.

Elkin, Rivka. *The Heart Beats On: Continuity and Change in Social Work and Welfare Activities of German Jews under the Nazi Regime, 1933–1945.* Jerusalem: Yad Vashem, 2004. (In Hebrew.)

Erpel, Simone. "Struggle and Survival: Jewish Women in the Anti-Fascist Resistance in Germany." *LBIYB* 37 (1992): 397–414.

Feidel-Mertz, Hildegard, and Andreas Paetz. *Ein verlorenes Paradies: Das jüdische Kinder- und Landschulheim Caputh (1931–1938).* Frankfurt am Main: Dipa-Verlag, 1994.

Feilchenfeld, Werner, Dolf Michaelis, and Ludwig Pinner. *Haʾavara-Transfer nach Palästina und Einwanderung deutscher Juden, 1933–1939.* Tübingen: Mohr, 1972.

Fink, Carole. *Defending the Rights of Others: The Great Powers, the Jews and International Minority Protection, 1878–1938.* Cambridge: Cambridge University Press, 2004.

Freeden, Herbert. *The Jewish Press in the Third Reich.* Providence, RI: Berg, 1993.

————. *Jüdisches Theater im Nazi-Deutschland.* Tübingen: Niemeyer Verlag, 1964.

Friedländer, Saul. *Nazi Germany and the Jews.* Vol. 1, *The Years of Persecution, 1933–1939.* New York: HarperCollins 1997.

Garbarini, Alexandra. *Numbered Days: Diaries and the Holocaust.* New Haven, CT: Yale University Press, 2006.

Gellately, Robert. *Backing Hitler: Consent and Coercion in Nazi Germany.* Oxford: Oxford University Press, 2001.

————. *The Gestapo and Modern Society: Enforcing Racial Policy, 1933–1945.* Oxford: Clarendon Press, 1990.

Graml, Hermann. *Reichskristallnacht: Antisemitismus und Judenverfolgung im Dritten Reich.* Munich: DTV, 1988.

Gruenewald, Max. "The Beginning of the 'Reichsvertretung.'" *LBIYB* 1 (1956): 57–67.

Gruner, Wolf. *Jewish Forced Labor under the Nazis: Economic Needs and Racial Aims, 1938–1944.* New York: Cambridge University Press in association with the USHMM, 2006.

———. *Judenverfolgung in Berlin, 1933–1945: Eine Chronologie der Behördenmaßnahmen in der Reichshauptstadt.* Berlin: Hentrich, 1996.

Harris, Mark J., and Deborah Oppenheimer. *Into the Arms of Strangers: Stories of the Kindertransport.* London: Bloomsbury Publishing, 2000.

Heim, Susanne. "Immigration Policy and Forced Emigration from Germany: The Situation of Jewish Children (1933–1945)." In *Children and the Holocaust: Symposium Presentations,* edited by USHMM, 1–18. Washington, DC: Center for Advanced Holocaust Studies Occasional Paper, 2004.

Hepp, Michael, ed. *Expatriation Lists as Published in the "Reichsanzeiger," 1933–45.* Vol. 1. Munich: K. G. Saur, 1985.

Hilberg, Raul. *The Destruction of the European Jews.* 3 vols. Rev. exp. ed. New Haven, CT: Yale University Press, 2003.

———. *Perpetrators, Victims, Bystanders: The Jewish Catastrophe, 1933–1945.* New York: Aaron Asher Books, 1992.

Hildesheimer, Esriel. *Jüdische Selbstverwaltung unter dem NS-Regime: Der Existenzkampf der Reichsvertretung und Reichsvereinigung der Juden in Deutschland.* Tübingen: Mohr, 1994.

Jewish Resistance during the Holocaust: Proceedings of the Conference on Manifestations of Jewish Resistance. Jerusalem: Yad Vashem, 1971.

Johnson, Eric A., and Karl-Heinz Reuband, *What We Knew: Terror, Mass Murder and Everyday Life in Nazi Germany—An Oral History.* London: John Murray Publishers, 2005.

Kaplan, Marion A. *Between Dignity and Despair: Jewish Life in Nazi Germany.* New York: Oxford University Press, 1998.

———, ed. *Jewish Daily Life in Germany, 1618–1945.* New York: Oxford University Press, 2005.

———. *The Jewish Feminist Movement in Germany: The Campaigns of the Jüdischer Frauenbund, 1904–1938.* London: Greenwood Press, 1979.

———. "Keeping Calm and Weathering the Storm: Jewish Women's Responses to Daily Life in Nazi Germany, 1933–1939." In *Women and the Holocaust,* edited by Dalia Ofer and Lenore J. Weitzman, 39–54. New Haven, CT: Yale University Press, 1998.

———. "When the Ordinary Became Extraordinary: German Jews Reacting to Nazi Persecution, 1933–1939." In *Social Outsiders in Nazi Germany,* edited by Robert Gellately and Nathan Stoltzfus, 66–98. Princeton, NJ: Princeton University Press, 2001.

Kaplan, Marion A., and Beate Meyer, eds. *Jüdische Welten: Juden in Deutschland vom 18. Jahrhundert bis in die Gegenwart.* Göttingen: Wallstein Verlag, 2005.

Kater, Michael W. "Everyday Anti-Semitism in Pre-War Nazi Germany: The Popular Bases." *YVS* 16 (1984): 129–59.

———. *The Nazi Party: A Social Profile of Its Members and Leaders, 1919–1945.* Oxford: Blackwell, 1983.

Kershaw, Ian. *Hitler 1889–1936: Hubris.* New York: W. W. Norton, 1998.

———. *Hitler 1936–1945: Nemesis.* London: Allen Lane, 2000.

———. *Hitler, the Germans, and the Final Solution.* New Haven, CT: Yale University Press, 2008.

Koonz, Claudia. *The Nazi Conscience.* Cambridge, MA: Harvard University Press, 2003.

Kulka, Otto Dov, and Esriel Hildesheimer. "The Central Organization of Jews in the Third Reich and Its Archives." *LBIYB* 34 (1989): 187–201.

Kwiet, Konrad. "Forced Labour of German Jews in Nazi Germany." *LBIYB* 36 (1991): 389–410.

———. "To Leave or Not to Leave? The German Jews at the Crossroads." In *November 1938: From "Reichskristallnacht" to Genocide*, edited by Walter H. Pehle, 139–53. New York: Berg, 1991.

———. "The Ultimate Refuge—Suicide in the Jewish Community under Nazism." *LBIYB* 29 (1984): 173–98.

Kwiet, Konrad, and Helmut Eschwege. *Selbstbehauptung und Widerstand: Deutsche Juden im Kampf um Existenz und Menschenwürde, 1933–1945*. Hamburg: Christians, 1984.

Lamberti, Marjorie. "The Jewish Defence in Germany after the National-Socialist Seizure of Power." *LBIYB* 42 (1997): 135–47.

Laqueur, Walter. *Geboren in Deutschland: Der Exodus der jüdischen Jugend nach 1933*. Berlin: Propyläen Verlag, 2000.

Lipstadt, Deborah E. "The American Press and the Persecution of German Jewry: The Early Years, 1933–1935." *LBIYB* 29 (1984): 27–55.

———. *Beyond Belief: The American Press and the Coming of the Holocaust, 1933–1945*. New York: Free Press, 1986.

Longerich, Peter. *Holocaust: The Nazi Persecution and Murder of the Jews*. Oxford: Oxford University Press, 2009. (Translated from *Politik der Vernichtung: Eine Gesamtdarstellung der nationalsozialistischen Judenverfolgung*. Munich: Piper, 1998.)

Maierhof, Gudrun. *Selbstbehauptung im Chaos: Frauen in der jüdischen Selbsthilfe, 1933–1943*. Frankfurt am Main: Campus, 2002.

Maierhof, Gudrun, Chana Schütz, and Hermann Simon, eds. *Aus Kindern wurden Briefe: Die Rettung jüdischer Kinder aus Nazi-Deutschland*. Berlin: Metropol, 2004.

Margaliot, Abraham. "The Dispute over the Leadership of Germany's Jews, 1933–1938." *YVS* 10 (1974): 129–48.

———. "The Reaction of the Jewish Public in Germany to the Nuremberg Laws." *YVS* 12 (1977): 75–107.

Maurer, Trude. "Ausländische Juden in Deutschland, 1933–1939." In *Die Juden im nationalsozialistischen Deutschland: The Jews in Nazi Germany, 1933–1943*, edited by Arnold Paucker, 189–210. Tübingen: J. C. B. Mohr, 1986.

———. "From Everyday to State of Emergency: Jews in Weimar and Nazi Germany." In *Jewish Daily Life in Germany, 1618–1945*, edited by Marion A. Kaplan, 271–373. Oxford: Berghahn, 2005.

Mayer, Michael A., ed. *Joachim Prinz, Rebellious Rabbi: An Autobiography—the German and Early American Years*. Bloomington: Indiana University Press, 2008.

Meyer, Beate. "Grenzgänger—'Mischlinge' ersten Grades' zwischen Normalität und Verfolgung (1933–1945)." In *Dimension der Verfolgung: Opfer und Opfergruppen im Nationalsozialismus*, edited by Sibylle Quack, 15–48. Munich: DVA, 2003.

———. "The Inevitable Dilemma: The Reich Association (Reichsvereinigung) of Jews in Germany, the Deportations, and the Jews Who Went Underground." In *On Germans and Jews under the Nazi Regime*, edited by Moshe Zimmermann, 297–312. Jerusalem: Hebrew University Magnes Press, 2006.

———. *"Jüdische Mischlinge": Rassenpolitik und Verfolgungserfahrung, 1933–1945*. Hamburg: Doelling & Galitz, 1999.

————, ed. *Die Verfolgung und Ermordung der Hamburger Juden, 1933–1945: Geschichte, Zeugnis, Erinnerung.* Hamburg: Landeszentrale für politische Bildung, 2006.

Meyer, Beate, and Hermann Simon, eds. *Juden in Berlin, 1938–1945.* Berlin: Philo Verlag, 2000.

Michman, Dan. *Holocaust Historiography from a Jewish Perspective: Conceptualization, Terminology, Approaches and Fundamental Issues.* London: Vallentine Mitchell, 2003.

Milton, Sybil. "The Expulsion of Polish Jews from Germany, October 1938 to July 1939: A Documentation." *LBIYB* 29 (1984): 169–99.

Mommsen, Hans. "Hitler's Reichstag Speech of 30 January 1939." *History & Memory* 9, no. 1/2 (1997): 147–61.

————. "The Realization of the Unthinkable: The 'Final Solution of the Jewish Question' in the Third Reich." In *The Policies of Genocide: Jews and Soviet Prisoners of War in Nazi Germany,* edited by Gerhard Hirschfeld, 97–144. London: Unwin Hyman, 1986.

Mosse, Werner E., ed. *Entscheidungsjahr 1932: Zur Judenfrage in der Endphase der Weimarer Republik.* Tübingen: J. C. B. Mohr, 1966.

Noakes, Jeremy. "The Development of Nazi Policy towards the German-Jewish *Mischlinge,* 1933–1945." *LBIYB* 34 (1989): 291–354.

Nicosia, Francis R. "The End of Emancipation and the Illusion of Preferential Treatment: German Zionism, 1933–1938." *LBIYB* 36 (1991): 243–65.

————. "Jewish Farmers in Hitler's Germany: Zionist Occupational Retraining and Nazi 'Jewish Policy.'" *H&GS* 19, no. 3 (2005): 365–89.

————. "Revisionist Zionism in Germany (II)—Georg Kareski and the Staatszionistische Organisation, 1933–1935." *LBIYB* 32 (1987): 367–400.

————. *The Third Reich and the Palestine Question.* London: Tauris, 1985.

————. *Zionism and Anti-Semitism in Nazi Germany.* Cambridge: Cambridge University Press, 2008.

Nicosia, Francis R., and David Scrase, eds. *Jewish Life in Nazi Germany: Dilemmas and Responses.* New York: Berghahn Books, 2010.

Ofer, Dalia, and Lenore J. Weitzman, eds. *Women and the Holocaust.* New Haven, CT: Yale University Press, 1998.

Paucker, Arnold. "Changing Perceptions: Reflections on the Historiography of Jewish Self-defense and Jewish Resistance, 1890–2000." In *Jüdische Welten: Juden in Deutschland vom 18. Jahrhundert bis in die Gegenwart,* edited by Marion A. Kaplan and Beate Meyer, 440–56. Göttingen: Wallstein Verlag, 2005.

————. *Deutsche Juden im Kampf um Recht und Freiheit: Studien zu Abwehr, Selbstbehauptung und Widerstand der deutschen Juden seit dem Ende des 19. Jahrhunderts.* Berlin: Hentrich & Hentrich, 2003.

————, ed. *Die Juden im nationalsozialistischen Deutschland: The Jews in Nazi Germany, 1933–1945.* Tübingen: J. C. B. Mohr, 1986.

————. *Der jüdische Abwehrkampf gegen Antisemitismus und Nationalsozialismus in den letzten Jahren der Weimarer Republik.* Hamburg: Leibniz Verlag, 1968.

Paucker, Arnold, and Konrad Kwiet. "Jewish Leadership and Jewish Resistance." In *Probing the Depths of German Anti-Semitism: German Society and the Persecution of the Jews, 1933–1941,* edited by David Bankier, 371–94. New York: Berghahn, 2000.

Pehle, Walter H., ed. *November 1938: From "Reichskristallnacht" to Genocide.* New York: Berg, 1991.

Peukert, Detlev. *Inside Nazi Germany: Conformity, Opposition, and Racism in Everyday Life.* New Haven, CT: Yale University Press, 1987.

Rabinovici, Doron. *Instanzen der Ohnmacht: Wien 1938 bis 1945. Der Weg zum Judenrat.* Frankfurt am Main: Jüdischer Verlag, 2000.

Reinharz, Jehuda. "The Zionist Response to Antisemitism in Germany." *LBIYB* 30 (1985): 105–40.

Rheins, Carl J. "Deutscher Vortrupp, Gefolgschaft deutscher Juden, 1933–1935." *LBIYB* 26 (1981): 207–29.

———. "The Schwarzes Fähnlein, Jungenschaft, 1932–1934." *LBIYB* 23 (1978): 173–97.

———. "The Verband nationaldeutscher Juden, 1921–1933." *LBIYB* 25 (1980): 243–68.

Richarz, Monika, ed. *Jewish Life in Germany: Memoirs from Three Centuries.* Bloomington: Indiana University Press, 1991.

Röhm, Eberhard, and Jörg Thierfelder. *Juden-Christen-Deutsche: 1933 bis 1945.* 3 vols. Stuttgart: Calwer Verlag, 2004.

Roseman, Mark. *A Past in Hiding: Memory and Survival in Nazi Germany.* New York: Metropolitan Books, 2000.

———. *The Wannsee Conference and the Final Solution: A Reconsideration.* New York: Metropolitan Books, 2002.

Roskies, David G. *The Literature of Destruction: Jewish Responses to Catastrophe.* Philadelphia: Jewish Publication Society, 1988.

Safrian, Hans. "Expediting Expropriation and Expulsion: The Impact of the 'Vienna Model' on Anti-Jewish Policies in Nazi Germany, 1939." *H&GS* 14, no. 3 (2000): 390–414.

Schatzker, Chaim. "The Jewish Youth Movement in Germany in the Holocaust Period (I)—Youth in Confrontation with a New Reality." *LBIYB* 19 (1974): 157–81.

———. "The Jewish Youth Movement in Germany in the Holocaust Period (II)—The Relations between the Youth Movement and the Hechaluz." *LBIYB* 33 (1988): 301–25.

Schleunes, Karl A. *The Twisted Road to Auschwitz: Nazi Policy toward German Jews, 1933–1939.* Urbana: University of Illinois Press, 1970.

Schorsch, Ismar. *Jewish Reactions to German Anti-Semitism, 1870–1914.* New York: Columbia University Press, 1972.

Silberklang, David. "Jewish Politics and Rescue: The Founding of the Council for German Jewry." *H&GS* 7, no. 3 (1993): 333–71.

Simon, Ernst. *Aufbau im Untergang: Jüdische Erwachsenenbildung im nationalsozialistischen Deutschland als geistiger Widerstand.* Tübingen: J. C. B. Mohr, 1959.

Stargardt, Nicholas. *Witnesses of War: Children's Lives under the Nazis.* New York: Alfred A. Knopf, 2006.

Steinweis, Alan E. *Art, Ideology and Economics in Nazi Germany: The Reich Chamber of Culture and the Regulation of the Culture Professions in Nazi Germany.* Chapel Hill: University of North Carolina Press, 1988.

———. "Hans Hinkel and German Jewry, 1933–1941." *LBIYB* 38 (1993): 209–19.

———. *Studying the Jew: Scholarly Antisemitism in Nazi Germany.* Cambridge, MA: Harvard University Press, 2006.

Strauss, Herbert A. "Jewish Emigration from Germany: Nazi Policies and Jewish Responses," *LBIYB* 25 (1980): 313–61; *LBIYB* 26 (1981): 343–409.

Tent, James F. *In the Shadow of the Holocaust: Nazi Persecution of Jewish-Christian Germans.* Lawrence: Kansas University Press, 2003.

Voelker, Karin. "The B'nai B'rith Order (U.O.B.B.) in the Third Reich." *LBIYB* 32 (1987): 269–95.

Volkov, Shulamit. "Old and New Approaches to the History of National Socialism: The Double Perspective of Jews and Germans." In *Jüdische Welten: Juden in Deutschland vom 18. Jahrhundert bis in die Gegenwart,* edited by Marion A. Kaplan and Beate Meyer, 457–75. Göttingen: Wallstein Verlag, 2005.

Vuletić, Aleksandar-Saša. *Christen jüdischer Herkunft im Dritten Reich: Verfolgung und organisierte Selbsthilfe, 1933–1939.* Mainz: Verlag Phillip von Zabern, 1999.

Walk, Joseph. *Jüdische Schule und Erziehung im Dritten Reich.* Frankfurt am Main: A. Hain, 1991.

Wegner, Gregory. *Anti-Semitism and Schooling under the Third Reich.* New York: Routledge, 2002.

Weiss, Yfaat. *Deutsche und polnische Juden vor dem Holocaust: Jüdische Identität zwischen Staatsbürgerschaft und Ethnizität, 1933–1940.* Munich: R. Oldenbourg Verlag, 2000.

———. "Jews in Germany and Poland: Changing Roles in Times of Adversity." *LBIYB* 44 (1999): 205–23.

———. *Schicksalsgemeinschaft im Wandel: Jüdische Erziehung im nationalsozialistischen Deutschland, 1933–1938.* Hamburg: Christians, 1991.

———. "The Transfer Agreement and the Boycott Movement: A Jewish Dilemma on the Eve of the Holocaust." *YVS* 26 (1998): 129–71.

Wildt, Michael. *Generation des Unbedingten: Das Führungskorps des Reichssicherheitshauptamtes.* Hamburg: Hamburger Edition, 2002.

———. "Violence against Jews in Germany, 1933–1939." In *Probing the Depths of German Anti-Semitism: German Society and the Persecution of the Jews, 1933–1941,* edited by David Bankier, 181–209. New York: Berghahn, 2000.

———. *Volksgemeinschaft als Selbstermächtigung: Gewalt gegen Juden in der deutschen Provinz, 1919–1939.* Hamburg: Hamburger Edition, 2006.

Yahil, Leni. *The Holocaust: The Fate of European Jewry, 1932–1945.* New York: Oxford University Press, 1990.

———. "Jews in Concentration Camps in Germany Prior to World War II." In *The Nazi Concentration Camps: Proceedings of the 4th Yad Vashem International Historical Conference,* edited by Yad Vashem, 69–100. Jerusalem: Yad Vashem, 1984.

Zimmermann, Moshe, ed. *On Germans and Jews under the Nazi Regime.* Jerusalem: Magnes Press, 2007.

Zucker, Bat-Ami. *In Search of Refuge: Jews and U.S. Consuls in Nazi Germany, 1933–1941.* London: Vallentine Mitchell, 2001.

Glossary

Abraham, Max (1904–ca. 1970) Abraham was a preacher (*Prediger*) in the small Jewish community—approximately 110 members in 1933——in Rathenow, Brandenburg, a town of 28,000 inhabitants. Arrested in June 1933 on fabricated charges, he was incarcerated for several months in Oranienburg and other concentration camps. After his release he escaped to Czechoslovakia, where in 1934 he published an account of his concentration camp ordeal. Before the war began, Abraham managed to emigrate to England.

See Irene A. Diekmann and Klaus Wettig, eds., *Konzentrationslager Oranienburg: Augenzeugenberichte aus dem Jahre 1933* (Potsdam: Verlag für Berlin-Brandenburg, 2003), 119–67.

Affidavit Sworn testimony provided on a voluntary basis to designated officials as part of a legal proceeding. During the emigration crisis of the 1930s and early 1940s, affidavits became synonymous with the legally binding guarantees of financial support given for would-be immigrants prior to their admission into a country and required by U.S. immigration regulations.

Aliyah (Hebrew: "ascent") In the context of the Zionist movement, this term describes the mass settlement of Diaspora Jews in Palestine to establish a Jewish homeland. After 1933 *Aliyah* organized by the Palästina-Amt and assisted by the Ha'avara Agreement became a prominent feature of Jewish emigration from Nazi Germany. In the period from 1933 to 1941, a total of more than fifty-two hundred Jews left the German Reich for Palestine; the Youth *Aliyah* organized by Recha Freier and others helped more than five thousand young Jews in the period up to September 1939. With British restrictions on Jewish settlement in Palestine increasing since the mid-1930s, the illegal *Aliyah*

(*Aliyah Bet*) became steadily more significant and continued up to the founding of the state of Israel in 1948.

See Brian Amkraut, *Between Home and Homeland: Youth Aliyah from Nazi Germany* (Tuscaloosa: University of Alabama Press, 2006).

American Jewish Joint Distribution Committee (AJJDC, also AJDC, JDC, Joint) Founded in 1914, the AJJDC provided assistance to Jews around the world, particularly in Eastern Europe. During the Nazi era this umbrella for aid organizations in the United States was involved in emigration planning and relief work in Germany, until 1939 providing an increasing share of the budget for German Jewish organizations such as the Zentralausschuß der deutschen Juden für Hilfe und Aufbau or the Reichsvertretung. The AJJDC's efforts continued after the war began and extended beyond the Reich into countries occupied or controlled by Germany.

See Yehuda Bauer, *American Jewry and the Holocaust: The American Jewish Joint Distribution Committee, 1939–45* (Detroit, MI: Wayne State University Press, 1981).

Anschluss ("joining," "connection") Euphemistic shorthand for the German annexation of Austria in March 1938. Although it constituted an act of aggression on the part of Germany against its independent neighbor that went hand in hand with mass arrests and anti-Jewish violence, the *Anschluss* met with widespread popular support, both in Austria and in Germany. Austria remained a part of the German Reich until the end of World War II.

"Aryan"; antonym: "non-Aryan" (German: *Arier, Nicht-Arier*) Originally a linguistic category in nineteenth-century ethnology, the term became firmly integrated into racial and eugenic discourse. Ideologues used the key, although not clearly defined, concept to support the thesis of the inequality of human races and the superiority of "Aryans" over other ethnic groups; the term often appeared synonymous with the equally amorphous term Nordic (*nordisch*), with Western European whites of Christian background at its core. Nazi ideology used the construct of an "Aryan" ideal type to denigrate "non-Aryans," particularly Jews, in the attempt to prevent miscegenation and the birth of "*Mischlinge*" and to create a racially homogenous *Volksgemeinschaft*. Racial segregation became legally codified in the Third Reich with the Civil Service Law, enacted in April 1933, and was developed further in the Nuremberg Laws and subsequent regulations.

See Michael Burleigh and Wolfgang Wippermann, *The Racial State: Germany, 1933–1945* (Cambridge: Cambridge University Press, 1991); Claudia Koonz, *The Nazi Conscience* (Cambridge, MA: Harvard University Press, 2003).

"Aryanization," "Aryanize" (German: *Arisierung, arisieren*) Derived from the vocabulary of *völkisch* antisemitism, the term denotes the process of expropriating Jews and excluding them for the purpose of establishing a racially "purified" economy. During the Third Reich, Nazi functionaries, government officials, and private businessmen worked toward this goal using legislative, administrative, and even terrorist means. Starting in early 1933, the process gathered pace over time. The *Anschluss* of Austria in 1938 triggered a wave of exclusionary measures that culminated in the forced "Aryanization" of the remaining Jewish businesses later that year.

See Avraham Barkai, *From Boycott to Annihilation: The Economic Struggle of German Jews, 1933–1943* (Hanover, NH: University of New England Press, 1989).

Baeck, Leo (1873–1956) A rabbi and scholar who held a number of prominent positions within German Jewish organizations during the interwar era. After the Nazi's rise to power, Baeck's ability to reduce friction between opposing factions and to provide moral leadership prompted his appointment as president of the Reichsvertretung in September 1933, a position he retained until the organization's replacement with the Gestapo-controlled Reichsvereinigung in 1939. Briefly arrested in the autumn of 1935, Baeck intervened repeatedly at the Gestapo for the release or emigration of other officials, especially after "*Kristallnacht.*" Baeck was deported to Theresienstadt in late January 1943, where he played an important, though largely informal, role in the ghetto community. He survived the war, emigrated to London, and continued his political, religious, and educational endeavors until his death. In 1955 an institute for the study of German Jewish history was created in his name, with branches in London, New York, and Jerusalem.

See Albert H. Friedlander, *Leo Baeck, Teacher of Theresienstadt* (Woodstock, NY: Overlook Press, 1991).

Balfour Declaration Statement by British foreign secretary Arthur James Balfour made on November 2, 1917, expressing that his government viewed "with favour the establishment in Palestine of a national home for the Jewish people, and will use their best endeavours to facilitate the achievement of the object, it being clearly understood that nothing shall be done which may prejudice the civil and religious' rights of existing non-Jewish communities in Palestine, or the rights and political status enjoyed by Jews in any other country." The statement resulted from the Zionist movement's pressuring the Allied powers and was made in the context of British plans for the post–World War I British presence in this strategically important region; it was later incorporated into the British mandate for Palestine issued by the League of Nations in 1920.

See Walter Laqueur, *A History of Zionism* (New York: Schocken Books, 2003).

Berliner, Cora (1890–1942) After receiving a doctorate in sociology and political science in 1916, Berliner began a career as a public servant in the Reich Economics Ministry and became a professor of economics in Berlin, while maintaining her involvement in Jewish organizational life. After her dismissal from her teaching position in 1933, Berliner played a lead role in the Centralverein and helped form the Zentralausschuß der deutschen Juden für Hilfe und Aufbau; she coordinated youth work for the latter organization. From 1934 to 1937 she was vice president of the Jüdischer Frauenbund and served on the board of the Reichsvertretung as well as its successor organization, the

Reichsvereinigung. In the summer of 1942, Berliner was deported, in all likelihood to Minsk in German-occupied Belorussia, where she was murdered.

See Gudrun Maierhof, *Selbstbehauptung im Chaos: Frauen in der jüdischen Selbsthilfe, 1933–1943* (Frankfurt am Main: Campus, 2002), 77–87, 190–93.

Block, Elisabeth (1923–1942) Living with her parents and two siblings in rural Bavaria, Elisabeth Block kept a diary with few direct references to the persecution of Jews. In the spring of 1942, she was deported with her family via Munich-Milbertshofen to Piaski in the Lublin district before they were murdered, presumably in Bełżec or Sobibór, in the summer of 1942.

See *Erinnerungszeichen: Die Tagebücher der Elisabeth Block*, ed. Haus der Bayerischen Geschichte (Rosenheim: Bayerische Staatskanzlei, 1993).

Bondy, Curt (1894–1972) A professor in Göttingen until his dismissal in 1933, when he dedicated himself to adult education for German Jews. In 1936 he became director of the emigration training farm (*Jüdisches Auswandererlehrgut*) located at Gross-Breesen and supported by the Reichsvertretung. Bondy directed the farm until its forced closure on November 10, 1938, when along with many of his staff, he was arrested and interned at the Buchenwald concentration camp. Upon his release in early 1939, Bondy fled to the United States, but he briefly returned the following year in order to aid fellow German Jewish refugees in their emigration efforts.

See Werner T. Angress, *Between Fear and Hope: Jewish Youth in the Third Reich* (New York: Columbia University Press, 1988).

Brodnitz, Friedrich (1899–1995) Son of longtime Centralverein chairman Julius Brodnitz, a physician by training, and a German Jewish activist in his own right. Holding several prominent positions within the CV, the Reichsvertretung, and the Zentralausschuß der deutschen Juden für Hilfe und Aufbau, after 1933 Brodnitz established and maintained clandestine contacts with U.S. and other foreign journalists and diplomats, updating them about state-sanctioned antisemitism in Nazi Germany. In the summer of 1937, the year following his father's death, Brodnitz left Germany via France for New York City, where he resumed his medical career.

See Friedrich S. Brodnitz, "Memories of the Reichsvertretung: A Personal Report," *LBIYB* 31 (1986): 267–77.

Brodnitz, Julius (1866–1936) A lawyer and leading figure in German Jewish organizational life during the Weimar era and in the early years of the Nazi regime. From 1920 until his death, Brodnitz served as the chairman (*Vorsitzender*) of the Centralverein and cofounded its weekly journal, the *CV-Zeitung*, as well as *Der Morgen* (published every two months). After Hitler's ascent to power, he oversaw the CV's attempts at transforming itself from a self-defense organization into a relief agency. In March 1933 he was among a small group of German Jewish leaders who met with Hermann Göring about the ensuing Nazi boycott movement. Brodnitz was killed in June 1936 in a Berlin traffic accident.

See Avraham Barkai, *"Wehr Dich!" Der Centralverein deutscher Staatsbürger jüdischen Glaubens (C.V.), 1893–1938* (Munich: C. H. Beck, 2002).

Bund Deutsch-Jüdischer Jugend (BDJ, Bund; League of German Jewish Youth) German Jewish youth organization formed in 1925, based on the ideals of the German youth movement and closely associated with the Centralverein. After 1933 the BDJ absorbed a host of other non-Zionist youth groups, increasing its membership to six thousand in the mid-1930s. Led by Heinz Kellermann, the BDJ maintained its close ties to the CV and Reichsbund jüdischer Frontsoldaten, as well as its opposition to Zionist goals; nevertheless, with the prospects for Jewish life in Germany diminishing, the BDJ increasingly supported emigration (to destinations other than Palestine) and tried to instill in its members an increased sense of Jewish identity. Renamed Der Ring Bund jüdischer Jugend in the spring of 1936, the organization was dissolved by the Gestapo at the end of the year.

See Chaim Schatzker, "The Jewish Youth Movement in Germany in the Holocaust Period" (2 parts), *LBIYB* 32 (1987): 157–81; 33 (1988): 301–25.

Centralverein deutscher Staatsbürger jüdischen Glaubens (CV; Central Association of German Citizens of Jewish Faith) Founded in 1893 as a result of both growing antisemitism and increasing assimilation of Jews in Germany, the CV sought to defend the rights of German Jews while fostering the "cultivation of German sentiment" among its members. Its membership figures (72,500 in 1924), well-developed organization (26 regional and 632 local offices in 1921), efficient head office in Berlin, and popular weekly journal (the *CV-Zeitung*, with a circulation of 55,000 in 1933) attest to the CV's broad appeal among German Jews. Claiming neutrality in matters of religious and political orientation, the CV nevertheless collided with the Zionistische Vereinigung für Deutschland before World War I and attracted comparatively few members from among Orthodox Jews and *Ostjuden*. Despite strong links to German Jewish youth groups with a similar ideological orientation, most notably the Bund Deutsch-Jüdischer Jugend, and to the women's movement (Jüdischer Frauenbund), the organization's leadership remained dominated by middle-aged men, especially lawyers. The radicalization of the German political landscape in the final years of the Weimar Republic and the massive increase in antisemitic agitation prompted the use of more aggressive means for combating the *völkisch* and Nazi threat, an effort coordinated from the CV head office in Berlin by Hans Reichmann. After 1933, the CV spearheaded the formation of the Reichsvertretung in September 1933 and, despite increased supervision by the police and shrinking opportunities, played a leading role in that organization's practical work. Moving away from its traditional focus on legal help, the CV reoriented its work toward assistance for emigration and material aid for those Jews remaining in Germany. Renamed in September 1935 as Centralverein der Juden in Deutschland and one year later as Jüdischer Centralverein, the organization was abolished by the Gestapo in the wake of "*Kristallnacht.*"

See Avraham Barkai, "*Wehr Dich!" Der Centralverein deutscher Staatsbürger jüdischen Glaubens (C.V.), 1893–1938* (Munich: C. H. Beck, 2002); Jehuda Reinharz, *Fatherland or Promised Land: The Dilemma of the German Jew, 1893–1914* (Ann Arbor: University of Michigan Press, 1975).

Cohn, Willy (1888–1941) Born in Breslau, Lower Silesia, Cohn was a historian, educator, and veteran of World War I. After he had lost his teaching position in Breslau in April 1933, Cohn contributed numerous publications to German Jewish periodicals in support of pedagogical endeavors while maintaining his extensive diary writing. A supporter of the Zionist cause, he and his second wife, Gertrud (Trudi, née Rothmann), visited his son from his first marriage, Ernst (b. 1919), in Palestine in early 1937; Louis Wolfgang (b. 1914), another son from Cohn's first marriage, had emigrated to France in 1934, and Cohn's eldest daughter, Ruth (b. 1924), escaped to Palestine in 1940. On November 21, 1941, Cohn, Trudi, and their two daughters, Tamara (b. 1938) and Susanne (b. 1932), were, together with over a thousand other Breslau Jews, summoned for deportation to Kovno in German-occupied Lithuania, where they were murdered on arrival.

See Norbert Conrads, ed., *Kein Recht, Nirgends: Tagebuch vom Untergang des Breslauer Judentums, 1933–1941.* Vol. 1 (Cologne: Böhlau Verlag, 2007).

Deutscher Gruss ("German greeting" or "salute") Originating in ancient Rome, the gesture of an outstretched arm found favor during the twentieth century with the Italian Fascist movement and was later appropriated by the Nazi Party, which added the phrase "Heil Hitler!" Commonly used by NSDAP functionaries already during the Weimar period, the salute spread throughout German society following Hitler's appointment as Reich chancellor. "With German salute" (*mit deutschem Gruss*) became the standard closing line for written communications, both official and private. Throughout the Nazi era, failing to use this salute was frequently construed as an expression of opposition to the regime. For Jews after 1933, the problem of how to greet others in public caused consternation and could trigger aggression from Nazi supporters. After the Nuremberg Laws, German courts increasingly targeted Jews and "*Mischlinge*" for applying a gesture meant to be used by "Aryans" only. While prohibitions increased after 1936 and 1937, their application vis-à-vis Jews and "*Mischlinge*" remained uneven.

See Tilman Allert, *The Hitler Salute: On the Meaning of a Gesture* (New York: Metropolitan, 2008).

Dienemann, Mally (née Hirsch; 1883–1963) Active in Germany's feminist movement and from 1904 married to Rabbi Max Dienemann, with whom she moved to Ratibor, Upper Silesia, and later to Offenbach, Hesse. Dienemann's diary notes, now located in the archive of the Leo Baeck Institute in New York, attest to the couple's work in the

Offenbach Jewish community between 1933 and *"Kristallnacht."* After Max's release from the Sachsenhausen concentration camp in late 1938, the Dienemanns followed their daughters Paula and Gabi to Palestine, where Max died only months later from the aftereffects of his imprisonment. Mally Dienemann later emigrated to the United States, and in 1946 she released *Max Dienemann: Ein Gedenkbuch, 1875–1939*, a memorial tribute to her husband.

See Margarete Limberg and Hubert Rübsaat, eds., *Germans No More: Accounts of Jewish Everyday Life, 1933–1938* (New York: Berghahn Books, 2006): 84–86, 183.

Ehrenkreuz ("Honor Cross") Medal retroactively awarded to German Word War I veterans on July 13, 1934, by order of Reich President Paul von Hindenburg. These medals were divided into three categories (awarded to frontline soldiers, noncombative servicemen, and military families).

Eichmann, Adolf (1906–1962) Raised in the Austrian city of Linz, in 1932 Eichmann joined the Nazi Party and the SS in Austria before he moved to Germany, where he joined Reinhard Heydrich's SD. Following the *Anschluss* of Austria, Eichmann started to play a key role as an expert for "Jewish affairs"; after the beginning of the war he became one of the chief agents of Nazi anti-Jewish policy that led to the systematic murder of the European Jews. In hiding after the war, he was abducted by the Israeli secret service in Argentina in May 1960 and put on trial in Jerusalem. Sentenced to death by the court, he was hanged in June 1962.

Elbogen, Ismar (1874–1943) Elbogen taught at the Berlin-based Hochschule für die Wissenschaft des Judentums from 1919 and was active in many academic disciplines, including sociology and art. He presided over the Reichsvertretung's education committee (*Erziehungsausschuss*) before he emigrated to the United States in 1938 and accepted a position at the Jewish Theological Seminary of New York the following year.

See Michael A. Meyer, *Without Wissenschaft There is no Judaism: The Life and Thought of the Jewish Historian Ismar Elbogen* (Ramat-Gan: Bar-Ilan University, 2004).

Erez Israel (Hebrew: "Land of Israel" with scriptural and historical connotations) The Zionist movement began using the term in the early twentieth century when referring to Palestine and the envisaged Jewish national home they sought to establish there.

Ermächtigungsgesetz ("Enabling Act") Short for Law for Remedying the Plight of the People and the State (*Gesetz zur Behebung der Not von Volk und Reich*) designed to grant Hitler's government full legislative powers by suspending the checks and balances provided for by the Weimar Republic's constitution. A two-thirds majority in the Reichstag approved the measure (against the votes of the Social Democratic MPs) on March 24, 1933. This law, in conjunction with the earlier suspension of personal freedoms in the wake of the Reichstag fire, effectively terminated the Weimar democratic system without formally abolishing its constitution and served as the foundation for the Nazi regime until its demise in 1945.

See Richard J. Evans, *The Coming of the Third Reich* (New York: Penguin Press, 2004).

Freier, Recha (1892–1984) A teacher and champion of child welfare and resettlement efforts, Freier created the Children and Youth *Aliyah*, which was officially recognized by the Zionist Congress in August 1933. Freier's organization aimed at resettling Jewish youth threatened by Nazi persecution, with Palestine as the primary destination. Between 1932 and 1939 she helped more than five thousand young Jews escape from the Nazi sphere of influence. Freier's work in the resettlement program continued following her emigration to Palestine in 1941.

See Recha Freier, *Let the Children Come: The Early History of Youth Aliyah* (London: Weidenfeld & Nicolson, 1961).

Frick, Wilhelm (1877–1946) A Bavarian state official who participated in the failed Nazi coup of November 9, 1923, and served as a Reichstag MP for the NSDAP since 1925. In 1933 he became Reich minister of the interior (Reichsminister des Innern) in Hitler's cabinet, a post that he held until the summer of 1943, when he was replaced by Heinrich Himmler. Particularly in the early years of the Nazi regime, Frick's expertise was essential for integrating state and party agencies and for passing landmark legislation (*Ermächtigungsgesetz*) that facilitated the transformation of Nazi rule into a dictatorship. Frick and his ministry also played a key role in drafting and administering racial legislation, including the Nuremberg Laws. In 1946 the International Military Tribunal at Nuremberg tried and sentenced him to death.

Führer ("leader") Commonly used to refer to Hitler, the term indicated, first, his function as head of the Nazi Party and, second, after 1933 and especially after the death of Reich President Paul von Hindenburg, Hitler's role as supreme authority within the state. Replicated throughout the state and party hierarchy, the "Führer principle" was meant to ensure clear vertical lines of authority, yet in effect led to the diffusion of responsibilities through Hitler's creation of special agencies and parallel authority structures.

See Ian Kershaw, *The Hitler Myth: Image and Reality in the Third Reich* (New York: Oxford University Press, 1987).

Gauleiter Resulting from the stratification of the Nazi Party (NSDAP) after 1925, the men serving as Gauleiter acted as the regional party heads in a *Gau* region (forty-three throughout Germany) and maintained a strong personal connection to Hitler, the party chief. From the beginning of the Nazi regime onwards, the office of Gauleiter became increasingly intertwined with state functions at the top regional level.

Gestapa (Geheimes Staatspolizeiamt, Secret State Police Office) Drawing from the Prussian political police of the Weimar era, the Gestapa was formed in April 1933 and subordinated first to Prussian Interior Minister and Police Chief Hermann Göring, then from 1934 to Heinrich Himmler. The Berlin-based Gestapa served as the central office of the Gestapo until the latter became established as police agency for the entire Reich in mid-1936.

Gestapo (Geheime Staatspolizei, Secret State Police) As the chief executive agency charged with fighting internal "enemies of the state," the Gestapo functioned—in many respects parallel to and in competition with the SD (see Reinhard Heydrich)—as the Third Reich's main surveillance and terror instrument, first within Germany and later in the territories occupied by Germany. After 1933, the Gestapo became part of a complex apparatus of state and party police agencies and maintained special administrative offices to supervise anti-Jewish policies. The Prussian Gestapa figured most prominently among its regional branches; after 1934 the Gestapo was placed under SS chief Heinrich Himmler, became part of Reinhard Heydrich's Security Police in mid-1936, and in September 1939 was merged with the SD into the Reichssicherheitshauptamt.

See George C. Browder, *Foundations of the Nazi Police State: The Formation of Sipo and SD* (Lexington: Kentucky University Press, 1990).

Goebbels, Joseph (1897–1945) After studying literature at university, Goebbels joined the Nazi movement in 1924 and was initially drawn to its revolutionary wing. Serving since 1926 as Gauleiter for Berlin and since 1928 as Reichstag MP, Goebbels became architect of the successful Nazi propaganda machine, with its radical antisemitism and mystification of Hitler as Führer. In March 1933 Hitler appointed him as Reich minister for public enlightenment and propaganda (Reichsminister für Volksaufklärung und Propaganda). Goebbels also directed the policies of the Reich Chamber of Culture (Reichskulturkammer), particularly in matters of race, and played a key role in the instigation of "*Kristallnacht*" and subsequent anti-Jewish measures, including the deportation of Jews from Berlin to ghettos, concentration camps, and extermination centers.

See Jeffrey Herf, *The Jewish Enemy: Nazi Propaganda during World War II and the Holocaust* (Cambridge, MA: Belknap Press, 2006).

Göring, Hermann (1893–1946) A World War I flight commander and participant in the 1923 Nazi putsch attempt in Munich, Göring provided an important link for Hitler's movement with Germany's conservative elite. Reichstag MP for the Nazi Party since 1928, Göring was one of very few party members originally within Hitler's new cabinet (Reich minister without portfolio, Prussian interior minister, and head of the Gestapa; after April 1933, Prussian prime minister). Göring amassed an array of functions, particularly in the area of rearmament and economic policy; for instance, he was named plenipotentiary for the four-year plan (Beauftragter für den Vierjahresplan in October 1936) and Hitler's official successor (September 1939). In 1941 Göring charged Reinhard Heydrich with development of a "total solution to the Jewish Question." The highest-ranking Nazi in the dock at the International Military Tribunal in Nuremberg, Göring was convicted and sentenced to death in 1946.

See Richard J. Overy, *Göring, the "Iron Man"* (London: Routledge and Keagan Paul, 1984).

Ha'avara (Transfer) Agreement An agreement concluded in August 1933 following negotiations between the Zionistische Vereinigung für Deutschland and Third Reich government officials to facilitate the passage of German Jewish émigrés headed for Palestine. It allowed them to retain a large enough percentage of their assets so that they qualified for visas ordinarily reserved for more wealthy emigrants (so-called capitalists). At the same time, the Ha'avara Agreement enabled the Reichsvertretung to use émigré assets tied up in Germany for relief work among the Jews who remained behind. Ha'avara allowed for the export of substantial amounts of German goods to Palestine, with the proceeds used to pay for emigrants' visa fees and provide start-up capital. For the Nazis, the agreement provided an instrument to speed up Jewish emigration and also created a market for German exports. In order to facilitate the terms of the agreement, German Jewish functionaries enlisted a number of prominent bankers to create the Palästina Treuhandstelle. Highly controversial within the Zionist movement and increasingly seen as potentially dangerous by German officials, Ha'avara nonetheless helped more than forty thousand Jews (until the end of 1938) leave Germany for Palestine. Adapted in 1937 into a different agreement to allow for Jewish emigration to other countries than Palestine, the Ha'avara Agreement remained in place until after the beginning of the war in 1939.

See Francis R. Nicosia, *Zionism and Anti-Semitism in Nazi Germany* (Cambridge: Cambridge University Press, 2008); Werner Feilchenfeld, Dolf Michaelis, and Ludwig Pinner, *Haavara-Transfer nach Palästina und Einwanderung deutscher Juden, 1933–1939* (Tübingen: J. C. B. Mohr, 1972).

Hachsharah (Hebrew: "preparation") The training and education of young Jews prior to their planned move to Palestine (*Aliyah*), especially as part of the Hechaluz movement. Several German Jewish organizations within and beyond the Zionist spectrum established training farms and other facilities for the purpose of preparing youth for emigration to Palestine.

Hechaluz The word *hechaluz* is directly translated from Hebrew as "the pioneer." The Hechaluz movement was founded in 1921 in Warsaw as an international association that in 1935 had roughly one hundred thousand members. Dedicated to the Zionist ideal of reestablishing a Jewish homestead, the Hechaluz organized professional training courses for European Jews as they prepared to leave for Palestine and create Kibbutz settlements there. Nazi persecution increased many Jews' interest in the Hechaluz movement in Germany, which grew from five hundred members in 1933 to around fourteen hundred just two years later.

Heydrich, Reinhard (1904–1942) After his dismissal from the German Navy in 1931, Heydrich, involved since the early 1920s in *völkisch* circles, received a commission from SS chief Himmler to create a secret service for the Nazi Party (the *Sicherheitsdienst*, or SD), which he headed until his death. Highly ambitious, Heydrich accumulated additional functions (head of the Gestapo in Bavaria and Prussia in 1933 and 1934) and in 1936 became head of the Security Police main office within the SS that combined the Gestapo and the Criminal Police. The Security Police, together with the SD, increasingly controlled the Third Reich's anti-Jewish policy. In the autumn of 1939,

Heydrich merged the two agencies into the newly created Reichssicherheitshauptamt, which became the single most important agency for the implementation of the Holocaust through ghettoization, deportation, and mass murder. Attempting to bring the ensuing "final solution" under his closer control, Heydrich invited leading officials from state and party agencies to the Wannsee Conference held on January 20, 1942. He died as the result of an assassination attempt by Czech partisans in Prague.

See Mark Roseman, *The Wannsee Conference and the Final Solution: A Reconsideration* (New York: Metropolitan Books, 2002).

HICEM Three Jewish advocacy organizations, the Hebrew Sheltering and Immigrant Aid Society (HIAS), the Jewish Colonization Association (JCA or ICA), and the Emigration Board (EM), pooled their personnel and resources in 1927 in order to form HICEM, based in Paris. After 1933 HICEM helped Jews in Nazi Germany and refugees by providing visa applications and securing transportation for them. Following the German attack on France in 1940, HICEM relocated to New York, where it was absorbed into HIAS in 1945.

Hilfsverein der deutschen Juden (Hilfsverein; Relief Association of German Jews) Established in 1901 to provide financial assistance and educational opportunities primarily for Jews living in Eastern Europe, the Hilfsverein became integrated into the chain of German Jewish relief agencies after 1933, first under the umbrella of the Zentralausschuß der deutschen Juden für Hilfe und Aufbau and, beginning in September 1933, under the Reichsvertretung. As the plight of German Jews worsened, its main focus began to shift toward fostering emigration. While the Palästina-Amt catered to Jews trying to escape to Palestine, the Hilfsverein assisted those heading to other countries (roughly 120,000 émigrés through the end of 1938) and in 1939 was absorbed by the Gestapo-controlled Reichsvereinigung.

See Salomon Adler-Rudel, *Jüdische Selbsthilfe unter dem Nazi-Regime 1933–1939 im Spiegel der Berichte der Reichsvertretung der Juden in Deutschland* (Tübingen: J. C. B. Mohr, 1974).

Himmler, Heinrich (1900–1945) A member of the *völkisch* movement and a participant in the November 1923 Nazi putsch in Munich, Himmler was appointed by Hitler in early 1929 to become the leader (Reichsführer) of the SS (which until 1934 remained subordinate to the SA). After 1933 Himmler advanced rapidly from his initially small power base in Bavaria (as police president in Munich in 1933) to become head of the Gestapo in Prussia (April 1934) and chief of the entire German police in mid-1936. During the war, Himmler further expanded his SS and police apparatus to uphold Nazi control in the Reich and in German-controlled countries and to play the key role in executing the genocide of European Jewry.

See Richard Breitman, *The Architect of Genocide: Himmler and the Final Solution* (New York: Alfred A. Knopf, 1991).

Hindenburg, Paul von (1847–1934) German military leader during World War I and from 1925 until his death the elected president of the Weimar Republic. Under pressure from ultranationalist groups in the German political elite, he appointed Adolf Hitler as German chancellor on January 30, 1933. In response to the economic crisis and dissolution of a functioning parliamentarian system in the early 1930s, Hindenburg invoked his constitutional powers to rule the country by presidential decree. He thus prepared the way for Hitler's sidestepping of the Reichstag by way of the *Ermächtigungsgesetz*, facilitating the consolidation of Nazi rule. Hindenburg's death in 1934 allowed Hitler to assume the president's powers, particularly as commander of the German armed forces.

See William J. Astore and Dennis E. Showalter, *Hindenburg: Icon of German Militarism* (Dulles, VA: Potomac Books, 2005).

Hirsch, Otto (1885–1941) A lawyer and government official in the German state of Württemberg from 1920 until his dismissal in 1933. Because of his extensive involvement in German Jewish organizational life and his great management skills, Hirsch in September 1933 became the director of the Reichsvertretung in charge of its practical work, while Leo Baeck served as its nominal head (*Präsident*). Hirsch remained in Germany even after his release from concentration camp imprisonment after "*Kristallnacht*" to serve in the Reichsvereinigung until his final arrest by the Gestapo in early 1941. He died in Mauthausen concentration camp on June 19, 1941.

See Paul Sauer, "Otto Hirsch (1885–1941)—Director of the Reichsvertretung," *LBIYB* 32 (1987): 341–68.

Hirschberg, Alfred (1901–1971) Hirschberg began his career with the Centralverein head office in Berlin after completing his legal studies in the years after World War I. One of the leading contributors to the *CV-Zeitung*, in 1933 he became this newspaper's editor in chief. Arrested in the wake of the pogrom of November 1938, Hirschberg managed to emigrate to Brazil in 1939.

See Avraham Barkai, "*Wehr Dich!*" *Der Centralverein deutscher Staatsbürger jüdischen Glaubens (C.V.), 1893–1938* (Munich: C. H. Beck, 2002), 163–64.

Jewish Agency for Palestine Established by the World Zionist Organization in 1922, the Jewish Agency for Palestine established offices in Jerusalem, London, and Geneva in order to facilitate emigration to Palestine (*Aliyah*) and provide representation to those Jews already in the British mandate until the founding of the state of Israel in 1948. In Germany before World War II, the Jewish Agency was in charge of the Palästina-Amt.

Jüdischer Frauenbund (JFB; League of Jewish Women) Formed in 1904 as part of the international women's movement, the league attracted followers from a wide spectrum within the German Jewish community. Its goals were to offer Jewish women a voice and advance their rights both in the Jewish community and in German society at large. Beginning in 1924 the JFB published a monthly journal, *Blätter des JFB*.

After 1933 the organization assisted in the training and retraining of Jewish girls as the employment landscape shifted dramatically for Jews. The organization remained popular, and in the mid-1930s its membership consisted of some fifty thousand women in numerous regional and local branches throughout Germany. The JFB was abolished after "*Kristallnacht*," when many of its functions and staff were absorbed by the Reichsvereinigung.

See Marion A. Kaplan, *The Making of the Jewish Middle Class: Women, Family and Identity in Imperial Germany* (New York: Oxford University Press, 1991); Marion A. Kaplan, *Between Dignity and Despair: Jewish Life in Nazi Germany* (New York: Oxford University Press, 1998).

Kahn, Bernhard (1876–1955) Former secretary general of the Hilfsverein, and after 1921, until his 1939 emigration to the United States, director of the American Jewish Joint Distribution Committee's European office in Geneva.

Kareski, Georg (1878–1947) Industrialist, chairman of the Jewish community of Berlin (1929–1930), and a member of the community's board (1925–1937). In May 1933 he founded the Staatszionistische Organisation, a breakaway from the Jüdische Volkspartei and the Zionist-Revisionist movement, through which Kareski tried to achieve his goal of promoting massive German Jewish emigration to Palestine with the support of the Gestapo. After his attempts to obtain a leadership role within the Kulturbund and the Reichsvertretung had failed, he emigrated to Palestine in 1937; the Nazi regime dissolved the Staatszionistische Organisation in August 1938.

See Yehoyakim Cochavi, "Georg Kareski's Nomination as Head of the Kulturbund: The Gestapo's First Attempt—and Last Failure to Impose a Jewish Leadership," *LBIYB* 34 (1989): 227–46; Francis R. Nicosia, *Zionism and Anti-Semitism in Nazi Germany* (Cambridge: Cambridge University Press, 2008).

Karminski, Hannah (1897–1942) A Berlin-based educator, Karminski formed close ties in the 1920s with several leading members of the Jüdischer Frauenbund, an organization she joined in 1924. In addition to serving as the JFB's executive secretary, Karminski also took charge of its publications (*Blätter des JFB*), business, and emigration branches. Holding a prominent position within the Reichsvertretung, she remained in Germany after "*Kristallnacht*" to organize Jewish relief work. In November 1942, she was deported to Auschwitz, where she was murdered.

See Gudrun Maierhof, *Selbstbehauptung im Chaos: Frauen in der jüdischen Selbsthilfe, 1933–1943* (Frankfurt am Main: Campus, 2002), 71–77, 193–95.

Kellermann, Heinz (1910–1998) Head of the Bund Deutsch-Jüdischer Jugend, Kellermann was involved in the Reichsvertretung's youth organization leadership until his emigration to the Unites States in 1937. Working closely with the Centralverein, Kellermann supported efforts to increase Jewish emigration from Germany to places other then Palestine (e.g., via retraining farms). In the United States, he joined the diplomatic service; after the war he was involved in the Nuremberg trials, then later in education programs in West Germany.

See Henry J. Kellermann, "From Imperial to National-Socialist Germany: Recollections of a German-Jewish Youth Leader," *LBIYB* 34 (1994): 305–30.

Kibbutz (Hebrew: "gathering") In the early twentieth century, the kibbutz was a form of collective settlement instigated by the Zionist movement in Palestine and based on ideas about shared forms of production, education, and ownership popular among reformist circles since the late nineteenth century. With increased numbers of youth making *Aliyah* from Germany, the proportion of German Jews among *Kibbutzim* (kibbutz settlers) grew; some kibbutz settlements (such as Givat Brenner or Beit Zear) were founded by German émigrés in the early 1930s.

See Michael Brenner, *Zionism: A Brief History* (Princeton, NJ: Markus Wiener, 2003).

"Kristallnacht" (also *"Reichskristallnacht"*; "[Reich] Crystal Night" or "Night of Broken Glass") A euphemistic reference to the pogroms, arrests, and destruction of Jewish property that swept through Germany on the night of November 9 to 10, 1938. Acts of anti-Jewish violence had preceded that date, but now they escalated. The Nazi leadership staged Reich-wide pogroms to express "the German people's outrage" at the assassination of a German diplomat in Paris by the seventeen-year-old Hershel Grynszpan, whose parents had been deported from Germany across the Polish border in late October, together with around seventeen thousand other *Ostjuden*. During *"Kristallnacht,"* synagogues, shops, and apartments owned or occupied by Jews were destroyed; at least twenty-six thousand Jewish men were arrested and incarcerated in the Dachau, Sachsenhausen, and Buchenwald concentration camps. The official death total of ninety-one people represents only a fraction of the actual casualties; after this event, a wave of anti-Jewish regulations swept Germany and forced more German Jews to emigrate.

See Walter H. Pehle, ed., *November 1938: From "Reichskristallnacht" to Genocide* (New York: Berg, 1991).

Kulturbund deutscher Juden (Kulturbund; Culture League of German Jews) Formed in June 1933, the Kulturbund quickly became the main building block for the performing arts in the Jewish sector and a venue for Jewish artists and audiences excluded from the nazified culture of the Third Reich. Under the close supervision of Joseph Goebbels's Propaganda Ministry, the Kulturbund conducted a host of theater and film performances, concerts, lectures, and other events open to members only. By 1936, the organization had a membership of nearly ninety thousand Jews and local branches in almost thirty German cities, each conducting its own programs. Beginning in April 1935 these branches were integrated into an umbrella institution called Reichsverband jüdischer Kulturbünde. Renamed Jüdischer Kulturbund in Deutschland in early 1939, the Kulturbund published the only remaining Jewish periodical in Germany (*Jüdisches Nachrichtenblatt*) and was merged into the Reichsvereinigung in September 1941.

See Alan E. Steinweis. "Hans Hinkel and German Jewry, 1933–1941," *LBIYB* 38 (1993): 209–20.

League of Nations Formed in the aftermath of World War I and based on the clauses of the Versailles Treaty signed by Germany and on similar treaties signed by the other defeated nations, the league represented an international project to prevent military confrontations and to ensure international stability through collective security. Promoted by U.S. president Woodrow Wilson (ironically, the United States never became a member state) and with its seat in Geneva, the league originally (1920) comprised forty-five nations that had either been affiliated with the Entente Powers (the victorious alliance led by Great Britain, France, and, after 1917, the United States) or had remained neutral in the conflict. Germany joined as a permanent member in 1925. As part of the league issuing mandates to member countries for the purpose of administering territories ceded by Germany and Turkey, in 1920 Britain became the mandate power over Palestine. The league took an active interest in the protection of minority rights, including civil rights for Jews, but could not override the sovereign powers claimed by its member states. Attempts to negotiate disarmament agreements failed in the face of aggressive territorial expansion projects staged by Japan, Italy, and later Germany. Germany left the league at the end of 1933. Powerless to prevent another world war, the league was officially succeeded by the United Nations in April 1946.

See Carol Fink, *Defending the Rights of Others: The Great Powers, the Jews and International Minority Protection, 1878–1938* (Cambridge: Cambridge University Press, 2004).

Lessler, Toni (1874–1952) A social worker and educator who ran a Montessori school in Berlin-Grunewald before emigrating to the United States after "*Kristallnacht*." She later opened a language school in the vicinity of New York City.

Maier, Ruth (1920–1942) The daughter of assimilated Jewish parents living in Vienna; her father died in 1933. Having experienced *Anschluss* and "*Kristallnacht*" in Austria, Ruth's sister Judith (b. 1922) left for England in December 1938 while Ruth escaped to Norway in January 1939. Unable to join her sister and mother (who fled to England in April 1939), Ruth was deported from German-occupied Norway together with more than five hundred Jews in late November 1942 and murdered on her arrival in Auschwitz. Ruth Maier's diaries attest to her great sensitivity in observing outside events and to her literary skills.

See Ruth Maier. "*Das Leben könnte gut sein*": *Tagebücher 1933 bis 1942*, ed. Jan Erik Vold. Stuttgart: DVA, 2008.

Maybaum, Ignaz (1897–1976) A World War I veteran in the Austrian army and rabbi for several Jewish Reform communities throughout Germany prior to and during the Third Reich. Arrested for some time in 1935, in 1939 Maybaum managed to escape the Reich for England, where he resumed his rabbinical work. In the postwar era he controversially claimed that God had brought about the Holocaust to punish Jews for the sins of mankind.

See Steven T. Katz, Shlomo Biderman, and Gershon Greenberg, eds., *Wrestling with God: Jewish Theological Responses to the Holocaust during and after the Holocaust* (Oxford: Oxford University Press, 2007), 401–8.

"Mischling" (pl.: *"Mischlinge"*; "mixed breed") A racial category rooted in nineteenth-century biological thinking and formally introduced into the Third Reich's anti-Jewish politics with the issuing of the Nuremberg Laws. *"Mischling"* was meant to designate an individual of both "Aryan" and "non-Aryan," particularly Jewish, descent; if that person's parents were married, their union would be considered a "mixed marriage" (*"Mischehe"*). The Nuremberg Laws divided *"Mischlinge"* into distinct categories and criminalized sexual contacts between "Aryans" and Jews (*"Rassenschande"*) in order to prevent the birth of "mixed breeds." This group's fate was the subject of intense, yet inconclusive, debates within and between Nazi Party and state agencies until the end of the war. During the war, especially in German-occupied Eastern Europe, *"Mischlinge"* were to a large degree treated like Jews and targeted for murder as part of the "final solution."

See Beate Meyer, *"Jüdische Mischlinge": Rassenpolitik und Verfolgungserfahrung, 1933–1945* (Hamburg: Doelling & Galitz, 1999); Jeremy Noakes, "The Development of Nazi Policy towards the German-Jewish '*Mischlinge*,' 1933–1945," *LBIYB* 34 (1989): 291–354.

Moses, Julius (1868–1942) A physician by training and, during the Weimar period, a member of the Reichstag for the Social Democratic Party of Germany. Moses disagreed with many of the proposed Nazi medical policies and was forced to retreat into private life in Berlin with Hitler's assumption of power. Moses had three children with his first wife, Gertrud Moritz. His son Erwin (1897–1976) left Germany for Palestine in May 1933 with his wife Trude and their two sons Gad (Gert, b. 1924) and Gil (Günther, b. 1927) and corresponded regularly with his father in Berlin. Moses's second son, Rudi (1898–1979), worked as a doctor until dismissed by the Nazis in 1933; in the summer of 1938, he escaped to the Philippines. Moses had a daughter, Vera (b. 1900), with his first wife, and a third son, Kurt (b. 1925), with his non-Jewish partner, Elfriede Nemitz (1893–1979). Kurt lived with his mother after the Nuremberg Laws forced the couple to separate. One day after his seventy-fourth birthday in July 1942, Julius Moses was deported to Theresienstadt, where he died a few months later. His former wife, Gertrud Moritz, and their daughter, Vera, were killed in 1942 after having been deported to Theresienstadt.

See Dieter Fricke, *Jüdisches Leben in Berlin und Tel Aviv 1933 bis 1939: Der Briefwechsel des ehemaligen Reichstagabgeordneten Dr. Julius Moses* (Hamburg: von Bockel, 1997); Kurt Nemitz, "Julius Moses: Arzt und Parlamentarier," *Jahrbuch des Landesarchivs Berlin* (2007): 135–49.

Nuremberg Laws Shorthand expression frequently used for the two basic pillars of Nazi antisemitic legislation—the Reich Citizenship Law (*Reichsbürgergesetz*) and the Law for the Protection of German Blood and German Honor (*Gesetz zum Schutze des deutschen*

Blutes und der deutschen Ehre)—promulgated, together with the Reich Flag Law (*Reichs-flaggengesetz*), on September 15, 1935, during the annual Nazi Party rally and a specially convened session of the Reichstag in Nuremberg, Franconia. The first law restricted citizenship (and thus full protection under the law) to those of "German or related blood," while the second measure proscribed marriage and sexual contact between this group and Jews. Subsequent regulations defined a "Jew" as someone with at least three Jewish grandparents (according to their religious affiliation) or someone descended from two Jewish grandparents who him- or herself practiced the Jewish religion or was married to a Jew. People with two Jewish grandparents, but without Jewish religious affiliations and not married to Jews, came to be defined as "*Mischlinge* of the first degree" (*Mischlinge ersten Grades*); persons with one Jewish grandfather or grandmother were labeled "*Mischlinge* of the second degree" (*Mischlinge zweiten Grades*). With later clauses added to facilitate the deportation, murder, and expropriation of German Jews, the Nuremberg Laws formed one of the basic laws of the Third Reich until its defeat in May 1945.

See Raul Hilberg, *The Destruction of the European Jews* (New Haven, CT: Yale University Press, 2003), 61–78; Karl A. Schleunes, ed., *Legislating the Holocaust: The Bernhard Loesener Memoirs and Supporting Documents* (Boulder, CO: Westview Press, 2001).

Ostjuden ("Eastern Jews") Prior to 1933, according to the prevailing image among the majority of German non-Jews as well as among German Jews, *Ostjuden* shared distinct characteristics, were less assimilated into the Gentile societies of Eastern Europe than their Western counterparts, practiced more traditional religious customs, and were recognizable by their outward appearance and (Yiddish) language. The real situation, however, in Eastern Europe as well as in Germany, with its sizeable number of Jewish foreigners—in mid-1933, roughly 20 percent of the approximately five hundred thousand Jews in Germany were foreign, and of these, more than 57 percent were Polish citizens—reflected a much more diverse image. Prior to 1933, the organizations of mainstream German Jewry such as the Centralverein tended to dissociate themselves from *Ostjuden* in the Reich in their attempt to stress their own German patriotism in the face of antisemitic allegations of disloyalty. German Zionists, by contrast, embraced the *Ostjuden* for their more developed Jewish identity and as allies in the struggle for control over Jewish communal institutions. In propagating a distilled stereotype of "the Jew," German antisemites relied heavily on a fictitious, highly racialized image of *Ostjuden* that reflected the economic, political, and social fears exploited by the Nazi movement. After 1933 *Ostjuden* were among the first targeted by the new regime's anti-Jewish measures; at the same time, organized German Jewry increasingly incorporated *Ostjuden* into their efforts to sustain Jewish life in Germany. With the beginning of World War II, *Ostjuden* in German-occupied Poland became the first victims of the evolving "final solution."

See Trude Maurer, "Ausländische Juden in Deutschland, 1933–1939," in *Die Juden im nationalsozialistischen Deutschland: The Jews in Nazi Germany, 1933–1943*, ed. Arnold Paucker, 189–210 (Tübingen: J. C. B. Mohr, 1986); Steven Aschheim, *Brothers and*

Strangers: The East European Jew in German and German-Jewish Consciousness, 1800–1923 (Madison: University of Wisconsin Press, 1982).

Palästina-Amt (Palestine Office) The German branch of the Jewish Agency for Palestine helped Jews prepare for and organize their emigration to Palestine. With its main office in Berlin, the Palästina-Amt maintained representatives in other cities throughout the Reich. In accordance with the requirements of British immigration policy, the Palästina-Amt offered advice, decided on emigration applications, and distributed certificates that permitted holders entry into Palestine. The organization thus played a key role in the successful emigration of more than forty thousand Jews out of Germany between 1933 and 1938. In the second half of the 1930s, the office struggled with a rapidly growing gap between rising demand and shrinking opportunities for emigration. In 1941, the Palästina-Amt was integrated into the Reichsvereinigung. Up to that time, roughly sixty-five thousand Jews had emigrated from the Reich, including from annexed Austria and Bohemia-Moravia, into Palestine; seventeen thousand more are estimated to have reached that destination illegally.

Palästina Treuhandstelle (Paltreu; Palestine Trustee Office) Established by a number of prominent Jewish bankers, including Max Warburg, as part of the Ha'avara Agreement, this organization held the assets of emigrating Jews in trusteeship, thereby minimizing some of the Nazi efforts to expropriate Jews. Due to currency restrictions imposed by the Nazi government on emigrants, most of these assets were paid back in the form of material goods.

"*Rassenschande*" ("race defilement") A key term for those in Nazi Germany who decried real or imagined sexual contact between "Aryans" and "non-Aryans" (especially Jews), viewing such contact as a moral and biological crime. The Nuremberg Laws provided the apparatus to make such relations punishable under the law.

Reichmann, Eva (née Jungmann; 1897–1999) In 1924, after earning her doctorate in philosophy, Reichmann began her career with the Centralverein as part of its team of advisors to the Jewish public, especially in matters regarding emigration. Based on her skills as a writer, she contributed regularly to the *CV-Zeitung* before accepting a seat on the editorial board of *Der Morgen*, which she retained until authorities shut down the monthly in the wake of "*Kristallnacht*." In 1930 she married Hans Reichmann, a colleague in the CV's Berlin head office, where she helped those seeking advice on problems of Jewish life in Nazi Germany. In early 1939 she escaped with her husband, first to the Netherlands, then to Great Britain, where she spent the rest of her life.

See Eva G. Reichmann, *Grösse und Verhängnis deutsch-jüdischer Existenz: Zeugnisse einer tragischen Begegnung* (Heidelberg: Verlag Lambert Schneider, 1974).

Reichmann, Hans (1900–1964) After gaining firsthand experience with the Centralverein's struggle against German antisemitism in the early 1920s in Upper Silesia, Reichmann joined the CV head office in Berlin in 1926 as syndic (*Syndikus*). Seeing the need for greater mass assistance in exposing the Nazi Party's aims and lies to the German public, Reichmann supported deploying new forms of agitation through the so-called Büro Wilhelmstrasse, which systematically collected all information available on Nazi activities. After Hitler's rise to power, Reichmann became one of the top CV functionaries, while writing frequently for the *CV-Zeitung* and traveling throughout the country to help those seeking advice. He continued these efforts until "*Kristallnacht*," when he was imprisoned at Sachsenhausen concentration camp. Following his release, he and his wife, Eva Reichmann, emigrated to the Netherlands before finally settling down in Great Britain in 1940.

See Hans Reichmann, *Deutscher Bürger und verfolgter Jude: Novemberpogrom und KZ Sachsenhausen 1937 bis 1939*, ed. Michael Wildt (Munich: R. Oldenbourg Verlag and Institut für Zeitgeschichte, 1998); Council of Jews from Germany, ed., *Zum Gedenken an Hans Reichmann* (London: Council of Jews from Germany, 1965).

Reichsbund jüdischer Frontsoldaten (RjF; Reich League of Jewish Frontline Soldiers) Formed in 1919 by Leo Löwenstein (1876–1956) in response to a new wave of antisemitism in Germany and as an expression of German Jews' contribution to the war effort, the RjF provided a sense of group identity, financial assistance, and medical services to its members, Jewish veterans of World War I. Sharing the Centralverein's ideological orientation, the organization retained its appeal even after 1933; in 1935, it had thirty thousand members organized in 16 regional and 350 local branches. The Reichsbund shielded many Jewish veterans and their families from the ill effects of Nazi legislation until the enactment of the Nuremberg Laws terminated earlier exemptions. The RjF also maintained a large-scale network of sports associations named (like the organization's journal) *Der Schild*. Like other German Jewish organizations, the Reichsbund was dissolved in the wake of "*Kristallnacht*."

See Ulrich Dunker, *Der Reichsbund jüdischer Frontsoldaten, 1919–1938: Geschichte eines jüdischen Abwehrvereins* (Düsseldorf: Droste, 1977).

Reichsmark (RM) Standard German currency between 1871 and 1945. Despite nominal growth of its exchange rate value during the prewar years of the Third Reich (in 1933, US$1 was worth RM 4.2; in 1938, it was worth RM 2.49), the RM declined in real value due to the Reich treasury's chronic shortage of hard foreign currency. Measures such as the "Reich flight tax" designed to remedy Germany's foreign currency crisis presented a major obstacle to Jews hoping to emigrate.

See J. Adam Tooze, *The Wages of Destruction: The Making and Breaking of the German Economy* (London: Allen Lane, 2006).

Reichstag The term refers to both the institution of the democratically elected German national parliament (established in 1871) and its physical location in Berlin next to the Brandenburg Gate. The Reichstag fire a month following Hitler's appointment as chancellor damaged the parliament house and gave the new regime a pretext for issuing the Reichstag Fire Decree and the subsequent *Ermächtigungsgesetz*. These measures destroyed the rights and freedoms guaranteed under the Weimar Republic's constitution. The Reichstag formally existed as a parliamentary institution devoid of all real political power until the end of the Nazi era: it was used to provide acclamation for the leadership's policy and as a forum for propagandistic grandstanding.

See Michael Cullen, *The German Reichstag between Monarchy and Federalism* (Berlin: Be.bra, 2004); Peter Hubert, *Uniformierter Reichstag: Die Geschichte der Pseudo-Volksvertretung, 1933–1945* (Düsseldorf: Droste, 1992).

Reichsverband christlich-deutscher Staatsbürger nichtarischer oder nicht rein arischer Abstammung e.V. (RVC; Reich Union of Christian-German Citizens of Non-Aryan or Not-Purely-Aryan Descent) Founded on July 20, 1933, this organization had branch offices throughout Germany and received support from groups within the Protestant and Catholic churches critical of the Nazi regime. The RVC provided its members, German Christians of Jewish descent, with financial, legal, and educational counseling and helped with emigration. In 1934 the organization changed its name to the Reichsverband der nichtarischen Christen (Reich Union of Non-Aryan Christians); in 1936 it added the prefix "Paulusbund." Following the Nuremberg Laws, which provided the legal basis for the concept of "*Mischlinge*," almost twenty thousand of the ninety thousand converts to Protestantism counted as "three-quarter Jews" or "full Jews"; among twenty-six thousand Catholics, six thousand fell into that category. Furthermore, forty-five thousand Protestants and thirteen thousand Catholics were deemed "*Mischlinge* of the first degree," and twenty-five thousand Protestants and seven thousand Catholics were deemed "*Mischlinge* of the second degree." In March 1937 the RVC was separated into a Vereinigung 1937 (for "*Mischlinge*") and a Büro Heinrich Spiro (for "full Jews"), named after the Reichsverband's director at the time. In the summer of 1939, the Büro Spiro was attached to the Protestant relief agency Büro Heinrich Grüber, while the Catholic Hilfswerk beim Bischöflichen Ordinariat Berlin continued the work of the St. Raphaelsverein and the Deutsche Caritasverband in catering to Catholic "full Jews." The Nazi regime disbanded the Vereinigung 1937 in August 1939 and the Büro Heinrich Grüber in early 1941.

See Werner Cohn, "Bearers of a Common Fate? The 'Non-Aryan' Christian 'Fate-Comrades' of the Paulus-Bund, 1933–1939," *LBIYB* 33 (1988): 327–66; Aleksandar-Saša Vuletić, *Christen jüdischer Herkunft im Dritten Reich: Verfolgung und organisierte Selbsthilfe, 1933–1939* (Mainz: Verlag Phillip von Zabern, 1999).

Reichsvereinigung der Juden in Deutschland (Reichsvereinigung; Reich Association of Jews in Germany) Gestapo-enforced successor organization to the Reichsvertretung, formally installed in July 1939. While it inherited many key officials from the Reichsvertretung, including Leo Baeck and Otto Hirsch, who could not or would not leave the country for a safe haven, the Reichsvereinigung became a tool for the administration and control of Jews remaining in Germany. Large-scale deportations of German Jews "to the East" started in November 1941; once the Reichsvereinigung had served the purpose set by the regime, it was dissolved in 1943 and its staff deported.

See Beate Meyer, "The Inevitable Dilemma: The Reich Association (Reichsvereinigung) of Jews in Germany, the Deportations, and the Jews Who Went Underground," in *On Germans and Jews under the Nazi Regime*, ed. Moshe Zimmermann, 297–312 (Jerusalem: Hebrew University Magnes Press, 2006).

Reichsvertretung der deutschen Juden (RV; Reich Representation of German Jews) Using the same name as a weaker body already in existence, the (new) Reichsvertretung was founded in September 1933 by a coalition of leading German Jewish functionaries, most prominent among them Leo Baeck (who subsequently served as the organization's president) and Otto Hirsch (its director). Intended as a coordinating umbrella organization for the many already established and newly founded German Jewish organizations in the Third Reich, the Reichsvertretung cooperated closely with the Centralverein, Jüdischer Frauenbund, Zionistische Vereinigung für Deutschland, Zentralausschuß der deutschen Juden für Hilfe und Aufbau, and others, as well as with Jewish organizations outside of Germany that provided a growing portion of its budget and assisted in its efforts to create opportunities for emigration. By 1935 the Reichsvertretung had become the core of the Jewish sector around which the works of other organizations increasingly gravitated. The Nuremberg Laws had an immediate effect on the organization's ability to protect Jews in Germany from persecution and resulted in the organization's stepping up its efforts to encourage emigration; the organization also changed its name to Reichsvertretung der Juden in Deutschland (Reich Representation of Jews in Germany). A significant percentage of the roughly 250,000 Jews that fled the Reich before the war did so with the help of the Reichsvertretung and its associated organizations, especially after the Jewish communities had lost their legally protected status in early 1938. The increasing pace of anti-Jewish persecution, the parallel disintegration of German Jewish structures, and criticism from within convinced Reichsvertretung leaders of the need to reorganize, which led to the formation of the more representative, yet ephemeral, Reichsverband. Further plans ended in November 1938 in the wave of violence, arrests, and closings of Jewish organizations triggered by "*Kristallnacht.*" While the regime demanded the reopening of the organization's offices soon after the pogrom, it had transformed the hitherto largely autonomous Reichsvertretung into the fully Gestapo-controlled Reichsvereinigung by the spring of 1939. Among the leaders of the organization murdered during the Holocaust were Cora Berliner, Otto Hirsch, Hannah Karminski, and Julius Seligsohn.

See Otto Dov Kulka, ed., *Deutsches Judentum unter dem Nationalsozialismus*, Bd. 1, *Dokumente zur Geschichte der Reichsvertretung der Juden, 1933–1939* (Tübingen: J. C. B. Mohr, 1997); Otto Dov Kulka and Esriel Hildesheimer, "The Central Organization of Jews in the Third Reich and Its Archives," *LBIYB* 34 (1989): 187–201; Herbert A. Strauss, "Jewish Autonomy within the Limits of National Socialist Policy: The Communities and the Reichsvertretung," in *Die Juden im nationalsozialistischen Deutschland: The Jews in Nazi Germany, 1933–1945*, ed. Arnold Paucker, 125–52 (Tübingen: J. C. B. Mohr, 1986).

Rosenberg, Kurt (1900–1977) Kurt Rosenberg practiced law in his native Hamburg for a number of years until dismissed on the basis of the 1933 anti-Jewish Civil Service Law. In his diaries he describes his reactions to the worsening conditions in Nazi Germany for Jews. Rosenberg emigrated to the United States in 1938 with his wife.

Rosenheim, Käthe (1882–1980) A German Jewish professional social worker and women's rights activist since before World War I, Rosenheim worked as the personal secretary to the Prussian minister of the interior, as well as for the Berlin police administration in the years leading up to 1933. After her dismissal from public service by the Nazis, she became active in the Jüdischer Frauenbund and the Reichsvertretung, where she directed its office in charge of Jewish children's emigration. On several occasions Rosenheim accompanied departing children to the United States and Britain. In 1941 she emigrated to the United States, where she renewed her career in social work.

See Gudrun Maierhof, *Selbstbehauptung im Chaos: Frauen in der jüdischen Selbsthilfe, 1933–1943* (Frankfurt: Campus, 2002), 204–6.

SA (Sturmabteilung; Storm Division) As the paramilitary wing of the Nazi Party, the SA, formed in 1921, initially comprised mainly German World War I veterans, militia members, and others opposed to both the democratic Weimar Republic and the Nazi Party's main competitor for mass support, the Communist Party. With the advent of the Great Depression, the SA attracted many new members, growing from seventy-seven thousand (in 1931) to roughly seven hundred thousand men in 1933. Its terror tactics against opponents—politicians on the Left as well as Jews and others outside the spectrum of the *Volksgemeinschaft*—increased the public visibility of the Nazi movement, both before and after Hitler's coming to power. Once the Nazi regime was established, it began to perceive the potentially disruptive tactics of the SA as a threat. Hitler acquiesced in the murder of the SA's top leadership in June 1934 (variously known as the "Röhm Purge" or "Night of the Long Knives"), carried out primarily by the SS. The SS, previously a part of the SA, now relegated that organization to a Nazi Party agency of secondary importance.

See Richard Bessel, *Political Violence and the Rise of Nazism: The Stormtroopers in Eastern Germany, 1925–1934* (New Haven, CT: Yale University Press, 1984).

Saar An industrial region in southwestern Germany, also referred to as Saarland or, in French, Sarre. France administered the Saar after World War I under a mandate issued by the League of Nations. Until its reincorporation into Germany in early 1935, the region served as a source of contention for *völkisch* groups in their condemnation of the Versailles Treaty. After Hitler's rise to power, it became a temporary place of refuge for opponents of the regime until the Saar's population decided overwhelmingly in a referendum on January 13, 1935, to return the region to the Reich, which was done on March 1, 1935.

Schacht, Hjalmar (1877–1970) A prominent German banker and chief financial functionary for both the Weimar Republic and the Third Reich, Schacht had since

1930 provided major support to the Nazi Party. He was rewarded by Hitler in March 1933 with the position of president of the German national bank (Reichsbank), a position that he had already held from 1924 to 1930; in addition, he became Reich economics minister from July 1934 to November 1937. Schacht served as one of the primary architects of the Third Reich's armament-oriented economy and of the "Aryanization" of Jewish businesses, while opposing measures that jeopardized controlled economic transformation. After his dismissal as Reichsbank president in early 1939, Schacht grew disaffected with the regime but never joined the opposition. Although found innocent of war crimes by the International Military Tribunal at Nuremberg in 1945, he was convicted on separate charges by an independent German court and served a prison term until 1950.

See Albert Fischer, *Hjalmar Schacht und Deutschlands "Judenfrage": Der "Wirtschafts-diktator" und die Vertreibung der Juden aus der deutschen Wirtschaft* (Cologne: Böhlau Verlag, 1995).

Schächten (Hebrew: *shechitah*) An essential component of Jewish dietary law, *shechitah* designates the slaughter of animals for food by a trained specialist, or *shohet*. Antisemites had since the nineteenth century agitated against *Schächten*, which they linked to the alleged "ritual slaughter" of Christian children ("blood libel"). Already outlawed in parts of Germany before 1933, it was abolished by the Nazi regime early on under the pretext of animal protection. The prohibition of *Schächten* first in the Reich and subsequently in other German-controlled countries posed serious problems for Jews who sought to maintain traditional practices in daily life.

See David Charles Kramer, *Jewish Eating and Identity through the Ages* (New York: Routledge, 2009).

Schoeps, Hans-Joachim (1909–1980) A staunch German nationalist and religiously minded Jew, Schoeps founded the Deutscher Vortrupp Gefolgschaft deutscher Juden in 1933. A numerically small organization, it agitated for a German Jewish revival based on a diffuse blend of authoritarian leadership, ill-defined Jewish sentiment, and disassociation from Zionists and *Ostjuden*. To spread his ideas Schoeps founded the Vortrupp-Verlag, one of several Jewish publishing houses active during the first years of the Third Reich. In line with its increasing suppression of Jewish "assimilationists," the Gestapo dissolved the Vortrupp in 1935; Schoeps emigrated to Sweden in 1938 and returned to Germany in 1946.

See Hans-Joachim Schoeps, *Bereit für Deutschland: Der Patriotismus deutscher Juden und der Nationalsozialismus* (Berlin: Haude & Spenersche, 1979).

Schönewald, Ottilie (1883–1961) A social worker by profession, Schönewald became active in the German Jewish women's movement and joined the Jüdischer Frauenbund in 1929, which she headed beginning in 1934. One of the few women within the leadership circles of organized German Jewry, she and her family fled in 1938, first to Holland, then to England, where she later led the Association of Jewish Refugees. After moving to the United States in 1946, she remained active in Jewish organizational work until her death in Chicago.

See Gudrun Maierhof, *Selbstbehauptung im Chaos: Frauen in der jüdischen Selbsthilfe, 1933–1943* (Frankfurt am Main: Campus, 2001), 87–92, 344–45; Marion A. Kaplan, *The Jewish Feminist Movement in Germany: The Campaigns of the Jüdischer Frauenbund, 1904–1938* (Westport, CT: Greenwood Press, 1979).

Schutzhaft ("protective custody") Initially employed in Germany in the second half of the nineteenth century for the purpose of putting down militant opposition, *Schutzhaft* became most infamous for its endemic use after 1933 against opponents of the Nazi regime. In late July 1933 more than twenty-six thousand persons were placed in custody under *Schutzhaft*, especially in concentration camps, but also in police prisons and jails. From early 1938 onwards, the Gestapo had a monopoly on employing *Schutzhaft* and used it widely to stifle dissent and implement the Third Reich's racial and social policies.

SS (Schutzstaffel; Protective Squadron) Established in 1925 as a protective service for prominent NSDAP functionaries (most notably Hitler), the SS grew under the stewardship of Heinrich Himmler into one of the most important tools for maintaining the regime's grip on political power through suppression and terror directed against real or imagined internal "enemies of the Reich." Many of these enemies landed in concentration camps run by the SS. Though a party branch, it increasingly overlapped with state agencies such as the Gestapo and other parts of the police subordinated to Himmler. In 1940 it added a military wing, the Waffen-SS. Himmler's apparatus, which by the war's end comprised more than one million men in a range of different agencies, played a key role in planning and implementing the genocide of European Jewry.

See Heinz Höhne, *The Order of the Death's Head: The Story of Hitler's SS* (New York: Coward-McCann, 1970).

Solmitz, Luise (née Stephan; 1889–1973) A native of Hamburg, Solmitz worked as a high school teacher and later married Friedrich Wilhelm (Fredy) Solmitz (1877–1961), an engineer and flight officer in the German army during World War I. Because Fredy was Jewish and Luise was not, the Nazi regime regarded their marriage as a "mixed marriage" ("*Mischehe*"); accordingly, their daughter, Gisela (b. 1920), became labeled first as a "non-Aryan," then, after the passage of the Nuremberg Laws, as a "*Mischling* of the first degree." As a partner in a mixed marriage with a child who had not been brought up as a Jew, Fredy was not deported during the war. The family lived in a small villa in Hamburg's Kippingstrasse 12, where after 1939 other Hamburg Jews were forced to move in an attempt to concentrate the remaining German Jews in so-called Jew houses (*Judenhäuser*).

See Richard Evans, "The Diaries of Luise Solmitz," in *Histories of Women, Tales of Gender*, ed. Willem de Blécourt, 207–19 (Amsterdam: AMB Press, 2008).

Stahl, Heinrich (1886–1942) Head of the Jewish community of Berlin, the largest in Germany, following the Nazi takeover in 1933. Although Stahl was an original member of the Reichsvertretung and on its governing board, he opposed attempts to centralize German Jewish organizational structures, which he saw as detrimental to the interests of his community, until the late 1930s. He was deported to Theresienstadt in June 1942, where he died six months later.

See Beate Meyer and Herman Simon, eds., *Juden in Berlin, 1938–1945* (Berlin: Philo Verlag, 2000).

Streicher, Julius (1885–1946) A schoolteacher from Bavaria, Streicher was actively involved in the *völkisch* movement before joining the NSDAP in 1922. He became editor of the Nazi Party newspaper *Der Stürmer* in 1923, and from 1925 he also served as Nazi regional party head (Gauleiter) in Franconia. Until the collapse of the Third Reich, *Der Stürmer*, a highly publicized weekly periodical, served as an outlet for the dissemination of the most rabid antisemitic propaganda. Tried at the International Military Tribunal at Nuremberg in October 1945, Streicher was found guilty and sentenced to death.

See Dennis Showalter, *Little Man, What Now? Der Stürmer in the Weimar Republic* (Hamden: Archon, 1982).

Verband nationaldeutscher Juden (VndJ; Association of National German Jews) Established in 1921 by Max Naumann (1875–1939), the VndJ outdid the mainstream Centralverein, as well as the Reichsbund jüdischer Frontsoldaten on the right end of the political spectrum, in its unflinching support for German nationalist goals domestically and internationally. The Verband hoped after 1933 to have found an ally in the new regime, with its anti-leftist agenda. Fiercely anti-Zionist, the Verband also antagonized most German Jewish leaders due to its opposition to the Reichsvertretung and was abolished by the Gestapo in 1935.

See Carl J. Rheins, "The Verband nationaldeutscher Juden, 1921–1933," *LBIYB* 25 (1980): 243–68; Matthias Hambrock, *Die Etablierung der Außenseiter: Der Verband nationaldeutscher Juden, 1921–1935* (Cologne: Böhlau Verlag, 2003).

Versailles Treaty Drafted by the victors in World War I and signed by Reich officials amid widespread German protests in June 1919, the Versailles Treaty laid out the conditions of the German defeat. The treaty imposed harsh financial sanctions, territorial demands, and military limitations on Germany, which fueled the *völkisch* movement that undermined the troubled democratic Weimar Republic. Many blamed the treaty's provisions for having provided the essential precondition for the NSDAP's success, but other domestic factors also proved critical in contributing to the demise of Germany's democracy.

See Conan Fisher and Alan Sharp, *After the Versailles Treaty: Enforcement, Compliance, Contested Identities* (London: Routledge, 2008).

Völkisch ("folkish") German nationalists appropriated this term in the nineteenth century to express their aspirations for a racially and socially homogeneous society (*Volksgemeinschaft*). They sought an antidote to what they perceived as leftist or liberal ideals of justice and equality for diverse communities. Starting in the 1920s the *völkisch* movement formed an important element of the hodgepodge of German right-wing, antidemocratic political groups and provided a central element of Nazi ideology.

See Michael Burleigh and Wolfgang Wippermann, *The Racial State: Germany, 1933–1945* (Cambridge: Cambridge University Press, 1991).

Völkischer Beobachter The official paper of the Nazi Party, it was created in 1920 and printed daily from 1923 until the collapse of the Third Reich in 1945. After 1933 the newspaper was published in different regional versions; at its peak in 1944, its circulation was estimated at over one million copies.

Volksgemeinschaft Beyond its literal meaning, "people's community," during the Third Reich the term denoted the utopian idea of a homogenous social and racial body of persons of "Aryan" descent integrated by Nazi principles of leadership (Führer). Like much of the regime's vernacular, the concept of *Volksgemeinschaft* had deep roots in German history and was popular among a broad spectrum of political groups, especially right-wing nationalists. In an attempt to garner support for the party in its formative years, Nazi propaganda claimed that a *Volksgemeinschaft* would remedy all social ills and form the basis for Germany's rise as a world power. Once in power, the Nazi regime evoked *Volksgemeinschaft* repeatedly in its propaganda around racial policy.

See David Welch, "Nazi Propaganda and the *Volksgemeinschaft*: Constructing a People's Community," *Journal of Contemporary History* 39 (2004): 213–38.

Warburg, Max M. (1867–1946) A German Jewish banker from Hamburg, activist, philanthropist, and member of the German delegation to the Versailles Peace Conference in 1919. During the Weimar Republic, in addition to his role in politics (advisor to the German government on reparation issues) and finance (board member of the German national bank), Warburg became one of the Hilfsverein's leading functionaries. After Hitler's coming to power terminated his participation in the public sector, Warburg was involved in the founding of the Reichsvertretung and accepted a leading position in the Zentralausschuß der deutschen Juden für Hilfe und Aufbau. After his banking business had been "Aryanized" in 1938, he emigrated to Great Britain before settling in the United States in 1939.

See A. J. Sherman, "A Jewish Bank during the Schacht Era: M. M. Warburg & Co., 1933–1938," in *Die Juden im nationalsozialistischen Deutschland: The Jews in Nazi Germany, 1933–1943*, ed. Arnold Paucker, 167–72 (Tübingen: J. C. B. Mohr, 1986).

Weimar Republic German federal democracy formed at the end of World War I and named after the city in which the national constitution was adopted in February 1919. The functioning of the democratic political system rested on the three major parties in the federal parliament (Reichstag)—the Social Democratic Party, the German Democratic Party, and the Center Party—that formed government coalitions, as well as on the constitutional authorities of the Reich president, among them executive powers in emergencies. Following a phase of relative internal stability, starting in 1929 the Weimar Republic underwent a massive crisis triggered by the worldwide economic downturn. Elite manipulations of the republic's constitution, combined with the economic crisis, produced the rapid erosion of political support for democratic parties. Against this backcloth, conservative elites negotiated Hitler's appointment as chancellor on January 30, 1933.

See Detlev J. K. Peukert, *The Weimar Republic: The Crisis of Classical Modernity* (New York: Hill and Wang, 1993).

Weltsch, Robert (1891–1982) A leading Austrian-German Zionist who, after World War I, became editor in chief of the *Jüdische Rundschau*, the official newspaper of the Zionistische Vereinigung für Deutschland. A prolific writer and journalist, he published his best-known editorial in early 1933, "Tragt ihn mit Stolz, den Gelben Fleck" ("Wear the Yellow Badge with Pride"), in response to the Nazi anti-Jewish boycott call of April 1. Weltsch emigrated first to Palestine, where he started a new German-language newspaper (*Jüdische Welt-Rundschau*). After the war Weltsch went to England and helped found the Leo Baeck Institute in 1955, for which he edited the *LBIYB* as well as numerous anthologies.

See Christian Wiese, "The Janus Face of Nationalism: The Ambivalence of Robert Weltsch and Hans Kohn," *LBIYB* 51 (2006): 103–30.

Wise, Stephen Samuel (1874–1949) A rabbi in New York City and American Zionist leader who forged a number of relationships with key policy makers, particularly within the Roosevelt administration. Wise became president of the American Jewish Congress in 1933 and of the World Jewish Congress three years later. In this capacity he orchestrated the boycott of German products in the United States. Wise attempted to increase the number of Jewish refugees allowed into the United States and, after the beginning of the war, to alert the American public to Nazi plans to exterminate European Jewry.

See Stephen Samuel Wise, *Challenging Years: The Autobiography of Stephen Wise* (New York: Putnam's Sons, 1949).

World Jewish Congress (WJC) The WJC was founded in 1936 in Geneva for the purpose of representing Jewry on an international level, regardless of political persuasion. Its first president was New York rabbi and activist Stephen Wise, who headed a similar body (the American Jewish Congress) beginning in 1933. The WJC staged numerous demonstrations against Nazi Germany and worked to solve the Jewish refugee crisis prior to and during World War II. Throughout the postwar period, the organization continued its relief efforts and also assisted in bringing Nazi war criminals to justice.

See World Jewish Congress, *Unity in Dispersion: A History of the World Jewish Congress* (New York: Institute of Jewish Affairs of the World Jewish Congress, 1948); Richard

Breitman and Alan M. Kraut, *American Refugee Policy and European Jewry, 1933–1945* (Bloomington: Indiana University Press, 1987).

Zentralausschuss der deutschen Juden für Hilfe und Aufbau (ZAHA; Central Committee of the German Jews for Help and Reconstruction) A German Jewish relief organization founded in April 1933 to facilitate interagency cooperation between the Centralverein, Jüdischer Frauenbund, Reichsbund jüdischer Frontsoldaten, and the Zionistische Vereinigung für Deutschland in providing social and economic help. The committee worked in close association with the Reichsvertretung, especially to foster the educational and vocational training of Jewish youth. ZAHA became part of the Reichsvertretung in 1935 and, like many other remaining Jewish organizations, was merged into the Gestapo-controlled Reichsvereinigung following *"Kristallnacht."*

See Salomon Adler-Rudel, *Jüdische Selbsthilfe unter dem Naziregime 1933–1939 im Spiegel der Berichte der Reichsvertretung der deutschen Juden* (Tübingen: J. C. B. Mohr, 1974).

Zertifikate ("certificates") In order to enter British-administered Palestine (see *Aliyah*), Jewish refugees needed entry permits from the British authorities, which in Germany were issued by the Palästina-Amt. These "Palestine Certificates" were divided into five categories to reflect the vocation, age group, and familial relation of their holders. One category allowed for the immigration of so-called capitalists, persons who arrived in Palestine with a minimum of £1,000; this category became important for emigration based on the Ha'avara Agreement.

See Bernard Wasserstein, *Britain and the Jews of Europe, 1939–1945* (London: Leicester University Press, 1999).

Zionistische Vereinigung für Deutschland (ZVfD; Zionist Association for Germany) The ZVfD was established in 1897, one year after the publication of Theodor Herzl's *Der Judenstaat*, and despite its small membership (between 1921 and 1932 it had on average around 17,500 members), it formed an important faction within the World Zionist Organization. Ideological clashes with mainstream German Jewish organizations such as the Centralverein and the Reichsbund jüdischer Frontsoldaten stemming from the ZVfD's agitation for *Aliyah* to Palestine, as well as the ZVfD's growing appeal to *Ostjuden* in Germany, increased the visibility of the organization and its influence within Jewish communities. After 1933 the ZVfD tried to gain concessions from the Nazi regime for increased Jewish emigration to Palestine (see Ha'avara Agreement, Palästina-Amt) while joining mainstream organizations within the Reichsvertretung in order to improve the lot of Jews remaining in Germany. The ZVfD's weekly *Jüdische Rundschau*, edited by Robert Weltsch, had a wide readership within and beyond the Reich. Nazi authorities abolished the ZVfD in the wake of *"Kristallnacht,"* a fate shared by most other Jewish organizations in Germany.

See Hagit Lavsky, *Before Catastrophe: The Distinctive Path of German Zionism* (Detroit, MI: Wayne State University Press, 1996); Francis R. Nicosia, *Zionism and Anti-Semitism in Nazi Germany* (Cambridge: Cambridge University Press, 2008).

CHRONOLOGY

THE DATES LISTED below form but a small selection of events impacting the life of Jews in Germany between 1933 and early 1939. This chronology is meant to provide additional context for the sources presented in this volume; it is neither comprehensive (especially in terms of anti-Jewish laws and regulations enacted in Nazi Germany) nor a substitute for integrated studies of the period like those referenced in this volume's chapters and bibliography.

1933

January 30, 1933: Reich President **Paul von Hindenburg** appoints Adolf Hitler as Reich chancellor in a coalition government. Among the members of Hitler's cabinet are initially only two Nazi Party officials, **Wilhelm Frick** as Reich interior minister and **Hermann Göring** as Reich minister without portfolio in addition to his appointment as Prussian interior minister (until May 1933; after April 1933, Prussian prime minister) and chief of the Prussian police, including the **Gestapo** (until November 1934).

February 1, 1933: Hindenburg dissolves the **Reichstag**; election is set for March 5.

February 4, 1933: Hindenburg issues the Regulation for the Protection of the German People (*Verordnung zum Schutze des deutschen Volkes*) allowing restrictions of personal rights and freedoms.

February 28, 1933: Following an arson attack on the Reichstag building on February 27, Hindenburg issues the Regulation for the Protection of the People and the State (*Verordnung zum Schutze von Volk und Staat*), which allows further restrictions of personal rights and freedoms, including "protective custody" (*Schutzhaft*), first in Prussia, then after March 5 in the other German states as well.

March 5, 1933: Reichstag elections are held; Hitler's NSDAP gets 43.9 percent of the popular vote, partly resulting from a massive propaganda campaign and intimidation by the **SA** and other Nazi Party organizations.

March 6/7, 1933: Local Nazi Party activists start a wave of anti-Jewish attacks, especially boycotts of Jewish businesses and assaults on Jewish lawyers, in Berlin and the Rhine-Ruhr area, then later also in Chemnitz (March 9), Breslau (March 12), Gleiwitz (March 27), Görlitz (March 28), and other German cities. These attacks continue with varying intensity at the local and regional level until early July 1933.

March 8, 1933: Reich Interior Minister Frick announces the creation of concentration camps for political prisoners and persons taken into "protective custody." That same month, the first prisoners start being transferred to camps at Dachau (near Munich), Oranienburg (near Berlin), and a range of other places, mostly on the basis of initiatives by local and regional party functionaries.

March 13, 1933: **Joseph Goebbels** is appointed Reich minister for popular enlightenment and propaganda (Reichsminister für Volksaufklärung und Propaganda).

March 17, 1933: **Hjalmar Schacht** is appointed president of the German National Bank (Reichsbank).

March 21, 1933: The newly elected Reichstag opens.

March 23, 1933: Representatives of all Reichstag parties—with the exception of the Social Democratic Party delegates, who oppose the measure—provide the required two-thirds majority to pass the Enabling Act (*Ermächtigungsgesetz*, or *Gesetz zur Behebung der Not von Volk und Reich*), which, despite a term limit of four years and assurances from the government to observe constitutional guarantees, effectively provides the basis for Hitler's dictatorship.

March 25, 1933: A group of German Jewish leaders, including **Julius Brodnitz**, meets with Göring to discuss the public protests against Nazi measures in the United States and other countries. In late March, many German Jewish organizations, including the **Centralverein deutscher Staatsbürger jüdischen Glaubens** (CV) and the **Zionistische Vereinigung für Deutschland** (ZVfD), publish appeals to Jews abroad to refrain from "anti-German demonstrations"; at the same time, these organizations intervene with German government agencies against anti-Jewish agitation and discriminatory actions in Germany.

March 28, 1933: The Nazi newspaper *Völkischer Beobachter* publishes an anti-Jewish boycott call. A specially appointed boycott committee, initiated by Hitler and headed by **Julius Streicher**, is established to organize regional and local actions.

March 29, 1933: German Jewish community leaders headed by **Leo Baeck** send a letter to Hitler protesting the anti-Jewish boycott call.

April 1, 1933: Under the official leadership of Streicher's committee, the SA and other Nazi organizations conduct boycott actions against Jewish businesses, doctors, and lawyers throughout Germany.

April 4, 1933: The **Reichsbund jüdischer Frontsoldaten** (RjF) appeals in a letter to Hitler against hardships facing Jewish veterans and their families as a result of anti-Jewish agitation.

April 7, 1933: The Law for the Restoration of the Professional Civil Service (*Gesetz zur Wiederherstellung des Berufsbeamtentums*), or Civil Service Law, calls, among other things, for the forced retirement of officials "not of **Aryan** extraction" with the exception for World War I veterans and their relatives. The Law for Admission as a Professional Lawyer (*Gesetz über die Zulassung zur Rechtsanwaltschaft*) facilitates the withdrawal of permission to work as a lawyer from a person of "non-Aryan extraction."

April 11, 1933: The first supplementary decree (*Durchführungsverordnung*) to the Civil Service Law defines as "non-Aryan" any person "who descends from non-Aryan, especially Jewish, parents or grandparents." Subsequently, this "Aryan clause" is increasingly adopted by private businesses, organizations, sports clubs, and so forth, throughout the German economy and society to exclude persons labeled as Jews.

April 13, 1933: German Jewish organizations found the **Zentralausschuß der deutschen Juden für Hilfe und Aufbau** (ZAHA; Central Committee of the German Jews for Help and Reconstruction) to coordinate relief work.

April 21, 1933: The Germany-wide Law on the Slaughter of Animals (*Gesetz über das Schlachten von Tieren*) outlaws the butchering of animals according to Jewish religious laws (**Schächten**; *shechitah*), which had previously already been disallowed in individual German states.

April 22, 1933: A new law (*Gesetz über die Bildung von Studentenschaften*) excludes Jews from membership in university student fraternities.

April 22, 1933: A new regulation (*Verordnung über die Zulassung von Ärzten zur Tätigkeit in den Krankenkassen*) terminates the admission of "non-Aryan" doctors (except war veterans) to the health-insurance-covered treatment of "Aryan" patients.

April 25, 1933: The Law against Overcrowding German Schools and Universities (*Gesetz gegen die Überfüllung deutscher Schulen und Hochschulen*) introduces a *numerus clausus* of a maximum of 5 percent for Jewish students. Exemptions for the families of war veterans protect roughly 75 percent of Jewish students.

May 10, 1933: Nazi activists organize public book burnings in many German cities and the screening of libraries for books written by leftist, pacifist, and Jewish authors.

May 17, 1933: A Jewish committee (Comité des Délégations Juives) submits the so-called Bernheim Petition to the **League of Nations** in Geneva regarding Jewish minority rights in Upper Silesia, a region in eastern Germany protected by international agreements until May 1937.

May 29, 1933: The first public statement is made by the association of German Jewish communal bodies (Reichsvertretung der jüdischen Landesverbände) protesting as a representative body against the denouncing of Jews in Germany and the danger of their loss of rights. On June 6, 1933, the protest is sent to Hitler.

June 16, 1933: The founding of the **Kulturbund deutscher Juden** creates an umbrella organization for Jewish cultural activities that caters to exclusively Jewish audiences, first in Berlin and later in many other German cities.

June 21, 1933: A proclamation by the ZVfD regarding the status of Jews "in the new German state" stresses its hope for a viable relationship between the Jewish and the German people.

June 30, 1933: According to official U.S. immigration statistics and based on the immigration laws of 1921 and 1924, which established maximum annual levels of immigration from each European country (quotas) as well as various qualifications for immigrants, between July 1, 1932 and June 30, 1933 a total of 2,372 Jewish immigrants were admitted to the United States, 3.04 percent of whom were German Jews.[1]

July 6, 1933: In a speech to his representatives in the German states (*Reichsstatthalter*), Hitler declares the Nazi "revolution" to be over and announces a shift toward further "evolution" of its principles.

July 14, 1933: The Law for the Prevention of Hereditarily Sick Offspring (*Gesetz zur Verhütung erbkranken Nachwuchses*) allows the compulsory sterilization of persons deemed hereditarily ill. Up to the end of the war, roughly four hundred thousand persons, including Jews, Sinti, and Roma, are sterilized under that law in Germany and the annexed territories.

July 14, 1933: The Law for Revoking Naturalizations and Withdrawing German Citizenship (*Gesetz über den Widerruf von Einbürgerungen und die Aberkennung der deutschen Staatsangehörigkeit*) allows the denaturalization of persons who became German citizens during the years of the **Weimar Republic**. The law and a decree, enacted July 26, 1933, is subsequently used especially against *Ostjuden*.

August 25, 1933: Representatives of Jewish organizations in Palestine and of the German government sign the **Ha'avara Agreement**, which facilitates the immigration of Jews to Palestine in combination with the transfer of funds from Germany to Palestine.

---

1. These and the following immigration figures for the United States are from *AJYB* for the years 1934–1935 to 1940–1941.

September 8, 1933: In a letter to the German Industrial and Trade Association (Deutscher Industrie- und Handelstag), Reich Economics Minister Kurt P. Schmitt claims his ministry does not differentiate between "Aryan" and "non-Aryan" businesses and stresses the damaging effect of anti-Jewish boycott actions on the German economy.

September 17, 1933: The **Reichsvertretung der deutschen Juden** is founded as the central organization of most major Jewish communal bodies and organizations in Germany. Leo Baeck becomes the organization's president, and **Otto Hirsch**, its director.

September 22, 1933: The Reich Culture Chamber Law (*Reichskulturkammergesetz*) excludes Jews from membership in professional arts associations.

October 14, 1933: The German government leaves both the League of Nations and the international disarmament conference.

November 12, 1933: The Reichstag elections, after the disallowance of all other political parties, give Hitler's NSDAP 92.2 percent (turnout 95.2 percent) of the votes. A simultaneously held referendum confirms Germany's withdrawal from the League of Nations and the international disarmament conference, with 95.1 percent voting yes, and 4.9 percent voting no (turnout 96.3 percent).

November 24, 1933: A regulation is passed by the Reich Labor Ministry against the laying off of Jewish employees in private companies. The regulation also confirms the nonexistence of "exclusionary laws" (*Ausnahmegesetze*) aimed against Jews; a similar decree is issued on January 17, 1934, by the Reich Interior Ministry. In reality, however, Jewish businesses and employees are discriminated against to varying degrees all across Germany on a daily basis.

December 16, 1933: A circular by the Reich Economics Ministry demands noninterference with Jewish businesses during the Christmas shopping season.

1934

January 24, 1934: A new national labor law (*Gesetz zur Ordnung der nationalen Arbeit*) excludes Jewish employees from holding leading positions in German firms and from membership in the German Labor Front (Deutsche Arbeitsfront)

February 26, 1934: The German army (Reichswehr) implements the "Aryan clause" of the Civil Service Law, which leads to the dismissal of roughly 70 servicemen, despite protests from the Reichsbund jüdischer Frontsoldaten to Reich President Hindenburg.

April 20, 1934: Göring appoints **Heinrich Himmler** as Gestapo head in Prussia.

May 1, 1934: Streicher's *Der Stürmer* publishes a special issue on "ritual murder." The Reichsvertretung had already protested against publication of this issue to the Reich Interior Ministry on April 26.

May 15, 1934: The Reichsvertretung (Baeck, Hirsch) writes a letter to Goebbels protesting against his May 11 speech blaming Jews for anti-German boycotts abroad.

May 18, 1934: An amendment to the existing law regarding the "Reich flight tax" (*Reichsfluchtsteuer*) reduces the amount exempt from taxation that émigrés are allowed to take out of the country from RM 200,000 to RM 50,000. On June 23, 1934, the amount of foreign currency that can be exchanged by persons emigrating is reduced from RM 10,000 to RM 2,000.

June 26, 1934: A circular by **Gestapa** chief **Reinhard Heydrich** reminds the political police not to allow "Jewish gatherings" without prior permission and reinforces the need for Gestapo surveillance of organized Jewish events.

June 30, 1934: According to official U.S. immigration statistics, from July 1, 1933 to June 30, 1934, a total of 4,134 Jewish immigrants were admitted to the United States, 43.20 percent of whom were German Jews.

June 30–July 2, 1934: Hitler orders the murder of the SA leadership and other conservative regime critics and dresses the event up as the squashing of an attempted coup (*Röhmrevolte*, "Night of the Long Knifes"). In some instances, these crimes coincide with local actions against Jews.

July 18, 1934: New guidelines by the Reich sports leader (*Reichssportführer*) restrict membership of Jews to the Jewish sports clubs Makkabi (affiliated with the ZVfD) and Schild (RjF).

July 30, 1934: Reich bank president Schacht is appointed Reich economics minister.

August 2, 1934: The death of Hindenburg allows Hitler to combine the offices of Reich president and Reich chancellor in his capacity as "**Führer** und Reichskanzler" and leads to the German army's swearing an oath of loyalty to Hitler. During a referendum held on August 19, the unification of the two offices is approved by an overwhelming majority of voters (yes, 89.9 percent; no, 10.1 percent; turnout, 95.7 percent; invalid votes, 2 percent).

August 16, 1934: A decree by the deputy of the Führer (Rudolf Hess) prohibits contacts between party members and Jews.

November 15, 1934: In interministerial discussions, leading state and party functionaries acknowledge the negative diplomatic implications of Germany's racial policy but reach a consensus that even intense diplomatic pressure should not lead to a revision of Nazi principles. To alleviate some problems, they suggest replacing the concept of "non-Aryan" with "Jewish" in future laws and regulations.

December 12, 1934: In a letter to the Reich interior minister and with reference to Frick's decree of January 17, 1934, Reich Economics Minister Schacht protests the new wave of anti-Jewish boycotts and other violent actions. As a result, two weeks later Frick calls on Göring as Prussian prime minister and chief of the Gestapa to end such actions.

1935

January 13, 1935: In a plebiscite held in the **Saar** on the question of whether the region should return to German rule, 90.8 percent vote yes. Subsequently, roughly five thousand regime opponents leave the Saar to avoid being targeted by anti-Jewish regulations and other discriminatory measures already valid in the Reich.

February–August 1935: A wave of grassroots antisemitic outbursts (boycotts, agitation against "*Rassenschande*," acts of physical violence) and state-sponsored measures sweep through the Reich, with regional variations in terms of intensity, as a result of heightened anti-Jewish propaganda and local pressures for action.

March 16, 1935: Compulsory military service is reintroduced.

April 1, 1935: ZAHA and other German Jewish relief organizations are voluntarily integrated into the Reichsvertretung for the purpose of increasing efficiency.

April 11, 1935: The deputy of the Führer (Hess) prohibits "individual actions" (*Einzelaktionen*) against Jews and reiterates the prohibition against having contact with Jews for all party members.

May 15, 1935: In an article on the introduction of compulsory military service, the **SS** journal *Das Schwarze Korps* predicts the exclusion of Jews in the coming Defense Law (*Wehrgesetz*).

May 18–25, 1935: During riots and anti-Jewish and anti-Catholic actions in Munich, the police arrest SA and SS men. Criticism by high-ranking Nazi officials (i.e., Frick, Reich Justice Minister Franz Gürtner) leads to a temporary turning down of violence by regional party officials.

May 21, 1935: The new Defense Law requires "Aryan" descent for military service. A decree issued on July 25, 1935, excludes "non-Aryans" from active military service under the new law.

June 14, 1935: The deputy of the Führer (Hess) orders the maintenance of "party discipline" in fighting "ideological opponents."

June 18, 1935: A German-British naval agreement is signed.

June 21, 1935: A decree by the Reich Interior Ministry orders the removal of anti-Jewish slogans from road and other official signs in preparation for the 1936 Olympic Games in Germany.

June 30, 1935: According to official U.S. immigration statistics, from July 1, 1934 to June 30, 1935, a total of 4,837 Jewish immigrants were admitted to the United States, 34.80 percent of whom were German Jews.

July 16, 1935: Frick advises local registrar officials (*Standesbeamte*) throughout the Reich not to perform "racially mixed marriages." These marriages are formally disallowed with the passing of the **Nuremberg Laws** on September 15, 1935.

July 22–28, 1935: Anti-Jewish riots by Berlin Nazi activists break out on Berlin's Kurfürstendamm. On July 30, 1935, the Berlin city administration agrees with party and police offices to disallow new Jewish businesses and to mark "Aryan" shops.

August 6, 1935: The Reichsvertretung issues a "word of consolation" (*Trostwort*) to Jewish communities for the first sabbath after the 9th of Av with reference to the recent "wave of abuse" (*Flut von Beschimpfungen*) and an appeal against depression and embitterment among German Jews.

September 6, 1935: A new Gestapo decree calls for the creation by the secret state police of a "Jewish file card catalogue" (*Judenkartei*) containing names of members of Jewish organizations.

September 15, 1935: During the Nazi Party congress, the Reichstag passes the so-called Nuremberg Laws comprising

1. Reich Citizenship Law (*Reichsbürgergesetz*): Article 1: "A 'subject of the state' [*Staatsangehöriger*] is anyone who enjoys the protection of the German Reich and who, in return, has particular obligations to the Reich"; Article 2: "A 'citizen of the Reich' [*Reichsbürger*] is only that subject who is of German or related blood and who, by his conduct, demonstrates that he is both willing and suited to serve faithfully the German people and Reich." This law forms the basis for a plethora of anti-Jewish measures based on thirteen supplementary decrees enacted over the period up to July 1943.

2. Law for the Protection of German Blood and German Honor (*Gesetz zum Schutze des deutschen Blutes und der deutschen Ehre*; *Blutschutzgesetz*): Article 1: "Marriages between Jews and nationals of German or related blood are prohibited"; Article 2: "Extramarital relations between Jews and nationals of German or related blood are prohibited"; Article 3: "Jews are not permitted to employ in their households female nationals who are of German or related blood and who are under the age of 45"; Article 4: "Jews are forbidden to display the Reich and national flag or the colors of the Reich" but are "allowed to display the Jewish colors."

September 17, 1935: The CV changes its name to Centralverein der Juden in Deutschland. On September 22, 1935, the Reichsvertretung changes its name to Reichsvertretung der Juden in Deutschland; other Jewish organizations adopt similar name changes in the wake of the Nuremberg Laws. The Reichsvertretung also issues a declaration expressing its will to help create, as announced by Hitler in his Nuremberg address, a basis on which a "tolerable relationship between the German and the Jewish people is possible" and calls for its acceptance as an "autonomous Jewish leadership" by the government.

September 25, 1935: Reichsvertretung president Leo Baeck circulates his speech for Kol Nidre (the night prior to Yom Kippur) criticizing "the lie turned against us; the slander used against our religion and its testimonies" to German communities. As a result, the speech is prohibited; Baeck and Hirsch are arrested by the Gestapo to be released after a short incarceration in early October 1935.

September 30, 1935: The forced retirement of all Jewish public servants until then exempt under the clauses of the Civil Service Law enacted on April 4, 1933, takes effect.

October 15, 1935: The Jewish Winter Relief (Jüdische Winterhilfe) is excluded from the national German winter relief system.

October 18, 1935: The Law for the Protection of the Hereditary Health of the German People (*Gesetz zum Schutze der Erbgesundheit des deutschen Volkes*) makes a premarital "marriage fitness certificate" (*Ehetauglichgkeitszeugnis*) mandatory.

November 14, 1935: The first supplementary decree to the Reich Citizenship Law (*Reichsbürgergesetz*) enacted on September 15, 1935, defines Jews and "***Mischlinge***":

- Paragraph 2: "A Jewish *Mischling* is anyone who is descended from one or two grandparents who are racially full Jews. [. . .] A grandparent is considered a full-blooded Jew if he or she belonged to the Jewish religious community."

- Paragraph 4: "A Jew cannot be a citizen of the Reich. He has no right to vote on political matters and he cannot hold public office. Jewish civil servants will retire by December 31, 1935."

- Paragraph 5: "A Jew is anyone who is descended from at least three grandparents who are racially full Jews. [. . .] Also deemed to be a Jew is a Jewish *Mischling* who is descended from two fully Jewish grandparents,

    a. who belonged to the Jewish religious community at the time this law is issued, or joined the community at a later date,

    b. who was married to a Jew when the law was issued or marries one subsequently,

    c. who is the offspring of a marriage with a Jew as defined in section 1 of this paragraph and which was entered into after the Law for the Protection of German Blood and German Honor became effective,

    d. who is the offspring of an extramarital relationship with a Jew as defined in section 1 of this paragraph, and was born out of wedlock after July 31, 1936."

- Paragraph 7: "The Führer and Reich Chancellor can grant exemptions from the regulations laid down in this supplementary decree."

November 14, 1935: The first supplementary decree to the Law for the Protection of German Blood and German Honor (*Gesetz zum Schutze des deutschen Blutes und der deutschen Ehre*), paragraph 2, prohibits marriage "between Jews and subjects of the state who are *Mischlinge* with one fully Jewish grandparent." Paragraph 3 stipulates that marriages between "subjects of the state who are *Mischlinge* with two fully Jewish grandparents," and a person "of German or related blood or a subject of the state who is a *Mischling* with one fully Jewish grandparent" require permission from the Reich interior minister (Frick), and the deputy of the Führer (Hess), or his delegated representative. Paragraph 4 prohibits marriages "between state subjects when each are *Mischlinge* with one fully Jewish grandparent." Paragraph 6 states, "No marriage shall be concluded if it is feared that its offspring will endanger the purity of German blood." Paragraph 11 extends prohibitions to "sexual relations." Paragraph 12 restricts the employment of "female subjects of the state who are of German and related blood" in "Jewish households" with a Jewish male as head or member to persons at least thirty-five years old on December 31, 1935. Paragraph 16 allows the Führer and Reich chancellor to make exemptions and calls for permission by the Reich ministers of justice and the interior prior to the criminal prosecution of a foreign citizen under the law.

November 26, 1935: A decree by the Reich Interior Ministry replaces "non-Aryan" (*Nichtarier*) with "Jew" (*Jude*), and "Aryan descent" (*arische Abstammung*) with "German and related blood" (*deutsches und artverwandtes Blut*) in legal and administrative texts.

1936

February 4, 1936: The Jewish student David Frankfurter assassinates Wilhelm Gustloff, Nazi leader in Switzerland (*Leiter der Landesgruppe Schweiz der NSDAP-AO*) as an act of protest.

February 5, 1936: The Reich Justice Ministry prohibits "individual actions" (*Einzelaktionen*) against Jews after the murder of Gustloff prior to the Olympic Winter Games, held from February 6 to 16, 1936, in Garmisch-Partenkirchen, Germany.

March 7, 1936: The German army (Wehrmacht) moves into the Rhineland area that had been demilitarized following the Versailles Treaty.

March 7, 1936: A new national electoral law (*Gesetz über das Reichstagswahlrecht*) excludes Jews from voting. An election to the Reichstag and referendum held on March 29, 1936, yields a 99 percent yes vote for Hitler's foreign policy.

June 17, 1936: Hitler appoints SS chief Himmler as head of the German police. Himmler appoints Heydrich as chief of the Security Police and SD (*Sicherheitspolizei und Sicherheitsdienst*) and Kurt Daluege as chief of the Order Police (*Ordnungspolizei*).

June 30, 1936: According to official U.S. immigration statistics, from July 1, 1935 to June 30, 1936, a total of 6,252 Jewish immigrants were admitted to the United States, 52.53 percent of whom were German Jews.

July 13, 1936: A circular decree by the Reich Education Ministry allows the establishment of retraining schools for Jews in preparation for their emigration.

August 1936: Hitler establishes the Office of the Four-Year Plan, to be headed by Göring, to coordinate and intensify the regime's preparations for war. Hitler's secret memo includes announcements of severe sentences, including collective Jewish accountability for crimes committed by individual Jews.

August 1, 1936: Hitler opens the Eleventh Summer Olympic Games in Berlin.

August 12, 1936: A decree by the Reich Interior Ministry announces the marking of hospitals and medical institutes owned or run by Jews.

September 8–14, 1936: A Nazi Party congress is held in Nuremberg, and the Four-Year Plan is announced.

October 25, 1936: The German-Italian alliance ("axis Berlin-Rome") is signed.

November 25, 1936: Japan signs the Anti-Comintern Pact with Germany.

December 1, 1936: A new regulation excludes Jewish welfare agencies from tax exemption.

December 30, 1936: The Gestapo dissolves the CV-affiliated Jewish youth organization Der Ring **Bund Deutsch-Jüdischer Jugend** (BDJ).

1937

January 30, 1937: In a pro forma vote, the Reichstag extends the Enabling Act passed March 23, 1933, for another four years.

March 18, 1937: The Gestapa Berlin decides on more strict supervision of "assimilationist" German Jewish organizations, especially the CV and the RjF.

April 15, 1937: A decree by the Reich education minister prohibits Jews from obtaining doctoral degrees at German universities.

June 12, 1937: A secret decree by the head of the Security Police (Heydrich) instructs local police to take Jews who have been convicted of "race defilement" ("*Rassenschande*") and released from prison into "protective custody" (*Schutzhaft*) and to incarcerate them in concentration camps.

June 30, 1937: According to official U.S. immigration statistics, from July 1, 1936 to June 30, 1937, a total of 11,352 Jewish immigrants were admitted to the United States, 59.46 percent of whom were German Jews.

September 5, 1937: Schacht takes a leave of absence from the post of Reich economic minister (resigning formally in November). Göring acts pro tem until the appointment of Walther Funk in February 1938.

September 13, 1937: A decree by Himmler (chief of the German police) allows the release of Jews from "protective custody" (*Schutzhaft*) in concentration camps if they can provide evidence of their imminent emigration.

November 4, 1937: The Reich Justice Ministry forbids Jews to utilize the "German salute" (***Deutscher Gruss***) vis-à-vis judicial agencies.

November 8, 1937: Reich Propaganda Minister Goebbels opens the anti-semitic exhibition "The Eternal Jew" (*Der Ewige Jude*) in Munich.

December 13, 1937: The Reichsvertretung forms a Zentralstelle für jüdische Auswanderung (Central Office for Jewish Emigration) to better plan and coordinate the work of already existing Jewish organizations that promote and facilitate the emigration of Jews from Germany.

December 16, 1937: A regulation by the Reich Interior Ministry restricts the issuing of passports to Jews to exceptional cases (e.g., emigration, travel in the economic interest of Germany, serious illness or death of next of kin, one's own illness, or visits of children in schools abroad).

1938

January 5, 1938: Himmler orders the expulsion of Soviet citizens from the Reich within ten days with the exception of accredited diplomats.

January 5, 1938: The Law on the Modification of Family and First Names (*Gesetz über die Änderung von Familien- und Vornamen*) prohibits the change of family names for Jews and "*Mischlinge*" in order to prevent them from hiding their ancestry.

February 4, 1938: As part of the planning for war, Hitler takes over the supreme command of the German armed forces.

March 12, 1938: German troops invade Austria (***Anschluss***), which triggers a massive wave of anti-Jewish actions, including arrests, assaults, and expropriations.

March 28, 1938: The Law on the Legal Relationships of the Jewish Cultural Associations (*Gesetz über die Rechtsverhältnisse der jüdischen Kultusvereinigungen*) reduces the status of Jewish communities from public law entities (*Körperschaften öffentlichen Rechts*) to registered associations (*Vereine*) by April 1, 1938. The new law has a massive effect on Jewish communal organizations in Germany and prompts the Reichsvertretung to restructure.

April 12, 1938: A new family law (*Gesetz über die Änderung und Ergänzung familienrechtlicher Vorschriften und über die Rechtsstellung der Staatenlosen*) allows state prosecutors to open court proceedings to establish a person's (Jewish or non-Jewish) ancestry.

April 22, 1938: A new regulation imposes penalties for "covering up" the Jewish owner-ship of a business.

April 26, 1938: The Regulation Regarding the Registration of Jewish Assets (*Verordnung über die Anmeldung jüdischen Vermögens*) requires all Jews to register assets exceeding RM 5,000 in value. Göring's Office of the Four-Year Plan is empowered to expropriate these assets "in the interest of German economy."

May 20, 1938: The Nuremberg Laws are officially introduced in annexed Austria.

May 31, 1938: Hitler orders the Wehrmacht to prepare for the invasion of Czechoslovakia.

June 1, 1938: A decree by the Reich Economics Ministry excludes Jewish schools from tax exemption.

June 13–18, 1938: Across the Reich, the police arrest more than ten thousand "work-shy" (*Arbeitsscheue*) and "asocials," including roughly fifteen hundred Jews, incarcerating them in concentration camps.

June 14, 1938: The Reich Economics Ministry revokes its earlier regulations on the nonapplication of the "Aryan clause" to the private economy.

June 14, 1938: The third supplementary decree to the Reich Citizenship Law (*Reichs-bürgergesetz*) introduces the concept of Jewish enterprises (*jüdische Gewerbebetriebe*) and stipulates their registration and marking.

June 20, 1938: A decree by the Reich Economics Ministry excludes Jews from attending the German stock exchange.

June 30, 1938: According to official U.S. immigration statistics, from July 1, 1937 to June 30, 1938, a total of 19,736 Jewish immigrants were admitted to the United States, 60.38 percent of whom were Jews from Germany and Austria.

July 6–15, 1938: An international conference at Évian-les-Bains, France, is initiated by U.S. president Franklin D. Roosevelt on the refugee crisis, with representatives from thirty-two countries and two dozen organizations. While doing little to remedy the plight of Jews trying to escape the Reich, the conference leads to the creation of an Intergovernmental Committee for Refugees headed by U.S. diplomat George Rublee.

July 23, 1938: A regulation by the Reich Interior Ministry orders German Jews to report to police by December 31, 1938, in order to receive special ID cards (*Kennkarten*). After this date, the IDs are to be presented in all dealings with government officials.

July 25, 1938: The fourth supplementary regulation to the Reich Citizenship Law (*Reichsbürgergesetz*) prohibits Jewish doctors from practicing and relegates a small num-ber to serve as "caretakers of the sick" (*Krankenbehandler*) for Jews only.

July 27, 1938: A decree by the Reich Interior Ministry orders the renaming of streets named after Jews and first-degree "*Mischlinge.*"

August 17, 1938: A supplementary decree to the family names law (*Gesetz über die Änderung von Familien- und Vornamen*) requires Jews to use the compulsory middle names Sara for women and Israel for men as of January 1, 1939.

August 20, 1938: The Viennese SD (**Adolf Eichmann**) establishes a Central Office for Jewish Emigration (Zentralstelle für jüdische Auswanderung) for the purpose of speeding up the forced emigration of Jews from former Austria.

August 22, 1938: A new police regulation (*Ausländerpolizeiverordnung*) allows the withdrawal of permissions to stay in Germany for non-German and denaturalized Jews.

September 1938: An international crisis over German claims regarding the Sudetenland in Czechoslovakia triggers a new wave of antisemitic violence in the Reich that culminates in "*Kristallnacht.*"

September 29/30, 1938: The Munich agreement forces Czechoslovakia to cede the Sudetenland to the Reich.

October 1–10, 1938: German troops occupy the Sudetenland; Jewish inhabitants flee across the border into Czechoslovakia.

October 5, 1938: A decree by the Reich Interior Ministry voids German passports issued to Jews and orders a restricted reissuing of passports stamped with the letter *J.*

October 6, 1938: The Italian Fascist Grand Council approves racial laws along German lines announced by Benito Mussolini in July 1938.

October 28, 1938: Fifteen to seventeen thousand Polish Jewish citizens are arrested and deported from various cities in Germany over the border to Poland. Thousands of deportees get stranded in the border area, some entering Poland, others returning to Germany.

November 7, 1938: In protest against the expulsion of Polish Jews from the Reich, Jewish student Herschel Grynszpan shoots German embassy official Ernst vom Rath in Paris.

November 9–10, 1938: "*Kristallnacht.*" The Nazi Party–instigated pogrom in Germany results in the murder of more than a hundred Jews, the mass arrest of at least twenty-six thousand Jewish men and their incarceration in prisons or concentration camps, the closing of Jewish organizations, and the massive destruction of buildings and other property owned by Jews.

November 12, 1938: A series of regulations calls for payment by German Jews of RM 1 billion as "compensation for damages" during "*Kristallnacht,*" excludes Jews from the German economy by closing all Jewish businesses and workshops, and bans Jews from public theaters, cinemas, and exhibitions. On November 15, 1938, Jewish children are banned from German schools.

November 19, 1938: A new regulation (*Verordnung über die öffentliche Fürsorge der Juden*) reduces public welfare for Jews to exceptional cases.

November 23, 1938: After the abolishing of Jewish periodicals in Germany, the first issue of the *Jüdisches Nachrichtenblatt* published by the Reichsvertretung informs readers about government regulations.

November 28, 1938: A police regulation restricts the mobility of Jews in public.

November 29, 1938: The Reichsvertretung officially resumes its work after the shutdown or abolishment of Jewish organizations caused by "*Kristallnacht*."

November 1938–February 1939: Negotiations similar to the Ha'avara Agreement take place between George Rublee, head of the Intergovernmental Committee for Refugees established at the Évian conference, and German government officials (especially Schacht) to facilitate large-scale Jewish emigration from Germany to destinations yet to be determined.

December 3, 1938: The Decree on the Use of Jewish Assets (*Verordnung über den Einsatz jüdischen Vermögens*) regulates the forced sale of Jewish businesses, real estate, and other assets.

December 12, 1938: A new foreign currency law (*Gesetz über Devisenbewirtschaftung*) restricts the possessions emigrants may take out of Germany (including money and jewelry) to items of personal use.

December 20, 1938: Moving beyond forced labor regulations initiated locally earlier on, the Reich Labor Ministry decrees labor duties for unemployed Jews.

EARLY 1939

January 16, 1939: In a conversation with the Hungarian foreign minister and against the background of the negotiations between Rublee and Schacht, Hitler suggests an international financial agreement for the purpose of removing "every last Jew" from the Reich.

January 30, 1939: In a speech to the Reichstag, Hitler states, "Today I will be once more a prophet: if the international Jewish financiers in and outside Europe should succeed in plunging the nations once more into a world war, then the result will not be the Bolshevizing of the earth, and thus the victory of Jewry, but the annihilation of the Jewish race in Europe [*Vernichtung der jüdischen Rasse in Europa*]!"

February 17, 1939: The *Jüdisches Nachrichtenblatt* announces the reorganization of the Reichsvertretung into the **Reichsvereinigung der Juden in Deutschland.** The regime officially recognizes the Reichsvereinigung in the tenth supplementary decree to the Reich Citizenship Law (*Reichsbürgergesetz*) on July 4, 1939, to ensure "the promotion of Jewish emigration" and to supervise the Jewish school and welfare system. All persons defined as Jewish under the Nuremberg Laws (with the exception of foreign nationals and Jewish female spouses in "mixed marriages" with children) had to join the Reichsvereinigung, which until its dissolution in 1943 was controlled by Heydrich's Security Police and SD.

June 30, 1939: According to official U.S. immigration statistics, from July 1, 1938 to June 30, 1939, a total of 43,450 Jewish immigrants were admitted to the United States, 69.27 percent of whom were Jews from Germany and Austria.

Index

Entries which appear in boldface can be found in the Glossary. Cities and countries are listed according to 1933 borders; references to variations on place names in other languages are also included.

ABOUT THE AUTHORS

Jürgen Matthäus, historian, research director at the Center for Advanced Holocaust Studies of the United States Holocaust Memorial Museum, Washington, D.C. Dr. Matthäus's publications include *Approaching an Auschwitz Survivor: Holocaust Testimony and its Transformations* (2009); (ed. with P. Heberer) *Atrocities on Trial: Historical Perspectives on the Politics of Prosecuting War Criminals* (2008); and (ed. with K. Kwiet), *Contemporary Responses to the Holocaust* (2005).

Mark Roseman, historian, professor in the Department of History and Pat M. Glazer Chair of Jewish Studies at Indiana University. Professor Roseman's more recent publications include (ed. with F. Biess and H. Schissler) *Conflict, Catastrophe and Continuity: Essays on Modern German History* (2007); *The Wannsee Conference and the 'Final Solution'* (2002); and *A Past in Hiding: Memory and Survival in Nazi Germany* (2000).